PRIVILEGE AND PREJUDICE

Privilege and Prejudice

THE LIFE OF A BLACK PIONEER

Clifton R. Wharton Jr.

Michigan State University Press | *East Lansing*

Michigan State University Press
East Lansing, Michigan 48823-5245

Printed and bound in the United States of America.

21 20 19 18 17 16 15   1 2 3 4 5 6 7 8 9 10

Library of Congress Control Number: 2015930556
ISBN: 978-1-61186-171-6 (cloth)
ISBN: 978-1-60917-460-6 (ebook: PDF)
ISBN: 978-1-62895-232-2 (ebook: ePub)
ISBN: 978-1-62896-232-1 (ebook: Kindle)

Book design by Charlie Sharp, Sharp Des!gns, Lansing, Michigan
Cover design by David Drummond, Salamander Design, www.salamanderhill.com
Cover photo by Bill Ray and is used courtesy of the photographer. All rights reserved.

Michigan State University Press is a member of the Green Press Initiative and is
committed to developing and encouraging ecologically responsible publishing
practices. For more information about the Green Press Initiative and the use
of recycled paper in book publishing, please visit *www.greenpressinitiative.org*.

Visit Michigan State University Press at *www.msupress.org*

Contents

Foreword

This is a landmark book that I wish every Black kid in America would read. Clif Wharton is an incredible role model, not just for Black youth but for white youth as well. They will see him being efficient, effective and open, and not allowing prejudice to interfere. They will see him going to the best schools, taking on tough jobs and doing well, growing along the way, not apologizing but just doing the job, and taking what came. Many Black youth will read this book and say *My God is this possible? Look at what this guy did. He led the way; all I have to do is be like him, use my brain, learn all the time, and be open to people.*

They will also find that he was growing all the time in each of his careers. Clif Wharton is one of those people I admire because he always learns from experience. Some people go through all kinds of experiences and they don't change a bit. But Clif was constantly changing and constantly learning and even in tough situations he kept a kind of serenity about him.

Another important dimension of the Clif Wharton story is his wife Dolores. She is a wonderful lady, was always with him, and was always supportive. Another university president once observed about his wife and marriage that "She and I cast a single shadow." I invariably think of Clif and Dolores casting a single shadow.

—The Reverend Theodore M. Hesburgh, CSC, STD,
President Emeritus, University of Notre Dame

You and Dolores have had a great partnership. Both together and independently, each of you have left a very strong mark on this nation in many ways.

At SUNY you were so successful in bringing a measure—not as much as you wanted but still a measure—of autonomy to that huge overregulated system.

And then there was TIAA-CREF. You really lifted that organization from the depths into which it had fallen by reason of becoming disconnected from its core constituency. You moved rapidly, forcefully, and correctly to restore its reputation.

You have been and still are a towering figure in American higher education. Through your writings, your speeches, and your leadership, you have exemplified the very best in our business and in our society. You will always be a hero to me and to countless others.

—Robert H. Atwell, President Emeritus, American Council on Education

Clifton Wharton is one of America's distinguished public servants. His great success as a university president, corporate chief executive, and foundation leader is anchored in his deep sense of compassion, enormous energy, personal courage, and intelligence. This inspiring book should be read to appreciate how much we can really achieve through uncommon commitment to the principles we live by.

—William C. Friday, President Emeritus, University of North Carolina

Preface

This book is about the life experiences and three careers of a Black American descended from several generations of high-achieving ancestors. My major motivation in writing my autobiography was to present a story that might serve as an example of one man's odyssey to achieve full equality and integration. This story occurred at a time of great social change, turmoil, and conflict, as our nation's diverse racial groups were striving to secure these goals. This story of a Black who integrated the American dream may give *all* readers a better understanding of this dimension of racial progress in our country.

Though privileged in some ways from my earliest years, I had no immunity from the pervasive racial prejudice of the era. Nevertheless, I never allowed racism to discourage or defeat me. My parents and my extended family prized individual accomplishment highly and always insisted upon the prerequisites of discipline, hard work, integrity, and a passion for excellence. They believed that education was the universal foundation for personal progress and a better life. At the same time, I was taught to believe in the importance of helping others through developing their human capital, particularly for potential future leaders from groups to whom the doors of opportunity had been closed historically.

I prepared the autobiography in two versions. The first was a long, detailed, chronological document useful for future scholars or historians using my large archives, as well as for my immediate family. The second version was based upon the long manuscript and became this book.

. . . .

My previous writings have dealt largely with economics and higher education. Autobiography proved to be very different. I quickly learned that memory is highly fallible—recollections are often inaccurate or distorted. With retelling over time, anecdotes melt, mutate, and sometimes become more flattering to oneself. Consequently, a demanding requirement in writing a personal history is the frequent checking and verification of facts and events. In my case I had the advantage of unusual archives of materials tracing my entire life from birth—ranging from my mother's diaries, my father's photographs, earliest school report cards, and college lecture notes, to later correspondence, office calendars, memoranda, reports, speeches, research materials, tape recordings, movies, videos, photographs, and newspaper clippings. All these were systematically used to produce a document that was as accurate and truthful as possible.

This writing was an eerie experience of reliving past events while simultaneously observing them from the vantage of the more mature viewpoint of the present. Because of this time perspective, there was a subtle shift in my understanding of each life stage.

This book is the result of the help and support of a large number of persons and institutions. I must begin with my thanks to President Lou Anna K. Simon of Michigan State University for her interest and encouragement. Also, Gabriel Dotto, director of the MSU Press, and his outstanding team deserve highest thanks for producing the final product.

Many individuals who contributed to my efforts are mentioned in notes. I taped interviews with several early childhood friends and contacted many past acquaintances and colleagues to get their views on specific events or to elicit facts that had become vague in my memory. Their willing responses were most helpful in developing the final text. Their names, along with certain institutions, are listed in an acknowledgments section with my most heartfelt gratitude for their assistance.

· · · ·

I would be remiss not to mention certain individuals who had very special involvement. Two early contributors were archivist Nancy Langford, who assembled and classified a majority of my archives, and Melissa Manikas, who performed a similar task on my photographs and videos and transcribed many interviews. In this age of high technology, my computer expert Juan Perez was my crisis responder. The former TIAA-CREF archivist Carolyn Kopp was ever ready with her unique research skills, as were Betty Klaviter and Chelsea Fristoe, both from Lansing, Michigan. Similar help was provided by the MSU Archives and Historical Collections staff. My highest praise goes to Kathryn Sartori, my TIAA-CREF executive assistant of twenty-seven years, who proved a diligent researcher and a committed professional throughout the entire endeavor, overseeing the myriad details involved. These persons quietly carried out the basic tasks for my work, thereby deserving my profound thanks.

Robert Perrin and James Harkness, both colleagues of long standing, took on the arduous task of reviewing and commenting on the initial long version throughout its development, and at times even rewriting some parts of the longer version. They gave superb attention and excellent editing help for which I am deeply grateful. I must apologize for having imposed upon them for almost three decades—a debt that I can never repay.

From time to time, other persons reviewed major sections or all of the semifinal manuscript, including Jim Spaniolo, Al Wilson, Tom Jones, Carl Taylor, Murray Block, and his son Paul Block. Their knowledgeable comments and perceptive observations helped make this a better book, although any remaining errors are mine alone. Their contributions were highly appreciated.

▪ ▪ ▪ ▪

The initial long version totaled 1,700 pages, requiring a skillful mandatory reduction to achieve a shorter autobiography. The key person who performed this challenging task was Jim Harkness. He amazingly condensed the manuscript by more than half for the Michigan State University Press, while miraculously preserving my main themes and my own authorial voice. He was the invaluable contributor to this effort. I will be eternally thankful to Jim because without him I doubt this book would ever have been finished.

Finally, Dolores lived most of the book with me for more than six decades and throughout the writing was my priceless muse.

Acknowledgments

An autobiography places upon the author a special demand for accuracy. This is not merely due to the dangers of fallible memory but also to the distortions and differences in perception between the author and other participants in the narrative. I have been especially grateful for the willingness of so many of my friends and colleagues to help. Whether it was formal taped interviews, correspondence, or telephone calls, their assistance was invaluable. My thanks goes to those listed below according to the major periods of my life. If I have omitted someone, I apologize. The final product could not have been completed without them.

Assistance in the first five chapters came from the following persons:

Carlos Blanco, George Branche, Matt Branche, Flor Brennan, David W. Brown, John Camp, Gelia Castillo, Michael Contompasis, Martha Dalrymple, R. Turner Dickerson, Joe Douglas, Ralph Dungan, Howie Edmonds, Bill Ellis, Court Ellis, George Forsythe, Edward Franklin, J. Price Gittinger, Pete Gosling, William Henessey, Stuart Ho, Betty Fitzgerald Howard, Ernie Howell, Kanianthra T. Joseph, Richard Kaye, Ray Lamontagne, Trai Le, Ron Lee, Emily Lippman (Robertson), Virginia Locke, Priscilla Mason, Harold May, Tom McHale, Richelieu Morris, Arthur T. Mosher, Gayl Ness, Norman Parmer, Florence Prioleau, Ignacio Rivero y Noble, Vernon Ruttan, Agoes Salim, Mary Wharton Sampson, Gene Schwartz, Myron Simon, Richard H. Smith, Robert D. Stevens, Chuck Stone, Phil Talbot, Augustine Tan Hui Heng, Grace Tongue, George Varghese, Wang Gung Wu, Elaine Wharton Weatherly, Abe Weisblat, Bill Welsh, Dan Wharton, Gretchen Wharton, William Wharton, Wong Nan Jang, and Arthur Young.

The individuals helpful with the chapters on Michigan State University and State University of New York were the following:

William Anslow, Bob Atwell, Charlie Baggett, Al Ballard, Ken Beachler, Don Blinken, Murray Block, Jim Bonnen, Carter Burgess, Joe Burke, John Cantlon, Alice Chandler, Darwin Davis, Marylee Davis, Nolen Ellison, Irving Freedman, Tom Freeman, Herb Gordon, Pete Gosling, Ruth Hamilton, Jim Harkness, Nancy Harrigan, Dale Hathaway, Vernon Jordan, Jerome Komisar, Ray Lamontagne, Ron Lee, Sanford Levine, Marvel Luykx, Jim Lyng, Peter Magrath, Phyllis Maner, Blanche Martin, Judith Moyers, Milt Muelder, Gayl Ness, Don O'Dowd, Vince O'Leary, Bob Perrin, Susan Reardon, Norman Rice, Shelly Segal, William Sewell, Roy Simon, Ralph Smuckler, Jim Spaniolo, Harry Spindler, Stuart Steiner, Don Stevens, Carl Taylor, Clarence Underwood, Jim Votruba, Chuck Webb, Robert Wenner, Roger Wilkinson, and Lee Winder.

The final chapters benefited from contacts with the following persons:

Marcus Alexis, Mike Armacost, Bob Atwell, Brian Atwood, Anna Borg, Andy Brimmer, Jock Covey, Kirk Dorn, Bill Friday, Marc Grossman, Jim Harkness, Father Ted Hesburgh, Tom Jones, Vernon Jordan, Samuel W. Lewis, Sol Linowitz, Mike McCurry, Alan Monroe, George Moose, Bob Perrin, Claire Sheehan, Phil Talbot, and Jim Wolf.

The institutions that provided welcome service were these:

The Michigan State University Archives and Historical Collections, the Rockefeller Archive Center, and the Jimmy Carter Presidential Library and Museum.

Prologue

A big day in Monrovia. Received at the Mansion from 11–1 by the President, Mrs. King, members of the Cabinet and their wives. This hour included only the Senators and the members of the diplomatic corps. The other folks according to rank came later, our group being the very first to be received by the President. We had lots of company all afternoon. Went to the ball at the Mansion in the evening and had a lovely time. I wore my old college evening dress, one pair of my Christmas stockings which went very well with my evening dress & shoes. I also carried my fan which created quite a bit of commendation. I danced almost every dance, including one with the new British charge d'affaires and one with the manager of the bank of British West Africa. . . . We did not get home until very late and were very tired.

　　　　　　　—Harriette B. Wharton, diary, Monrovia, Liberia, December 16, 1925

Did not feel so well today. . . . Spent some time sewing. Went for a walk in the afternoon.

　　　　　　　—HBW, January 15, 1926

Still on the sick list.

　　　　　　　—HBW, January 19, 1926

I went to see the doctor as I am sick so much of late. He said nothing strange and would give me nothing, only to return in another month. All symptoms point toward one thing!

　　　　　　　—HBW, January 20, 1926

CHAPTER ONE

The Beginning: Genesis and Youth

I was conceived in Monrovia, West Africa, on December 16, 1925, after a pre-Christmas ball hosted by the president of Liberia. We all know we were conceived, though rarely exactly how or when. But my mother kept a diary that described the ball, her almost immediate onset of morning sickness, and the doctor's diagnosis weeks later.

. . . .

Infant memory can be chimerical, a dreamy movie watched from a great distance. Yet the images abide as tangled threads of what you truly recall and what your parents have told you. Among my earliest recollections are the smell of the sea, cold spray, and a tangy salt breeze. The ship is the SS *Highbo*, en route from the United States to Liberia in October 1927, a year after my birth in Boston. Holding my mother's hand, I am walking the deck. The ship rolls on a vast swell of green water under empty blue washed sky this picture is imprinted on my senses permanently. Ocean travel would become a lifelong pleasure.

I recall as well being on another ship, this time as a three-year-old, returning to the United States from Africa with a cargo of wild animals. I was familiar with animals—small aggressive monkeys infested the trees behind our home in Monrovia, sometimes leaping onto my back to snatch food from my hand. On the ship I soon noticed a baby gorilla that the sailors had made a pet. He was bigger than my backyard monkeys, but I was not afraid of him. One day, the baby gorilla unexpectedly broke away from the sailors and knocked me down to get a piece of fruit I had been eating. I can still remember his smell and breathing as he crouched over me. Except for a few scratches, I was unhurt.

In our backyard in Monrovia I can picture an enormous cashew tree whose fruit I was

FRANCIS WHARTON AND MALE DESCENDANTS IN ACCOMACK

FRANCIS WHARTON SR. (b. 1641 England)
↓
FRANCIS WHARTON JR. (b. 1665)
↓
JOHN WHARTON SR. (b. 1698)
↓
JOHN WHARTON JR. (b. 1733, d. July 30, 1776)
↓
JOHN WHARTON 3ʳᵈ (b. November 25, 1762, d. February 25 1814)

forbidden to eat when it dropped to the ground. One day nonetheless I bit into a fallen green cashew nut, and the acid burned my lips badly—I learned the penalty for disobedience.

Because fresh milk was unavailable, my mother fed me from a powdered product called "KLIM." Photographs of me with the large KLIM cans went back to relatives in the United States.

· · · ·

In my mind's eye I still conjure my parents dressing for formal dinner parties, my mother humming happily all the while. I had a child's tennis racquet that I treasured, though I could not hit very well. I loved even better my pint-sized pith helmet, like my father's. And I remember an afternoon standing with him on the edge of a large open field, watching a medicine man (a "juju") haranguing a large group of local people. I was puzzled that neither of us felt the mass hypnotist's spell, and wondered if our immunity came from being Americans and outsiders.

From my earliest days I always understood that my background was to a degree privileged—I suppose the impression came from my father, Clifton Reginald Wharton Sr., and his heritage. Peter Wharton, my paternal great-great-great-grandfather, was a "Freed Negro" from Accomack County, Virginia, in the late 1700s. In the early and mid-nineteenth century, freed Negroes owned land and earned their living with skills in numbers considerably larger than many people today realize. For example, in 1830 the three states with the largest free Negro populations were Maryland (52,938), Virginia (47,348), and New York (44,870).[1] Peter was a "dark copper colour" mulatto, 5'1¼" tall, and "having a scar on the left hand and a scar on the end of the fourth finger of the left hand."[2] My father said that Peter, a baker, was the son of a white man, John Wharton, who lived during the American Revolution. An article in a 1963 issue of *Ladies Home Journal* has a photograph of a "Wharton mansion" built by a John Wharton 3ʳᵈ, still standing in Mappsville, Virginia.[3] My father strongly suspected that

My paternal grandfather, William Bowman Wharton (b. July 15, 1877, d. November 28, 1972), was Maria Wharton's fifth son.

this was his ancestor, a descendant of the Whartons from England. Francis Wharton Sr. was born in England, emigrated to Philadelphia, and then traveled to Accomack County before 1669.[4] Born a slave, Peter was freed by John 3rd's widow, Elizabeth Williams Wharton, through her will in 1831. This was three decades before the 1863 Emancipation Proclamation. Peter's granddaughter, Maria (b. 1850) was my great-grandmother.

▪ ▪ ▪ ▪

I don't know much about the early years of my paternal grandfather, William Bowman Wharton, Maria's son (b. July 15, 1877). His father was Louis C. H. Finney, a white lawyer and lieutenant colonel in the Confederate Army, from a distinguished family in Accomack County. All Maria's children, however, kept the surname Wharton, not Finney.

My grandfather left home at age sixteen for Baltimore. There he joined his brother Heber, a public school supervisor, with his son Heber Jr., a physician, and his three daughters, all schoolteachers. William was light-skinned enough to "pass" for white, and he worked for a time as a hotel bellman, then a clerk. In 1895 he married Mary Roselind Griffin, of the prominent Negro O'Neill family. Roselind, or Rosie, had bronze skin, strong Indian features, straight jet-black hair, and limpid dark eyes. After six years in Baltimore, William and Rosie moved to Atlantic City, then in 1903 to Boston. By then the couple had seven children, of whom only my father Clifton (born May 11, 1899) and his older sister Ianthia Enola (November 10, 1897) lived beyond age three.

Because my grandfather could easily have passed as white, I can't say to what extent my grandfather's odyssey was shaped by discrimination. He left no recorded opinions of the Jim Crow era, though in a small town such as Accomac (the town nearest his Accomack County home) his Negro blood would have been common knowledge. Over the decades after the Reconstruction, dogged racial progress had taken place in the South, and substantial numbers of Negroes became successful artisans, established profitable businesses, and accumulated wealth. Some were even elected to public office, such as Jasper Wright (the South Carolina Supreme Court) and P. B. S. Pinchback (governor of Louisiana).[5] By the 1880s, however, a series of court decisions had begun to erode the rights of former slaves, and the U.S. Supreme Court had held that the Fourteenth Amendment restricted states but not individuals or private organizations from discriminating against people on the basis of race. By 1896, when my grandfather and his family reached Baltimore, the Court held in *Plessy v. Ferguson* that "separate but equal" accommodations were sufficient to ensure Negroes their constitutional rights. Alongside resurgent discrimination was also the pervasive violence of the period, the beatings, shootings, and lynchings that, the Tuskegee Institute estimates, took the lives of 4,730 Negroes between the early 1890s and 1951.[6] White southerners institutionalized lynching as a means of terrorizing, intimidating, and controlling Negroes after Reconstruction. Most lynchings involved hanging, but other victims were shot, burned at the stake, dismembered, castrated, or in other ways tortured to death. Racism was the major force behind most lynchings. These numbers cannot adequately capture the horrific acts of destroying so many human lives through racial hatred.

Such forces must have buffeted my grandfather, despite his light skin and the modest prosperity he had accumulated in Accomack and Baltimore. Better jobs and education for the children may have been even more powerful lures in his steady northward exodus. In Boston, then known as the Acropolis of American education, primary and secondary public schooling was available to people from all backgrounds and walks of life, a fact in which the city took great civic pride and which was by no means lost on Negroes who migrated there.

When my grandfather (along with his oldest brother Charles and younger brother Samuel) arrived in Boston in 1910, Negroes or "coloreds" numbered 13,564, some 2 percent of the population—though the census certainly missed many who were clandestinely blending among the majority. As in the South, there was undoubtedly prejudice, but the range of opportunities was decidedly wider in Boston. Moreover, my grandfather had accumulated some financial assets in Baltimore, and the fact that his brother, my great-uncle Charles, could immediately start a grocery store in Boston indicates that he had brought capital as well.

Only a year after settling in Boston, the William Whartons were struck by tragedy. On March 11, 1911, both Rosalind and my father's sister Enola died in a house fire that raised front-page headlines in the *Boston Globe*—"Two Women, a Girl and an Infant, Cut Off by Rapidly Spreading Midnight Flames."[7] My grandfather saved my father Clifton, then eleven, but he could not save his wife and daughter.

"Pop," as we grandchildren called him, never completely recovered from the calamity. He lost his ambition. Ever mild and pleasant, he always avoided any conversation about the fire, but you could feel his constant underlying pain. For the rest of his life he worked as a building superintendent in the Boston suburb of Alston.

. . . .

My father was undoubtedly aware of the accomplishments of his relatives, especially the Baltimore Whartons, such as his uncle Heber's family. Pop's working-class status didn't seem to have mattered to Dad, and he was an unfailingly dutiful son. But my father had an incredible intellect and a desire to prove himself in everything he undertook.

A few years after the fire my father enrolled in Boston's English High School. He took after his light-skinned father rather than his bronzed mother Roselind, with straight hair, thin lips, and a Hispanic or Spanish sort of complexion. For pocket money he worked as a hotel bellboy and for a time as a fishmonger, which explained his lifelong aversion to seafood. He learned to play piano and trumpet, and ran track at 600 yards. In June 1917 he graduated with honors and as battalion adjutant of the high school's Cadet Corps. He never spoke to me of any racial unpleasantness during his youth, though given his temperament he wouldn't have.

. . . .

Following a path that was not unusual at the time, Dad skipped a bachelor's degree program and enrolled directly in Boston University School of Law. I never was able to determine if my father knew that his white paternal grandfather, Louis C. H. Finney, was a graduate of Harvard Law School. If he had, this may explain my father becoming a lawyer. Both in high school and law school, he lived in the Back Bay, neighborhoods quite integrated at the time. He was one of two Negroes in a BU law class of eighty-eight—interestingly, there were six women. Since Pop could provide only modest help, my father took a part-time job as a hotel bellman and a full-time position as an evening elevator operator—the infrequency of nighttime passengers made it easy to study on the job.[8] He was on the swimming and boxing teams and was captain of the track team.

Two months after completing his LLB cum laude, he passed the Massachusetts bar, on September 24, 1920. His cum laude honor was due to outstanding grades. On exams he hardly ever received less than 85 percent, and in twenty-four courses his grades were 90 or higher; he even received a 99 in a bankruptcy class.[9] While in law school, my father joined the army during World War I. He served only three months and, when the war ended, was discharged without fighting abroad and returned to law school. I don't know whether he served in a segregated unit.

Both in high school and the university, I suspect that my father honed his lifelong practice of not denying his racial heritage, but not flaunting it as a flag or banner. Hence he moved easily in two worlds. At the turn of the century, Black fraternities were a newly emerging social institution at both Black and predominantly white colleges and universities. The first Black fraternity, Sigma Pi Phi, or "Boulé," was founded in 1904 and was followed over the next ten years by the creation of another five Black fraternities. In 1923, my father helped found and was the first president of the Boston Sigma Chapter of the national Negro fraternity Alpha Phi Alpha.[10] The chapter was composed of twenty-one Negro men then enrolled in major New England universities including the Massachusetts Institute of Technology, Boston University, Suffolk University, Tufts University, and Dartmouth College. Often the only Negroes on their campuses, they formed an elite group of their day—five of the fraternity brothers were studying medicine, four law, and two dentistry.

· · · ·

At BU my father met my mother, Harriette Mae Banks, born in Portsmouth, Virginia. Unlike the Whartons, she was dark-skinned, with tightly curled hair, a large nose, and strong features. She took after her father, Albert R. Banks, a large dark man who had played high school football in Virginia. I never met him, though years later I found that he and his brothers had operated a restaurant in Harlem until his death in 1939.

My maternal grandmother, Mary Magdalene Pratt, was born in 1882 in Edenton, North Carolina. She was light-skinned, what Negroes often call "high yellow," with wavy hair and sharp facial features—nose, chin, and forehead. Her most distinctive feature was her amber eyes, which could love you or cut you to the quick. She had married Albert when he was twenty-five and she was seventeen, but in 1905 she left him to move to Boston with Harriette and her younger brother Hubert. In Boston she worked for a while as a live-in cook in a white residence where she couldn't have her children with her. She first placed them in a children's home, then boarded them with a Negro family in nearby Medford.

In 1911 my grandmother legally divorced Albert Banks; a year later she married Thomas Hicks, a steward first class in the navy. "Pa," as the children were to call him, was a man of medium height, coffee-skinned, with a heavy mustache and a dour view of life. After the wedding, the new family of four settled at 96 Camden Street. Although Pa and my grandmother seemed always to be bickering, they remained married for fifty-one years, until he died in 1963.

"Nana," as all the grandkids later called her, was a disciplinarian. Woe unto any of us who scuffed our feet while walking. "Step smartly!" was a command that galvanized us all. In contrast, my mother was sweet and gentle. Slightly pigeon-toed at her right foot, my mother always walked as if tip-toeing. She was such a fine student that when she was about to graduate from Girls High School in June 1919, Elizabeth Richardson,[11] her white math teacher, urged my grandmother to send her to college—something rarely dreamed of at the time by women, Negro women especially. As a result, my mother applied and was admitted to BU. My grandmother, typically, pledged the needed financial support.

GRADUATION PHOTO, GIRLS HIGH SCHOOL, BOSTON, MA, JUNE 1919.

Left: My maternal grandmother, Mary Pratt Hicks's (b. November 4, 1882, d. October 10, 1968) first husband was Albert Banks. She later married Thomas Hicks. *Right*: My mother, Harriette Mae Banks (b. August 6, 1900, d. October 5, 1991), received a BA degree in chemistry from Boston University at the same 1923 commencement that my father received his LLM. She later earned a master's degree in social work from Simmons College.

My parents' courtship began during their college days. At BU my mother majored in chemistry. She was 5′6″, very thin, with straightened black hair worn slightly over the right side of her face. Dad was two inches taller, wiry but strong. He wore black horn-rimmed glasses and soon grew the thin triangular mustache that he would have for the rest of his life. Before long my father became a favorite of Nana's; his letters to her sounded like those of a loving son. In July 1923 my parents received their BU degrees in the same ceremony, a BS for my mother and an LLM for my father. My father proposed to my mother while they sat on the rock fence of a graveyard in Arlington.

In the final year of study for his first law degree, my father's torts class had been visited by the head of a small Boston law firm, who had magnanimously offered to consider for employment any of the students who later got over the hurdle of the Massachusetts bar. Two months later, my father didn't hesitate to show up at the surprised lawyer's door. After being hired, he began immediately to work on his second law degree.

Four years later, frustrated by a lack of advancement, my father decided to explore federal government employment. In 1924 he quit the law firm to become an examiner in the Veterans Bureau in Washington, D.C. But he also applied to the U.S. Department of State, and in August he was appointed a law clerk in the Consular Commercial Section at a salary of $1,860 per annum.[12] Meanwhile, Harriette had joined the faculty of Virginia Normal and Industrial Institute, a historically Black college that eventually became Virginia State University. Despite her degree in chemistry, she was assigned to teach Latin and French.

Perhaps Dad's new position was the catalyst. At any rate, the two eloped on September 11, 1924, to Providence, Rhode Island, where they were married.

My parents' courting and wedding caused comment within Boston's "colored" community. In a social space where skin color often determined standing, their union was so odd that an author wrote about it later in *American Mercury*:

> Clifton Wharton . . . resembles a Caucasian sufficiently to enable him to sleep above a Grand Goblin [i.e., Ku Klux Klan leader]. . . . "Of course, he's merely kidding her," the cream-colored feminine Bostonians told one another. "Boston's going to see a heart-broken brown baby when Clif drops her and takes one of us for his wife." But Clif married the brown lady. . . . In the last analysis, every explanation came back upon itself in the plaintive wail, "What *did* he see in her?"[13]

My mother must have been deeply pained. Still, she maintained an apparent equipoise. After all, *she* was the one my father had chosen.

At the time he joined the State Department my father was the first and only Negro professional in the entire headquarters. There were also three Black political appointees to overseas posts:[14] James Garneth Carter, U.S. postal clerk and newspaper manager, consul to Madagascar (1906); William J. Yerby, medical doctor, consul to Sierra Leone (1906); and James Weldon Johnson, songwriter,[15] educator, and poet, consul at Puerto Cabello, Venezuela, and later to Corinto, Nicaragua.[16] The only other Negro employees in the department were messengers and cleaners. Only once during my father's entire tour at State did a white fellow employee invite Dad to lunch. I learned this fact after his death—typical of my father's stoic courage in the face of racism.

Congress had just passed the Rogers Act, which aimed to make the Foreign Service appointments merit-based as well as to merge the politically appointed Diplomatic Service and the professional Consular Service into one. Along with 144 others, my father sat for the first examination after the act took effect. Twenty people qualified, my father among them. Under Secretary of State Joseph Grew wrote to a colleague that the twenty who had passed the test included "one negro, who will go at once to Liberia."[17]

There had been much resistance to Negroes and women entering officer levels of the State Department, and after the Rogers Act the executive committee of the Foreign Service

GRADUATED BEFORE HE ENTERED

The "Graduated Before He Entered" cartoon depicts the Foreign Service Institute denying my father admission after he was the first Negro to pass the Foreign Service examination.

Personnel Board even wrote a memo suggesting subterfuges to avoid the problem. Fortunately
Secretary of State Charles Evans Hughes disregarded it.

On March 25, 1925, President Coolidge named my father a foreign service officer, the first
person of his race to become a career American diplomat. The persistence of prejudice and
discrimination in the Foreign Service is dramatically demonstrated by the fact that between
1925 and 1945 not a single Black became a career foreign service officer. My father stood alone
for twenty-one years.

After my father became an official foreign service officer, the State Department declined
sending him to the newly created Foreign Service School, which all new appointees were supposed to attend for a year before going overseas. Instead, the department's faceless leadership
declared him the school's "first graduate," awarding a diploma without his ever attending a
class. On March 31 he was hurriedly named third secretary of the U.S. Legation (Embassy) in
Liberia. The justification for this obvious discrimination was that he was "urgently needed"
in the field.

The *Afro-American*, a Negro paper in Baltimore, pilloried the department for discrimination, pointing out that by excluding my father the school was able to stay "lily white."[18] Under
the headline "Graduated Before He Entered," an editorial cartoon showed my father knocking
on a schoolhouse door as someone inside tosses a diploma out the window, saying, "Here's
your diploma, and we have a ship waiting to take you to Liberia." The newspaper's role in the
controversy was not a coincidence since the Wharton and O'Neill families were well known
in the Baltimore Negro community as distinguished citizens and leaders.

• • • •

My father thus began without training in the art of everyday tasks of diplomacy. But the
department had badly underestimated his mettle. When informed, for example, that he and
my mother would go to Africa on a cargo ship offering only two primitive cabins, he told the
department that he didn't need the job that badly. Probably fearing further critical commentary
in the Baltimore *Afro-American*, the department abruptly reversed tack. On April 28, he and
my mother left the United States on the *Adriatic*, a White Star–Cunard liner headed for
Amsterdam by way of Liverpool and London.

My mother's diaries describe that first trip overseas in the mid-1920s. She soon discovered
that she wasn't a natural sailor—she got seasick at the slightest ship's roll. Other passengers
stared at the couple, undoubtedly because of their contrasting skin colors or because of
the rarity of well-dressed, educated, professional Blacks traveling abroad. Disembarked in
London, they visited Westminster Abbey, Parliament, and Big Ben, gawking at cars driving on
the left, buses with outside advertising, and the bizarre traffic "circuses." In the Netherlands
they took a train from Hook of Holland to Amsterdam, enjoying glimpses of the countryside
and daily life of the Dutch.

From Amsterdam they traveled down the European coast toward West Africa. In the

Canary Islands they stopped in Tenerife. Passing Las Palmas, they continued on; with binoculars they could see Dakar from the ship. After three days docked in Freetown, Sierra Leone, they steamed on and reached Monrovia on May 25, 1925.

▪ Liberia

The nation of Liberia originated with the American Colonization Society, founded in Washington, D.C., in 1816.[19] The Society's motives had been mixed. Some members genuinely sought a "natural" African home to which freed slaves could repatriate. Others hoped to avoid responsibility for free Negroes who might prove unable to fend for themselves. Still others wanted to forestall the horrors of "race mixing." In 1820 the Society's first shipload—eighty-eight men, women, and children—sailed from New York for the new land of liberty, hence "Liberia." Twenty-three died in the initial venture, along with two white "agents." Even so, by 1847 the country had solidified, declared nationhood, and adopted a U.S.-style constitution. U.S. emigration continued well after independence—as late as 1878, for example, 206 people arrived from Charleston, South Carolina.

Liberia is roughly the size of Pennsylvania. In the mid-1920s it had about two million people, of whom fifty or sixty thousand were so-called Americo-Liberians. Four hundred or so whites lived there, almost entirely in Monrovia (named for President Monroe of the United States). The bulk of the population consisted of indigenous tribes—eleven around Monrovia alone—and although the official language was English, the different tribal tongues made communication difficult in the hinterland. Most of the country was covered in forest and bush. The climate was mainly tropical, with heavy rains from April to November. The main export was rubber, while imports included cloth, tobacco, petroleum, galvanized iron sheets, and soap.

Monrovia was a relatively backward town, and living conditions could be difficult. There was a small ice plant and an electric plant. With only thirty or so cars and trucks in service few streets were paved, though the government was gradually installing curbs. There were no public waterworks or sewage facilities. Physicians were rare, there were no dentists, and only three poorly equipped hospitals served the entire country.

The U.S. minister, under whom my father would serve as secretary, was Dr. Solomon Porter Hood. My mother's diaries refer repeatedly to his chronic illnesses, which immediately settled an unusual amount of work and responsibility onto my father.

My mother threw herself eagerly into her first overseas post. She traveled to upriver villages and met dignitaries and their wives. She shopped at "Waterside," the local market, started French lessons, and read avidly during the sodden afternoons of the rainy season. In her diary she routinely tracked local health crises—food poisoning and heat prostration seemed

This picture was taken in Monrovia, Liberia, in March 1929, when I was two and a half years old.

to affect everybody at some time. But both my parents thrived on the exotic locale and the excitement of their new life and responsibilities.

From my mother's diaries it is clear that my mother was overjoyed at the prospect of a child. Although her pregnancy had been attended by a degree of malaise from the start, she had strenuously resisted having to return to the United States for my birth. On Easter she had come down with malaria. The doctor said she could remain in Monrovia provided she took quinine regularly. But her weakness persisted, and eventually both she and my father agreed that she should go home. She left Liberia in late June and after a brief stop in the Grenadines arrived in New York on July 16. The next day she took a train to Boston. There I was born on Monday, September 13, 1926, in the Lying-In Hospital just off Pasteur Avenue.

After a year in Boston, Mother went back with me to Monrovia. Overall, my hazy memories of our first two years there are of being happy and loved, my mother and father a warm, secure world unto themselves. My small circle was filled with Africans of many miens and hues.

Richelieu Morris, a playmate four months older, would become a lifelong friend. He was the son of an Americo-Liberian planter and an American mother Maud, whose father, Dr. Ernest Lyons, had been U.S. minister resident and consul general to Liberia in 1903. The Morrises belonged to a privileged group of American Negroes who had returned to the "motherland."

· · · ·

However idyllic in nostalgia's eye, in fact my Liberian infancy was full of threats. In the 1920s illness was a constant. Dysentery, boils, diarrhea, infections, mosquitoes, ticks, and leeches were facts of daily life. Both my parents contracted malaria, and they made me take bitter quinine pills as a precaution. Other hazards included snakes and dire insects. I still have a picture of myself in front of a fire-ant hill three times my height near our home.

My father's first assignment for the State Department was in Monrovia, Liberia. In February 1929, when this picture of my father, my mother, and me was taken, I was two years and five months old, and I had my own pith helmet.

In 1929, at least in part because of their growing concern for my future health and safety, my mother took me back to the United States once more. My father stayed behind, tending his duties and waiting for State Department action on his request for transfer to a better climate.

In Boston again we moved in with Nana and Pa Hicks in Roxbury, where red-brick houses lined Highland Street with a sedate and respectable air. Here Pa had used his navy separation pay to purchase a three-story apartment (No. 69) in a block of similar buildings. We lived in the second-floor flat, narrow and running straight from the front to the rear of the building. Above the street front were an alcove and living room. A corridor led back to the two bedrooms, then the dining room and kitchen. The entry, hallway, and stairs were dimly lit—Pa used low-watt bulbs to save money. Every Saturday he polished the brass street numbers and kick-plate on the front door, then scrubbed the white marble steps by hand.

The neighborhood was ethnically mixed, with mainly working-class and middle-income families—Irish, Italians, Poles, Scots, Swedes, Armenians, and several Jews. We had regular friendly contact and social interaction with several white families, and regularly rented to them the first-floor and third-floor apartments in Pa's building during these years.

I have an early memory of a Mrs. Hart, an elderly Irish lady who lived next door on the second floor. She would sit in her rocking chair and play peek-a-boo with me through the low slatted fence of her back porch, while I hid behind our own. Exacerbated by badly fitted false teeth, her thick Irish brogue was difficult for me to understand.

As I absorbed the curiosities and lore of the neighborhood, my father arrived home from Liberia. In March 1930 we went down to Washington so he could lobby in person for a better post. At three-and-a-half years, I was as yet oblivious to segregation, but Washington was very much a southern town, with few hotels for Negroes. We stayed with Ed and Jo Simmons, friends of my father. Ed was a messenger in the State Department, where he and Dad had met in the nonwhite cafeteria.

In Washington, D.C., I met my great-great-uncle Frazier Wharton, who was visiting some of his children there. He was the richest and largest landowner of the Accomack Whartons; my great-grandmother Maria was his older sister. When I was introduced, he called me over for a hug and noticed that my lips were chapped. To my astonishment, he pulled a small jar of Vaseline from his pocket and rubbed the ointment over my mouth, saying to my father, "Clif, what are you *doing* to this fine boy?"

There was a lot of wrangling over my father's next job. The department first suggested Calais, France, which sounded promising. Then they back-pedaled to Martinique, where Negroes had served already. My father insisted on somewhere more temperate. Finally the department agreed to name him vice consul to the Canary Islands, Spain.

While Dad headed overseas again to take up his duties in Las Palmas, Gran Canaria, I started kindergarten at the Nathan Hale School on Cedar Street back in Boston.[20] My first teacher was Miss Cecilia Tishler, a rather plain but dedicated and caring woman. I found that

This picture of my mother and me, age three years and seven months, was taken in Washington, D.C., on April 19, 1930, around the time of my father's departure to his new post as U.S. consul in Las Palmas, Canary Islands, Spain.

I loved both being with other children and doing the assigned work. When I brought home a drawing, a modeled Plasticine (clay) figure, or a tracing of the alphabet, my mother's delight was palpable, and her unfailing admiration always spurred me on for the next day's class. High expectations were common among Black families (as among many immigrant groups as well), and I suspect the intensity was even greater because both my mother and father were college graduates. In any event, being praised both at home and at school was critical to my early upbringing, a precious gift from my teachers and my parents alike. Decades later, my mother remarked to a reporter that seeking and trying to live up to her approval was a pattern I had followed throughout my life.[21]

At Christmas my first sled was an old one my step-grandfather Pa found in the basement. I remember asking Mother why the hardpack snow squeaked when you walked on it, and why it smelled different when it was very, very cold. But the days of modeling clay and buckled galoshes weren't to last long. After only four months in kindergarten, I left with my mother in January 1931 to rejoin my father in the Canary Islands.

Canary Islands, Spain

The seven islands making up the Canaries are in the Atlantic along the Tropic of Cancer, about seventy miles northwest of the African coast. My first glimpse there of my father was around midnight, when he rode out in a small pilot boat to meet our passenger steamer. Caught in a floodlight, he wore a tan suit and a white straw hat. As I peered over the ship's rail, my mother exclaimed, "Clifton, that's your father!"

Was it really? I couldn't remember his face. He had to be important, though. The ship was not due to tie up until the next morning, but my father was determined to greet us immediately and take us home. Passengers stared as the captain welcomed him aboard. With everyone buzzing, he hugged and kissed my mother, then swung me exuberantly aloft. When he beamed up at me I recalled that his two front teeth overlapped and had serrated edges, and for some reason the sight instantly assured me that this was indeed my dad.

The home on Paseo Madrid to which he took us was newly constructed in what was then the sparsely settled Ciudad Jardin, between the port and downtown Las Palmas. Nearby, the Parque Doramba contained a lovely old wooden hotel, the Santa Catalina. Our own house was Moorish in flavor, two and a half stories of off-white stucco walls, with a foyer of crushed terrazzo. On the first floor were a living area, a large dining room, a smaller dining or playroom, and kitchen. Upstairs were several bedrooms, including mine, as well as front and side verandas. The top floor offered a sweeping view of the ocean; below, lush gardens crowded the house on three sides, bright with red geraniums.

My mother had shipped some western-style chairs and ottomans from home. Otherwise the furniture was local, including hand-carved folding end tables and ornate carpets bought from the itinerant Moors and Asian Indians who regularly visited the islands. There was a piano at the rear of the hall, and in the living room hung two Italian wall tapestries: *Venice* showed an aristocratic family beside a canal, while *Hunting* depicted an Arab horseman with a rifle.

For more than a decade this was to be our home.

. . . .

Las Palmas is at the northeast tip of Gran Canaria. El Puerto de la Luz, where we had landed, was due east of the city. Of volcanic origin, all the islands boast looming cliffs and spectacular beaches. One island, Lanzarote, is famed for its otherworldly lava-scapes. Daily high temperatures ranged from the low seventies in January to mid-eighties in August, with winter lows rarely falling into the fifties. Swimming was possible almost year around. Occasionally sirocco winds blew sand and dust out from the mainland, but the haze usually cleared by afternoon.

The islands had a rich history—an indigenous neolithic race of blond and blue-eyed seven-foot giants named *Guanches* who lived in small caves and refused to surrender, so eventually were extinguished by the conquering Spaniards; a peoples who developed a whistle language *silbo* enabling them to communicate from the mountain of one island to the next; and the last port of departure for Columbus on his 1492 voyage to discover the new world—America!

In the 1930s the Canary Islands had an export-driven economy heavily dependent on tourism—English, Germans, and a few Scandinavians. The major exports were bananas, tomatoes, and a red dye made from cochineal, a small red insect that grows on the leaves of a prickly pear cactus, and used for lipstick. Because of its accommodating large harbor, Las Palmas had a natural advantage. It operated virtually as a free port, attractive for transshipments. As a result the city had become more cosmopolitan than the other islands.

The community into which my mother and I were now introduced included a number of foreigners, mostly diplomats and businessmen, but the majority of residents were Spanish-speaking *Canarios*. My first friend was Ignacio Rivero y Noble, whose family lived just across the street from us. Owners of a large wholesale dry goods store, they were among the city's wealthy elite. Ignacio was the youngest of seven children, six of them boys. Soon we were "Ignacito" and "Clestoncito," the diminutive endings a mark of our closeness. Through Ignacio I soon met other boys in the neighborhood. We were in and out of each other's houses constantly, like a single large family. Our play seemed to involve mostly toy soldiers, tricycles, wagons, and carts. To Ignacio and the boys I was at first considered strange. "All that American stuff sounded to us like the moon," Ignacio would recount to me many years later. For example, "New York City . . . was a hundred times larger than Las Palmas, or a thousand times larger. . . . You would tell us, and we'd tell you it was a lie. . . . This Coca-Cola thing . . . At the beginning I think we didn't like it very much, but later we would spend the whole day trying to go over to your house to get some . . . Coca-Cola."[22]

My parents' social life seemed a constant stream of visits, teas, and dinners; there were endless occasions for diplomats to entertain the locals, and vice versa. Mother and Dad seemed to be in formalwear every other evening. Bridge and other parties were regular fare at the Club Nautico or the nearby Hotel Metropole. I always told my mother she would be the most beautiful of the guests, and my father would be most *guapo* (handsome).

In the early years both my parents studied Spanish. Mother studied French as well, becoming quite proficient and joining the Alliance Française. My own Spanish was soon effortless, with no American accent. Thus I became fully bilingual.

. . . .

The island was strongly Roman Catholic, though my parents and I attended the Episcopal Holy Trinity Church founded by British residents in 1897. Apparently I went to Sunday school, though I don't remember it. I do recall uncomfortable Sunday clothes and the sonorous drone of the interminable sermons. I rarely listened past the first five minutes. Once, though, the chaplain was enlarging on "redemption," a big word for me at the time. As he spoke I began to wonder what I might have done so sinful that "redemption" might be called for. In town, the Catholic faithful sometimes paraded *La Virgen de la Candelaria* over carpets of flower petals through the streets—interestingly, a Black Madonna. Why was she black? I wondered. Did it make her special to her celebrants? Was there some mystery or secret to her blackness? Was I supposed to have some special bond with her?

A particularly vivid rite was the annual procession of the *penetentes*, who crawled on their knees from the mountain town of Teror several miles down to La Iglesia del Pino in the city. By the time they reached Las Palmas most were raw and bloody about the knees, an appalling sight. Did God think it was good for people to hurt themselves? I asked Mother. She explained that the ritual was the penitents' way of proving their devotion, though she didn't sound entirely convinced, herself. It was the first serious nagging I felt about some elements of organized religion that would bother me increasingly as I got older.

Sometimes my father drove our Willys-Overland sedan into the mountains for picnics, creeping around hairpin curves up the steep sides of extinct volcanoes. We also loved the beaches, like the spectacular Playa de las Canteras. Usually we went with a crowd of friends, carrying huge baskets of food and drink. The Argentine consul DeGamas family were regulars, as well as the local Dominguez family—Juan was one of my father's closest comrades. He had a daughter nicknamed Pepa, who annoyed me by constantly following me around. One day at the beach my father tucked me into one arm and swam out into the surf. I couldn't swim, and the waves looked cold and enormous, but Dad asked me to trust him. It seemed as if he swam with me forever. By the time we started back, my mother was standing like a tiny doll a foot or two into the sandy foam. She was shaking, and her face was furious. What had he been thinking of? she shouted. Taken aback, my father reminded her that he was an accomplished swimmer. What if you'd gotten a cramp? she shot back. What if there had been a riptide?

Despite the argument, I always remembered how secure it felt to place my complete trust in my father's love.

Although I didn't know it at the time, the years 1931–36 would be my longest continuous stay with my father, and his presence filled me like a vessel. Most of the time Dad was a jovial figure, full of fun. He loved to horse around, and his intelligence and quick wit made him a wonderful companion. He was a very loving father, with me as well as my siblings yet to come.

Evenings he smoked a pipe, had a gin and bitters before dinner, and often helped me practice reciting a poem—"recitation" was important in a child's deportment in the era, especially with guests. He played the piano quite well, always ending with "Danny Boy," which he sang with a mournful feeling. I asked him several times why he liked such a sad song, but he never really answered.

Although he played tennis desultorily, golf became his passion. In the tweed plus fours of the day, he played at the course on the hill at the end of Paseo Madrid almost daily, with Juan Dominguez or diplomatic colleagues, followed by lunch and a siesta. Occasionally he took me along, and he even bought me a miniature club, though I never really took to the game.

He entered tournaments regularly. Once he was a finalist for the "Bagan Cup," recorded for posterity with many photographs.

As U.S. consul, Dad supervised a broad range of activities, from providing commercial liaison, to issuing American entry visas, to rounding up errant sailors who had jumped ship. He also greeted distinguished visitors. There weren't a lot, actually, with two notable exceptions. In early 1931 playwright Eugene O'Neill and his wife Carlotta spent three months in Las Palmas while he put the finishing touches on *Mourning Becomes Electra*. And in late 1933 Charles and Anne Lindbergh showed up. Still a celebrity six years after his historic transatlantic solo, Lindbergh was flying down the European coast and into Africa in a modified Lockheed Sirius named *Tingmissartog*. His wife had traveled separately to meet him on Gran Canaria, where the famous visitors captivated the capital. Anne Lindbergh was reserved and quiet. When they stopped by our home for an hour, one of the maids brought in my seven-month-old brother William. Mrs. Lindbergh shyly asked if she could hold him, and as she took him she started silently to cry. My parents pointedly didn't notice. After they left I asked Mother what was wrong. She explained that the Lindberghs' twenty-month-old baby had been kidnapped the year before and was presumed murdered.

My father taught me discipline and respect for others. One day I decided to ride my toy automobile in the street to avoid the cement sidewalks with small squares, which were very bumpy. There was hardly any traffic, but a local Guardia Civil came along and told me to get back on the sidewalk. He couldn't make me, I told him arrogantly. *Soy hijo del consul americano!*

My father overheard, and called me inside. "Clifton," he said, "I'm glad you're proud of me and my position. But you don't have the right to ignore the laws of this country, or to treat anyone here with disrespect. I don't care whether it is that police officer or Augustin the gardener, someone rich like the Riveros or poor like the beggar who comes to the gate every day. They're all human beings, just like you."

Dad could be hard sometimes. He took me to my first bullfight, in an open amphitheater half a mile from our home. He tried to explain the niceties of the "sport," but the more the blood spurted, the more upset I got. When I slumped down, covered my eyes, and fought back tears, Dad upbraided me intensely. Did I want to be a sissy? he demanded. When the second bull came out, I forced myself to watch. By the third bull, I was cheering the matador just like the Spanish fans all around us.

. . . .

My mother's discipline pattern was explaining to me what I had done that was wrong, followed by punishment that ranged from sitting in the corner to a day without friends or toys. One of my early failings was a tendency to tell white lies. My mother said that I should always tell the truth, even when it hurts. "Telling lies," she told me, "is like hammering a nail in a piece of wood." She then got a piece of wood, hammered a nail into it, and then took the nail out, leaving a hole. "Clifton, you can repent the lie, which is pulling out the nail, but the hole will always be there in the wood. So don't lie in the first place." I took this seriously to heart. Then came the watch incident.

When I was five my grandmother Nana's Christmas gift was a beautiful wristwatch from Boston's Waltham Watch Company, where she was then working. It was my pride and joy, but Dad insisted that it should be wound by an adult to avoid my breaking it. Yet one day it stopped. Dad asked me if I had tried to wind it, and I said no—repeatedly. Angry with my persistent denials, he decided that a strap was the only way to teach me to tell the truth. He took me into my room, closed the door, and whipped me with an old belt until I screamed and cried. Then he left me alone, sobbing.

That evening our cook Maria returned from her day off. When she found me confined to my room and denied dinner, she asked my parents what I had done. Told, she instantly confessed that she was the one who had accidentally overwound the watch.

My father never physically punished me again.

Even if he had, I doubt it would have mattered. I had come to love him deeply—and also to admire him. Brilliance, determination, and drive shot through his personality like seams of bright ore. And even at my age I was vaguely aware that his position in Las Palmas represented some sort of pioneering or breakthrough.

· · · ·

It was my mother, though, who was the dominant force in my education. For her, learning was the foundation for everything—what you could achieve, the life you would lead. Having taught in college, she decided to tutor me herself—there was really little choice, since there were then no American or international schools in Gran Canaria (or elsewhere). (Though I had become perfectly fluent in Spanish, my parents didn't want to enroll me in the local schools because they were run by Catholic orders.) So when I was four and a half years old, Mother took on the task of teaching me reading, writing, and arithmetic. She also began teaching me to play the piano.

I loved books—especially J. H. Stickney's edition of *Aesop's Fables* and James Baldwin's *Old Greek Stories*, the latter with its rich gray cloth cover and vivid red lettering. One day, reading aloud the myth of Perseus, I struggled with a difficult passage. "Clifton," my mother suggested, "don't read with your ear. Read with your eye—and see them." Huh? I thought. But I looked down at the words on the page and tried to see them as images in my mind. For a second it was just a blank screen—then the picture was suddenly and fully there: the Medusa's writhing serpent locks, the desperate hero, the shield's reflecting mirror, the hissing sweep of the sword. From then on reading was altogether different, a passionate and consuming joy.

Mathematics, not so much. With numbers my difficulty was stony. Mother tried to get me to picture numbers in my head just as I had with words. But how could I? Words transformed themselves into images effortlessly, but numbers were just . . . numbers. It was easy to turn "chair" into the thing at the dinner table, or "running" into what I liked to do along the tide line at the beach. But a number? I couldn't *see* it. One day in desperation Mother said, "Clifton, look at the clock." On the wall was a large banjo clock ringed by Arabic numerals from one to twelve—but that made things more frustrating yet. From one to twelve, fine—but what came after that?

At age five and a half I just couldn't get hold of the problem, much less explain it to my mother. Finally, though, I solved it on my own. Mentally I "broke open" the clock into a progressive series of half-circles, each containing a decanal digit group (that is, one to ten, eleven to twenty, twenty-one to thirty, and so on), with each group of numbers arrayed in the lower half of the loop. I still see any long series of numbers under one hundred as decanal digit loops. Had anyone else come up with such a bizarre idea, much less actually made use of it? Even today, I barely understand it myself.

Mother also enrolled me in French classes taught by an émigré family of White Russians, the De Reschos. At first the daughter Gabrielle taught me at home. Later I took group lessons at their house. I learned enough French for simple conversations. A couple of my neighborhood Spanish buddies also attended, which made it more fun.

· · · ·

When I was six Mother signed me up for the famous Calvert Correspondence School. Based in Baltimore, the Calvert program was widely used by the children of U.S. diplomats abroad, but it was an awkward tool. With no commercial airmail, the lessons and exams took two weeks to travel by ship from America to the Canaries. Once they were in my hands, I read the books, did the assignments, and took the tests, which then went back to Baltimore to be graded and corrected—still more weeks to get the results and new materials.

A lot depended on the quality of the tutor at home. Luckily, my mother had taught at the college level and was a natural. Even so, my first Calvert report wasn't particularly glowing. An example was my low grade in composition. "[Your essay] was a disappointment," Ms. Bassett, my Calvert teacher, wrote. "You started out beautifully, but your first sentence was the only good one. I do not see how you could have spent forty-five minutes in writing those four sentences. . . . I want you to rewrite the story. . . . I want you to do justice to yourself and to show me that you can turn out a very much better story of *Sleeping Beauty* than you did."

My problem? My young brain was puzzled by the term "essay." I thought that since the story was already written, how could you write about *Sleeping Beauty* without writing it exactly the same way over again? In my frustration I had written the five sentences that drew my teacher's scorn. Eventually, I rewrote the essay and received her approval.

But then from grading period to grading period, I worked doggedly and saw steady improvement. By grade 3 my absentee teacher in Baltimore, a woman named Mildred Phillips, called me a "capable and ambitious pupil"—it may have made me a little cocky about my burgeoning academic prowess.

Thus were laid the early foundations of my education. In retrospect it seems quaint and

This picture, taken at age six and a half, shows me driving my 1932 Christmas present, a pedal automobile, in the garden of our home on Paseo Madrid, Las Palmas.

haphazard, if not a bit dubious. But I had the priceless example of two rigorously educated, high-achieving parents before me. And I equated successful learning with pleasing my mother, recoiling from her scowl when I didn't.

· · · ·

I don't recall much racism in the Canaries. Swarthy skins were common among Spaniards, and the Moors who occasionally visited the islands were treated with deference as former rulers.[23] When we first arrived in Las Palmas, in fact, my mother's darker complexion caused many people to mistake her for a Moor.

There was some racially based tension between my parents in the year we arrived in Las Palmas. With his own light skin, my father had been vocally uneasy about the potential for discrimination against my mother, and she was wounded by what she called his "complex." As so many *Canarios* became her close friends, his uneasiness apparently abated. No one ever mentioned the problem in my presence, and I learned of it from my mother's diaries only decades later, after she died. In public and in private, Mother adored my father and supported him wholeheartedly. As far as I could see, he felt and behaved toward her exactly the same way.

My mother strongly embraced our Negro heritage, to the point of systematically stressing the role and contributions of Black figures in the history lessons she taught me. From her I learned about Hannibal, the ancient African kingdoms of Ghana, Mali, and Songhay, and in the United States about Frederick Douglass, W. E. B. Du Bois, George Washington Carver, Benjamin Banneker, Booker T. Washington, and Mary McLeod Bethune. All were skillfully meshed into my lessons wherever she felt it appropriate. One day she even spoke proudly of the pioneering of my father, and my heart burst to think that he had made history. Thus, for me, American Negroes were an unquestioned, important, long-standing part of the United States from its very beginning and had made tremendous contributions throughout its history.

. . . .

Mother wanted more children desperately, and after two miscarriages, a third try proved successful. As she reached term in May 1933, all the women in Las Palmas seemed to be camped in our house, knitting baby clothes and festooning the waiting crib. When she went into labor Mother dispatched me up the street to visit neighbors. Attended by a Spanish doctor and an English nurse, she had to act as interpreter during the delivery.

William Bowman Wharton 2nd was born around noon May 7. When word came that I had a new baby brother, I rushed back to see him. "Mother," I cried, "his face is all red!" And so it was, under a scalp covered with flossy straight blond hair. My father later traced Bill's ruddiness to his paternal grandmother's Native American lineage. To this day, Bill always tans to red-bronze.

At that time, I was only vaguely aware of the looming political storm in Spain, although there had been some work stoppages and other minor disturbances. The *Rojos*, Communists and anarchists, waved red flags, and the rightist *Falangistas* waved blue ones—both groups were big on loud songs and street chants. Even at a remove from the mainland, the atmosphere in Las Palmas was taut. My father advised me to watch what I said at mealtimes—he suspected that a couple of our servants might be spying for one side or the other. "It's never a good idea to treat people as if they aren't there," he remarked. At my age it wasn't so much a life lesson as a conjuration of melodrama. I felt like I was living in a spy movie.

My friend Ignacio's family sometimes took me on holiday to one of their country farms, where I milked a cow for the first time and rode on the back of a young bull. I loved the hearty, rustic fare of homemade *chorizos*, sweet cakes, and cheese. One day Julio Gomez Carlos, another young houseguest, joined me in stomping grapes for wine with our bare feet. Ignacio had a cold and wasn't allowed to help, so he stood outside, crying.

It was during a visit to the Riveros' *finca* (farm) that I first had difficulty with my breathing. The adults thought my wheezing might be caused by something I ate—in fact it was my first attack of asthma. Back home, my parents wrung their hands and tried a string of remedies without success. The cook Maria recommended upending glasses full of flaming alcohol onto my chest—they were supposed to suck the illness from my lungs. Eventually a doctor suggested I try smoking menthol cigarettes. When Ignacio, Luis, and Julio came round to see me, I puffed like a veteran, blew smoke from my nose, and tried to make smoke rings—childhood one-upmanship at its best! But my parents fretted and thought I should see an asthma bronchial specialist on our next return to the United States.

The opportunity came sooner than expected. Near year-end Mother found that she was expecting again, and this time she wanted the birth to take place in Boston. My father agreed, arranging home leave for all four of us via the *Magallanes* out of Cadiz, Portugal, scheduled to arrive in New York on December 3, 1934. Our family did not take regular "home leave" tours as is now done by foreign service officers because in those days, the officer had to pay for his and his family's travel from his own pocket (in our case with help from mother-in-law Nana). In retrospect, I was amazed that despite the Great Depression, Nana had continued her position at the Waltham Watch company, giving her financial resources.

As always, my mother got seasick immediately on setting foot on the ship. The voyage was even worse than usual because of her pregnancy, and she remained in bed throughout much of our crossing.

For myself, I still loved being on the ocean. No color was so glorious as the iridescent green of the sea, and I spent hours gazing down at the pounding bow wave, or from the stern as the hidden propeller churned yellow-white foam behind. From time to time I had to tend my toddler brother William. Once while in port, with my mother recovering in a deck chair, he eventually got away from me. When I heard him crying inside a compartment, I raced for the door, tripped, and sprawled across the threshold. My forehead struck the metal strip along the raised base of the doorway, which cut the arch of my nose and my right eyebrow to the bone. Miraculously, a doctor was sitting nearby, who rushed me to the ship's infirmary, where my wound took thirty stitches. Afterward the doctor wrapped my entire face so that I looked like a wounded soldier or an Egyptian mummy. My head ached for several days, but I was still happy to be at sea and was sad when we finally docked in New York.

After we reached Boston, Dad scouted around and rented the second half of a duplex on Highland Avenue, just around the corner from my grandmother Nana and her husband Pa. The owner apparently didn't recognize my father as a Negro; when we came to move in and she saw my mother, she tried to refuse us entry. There was a lot of bluster, the owner proclaiming over and over that she didn't rent to Negroes. But a contract had been signed, and Dad had been a practicing attorney. When he icily ran through the possible consequences of breaking the deal, the owner bitterly backed down. We moved our trunks off the sidewalk and into our new temporary home.

. . . .

Almost as soon as we had unpacked, Mother hustled me right into school—I was downcast but hardly surprised. She took me back to Nathan Hale, where my placement scores created confusion: I read at sixth-grade level, with fifth-grade proficiency in history and geography, fourth-grade spelling, and third-grade arithmetic. Ms. E. K. Kennedy, acting principal and fourth-grade teacher, placed me temporarily into her fourth grade, while I took third-grade math to catch up—which I did. I ended up a year ahead of where I would have been normally, and afterward I was almost always the youngest student in my classes.

At Nathan Hale I got my first personal dose of race prejudice. During English class Ms. Kennedy asked me to read in front of the class—she knew it was my forte, and she wanted to put me at ease among the other students. Afterward, during recess, a white boy came up to me and said, "You think you're smart, don't you? But you're still just a nigger!"

I hadn't heard the word before, but its meaning was obvious—and I knew it was no compliment. When I reported it to Mother, she sat me down, held my hand, and said solemnly, "Clifton, this is the way some people try to put you in a box and label you inferior. Don't let them do it. Be proud that you are a Negro, and never see yourself only as a Negro or as inferior because of it. Be proud of *everything* you are!"

It was the first time I realized that for many people being Black was somehow less than being white. But my mother's forceful admonition provided an early and powerful immunization against the insidious virus.

· · · ·

In Roxbury, I got to know for the first time my three Banks cousins, children of my mother's brother Hubert—June, the eldest; Mary Ellen whom everyone swore was my grandmother's twin; and Hubert Reginald Jr., called Sonny. Usually we saw each other on Sunday after church, when we went to Nana's to read the newspaper comics and feast at her table groaning with delicious food. Dinners were as memorable for the discipline as for the food—"Sit up straight!" Nana would bark. "Keep your elbows off the table!" Out of her earshot we echoed her commands laughingly: "Step lively! Stop scuffling!"

Our step-grandfather Pa had some eccentricities of his own, and they sparked even greater hilarity. He was always unplugging the radio and lamps, unshakably convinced that they continued using electricity even when they were turned off. Also, you had to make a high court pleading to use the party-line telephone.

Pa's pride and joy was his new black Plymouth, which he washed and polished religiously every Saturday. He hated to get caught driving it in the rain, and when he did he rushed it back into the garage, where he wiped it dry from top to bottom. After church on Sunday he sometimes drove us out into the country, or to visit friends in Providence or West Medford. But he never learned to use the clutch! Starting out in first gear, he would jam into second and third with a great metallic clashing, while the car bucked down the street like a bronco. Even worse was his creeping around turns without downshifting, stalling, shaking, and holding up traffic behind. Nana's agitated remonstrances were the very embodiment of the phrase "backseat" driving, while we children squeezed shut our eyes and held our sides to avoid bursting into gales of laughter.

Living around the corner from Nana and Pa, I often came into contact with three Negro families who lived next door to them: the Garrett-Ridgely boys, who used to escort me to kindergarten, the Branches, and the Forsythes. The Forsythes had a son George who befriended me, introducing me to street and back-lot games. George had a mild stutter and wore glasses, which made him the object of frequent teasing by the other kids. To him and the rest of the neighborhood, apparently, my exotic background made me quite an oddity. "You were strange," George told me much later. "You spoke all these languages and had lived in foreign countries. The other kids would listen on the radio to Buck Rogers, or Amos and Andy, or Bobby Benson and the 'H-Bar-O Ranch.' You'd go into the house to listen to Lowell Thomas [news broadcasts]." When Forsythe became a successful reporter for the *Boston Traveler* and Boston's TV Channel 5, he realized that Mother was giving me preparation in current events.[24]

One afternoon Mother took me over to a branch of the Boston Public Library at nearby 47 Millmont Street for my first library card. After the librarian showed me how to fill out a book request slip, she asked had I ever read the sea stories of Nordoff and Hall? When I said I hadn't, she had me check out my first book, *Mutiny on the Bounty*. I was hooked. From then on, I regularly visited the library, bringing back one Nordoff and Hall sea adventure and checking out another. It was all a great delight. More significantly, it opened up for me the workings and joys of a library.

Shortly after starting school, I went to the Lahey Clinic for a full assessment of my asthma problems. Allergy tests were done on the skin of my arm, but all that showed up were the usual sensitivities to dust and mold. Strangely, in the United States I had had no attacks at all. The doctors told my parents it must be some childhood malady that I would probably outgrow.

My second brother, Richard Gilbert Wharton, was born June 16, 1935, a fat happy baby we all loved. There were now three sons, though my mother still longed for a daughter.

In October I entered the fifth grade at a new institution, the Dudley School, where my mother mortified me by sending me off in knickers. After a teacher-parent conference during which she saw that none of the other boys wore them, she relented and bought me long pants.

From Dudley I remember mainly my problems in penmanship, taught there by the old Palmer method that required practicing "push-pulls" and "ovals" with a squib pen and inkwell. You had to hold your hand stiffly and write with your forearm, making slanted lines or overlapping concentric circles. I must have scratched and ripped my way through a dozen reams of paper, but though I finally made the honor role for the regular subjects, I never won any prizes in penmanship.

By early 1936, at any rate, our leave was nearly over, and it was time for us to return to the Canary Islands. This time my grandmother Nana, who had never before been abroad, decided to come along for a visit.

Her arrival in Las Palmas made a great excuse for our friends to give parties. There were picnics, *paellas*, and *bailes* (dances) almost every other day. I had never seen my grandmother so carefree. She had been like this as a young woman, Mother confided, before the divorce. Now Nana was suddenly charming, full of fun, and though she could not speak a word of

Spanish she managed to banter with the women and flirt mercilessly with the men. Everyone loved her. "Why couldn't she couldn't stay on indefinitely?" they wanted to know.

. . . .

Meanwhile, the Canaries remained embroiled in the escalating warfare between the "Reds" and the "Blues"—in a matter of weeks the Spanish Civil War would begin. Truckloads of partisans careened around Las Palmas, brandishing standards and sometimes rifles. The election of the socialist-leaning Popular Front had split both Spain and her islands. Franco had made one unsuccessful try at breaking his troops out of North Africa; soon he would try again. In mid-July Emilio Mola led a group of generals, including Franco, in issuing the Navarro proclamation, the start of a coup against the Spanish president, Manuel Azana. Franco flew to Morocco to take over the Army of Africa and launch an attack on Spain's southern flank. By September he commanded the Nationalist Army and had become "chief of state." Russia was supporting the Republicans, but Franco was backed by fascist Germany and Italy. Spain's bloody civil strife was becoming the training ground for the opposing forces that would eventually fight the Second World War.

Of such matters I knew hardly anything, but actual dangers were encroaching. One evening a year later my parents were tending William, in bed with an earache. Just as they bent to comfort him, a stream of bullets stitched the wall above his headboard. But for that providential leaning down, my brothers and I might have been orphaned. The next morning they could clearly see the machine gun nest in an open field across Paseo Madrid.

It was time for Nana to return home, and as my bronchial attacks had returned with a vengeance, my parents decided to send me back to Boston with her. Undoubtedly more than my health was at stake. My parents felt I had reached the point of needing more than Calvert's correspondence training. Already some of my local friends who were offspring of expatriates were being sent back to attend school in their home countries. My parents wanted me to go to a regular school, too. And to become, perhaps, "more American."

Nana had never traveled before and suspected she might not again, so she wanted to visit Paris on the way back. She spoke no French, but I was fluent enough for ordinary matters. We landed in Dieppe on June 22 and took the train to Paris. A syndicalist strike was on throughout France, so the hotels had no maids or porters, and the dining rooms were closed. We had to eat in restaurants. For two days, meal after meal, I perused the menus intently, paused thoughtfully, then ordered the same thing—lobster! My favorite.

"Clifton," Nana said finally with a sigh, "I see people at the next table eating a very attractive chicken. Today you will please ask for *that*."

For the rest of the voyage we maintained a restrained truce.

In my first ten years, I crossed the Atlantic Ocean six times, often changing ships mid-course. Whenever I boarded a ship, even before it left port, I always examined it from top to bottom. Because I was a child, all the sailors, seamen, and officers indulged me. On most ships I even went down into the boiler and engine rooms and up to the bridge, areas normally forbidden to passengers. From my ship tours, I quickly got to know the entire crew and where everything was on board. In retrospect, I believe this propensity of fully examining any new "territory" or situation to know it as well as possible at the outset spawned my similar adult practice.

▪ Boston

When we got back to Boston I couldn't for the moment stay with my grandmother, because my cousin June Banks was already sharing her home. Instead I went to board with Mr. and Mrs. William Roper. Lottie Roper had been in the same classes with my father from the second to the eighth grade. She was one of my mother's best friends and one of the few people she would trust to care for me. Much to their sadness, the Ropers had been unable to have children.

It was my first time away from both of my parents for an extended period, but I wasn't especially lonely or homesick. I didn't even "write home" very often—certainly less frequently than my parents wrote to me. In retrospect, I think that I was always a secure child and my absent mother encouraged me—she always addressed her letters to me "My Dear Little Man." This was a proud emblem.

· · · ·

In August 1936 my paternal grandfather, "Pop" Wharton, invited me to join him in a visit to the Wharton family homestead in Accomack County, Virginia. The trip was the result of my persistent curiosity about my Wharton forebears. As a ten-year-old I had a highly inquisitive nature and had kept asking my grandfather to tell me about my Wharton ancestry. Before the trip he finally described some of my family ancestry, and my father subsequently corroborated all these facts.

My grandfather had previously told me that his great-grandfather was Peter Wharton, a "free Negro" who lived most of his life in Accomack. (The 1860 Accomack County mortality list showed that one-third of the Negroes who died that year were free.) Pop then repeated that Peter's father was John Wharton 3rd, who built the Wharton mansion described in the photographic article that my father had sent to me. According to my grandfather, Peter Wharton bought his daughter, my great-great-grandmother Tabitha, out of slavery. My grandfather's discussion tried to skirt the fact that the fathers of both Tabitha's and her daughter Maria's children were white men,[25] but that both women and their children kept the Wharton name, a not unusual practice during racial miscegenation laws in that era.

Dr. Dan Wharton's genealogical research uncovered documentation correcting my grandfather's oral history. Peter's wife, Sarah, and their two daughters, Tabitha and "Easter"

(Hester), had lived next to the Whartons on the plantation of William Drummond Cropper (b. 1776, d. 1834). All three women had been freed in 1829 not by purchase or will but by deed of manumission. The freedom of Sarah and her daughters could have easily been via Peter's efforts at buying them while he himself was still a slave of Elizabeth Williams Wharton.

During slavery throughout the South Negro children were often the offspring of master-slave relationships. Such miscegenation also took place between white men and free Black women even before Emancipation. The racial tinctures of the resulting "coloreds" ranged from almost pure white to yellow, ivory, tan, beige, mocha, brown, and black. Before the war, those with paler skin tones often had better treatment and more opportunities as "house servants," in some cases even passing into the world of whites themselves. In post–Civil War years, miscegenation hardly abated, and white men often kept Negro women outside of marriage.

My "free" great-grandmother Maria was a striking golden-hued woman with an oval face, aquiline nose, deep-set brown eyes, and auburn hair. She had at least two white men in her life, who fathered my grandfather, great uncles, and great aunts.

According to Pop, his white father (my great-grandfather) was L. C. H. "Louis" Finney, born in January 20, 1822, a wealthy attorney-at-law who lived in St. Georges Parish in Accomack County. I later learned that Finney received his A.B. from Washington College in Pennsylvania[26] in 1841 and graduated with an LLB from Harvard Law School in 1843.[27] A senator in the State Legislature (1845–55), he was elected to the 1850 convention to revise the Virginia state constitution. At the convention he was prominent in producing a compromise that lowered the tax paid by slave owners like him to appease the western region over voting balance.[28] Finney's role offers a fascinating insight into his pro-slavery views and provides a striking backdrop to his contrasting personal behavior when it came to racial miscegenation. He died May 21, 1884.

What puzzled me later was how the two met or why they were attracted to each other. Louis was apparently a bachelor—in none of the U.S. censuses is a wife listed, and he lived mainly with his two older sisters. There were slaves in the Finney siblings' household, but why would Louis choose to have an extended assignation with a Negro woman who was born free? Louis and Maria's relationship appears to have begun prior to the birth of Maria's oldest son, Charles, on August 10, 1869, when Maria was 17, and to have continued until around July 15, 1877, when my grandfather was born. Maria named my grandfather William Bowman Wharton, which suggests his lineage in that Louis's mother's maiden name was Bowman, and his older brother was William Bowman Finney. The use of these family names perhaps represents the most thoughtful and explicit recognition of my grandfather's paternity that circumstances would allow.[29]

All this ancestry information filled me with excited anticipation as we boarded the train in South Station. From Boston the train first went to Washington, D.C., where we would change to another line for Accomack. Before that change as we approached northern Maryland—the

Mason-Dixon Line, I later learned—Pop turned to me and said, "Clifton, what's the Spanish word for *yes?*"

"*Sí*," I told him.

"Well," he went on, "when the conductor comes along, I want you to speak to me in Spanish, not English."

When I asked my light-skinned grandfather why, he didn't answer. Nonetheless I did as he asked. Taking our tickets, the conductor looked at me oddly but said nothing and moved on. Other Negroes had already begun leaving their seats, moving to what I later learned were the "colored" coaches.

In Washington's Union Station I became obstinate for some reason and refused to speak Spanish, much to my grandfather's annoyance. En route to Accomack, we ended up in the "Negro" car, right behind the smoke-billowing engine.

Especially in the South, Pop told me resignedly, Negroes had to tolerate separate, poorer accommodations. Whites held themselves apart, he explained. Negroes had to use different public lavatories and different water fountains, cracked stained basins labeled "Colored Only." We couldn't eat in "white" restaurants, though sometimes we could buy food passed from a back door and eat it outside. We weren't even supposed to enter white homes through the front doors.

I was dumbfounded. I had never even heard the term "segregation." Most of my Spanish friends, I told Pop, had tan skin, often darker than mine. It's not the same thing, he said sadly. And he made sure I understood that if I didn't watch it I could get us both into real trouble. He did not mention the ever-present dangers of violating racial codes below the Mason-Dixon Line—the beatings, killings, and lynchings of Negroes in the South, sometimes for far less than choosing the wrong train seat. These were horrific acts outside the law and courts after the end of Reconstruction in 1877. Thousands of Black men, women, and children met their deaths in the grasp of white southern mobs,[30] often organized by the white-hooded Ku Klux Klan secret society.

In Accomack, a county near the southern tip of the Delmarva Peninsula, we stayed with my great-aunt Susie, Pop's younger sister, and her undertaker husband Edgar Thomas. In my memory three things stand out—first was meeting so many Whartons! On the first day as I was going out to play, my grandfather told me strongly to be polite because in the South everyone greets each other. I asked him how I could greet people if I didn't know them? He said that since most of them would be my cousins, "Just say, 'Mornin' cousin.'" I did, and I was amazed—most of those whom I saw *were* my cousins! The road was a small community filled with Whartons. My grandfather told me that his mother Maria had bought the original land for the family homestead, buying her first two acres of land for $100 in 1873 with her sister Susan, at the age of twenty-one. How she came by the money for the purchase I don't know. But the family had already found the resources to acquire substantial farmland—how much before and how much after the Civil War I haven't been able to determine. One of Maria's younger brothers, James Frazier Wharton, had a very large farm and at one point is reported to have owned much of Cape Charles south of Accomack.[31] In 1921, Frazier donated land to build the first public school for Negroes in the county.[32] Family photographs of the period, especially of Maria's children, reveal most, though not all, to have been quite light-skinned, virtually white.

Thus, by the end of the Civil War and into the immediately following decades, the Whartons of Accomack had become reasonably prosperous farmers and community leaders—not uncommon in mid-nineteenth-century Virginia, despite what must have been persistent, if not overwhelming, adversity in the milieu. As is often the case, this early prosperity led to further success of subsequent generations.

My second strong memory was the food! Never before—and never, I sometimes think, afterward—had I eaten such meals. Mornings broke to the heavenly aroma of just-laid eggs, sausage, chicken livers, hominy grits, sliced ham, sometimes even soft-shelled crabs. Dinner might bring fried chicken, yams, collard or mustard greens, at least two kinds of pie. Pop threatened to enter me in the Tasley County Fair eating contests.

The other thing I remember most vividly was the fair itself. Since the Whartons were on the organizing committee of the separate Negro Tasley fair, I could roam the grounds with impunity. The sulky races in particular were riveting. I learned how "pace" horses moved their legs on each side in unison, while "trotters" moved left-front and right-rear legs together, followed by right-front, left-rear. The horses' rippling muscles filled me with awe—how I yearned to become a driver, crouched over two whirling wheels behind their flying hoofs!

. . . .

In September I went to the Henry L. Higginson School. At first they put me in the fifth grade for having been so long out of the country, but after a few days they bumped me up into the sixth grade. The class was polyglot: a third or so Negro, a third Jewish, and the rest a mix of Irish, English, and Italian. Our teacher, Miss Finneran, didn't tolerate much cutting up, and if she didn't know who had started trouble, she was happy to round up "the usual suspects." I once worried about my grades in conduct, although in any event I came out all right.

My two best friends were Courtland Ellis and Joseph Mitchell Jr. Court was a wiry bundle of energy with a grin made interesting by a missing front tooth. Son of a U.S. postal clerk, he had the look of someone who could take care of himself. His oldest brother, Bill, was at Boston Latin School. Joe was the son of Joseph and Lucy Mitchell, friends of my parents. Joseph senior worked in state government—at various times he was a Massachusetts assistant attorney general and executive secretary of Leverett Saltonstall's Governor's Council. Lucy had degrees from Talladega College in Alabama and BU. She was what would later be called an activist, involved in many causes: the YWCA, the NAACP, the Boston Community Council, and various child and family support groups.

I attended Henry L. Higginson School, in Boston, Massachusetts, in sixth grade. This picture, taken in June 1937, includes me, age ten (*top row, 6th from left*), and my friend Courtland Ellis (*3rd row, far right*).

Court, Joe, and I were inseparable—playing "King of the Castle" in Harris Park, throwing our sleds down the snowy hillside of Washington Park, roughhousing everywhere to the adults' considerable consternation. Saturdays usually saw us at the Humboldt Theater. We watched Tom Mix, Buck Rogers, Tarzan, and Flash Gordon movies, eating Necco Wafers, Root Beer Barrels, and Jujubes, a tiny, rock-hard candy that always threatened to crack your tooth. If you sat through the feature twice, you could really stuff yourself.

▪ Life with Nana

In the spring of 1937 my cousin June went back to live with her father, and against all odds Lottie Roper had become pregnant. Now I would go to live with Nana and Pa.

My grandmother was a formidable woman. She believed that certain patterns of behavior were important in defining who you were and where you were going. For example, one of my regular Saturday duties was to wash all the windows in the apartment and to polish the brass faucets and fittings over the kitchen sink. (The windows were very difficult small square panes.) After I finished, Nana would carefully, almost minutely, inspect everything. If there was a single missed spot or smudge—even just in one single square of a pane—she would make me do over the entire job, not just correct the area improperly done.

She was also frugal and shrewd. Working by now as the main chef in the executive dining room at Waltham Watch Company, she listened attentively to table talk and invested systematically in stocks she heard the moguls praise, especially AT&T. I doubt she ever earned more than $3,000 in her best year—yet she lived well, bought clothes and sundries for her seven grandchildren, supplied emergency funds as needed, and unfailingly lavished holiday presents on the entire family. She also had lots of "cookie jars" for unexpected needs. Years later, when I graduated from high school, she handed me a savings book in my name with $800 (about $10,800 in 2015 dollars) that she had secretly saved for my college tuition.

. . . .

Perhaps Nana's greatest influence on me was scholastic. Although she had only an elementary school education, she attached overwhelming importance to education. She would accept nothing but utmost educational effort. When I came home from Boston Latin with a failing grade in math for the first month, she upbraided me unmercifully. The next month I passed math but failed Latin—and she really lit into me. She hired a tutor and I worked very hard. Two months later, when I got an 82 in Latin, I was thrilled and rushed home. When I proudly presented my grade sheet to Nana, she looked it over carefully. "Did anyone in the class get anything higher?" That epitomized my grandmother. It wasn't enough to do well. You had to be the best!

. . . .

In Liberia and the Canaries I had been largely insulated from racism, but now that I was living permanently in the United States I couldn't escape a growing awareness of the peculiar "American Dilemma."[33] Initially galling was that whites considered Negroes to be shiftless, lazy, stupid, and without any redeeming feature, other than as a humorous foil for the enjoyment of whites. Most offensive to me were the white-created stereotypes, where the archetype was white Al Jolson in blackface with exaggeratedly large white painted Negroid lips, singing "My Mammy" as the happy, dancing "darkie" wearing white gloves.[34] This was the demeaning image of Negroes fostered by a white actor to conform with white prejudice while becoming famous and wealthy.

Even more annoying and puzzling, I couldn't help wondering why whites so often treated Negroes with contempt, even hatred. Did they—at my age, for that matter, did I?—even know what a Negro was? Gradually I came to grasp that "Negro" and "colored" weren't ordinary words, descriptive and neutral—encompassing multiple objective traits such as color, hair, and facial features. They were, rather, terms of a malign *proscription*: an exclusionary verbal turning of the back. The focus on color was simultaneously preemptive and empty. It dismissed the entire complexity of your existence on the single basis of the hue of your skin—and even then not necessarily your real hue, but rather the ghostly and subjective hue imagined to have been derived from only one group of your ancestors. In the formula of the day, anyone with a single drop of "Negro blood" was automatically Black—even if the individual looked completely white.

It perplexed me to realize that many, maybe even most of my compatriots would gauge my worth on a single dimension—my color! What was the point? What good did it do, other than to foster a wildly fantastical erroneous sense of their superiority over a whole group of people? Or was it an ingrained reaction from the legacy of Black slavery and the white justification of their heinous inhuman practice—their refusal to acknowledge any moral guilt?

Though it never went away, over time my indignation cooled to small, diamond-hard ire I could usually disregard. After all, race wasn't *my* straitjacket, but theirs. I resolved to hold fast to the pride in my heritage that my mother had done so much to nurture, but never to collude in anyone's attempt to define me by one thing alone.

. . . .

Ironically, the color pathology wasn't confined to racist whites. Although differences in skin tone among Negroes were ubiquitous, I had never given much thought to the practice of "passing." One day while shopping with Nana at Jordan Marsh, I spotted my father's cousin Grafton Wharton and his son Jackie (Grafton was a son of my great-great-uncle Frazier). As I started to go to greet them, my grandmother caught my sleeve, pulled me back, and insisted sotto voce that I pay them no attention. Later she explained that Grafton, who was blue-eyed, blond, and had a Caucasian wife, was "passing." He lived publically and most of the time in the white world, though he maintained contact with friends and relatives in the Negro community. It would have been bad form to reveal his Negro ancestry, Nana said, in such a setting.

The most common reason for passing was to get a better job, though even as a youngster I observed that such hopes didn't pan out all that often—at best you could perhaps elude some of the most corrosive effects of daily racism. But a few who passed gave up and even denied all connection to the Negro world. A handful even became rabidly anti-Black themselves, joining the front ranks of the anti-Negro phalanxes. It was as though they were frantic to prevent themselves from being "mistaken" as Black. Their self-loathing must have soured them to their very core.

I began to form a new appreciation of my parents' deep-seated commitment to the highest standards of achievement—for me no less than for themselves. It wasn't that they wanted to act or be white, or adopt white ways. It was that they wanted to meet whites openly on their own ground, to prove that as Negroes they could do as well as or better than anyone else—regardless of the color of their skin.

- Camp Atwater _____

In the summer of 1937 I went happily off to Camp Atwater, on Lake Lashaway, in East Brook-field, Massachusetts. I had first attended in 1935, while we were on home leave in Boston for the birth of my second brother, Richard. Founded in 1921, the camp was named for Dr. David Atwater, whose daughter Mary had donated the initial fifty acres to establish it. Its founding director was Dr. William DeBerry, then pastor of St. John's Congregational Church and head of the Urban League in Springfield. At the time most summer camps excluded Negroes, but in DeBerry's steady hands Atwater quickly became a summer Mecca for young Blacks from families up and down the Eastern seaboard. Boys attended in July, and girls went in August. Every year a number of slots were set aside for youth from low-income households, but you could hardly ever tell who was who.

When I first arrived at Atwater there were ten or so buildings: the Lodge, Beebe Rec Hall, and the laundry, plus cabins with names such as Goodwill, Harris Bath House Annex, Maple Grove, and the Dunbar Tent. New campers shared a huge, dorm-style building, our beds crowded side by side into long rows—a big change from the private room and bath I was used to. (Returning campers were assigned to cabins mostly by age groupings.) The sudden plunge into quasi-communal living was bracing, for lack of a better word.

During most of the years I attended, the assistant directors and senior counselors ran the camp on a day-to-day basis. Director R. Turner Dickerson, a New Jersey public school teacher, was practically the personification of Camp Atwater: a handsome, energetic man with a palpable air of fairness. His specialty was juggling Indian clubs, which he could twirl into a spectacular dance. The older counselors were an obviously elite group, too, most of them college undergraduate or graduate students. Some came from Black campuses—Morehouse, Fisk, Howard, and Meharry. An even larger number were studying at predominantly white schools such as Harvard, Bowdoin, Bates, Temple, and Syracuse University.

Dr. DeBerry lived with his wife in White Cottage, just outside the camp entrance. He was a quiet, imposing, jet-black man, totally bald, who spoke with a pronounced sibilant *s*. "Boys," he would say, "Pleassse do not pick the bark from the treesss. Our birchessss are our most treasssssured beauty."

The camp program didn't differ much from those at the all-white camps of the era—reveille and flag-raising at the crack of dawn, breakfast, then making our beds and collectively policing up the grounds. After that we could choose among organized activities such as music, nature hikes, archery, crafts, tennis, and dramatics. At eleven we went for an hour of swimming in Lake Lashaway, our bathing caps color-coded to track our proficiency in the water. At 12:30 the bugle for lunch triggered a mad dash first to the dining hall, then to our assigned tables. If you were a waiter that day, the group's ravenous appetites made for a demanding job—but with compensations, because campers with table duty got bigger portions in the kitchen when the work was over.

After lunch campers went to rest before the day's second round of activities, followed by another hour-long swim. Then there was free time before the flag was lowered at 5:55 in the afternoon. Following dinner the canteen opened, where we paid for our goodies from "accounts" deposited by our families—cash was forbidden during our stay. At 8:30 P.M., flashlights in hand, we converged on Beebe Hall to sit on long backless benches and sing camp songs—"Camp Atwater," "Tell Me Why," and other standards such as "Day Is Done." When Dr. DeBerry asked me once to sing in Spanish, I gave them "La Paloma" to a chorus of rowdy, good-natured hoots.

Fads came and went at camp at an amazing pace—often with a distinctively Black angle. One was "playing the dozens." Usually it began after taps with one camper tossing off some outrageous characterization of another's mother. The insulted party had to respond instantly with a slander even fouler. From there the insults escalated, the success of each new sally gauged by the volume of catcalls from the audience, until one boy or the other gave up or a counselor broke up the contest.

Never before had I heard such language! And yet the spontaneity and creativity of the insults were awe-inspiring, and the aplomb with which the antagonists went at it was astonishing. Not losing your cool, of course, was the whole point.

Now and then we had fights, myself included. One day a boy named Scott and I got into a confrontation for some reason, and we were soon thrashing around on the floor between the cots. Howie Edmonds, a counselor, pulled us apart for a few seconds, jammed our hands into bulky padded boxing gloves, and let us have back at it. Aside from one abortive lesson with my father years before, I had never boxed in my life. Scott gave me a thrashing. No serious damage was done, but I saw stars intermittently for the rest of the day.

Later Howie asked me if I had ever learned to box. When I said no, he started teaching me the basics. A week or two afterward one of my camp mates hit me in the back of the head with a tin can he had thrown at someone else. I went after him, and this time acquitted myself fairly well. I had no more trouble with him or for that matter with Scott, and I owed Howie a debt (he had also taught me to swim in my first Atwater session).

• • • •

In its own oblique way, Camp Atwater helped clarify my nascent thinking about race in the country where I was just settling in. It was at Camp Atwater that for the first time I found myself in a large group of American Negroes, largely of my own sex and age. Most campers came from middle-class, fairly comfortable Negro families, and at home we were viewed by whites as anomalies. On the shores of Lake Lashaway we found a couple of hundred others just like ourselves. No need, here, always to pick the scab of race. In sports, camp activities, social life, and more our exuberance was fierce, but our rivalries were friendly—we really wanted each other to excel. At Atwater everyone was just who they were, and did what they did—without the perpetual miasma of race as the sole touchstone. If you were a star at track, it was because you could run fast and jump high, not because as a Negro you were "naturally" good at sports. If you were a virtuoso musician, it was because you practiced long and hard, not because you "had rhythm." If you were a budding scientist, it was because you were fascinated by physics or biology, and it wasn't "despite" your being a Negro. Atwater was a wonderful retreat from the racial knocks and bruises of the outside world. It added further strength to my sense of self-worth and pride in who I was and in being an American Negro.

Only after being so fully, uncomplicatedly, and wholeheartedly surrounded by and involved with a host of other Negroes did I slowly begin to realize both the pervasiveness and the complexity of discrimination in the "outside world." I wasn't stupid, nor insensible to the nature of the slights I had begun to hear about and see for myself almost as soon as I had settled in with Nana and Pa. I already had a dawning sense of how overwhelming racism could be for most American Negroes. Walking down the street, entering a store or a movie, going to school, riding a train, working in an office or factory—for most, I was understanding, the next sneer or slap might be just a blink away.

At Atwater I first began to grasp the strange and subtle nexus of privilege and prejudice within which my own life would unfold. Even without yet having been the object of much overt unpleasantness, I saw that my racial identity was and always would be fundamental—and no power of differing circumstances could deny or fully dispel it.

▪ The Junior Assembly

In June 1938, several Boston Negro families decided to organize a social club, dubbed the "Junior Assembly"—probably aiming to contain the too-obviously stirring adolescent juices of their Negro youth within a safe channel. Members ranged in age from about ten to fourteen. Some of us were on the brink of puberty; to others adolescence was yet a bit of a mystery.

The first all-Negro social event took place in a large brownstone owned by the Women's Service Club, which had originally bought it to house Black female college students for whom there "weren't enough dorm rooms" at local colleges. Many of the neighborhood mothers were members. At the Assembly's inaugural dance the boys wore suits and ties, the girls long dresses. We danced to music played over the PA system, though many stood around shyly, uncertain what to do. I remember being impressed by a friend named Junior Lippman, who sang "A Cottage for Sale" with great verve. I was even more impressed by his sister Emily, a pretty girl with fetching "sloe" eyes. But she made it clear she had set her cap for another boy. Many in the group later became our teenage and lifelong friends with whom we socially interacted over the years.

The Junior Assembly of Negro youth held a social gathering in Boston, Massachusetts, in June 1938. (*Left to right,
row 2, 10th*) Emily Lippman; (*row 3, 13th*) Elizabeth Fitzgerald (Dolores's cousin); (*far right*) Joseph Mitchell Jr.
(my childhood friend); (*row 4, 6th*) Jackie Wharton (my cousin and Grafton's son); (*7th*) me (age 11); (*9th*) Coco;
(*10th*) Romeyn Lippman; and (*row 5, far right*) Courtland Ellis (my childhood friend).

▪ Boston Latin School _____

In mid-1936, while I was winding up sixth grade before heading off to Camp Atwater in July,
Nana and my teacher Miss Finneran urged me to apply for admission to Boston Latin, the
city's famous, ultracompetitive public school.

In a period when Boston schools saw themselves as the academic Athens of the nation,
Boston Latin was the jewel in the crown. Founded in 1635, it was the oldest public school in
the country, older in fact than Harvard, the first American college. It offered a dauntingly
rigorous six-year program, corresponding to what today would be the middle- and high-
school grades. Admission was based on your prior academic performance and a letter of
recommendation from your grade-school principal. The curriculum stipulated Latin and
English study for all six years; four years of history and math; two of natural science, physics,

or chemistry; two of French; and any combination of Greek, German, or French courses in your final two years.

Despite the rigor of its admission process, Boston Latin drew students from all over the city and from all walks of life. The classes were extremely diverse, the proverbial rainbow of race, ethnicity, class, and religion. Even so, not many Negroes had attended and graduated—on average, three or four a year before and for quite a while after my own matriculation.

On my first day in Boston Latin I felt like I had fallen into the pages of a history book. Around the ceiling of the auditorium ran a top frieze of the school's great luminaries: Samuel Adams, Benjamin Franklin, Ralph Waldo Emerson, John Hancock, Henry Ward Beecher, George Santayana—these were the minds I was supposed to live up to? At a second glance I noticed Henry Lee Higginson, the namesake of the school I had just left. It gave me a mild sense of personal identification, though not perfect confidence for myself in what lay ahead.

Unlike in the primary schools, Boston Latin's teachers were all men. We addressed them all as "Master," a title they almost universally deserved. We "boys," as we were called, were theirs to nurture and mold. For the most part they treated us quite impartially. In my six years there I had only two teachers who irritated me by appearing to treat me with special consideration or to grade me more leniently than my classmates due to my race. And there was only one who, consciously or otherwise, seemed to want to prove me inferior, unable to meet the school's vaunted standards.

A memorable personality was Max Levine, who taught French. Looking incredibly Gallic, though an American, he had a rooster-like crown of black hair with a widow's peak in front, intense eyes behind rimless glasses, a French-type moustache, and, yes, he wore a French beret. In those days most colleges required a foreign language to complete an undergraduate degree program, and students usually opted for French, German, or Spanish. Max always began his class each year with the phrase, "Students, we must begin with the two most important verbs in the French language—*avoir* and *étre*." The blackboards in his class were permanently filled with long columns of regular and irregular verbs. He drilled us incessantly on grammar and vocabulary, as well as the nuances of the French language. Year after year Levine set out to protect his record that every senior who studied with him achieved a score on the College Board tests high enough that they did not have to take the required language courses at the college level. Our class was predestined to join his roster of success.

By a modern yardstick many of the Boston Latin masters would be judged martinets. One of the scariest was Mr. Roche, a Latin teacher. He had a distressing method of going through the classroom, seat by seat, row by row, calling upon each student in turn to stand for the day's translation. One mistake, and down you sat, a zero for the day. As we were seated alphabetically, being a Wharton was a great advantage until my mother returned to Boston. Having taught Latin herself, she figured out I was relying on memorization rather than really learning the language. Taking matters in hand, she visited Mr. Roche without telling me and outlined to him my weakness. That night she said, "I told Mr. Roche you *didn't know* Latin at all." "You did *what*?" I howled. She continued calmly, "So he will call on you first from now on, and send me a note home each day telling me how you have done." Betrayed by my own mother. After that, Roche called on me first every day!

Thanks to that martinet, Mr. Roche, I *did* learn Latin—though the first few lines of Caesar's *Gallic Wars* make my palms sweat to this day.

I mentioned this incident in my 1985 keynote speech at the Latin School's 350th anniversary and learned that Roche, then ninety, was still alive. When I sent him a copy of my speech, he responded: "It is an honor to be remembered after so many years.... A teacher's only reward is the success of his pupils; if I was ever of help to you, I am amply rewarded. Sometimes, I think that I drove my students too hard. I can plead in defense only that I was trying to give them a love of learning and of high emprise. In view of your distinguished career, I am encouraged to hope that my endeavor was not wholly unattended with success."[35] Only then did I learn that his first name was William!

Often the alphabetical seating arrangement influenced our friendships. For example, two of my lifelong friends are Ben Soble and Myke Simon—since the Ss sat in the row next to mine. Many classmates had the same last name. In my class, we had five Cohens, three Dunns, two Hennesseys, two Kaplans, two Kellys, three Levines, two Markses, two Monahans, two Murdochs, three Murphys, two Rileys, three Sullivans, two Walshes, and two Weinerts. In my Class VI homeroom, three of the five Cohens were enrolled, distinguished as "Big Cohen,"[36] "Little Cohen," and "Quinn." Although his real first name was "Merrill," he had been given a new name by Roche, who said, "There are too many Cohens in this class, so from now on your name is Quinn!"

My most impressive memory of the school is the diversity of the students. When I returned to Boston Latin years after graduation, I was asked by a student reporter what I considered the most important subject that I had studied during my six years there. I told him that the most important was not a subject but a lesson. I learned that "innate ability is randomly distributed in society. In any given class . . . the best Greek student might be a middle-income Jewish youth; the best French, a middle-income Black; the best English, a high-income Irish; the best Latin, a low-income Italian. . . . It made little difference where you lived or your station in life." From this I learned the importance of excellence and of equity and the profound complementarity of the two.[37]

• Track

Boston Latin had extensive extracurricular activities. I believe it was Court Ellis who during our first year at Boston Latin suggested I go out for track. He told me about tryouts for what was then called the "midget relay" of the Boston Athletic Association Track Meet, held in the Boston Garden, which drew track and field stars from colleges around the country. As a warm-up entertainment, there were relay races among three or four teams of local school kids, most of them under the age of twelve. Each leg of the race was 110 yards, a quarter around the oval. Runners wore numbers on our backs, just like the older boys. The three-digit identifiers made the number cards wider than our backs, so the crowds got a kick out of watching us flying around the track, legs pumping, while the cards flapped behind us like capes.

But everyone cheered, no matter who won. And after the midget races we could roam the floor freely for the rest of the meet. Even the superstars were usually friendly. I remember being first in line to get the autograph of John Borican after he set a new meet record in the 1,000-yard race. And at another meet there was the red-letter day when I collected the signature of the "Flying Dutchman" Cornelius Warmerdam after he broke the world indoor record in the pole vault.

The "midget relays" taught the rudiments of running form and of how to pass the baton—though we often missed or dropped it. After eventually winning a first medal—our team came in second to English High, with a time of one minute, 25.8 seconds—I was hooked on track. For the next five years it would be a big part of my life at Boston Latin.

. . . .

At the end of March 1939 the Spanish Republicans surrendered to the Nationalists in Madrid, and General Franco formed what would become his Fascist dictatorship. While many hoped a wider conflict could now be averted, my father wasn't sanguine. German rearmament was burgeoning. Hitler had already annexed Austria, and Neville Chamberlain's infamous Munich Pact soon cleared the way for worse.

Despite my father's diplomatic "immunity" on Gran Canaria, strife had several times come too close for comfort, such as the machine gun incident. Reluctantly my parents decided it was time to bring the family back to the United States. Besides the imminence of a world war—certainly the major factor—they also agreed the time was opportune for my brothers and sister to join me in attending school on American soil.

On July 15, in the Island Cabin at Camp Atwater, I got word that my mother and siblings were waiting for me on the other side of the lake. Recovering from my shock, I leaped into a rowboat and plowed across the water faster than I had ever rowed. There they were—brothers William and Richard, and my mother holding my new little sister Mary, whom I had never seen before. At fourteen months she wouldn't come to me, but with her tiny earrings and short pinafore dress, I loved her at first sight.

Accompanying the family was Encarnación, our Spanish maid, whom Mother had brought from the Canaries. Step-grandfather Pa, who had driven them out from town, stood aside with his usual air of quiet disgruntlement.

My father wasn't there because he was debriefing at the State Department in Washington.

But several weeks later he was free, and since he had never been to Camp Atwater I insisted that he go with me for a visit during the girls' season. I wanted him to see for himself why I loved the place. After we had walked around a bit, I went over to Beebe Recreation Hall and put on my trunks for a swim. From the lake I could see Dad sitting on a bench, and soon he was surrounded by several attractive young women. When I emerged from the water, he called out, "Clif, come over and meet these girls."

"No, Dad," I said, heading quickly back to Beebe. As I hurried away I heard one of the girls protest good-naturedly to my father, "But you told us he was your younger brother!"

As I changed out of my bathing suit on the screened second floor balcony, there was a commotion down below the balcony. Parting the window curtains I could see my father surrounded by a dozen female campers, all starting to chant: "Come down, Clifton, come down."

I was paralyzed, and in my shyness just stayed put. The standoff lasted a good fifteen minutes, until the camp director, Dickerson, came up and told me laughingly that if I didn't go downstairs, he would let the girls in to come up. That did it! I dashed down the stairs and streaked for our car, with the girls shrieking behind me. Jumping in, I locked the doors and sat there staring through the windshield at my tormentors.

Dad sauntered up. "Clif," he smilingly lectured, "I'm surprised at you." He then introduced the girls one at a time. Even after my years in Spain, at thirteen I was no Don Juan. Years later I met several of the same girls at a party where this time I showed them my Don Juan "moves."

· · · ·

After a lot of looking, my parents found a three-story house at 285 Walnut Avenue in Roxbury, just a block from my old Higginson School—it would become the family "homestead" for the next three decades.

I moved out of Nana's to join the others. Then I went back for my "high school freshman" (Class 4) third year at Boston Latin. William and Richard enrolled in the David A. Ellis School, literally just across the street. The toddler Mary stayed home with Encarnación.

I had been reunited with my family for hardly any time at all when Hitler signed a nonaggression pact with Russia, thus proving correct my father's pessimism about things to come on the international front. On September 1 Germany invaded Poland. Two days later England and France declared war. The same day, thirty Americans died when a German U-boat sank the British passenger ship *Athenia*. The ship's route was one on which we had regularly taken passage.

After my father left once again for Las Palmas, my mother and Nana seemed to grow closer than ever. They spoke daily by telephone, even when they had seen each other in person just a few hours before. They talked about everything, from the children's petty scrapes to the latest chatter about their friends.

Mother also began a tradition of evening dinner conversations with all four of us children. She orchestrated a lively give-and-take, paid close attention to each of us in turn, and took our comments seriously—whether they deserved it or not. It made us youngsters feel interesting and rather grown up.

Mother believed strongly in cultural enrichment, especially music. She took us regularly to Boston Symphony concerts. For piano lessons mother had engaged Marie Wharton, daughter of my great-uncle Charles. Then she shifted me to Doris Dandridge Harris, a graduate of New England Conservatory of Music, to teach me piano. In an era when it was hard for a Black woman to earn wide recognition as a performer, Miss Harris supplemented her income by giving lessons to the children of upscale Negro families. All her students performed annual recitals in a concert hall before adoring parents and friends. I continued my lessons with Miss Harris until June 1943, when I left for college. My siblings also took piano lessons and eventually added other instruments—William, the drums; Richard, the violin; and Mary, later, the viola. Sometimes I played solo piano and the others performed as a trio at St. Monica's Home for the Aged on Highland Street, where my grandmother Nana was a volunteer of long standing. Although it seemed to us a chore, the elderly audience was loudly appreciative, and after the final number their applause made us feel warm all over.

Despite my poor showing at Camp Atwater not so long before, it was in this period that the subject of girls was taking on increasing urgency to all my male friends—and to me, too. Eventually the members of the Junior Assembly took charge of the social calendar, organizing parties in their own living rooms or decorated basements. Those with good collections brought their records—I specialized in Nat King Cole and Duke Ellington. Once the parties got going, we moved the rugs and furniture back for dancing. Somebody usually swapped out the regular light bulbs for dim reds or blues to make a romantic mood. But parents made it a point to drop in from time to time to "fluff up the pillows on the couch."

Jitterbugging was popular, and Court Ellis and I were pretty good at it. When we danced with my next-door neighbors the Tynes sisters, who were a bit stout, we slingshot them around rambunctiously, knocking everybody else off the floor.

▪ ▪ ▪ ▪

The family always attended Sunday services at The Church of St. Augustine and St. Martin, at 31 Lenox Street in Boston. The congregation was made up almost entirely of Negroes. The Cowley Fathers who were our priests, on the other hand, were white, and—shades of past colonialism!—usually British citizens. St. Augustine's pastor was then the rather hot-tempered Father Frank Fitz. When displeased he ground his teeth visibly and his eyes rolled upward, shooting sparks. The rumor was he had gotten his pastorship because the church fathers could cajole only our predominantly Black church into accepting him.

During my fourth year at Boston Latin I took confirmation classes with Father Fitz at St. Augustine's. I had a good memory and enjoyed learning the catechism and chants. Since I knew Latin, Fitz took an interest in me, often calling on me to answer the more difficult questions. One day, as the end of my group's preparation period was nearing, Fitz invited all the boys back to the residential quarters attached to the church. There he boldly told us to drop our pants. I was dumbfounded—but all the others complied, so I did too. Thereupon Fitz gave each of us four resounding whacks across our bare buttocks with a ruler. Then he brusquely sent us on our ways.

When I told Mother about it, she stormed immediately to St. Augustine's inner lair. What she said during her interview with Fitz she never repeated, but I wasn't surprised that nothing like the incident ever happened again.

In December 1940 I was confirmed in the Episcopal Church by the suffragan bishop of Massachusetts, Raymond Heron. My fellow confirmands and I stifled our laughter at the white bishop's dilemma in the "laying of hands" on all those Vaselined Negro heads. Soon enough I became a "server" at St. Augustine, one of two acolytes who worked directly with the priest. It meant learning the liturgy and the requirements of the masses. But it also meant coming without fail to the 7:00 A.M. Sunday mass, and often Sunday evening vespers—plus weekday duties during Lent. Among other rituals, you had to follow the twelve Stations of the Cross, at each of which the priest and acolytes knelt and prayed at length. All around the Stations the church floor was bare hardwood. By the time I returned to the altar my knees were stiff and aching.

Being in the "back offices" of church tended to debunk my religious celestial mysteries. It was hard to feel holy awe after glimpsing a priest gulping down the wine left over from communion—with more gusto than sacrificial reverence—and the petty jealousies of the robing room made me muse about the difference between faith and the faithful. What I had once seen in an ethereal spiritual light resolved all too solidly into a creation of fallible men.

Nevertheless, St. Augustine strengthened my sense of right and wrong, shaping my views of organized religion in ways that continued to evolve later in life. Eventually I even took over one of the Sunday school classes. I used all the orthodox texts and materials, but I also tried copying some of the methods I had observed among the teachers I liked best at Boston Latin. The children were a delight, and even though they knew there were no grades, they often responded with genuine enthusiasm.

It was my first attempt at teaching, and I loved it.

· · · ·

One master who made a great impression on me at Boston Latin School was Mr. Cray, who taught my Class III (high-school sophomore) Latin during the 1940–41 academic year. Tall, gangly, with a hooked nose and twinkly blue-gray eyes, Cray almost always seemed to wear a slight grin. He was friendly but intellectually demanding, and his pedagogic style set him apart. Rather than have us just translate passages from Latin into English, he would often point to a few lines or even a picture in the book and ask us to reflect aloud on them. He wanted to know what we *thought* about a particular Roman figure or writer, for example. Was he a good man or bad? Were his ideas right or wrong—not just in his own day but now? Cray once

While my brother Richard and I were born in the United States, my other siblings, Mary and William, were born in Spain. Mary and William were automatically granted U.S. citizenship given our father's status as U.S. consul. This picture, taken on Christmas 1941, shows the Wharton siblings: (*left to right*) me, age fourteen; Mary, age one and a half; William, age seven; Richard, age five.

sent me off to research the significance of the constellation of stars observed by a character in Ovid's *Metamorphoses*. It was a weird but exciting assignment, requiring me to shift from the easy, passive regurgitation of simple translation into a more expansive and challenging engagement with the subject matter.

That same year, there might have been a racial tinge to an exchange I had with my homeroom and English teacher Mr. Mahan, who asked me about General Franco's inauguration of the Spanish Civil War. Which time? I had replied. Scathingly, Mahan told me there had been only one civil war, hence only one beginning. But, I protested, Franco had in fact tried to start the war twice. Mahan waved me off contemptuously. After class was over and the other students had gone, I approached Mahan and diffidently explained that it had only been on Franco's second attempt to leave the Canary Islands, where he had been exiled, that he successfully escaped to Morocco and took command of the Moorish and Spanish troops.

After all, I said, my father had been the American consul there at the time, so I thought I knew something about the matter.

Mahan didn't apologize, just murmured about not having realized I had any firsthand information. He then asked me a few questions about what I wanted to do in life. When he suggested rather superciliously that I must think about going down South as a teacher, where I could "help my people," I told him flatly that I had always planned to follow in my father's footsteps as a diplomat. The look on his face could have come with a thought-bubble: *Aren't you getting a little uppity, boy?*

▪ Track Star

Being on the track team took up more of my time as I moved up in and through Boston Latin. I always had a lot of energy, running constantly as a child. An individual sport, track was a natural for me—it didn't demand the grueling team drills required for football or basketball, and winning or losing usually depended on your own effort. Luckily my asthma problems hadn't recurred since leaving the Canary Islands, and my stamina was strong.

In the first meet of the 1939–40 season I graduated from "midget" status and ran the 176-yard race, once around the indoor track. I was the smallest boy in my heat, and as I reached the first banked turn, flying elbows pummeled me from all around. I finished the race with my mouth bleeding, suspecting that the 176 might not be my cup of tea.

In the next meet I decided to try the 50-yard dash. I did well in the first two heats. In the final, as we crouched for the start, my left hand touching that of the runner beside me. At pistol's report he sharply swiped my hand out from under me, and I fell flat on my face. The official starter was a Boston Latin master, but there was no disqualification for the blatant foul. Another athletic failure.

Court Ellis had been doing well in the high jump and hurdles, so I thought I might give the 50-yard low hurdles a try. I also signed up for the high jump. In my first class D meet I won both events. That, I thought, was more like it.

I trained so hard that year I got bad shin splints. Charlie Fitzgerald, the coach, was an amiable man who also taught French. Though he insisted on rigorous daily workouts, he otherwise took an almost laissez-faire approach. Almost every day we trained running through the school basement, ducking under the overhead pipes and whacking them with our palms. After class we dashed and sprinted and jumped until at dusk we could barely manage to stagger off home.

The 1941 annual regimental meet was viewed as the city championships. Court and I were competing against each other in the high jump. The *Boston Herald* said, "Ellis and his Latin School buddy, Clif Wharton, might tie in the high jump, and both are expected to break the record of 5 feet one and ⅝ inches. They have done better than that in every meet this year."[38] So we did. We tied, setting a new Boston high school record for Class D at 5'3½".[39] A photograph of the two of us going over the high jump together was printed in the sports pages of the *Boston Daily Record* to the delight of the Ellis and Wharton households.[40]

The next year I switched from the hurdles to the 220-yard dash. In the first two indoor meets of the season I won my event and was part of Boston Latin's winning relay team. But as the weeks went by the local sports pages were full of another boy, Roland Doherty—from our archrival English High School—who was winning the 220 in times faster than mine. I wondered how I would do when the two of us finally ran side by side. My teammates slapped my back encouragingly, while my "friends" at English crowed that Doherty would run me off the track. My pal Court Ellis, who by now had transferred to English High, needled me playfully, though I sensed that in fact he hoped I would win.

Then the stakes skyrocketed when I learned that my father would be there to see me run. Unexpectedly, Dad had returned from Las Palmas for consultations at the State Department. It was wonderful to have him home, however briefly, and he seemed happy and relaxed to be there. A varsity track man himself, he had won medals and ribbons in school and captained the team while studying at Boston University. As an English High alumnus he couldn't resist ribbing me good-naturedly before the race. For my part, I kept trying to manage his expectations, reminding him of Roland Doherty's faster times. It would be the first time my father had ever seen me in a meet, and I wanted desperately to win.

On Friday, February 6, 1942, the two schools met for their annual showdown. When the gun went off for the 220 dash, Doherty exploded from the blocks and tore through the first two turns like a rocket. On the back stretch he pulled even further ahead, and into the third turn he led by five or six yards.

During hot competition something happens that many athletes have noticed. However loud, the all-enveloping roar of the spectators just fades away into silence—it's almost like you're wearing earplugs, and you hear if anything just your own breath and pounding footsteps, and maybe the gasps of the other runners. But this time it wasn't so. As I rounded the last turn my father was standing in the crowd, and suddenly I could clearly hear him yelling—"Go-o-o, Clif! *Get him.*" Doherty drifted a little right, and with a sudden harsh burst of effort I took the inside lane. A few steps before the finish line I went past him to win the race.

The exultation among the Boston Latin side was tumultuous, and my father greeted me with a big hug. "See," he said quietly. "I knew you could do it." I beat Doherty the same way every time that year.

▪ The Wonderspool Factory _____

For most of my childhood my father had regularly given or mailed me an allowance of five dollars a month, but when I was fourteen he stopped. At his age, he wrote me from Las Palmas, he had earned his own pocket money. Now it was time for me to do so as well.

I was irritated, but his mind was made up. For a while I took odd jobs in the neighborhood—mowing lawns, clipping hedges, washing windows, and waxing and polishing floors. But it was mostly seasonal work, and I wanted a steady income. Moreover, my mother had begun to substitute-teach in the Boston public schools, and I felt I ought to do my part to help make ends meet, especially since my parents maintained two far-apart homes. My mother later told a reporter that during this period I mapped out a work schedule for the family to maximize everyone's time—my early penchant for organizing.

Court Ellis had found a job at a factory downtown, in Boston's harbor area, working after school and on Saturdays. When I asked, he recommended me, and shortly afterward I was hired.

Atypically for the time, the Wonderspool Company was run by a woman, Miss Lebeau. It made spools for everything from shoelaces and twine to the thick hemp ropes for ships' hawsers. The tubes or cylinders were formed from sulfurized cardboard. The smallest were about four inches long and an inch or two thick; the largest (sometimes made of wood) might be four feet in diameter. The end pieces were fixed to the tubes with glue, then machined into place. Keeping the spool from spinning while aligning the end pieces frequently led to burns and blisters on your hands.

The minimum wage was thirty cents an hour, but Court and I made more doing piecework with the very small spools. We sang, joked, and raced to see who could do more spools in half an hour. The work got so automatic that after a couple of weeks the regular employees complained that we were too fast. Miss Lebeau reduced our piece rate, but Court and I were enjoying ourselves so much we didn't really care.

We worked almost every afternoon, unless there was a track meet. On Saturdays we brown-bagged it and ate with the other workers, with whom we gradually got on relaxed and friendly terms. They were all white—Irish, Italian, Portuguese, and one Greek—but there wasn't any racial tension. Mild ethnic epithets flew back and forth all the time, but with much the same air as similar bantering among Negroes. There was also the usual off-color skirmishing between the men and women, never seriously vulgar. Once Court was working with an Italian girl named Angie, who had a crush on him. At some tease by her, Court swatted her rear—not noticing Miss Lebeau standing right behind them. Court was banished to the horrendous sulfur room, where he spent the rest of the day dumping heavy bags of the chemical into huge smoky vats. His hair, skin, and clothes reeked all the way home.

I liked having money in my pocket and being able to contribute at home. I was also a bit

In 1943 I was captain of the Boston Latin School Track Team. (*Left to right, seated in chairs, 3rd*) Matt Branche; (*4th*) Carl Parsons; (*6th*) me; (*7th*) Art Collins; (*standing, 1st*) Coach Charlie Fitzgerald; (*far right*) Alan Munroe, manager.

awed by the endurance and the fortitude of people who could labor without complaint at the same hard tasks, day after day. But the Wonderspool Company convinced me as nothing else could have that I did not want to spend my life working shifts on a factory floor. Long before I left the job, I knew I was *definitely* going to go to college and to get a degree.

· · · ·

In my senior year at Boston Latin I was named captain of the track team—certified by my purple and white windbreaker with the big *L* and the double white "stripes of office" on the sleeve. While I felt understandable pride, the positive reaction of my teammates affected me more.

Early the same year, for reasons I don't recall, I got the idea of forming an athletic club for young Negro athletes from all the different high schools in Boston. We knew each other from meets and often socially as well. I knew there were other interschool clubs, and I thought it would be fun for us to have one, too.

We registered as the Meteors Athletic Club, with twelve members. For a while we mostly met in each other's homes and talked about all things track-related. We also raced in a couple of statewide meets, including one sponsored by the American-Scandinavian Athletic Association in May. Then we signed up for a meet sponsored by the New England Association of the Amateur Athletic Union (NEAAU) on June 5. Though almost the entire club entered, only a few of us actually planned to participate. It didn't matter that much—we were doing it mainly for the experience and the fun.

First, Court Ellis placed third in the high jump. Then we entered the mile relay against teams from Boston College, Hope AA, and Phillips Exeter Academy. Harry Murphy led off and kept us near the front, and in the second leg I moved us up. After taking the baton from me, Court caught the leaders, and anchor Carl Parsons, with his famous finishing kick, brought us home the win. For a few minutes we were exultant—until the NEAAU told us we wouldn't be getting any medals.

We were not an official organization, they claimed. We had not paid the registration fee. In fact, they scolded, we were really just a "getup" group with no standing to compete.

We were stunned, and then furious. We protested, to no avail. The second-place Exeter team got just as angry, refusing to accept the prize they hadn't won. Showing far more sportsmanship than the NEAAU officials, they even offered to reimburse us for our entry fee.

I may have been a callow sixteen-year-old, but I had a pretty good idea about what had just happened. Seething, I went to the NEAAU headquarters the next day and slapped down the registration form proving we were in fact a legitimate club. The organizers sputtered and muttered. Finally, grudgingly they agreed to give us our medals—red, white, and blue ribbons topped with a metal legend *Championship*.

· · · ·

I sat my college entrance exams on April 10, 1943, in an assembly room at Boston Latin. The familiarity of the setting helped settled my nerves, but it was nonetheless a tense few hours. Boston Latin boys had a reputation to live up to, and our class was no exception. The tests were not easy, but on the whole I felt I had done well.

Once the boards were past there was little incentive to keep up the pace of the last six years. Never one to lose an opportunity, Mother decided I should take a short leave from Boston Latin to enroll in "secretarial school"—she wanted me to learn to type and take shorthand! During her own college days she had found that these were skills that would prove an advantage in other course work. I was nonplussed, but not offered a vote. Over six weeks or so I got my typing speed and accuracy up to "professional" level—having played the piano so long probably helped. There wasn't enough time to learn shorthand by either of the traditional Pittman or Gregg methods, so my instructor introduced me to the then-new method of Speedwriting.

Meanwhile, I was still "waiting for the envelope." In the 1940s you applied through the College Board itself, not directly to colleges, and initially you could select only three schools, ranked by order of preferences. I was intent on Bowdoin College, a small campus George Branche had recommended. For some reason, too, I thought it would be great to live in Maine.

My mother had other ideas. She had always wanted me to attend Harvard—so I *had* to include it on my list. She also strongly counseled me to include Boston University, her and my father's alma mater, as my "backup" choice.

Ultimately I ranked Harvard first, Bowdoin second, and BU third. One complication was that Harvard was known to have an unwritten quota system for Jews and minorities. It was also supposed to allocate places geographically. If you were Jewish, but did not have a name that sounded Jewish and you came from Fargo, North Dakota, you might have a better shot than if you lived in Boston, almost around the corner from Cambridge. Anyway, I had heard that Harvard routinely capped Negro admissions at three or four per year, so I did not think I had much chance of getting in.

The first reply I got was from Bowdoin—a fat envelope of forms and information, not a thin one of rejection. My relief surprised me—at least I had one place to go. Then in May, two envelopes arrived, one after another—both thick, a surfeit of riches. When my head stopped spinning, I wrote thank-you letters to BU and Bowdoin, and sent my signed registration forms to Harvard Yard. Our Boston Latin School class met the test of excellence: out of 622 who enrolled, about 260 graduated—more than half fell by the wayside. Each year the public Boston Latin School vied to secure more admissions to Harvard than the leading private school, Andover, and our class beat Andover that year with forty-seven.[41]

Military drill was a requirement at all the Boston public schools in the 1930s and 1940s, and near the end of every school year there was a huge citywide parade. It was a holiday event. Families and friends lined the downtown streets, cheering as students dressed in khaki uniforms (with puttees!) marched through town to the Boston Common. After Pearl Harbor, of course, the party atmosphere faded somewhat. There were still drums and cheers, but everyone knew the drills were no longer a game. Some of our classmates had volunteered or been drafted already, and we guessed our own time would come soon enough.

In my senior year I had been pleased to have been appointed a second lieutenant in the Eighth Company, First Regiment, at Boston Latin. To my mother's and sibling's delight, I led my platoon in the annual parade. And at year end I was promoted to captain in the First Regiment of the "Boston School Cadets."

My graduation took place on June 4, 1943, in the Latin School auditorium. It was a formal but festive day, stretched interminably with the usual citations and excellences. About half the awards seemed to go to a single classmate, Francis James Riley—after a while it got to be funny, with groans and suppressed giggles each time the headmaster intoned Riley's name. Another big winner was Victor Kimmel, a serious, gimlet-eyed student who for six years had intimidated us all.

Midway through the ceremony, my name was called, and my award announced—for six years at Latin School without a "misdemeanor mark" or demerit. My family and the other parents beamed with pride—my classmates just hooted and booed. They knew that if you only got two or three conduct demerits a month, they were always expunged from your record.

So there I stood before my friends, my family, and the world, a Boston Latin graduate, about to enter Harvard University the following fall—undeservedly yet indelibly branded a "Goody Two-shoes." It helped not at all that in my senior yearbook, the caption under my picture read: "Unto the Pure All Things Are Pure." But I didn't mind, I had successfully met the competitive challenge of Boston Latin and was about to enter Harvard College at the age of sixteen.

CHAPTER TWO

The Student: College Years

Because World War II was now well under way, my start at Harvard was in June rather than September. The welcome assembly was in the classic Victorian building Memorial Hall, erected in 1874 to honor Harvard men who had died in the Civil War. Sitting there I wondered if the alumni who paid for it ever expected the descendants of the slaves for whose liberty their classmates fought might one day join their ranks.

There were only two other Negroes in my freshman class. One day when I was walking across the Yard, a light-skinned fellow called out to me and strode over to introduce himself. "I'm Ernie Howell, from Bettendorf, Iowa!" he declared. He lived in Dunster House, he added, with our other Negro classmate, an Andover graduate from Chicago, Bill Jackson. Eventually a fourth Negro, Harold May, would join the class. At the time, in most private New England colleges, Negroes were strikingly few, not too different from our parents' college years.[1]

As a commuter student I still lived at home. With Dad abroad and maintaining residences in both Las Palmas and Boston, his Foreign Service salary was stretched thin. Harvard's tuition alone ran $200 per term, so Nana's surprise gift of $800 ($10,800 in 2015 dollars) would cover at least two years.

World War II had jumbled up class vintages quite a bit, with some students drafted into the service midway through their studies and others returning after their discharge. To ease the disruption Harvard allowed students to matriculate into any of three semesters, including summer. Each class year had a suffix—*A* for summer, *B* for fall, and *C* for winter. My class was 1947A.

As a freshman I took five courses—English, biology, French, history, and Spanish—instead of the usual four. To accelerate their studies during the war, students could take a full course load during the summer, offering in effect three full semesters per academic year rather than only the usual two with a summer vacation. Students also could take five instead of four courses per semester. My intended major was history, as likely the best preparation to follow my father in the diplomatic service. Thanks to Encarna's presence at home, my Spanish fluency was still strong, so Spanish 1 would be good for "grade protection." The same was true of advanced (conversational) French because of my study with Madame de Rescho in Las Palmas and Max Levine at Boston Latin.

Introductory Spanish was taught by Robert Jordan Carner. Though American, Carner looked Spanish—dark, with soulful eyes and a brushy mustache. He also had an artificial leg below one knee. The rumor was that he had lost it in the Spanish Civil War and that he had been Hemingway's model for the main character in *For Whom the Bell Tolls*. Whenever we tried to get the truth, Carner flicked the query deftly away.

I didn't initially admit that I already spoke Spanish, but was soon unmasked. Carner had a habit of telling jokes in Spanish, often involving a play on words. About the third week into the class, he told an off-color joke; unfortunately, I was the only student who guffawed.

"Mr. Wharton," he said mildly, "may I see you after class?" Dutifully I stayed behind, whereupon he asked where I had gone to high school. "Boston Latin, sir," I replied. Well, he inquired, had I had intensive language training?

By now confession seemed wise: "Sir, I know what you want to find out. *Me gusto su chiste verde*" (I liked your green [bawdy] joke).

"Ah," he said, breaking into a big smile. I explained my childhood in the Canary Islands, but that I had never formally studied Spanish or Spanish grammar. Carner had no problem with my taking his class. It was no different, he pointed out, from Americans choosing to take English even though they had spoken the language all their lives.

My other freshman courses were not so congenial. History 1, required for all freshmen, almost ended my Harvard career before it began. It was a world history survey, taught in large lecture sessions supplemented by small tutorials. Besides the textbook you had to buy a big chronological chart on two pieces of paper, each two feet by three, covered on both sides with major dates and key events in tiny black type. Page 1 covered from 399 BC to AD 1453—"Rome, Holy Roman Empire, Germany" to "Greece, Byzantine Empire, Muslims, Spain, Near East, and Russia." The second ran from 1453 to 1815, with even more detail.

Socrates's death in 399 BC and Joan of Arc being burned at the stake in AD 1431 was fine, but they lost me on the Theodosian Code and the Albigensian Crusade. Putting the charts up on the wall didn't really help, and memorization was impossible—there was just too much information to process it all.

The professor who taught the lecture session was often hard to hear, and my section instructor—named Mr. Cram, believe it or not—was a fearsome man who paraded back and forth in basement room No. 5, New Lecture Hall, wielding a long window-opening pole like a Saxon's pike, stabbing the end into the floor to emphasize every point. He had a fierce eye, and his comments about his students' "pea-sized brains" dripped sarcasm. It was like being back at Latin School with a much meaner version of Mr. Roche.

Boston Latin had not taught note taking, and by the time I decided what to write the lecturer often had moved on. In history, knowing what was important required a sense of context and relevance I often lacked. Teaming up with several classmates was tried, but collective note taking wasn't an easy skill to master. After failing some quizzes, my first semester ended with a D. But thanks to an A in Spanish, I was still in school.

Though racism was undoubtedly present, for the most part the treatment of Negroes at Harvard was not overtly discriminatory. At the time there was no such thing as affirmative action, hence no perverse presumption that Black students were somehow "special admits" not subject to ordinary academic standards. There were occasional remarks about our being on "scholarship," but scholarships were then merit- rather than need-based. The exceedingly small number of Negroes on campus, which remained roughly the same year after year, was certainly evidence of a tacit quota system. But in some fashion it also created a perception that we had to have been exceptional to have been admitted at all to Harvard's hallowed halls.

An animus toward Jews was probably more blatant than race prejudice per se—the quota system for them was well known. Because Jewish immigrant families often changed their names, the college Admissions Office routinely conducted spot checks on students from places populated disproportionately by Jews. (Those from the Midwest, say, or the South could often elude the quota system, especially if their surnames sounded Anglo-Saxon.) Because of the competition among Jewish hopefuls for an artificially restricted number of slots, ironically, those who were admitted raised the intellectual stakes across the campus.

Although there was no preferential admissions policy for Negroes, there certainly was for the sons of wealthy establishment alumni—not all of them the best and brightest, to say the least. Despite President James Conant's announced intention of increasing student diversity, Harvard was still a WASP citadel.

The subtle social and class/income differentiation among the students was striking. At the top of the heap was the Hasty Pudding Club, founded in 1795, initially a secret social club to cultivate "friendship and patriotism." It became the country's oldest dramatic institution where men performed both male and female parts. In the 1940s its membership tended to reflect strongly the social elites. The other fraternities weren't much better. I never joined a fraternity. I could not understand how one could belong to an organization whose very name meant brotherhood when its exclusivity was a denial of brotherhood. The Alpha Phi Alpha Negro fraternity chapter founded by my father tried to persuade me to join, but I was adamant. I wanted to be a brother to all, not just a few.

Because of my first-term difficulties in history, my mother suggested my changing majors, but the challenges just made me more resolute. History encompassed economics, politics, sociology, science, culture—the long factual chronicle of the peoples and nations of the world—and it would prepare me well to follow in my father's footsteps. In the second semester, as my note taking improved, my history grade went up to a C, again with an A in Spanish and respectable Bs in my other courses.

During the winter term I joined the Spanish and French clubs, and again indulged my penchant for overcommitment by going out for track. During the war years college athletics tended to be improvisational, and varsity track teams often competed with high school and club groups. At Harvard the winter track season was uneventful, though competitively much tougher than my previous experience. Coach Jaako Mikkola, a Finnish former pole vaulter who had been an Olympic star, made me a member of the mile relay team, and also had me run a few times in the 50-yard dash and 300-yard race. In a meet at Andover I won the high jump, and in another at Tufts took second in the broad jump.

• • • •

After completing my freshman "year" in six months, I moved out of our home on Walnut Avenue into a dormitory—my mother thought that living on campus would benefit both my studies and my extracurricular activities. When I applied for housing, I was assigned F-3, a three-person room on the ground floor of Adams House. Our windows looked out on the *Lampoon* (humorous student magazine) building across the street. My roommate was Harold May from Poughkeepsie, New York. One of a minister's twin sons, Harold had graduated from high school early and entered college midyear. He was ever-pleasant, with a cherubic face. He believed in the inherent goodness of all creatures and read his Bible every night.

For a few weeks the third bed in our suite remained empty, wartime housing demands notwithstanding. When I asked Mrs. Dallas Hext, the House secretary, when we would get a third roommate, she hemmed and hawed. But she was a nice woman, and I resisted the suspicion that she thought Blacks and whites should not live together. After chatting with her innocently for a few minutes about my childhood in Spain, I mused that it might be nice to have a Spanish student join our room.

Mrs. Hext looked nonplussed, but soon enough Carlos Blanco turned up. Scion of a Basque family that had emigrated to Mexico after the war in Spain,[2] Carlos fit F-3 and us like a hand in a glove. In short order, ours had become one of the most congenial, hospitable rooms in Adams House—a gathering spot for classmates from many different backgrounds. If our friends didn't want to traipse off to their rooms upstairs before lunch, they left their books in our room. If they needed to use the facilities, ours were right on the way to the dining room. We even hosted regular pre- and post-football-game parties, garnering much social cache.

Whatever Mrs. Hext had actually been thinking, we were well content with the result. By fighting stereotypical thinking that might have imposed limits of choice, we came out happier and richer.

Because of Carlos, our room also became a magnet for Spanish and Latin American students, and for a semester we had a roommate from Cuba, Pepe Massip Ysalgué. Pepe's fractured English often broke us up, as on the winter evening he came rushing back from the riverbank exclaiming, "*El Charles esta frozeado!*"[3]

Carlos treasured a painting given to him by classmate John Paul Manship, son of the famous artist who had sculpted the golden Prometheus that looms above the Rockefeller Center skating rink. One afternoon David Schine, who was in one of my classes, stopped by to pick up some notes. When he saw the Manship painting in its place of honor over the fireplace, he immediately wanted to buy it. Carlos said it wasn't for sale. Schine persisted, raising his offer again and again. Carlos's pent-up anger was obviously on the rise, too. After Schine finally left without the painting, Carlos told me furiously that if I ever let that "pompous, arrogant, money-throwing bastard in the room again," he would move out. In 1953–54 Schine joined Roy Cohn as a handmaiden to Senator Joe McCarthy's anticommunist inquisition.

▪ ▪ ▪ ▪

Mischief is the one inexhaustible commodity of undergraduate life. At the dorm's first get-acquainted party, one student played the piano and sang some hilarious ditties with a straight face. His name was Tom Lehrer. Little did we realize that years later his recorded humorous songs would become national best sellers. My two favorites were "The Old Dope Peddler" ("doing well by doing good"), and "Lobachevsky" ("Plagiarize, plagiarize, plagiarize . . . only be sure always to call it please "research").

One night two Adams House residents snuck in a couple of strippers from the Old Howard burlesque theater, famous for featuring such luminaries as Sally Rand, Fanny Brice, Gypsy Rose Lee, and Sophie Tucker. The boys took their guests to the dorm pool, where naked swimming was the rule. The screeches and laughter attracted the night janitor, who caught them in all their naked glory. Both students were suspended. The two went to Alaska to work on the new Alaska Highway. Only one stuck it out and returned—he later graduated with honors.[4]

Our room wasn't immune to shenanigans. One conversation-stopper was a long trail of male and female footprints we had cut from cardboard and pasted in our rooms. Starting on either side of the fireplace, the footprints continued up the wall and met—now as bare feet—on the ceiling. Just outside the bedroom the female footprints disappeared (obviously the man had lifted her up), while the male footprints continued on to the bedside. We always watched closely the reaction to the footprints by any woman visitor to our room. A scowl, a grin, laughter outright—it was a pretty good hint what kind of girl she might be.

Rules for women visitors were fairly strict; they were permitted in the dorm only for dinner meals on weekdays and in the afternoons on weekends. As I recall, evening visits until 10:00 P.M. could only take place on Fridays and Saturdays. Whenever a student had a female guest, he was supposed to complete a buff-colored "sign in" slip with her name, his name and signature, and his room number. A blue sign-out slip was to be completed upon departure. Both slips were placed in a box located near dorm entries.

Our room on the ground floor was next to a main entry into our building. Hence, one of the boxes for these transactions was in the corridor immediately outside our room. The result was that our classmates soon insisted that we forge their signatures on slips when they forgot to deposit them or even when a visitor was still in a room after the deadline.

Not all our classmates dragooned us into becoming forgers. Shaw Livermore, a next-door mate in F-2, was regularly dating a student from Wellesley College. On one occasion Shaw had failed to sign her out by 10:00 P.M. When the janitor came to collect the various slips from the box, he noticed that Shaw's guest had signed in but not signed out, causing him to bang on Shaw's door asking if she were still there. Quickly, Shaw hid his guest in the narrow passageway that connected our two rooms. With total composure he reported that she had left, and he had merely forgotten to sign her out.[5] Afterward, we told our friends, just don't sign them in—then there will be no knocks on their door or ours. Shaw later became a professor of history at the University of Michigan (1964–2007). His other roommate, William "Red" Liller, became a world-famous astronomer and incredibly the master of Adams House (1969–73).

· · · · ·

But life at Harvard was mostly hard study, with escapades generally confined to weekends. Carlos maintained that I had every minute of my days and weeks organized on a chart on the wall over my desk. Apparently it was then that I began to learn the value of time allocation and the importance of prioritizing my activities—a practice I followed the rest of my life. I still don't know where the impetus came from.

As a sophomore I dropped back to the standard four-course load, including Economics A and the Government 1 course taught by William Yandell Elliott. A bear of a man with bristling eyebrows, Elliott affected a black string tie and spent most of his lectures dropping the names of important political figures he had visited during his latest trip to Washington, D.C. He loved to sit on the corner of his desk, foot swinging, then stride around the stage like a Shakespearean actor.

▪ The Sunday Evening Group _____

One day, Ernie Howell told me about a group organized by the Old Cambridge Baptist Church at the corner of Harvard Street and Massachusetts Avenue. It was an interracial, coeducational group of students from major universities in the greater Boston area. The focus was twofold: a broad, nondenominational religious exploration of life and the self-examination of personal values. He found the meetings thought provoking and enthusiastically suggested that I join the "The Sunday Evening Group."

The student pastor, Prentiss L. "Pem" Pemberton, had a highly effective way of nurturing leadership among young people. He provided a framework for each person to display individual insights or perspectives to the rest of the group. Many of the students were bright, sensitive, thoughtful, and caring. Pem did everything that he could to provide them a forum in which leadership qualities could be further developed.

I began to attend the sessions regularly and made many friends. Although most came from Harvard, Radcliffe, and Boston University, there were also a few from Tufts and Wellesley. A young woman from Wellesley College, Virginia "Ginny" Pierce, attracted my special attention as well. A tall brunette who resembled Katherine Hepburn, she was a senior, but I was quite taken, and we started to have regular dates. The interracial aspect was far less significant in our relationship than the anomaly of a Harvard freshman dating a Wellesley senior (class of 1944). It did not last long, but we continued to be friends.

· · · ·

In my second sophomore semester I signed up for two additional history courses (5a and 42b). Although my grades were a B in one, a C in the other, I was still determined to major in history, even if it were the subject where my grades were lowest.

My other worry was money. After moving into the dorm I had taken a short-lived job in the main student dining hall, then a couple of weeks later managed to get back my old spot at Wonderspool Company. The spool factory was harder work than the dining hall, but it paid better and didn't leave my clothes smelling like cooking oil. But since I still needed more financial help, Ernie suggested another part-time position as an assistant to Gordon Allport, a faculty member doing research on the psychological aspects of wartime rumors. In one experiment my role was to stand at the front of the room, describing pictures projected on a screen that the other students in the room couldn't see. Once the picture was of a subway car containing an old man with a hat and long beard; a young, well-dressed Negro sitting adjacent and reading a newspaper; and a young white woman, hanging by a strap and reading a poster advertisement for Gillette razor blades. After I described the picture minutely, each of the other students went into separate rooms, where they repeated what I had said as best they could to three or four new people. Then everyone came back to hear what the new group remembered and compare it with the actual scene. The most frequent reports were either that a Negro youth was attacking a rabbi, or that he was robbing the young woman with a razor in her face.

My job with Dr. Allport paid $15 a week. Another part-time job for a while was in the acoustical lab, testing microphones and earpieces for use by Army Air Corps pilots. I earned enough to cover dorm costs, meals, and books (my budget for a three-semester year was $1,275). I also won $200 scholarships from Harvard for summer 1944 and winter 1945. Learning that the American Foreign Service Association offered student aid to the children of professional diplomats, I applied for and got one-half of the Oliver Bishop Harriman Memorial Scholarship for 1944–45, adding $500. The Harriman award, luckily, didn't affect my support from

Harvard, which "should be regarded as a prize," assistant dean Sargent Kennedy wrote to the university's committee on scholarships.

- ## Harvard Crimson Network (WHCN)

With backing from the *Harvard Crimson*, two student "hams" had set up a radio station (WHCN) in Shepard Hall that used the campus-wide heating pipes as a medium of transmission.[6] Regular evening broadcasts of the Crimson Network began in December 1941, students listening in by wiring their radios to the pipes in their rooms.

Bill Lippman, nephew of columnist Walter Lippmann, had become a friend while studying Spanish with Carner. Bill had gotten involved with the Crimson Network in 1943, and he soon urged me to try out as a "candidate" for membership. I thought it would be fun. By that time the station was struggling because of the wartime turnover in students. Though still student run, it had also become independent of the *Crimson* newspaper. As our competitor for campus attention, the paper no longer allowed the radio station to use their wire service machine for news broadcasts, so my candidacy consisted in large part in taking the subway from Harvard to downtown Boston's AP office, ripping the latest copy from their newswire, and rushing back to WHCN just in time for it to be edited and read over the air.

There were two divisions, production and technical, each with a director—on one side production managers (or "PMs"), scriptwriters, and announcers, and on the other "technicals," who operated the equipment and kept it running.

In April 1944 I was elected a full member of the station, along with three others (Alan Rich, William Sullivan, and J. D. Kettelle). Every member had a code signature. Bill Lippman was "WJL," for example, and Bill Sullivan was "wes." I was going to be "CRW" but it turned out there had already been one, so it was changed to "CLIF." Although I was the first Negro to join, I was treated just like everyone else. My first announcing slot was with Bill Lippman and two others on jazz. I also worked on the foreign language series and occasionally filled in on the daily saxophone program.

Frequently we talked celebrities into stopping by. In September 1944, at Boston's "Tic Toc" club, I heard singer Billy Eckstine and trumpeter Dizzy Gillespie and immediately begged the two Negro stars to come to the station. It was the period when Gillespie and Charlie Parker were at the forefront of the frenetic new "be-bop" movement. Dizzy took me up on the invitation—it was one of my most memorable radio interview sessions. We also rebroadcast Orson Welles's *War of the Worlds*, from 1938. It caused a flap on campus, though it was hard to believe that Harvard students wouldn't have known the story long before.

In mid-July 1944, Bill Lippman resigned as production director to take a job announcing on a local commercial station, and I was elected to replace him. One of my first acts was writing

In July 1944 I was elected production director of the student radio station, Harvard Crimson Network (WHCN), where I also continued to announce.

a page and a half memorandum in the comment book[7] outlining the various organizational changes that should be made to help the station "become better and worthy of the standards which have been made by other members" and to propose steps "making our procedures even better." (Reading this entry sixty years later I was struck that the new CEO taking charge was only eighteen years old at the time.)

The Crimson Network had a sister station, Radio Radcliffe. With a staff even smaller than ours, they used a lot of our programming, and we occasionally did joint productions. One was a quiz show, with four Harvard freshmen and four first-year ladies from Radcliffe. The prize for the two winners was a dinner-and-a-movie date, paid for by the station. There was a host announcer for each team. As production director for the station, I unabashedly assigned myself to the Radcliffe group, and before long I got to know some of the most attractive young women on the campus. One day I called Betty Fitzgerald, now a freshman who with her sister had studied piano with my cousin Marie, to ask her to dinner at Adams House. Her roommate got onto the phone and wanted to come, too. Then the switchboard operator, who had been listening in, asked could she come, too! When I went over to pick them up, Betty wasn't quite ready, so I went into her dormitory's living room and sat down at a piano there. The tinkling of music soon drew a few other girls, including three who had been on our Crimson Network quiz show. Before long one more had invited herself along to the party.

Into the room now came Harry Murphy, a friend and former high-school track competitor, currently a freshman at MIT. With blue eyes and auburn hair, Harry was "passing." I had run into him a few weeks before on the Boston transit surface train with his friends, and as they had gotten off he had told me that he would appreciate my not blowing his "cover." So now I obligingly ignored him and returned to playing more piano tunes. When the women finally drifted away to get ready, Harry came over and asked how in the world I knew all these good-looking white women. "Sorry," I told him wryly, "since I don't know you, I can't really introduce you around."

At the beginning of the fall semester in 1944, once again I had overburdened myself with extracurricular activities. Between the Network, track, the Sunday Evening Club, and the Spanish Club, my grades were starting to slip.[8] I hated to do it, but reluctantly I resigned as production director of WHCN.

The Network, later named WHRB, with its team of "high achievers," was an important and enjoyable influence during my Harvard years. Hartford Gunn served for many years as head of Boston's WGBH, the country's premier public radio station. Marty Bookspan later became an announcer and program director at New York's WQXR classical radio station, director of classical music at ASCAP, vice president of VOX Records, and best known as the voice of Lincoln Center for thirty years (1976–2006). Alan Rich later served as the chief music critic for the *New York Herald Tribune* and the *New Yorker* magazine. Dick Kaye's subsequent career extended his Crimson Network interests; he became president and chairman of WCRB in Boston, cofounder of the Concert Music Broadcasters Association, and the announcer, producer, and syndicator of the Boston Symphony Orchestra radio broadcasts. Phil Stern became a successful author and a member of President Kennedy's White House staff. Bill "Liam" Sullivan performed on Broadway, then became a successful character movie actor, songwriter, and playwright in Hollywood.

▪ ▪ ▪ ▪

The War was a constant undercurrent among many students, though rarely discussed. The campaign in North Africa and Italy plus the naval battles with the Japanese in the Pacific heightened awareness of the impending involvement of my classmates and myself.

▪ Beauty and Brains _____

One day Betty Fitzgerald called. A freshman at Radcliffe, Betty was the daughter of friends of my parents. Her cousin, Dolores Duncan, was coming from Danbury, Connecticut, for a visit. Would I be able to take her to a formal dance at Radcliffe?

"Sorry," I apologized, "but I never go on blind dates."

"But you met her last winter at my house," Betty reminded me. "She's very beautiful."

Vaguely I recalled a petite sixteen-year-old girl who had made a grand entrance, down the stairs of Betty's home into a thick cluster of strutting, panting young males. Dolores recalls that she was wearing a pink, blue, and beige plaid wool skirt, topped by a baby blue cashmere crew-neck sweater. She wore pearls, contrasted with loafer shoes and Angora bobby socks. I did indeed remember her casual elegance, which seemed a marked contrast to the stiff taffeta and organza dresses of the other girls, whose jealous reaction was obvious.

That Saturday—December 16, 1944—the girls met me at Harvard Square and I led them off to a pre-dance dinner at Adams House. "Ma" Reardon, the doyenne of the line servers in the cafeteria, always made a point of evaluating my dates. She took one look and said, "Now *that* girl is special!"

There were about 150 couples at Radcliffe's Cabot House for the dance. Dolores's shining black hair was parted in the middle and fell down her back to her waist. Every time she smiled I was enthralled by the single dimple in her right cheek. She was alluring, intelligent, and mischievous, and with her near translucent skin she looked like a porcelain doll.

I should have been captivated—I was, but I wouldn't admit it to myself. Not surprisingly, Dolores had another take on things. She later told me she thought I was an eighteen-year-old sophomore BMOC (big man on campus) and acted like I knew it. I was a lofty "Hahvahd" sophomore, while she was just a high school student from the Connecticut "sticks." Dolores's version of me was probably closer to the truth.

I knew she came from a successful, affluent Negro family—"a Bradford from Baltimore and Philadelphia"—a recognizable elite multigenerational heritage. Anyone attracted by her beauty could easily miss that underneath she was extremely bright and intellectually quick.

The next day I invited both Betty and Dolores to St. Augustine's Church, where I was an acolyte for Sunday mass. At the church I went into the sacristy to get ready, leaving them behind. As I finished robing, Father Fitz roared into the room in high dudgeon, thundering about two young women he had found in grave transgression. "They were speaking aloud in the house of God!" he spat. His bulging eyes rolled toward the ceiling. I knew exactly who he meant.

After the service I tried to introduce Dolores to my mother, who barely acknowledged her before dashing off to corral my siblings from Sunday school. A few minutes later Mother came back and pulled me away peremptorily to meet another parishioner.

I resisted further relationships with Dolores—probably due to a slight trepidation at the challenge of her beauty and brains. My roommate Harold May stopped off in Danbury regularly on his way home to Poughkeepsie, however, and he ended up bringing Dolores to a dance at Harvard. Again she was the most striking girl at the dance, wearing a black ribbon choker around her neck, dangling a single pearl. I couldn't resist teasing her that she looked like a puppy with a collar around its neck. "Where's your leash and master?" I taunted.

Delores smiled back at me sweetly. "Not you!" she laughed. If I ever took a serious interest in her, I thought, she would be a worthy opponent. I didn't know it then, but the spell had been cast and I was fatefully bewitched.

For a while my romantic interests took another turn. Richelieu Morris, the childhood friend with whom I had romped as a toddler in Liberia, had looked me up after arriving in Boston to enroll at Tufts University. Sometimes the two of us traveled to Wellesley College, where I visited Ginny Pierce. Richelieu was an accomplished musician, and the two of us enjoyed playing and singing songs for Wellesley women in Tower Court dormitory, with its majestic open center room under a twenty-foot ceiling. A balcony ran around the second floor, where some of the girls would lean over and float sheet music down for Richelieu to sight-read. Sometimes we played romantic songs we had written ourselves, with titles such as "Raindrops," "I Understand Now," and "Like This in the Night." It was a time when eighteen-year-olds were entitled to be dreamy-eyed and sentimental in the presence of the opposite sex.

Also at Wellesley I met Rita Buckner, an attractive Negro freshman from Washington, D.C. We had a few dates, but she kept me at arm's length. Rita also attracted the interest of Ernie Howell and Chet Pierce, my Atwater acquaintance who had enrolled at Harvard that fall and was on the football team. Rita made it plain that she would only be friends and nothing more. So I continued to play the field.

Although I was taking a five-course load, my hard work was starting to pay off, and I wrapped up the junior semester with all Bs—the first time. My track performances were improving, too. In a winning mile relay against Rhode Island State I ran the third leg and turned in a 52.1 second quarter. In the next meet, against Exeter, I won the 40-yard dash and 300-yard race, and was beginning to attract some notice from the regional sportswriters—a headline trumpeted, "Wharton's 10 Points Highlights 41–13 Rout."[9] And with my academic standing firmer, I was again elected production director of the Crimson Network.

But now such things seemed to matter less, as the world war and the draft machine ground ever closer to home.

• Tuskegee

By mid-1944 the tide of war was near its crest. The Allied invasion had bloodied the Normandy coast, Patton's Third Army was pressing toward the Rhineland. MacArthur was brooding over his pledged return to the Philippines in the Pacific. At that juncture, my Negro friends all maintained, letting yourself be drafted was the worst thing you could do. It wasn't a matter of not wanting to fight—rather of avoiding the "cotton toting" jobs usually assigned to Blacks. As a draftee, you automatically went to a segregated unit, almost always commanded by white officers. Regardless of your background and abilities, you would end up working as a cook, a stevedore, or some other menial job.

Nevertheless, my friends and I were loyal and willing to do our part—just preferably not something degrading. The best idea seemed to volunteer—you could at least hope for a decent assignment, though your choice didn't always come through.

My decision was to try for air cadet training at Tuskegee Institute. I had been impressed by Tuskegee airmen's "double V" campaign—using two fingers on both hands to signal two "Vs"—victory over fascism abroad and victory over racism at home.[10] Since early 1941 Tuskegee had served as the home base for the army's new (but segregated) Ninety-Ninth Fighter Squadron. Early on the program had faced stiff opposition, first from whites who thought Blacks were unsuited to serve as officers and to fly warplanes, later from those who wanted to prevent them from serving over Europe and North Africa. But it had great support from Eleanor Roosevelt and Mary McLeod Bethune, the civil rights leader and founder of Bethune-Cookman University, among others. After visiting Tuskegee and taking an hour's flight with instructor Charles Anderson, the first Black American to earn a pilot's license, Mrs. Roosevelt persuaded her husband, the president, to task the Ninety-Ninth for overseas combat. By fall 1944, when I was ready to apply, Tuskegee had produced the legendary 332nd Fighter Group, whose Red Tails' exploits over Europe were generating pride throughout the Black community and even in the mainstream white press back home.

To qualify for Tuskegee it was necessary to pass a written test and a physical. The exam was easy. My score was 128 or "superior" in the Wechsler-Bellevue Intelligence Scale, which my Dad boasted about. But the physical, taken at Grenier Field in Manchester, New Hampshire, presented a problem. With 20/20 vision required in both eyes, I doubted my right eye would make the cut. But standing in the queue for the vision test, I noticed that the examiner was using only two charts, and not even randomly. Moving up, I listened closely to those ahead of me, memorizing the lines as they read them aloud. When my turn came, I just repeated what I had heard, and readily passed. When I got to Tuskegee my eyes were retested, with no chance to reuse the ploy. Since I had come so far already, apparently, they passed me once again.

Shortly before leaving college, Court Ellis's brother Bill moved in with us in Adams F-3. Bill had enrolled in Harvard in 1940, then left in 1943 to join the army. At the end of 1944 he was honorably discharged because of poor eyesight, after which he reapplied for school. My roommate Harold was later heading for Tuskegee also, so we hoped Bill and Carlos would hold the fort in our room until we got back.

On March 13 my orders came. I was to leave campus on March 26 for induction at Fort Devens, thirty miles west of Boston, then travel south to Biloxi, Mississippi. With her eldest son facing the prospect of lethal fighting, my mother tried to be strong, but the morning I left she broke down in tears.

That afternoon, after a short, surprisingly moving swearing in at Fort Devens, I left Ayer, Massachusetts, by train, routed through Albany and Cleveland. In Cincinnati I caught the *Azalean* for Biloxi. My papers labeled me "colored," but the ticket combined first- and coach-class seats, allowing eight meals en route—overall a marked improvement over my childhood trip across the Mason-Dixon Line with my grandfather. It was a long, tedious, uneventful journey. We arrived at Keesler Field around five o'clock and were assigned to temporary barracks by the time it was dark.

The next morning I fell out at reveille to be greeted by three genial representatives of the Mississippi delta—the heat, the humidity, and a spit-and-polish drill sergeant. After breakfast we marched to a large building for intake processing. Each of us carried our records in a sealed manila envelope. White recruits went first, Negroes second. We lined up in alphabetical order and moved from one table to the next. At each station sat a white noncom, who would pull a sheet or two from our records, check something off, and point us onward. At one table a red-faced sergeant goggled comically at my forms, then shouted, "Where did you get this filled out!"

"Fort Devens, Sergeant," I blurted, taken aback.

"Wall, do you know we can *court*-martial y'all for falsifying yo' record?" he sputtered.

Dire visions flooded my imagination. In the army not even a week, in deepest Mississippi no less, and already headed for the stockade! An officer sitting nearby heard the commotion, rose, and came over. "What's the problem, Sergeant?" he asked.

"Wall, sir, this hyah Neegero has lied on his forms. Says he has lived in all kinds of foreign countries. Says he speaks Spanish an' French. Eighteen years old, and s'posed to be a junior in college!"

The officer looked at my form for a minute. Turning to me he said, "So you studied at Harvard?"

"Yes, sir," I replied.

"Did you live in one of the houses?"

"Adams House, sir."

"And how is Dr. Little these days?"

"Still hasn't missed a name, sir," I countered, thinking with a grin of the house master and his legendary memory.

The officer turned back to the apoplectic noncom. "There's nothing wrong here, Sergeant," he stated.[11]

Next in line alphabetically was Howard Williams. I turned to him—an eighteen-year-old summa cum laude and Phi Beta Kappa in math from Howard University—and whispered, "Wait till he sees *your* record!" The sergeant took one look at Williams's form and threw it in disgust to the next person.

For the next few days Fort Keesler kept us recruits busy with drilling and tests, including firearms training. I wasn't a very good pistol shot but scored marksman with a rifle. I also did well in typing, which might have been useful had I washed out of flying.

Bizarre as the base in Biloxi struck me in so many ways, what most often comes to mind is that I had to drink coffee for the first time ever. There was no milk in the kitchen, nor water in the mess hall. When I asked, the Negro mess sergeant stared at me and explained with slow deliberation, "Looka here, you pissant 'cruit. Got no milk, no water. All we got's coffee. Know what's good for you, you damn well bettah drink it!" So I drank my first black coffee from a white mug with no handles—and it wasn't too bad.

From Keesler the Blacks slated for pilot training shunted over to the 2164th Army Air Base in Tuskegee, about 270 miles away. We got in late at night. They gave us blankets and pillows and made us sleep on bare mattresses on the floor of a partially empty barrack.

Early the next morning I awoke before reveille to find an extremely large man looking down at me. He smiled and chuckled, "Hello cuz." Murdock Wharton and his older brother Ulysses, Dartmouth graduates, were the sons of Dr. Ulysses S. Wharton Sr., a prominent Negro physician in Washington, D.C., whose father was the son of George D. Wharton, my great-grandmother Maria's younger brother. Murdock was in an Advanced Tuskegee class.

Our class was 46A, expected to graduate in early 1946. The Tuskegee program aimed to train a pilot in ten months. There were four ten-week segments: Preflight, Primary, Basic, and Advanced. Preflight consisted of ground school, with classes in physics, aerial identification, navigation, and so on. In Primary you actually got to fly, always at first with an instructor, in Stearman PTs, two-seater biplanes with open cockpits. Primary included the rudiments of airborne maneuver—takeoffs, landings, turns and banks, stalls, and simple acrobatics such as snap rolls, slow rolls, chandelles, split-Ss, and Immelmanns. After soloing at the end of Primary, you would go on to Basic, flying AT-6Ds, then Advanced training. At the end successful cadets would get their wings and second lieutenant's bars before heading to either single-engine school or twin-engine school.

Thanks to my years at Camp Atwater, I adjusted to barracks living and made friends fairly easily. The difficulty was hazing, or "bracing"—the military's practice of instilling discipline by pounding raw, square recruits into round holes. The activities were designed to harass, abuse, or humiliate, ostensibly as a way of initiating a person into a group. At Tuskegee as everywhere else, the power hierarchy ran downhill: Advanced cadets "braced" the Basic students, Basic the Primary, and so on. Preflight cadets were fair game to all. Sometimes the hazing was fairly harmless, such as the farcical "claims to fame" we were assigned by upperclassmen—mine was "performing Caesarean operations on pregnant mosquitoes." Some upperclassmen noticed that I did not shave, a convenience probably inherited from my paternal grandmother's Native American genes. A very light fuzz above my upper lip was barely noticeable, and my cheeks or chin were totally bare. Nevertheless my bracers insisted I shave every day. Eventually I developed a reasonably normal amount of hair on my upper lip and chin. But often enough the baiting turned uncomfortable, even near sadistic. You could be ordered to "grab a brace," standing at rigid attention, and then told to sit on an imaginary stool, with or without your back against a wall. Or you might have to hold a heavy rifle or even a full duffle bag at arm's length until your muscles fairly screamed, or you were ordered to run around the complete perimeter of the airfield carrying this load.

The first commandant of cadets at Tuskegee had been Lt. Col. B. O. Davis, who had also been the first Negro to enter West Point in the twentieth century (1932). While a cadet himself, Davis had been brutally hazed. For four years his fellow West Pointers would speak to him only to convey an order and would not sit with him to eat unless specifically assigned to his table. I often wondered if his tolerance for hazing at Tuskegee came from some notion of its being a means to the mental toughness needed to challenge racial discrimination.

For me and some others in my Preflight group, one kind of harassment always seemed to take place just before meals. Our lowly status meant we went last to the mess hall, and somehow several upperclassmen found out that a few cadets in 46A were supposed to be "brains"—Edgar Williams, Alfred Woodland, William White, and me, known as the "Warm Ws" for our last names. When we lined up for chow, the upperclassmen invariably showed up and ordered us to fall out to their barracks, where they made us do their ground schoolwork. Often they kept us past the end of dinner, and on several days we missed meals. It became a major problem until the intervention of my cousin Murdock. When he discovered what was taking place, he confronted the upperclassmen and told them that I was his cousin, and to "cease and desist."

But there were worse things than hazing. When I arrived at Tuskegee there were a few Negro officers, mainly pilots back from fighting in Europe. But most officers were white, usually from the Deep South.[12] Because the majority of American Negroes still lived in the South, the military mistakenly believed that white southerners were better at dealing with Negroes—a deeply perverse misconception. When President Roosevelt died in April, I wondered if this would mean an increase in racial harassment at the base, especially with the loss of Eleanor's influence upon the president.

On one occasion a bunch of drunken white officers barged into our barracks just before taps. They forced us to grab a brace, then staggered around yelling profanities and racial slurs at us. One officer, who had heard that I was a Harvard student, put his face into mine and sneered, "You're smarter than me—right, nigger?" "No, sir," I answered. He asked me a second time more loudly, "I'm ordering you to say you are smarter than me!" I gazed straight ahead and shouted at the top of my voice, "I'm smarter than you, sir!" "Gawd damn black sonuva f——king bitch!" he snarled back. At taps the officers ordered us into our beds and, bellowing with laughter, made us "march under the covers" for the next quarter hour. Rubbing our knees and ankles against the rough sheets gave us abrasions that lasted for days.

Unpleasant as it sometimes got, interclass hazing, after all, was in a sense self-inflicted

—sooner or later you would be on the giving instead of the receiving end. Our officers' racism was something else again. You were under the total control of someone who could force you to do almost anything—someone who didn't consider you an equal, or even a human being. You were just a dark-skinned Negro eighteen-year-old nonentity to be toyed with, terrorized, and all too often reviled. One just had to take it. There was no recourse, and it wasn't going to go away. I had never experienced such racial humiliation, and it opened my eyes to why Swedish economist Gunnar Myrdal[13] found the United States to be a sick and troubled nation. It also gave me a glimpse of what slavery probably was like.

Nevertheless, the sense of solidarity within my class was extremely strong, especially since hazing created a sense of "us against the world." I formed several close friendships within the group, with many men destined to become future Negro leaders and professionals. By this time, my former roommate Harold May had arrived in Class 46B in lower pre-flight training.[14]

• • • •

In Preflight, of course, we never got off the ground. It was all classroom instruction, meant to weed out cadets not up to the job ahead. A lot of the work was downright boring—aircraft identification, for example, in which we fought to stay awake in a dark humid room as the silhouettes of different planes, friendly and enemy alike, flashed rapidly one after another on a screen. Oddly enough, most cadets enjoyed learning Morse code. Every evening for the first few weeks the barracks clattered *dah-dit-dit-dit-dah* as Preflight ranks practiced signaling each other.

When we graduated to Primary, we would at last start learning really to fly. It didn't take long to discover I loved flying an airplane. There was just nothing like it—thundering up and across the empty blue sky, the grid of fields and farms below, prop wash in your face. The speed and freedom were exhilarating, the adrenaline rush electric. It was even better—much better!—than being on a ship on the sea.

Actually, our bi-wing Stearman PTs almost flew themselves. The dowdy old biplanes were ideal for novice pilots. Doing anything seriously wrong in them was almost impossible—though not quite. One of our first basic flying lessons was how to stall the airplane (that is, lose lift under the wings by pulling the stick all the way back), then hit right rudder, and fall off into a rightward spin. To get out of the spin, hit left rudder, break the spin by hitting left rudder and recover by "dumping stick"—pushing it all the way forward, then pull up to regain normal speed and lift to level flight. Before going up, my civilian flight instructor, Perry Young,[15] had explained the mechanics patiently and repeatedly: stall, hit right rudder, fall into a rightward spin—get out by hitting left rudder, dump stick, pull up. In the air I was sure I had it down pat. At Young's command I stalled the plane and spun right—perfect! As we plummeted I hit the opposite rudder, broke the spin, and dumped stick—with a vengeance. I pushed it so hard it banged into the back of Young's own seat, and the plane bucked into a forbidden "outside loop."

Perry took over instantly and, at the cost of a few G-forces, got us straightened out.

Afterward he was remarkably calm. "Only move the stick slightly forward—just a little pop." In fact, Perry explained, most of the time the stick should move within a circle no larger than you can make by putting together your two thumbs and index fingers.

Back on the ground, when I walked into the hangar dayroom, someone had drawn on the blackboard a quite professional cartoon of a Stearman in an outside loop, with the legend "Wharton Dumping Stick."

· · · ·

In the early days of Preflight training cadets weren't allowed to go into town. It was irritating, especially when upperclassmen came back from town full of talk about the lovely ladies of Tuskegee. As another lonely, base-bound weekend approached, I heard about a party being planned at the home of a Negro doctor named Davis, who practiced at the local veterans hospital. Fortuitously, Davis lived next door to a Lt. Col. Branche, who was the father of George and Matt, friends from my Boston childhood. I called the colonel, introduced myself, and asked if he could help get me out from under the no-pass rule. Sure, he said, delighted to. Then he asked about my parents, and reminded me that he had gotten his MD from Boston University at the same ceremony where my parents had received their own degrees.

When I arrived at the party, Mrs. Davis met me at the door with southern courtesy, introducing herself and her daughter. When I told her my name, she looked at me in surprise and asked, "Are you Clif and Harriette's son?"

"Ah . . . yes," I blurted.

"I declare! Harvey," she called to her husband, "come meet Clif and Harriette's boy." Dr. Davis, it turned out, was yet another BU alumnus. He too had graduated at the same ceremony as my parents!

Over the next few weeks after the party, word apparently spread throughout the local Negro community. One mother after another encouraged me to ask their daughters for a date, confident that "Clif and Harriette's boy" would be a gentleman at all times.

My dreams of incognito trysts with Tuskegee city maidens were evaporating before my eyes, but things improved after the start of Primary. We cadets moved from the air base to Sage Hall, living on the Tuskegee Institute campus, near the center of town. One side of Sage faced a girls' dorm, which set off nightly battles over the few available binoculars. Rules for the Tuskegee Institute students were almost as strict as the army's. The only "fraternization" allowed between the male cadets and the institute girls was Saturday evening movies in Logan Hall. Even then the controls were Draconian. The minute the lights came up at the end of the movie, the dean of women got up to remind the girls that they had exactly ten minutes to get back to their houses. Remarkably, several girls, freshmen especially, managed to get sent home with swelling bellies during the term. Human nature, I guessed, somehow found a way.

In Primary, I started dating Charlotte Gibson, the daughter of an employee at the veterans hospital in town. Charlotte was shaped like a Jane Russell pinup, with a slow rolling walk that drew whistles and groans wherever she went. She had a great sense of humor and took herself not too seriously. Since she wasn't a student, she wasn't subject to Tuskegee's strict supervision. Although we went to the movies every Saturday night, I don't remember a single film we saw.

• • • •

Shortly after soloing came our first flight test, in which an outside officer would fly with us to decide whether we would continue or "wash out." Our reviewer was a white captain named Stanley Kominic. Although I believe he was from somewhere in Ohio, one look was all you needed to know there was trouble ahead.

We all watched as my first Primary classmate cleared the traffic pattern, maneuvered, circled a bit, and landed. The instant the plane rolled to a stop on the apron, Kominic leaned forward and growled, "You're *out*—next!"

When a second cadet met the same fate, I caught him and asked what in the world had happened. Both cadets were good pilots—I knew them well. The second cadet said that as soon as he cleared the traffic pattern, Kominic had begun to spit racial slurs, epithets so offensive that the cadets reacted either with rage or, rattled, by fumbling their maneuvers. Either way, Kominic immediately ordered them to land—washed out.

Soon came my turn, and the minute we leveled from taking off, the abuse began.

"Your mother is a juicy black c——t. Make a left turn. . . . How many nigger whores have you f——d at Tuskegee! Do a chandelle . . ."

At every jab I gritted my teeth and kept silent. I thought fleetingly of Camp Atwater, where "playing the dozens" had taught me to keep my cool. This was a lot worse and much more serious. I wouldn't, I told myself, let him get under my skin.

When we landed and I was standing at attention, expressionless but steaming, Kominic glared at me and intoned in a flat voice, "Okay. You pass."[16]

• • • •

In Primary we were not supposed to experiment with aerial acrobatics, though we all did it surreptitiously at times. One trick I *hadn't* tried, however, was the slow roll, taking the plane through a gradual 360-degree rotation while flying parallel to the ground—without, of course, losing too much speed or going into a stall. It contrasts with a "snap roll," done more quickly and at a faster forward velocity with sufficient G-forces to keep you in your seat. When Perry Young took me up to show me how, he asked over the intercom if I had fastened my seat belt.

Sure," I replied, even though you could get casual, if not sloppy, about strapping in. Meanwhile Perry had lowered his seat so only the tip of his head was visible, which seemed odd.

"Follow the controls," Perry said, meaning for me to keep my hands on my stick to feel his own movements to execute the maneuver.

As the plane rotated gently to the right, something felt . . . peculiar. I was surprised, then quite distressed, to find myself sliding steadily to one side of my seat. By the time the plane

In September 1945 I graduated from the Tuskegee Army Air Primary School in the 46A class. (*Left to right*) Alfred Woodland, highest ground school grade average cadet award; Perry Young, flight instructor; Clifton Wharton, outstanding cadet award.

Taken in September 1945, this graduation picture shows the Tuskegee Army Air Primary School 46A class. (*Left to right, standing, 4th*) Alfred Woodland; (*7th*) Joe Douglas; (*seated, 3rd*) me, first lieutenant; (*seated on ground, 6th*) Clinton Jones; (*7th*) Edgar Williams.

was upside down, I was hanging halfway out, my chest at the open-cockpit windshield's rim. Pens, coins, and notebooks spilled from my pockets, past my face on their way to the ground below. Only my seat belt kept me in the cockpit—loosely.

"Stop swinging the controls!" Perry yelled over the intercom—I was holding the stick for dear life. When we finally got through the roll, Perry was trying not to grin, and I could tell he had gotten a big charge out of the whole thing.

. . . .

There were twenty-six of us left when we finished Upper Primary and received Elementary Flying Certificates on September 11. Woody Woodland won the prize for the highest ground school grade average, and I the prize as the "Outstanding Cadet." Three others and I were appointed second lieutenants of our class.

For our next level, Basic, we moved back from the Tuskegee campus to the air base, where we would fly North American AT-6Ds 650-horsepower planes that had previously been used only in the last stage of pilot training. My flight instructor was Captain Lowell Steward, a Negro "Ace" who had flown 143 missions in Europe with the One Hundredth Fighter Squadron, 332nd Fighter Group. He had also earned a Distinguished Flying Cross and an Air Medal with four oak clusters. I felt lucky to have drawn such a teacher.

Steward was tough but fair, and on the whole we got on quite well. Once, though, we tangled. During ground instruction, Steward had insisted that we always take off and land using the reserve fuel tank of our AT-6Ds—in effect, the lowest part of the left-wing tank. The manual said we should use either the reserve or the right-wing tank, whichever was fuller. When I questioned him about it, Steward brushed me off. "It's *always*," he insisted, "the reserve."

One day we were doing touch-and-goes, multiple landings and takeoffs. Because Steward insisted on using the reserve, much of the fuel in that tank was gone. When I executed a particularly bad landing, Steward shoved the throttle forward hard to take us back airborne. He then showed his annoyance in his habitual way by jerking the stick hard to the right and left, cracking my knees painfully. Because of a hill at the end, we were 200 feet less than the altimeter-indicated altitude. Steward's abrupt gesture sloshed sideways the little fuel remaining in the reserve tank, and the airplane's engine stalled. As the heavy AT-6D started to sink, Steward switched instantly to the other gas tank and furiously pumped the choke. Gas surged into the engine, which fortunately caught.

Back at altitude, Steward didn't say a word. I took the controls, flew the scheduled maneuvers without making further errors, and landed. Then after taxiing to a stop, I climbed out of my side of the cockpit, and stood at attention.

Steward glared at me. "Cadet," he intoned carefully, "if you want to kill me, do it on the ground!"

All the cadets had "hot shot" photos taken to send back home. I had two—one in my flight helmet with goggles, the other in my lamb-lined collar leather jacket with dress cap.

(My pilot "Smiling Jack" comics imitation.) I ordered a lot of prints, autographed them, and sent them to family and certain special friends, including Dolores Duncan.

· · · · ·

When the "Tuskegee Experiment" was first proposed, there were predictable objections claiming that Negroes were intellectually incapable of piloting airplanes. This myth about Blacks being mentally deficient and even subhuman were the same arguments that had been used to justify slavery. Stanine test results were used to buttress this contention. In 1942 and 1943, the Army began using stanine scores (1 to 9) as a measure to admit cadets for training. A 1943 study found that 79.3 percent of Negro youth scores "fell in the stanine group of IV and V, in contrast to 14.6 percent for white applicants."[17] The Black intellectual leaders and academicians vigorously countered these findings, pointing to the inherent inadequacies and biases of the tests—an argument that would grow over the next years regarding similar tests.[18] "By February 1944 the [stanine] scores needed for all aircrew trainees [Blacks and whites] were the same—5 for pilot training, 6 for navigator, and 5 for bombadier."[19] But the racists' arguments of inferiority persisted.

The irony was that racial segregation was creating a higher quality talent pool at Tuskegee. Class 46A exemplified this development. Edgar Williams, with his summa cum laude at eighteen, would return to Howard University as a professor of mathematics. Joe Douglas, an undergraduate in electrical engineering at Purdue University, became the first Black professor of electrical engineering at Pennsylvania State University. Harold K. Hoskins left Tuskegee to enroll and complete his undergraduate degree at Portland State University. He then rejoined the Air Force, graduating as a pilot from Randolph Air Force Base. He fought in the Korean War, winning an air medal with oak leaf clusters, and became a lieutenant colonel, retiring to serve as vice president for student affairs at California State University in Hayward. John D. "Dusty" Rhodes from Orangeburg, South Carolina, later became a surgeon in Milwaukee, Wisconsin. Bob Church became a dentist in Detroit. Clinton Jones, who was older than most of us and had been one of the developers of the E6B computers used in air navigation, became a professor of physics at Tennessee State University, then a professor and director of the Computer Center at Fisk University. This was a strong group of Black "high achievers" who would make their mark.

Another less obvious irony is that Tuskegee Institute, the creation of legendary Booker T. Washington, had become a magnet for outstanding talent—more like W. E. B. Du Bois's "Talented Tenth" than Washington's own "industrial arts students who became tradesmen and artisans."[20] I found this a fascinating sequel to the earlier debate between these two Black legends over which should be the preferable approach for Negro liberation.[21]

· · · · ·

As time went on it got harder to resist a little showboating in the air. We weren't supposed to, but cadets flew over the town all the time. Tuskegee was small, and identifying residences from the air was easy. Sometimes we would go into a dive directly over a girlfriend's house, then pull out with a roar. Many girls loved it and couldn't wait to find out who was the culprit.

Once I nearly had a real accident. There was an empty farmer's field where we practiced landings and which was just long enough to take off from. Just before takeoff a ditch cut across the field perpendicularly. Hitting the edge at speed caused your plane to bounce sharply into the air, which we hotshots incorporated into our moves. Standing on the brakes, we would rev the engine to a critical pitch, then suddenly let go, sending the plane hurtling forward while pumping the hydraulics to raise the wheels. Because of the plane's weight, the wheels wouldn't retract—until they hit the ditch. Then they would come up with a snap. The plane would give a vertiginous little drop, catch air, and soar upward—just like we had seen in films of navy pilots goosing their F6F Hellcats off the back of a carrier.

That morning I didn't start far enough back. When the wheels hit the ditch they snapped up, all right, but the plane dropped fast and hard, and for a few seconds my propeller was mowing grass and hurling clumps of dirt in every direction. I managed to pull up, but it was a lucky break. I could have spun in and cracked up.

For all the hijinks, we knew full well we were preparing to fight a war. In August, news of the devastating atomic bombing of Hiroshima and Nagasaki suddenly brought the distant conflict a lot closer—the possibility of our own deaths rose up out of the subliminal depths where we usually managed to bury it.

A week later, on August 14, 1945, President Truman announced Japan's unconditional surrender. The elation was general and cacophonous. But even as we cheered the signing of the articles of surrender in early September, we couldn't help wondering what it meant for us—our training, our service, our future in the Army Air Corps. With no clear idea about the future, we continued to study, march, and learn to fly.

A few weeks later, those still active got word that we could either continue through Advanced training or opt for an immediate honorable discharge. The catch was in the fine print: If we mustered out, we could be redrafted. In effect, the personnel sergeant explained, going on meant signing up for three more years, regardless of whether we won our wings.

It was a painful dilemma—I adored flying, and Captain Steward said I was a good pilot. In fact, he promised to recommend me for the highly prized twin-engine school—a gleaming temptation.

But a college education wasn't something to turn away from lightly, as even Steward conceded. With so many pilots coming home from the war, what would my career prospects be, either in the Air Corps or even in civilian aviation? Moreover, although the Tuskegee Airmen and tens of thousands of other Negro soldiers had pushed the country a giant step down the path to change, the military remained a massively segregated institution, drenched in racial discrimination. Did I really look forward to a future where insult and degradation lurked around every corner?

My own opportunities, I realized, would lie elsewhere, and laying the foundation for a meaningful future meant finishing up my degree at Harvard.

My final discharge papers came through around Thanksgiving.

Before heading north I made a brief pilgrimage to the campus to see the laboratory of George Washington Carver, whose botanical studies had made him legendary. He had died only two years previously, and I didn't want to leave without paying my respects. I don't know what I was expecting—an airy, fully equipped modern facility, I suppose. When I found it, the Carver laboratory (by now a museum) was a shock. The room was small and dark, on the slightly sunken first floor of a rickety out-of-the-way building. Amid the musky shadows, the old beakers, test tubes, and microscope looked like junk—laughable at any self-respecting high school. Was this where the great Carver had conducted his groundbreaking research? This lowly clutter the spring from which had flowed 325 papers and reports on the peanut, 108 uses for sweet potatoes, and seventy-five by-products from pecans?

I was dumbfounded—but the realization I had stumbled onto was profound. It wasn't Carver's lab or equipment that mattered. The means were secondary at best. Carver's lifetime of invention and discovery had been in spite of, not because of, the tools available to him. His own innate intelligence, curiosity, perseverance, and drive—those were the real instruments of his success.

I left Tuskegee for Harvard thinking that flying an airplane wasn't the only way for someone to soar. I discovered that I could deal with the most virulent manifestations of racism without losing self-control—and succeed. I learned that racial prejudice is an insidious fog which enters your pores to pierce your soul by destroying your self-worth and denying your humanity—but that succeeds only if you let it.

▪ Back to Cambridge

Back in Cambridge I was a second-term junior who had already taken twenty-three of the thirty-two courses needed to graduate. Accelerated placement and high course loads had put me ahead despite the Tuskegee interlude, and in just three more semesters I could graduate.

But at Tuskegee I had learned a few things. For one thing, I knew I needed more time for seasoning, to grow to greater maturity. I also had a sharper sense of my academic priorities. Earlier, I admitted to myself, I had spent too much time in outside activities. Now I would buckle down and wait to graduate until 1947, on time with my class. My plan was still to follow my father into the Foreign Service, so I stayed with my history major.

Tuskegee had schooled me as nowhere else about racism. Back at Harvard, I found myself gradually revising my earlier impressions about how well Negroes really fit in. I wondered how I could have missed before the extent to which your place at Harvard depended on things entirely outside yourself, or even your academic performance. The forces involved were how much money you had, how you dressed, where you had been born and grown up, what schools you had attended or "prepped at," the social standing of your parents and forebears, and—surprise—the color of your skin.

Even among those who seemed most amiably accepting, there was all too often an insidious, unspoken assumption that Negroes were different—and inevitably lesser. At Tuskegee, the racists had been all too blatant, often semiliterate crackers. In Cambridge, many of the supposedly enlightened liberals still carried around the invisible baggage and secret codes of discrimination. Here it might come not as a curse or a sneer, but as thoughtlessly well-meant praise—"You're not like other Negroes"—or fastidious condescension—"Your white blood must make the difference."

The unspoken expectations were negative. In class and out, you were *not expected* to perform, *not expected* to know how to behave, *not expected* to aspire. During a dinner in Adams House not long after I had returned, a classmate from another dorm sat down at our table. As we ate, he mentioned that he hoped to become a diplomat. When I asked him to tell me more, he seemed surprised—then increasingly chilly and patronizing. Puzzled initially, I explained that my father was a career foreign service officer. I had spent a lot of my childhood abroad, and I added that I also planned to become a diplomat. By then the classmate was so angry he could barely speak. Without finishing his meal he left the table. The conversation was over—it was as if I had an ebony letter stamped on my forehead—a Negro counterpart to Nathaniel Hawthorne's Hester Prynne.

The problem did not stem from paranoia on my part, because I had full confidence in my own abilities. It wasn't that I felt that I was being persecuted, but rather that I had to confront on a daily basis a set of negative expectations from those who knew nothing about me. If you mention to someone that you are a graduate of "Harvard," because they see a Black face they hear "Howard," the predominately Black university. When they realize it *is* Harvard, they quickly change their approach. You have to help them see beyond the automatic Black stereotypes. In later life, I found that even a strong record of accomplishment was not enough; when you moved into a new situation, you had to deal with the negative expectations syndrome all over again and start from scratch to eliminate it. One effective method for dealing with such situations I found was through humor. Racist jokes about Negroes were common, but my telling a reverse anti-white joke often proved especially effective in squelching a biased bore.

Of course this experience is not unique to me. High-achieving Blacks confront it regularly throughout the United States. Occasionally younger Blacks ask me whether the problem disappears when you reach the upper strata or power levels of society. They are always disappointed when I tell them that it has recurred in all my careers throughout my life.

▪ New England Student Christian Movement _____

One outcome of my continuing involvement with the Old Cambridge Baptist Church Sunday Evening Club was my introduction to the New England Student Christian Movement (NESCM), a regional offshoot of the Student YMCA and YWCA. The annual conference, held at Camp O-At-Ka on Lake Sebago, Maine, drew student leaders of the YMCA and YWCA from all the colleges and universities in New England for discussions on religious and social issues. Participants included a number of my Harvard-Radcliffe colleagues such as Ernie Howell and my childhood friend from Roxbury Joe Mitchell, who was attending Bates College. Also, it was there I met Charles Sumner "Chuck" Stone from Wesleyan, who became a lifelong friend.

I attended my first O-At-Ka conference June 19–26, 1944. Each meeting had a major theme, with a carefully structured program of morning worship, followed by addresses heavily weighted toward religious subjects, afternoon seminars, hours of meditative silence, recreation, late afternoon speeches or panels, and finally evening programs. Speakers usually were leading religious or political figures of the period such as Reinhold Niebuhr, Norman Thomas, Liston Pope, Kirtley F. Mather, and James H. Robinson.

Bill Ellis, Court's brother, was the cochairman of the 1946 NESCM conference, and I became conference cochairman with Kitty Cochran (Smith) in 1947 (June 16–23). The experience was valuable as a training ground for the future. I was able to cultivate my interpersonal skills and leadership experience. Equally important was developing the ability to articulate my views and to give informal speeches. This was something I had not done previously, and O-At-Ka was a natural testing and early training ground.

The religious leader who had the greatest impact on me was the Reverend Herbert King from New York, pastor of Grace Congregational Church in Harlem. Herb was about 6'5" tall and heavily built. He had the deep, rich, resonant voice common among Negroes, with a booming laugh that welled up from his diaphragm and could fill any room. Whenever he laughed, it was with great abandon and joy, and no one around him could fail to join in. He was also extremely perceptive, sensitive, and wise. I respected him tremendously, and we became good friends.

One day Herb invited me to walk with him along the white sand lakeshore. We talked about a variety of issues, until he stopped, looked at me intently, and asked, "Clif, what do you plan to do with your life?"

"I have always planned to become a diplomat like my father. But I have also thought about the ministry."

Herb then told me something I had never realized about myself. "Whatever you do and wherever you are, you do not behave as though you are solely a Negro. You recognize and accept that you are a Negro, but your attitude and behavior are that you are a person to be accepted on your own merits. You are able to acknowledge a duality—the fact that you are a Negro in a racist society, while simultaneously functioning like any other human being."

"Too many Negroes," he added, "begin everything from the standpoint of their Blackness and never break out of it in their entire lives. You break out of it automatically every single day. When you walk into a room, you walk in just like anyone else, not as though you were a Negro expecting to be treated as a Negro."

He then planted a seed. "You should think long and hard about whether you should use your natural gift on a broader canvas other than going into the Foreign Service like your father. You have the opportunity to do much, much more than most of our people." Herb concluded, "You can be a pioneer for our people, and you can break barriers in whatever field you choose."

Herb gave me a great deal to think about because he saw me in ways I could not see myself. He revealed how I was unconsciously handling the "duality"—being a Negro *and* a human being.

. . . .

Having missed the 1943, 1944, and 1945 seasons, I decided to return to Camp Atwater one last time before graduating from college. Mr. Dickerson was kind enough to invite me to return as senior counselor for the Island and to stay on through the August girls' season. They also invited my childhood Liberian friend Richelieu Morris to serve both seasons, along with Matt Branche, now at Bowdoin.

The highlight of the girls' season was a musical comedy that Richelieu and I wrote called *Tilt*. During the boys' season, Matt Branche, who had a great penchant for starting fads, had begun greeting people by standing stock still on one foot with a bent leg and with one arm extended in front and another behind, somewhat like a teapot, while saying "Tilt!" Everyone in camp began greeting each other that way. The girls quickly adopted the fad as well. So Rich and I wrote our musical comedy *Tilt* for one of the evening assemblies. The title song "Tilt" was based upon Matt's pose. We also wrote two other songs, "Don't Do It" and "Suffer," evoking favorite camp expressions that summer. "Suffer" especially broke up the audience, since it dealt with female Negro hair.

The summer was a fitting conclusion to this phase of my youth.

. . . .

In spring 1946 I applied to the Foreign Service Association for the remainder of my Harriman scholarship, since only one semester of it had been used. It came through and supplemented my GI Bill stipend.

I also took the comprehensive exam in history, scoring 78.6. That qualified me preliminarily to graduate "magna" or "cum laude," depending on the rest of my grades and especially my honors thesis. Then as now, senior honors candidates were assigned tutors, after the British practice. I signed up for tutoring over the next two semesters. To oversee my thesis preparation I drew Wallace E. Davies, who set up regular meetings for me, as well as three or four others,

Taken in August 1946, this picture shows the waterfront crew for the girls' season at Camp Atwater. (*Standing, 7th*) Lois Higgenbotham; *(middle row, 8th)* Joyce Burrows; (*seated, 4th*) Howie Edmonds; (*6th*) me. My first camp counselor, Howie Edmonds, taught me how to swim at age eight. Lois Higginbotham later married Romeyn Lippman, and in 1953, during the Eisenhower administration, she became the first Black secretary in the White House. Joyce Burrows later married David Dinkins, who became the mayor of New York City (1990–1993).

to discuss assigned readings. In the group was Brad Perkins, son of Harvard history professor Dexter Perkins, who became a friend. With Brad the question wasn't whether he would get honors, just how high.

Also that spring I got back into track, where Coach Mikkola hoped I had regained form. My first meet was outdoors with Yale, Harvard hosting on a cold raw day. Jaako asked me to run the hurdles as well as the 440 and the high jump—if I placed, we would gain a valuable margin in the points. Thinking about the extra events ahead, I didn't warm up as much as I would have normally before the hurdles. Over the first jump I suddenly felt a searing bolt in my left leg and tumbled onto my hands—I had pulled a hamstring. Unlike today, doctors in the forties didn't have the means to rejuvenate the muscle—my track performance would never be the same afterward.

- The National Student Conference in Chicago _____

Bill Ellis, former roommate, had graduated in June 1946. He was selected by the YM/YWCA's National Intercollegiate Christian Council as a delegate to the August meeting of the World Student Congress in Prague. Bill and the other Americans who attended the congress were surprised to discover that of major Western nations only the United States had no national student organization.[22] The Americans were determined to change that. Returning home, they soon formed a committee to sponsor a founding conference in Chicago in late December. The prospectus for the meeting declared, in part:

> Experiences . . . among students of many nations have brought home . . . that a new segment of society is emerging . . . which often transcends national differences. . . . One way in which [the] responsibility of the American student can be realized is by the establishment of a nonpartisan organization . . . devoted to the needs and problems of students.[23]

Bill came back having been elected vice chair of the new International Union of Students (IUS) that had been created there. In the short time he was home preparing for long-term residence abroad, Bill talked to me about his efforts in Prague and the prospects for a nationwide student organization here in the United States. The idea, he said, was to promote public awareness of issues that students cared about, and to nurture formal relationships among students across the globe. Veterans were already flooding American campuses under the GI Bill. Shaped if not scarred by wartime experiences, many favored greater international engagement to avoid future wars and make the world a better place. A dawning was also going on. Students were awakening to their underlying mutual interests as a social group, and perhaps as well to higher education's changing role in the world at large.

Bill's report intrigued me greatly, and so did the prospect of the new organization. First, it would have a significant international element, which might prove relevant to my intended career. Second, although I had until now largely avoided campus politics, the new venture seemed to offer a chance of getting some leadership experience, possibly beyond the local or even regional level.

Although I was busy with my senior thesis and thinking about graduate school as well, I decided to run for one of Harvard's three undergraduate delegate slots to the December convention. In a December 12 campus-wide vote[24] on ten candidates, Douglass Cater came in first, with 1,093 votes. With 600, I squeaked in third, probably helped by my "name recognition" through WHCN.

No sooner had the delegates been named than controversy erupted. Ten days before the Chicago convention, professor of government William Yandell Elliott told the *Harvard Crimson* that the university's representatives should "keep a sharp lookout for Communist control bids. He blasted the IUS as an organization "beyond doubt in the hands of Russian oriented leaders" who wanted it to be a Soviet propaganda arm.[25] Citing information he had gotten from Georgetown University students who had been in Prague, he claimed that the IUS executive committee was weighted three to one in favor of Communist bloc countries, with only one American (Bill Ellis). He also charged that the driving force behind it all was the World Federation of Democratic Youth, "widely considered the successor to the Young Communist League." Elliott based his credibility as a critic on his role as a founder of the ill-fated Confédération Internationale des Étudiants, organized after World War I.

Elliott's bombast drew a quick reaction from senior student Doug Cater, who had learned his political infighting early and well.[26] Condemning Elliott for using unverified information from a single source (and identifying the Georgetown student who had passed it on), Cater rebutted every allegation with factual detail. To Elliott's scornful charge of the American students' "naïveté," he countered, "If we are so naive that we must fail every time we come up against representatives from Communist countries, then let us withdraw from the IUS and the United Nations and send the first bomb on its merry way."[27]

Chicago, I thought, was going to be interesting.

Held in Mandel Hall of the University of Chicago campus, the National Student Conference was attended by 672 delegates and observers from more than 300 U.S. colleges and universities. In a way it was my baptism in student politics.

The yearning for a student voice was fervent. But a certain anxiety permeated the meeting. Most of the delegates had no prior experience in anything of the kind, and the few who did tended to be seen as "professional students." Tossed into the mix were escalating Cold War tensions and growing distrust of the American Left, not least by students representing conservative Catholic organizations. Because the meeting was brief—only two days—the most participants could hope to do was determine whether there was genuine interest in taking the slow steps that would be necessary to bring a real organization into being.

Behind the scenes, left-wing students worked hard to dominate the agenda. Among other tactics, they pushed for all-night sessions, hoping that ordinary delegates would gradually slip away while the radical ranks held firm. One evening discussion dragged on until nearly 4:00 A.M. Everyone was groggy, out on their feet. At a seeming impasse, we broke for coffee in a lounge where there happened to be a piano. I sat down and began to play, and others gathered around to sing. After a while, we felt better and went back to work.

In addition to bureaucratic wrangling—governance structure, membership, finances, affiliations—race was an abiding, thorny issue for the meeting—so contentious it almost prevented the new student organization from being born.

While almost every delegate agreed "in principle" regarding racial equality, what that meant in concrete terms was nowhere near as easy to define. At the time poll taxes, "separate but equal," and Jim Crow segregation were the laws of the land, not just in the South. It would be almost a decade before the Supreme Court desegregated public schools, and even longer before Martin Luther King Jr.'s boycott opened the front seats of buses to Blacks in Montgomery, Alabama. Noting that the new organization would likely meet in all regions of the country, a group of Negro delegates proposed a resolution that it should "take every means within its power" to repeal state enforcement of segregation in education. But the southern white delegates fired back that a "Yankee-drafted" statement would work against itself, arguing that they must be allowed to work out measures to accommodate local situations.

I then offered a compromise, proposing to modify the language of the proposed constitution based upon the two conflicting positions. My double proposal was, first, strengthening the equal rights section of the preamble by stating "that racial and religious bigotry and discrimination be totally disavowed by this National Student Organization," and, second, inserting seven specific action steps under the third organizational "aim": "to secure for all people equal rights and possibility of primary, secondary, and higher education regardless of sex, race, religion, economic circumstance, social standing, or political convictions." Using Allan Ostar as my "floor manager," I contacted key leaders of larger student delegations to push the compromise forward.[28] The compromise passed as a temporary measure until the constitutional convention.

At the end of 1946, racism was a cancer much of America still didn't know it had. But a sense of humor helped a bit. When tempers flared in the midst of one tense discussion, a delegate from North Carolina jibed, "Mr. Chairman, I suggest we divide the conference into those with drawls and those without."

Among the most prominent leaders at Chicago were several students who had attended the Prague congress—Bill Ellis, Wally Wallace, Curt Farrar, and Doug Cater. Cater was certainly the most colorful and probably the most effective. Standing at the back of the Mandel Hall auditorium, he would wait until precisely the right moment in a debate, then raise his stentorian Alabama voice: "Mr. Speakahh. Mr. *Speak*ahh!" As all heads swiveled to see, Cater would stride ponderously, theatrically down the aisle. By the time he reached the mike, the entire audience was in his hand.

In preparation for a founding convention, officers and members of a National Continuations Committee were chosen. Jim Smith (University of Texas), who was a mature, calming voice during the meetings, was elected president; Russell Austin (University of Chicago; Young Socialist League) was chosen vice president; John Simons (Fordham University and the Young Catholic Student Organization) was elected treasurer; and I was elected secretary.

Well before the meeting's end, we knew the FBI was paying close attention—the Harvard delegation was sure it was because of William Yandell Elliott's extensive connections in Washington. It didn't help that the only national press coverage of the Chicago meeting was a picture of our elected officers (including me) on the front page of the *Daily Worker*,[29] the official organ of the Communist Party in the United States. When my father heard about it in the Azores, his bellow of outrage rolled all the way across the Atlantic Ocean.

Nor was that my father's only bombshell. When I got back to Boston from Chicago, I found my mother in tears. Returning home unexpectedly from his new post in Ponta Delgada, Azores, he had informed my mother that he wanted a divorce. *Divorce*? It was beyond comprehension to me. My parents' marriage had seemed nothing less than ideal, a model in every way: two people who loved each other without reservation, absent the slightest rift. My father, my hero, had been a perfect father, a perfect husband—and I worshiped my mother. Yes, they had been long apart because of the war. But that had been a deliberate, reasoned decision. What now could have gone wrong? How could he possibly do such a thing . . . and why?

There was another woman, my father admitted stonily to my mother. But he would take care of mother and us children, he promised.

My mother begged him to reconsider. He could even keep his woman if he had to, she said—if only the marriage could survive. But my father was adamant, and mother was devastated.

I took it all very hard. When we met, my father's face was implacable, his teeth clenched so tight his jaw muscles bunched. While he still admired and respected my mother, he said, their differences were irreconcilable. She was the one, he argued, who had wanted a big family. So many children had made it necessary and right for her to stay in the United States. But he could no longer live in such a way.

Desperate, I asked if he would change his mind if I went to law school. Then we could start a father-son firm, an idea we had tossed around occasionally as I was growing up. No, he insisted. My father would stay in the Foreign Service, and he and my mother would divorce.

News of my parents' impending split hit the local Negro community like a thunderbolt. Most of my mother's friends rallied round her—though a few crowed it was no worse than she deserved for her self-assurance in her marriage. Grandmother Nana was like a lioness whose cub had been clawed. She was especially angry because she had been fond of my father and done much for him over the years. She even contacted John McCormack, her congressional representative and Speaker of the House at the time. McCormack waffled and did nothing—what, for that matter, could he have done?

My siblings were stunned—William, then a just-adolescent thirteen, and Richard, eleven. William had always been thought the brightest of the children. Because of William's love of boats my father always called him "Admiral," invariably taking him along on official tours of warships visiting Las Palmas. For William the trauma was so severe that his grades slipped badly, and he had to transfer from Boston Latin to English High.

At eight, little Mary only partially understood what was happening, but as my father's "princess" she felt inexplicably abandoned. As for me, when I told Bill Ellis about the divorce, I cried for the first time since my childhood.

In addition to everything else, Mother was now experiencing financial problems—had it not been for the children, she admitted, she might have committed suicide. Everything seemed to be imploding on her. She couldn't help looking to me, the eldest child, for comfort—telephone calls came to Adams House almost nightly.

Two years later my father flew to Reno and filed for divorce, alleging "cruelty." My mother filed a counteraction in Boston, charging abandonment. The divorce settled in her favor four years later, in September 1950.

Awful as it was at the time, ordinary life went on—school foremost. By now I was well into my senior thesis. I had looked for a topic dealing with U.S. diplomacy in Latin America. My tutor Davies and I agreed on "Argentine Beef: A Frictional Factor in United States–Argentine Relations, 1939–1941." The focus was a ban America had levied on Argentine beef because of *aftosa* (foot-and-mouth disease) infecting Argentine cattle. Seen by many Latin American nations as a test of our vaunted "Good Neighbor" policy, the embargo had undercut U.S.-Argentine relations for several years.

My thesis was thoroughly researched, filled with relevant footnotes, charts, citations, bibliographical sources, and even tastefully reproduced political cartoons. But I made a fateful mistake: I failed to include any reference to a book by Professor Hubert C. Herring, one of three readers who would evaluate my work. Herring's publication was almost entirely irrelevant to my subject, but I would have been smart to mention it. Later Wallace Davies told me that the other two readers recommended me for a "magna," but Herring wouldn't have it. Instead I got a "cum laude" and my first lesson in academic politics. My fellow tutee Brad Perkins got a "magna" and my sincere congratulations.

During his few months in the United States before returning to Prague, Bill Ellis had been dating an attractive Radcliffe doctoral candidate from Detroit, Dorothy Anne Hicks. When he left for Europe, he asked me to look in on her from time to time. Dorothy Anne was a statuesque young Negro woman with limpid eyes, sensual lips, and long auburn hair. She was also warm, funny, and smart. From the beginning the attraction between us was irresistible. I saw her almost daily, often meeting her after class. She was also a practicing Christian Scientist. That didn't matter, but we both felt guilty because of Bill.

Making the situation worse, Dorothy Anne and my mother hit it off instantly—the first of my girlfriends she had liked unequivocally. But the guilt over Bill didn't abate, and anyway Dorothy Anne was going away for the summer. By the time I invited her to my graduation, I had already decided we should put the relationship on hold until Bill Ellis returned. That would give us both time to decide what we were really feeling.[30]

▪ ▪ ▪ ▪

I graduated from Harvard University on June 5, 1947.

The dewy early morning soon warmed under sunny skies to a balmy 68 degrees. Beneath the trees on the grassy quadrangle, folding chairs were set up in ranks facing the Chapel. The soon to be graduates sat in front of the stage, with family and friends behind. Following tradition, the sheriff of Middlesex County called the ceremony to order, a solemn request that we "draw nigh . . . and [be welcomed] into the ranks of learned men." The undergraduates rose and moved forward in a sea of black robes.

Our valedictorian was Doug Cater, my Chicago co-delegate, who gave his oration in the traditional Latin.

The commencement speaker was General George Marshall, hero of World War II and now secretary of state. His speech centered on the need to rebuild Europe—an early herald of what would become the famous, pathbreaking Marshall Plan. I listened to his talk with great concentration and interest. The idea of enlisting economic assistance in the service of national foreign policy was new to me, and powerfully persuasive.

My commencement guests were Mother, Nana, Pa, Pop, Cousin Marie, and Dorothy Anne Hicks. My father wasn't there, nominally because of the high cost of traveling from the Azores. All considered, it was probably for the best.

As a new family tradition my brothers, William and Richard, later also attended Harvard (classes of 1955 and 1957). William majored in government and was cox of the 150-pound crew; Richard majored in German and was captain of the track team. In 1957, the three of us purchased a Revere sterling silver bowl engraved with our first names and graduation years. We filled the bowl with many of the Harvard bills our mother had paid and a letter on top with a check as a small thanks. "We hope it is something you will treasure in your heart, as we do the many sacrifices which you have made to realize your dream and ours," we wrote. "You made it possible for us, and we did our utmost to succeed as best we could." She cried at our appreciation for what she had done as a single mother—three Harvard sons.

In 1961, our sister Mary received her BA in English from Suffolk University. All three of my siblings would eventually earn advanced degrees—William an LLB, Richard a PhD, and Mary an MA.

▪ Agony in the Azores

The other woman in my father's life was Evangeline "Leonie" Sears Carter, former wife of James G. Carter, a politically appointed (noncareer) Negro diplomat. Carter had retired from his post in Madagascar at the end of 1942, with World War II raging. While her husband returned to the United States, Leonie and her children had remained on the island.[31] After my father arrived in Tananarive as consul, she had gradually assumed an informal role as "hostess" at the consulate. Leonie was very fair, with reddish hair and Caucasian features. She spoke French, knew her way around diplomatic protocol, and could play her part perfectly. Over the next few years, in both Madagascar and later the Azores, the course of their relationship had developed predictably, perhaps inevitably.

Only days after my graduation from Harvard, my mother decided to make one last try at saving her marriage—traveling unannounced to see my father in the Azores. She took my sister Mary with her. Over her five-week stay in Ponta Delgada my mother repeatedly tried to persuade my father not to file a divorce. But he was adamant, determined to marry Leonie Carter. By this time Dad was almost totally blind. Deterioration of his central vision had begun soon after he left the Canary Islands. For almost half of his forty years of service, he successfully concealed from the State Department that he was virtually blind due to severe macular degeneration. There is some indication that this is a genetic trait. My father's great-grandmother, Tabitha Wharton, and his uncle, Ben Wharton, both became blind early in life.

Mother's letters to me were anguished, filled with her pain. Even though their protracted separation had been a mutual decision, perhaps she should have recognized the danger in it. But in my eyes, no amount of naïveté was sufficient to explain, much less justify my father's treatment of my mother. He was not the man I had known, admired, and loved.

After Mother returned from the Azores, convinced at last that the breakup was irreversible, her personality underwent a slow but profound change. She grew sadder, less cheerful. She had always possessed an inner strength and will—now the steel had been tempered by losing the love of her life. Financial straits brought added stress—she quickly decided to create a downstairs apartment at 285 to rent out for extra income.

Then and thereafter, amazingly, she insisted that we children should continue to write Dad and even, when possible, see him in person. He was our father, she reminded us constantly, and we owed him our love and respect. I obeyed reluctantly, but bitterness rendered any contact with my father infrequent and perfunctory. She herself would not see him again for the next four decades.

▪ NSA Convention in Madison _____

Eight months after the Chicago organizational meeting, came a weeklong founding convention (August 30–September 7) for what would become the National Student Association.[32] The meeting took place on the Madison campus of the University of Wisconsin, a beautiful spot in the American heartland. Some of my college friends attended, including my Walnut Avenue neighbor Janice Yates (Jackson College, Tufts) and Harvard classmate Ernie Howell, just elected cochair of the National Intercollegiate Christian Council. At the opening ceremony, greetings were read from President Truman. The keynote speaker, Dr. Homer P. Rainey, president of Stephens College, exhorted students to "slough off the protective shell

DAILY WORKER, JANUARY 3, 1947. PHOTOCOPY OF NEWSPAPER BY MANFRED WEIDEMANN, COOPERSTOWN, NEW YORK.

Taken in January 1947, this picture shows the U.S. National Student Association officers' convention founding committee. (*Left to right*) Russell Austin, vice president, University of Chicago; Jim Smith, president, University of Texas; John Simons, treasurer, Fordham University; me, secretary, Harvard University.

of ivory towers . . . and mix in with the realistic, hard-bitten world of politics, economics, and conflicting ideologies." He also counseled us to avoid partisan politics.

While plenary session votes never exceeded 581, press releases reported that some seven hundred delegates representing 350 colleges and universities attended. There was a heavy representation of World War II veterans, giving the conference a mature cast. Delegates made a broad geographic representation of the country, in part because so many came from state colleges and universities—a feature I could personally attest because I was in charge of seating the delegations and saw it from my regular seat on stage as convention secretary.

An issue that came up early was whether independent student organizations, such as the YMCA/YWCA, the Students for Democratic Action, the Young Communist League, the Student World Federalists, and the Newman Club Federation (Catholic) should be legal members of the proposed association. The university-based elected delegates were suspicious of the motives of the independents—because few attendees knew each other, it was hard to tell who outnumbered whom. There was also considerable concern that some student organizations might be Communist "fronts," whose scheming would poison the association in its cradle.

When the question was called, membership of student organizations was soundly rejected, and a sigh of collective relief was audible throughout the hall. The conference then created four panels to work through the thorny issues of membership eligibility, participation in domestic politics, joining the International Union of Students, and educational opportunities (i.e., the race issue). Their recommendations were presented to the plenary sessions for action.

My role as secretary was not solely perfunctory; my position allowed me to impact the mood of the sessions. New York was split into two delegations: New York State (upstate) and Metropolitan New York (city). During the early votes, the New York State delegation had adopted a "unit rule" where all of the delegation votes were cast in favor of the majority position, regardless of any internal split. "New York casts thirty-four votes for and zero votes against" was the roll call announcement. As the vote recorder, my vantage point on the stage enabled me to see that this unit-rule vote was causing negative reactions among the other delegations. After this happened a couple of times, the tension was palpable.

I realized that the strain need to be dramatically countered—with a bit of humor. I had glimpsed an old bullwhip in the back of the theater. Concealing the coiled whip under my jacket, it was slipped on a shelf under the podium. At the next roll call, when the New York State delegation announced their unit rule vote, out came the bullwhip and I cracked the whip loudly across the stage, to the approving laughter of the delegates. The embarrassed New York State delegation avoided unit rule votes thereafter.

At another strained moment, I eased the tension by taking the delegates on a "Lion Hunt," which I had previously introduced at the Chicago meeting. Sitting in a straight-backed chair on center stage, I led the audience through the steps of an imaginary hunt. "I'm going on a lion hunt!" I said as I stomped my feet in a simulated walking motion while simultaneously slapping my open palms on my thighs. The audience chanted back, "I'm going on a lion hunt," and they slapped their own thighs and stomped their feet. The audience followed along as I lifted a rifle, climbed a tree, crossed a swamp and bridge, parted the deep grass, and took other elaborate steps to try to find the elusive lion. Upon sighting the imaginary lion in a cave, we all "fled" in terror, rapidly repeating the entire process in reverse and at high speed. The resulting laughter suggested there was nothing better to reduce tension than a lion hunt. At times humor has a role in leadership.

Another contentious matter was whether the association should participate directly in politics. For some that seemed fundamental, a key function of student unions around the globe, and proponents argued that it was only through direct political action that student interests could be served. The counterargument was that political partisanship would inevitably split the organization along sharp ideological lines, hindering its ability to represent the broadest possible swath of American students. When the National Student Association (NSA) constitution eventually prohibited direct political action, it further weakened the commitment of a number of independent student organizations.

While most delegates agreed that U.S. students needed to involve themselves in international activities, the issue of affiliating with the International Union of Students was still controversial. Again, the concern was ideological. The IUS had traditionally stressed left-of-center political expression and action, eschewing any claim to nonpartisanship. Many worried that the infant NSA might be effectively smothered within an organization dominated by Soviet-bloc countries, pushing agendas more radical than U.S. students would accept. In the end, a delegate panel on internationalism extended a friendly but wary hand. It accepted the prospect of IUS affiliation, but stipulated the NSA's permanent political and administrative autonomy within the larger organization—as well as the right to repudiate specific IUS positions and decisions. The agreement also provided that affiliation with the IUS would have to be ratified by individual NSA campuses. Approval would require at least half of the member colleges, representing two-thirds of member students.

The Madison convention included numerous delegates from predominantly Black colleges. The southern Negroes tried to introduce several constitutional provisions condemning racism and discrimination in higher education. In support were some liberal white students, including left-wing extremists such as those from the Young Communist League. For a while the YCL often seemed a virtual echo of the Black delegates' positions.

The issue came to a head in the panel on educational opportunity, which I chaired. Because of my position, southern Negroes sought my support. But I suspected that they were at risk of being exploited by the YCL, whose positions seemed to me to reflect political expediency rather than real commitment. When I told them so, the Negro students disagreed strongly—some called me a "traitor to the cause."

Meanwhile, a southern white group opposed bringing any racial dimension into the NSA constitution at all—at one point, threatening to walk out of the convention. Soon the two groups had locked themselves into rigid positions. The situation was explosive, and the NSA's very future looked in doubt.

On the afternoon of September 4, after three full days of turbulence in corridors and committees, Jim Smith, chairman of the steering committee, introduced a compromise hammered out during the previous all-night meeting. When it came to the floor in plenary session, things boiled over again, and a solid two hours of contentious debate followed. The wrangling came down to a call to work toward eliminating discrimination at the regional level only. After a series of amendment proposals and challenges, Smith proposed committing the NSA to "take action on national, regional, and campus levels . . . with regard to the legal limitations involved."

When it was clear that the language had enough votes to pass, the leader of the YCL group jumped up to speak enthusiastically in favor of the compromise. I glanced over at the southern Negro leaders, who were obviously dumbfounded. It was hard not to sympathize with their evident sense of betrayal.

The final vote was greeted with a burst of applause that shook UW's Memorial Union Great Hall. Regional suspicions and antagonism dissolved as students celebrated settling, as the university press release put it, "the knottiest problem before the convention. . . . The Southern-Yankee conflict was whiffed away when the large New York delegation broke into the singing of 'Dixie.'"

In the founding convention's last action, the NSA delegates elected its first president: Bill Welsh,[33] a twenty-three-year-old senior majoring in history at Berea College. Bill and I had roomed together in Madison, and I had come to like and respect him. A veteran of three years in the army infantry, Bill was more seasoned than most of the delegates. He was unquestionably committed to social progress, including the elimination of racial discrimination. His political acumen drew admiration from the northerners, and because he came from the border state of Kentucky, he was acceptable to southern students as well. His charisma and natural leadership made me happy to be the one who gave his nominating speech.[34]

Heading back to Boston, I felt that the NSA experience had fully repaid my investment in it. On the personal level, I had made a good number of friends and learned a lot about what other students, more or less like myself, thought and believed.

But the experience had a broader significance. My original motivation for involvement was because it might offer me a new, broader chance to explore and possibly gain national leadership experience. It did so, but provided me with a great deal more. I was exposed to student issues that would later prove invaluable, to national issues about civil rights and solutions to white-Black racial problems, to the conflicting views of domestic isolationism versus internationalism, and to the politically explosive issue of communism and civil liberties.

Being part of the founding also was a priceless experience in the minutiae of successful leadership ranging from drafting legislation to negotiating its passage, learning and mastering Robert's Rules of Order, the art and value of public oratory, the tactics and strategy needed to forge alliances in any group to achieve a desired outcome, and the opportunity to test my political skills. Yes, even discovering humor as a leadership gambit. It was intellectually challenging and exciting.

Much of what I had seen and done in one short, intense week would prove invaluable later in life.

▪ School of Advanced International Studies ──────────

At the beginning of my senior year at Harvard, and before the shock of my parents' divorce, my father had encouraged me to consider graduate work in international affairs in preparation to follow in his footsteps. He had suggested three possibilities. One was the Fletcher School of Law and Diplomacy, then run jointly by Harvard and Tufts University. Another was

Georgetown University's foreign service program. The last was the new School of Advanced International Studies in Washington, D.C.[35]

Applications were sent to Fletcher and SAIS. To my surprise, Fletcher turned me down. Maybe my grades didn't meet their standards, despite my Harvard honors degree. Unknown to me at the time, my application had created a firestorm at SAIS. When in the school's early days Halford Hoskins, the founding dean, had appeared before the Washington, D.C., Board of Education, a Negro board member had asked whether the school would be open to Negroes. Yes, Hoskins had replied grudgingly, "if any qualified ones apply." Then along came my application—son of a career diplomat, bilingual, a Harvard honors graduate, and recipient of a scholarship from the U.S. Foreign Service Association. A near panic had ensued, but finally, I was admitted—SAIS's first Black student.[36] I also was the youngest person in my class.

The master's degree program at SAIS consisted of only two very intensive semesters. From the outset, I determined to avoid extracurricular activities and concentrate on my studies. It was not just my own ability that was on trial. My performance might influence whether other Negroes would have the opportunity to follow me at the school.

The school's formal classes were often supplemented by lounge discussions and drop-in talks by people from Congress and the White House. Many were friends and colleagues of the SAIS principals, who persuaded them to come by. Scotty Reston, then in the *New York Times* Washington bureau, was one. Another was a newly elected congressman from California, Richard Nixon. He was bright and articulate, but we just didn't like him. No one could say exactly why.

One of my most important classes was taught by Simon Hanson, whose area of expertise was Latin America. Hanson wasn't a member of the SAIS regular faculty. Most of his income came from consulting and his *Latin American Newsletter*. He was brilliant and outspoken, with a reputation for irascibility. He was a loner—somebody once said he should live at the bottom of a well with only his typewriter.

But I always found him interesting and responsive. He was a superb teacher who insisted that we think deeply about problems and issues, not just read about them. Hanson often brought to class an article from the day's *New York Times* or *Washington Post*. After reading it aloud, he would challenge a student to play the role of a State Department staffer, preparing a verbal memo for the secretary or even the president—all without advance preparation. His classes were both lively and educational. We also got used to reading the day's newspapers *before* class, just in case.

• • • •

Almost all of SAIS—men's dorms, classrooms, library, offices, and dining facilities—were in a single building at 1906 Florida Avenue N.W. Women lived in a separate building next door. In segregated Washington, with classmates including several from the Deep South, I wasn't surprised that some of my supposed peers avoided me, even getting up when I entered the dining room and sat down at their table. Dean Hoskins, who made a point of having all the students dine with him on a rotating basis, must have forgotten to mail my invitation.

Sunday evenings the dining room was closed, so some of us often got together to go out to eat. Once my classmates Jim Walsh, Hans Tuch, Mimi Lord, and I went to a Middle Eastern café, where we were served without incident. But when Jim and Hans went up to pay the bill, the woman behind the cash register pointed to me and asked, "What is he?"

"I don't know what you mean," said Jim, "but I know he has a lot of Irish in him."

A group of my classmates then organized a boycott of local restaurants where I could not join them for Sunday dinner or drinks.[37] This was an unusual and bold act in the nation's capital in that era.

A few months before these incidents, Jim Smith, president of the NSA founding convention, called to say that he and his new bride Kathy were in town from Texas. Could we get together for dinner? They were staying at the Willard Hotel, a few blocks from the White House, and I agreed to meet them there.

The Smiths were out when I arrived, so I sat in the lobby to wait. Not for long—soon the consternation was palpable across the ornate room. Guests, bellhops, desk clerks—everyone was staring and whispering over the Negro who had the audacity to intrude on the Willard's Tiffany-lit, leather-upholstered gentility.

Finally a manager came over and demanded to know what I wanted. From there, things went downhill. As I was about to be thrown out, the Smiths arrived. We all left quickly for Harvey's restaurant in the Mayflower Hotel, where we had dinner without further incident.

A few months later, undaunted, I went back to the Willard to say hello to Bill Welsh, the first NSA president. This time the hotel told Bill that if I came again, I must use the service elevator.

▪ ▪ ▪ ▪

In Simon Hanson's class my friend Robert Willis and I got permission to work together on a paper. Hanson suggested the topic: the *Flota Mercante Grancolombiana*, a new merchant fleet that Venezuela, Columbia, and Ecuador were establishing jointly. It was interesting because the *Flota* was the first serious effort at economic cooperation among three Latin American nations. There also were intriguing side issues concerning the joint fleet's dependence on foreign ships, especially U.S. ones.

Armed with introductions from Hanson, Bob and I visited the State Department several times. Our project had the department's informal blessing—staff there thought we might come up with some useful independent insights. On one visit we were talking with an officer in the policy-planning unit when we noticed he had been looking at a clipping from the *New York Times*. We innocently asked if we could have a copy. No, the officer said, looking unsettled.

"Why not!" we pressed. "It would show the department has an interest in a particular article," he said—an interest he did not want known publicly.

Later Bob and I skimmed through the *New York Times* for the last few weeks. When we found the article, we couldn't believe how bland and innocuous were its contents.

In the course of our research we got wind of a letter that the U.S. charge d'affaires in Bogotá had sent to a Colombian ministry, objecting to the Colombian Coffee Growers Federation's preferential treatment of the *Flota Mercante*. The letter and the controversy that had attended it strongly supported the case we were making in our paper, so at the State Department we asked if we could possibly see a copy. They refused, of course. After some grumbling, we waited around until the lunch hour, when the only one left in the office was a junior secretary. With great self-assurance we asked for the file we believed likely to contain the démarche in question. The secretary looked at us oddly, but since she knew we had been working with the department and obviously had the right name for the file, she handed it over. We found the letter and copied it as fast as we could.

Weeks later, when our project was finished, Bob and I sent one copy of the paper to Professor Hanson and one to the Department of State. In no time Hanson got an anguished call from State, wanting to know how we not only knew about the letter but referenced its actual, detailed text. Eventually a department officer sat us down and demanded to know how we had gotten the information. Of course we could not "reveal our source" without also disclosing our own somewhat unconventional research tactic. The officer then insisted that we expunge the "confidential" material from our paper. When he assured us that he would do the same with his own copy, I innocently asked him why. Didn't he already have the original letter in his files?

Our report led to an article in Simon Hanson's publication *Inter-American Economic Affairs*.[38] It was my first contribution to a professional academic journal.

My social life at SAIS wasn't nonexistent, though for a while it was close to that. I did socialize with a couple of white female classmates. Phyllis Weikart (later Greene) went out with me to hear the honey-voiced Sarah Vaughan, who was then just starting her career. I also took Mimi Lord to hear Nellie Lutcher play piano at a bar in a mostly Negro area. Squiring two blonds around segregated Washington was not exactly smart, but the relationships were entirely platonic. For the first time in my life I began to smoke, which seemed de rigeur with afternoon sherry in the student lounge.

Around Thanksgiving I got back in touch with Rita Buckner, whom I hadn't seen since leaving Boston. She was in Washington finishing her undergraduate studies at Catholic University. Over the weeks we drifted back together. Many evenings we studied together in the basement recreation room of her home. Rita even typed a couple of my papers, over the objections of her mother who (rightly) thought Rita should spend her time on her own work.

For a while things got serious enough with Rita that I agreed to see a priest for premarital instruction in Roman Catholicism. The meetings didn't go well—I raised all the paradoxes and conundrums of orthodox religion that had always bothered me, while the priest just tried to get on with it. Rita and I went on acting as though we were "semi-engaged," though perhaps neither of us were quite certain what that meant.

In the waning days of my year at SAIS I began to think seriously about getting a job. For all my tendencies toward open-minded thinking, my religious upbringing had been conscientious, and I sometimes had thought about a career in the ministry. My interest had increased through the New England Student Christian Movement. The church offered a passage to moral and intellectual leadership and a chance to pursue good works in a systematic way. But my doubts about religious orthodoxy and its institutions remained strong—hardly a ringing call to pastoral service.

Although I still thought about taking the competitive Foreign Service exam, I had begun to have reservations about the Foreign Service itself. Did I really want to follow in my father's footsteps—basking in the glow of his reputation or (more likely) struggling to escape it?

Previously when in Washington for consultations, my father had taken me to the U.S. Department of State and introduced me to some of his friends—among them Henry Villard, the first head of the department's Africa Division and later ambassador to Libya and Italy; Joseph Grew, former ambassador to Japan and an SAIS trustee; and the legendary Loy Henderson, for whom the department's main auditorium is now named. Each of them said essentially the same thing: "You're Clif's son? So when are you coming in?"

Especially after my parents' divorce, I didn't appreciate my father's colleagues' easy assumption that I would automatically emulate him. At twenty-one years old, I was starting to assert my own identity. And if I did succeed in the diplomatic service, I would never be quite sure whether it was in my own right or because I was my father's son—and bore his name.

I decided to make one last effort to reverse my father's divorce decision. I repeated my earlier idea to my father—if he would leave the Foreign Service to set up his own law firm, I would go to law school and prepare to join him. Naively, I thought that perhaps the opportunity to return to the United States and to join with his son might "bring him to his senses." But my father had too much invested in the Foreign Service. His lot was firmly cast with the other woman; a final divorce was inevitable.

My father's refusal tipped the scales against my entering the Foreign Service. Still seething over the divorce that I perceived as his rejection of my mother, my siblings, and me, following in his footsteps was no longer my choice. I would strike out on my own, beyond his reach—and hopefully still succeed.

An international career continued to be my first choice; but if not the Foreign Service where? In the United States, opportunities for young Negroes were still restricted, such that several of my college friends had gone abroad to avoid discrimination, making fuller use of their abilities.[39] It wasn't that other countries were entirely devoid of racism, of course, but their problems seemed significantly less pervasive both institutionally and in daily life. In the postwar world, moreover, regions and nations just emerging from colonial rule were places where a background in history and the social sciences could be a strong credential—especially for someone who had already lived outside the States and wasn't intimidated by the need to learn new languages.

Both government agencies and private businesses regularly scheduled interviews at SAIS. My first interview was with the Central Intelligence Agency. The recruiter seemed only mildly interested in me. I might be useful somewhere in Africa, he said, if anything happened to open up. "What about Latin America?" I asked. I knew little about Africa, but had lived in Spanish cultures and was fluent in the language. The recruiter didn't think Latin America was a good option—since I was Black, Africa was the "obvious" choice. Prejudice, here we go again, I thought. I remarked that there were significant Negro or African ethnic populations in several Latin American countries—Brazil, Cuba, Haiti, Jamaica, and even parts of Colombia and Venezuela. But the CIA interviewer would have none of that, and I could tell that my comments were making him quite uncomfortable.

Next was a personnel officer from the oil company Esso—he tightened up as soon as I walked in. Esso had extensive operations in Latin America, so it was obviously a region of corporate interest. But despite my bilingualism and my academic concentration on Latin America, Esso's interviewer didn't think I would be "comfortable" there. I doubted that it was my comfort he was worried about.[40]

One day Simon Hanson asked if I had given any thought to joining one of Nelson Rockefeller's organizations. Hanson had worked with Rockefeller in Washington, D.C., when he was coordinator of inter-American affairs in the Office of InterAmerican Affairs (OIAA) during 1940–45, appointed by President Roosevelt. As coordinator Rockefeller oversaw a program of U.S. cooperation with the nations of Latin America to help raise the standard of living, to achieve better relations among the nations of the Western Hemisphere, and to counter rising Nazi influence in the region. After serving briefly as an assistant secretary of state, Rockefeller had left Washington to return to New York as a private citizen. With a long-standing love of Latin America, he was committed to improving the region's economic development. Building on ideas he had conceived before the war, he set up three organizations, two in business and one nonprofit built around applying technical assistance to rural needs, especially in agriculture, food, and nutrition. The last was the American International Association for Economic and Social Development—known universally as AIA to avoid the jaw-breaking name.

When Hanson described Rockefeller's work in foreign development programs, I was immediately struck by their resemblance to the kind of efforts George Marshall had talked about at my Harvard commencement exercises. I told Hanson that I was definitely interested.

Hanson helped arrange an interview in New York City, scheduled for early February. Stepping out of the elevator on the fifty-sixth floor of 30 Rockefeller Plaza, I marveled at the deep carpets, the modernistic paintings, the glowing curvilinear halls. I was to discover later that the section of the floor occupied by the father, JDR Jr., was quite traditional compared with the tastes of his five sons—including oil tycoon JDR Sr.'s original plain wooden desk.

Excited, but nervous, I wanted to present myself in the best possible light. In my mind I ran through everything I wanted to mention about my abilities and my interest in Latin America. Though I was supposed to be interviewed by Frank Jamieson,[41] the Rockefeller family's top public relations officer, he was ill and had not come to work. Instead I met Lawrence Levy, a lawyer and one of Nelson Rockefeller's close associates. As soon as he showed me to a chair, he said, "You're Clifton Wharton. I understand you're looking for a job?"

"Yes, sir."

"So what can you do?"

The question was blunt, not one whose answer I had composed ahead of time. For a moment I was at a loss. How to respond? I was a Harvard graduate, soon to get my master's from the School of Advanced International Studies. What, in fact, *could* I do?

"Well, sir," I blurted out, "I can *think*!"

Levy let a smile cross his face briefly. "Well," he said, "there's a job opening up in June in our public relations department. It'll be yours if you want it, but I wouldn't advise you to take it. It's a pigeonhole with no prospects for promotion."

I thanked Levy and started to get up. "No, sit down," he said. "Let's talk a while."

So for the next half hour we talked—mostly, I did. Levy asked me question after question about myself, my family background, my academic work, and my outside interests. By the time I walked out of his office thirty minutes later, he had gotten more information out of me than I had expected.

Nonetheless I went back to Washington disconsolate. I was convinced overseas technical assistance was the coming thing in international affairs, and I was eager to get in right away. But had I convinced Levy that I might have what it took to be part of the venture that lay ahead? Hanson didn't seem too worried. He told me to keep looking for similar opportunities and suggested I write Levy a thank-you note. I did—including in it a summary of my background and a fervent declaration of my eagerness to join Nelson's organization at the earliest possible moment.

A couple of weeks later a call came from Robert W. "Pete" Hudgens, just named president of Nelson Rockefeller's nonprofit American International Association. My letter and resume had landed on his desk, and he was interested in meeting me.

Hudgens was a fascinating man. As an army captain (1915–22), he had been wounded badly in World War I, received a Purple Heart, and spent three years hospitalized. He never regained much use of his left arm and was in almost constant pain, though he rarely showed it. After the war he became an investment banker in Greenville, South Carolina, where he was also an official of the South Carolina and American Red Cross organizations. In Greenville he developed a "supervised credit" program that combined loans with technical assistance to help Depression-era farmers. It later became the model for efforts by Roosevelt's Resettlement Administration and Farm Security Administration. His years of success in outreach to impoverished farmers made him particularly suited to lead Rockefeller's new technical assistance initiative.

I hurried back to New York to meet with Hudgens, with whom I hit it off instantly. He was warm, thoughtful, and considerate. His empathy for the poor and disadvantaged was manifest. He was also one of those unusual whites whose upbringing amid southern prejudice and discrimination had given him a clear-eyed understanding of racism at its worst.

Because he was just setting his new office in order, Hudgens told me, he did not know if there would be a position for me. He would stay in touch, and we would see what turned up. Once again I traipsed back to Washington, not optimistic. Two weeks later Hudgens called to tell me that Nelson Rockefeller wanted to assign an "executive trainee" to each of his three new organizations.[42] The trainees would be generalists who would learn the ropes and might later be offered permanent jobs. The AIA traineeship would start on June 1, two days after I was scheduled to graduate from SAIS. The salary was $3,200 per year. Would I be interested?

The compensation was about $500 less than the average offer to my SAIS classmates, but that was far outweighed by the prospect of working in an area that held tremendous excitement for me. I was thrilled, I told Hudgens, to be on board.

When contacted with the news, my father reacted predictably—badly. My idea that economic aid and technical assistance would become important elements of U.S. foreign policy was just idealistic "do-goodism," he snorted. But I was young yet, he allowed. It wouldn't hurt me to try my wings before coming to my senses and taking my rightful path through the Foreign Service.

Fat chance, I thought.

• • • •

My hard work at the school paid off—I received As in all my classes except professor Philip W. Thayer's three law classes, where the only As went to two Texans who already had law degrees and had passed the bar! On May 22, 1948, the oral examining committee certified me for a master's degree from SAIS. I graduated a week later, on May 29. The commencement speaker was CIA director Allen Dulles; his topic was "The Responsibilities of Power." Christian Herter, chairman of the SAIS trustees, presented my degree, murmuring something about our being "fellow Bay Staters." (At the time Herter was U.S. representative from Massachusetts.[43]) Priscilla Mason, secretary to the SAIS board, whispered to me that my grades put me second among the forty graduates in my class. If it were true, I thought, at least I hadn't done anything to cloud the prospects of other Negroes who might come to SAIS in my wake.[44]

Just before the ceremony, Professors Thayer (commercial law and maritime law) and

Donald Hiss[45] (international law) came up to my mother separately. Both told her that they felt strongly that I should go to law school.

"He has a natural legal mind and the makings of a fine lawyer," said Thayer.

Really? I wondered silently. So why didn't you give me an A in your courses?

It didn't matter now. My choice had already been made, and I had no intention of changing course.

CHAPTER THREE

The Young Economist: The AIA, Dolores Duncan, and Chicago

Since my new job started immediately, I needed housing quickly. I called up Hal Bowser, a New York acquaintance who had been the second Black to join the Harvard radio station.[1] Hal knew about a tiny apartment on 112th Street, on Harlem's southern fringe at the north edge of Central Park. The building once had one flat to a floor, but now it was chopped up into one- and two-room units. The only furnishings were a bed and a bureau. Rent was on a weekly basis until something permanent was found.

I couldn't believe how many locks, bolts, and bars there were just on the building entrance—not to mention individual locks for each room. It was like living in a fortress. When the owner handed over the keys, she ran through the rules: No cooking, no women, no loud noises, and be sure to lock up behind you!

A few weeks after I moved in, my friend Joe Mitchell spent the night on his way to Philadelphia. A Bostonian like me, Joe naively left his bags overnight in the trunk of his car. Next morning, the car was clean as a whistle.

This painful lesson in urban living motivated me to look for better digs. Eventually Rita Buckner put me in touch with the Harrises, a charming elderly couple who lived in the Paul Laurence Dunbar Apartments on 246 West 150th Street, New York, NY.[2] The buildings wrapped around a U-shaped garden courtyard. The apartments were small, but tidy and attractive. Most of the families who lived there were middle-class Negro professionals, and the atmosphere was peaceful and pleasant. The Harrises rented me a bedroom without cooking privileges, which suited me fine. At my age, I didn't mind eating all my meals out.

Each morning after breakfast at one greasy spoon or another, I walked to the station for the Eighth Avenue Independent line and caught the D train for Rockefeller Center. At 125th

Street I changed for Columbus Circle, then crosstown to Park Avenue. Nearly every trip was an adventure. One day in a packed car the young woman in front of me suddenly jabbed her elbow into my stomach and hissed, "Keep your hands to yourself!" "Miss," I said as politely as I could, "if you look, you'll see I have a newspaper in one hand and the subway strap in the other." Swiveling angrily around, the woman spotted a short, unkempt man leering at her—whom she promptly whacked in the face with her other elbow.

Another day when I just barely made the train at 145th Street, the doors closed directly behind my shoulder blades. I was squashed on both sides and in front by four hulking passengers. When the train arrived at 125th Street, the next stop, I was horrified to see a large crowd waiting, all determined to get on. The train stopped in front of two large men, with an equally huge rather buxom woman between them. With the customary subway "etiquette," they bent their knees and shoved themselves upward and inward, carrying me along—lifting my 155 pounds up into the air. As the door closed, my toes barely touched the floor. Over my shoulder I pleaded to the woman whose large bosom held my shoulders aloft, "Madam, my feet can't touch the floor!" "They ain't?" she replied, and began to laugh heartily, as my feet bounced on the floor with each guffaw!

Then as now, New York City was a brash and boisterous melee, pounding and electric. Everyone was hurrying to get somewhere and do something. Pretty soon I found myself rushing along like everyone else.

· · · ·

Notwithstanding the overweening name, the American International Association for Economic Development[3]—universally abbreviated AIA—had modest offices on the fifty-first floor of Rockefeller Plaza,[4] five floors below the Rockefeller family offices. In addition to Pete Hudgens, who had hired me, the small staff included Rosemary Rockford, a Smith graduate, the personal secretary; Charlie Power, general office and travel manager; Carrie McKinstry Grogan, transferred from IBEC, the accountant; and Sonia Schultz, receptionist and general purpose secretary. Not long after I arrived, Pete hired Dr. James Maddox as his second in command. Jim had taken his undergraduate degree at the University of Arkansas, then his master's from the University of Wisconsin. In the late 1930s and early 1940s he had worked for several federal agencies, including the Farm Security Administration, where he met Hudgens.

· · · ·

When he joined AIA Jim Maddox had just finished his PhD in agricultural economics at Harvard. With owlish eyes behind rimless glasses and straight hair parted in the middle, he brought tempered intellectual rigor to the office. He had a quiet, firm dedication to helping the poor. Pete Hudgens had the vision and could articulate the plight of hardscrabble farmers and their families. Jim Maddox pulled together the data and analysis of alternatives that might lead to improvements.

AIA had initially been conceived as a catchall for Rockefeller's efforts to better the economies of certain Latin American countries, principally Venezuela and Brazil. A few early projects were remnants from Nelson's years as coordinator for inter-American affairs in Washington. Pete Hudgens brought a special vision to AIA based upon his experience with the U.S. Farm Security Administration, a rural supervised credit creation of the New Deal. In Venezuela, he developed two main AIA programs: Consejo Interamericano de Educación Alimenticia (CIDEA), or the Inter-American Council on Nutrition Education, and the Consejo de Bienestar Rural (CBR), or Council on Rural Welfare.

CBR was a supervised credit program adapted from the U.S. Farm Security Administration (FSA) model. In Venezuela's rural areas, CBR placed dual teams of farm and home technicians who helped poor farmers develop a Farm and Home Plan to improve their operation. The written plan would become the basis for a credit application to carry out the improvements designed to increase the productivity of the farmer and his family, making a loan feasible. This idea is a direct antecedent of today's microcredit programs so popular around the globe in less developed countries and regions.

In developing an individual plan, the two visiting technicians offered technical help ranging from seed selection and plant spacing to improved meal planning and kitchen organization. The size of the loans was quite small, but their impact was often very dramatic. Hudgens used a catchy phrase to describe this approach, "A Man, a Woman, and a Jeep"—reflecting the way in which the two-person teams traveled around the unpaved roads in the plains or on the steep mountains of the country.

In a typical case, a farmer's loan application would be recommended by the CBR technician and submitted to a local citizens' committee for approval and then made by the Venezuelan Banco Agricola y Pecuario. Loans could cover such items as a harness for the farmer's mule, better seed and fertilizer for crops, a corn sheller, or even a roof for his house. Throughout the farming season, CBR technicians provided continuing extension educational service. The home technician might instruct the wife how to improve family nutrition or improve sanitation, or even how to sew—all aimed at improving the farm's productivity and the quality of life of the family.

Given the initial shortage of technicians in Venezuela, most early experts came from the United States, often with FSA experience. To provide in-service training, Venezuelan assistants were assigned to the U.S. experts, with the expectation that they would eventually operate independently.

CBR also initially accepted responsibility to provide farm assistance in Valencia where an extremely large farm, or *latifundio*, had been confiscated by the government and subdivided into small farms for the former farm laborers.

The CBR program soon expanded beyond farm/home management and supervised credit into other areas of need identified by the government—farm-to-market roads, community services programs, land settlement projects, and training in farm management. The CBR technicians in their jeeps quickly recognized the isolation of their farmers and the need for easier access to markets. The road program started in the Andean mountains in the state of Táchira and proved extremely effective.

The second AIA program, CIDEA, was designed to correct the endemic hunger and malnutrition in Venezuela. Inadequate Venezuelan food production, coupled with high food import costs, was exacerbated by the lack of knowledge about proper nutrition and extremely poor eating habits of the populace. CIDEA undertook a massive national campaign. Large vans or mobile units toured the countryside distributing specially prepared pamphlets, showing motion pictures on the sides of church walls, using loudspeakers mounted on top of the vans to broadcast nutrition information, distributing records to radio stations, and providing lecturers to community groups. Special courses on nutrition were introduced into the regular curriculum of schoolteachers, and nutrition clubs were organized among schoolchildren throughout the nation.

AIA's general financing came from four U.S. oil companies operating mostly in Venezuela—Creole Petroleum Corporation; the Shell Caribbean Petroleum Company; the Mene Grande Oil Company, C.A.; and the Socony-Vacuum Oil Company. The companies initially committed $2.5 million over five years. This decision was an early instance of enlightened corporate social responsibility. The motivation was that "the oil companies in Venezuela cannot expect to continue their operations . . . in an atmosphere favorable to the maintenance of their business with satisfactory earnings, unless some solution can be found to the basic problem of raising the standard of living of the Venezuelan people."[5] Funding for programs in Brazil came primarily from Nelson Rockefeller and the Rockefeller family. From AIA's inception in 1946 to 1953, the Venezuelan oil companies contributed $4,152,210 and the Rockefeller family $1,138,087. Of these totals $2,607,491 was spent in Venezuela and $595,125 in Brazil (two-thirds in Associação de Crédito e Assistência Rural [ACAR]).[6]

· · · ·

One great advantage of life as an "executive trainee" at AIA was that both the organization and its programs were new. With virtually everything yet to learn, I had the luxury of working from a nearly blank slate. I was eager to jump to every task—writing reports, personally drawing graphs and charts, even cranking the office Gestetner mimeograph. Purple ink on my fingers was a badge of honor.

Besides my regular job assignments, I deliberately used my "trainee" status to learn as much as possible about different aspects of the Rockefeller apparatus. Carrie McKinstry Grogan, for example, let me delve into nonprofit-style accounting, and into for-profit accounting with higher ups at the International Basic Economy Corporation. I also spent a lot of time on the fifty-sixth floor with Martha Dalrymple, in Frank Jamieson's office, who showed me how public relations worked.[7] She was especially helpful with lessons about writing, communications, and handling the media that would serve me well for a lifetime.

Another learning opportunity was my exposure to the AIA board of directors meetings, especially when a memo or report I had drafted was to be discussed. The interplay between Nelson Rockefeller and colleagues was fascinating. Watching how different people at a board meeting used different approaches to make their points was fine theater but also great on-the-job instruction. I saw which tactics seemed to work and which did not; the arguments that had an effect or failed; and most important, the verbal skills that succeeded in winning support. Heady experience for a twenty-two-year-old, and extremely valuable lessons for the future.

I was intrigued by the "Lions at the Gate"—the Rockefeller brothers' closest advisers. Among them at the time were John Lockwood, Dana Creel, Lawrence Levy, Edgar Young, Arthur Jones, and later Datus Smith. Through these "imperial guards" all major issues and questions were channeled. Their roles were rarely public, but they were extremely powerful. Flor Brennan, a Venezuelan assistant in Nelson Rockefeller's office, helped me get a sense of their behind-the-scenes style.

Nelson Rockefeller himself struck me as a dynamo. Even sitting still, he was like an idling engine, waiting at the starting line for the green flag. Though he never flaunted it, he was clearly in charge. He left no doubt that he knew what he wanted, and he was comfortable with whatever it took to reach his goals. But he also valued intellectual exchange with those who knew more about any subject than he. A buoyant personality in a compact body, he had the openness to new ideas and experiences that came from formidable self-confidence. But he lacked arrogance or any evident excess of self-esteem.

Pete Hudgens, my boss, was a great teacher. He had an ex-boxer's battered face, a receding hairline, sparkling eyes, and a ready side-of-the-mouth grin. Everybody he met seemed genuinely to interest him. Pete often had me draft his memos for AIA board meetings. Once when a subject was very difficult, I labored for the better part of a week, then turned it over with much trepidation. Pete read it over carefully, then looked up. "Well, Clif," he said, "you've got all the points I wanted." I sighed with relief. "But there's a slight problem," and my heart leaped into my mouth. "Thing is, this memo sounds like Harvard, not like South Carolina." Pete then grinned his sideways grin, and I got it. I had to smile, too—but I never made the same mistake again.

. . . .

I experienced no overt racism among my white AIA colleagues—indeed, in anyone working in the various enterprises of "Mr. Nelson," as he was affectionately called. There was only one other Negro professional in the Rockefeller family offices, E. G. Spaulding, an accountant.[8] All the other Negro male employees were messengers. Most messengers were old enough to be my father and in positions inferior to mine. Initially, I sensed their embarrassment, and it took some time before our relationships became comfortable—eventually, friendly.

As my rapport with the messengers grew, I became irritated by the fact that they were invariably called by their first names. I thought it demeaning that grown men who were performing a necessary function would be patronized by overfamiliarity. I doubted that the practice was a hangover from slavery, but decided not to follow suit. This is why thereafter I followed the same practice with anyone in a presumed lesser position. I addressed messengers—and all secretaries, assistants, clerks, and lower staff whether white or Black—as "Mister" or "Miss" or "Mrs." followed by their last names. This became a practice for the rest of my life. Sometimes people were initially discomfited by it, but most soon adjusted, realizing that I was treating them with respect, regardless of their relative station.

In retrospect, I realize that subconsciously my position was based upon the memory of my maternal grandmother, Nana, who as a cook was always called by her first name. Although she never showed it, the practice angered her considerably. Her white employers could use her first name, but she had to use their last names with all appropriate courtesies. She once said to me, "I am a cook and proud of it, because I do it well. And I am a woman and a human being. So why can't they treat me respectfully the same as everyone else?"

One racial incident did take place during this period, which was unrelated to AIA. In early December 1948, I received a visit from Mr. John Buffett Keogh, Harvard class of 1925, a foreign service officer then stationed in Lisbon and a colleague of my father. In a fit of exuberance, Keogh asked if I belonged to the Harvard Club of New York. When I said I didn't, he asked if he could nominate me. Intrigued, I agreed. His letter to the Admissions Committee of December 7 referred to me as "an outstanding lad with a splendid academic record at Harvard and the son of my intimate friend the American Consul for the Azores." He mentioned my role in founding the National Student Association and my current work for Nelson Rockefeller, concluding, "I trust the members of your Committee will see to it that this rising star in the field of international affairs shines among us."

A few weeks later I learned that the committee had "blackballed" my nomination—an apt term in this case of prejudice. With no Negro members at all, they clearly did not want any Black to shine among them. I swore to myself that I would never join the Harvard Club of New York—and never did.

Years later I was indirectly involved in Clifford Alexander's becoming the first Black member of the Club. Clifford's parents and the Harvard admissions office had asked me to help persuade him to attend Harvard instead of his preference, Yale. Clifford did attend Harvard (class of 1955 with my brother Bill) and later Yale Law School (1958). Upon graduation, he became an assistant district attorney in New York City and in 1961 was nominated and elected as the first Black member of the Harvard Club of New York.[9]

. . . .

My parents' impending divorce was still hard for my mother, not only emotionally but financially. She had to be both mother and father to two teenage sons and a young daughter while trying to make ends meet. Nana helped, as she always had, but it wasn't enough. In addition to carving out a rental apartment on the first floor of her home, Mother took a job as a substitute teacher in the Boston school system. She loved teaching, but additional income was her overriding motive. Moreover, my brother William would soon enroll in college, which could only intensify the strain.

My semi-engagement to Rita Buckner had ended in the late summer of 1948. Given my responsibility to help my mother and siblings financially, I didn't see how I could afford to get married, even though Rita said she was prepared to help. With further reflection, I also admitted to myself that religion was the main problem. Rita was Roman Catholic and I was Anglican Catholic (High Episcopalian), and though the churches were in some ways quite similar, there were also fundamental differences I doubted could ever be reconciled. Under the circumstances, matrimony looked a long way off. Playing the field seemed the sensible choice, even the only one.

In such frame of mind I took a call in late March 1949 from Betty Fitzgerald in Boston. She and her cousin Dolores Duncan had weekend dates with two West Point cadets. Would I pick up Dolores, then bring her to meet Betty's train at Grand Central Station?

I had not seen Dolores for about five years, though she and a dozen other girls had been sent one of my "hotshot" Tuskegee pilot photos. Much had happened in her life during the intervening period. She had enrolled as a New York University freshman at the Washington Square campus, just blocks from the famous Little Red School House (Sixth Avenue at Bleecker Street) she had attended as a child. Her mother Josephine's inheritance from her Aunt May was the main source of funding. Her ambition at NYU was to become an English teacher. Predictably she absolutely loved the Western Civilization course whose professor regularly sent the students to the Metropolitan Museum of Art. Building upon her earlier Little Red School House museum visits, she was able to further expand her profound love and knowledge of the arts.

During World War II, her brother, Jackie, and her stepfather, James Owens, had enlisted in the army. Being alone, her mother wanted Dolores to return home; accordingly after completing her first year in good standing, she left NYU to enroll in the then Danbury State Teacher's College. When her stepfather returned to Danbury, Dolores left again. At the strong suggestion of her mother, herself enamored with the performing arts, and a neighbor professional actor and director, Dolores's new temporary goal was to pursue a possible acting career by enrolling in the famous Neighborhood Playhouse in New York City. The school, renowned for teaching "method acting" and led by Sandy Meisner, was the training grounds for such future stars as Marian Seldes, Darren McGavin, Richard Boone, Leslie Nielsen, Gregory Peck, and Robert Duvall. At the Playhouse, Dolores also studied modern dance with legendary Martha Graham and choreography with Louis Horst. Dolores loved Graham's classes and soon left the Playhouse to devote her full time to studying modern dance—though with the ever-present intent of returning to school for her BA.

When I called at Dolores's apartment, she was even more attractive, with flashing eyes and that mischievous one-dimple grin. On the subway to Grand Central, we talked the whole time, and it was obvious that the high-school teenager with whom I had briefly fenced had transformed herself into a graceful young sophisticate. She was self-confident, sensitive, refined, and well spoken—in a word she had "class." She was also deeply schooled in the fine arts. On top of it all, she was very intelligent. In sum she had become a phenomenal young woman. No wonder she was constantly surrounded by intelligent men—Black and white. After meeting Betty's train and helping with the bags, I was decidedly let down to have to drop the girls off back at Daisy Hamer's apartment, where Dolores was staying.

On Monday I called Dolores, who immediately began bubbling about the West Point weekend and recounting stories of her and Betty waltzing around Manhattan with their cadets in full dress uniform. When I could get in a word, I asked her to have dinner with me that evening. To my surprise, she agreed.

During dinner Dolores told me that her West Point date Billy Woodson had given her his academy "A pin"—a recognized "pre-engagement" step. Woodson was the grandson of Carter G. Woodson, the Black historian who led the drive to create the National Negro or Black History Month. Woodson's mother was already greeting her as "my daughter," and Daisy Hamer was encouraging the match. But evidently the pin wasn't a significant gift. Dolores explained that Billy was just "a nice young man with a crush."

If that was how she felt, I asked, "Why don't you send that little boy back his pin?" Dolores feigned surprise, but during the rest of the evening she managed to drop the names of at least three other young men she was seeing.

Before long I was calling Dolores every morning from my office, arranging a dinner date or planning some weekend event. As a native New Yorker, she skillfully exposed me to the joys and beauty of her city. We saw dozens of movies and had the rare pleasure of seeing the 1948 *Hamlet* starring Laurence Olivier in a Harlem movie theater, with the audience's spontaneous counter-participation in every scene. It was Shakespeare as I had never heard, before or since.

Soon Dolores and I were dating only each other. We craved one another's company and wanted to be together constantly. Surprisingly, neither of us professed much interest in getting married. But because of that we found it easy to be candid with each other about everything, from politics and religion to theater and fashion. We never fell into the common temptation to dissemble, muting our opinions to avoid disagreements.

Dolores came from a distinguished Negro family. Her mother, Josephine Bradford, had first married V. Kenneth Duncan, cofounder of the Duncan Brothers Funeral Home in New York (2303 Seventh Avenue, just north of 135th Street). With a premier business in the community, the Duncan family was well known and respected. Dolores and her older brother Jackie enjoyed all the benefits of an upper-middle-class life. The patriarch of the Bradford family was James T. Bradford Sr., Dolores's great-grandfather, a wealthy merchant in Baltimore and then Philadelphia in the latter half of the nineteenth century (b. May 8, 1842, d. February 10,

1913). His father, Thomas Bradford (b. 1815), was a "free Negro" and had been the personal valet of Thomas Swann, governor of Maryland (1866–69), who opposed slavery and favored full emancipation.[10]

Beginning as a butcher boy, James T. rapidly became a successful greengrocer and then highly successful caterer in Baltimore. He was a man of elegant taste, as shown by his family heirlooms, and eventually owned homes in Washington, D.C., Baltimore, and Philadelphia. Josephine, his granddaughter, had been raised in Philadelphia by her two aunts.

After a few months of dating, Dolores invited me to meet her mother and stepfather at their home in Danbury. Until she was twelve, she and her older brother Jackie had lived with their parents in New York City, where the children attended the progressive Little Red School House. Then her father and mother separated, and Josephine moved with the two youngsters to Bethel, Connecticut. A year after the divorce was final, she married James W. Owens, a Juilliard graduate who had inherited substantial wealth from his father, a well-known "horse-clocker" who once "broke the bank" at Saratoga Race Track, winning more than the track had in the cash drawer to pay out. On eleven acres on Lake Kenosha, the couple's beautiful estate included separate guest cabins and a two-story caretaker's residence near the entrance.

James and Josephine Owens made quite a pair. He was phlegmatic and rarely smiled, a real grouch. He asked the two Duncan children to call him "Partner." Besides horses, his other passion in life was automobiles. During the first year of my courtship of Dolores, I can recall his purchasing in sequence a red MG, a green Riley, a black Jaguar, and a green MG. He also bought a fine Rover saloon for Josephine.

Josephine was spirited, charming, and naturally gay—a few decades before, she might have been considered a flapper. Josephine was also fifty years old, while James was thirty-two, just seven years older than Jackie, Dolores's older brother. The age difference usually went unremarked because Josephine was so young looking and as beautiful as her daughter. She and Dolores could have been sisters, and were regularly mistaken as such.

That first weekend Josephine prepared a lunch of baked stuffed lobster. Later she made orange frappes with shaved ice, gin, and Cointreau, then brought them down to the lakeside, where we were swimming off the dock. After a trip or two back to the house to refresh the drinks, she sat down to chat. Dolores had paddled her canoe out in the lake, and Josephine and I were alone.

"Clifton," Josephine said, looking at me directly. "I don't want Dolores to get married."

I looked back. "Mrs. Owens," I said with sincerity, "I don't want to get married, either."

Since I was helping my mother support our family, I explained, I wasn't in any position to be thinking about marriage—much less to do anything about it. Josephine looked dubious, but smiled brightly and changed the subject.

Later Dolores told me that her mother had made a long practice of insisting that she bring her beaus to Danbury. In that lavish and luxurious setting, with all the trappings of the family heritage, what prospective suitor wouldn't be intimidated? And for her own part, how could Dolores fail to recognize the limited prospects and social unsuitability of her jejune guests?

For a while Josephine continued to do her best to discourage Dolores and me from getting any more serious. Who could blame her? Her daughter was her princess, for whom she envisioned a bright life of acclamation in theater or dance. But Dolores and I grew ever closer. The following splendiferous spring and summer seemed all brilliant sunshine and cotton-ball clouds—perfect weather for a perfect love story. Everyone and everywhere was glorious. What proved to be our marvelous courtship made passersby smile at the entranced couple. We took trips on the Staten Island Ferry. We traveled to the Statue of Liberty and the Bronx Zoo. We visited the top of the Empire State Building (Dolores, a native New Yorker, confessed that it was her first time). We went to the Apollo Theater in Harlem for the incomparable talent shows. Our lives were entwined, and we savored every moment together. At least that was how it felt to us. And I guess gradually Josephine began to resign herself to the inevitable. After a while she even asked me to call her "Aunt Joe."

· · · ·

In mid-1949 Pete Hudgens wanted me to go to Venezuela. My job title had been bumped up to "program analyst," and Pete thought observing AIA's programs on the ground would be of value to the organization. I was now charged with developing a system of record-keeping for all the programs in Venezuela and Brazil without ever having actually seen the activities.

There was a lot of trouble about getting my visa. At first it wasn't clear why—it wasn't as if I were asking to emigrate. One friend wondered half-seriously whether, since Americans discriminated against Negroes at home, maybe the Venezuelans thought they should do the same. Once in Venezuela I learned that *pardos*, dark-skinned and of African or Amerindian ancestry, were generally looked down on by the *mantuanos*, educated upper-class people with white European features, often descendants of colonial rulers. Pete pulled out all the stops, noting that I was an employee of a Nelson Rockefeller organization, and that any public controversy would be unhelpful to the three-man junta then in control of the country. But in spite of his efforts and those of AIA representatives in Caracas, no visa appeared.

Then Luis M. Chafardet Urbina, Venezuela's new permanent representative to the International Civil Aviation Organization, arrived in the United States on an emergency visit. His infant son was afflicted with an undetermined but dire brain disease (later I learned it was spina bifida). Since the Chafardets spoke no English and their search for medical help was being facilitated by Rockefeller, Pete Hudgens asked me to act as guide and interpreter for them. I met them at the airport, took them to their hotel, and afterward did everything I could to ease their distress during their weeklong stay in New York. The unexpected result was that when Chafardet returned to Venezuela, he intervened personally with the junta. My visa was issued on July 6, and I left for Caracas the next day.

The purpose of my trip was to observe AIA programs in the field. Over nine weeks I would tour the entire country. I would have the chance to see how things were actually done, and to translate what I had read and written about into reality.

Initially I stayed in the suburb Altamira, in a villa the Rockefeller organizations rented for staff and other visitors from the United States. The head of AIA in Venezuela was John R. Camp, a forestry graduate of Cornell, who had worked previously with Nelson Rockefeller when he was coordinator of inter-American affairs. Camp greeted me warmly, as did Bernardo Joffé, a special consultant in public relations. Bernardo, a Spaniard originally from the island of Majorca, was an engaging companion, full of insights, reminiscences, and gossip. He had nicotine-stained fingers and a deep liquid voice. Heavy set, he somehow contrived to squeeze into his boxy little Renault, smoked while he drove, talked with both hands, and completely ignored the traffic—dangerously on the steep mountain roads without railings.

The military junta had recently overthrown the government of Romulo Gallegos, a novelist who had been elected president in Venezuela's first democratic election in 119 years. Gallegos's Democratic Action Party had promoted itself as liberal and populist, but its land reform program and reduced support for the military alienated wealthy landowners and the armed forces. In November 1948 he had been ousted in a military coup by Lt. Col. Carlos Delgados Chalbaud, Lt. Col. Luis Felipe Llovera Páez, and Major Marcos Pérez Jiménez.

Bernardo gave me an earful about contemporary Venezuelan society and politics, especially the ongoing battles between liberal reformers and conservative elites. Like so many Latin American countries then, Venezuela's regime was autocratic, ruling by military might. The nation had vast oil deposits, and the government proclaimed as its dictum *sembrar el petroleo*—"sow the oil," that is, invest its petroleum revenues to produce wealth for the nation as a whole. But most resources stayed in the hands of a few very rich grandees, with little trickling down to the people. On large tracts held by absentee landlords, poor and usually illiterate sharecroppers worked long hours with primitive tools, paying oppressive crop-share rents that kept them and their families in near-subsistence bondage. Malnutrition was endemic, and public health a vapor.

The presence in Venezuela of AIA and other Rockefeller organizations wasn't in support of its undemocratic regime, but rather a broadly conceived effort to help solve problems that exacerbated the gap between the country's rich and poor. The country's dependence on oil exports had undercut its agricultural development, so that it imported much of its food from abroad—at a high cost. For instance, most of Venezuela's wheat flour came from the United States and was sold largely in Caracas. Outside the capital most people made do with maize. The need to improve agricultural practices and build farming competency in rural communities was exactly the sort of problem the Rockefeller organizations had been established to address.

To some outsiders—and particularly back in the United States—it was easy to mock the efforts of the forty-year-old scion of the family that founded Standard Oil as a cynical public-relations ploy—at best, a halfhearted sop to collective bad conscience. But Nelson

Rockefeller's concern with the plight of the poor was no capitalist guilt trip. You had only to see him chatting animatedly in Spanish with any *conuquero* about seed or tillage to know that he was not a preening, self-involved multimillionaire. The vivacity, drive, and authenticity that would become his political stock in trade were evident even then.

I had not been in a Latin setting or culture since childhood, and to be reimmersed in a Spanish-speaking community was delicious. My fluency came back quickly, and by the second week I could understand and take part easily in conversations. My accent made several Venezuelans think I was Cuban, though few were surprised to be told I had learned the language in the Canary Islands.

Traveling was an adventure. Roads were paved only in Caracas, the port city Maracaibo, and San Cristóbal, in the Andes. Everywhere else the roads were dirt, dust, and more dust, billowing over potholes deep enough to snap axles. At every provincial border guards demanded our ID cards or passports; sometimes they even checked our vaccination records, as though we were crossing to another country.

· · · ·

On my first venture out of Caracas I was accompanied by Mario Gutierrez and José Cardenas, two young technicians who worked for AIA's CBR. We stopped first in Valencia, where large tracts of land had been confiscated from absentee landlords to be divided among the property's formerly landless laborers. CBR hoped to help the new landowners learn to manage small individual plots more effectively—the goal was a model that might be copied throughout the country. CBR had also set up a central pool for farm machinery and taught the workers to operate it. The program also included the new supervised credit approach. Farm management specialists showed them how to increase productivity, while home economics agents worked with women on better home management. Modest loans were available, hinging on approval of farming plans the farmers themselves developed with the technicians. Though most of the farmers were functionally illiterate, my direct conversations with them convinced me that their skills and innate acumen were more than enough for them to succeed. The Valencia experiment proved short lived. When the military dictator General Pérez Jiménez seized sole power a few years later, he returned the land to the original owners.

Bouncing along over the flat Venezuelan *llanos*, I had several recurrences of my childhood asthma problems. I was surprised and greatly puzzled. I had had no attacks since leaving the Canary Islands, and doctors had assured me that it was a childhood malady, now supposedly outgrown. I decided it must be the long travel over boiling dusty roads, and discounted the episodes.

At night we usually stopped in small villages, where shy children always rushed the van—not begging, just looking mournful until you gave them something. For dinner we ate *pernil* (roast pork shoulder), *asado* (roast beef), and the national dish *pabellón criollo* (black beans, fried plantains, white rice, and *carne mechada*, or shredded meat). When the church

Nelson Rockefeller with John Heilman, director of CBR (Consejo de Bienstar Rural). The farmer learning to drive a tractor was a participant in the CBR program teaching previously landless *conuqueros* in Valencia and Guacara, Venezuela.

bells rang at sunrise, we rose to enjoy *bistec a caballo*, "eggs on horseback"—fried eggs on top of a large steak. I never developed much taste for *chicha*, a local drink made from ground rice, salt, condensed milk, sugar, vanilla, and ice.

Our last stop was in Táchira, a state in the western Andes near the Colombian border. The natives called themselves *Tachirenses*—and, proudly, *los que mandan*, "those who rule." Here CBR ran a more traditional program of farm management, home economics, and supervised credit, along with building farm-to-market roads. Arturo Ortiz, originally from New Mexico, was the farm management expert. His Venezuelan assistant, Fernando Rondon, showed me around several scraggly farmsteads clinging precariously to the mountain sides. The corn crops were on hills so steep that the joke was that you had to plant the seed with a shotgun.

On the plane trip back to the United States, I couldn't help thinking about the stark contrast of Venezuela's physical and cultural landscapes—majestic mountains towering into crystal blue skies, and below the peasants toiling in abysmal poverty. I remembered the conversations I had had with Bernardo Jofre about the delicate role of outside organizations or individuals working under a dictatorship. Did the positives outweigh the negatives? If you succeeded in improving things, did it merely mollify popular discontent that might otherwise build against the regime? If the host country followed policies antithetical to your values, what could you do about it? You didn't speak on behalf of the United States—to some degree the State Department might not even be altogether happy about what you were doing there. To stay and work quietly from within—or to stand firm against oppression by pulling out? It was a dilemma that wasn't going to go away.

· · · ·

Dolores and I had written to each other almost daily, and I had missed her terribly. By now Dolores and I were completely absorbed with one another, and we admitted to ourselves that our relationship was more than a passing infatuation. I would go to watch her rehearse at Martha Graham's studio at Twelfth Street and Fifth Avenue, sitting on the second-floor fire escape and watching through the window as she went through her modern dance exercises.

Our favorite restaurant was the Pink Elephant Room in the old Hotel Bristol on Forty-Ninth Street, around the corner from Rockefeller Center, where the waiters were kind to us and gave great tables to the cooing lovebirds. Another haunt was the Headquarters Restaurant, whose owners had catered for General Eisenhower during World War II. John Schwartz, the owner and maître d', was always solicitous to the young lovebirds. We were living the Rodgers and Hart love song "Manhattan," "turn[ing] Manhattan into an isle of joy."[11]

Occasionally Dolores and I attended St. Philip's Episcopal Church on 134th Street,[12] the largest Episcopal congregation in New York City. Rev. Shelton Hale Bishop, the rector, had baptized both Dolores and her brother Jackie. With piercing eyes, a stately walk, and a magnetic oratorical manner, he was an extraordinary and charismatic priest.

From his new post in Lisbon my father returned briefly to the United States. Notwithstanding my lingering resentment over the divorce, I insisted that he meet Dolores. He joined us for lunch at the Headquarters Restaurant, and the two hit it off famously. He found her bright, energetic, and classy.

Aside from noting that Dolores hadn't yet finished her undergraduate degree, my mother never said anything overtly negative. Still I sensed her reservations. Of course, she had reacted similarly toward almost every girl that interested me. Given her feelings about me as her firstborn, I doubted any woman would ever be fully acceptable to her.

There were, to be sure, substantial differences between the families. Socially, Dolores's mother and mine were almost polar opposites, and my father's life and career had little in common with those of Dolores's father and stepfather. But the relationship was between Dolores and me, not our parents. Contrary to expectations, my grandmother Nana liked Dolores instantly. I suspected that she saw in Dolores an inward drive and mental toughness that matched her own.

By early November, without our discussing it directly with our families, it was clear that the only way Dolores and I could be even closer was to marry. I proposed on a wooden bench at the northeast corner of 30 Rockefeller Plaza and Fiftieth Street outside of the 650 Avenue building. Dolores had been expecting it and said yes without hesitation.[13]

When I asked Dolores's father, V. K. Duncan, for his blessing, he said little, just for me to "take good care" of his little girl. Josephine Owens was unsurprised, though I had no idea what her husband Partner thought. My mother was probably just resigned, but greeted the news with a smile and a hug. When I introduced Dolores to my grandfather, he revealed his friendship with her grandfather Gray Bradford when both were living in Baltimore.

After a lot of subterfuges aimed at getting her ring size, I spent hours at Macy's looking at engagement rings. The one I liked was more than my budget, so I bought it "on-time," the first time I had ever purchased anything on credit. I made monthly payments for around two years—so tight were my finances during this time. Dolores had been captivated by a toy she had seen in a shop window, a little lamb with black imitation karacul fur. I purchased the toy and bow-tied the engagement ring around its neck. The day I planned to give her the ring, I was home at the Dunbar with a bad cold. When Dolores came by my room to see how I was feeling, I told her I had an early Christmas present. She lit up with delight and immediately dubbed the lamb "Beebitz"—why, I have never had any idea.

· · · ·

Dolores's mother Josephine had been friends since childhood with Miss Marian Anderson, who also had a Danbury estate, Marianna Farms, three miles down the highway from the Owenses. I met the legendary Black contralto several times while visiting the Owenses and had come to like her and her husband "Razzle" Fisher very much—no one called the architect by his first name, Orpheus. Despite her ever-present gracious demeanor, no one could ever forget the 1939 national drama of her exclusion by the Daughters of the American Revolution, and her standing outdoors on the steps beneath the statue of President Abraham Lincoln to sing "My country 'tis of thee, sweet land of liberty, of thee I sing."

For the upcoming marriage ceremony, Miss Anderson and Razzle offered the use of her studio on her estate grounds, and Josephine happily accepted.[14] The date was set for April 15, 1950. The wedding was described as the "top society wedding . . . of two of the country's most distinguished families."[15] With telephone calls and pleading letters pouring in from Boston, New York, Philadelphia, Baltimore, and Washington, winnowing down the guest list was painful.[16] All the families were well represented—the Duncans, Bradfords, Whartons, and Bankses. My brother William was my best man. The ushers were my new brother-in-law Jackie Duncan, my college roommate Bill Ellis, childhood friend Joe Mitchell, and Ira Aldridge. Mary Aldridge was Dolores's maid of honor, and the bridesmaids were her cousin Betty Fitzgerald and a friend, Betty Peters.

Dolores looked ethereal in her wedding gown, which had first been worn fifty years earlier

A

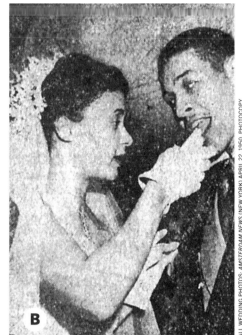

B

C

The Wharton-Duncan Wedding was held at Miss Marian Anderson's studio in Danbury, Connecticut, on April 15, 1950. The wedding photographs include: (A) Dolores's mother, Josephine Bradford Owens, kissing the bride; (B) the first piece of cake given to the groom by the bride; (C) Miss Anderson with Josephine's two Bradford cousins; and (D, *opposite page*) the wedding party (*left to right*): Jackie Duncan, Dolores's brother; Bill Ellis, my college roommate; Mary Aldridge, the maid of honor; Ira Aldridge; Joe Mitchell, my childhood friend; Betty Peters, friend of Dolores; Betty Fitzgerald, Dolores's cousin. My brother William, the best man, was not in these pictures.

by her great-aunt Blanch Bradford Dorsey of Philadelphia, and in turn by her own mother, Josephine.

Just before the nuptials were to start, Dolores's mother discovered that she did not have the right necktie for Partner's frock coat, and she insisted he go into Danbury for it—taking forty-five minutes. All the guests sat in Miss Anderson's studio, squirming restlessly as they waited. After a while Jackie Duncan, who had a wicked sense of humor, stood up. "Ladies and gentlemen," he announced, "I apologize for the delay. Our house on Lake Kenosha has only one bathroom, and there's a line ten people long waiting to get in."

Laughing uproariously, the crowd sat back and relaxed.

For Dolores and me it was an unforgettable day, and nothing could spoil it. The service was performed by two priests—Rev. Shelton Hale Bishop from Dolores's St. Philip's Episcopal Church in New York, and Father Oliver B. Dale, from St. Augustine's Episcopal in Boston.

When Dolores and I looked into each other's eyes to exchange vows, everyone else disappeared.

· · · ·

Before the wedding we had leased apartment 10D in the Riverton,[17] the same complex where Dolores had stayed briefly with the Aldridges. We bought furniture from the Henry Dick store in Danbury. Dolores picked a white French provincial bedroom set, a "tuxedo" sofa in olive fabric with gold thread, a Chinese-style cocktail table—and that was it. For end tables we used two packing boxes some wedding gifts had come in. On them we placed two tall brass lamps, a wedding gift from Dolores's maternal aunt Rose.

Dolores fixed up the apartment inexpensively but creatively. She was determined to convert our spare space into a cozy, attractive home. I was pressed into service painting the walls—white in the living/dining room, light coral in the bedroom. Using bolts of chocolate-brown raw silk, Dolores curtained the living room windows in valance style, then did the same in baby blue in the bedroom. Later, when a bit more money came in, she bought white, wall-to-wall WundaWeve carpet, brushing aside my jibes about the practicality of a white shag rug in New York City. Whenever people came to visit, they had to leave their shoes at the door.

Although we had white friends and acquaintances, we spent a good deal of time in the city's Black community. We went to the Black and White ball at the Savoy, and the "coming out" cotillions held in the 369th Regiment Armory for young women from affluent families in Harlem. At the first cotillion Dolores and I attended as "young patrons." I was moved by seeing Ralph Bunche, under-secretary-general to the U.N., leading Mary McLeod Bethune, the renowned founder of Bethune-Cookman College, in a high-stepping parade around the floor.

· · · ·

Now that I had a wife, I began to think more seriously about my career. I had been at AIA for a little more than two years, and wondered whether it was really my calling. At one point I toyed with the idea of moving into broadcasting. Some of my former colleagues from the Harvard Crimson Network were making names for themselves in radio—Alan Rich, Marty Bookspan, and Hartford Gunn[18]—and wondered if it might be worth a try for me, too. Bill Lippman suggested my contacting Kenneth Banghart, a well-respected announcer at NBC's New York station. Banghart explained gently that he doubted the radio would hire a Negro as an announcer. Why? I wanted to know. After all, it was radio, not television. Though my voice wasn't detectably Black, Banghart said, he expected that the other station personnel would make me "uncomfortable." I always despised this insipid racist euphemism.

With AIA up and running, at any rate, I got a raise and promotion to director of reports and analysis. I oversaw internal reporting from all AIA field projects, as well as the monthly operating report to the AIA board of trustees. My other responsibilities were special studies and annual reports, plus helping Pete Hudgens and Jim Maddox with proposals for new projects.

· · · ·

In February 1952, a few months following a second visit to Venezuela, I traveled for the first time to Brazil.[19]

I was immediately struck by the racial contrast of Brazil. The country had a reputation of being racially liberal—the African heritage was accepted and celebrated. These views were pushed by the author Gilberto Freyre, whose book, *The Masters and the Slaves*,[20] countered the belief that white races were superior to other ones. Freyre changed the mentality of people, especially of the white Brazilian elite, who considered the Brazilian people as "inferior" because of their African and Amerindian ancestry due to race mixing. The population was 62 percent white and 37 Black or *pardos* (mulatto). What I saw was that while the lower-income population was predominantly darker skinned, there still were a few Black or brown complexioned in middle-class and leadership roles. Brazil was a much more comfortable racial atmosphere that was less tense and more accepting of diversity than the United States.

Like the preceding trips, my main purpose was to familiarize myself more closely with the AIA's field projects within the country, and to get to know some of the program officers and specialists who were working there. After changing planes in Rio de Janeiro, I flew to São Paulo, the country's bustling industrial center. There AIA's J. B. "Dad" Griffing and his wife met the plane and drove me to the Lord Hotel. Griffing ran an interesting program aimed at controlling dairy cattle ticks, a major problem in Brazil, based on advanced U.S. insecticides and portable knapsack sprayers. The old local method of immersing cows fully in large walk-in vats led to lower animal body weight and reduced milk production. Griffing's portfolio in Santa Rosa included regular spraying services for thirty-five herds, several construction projects for trench silos, and an active agricultural extension program. There were also a thriving public health service with a full-time physician and ten boys' and girls' clubs for planting vegetable gardens and fruit trees.

By chance another visitor to São Paulo at the time was the Pulitzer-winning novelist Louis Bromfield. A farmer's son, Bromfield had begun using radical cultivation practices on his farm in Ohio—what today is often called natural farming.[21] With funding from Braniff Airways, Bromfield had brought thirty-five American farmers to visit the Agronomical Institute at Campinas, as well as several dairy farms throughout the region.

Invited to accompany them, I was quick to sign on. It was a chance to see Brazilian agriculture firsthand. I enjoyed getting to know Bromfield, a lion of U.S. letters and one of the early leaders of environmentally oriented agriculture. While the American farmers spoke no Portuguese and the *Paulista* farmworkers knew no English, they got along fine with ad hoc sign language. Most of the operations we visited, though, were atypical for the country. At one very well-to-do dairy farm the barns were spotless, the milking parlor was electrified, and the feeding troughs were semiautomatic. "This is how they farm in Brazil?" exclaimed one U.S. visitor. "Hell, we don't have this in the U.S.!"

Two weeks later I flew to Belo Horizonte, Minas Gerais, where I met Walt Crawford and his wife Nadine. As head of AIA's new Associação de Crédito e Assistência Rural, Walt had established a supervised credit program predicated on clients having established farm/home plans, coupled with farm management technical assistance. By that time ACAR was in full stride. Walt had an impressive team of both U.S. and local experts, including Sue Taylor (home economics), Jimmy Apodaca (farm management), and Eduardo King Carr (farm specialist). Carr in particular piqued my interest. He was a native Brazilian descended from U.S. Confederates who had emigrated to South America after the Civil War. Blond, blue-eyed,

COURTESY OF THE ROCKEFELLER ARCHIVE CENTER.

Carlos Tavares, head of the state bank, embracing Robert W. "Pete" Hudgens, President AIA, on the signing of the first farmer supervised credit loan under the ACAR (Associação de Crédito e Assistência Rural) program in Minas Gerais, Brazil. Hidden in the photograph on the right is Walter Crawford, director of ACAR, in the shadow of Santiago "Jimmy" Apodaca, Senior Farm Management Specialist for ACAR. The program subsequently was broadened into a national program ABCAR (Associação Brasileira de Crédito e Assistencia Rural) promoted by President Juscelino Kubitschek de Oliveira who, when governor of Minas Gerais, had been instrumental in the launch of ACAR. The ACAR program became the core of my 1958 Ph.D. economics thesis at the University of Chicago, *A Case Study of the Economic Impact of Technical Assistance.*

and lean, Eduardo looked like he had just stepped off the porch of some antebellum plantation home. He spoke Portuguese and English with equal fluency, the prior generations having extinguished any trace of a southern accent.

In Belo Horizonte Walt Crawford took me to a restaurant serving *churrasco* (beef barbequed on a long skewer and basted with a distinctive sauce), which was the rage at the time. As we stood in line outside one of the most popular places, the Brazilian owner rushed out and threw his arms around Walt. "Senhor Crawford," he exclaimed, "Do you remember me?" When Walt looked blank, he went on, "I was a poor farmer who tried to get a loan from you. Your experts convinced me that with only half a hectare, I could never succeed. I gave my land to my brother, came to Belo, and opened my restaurant."

He beamed. "So you are responsible for my good fortune. If you had given me a loan, I would still be back on that godforsaken farm!"

▪ ▪ ▪ ▪

During my monthlong stay in São Paulo and Minas Gerais, I learned a good deal about the politics of agricultural development. Walt Crawford explained, for example, that while the state's governor was a strong supporter of ACAR, the secretary of agriculture, a member of a different party, dragged his feet. Consequently AIA set up the program outside his department to avoid its being sabotaged. Pete Hudgens later remarked, "We had to put it where it could hold still long enough to take root."

Something similar happened with the program's line of bank credit. The governor had promised that short-term financing would be available through one of the state banks. But the supervising cashier was a middle-aged banker who had "come up the hard way" and who was sure no one from the United States could tell him anything about his credit practices. After Crawford accumulated a big backlog of applications, he called the governor's attention to the absurdity of one man's being able to stymie the struggle of sixty farmers to improve their lots. All those small voices were too much for the governor, who transferred the program's credit line to another bank.[22]

Walt Crawford insisted that before I left Brazil we should spend a weekend at Copacabana Beach—an experience not to be missed, he promised. Joining us would be Art McLawhon, a former FBI agent Pete Hudgens had hired to help straighten out some problems he thought had crept into the administration of AIA field offices. But the weekend was for fun and sun, not audits and inspections.

We stayed at the Hotel Regents, on Avenida Atlantica. After Sunday breakfast, we donned swimming trunks and sat in the sun on the street-level veranda. After a while we would cross the street for a swim in the ocean. After drying off, back we went to the veranda. Then back to the ocean . . . and so on. After that everybody took a siesta, got redressed, and went downstairs for late-afternoon cocktails of *caipirinos* (a refreshing, potent drink made from sugarcane rum and lime). I flew out of Rio that night at 9:30 P.M., asleep before the wheels were up.

• • • •

On September 4, 1952, our first son was born—Clifton R. Wharton 3rd. Together with Dolores's mother Josephine I visited him in the New York Park East Hospital. When the nurse held him up I saw through the window a big baby, squirming, his large bobbing head seemingly without a hair. Like so many fathers before me, I thought him perfect and beautiful.

For a while Clifton was a colicky baby—there was nothing like it to introduce first-timers to the joys of parenthood. The only thing that seemed to help was bouncing him as we paced, taking turns at sleeping. During pregnancy Dolores had watched her diet fanatically, and nine months later we found ourselves with a very large child. He wasn't fat, but during his first ten months he was so heavy that he couldn't crawl on his hands and knees—just writhed along the floor as if swimming. When not colicky, he was a happy child who laughed often and was alert and responsive. Dolores and I doted on him, and she hung a Harvard pennant over his crib.

Little Clifton's arrival brought more anxiety over the future. After several years of work, I still had few marketable skills. I wondered how much better I would now be able to answer Larry Levy's question, "What can you do?"

Predictably, my father tried to step into the breach. Dolores had been working persistently to foster rapprochement between Dad and me, and despite my lingering unhappiness over the divorce, my relationship with him had gradually rewarmed. For years my father had a habit of sending me photographs from diplomatic events, plus copies of articles ripped from journals or magazines, usually with a brief handwritten note. Especially when I was younger, they had often seemed odd or pointless. Now I came to recognize them as sort of "love notes," my father's way of staying in touch, reaching out for contact and acknowledgment.

Once again Dad urged me to consider the U.S. Foreign Service. But I was determined to succeed on my own terms.

At AIA I was unsettled that Nelson Rockefeller seemed to be pulling back his support. As Pete Hudgens increasingly pushed AIA to expand through government contracts, Nelson's interest began to wane.[23] Consequently, Pete and Jim Maddox drew up the blueprint for a new organization, independent of Rockefeller, one that would undertake overseas assistance through both foundation and government sponsorship. When launched, it was called International Development Services, and all AIA employees moved to its payroll.

Now I was even more concerned. All our fortunes would depend on securing contracts and grants. Any reduction in funding could bring budget cuts, which in turn might mean fewer staff. Still near the bottom of the totem pole, I might well be among the first to go.

When I went to Jim Maddox for a talk about my future, he took the conversation in an unexpected direction. Had I given any thought, he asked, to going back to school for a doctorate? Not much, I admitted. He was sure I had the intellectual capacity and thought a PhD in economics in particular could be invaluable for a career in overseas development.

I was a bit surprised, but intrigued. Maddox and I talked for a while longer, and he began to lay out what might be the best academic options. One was Harvard, where Maddox's old mentor, John D. Black, was running practically a one-man department of agricultural economics. Another was the University of Wisconsin, with a deep and long-standing institutional orientation toward economics. The third was the University of Chicago.

Especially since I had been an undergraduate at Harvard, Jim thought I would learn little that was new and different there. He also had reservations about whether Wisconsin's programs would foster the kind of skills most useful for development work. Chicago, on the other hand, might be just the place. It was at the forefront of the newly emerging school of mathematical and econometric analysis. It had a well-deserved reputation for intellectual rigor, and it had just launched a new program that would lead to a PhD in economic development and planning.

Jim thought I could matriculate into either the new curriculum, headed by Professor Bert Hoselitz, or the regular economics one. Think it over, he advised. In the meantime, he suggested I read an article in Bert Hoselitz's new journal, *Economic Development and Cultural Change*.[24] The author was Theodore W. Schultz, chairman of Chicago's Department of Economics.

A few days later Maddox called me into his office and introduced Schultz himself—a tall, imposing man with piercing eyes.

"I just tried to read your article," I gushed, and in my excitement blurted out, "I had a hard time understanding it."

Schultz smiled. "Lots of other people feel the same way. Just read it again."

It turned out that Schultz was organizing a project to survey the state of U.S. technical assistance in Latin America, with funding from the Ford Foundation through the National Planning Association. A few days later I got a letter from him, asking if I would be interested in a research assistantship in the project while I studied part-time for my PhD. I was ecstatic.

After the last several years at AIA, I certainly had the necessary background in technical assistance, while the financial support would be a godsend. Jim Maddox, of course, had been my "angel." As I sent off my application to Chicago I was full of gratitude to him.

Though I didn't know it, I was on the verge of membership in a small, dedicated band that styled itself CBCBCRAEA—the "city-born, city-bred, city-raised agricultural economics association." Few of us had studied agriculture. Many had never seen a farm, much less run one. Now we were somehow to become agricultural economists.

My official departure from AIA/IDS was on August 3. My colleagues from the fifty-first and fifty-sixth floors gave me a surprise reception, presenting an engraved wristwatch. It was a generous gesture, though I couldn't help feeling that such a traditional retirement present might be a little premature.

▪ The University of Chicago

Over the summer of 1953 Dolores and I planned our move to Chicago. We would store most of our belongings in New York City and live in a furnished student residence. We had been told the housing units were prefabricated one-story army surplus units, vintage World War II, but we had no idea what our new home might be like.

I will never forget Dolores's expression when she saw her first prefab. Used initially to house GIs during the war, the old huts had subsequently served several intakes of hard-living married students. Each hut had a nine- by eighteen-foot living room open to the kitchen, two small bedrooms, and one bathroom with toilet, basin, and shower—no bathtub. The unit temporarily assigned us had been empty for months and was in an appalling state. The floors were grimy, the mattresses were stained and lumpy, and the furniture was institutional at its worst. The only source of heat for the entire unit was a single kerosene stove in the middle of the building.

Waiting for our unit to be readied, Dolores, ten-month-old Clifton, and I instead stayed over in the nearby Evans Hotel—a sleepless night during which I seriously wondered if we should head right back to New York. But the next morning Dolores was having none of it, and her resolve persuaded me to forge ahead. After we moved into 1121 E. Sixtieth Street, Dolores miraculously transformed the drab little hovel into one of the coziest, most attractive homes in the area. She had done it in Riverton, and now she did it on Chicago's Midway.

The graduate adviser in the department was H. Gregg Lewis, professor of labor economics. After I settled into a hard chair in front of his desk, Lewis pulled my admissions file and silently read it through.

"Beyond freshman economics," he asked, "what economics courses have you had?"

I said I had taken international economics at SAIS, then mentioned a Harvard course taught by Seymour Harris.

Lewis winced, then sat looking at my papers for several more minutes without saying a word. He then surprised me by recommending that I take no economics courses at all during my first year in the program, only math and statistics. When he saw my puzzlement he added, "I'd be pleased to have you audit my course on intermediate economic theory. Then you can see what it's all about before you enroll in it."

I was astonished, but I soon learned the wisdom of his advice. In the first lecture, Lewis rattled on like a machine gun, simultaneously chalking line after line of calculus partial derivatives on the blackboard. The words were English, but they might as well have been in a foreign language. Mathematical economics? At the lecture's end I turned to the student next to me and asked if he had followed the argument. The student looked back at me with raised eyebrows and said mockingly, "You didn't?"

In a department preeminent in econometrics, where mastery of math and statistics were critical, I had been blissfully unaware of my lack of preparation. Lewis's gentle recommendation effectively saved my career from an early ignominious outcome. In my first fall term (1953), I earned a 49.5 out of 50 on my statistics final with Allen Wallis, though only 86 percent in math.

I audited Milton Friedman's famous section on basic price theory twice. Friedman's analytical power was awesome, and his lectures were like none I had heard before. Once you granted his basic assumptions and premises, you were predestined to lose any argument. His radical free-market conservatism was supposed to be counterbalanced by Professor Lloyd Metzler's Keynesianism. But Metzler had recently undergone an operation for a brain tumor and was only partially his former self intellectually. So Friedman's ideological dominance went largely unchecked.

The atmosphere in the economics department at Chicago was the most stimulating and challenging I had ever encountered, and in the early days I often felt as though I were hanging on by my fingernails.

The emphasis on empirical data, coupled with sophisticated theory, econometrics (mathematical/statistical tools), and analytical rigor, meant you risked your life the minute you opened your mouth. Outwardly the discussions might have sounded low-key, but the cut and thrust of the debate was razor sharp, not for the fainthearted. The toughest challenges, interestingly enough, often came not from the faculty but from your classmates. Among my own cohorts were several absolutely brilliant students, including some from Israel affectionately referred to as "those damned Israelis." I became especially close to Zvi Griliches and his wife Diane. A Lithuanian, Zvi was sent to the Dachau concentration camp during World War II. In 1947 he moved to Palestine, where he learned Hebrew and served in the Israeli army. After studying for a year at Hebrew University of Jerusalem, he migrated to the United States, where he earned a BS in Agricultural Economics from the University of California, Berkeley, ending up in Chicago. I was amazed at his peregrinations as well as his brilliance. After graduation, Zvi won the John Bates Clark Medal for his doctoral dissertation on the economics of technological change. He became a professor of economics at Harvard in 1969, serving for thirty years until his death in 1999.

I recall one telling incident with another Israeli in professor Carl Christ's econometrics course. Christ was writing a series of equations across the board. When he reached the end of the first line, Yehuda Grunfeld raised his hand. "Carl, don't you mean A bar, B bar, C bar?" Christ looked at what he chalked, acknowledged that he had omitted the bars, and added them. Then he began writing the next two lines—Grunfeld interrupted again, "That should be double A bar, double B bar, double C bar." Christ made the correction and continued. Halfway through the last line he stopped abruptly, went back, and slashed the appropriate bars into the equation, crowing at Grunfeld, "Caught ya!"

In the hallway after class Grunfeld remarked to the professor, "Carl, that was very good teaching technique, pretending you forgot the bars to see if the class was alert." Christ looked around at the rest of us. "Is he kidding?" he asked to general laughter. Grunfeld was probably the most brilliant student in the department. Several years later he died tragically, saving his son from an undertow off the coast of Israel, two weeks before he was due to return to Chicago as a new full professor.

. . . .

As department chair, Theodore Schultz was a force to be reckoned with, and as his research assistant I had the great fortune to work closely with him throughout my four years at Chicago.

Schultz had been raised in a tight-knit German family on a farm in South Dakota. He never went to high school, but against the family's wishes attended South Dakota State College, where he got a bachelor's in agricultural economics (1927), followed by a PhD from the University of Wisconsin (1930). Tall, with a large head, long face, and close-set eyes, he had a sharp sense of humor. In class he often spoke so elliptically that it took a while to see what he was getting at.

Schultz had gained national prominence while chairing the Department of Agricultural Economics at Iowa State. In a wartime study, a fellow professor had concluded that the nutritional properties of oleomargarine were no different from those of traditional butter, and that in some ways oleo might even be better. In recommending that oleo be used widely to conserve national resources, the report sparked a storm of controversy within the state's dairy industry, which pushed hard that the study be squelched. Citing academic freedom, Schultz stood firm against censoring the research. The report was published, the dispute escalated, and the college administration pushed for the article to be withdrawn. After speaking out unsuccessfully against the action, Schultz resigned in protest.

In 1943 Schultz joined the economics department at Chicago; in 1946 he became its chair, a post he would hold for fifteen years. From the 1940s to the 1960s, he specialized in the issues of economic development in the so-called Third World. His work on human capital theory, particularly *The Economic Value of Education* (1963) and *Investment in Human Capital* (1971), were the basis for his being named Nobel laureate in economics in 1979.

Along with his wife Esther, Schultz genuinely cared about students and their families. When you visited them at home, the warmth of their hospitality was a bracing tonic to all your doubts and fatigue. Human capital was more than just an academic idea for Schultz—he saw its embodiment in the hundreds of students who passed through his life. He promoted us and supported our work, showcasing the next generation whenever he could. And he followed up faithfully throughout the decades, sending around drafts of his latest articles and commenting in turn on those we sent him. Ever the teacher, he believed in human capital, and he invested his own productively throughout his life. I used to joke, not so facetiously, that you could always tell who Schultz's current graduate students were by seeing their names in the footnotes of his articles.

Schultz had a commanding presence—not physically intimidating, but imposing in his intellect, and especially his integrity. I personally witnessed a powerful example of the latter. One day, while I was waiting to see Schultz, a stranger came in and insisted on speaking to him immediately. Schultz asked me to wait, then ushered the man into his office, leaving the door ajar so I heard their conversation. The early 1950s in America were a time of allegations of communist infiltration in government led by Senator Joseph R. McCarthy and by the House Un-American Activities Committee. The senator's horrific tactic was to use demagogic, reckless, and unsubstantiated accusations, as well as public attacks on the character or patriotism of political opponents, celebrities, artists, and academics. Publicly televised committee hearings where individuals were accused of being Communists or had their loyalty to the United States questioned had created national paranoia. Loyalty oaths and witch hunts created an atmosphere of distrust, even fear. A careless comment—or anonymous accusation—could ruin a career in academia even more thoroughly than in Hollywood.

On this occasion, Schultz's visitor was conducting a "security check" on a former economics student. After looking over the visitor's credentials Schultz asked him whether he wanted an opinion of the former student's character, his competence as an economist, or his loyalty to the United States. All of that, the visitor confirmed.

"Well," said Schultz, "I'll be happy to tell you. But you'll have to keep notes. When we're done, I'll find a room and typewriter for you to write down a summary of what I've said, and an affirmation that I'm prepared to testify to my statements in a court of law, in the presence of the individual. Then I'll sign the document with you as witness, and we'll both keep a copy."

The visitor was stunned. He said he wasn't sure he could do that. Schultz handed him a telephone. "Why don't you check with your supervisor?" The flustered visitor reluctantly complied. Back came the exasperated reply something like, "Oh, Schultz—skip *him*!"

That was an unforgettable lesson in integrity.

· · · ·

Life in the prefabs was spartan. As a research assistant my stipend was low, and our rent was $55 per month. After housing, tuition, and books, our budget allowed $15 a week for food. Even in the early 1950s, that was a pittance, and how Dolores managed to feed three of us with tasty, nourishing meals, I never understood. We had only a two-burner hotplate, a portable electric oven (24" × 27" × 9"), and a fourthhand refrigerator. Like many neighbors, we planted a garden out back. No one had told us the topsoil was just an inch deep—the lettuce was fine, but the carrots were all tops.

Winters were brutal. Over the years the prefab's plywood walls had warped, and the insulation slid down between the risers. Through the cracks you could see the daylight outside, and Chicago's notorious wind—"the Hawk"—came slicing through.

One afternoon during our first spring in Chicago, Dolores found a recipe for dandelion wine. We could rarely afford alcoholic drinks, so Dolores and young Clifton went to the Midway, outside our door, which was carpeted with dandelions, and picked several baskets full. Dolores put them into a big ceramic crock and poured in boiling water with yeast. The crock then went into a shed outside to ferment.

Before long a noticeable odor was wafting from the shed, and all our neighbors knew just what we were up to. "Ready yet?" they would call as they passed by. We invited them all to our debut tasting. When we poured out the first glasses, the liquid was thick and smoky—we hadn't known you were just supposed to pour water over the blossoms, not leave them in the pot! But everyone agreed the wine wasn't bad, and its kick was wicked.

· · · ·

Anxious to finish her own degree, in late 1953 Dolores enrolled in evening classes at a branch campus of the Chicago Teachers College (later Chicago State University). Her courses met during the evening, while I stayed home with young Clifton. Predictably, given Dolores's intelligence, she kept getting As in all her classes.

At about the same time she was asked by Acrotheater, a University of Chicago extracurricular group, to offer instruction in modern dance. Although the group was mainly for gymnasts, the director persuaded Dolores to provide basic training in the techniques of modern dance performers such as Martha Graham, Louis Horst, and José Limón. For the

Acrodeo. In spring 1954 she choreographed the "Sunset" movement to Grofé's *Grand Canyon Suite*. The program drew rave reviews. Though I was euphoric at her performance and the applause it drew, I was also guilt-ridden that she was sacrificing her artistic talents to be my partner in life.

Dolores read aloud to Clifton constantly, and he quickly graduated from *Winnie the Pooh* to *The Cat in the Hat* and *The Wind in the Willows*. At three he had his own library card. But when we enrolled him in nursery school, it proved traumatic. Clifton did not like being left at school, even though the time there was only 9 to 11:30 A.M. Day after day, Dolores sat where he could see her on a bench at the back of the playground. After a long time, he began to tolerate it when she left. Clifton's teacher warned us that his abandonment anxieties might well persist into adulthood—words we were to recall many times later on.

At home, though, Clifton was a happy, friendly child. He liked to sit on the front steps, waving at passersby and calling a cheery "How do you do! Fine!" He got on especially well with Chi-chan, the daughter of Kelly and Yo Roberts, a white and Nisei couple, who lived in the prefab opposite ours. He loved to ride his hobbyhorse in the front yard while Chi-chan rode her own in syncopation across the way—the two bouncing up and down giggling merrily.

One lasting memory of our Chicago years was my daily "commute" from and to our prefab, across the grassy Midway, to the building (1126 E. Fifty-Ninth Street) on the other side where the economics department was housed. There were times when I thought I had worn a deep, rutted path across the Midway that should have been named for me. In 1956 when the prefabs were scheduled to be torn down for the construction of the university law school, we moved into a university apartment complex at 5428 S. Woodlawn Avenue (apartment 2B). We loved finally being in a real building even though Clifton had to sleep in a windowed alcove. At last we had a real bathtub instead of a shower stall.

The greatest learning impact came from my fellow students. Despite the competition, many students organized small study groups around particular courses and exams, especially before the prelims. Usually the groups consisted of four or five students who met and reviewed rigorously the material. We would challenge each other, explain what someone did not fully understand, or give an oral test on a range of topics. Being invited into a particularly competitive group sometimes lent indirect status among my fellow students. Some of the regular participants were Zvi Griliches, Alan Strout, John Dawson, and John Deaver. These groups certainly helped me develop and refine my own skills and competence. It was here that I began learning to think like an economist.

My classmates elected me president of the Economics Club for the 1955–56 academic year, with a board of Zvi Griliches, Steve Hastings, Walter Oi, and Bob Snyder. One major annual activity was the "post prelim" event whose centerpiece was a skit that lampooned professors and students alike, often playing with economic arcana. In 1956–57, I was reelected for a second year as club president, rewarding my rejuvenation of the club.

There weren't many other Black students in Chicago's graduate programs.[25] One was Hugh Lane, who was working on a doctorate in educational psychology. Another was Chuck Stone, a close friend from Wesleyan and the New England Student Christian Movement (NESCM), who had just finished a master's in sociology. Chuck had just been the first Black hired as a manager at the Carson Pirie Scott department store in downtown Chicago, though he seemed uncertain that this was the career he wanted. Chuck became a representative of CARE in India (1956–57) before returning to New York to edit *New York Age*. Later he was an aide to U.S. Representative Adam Clayton Powell before resuming his journalism career with the *Afro-American,* the *Chicago Defender*, and the *Philadelphia Daily News*. In 1991 he joined the University of North Carolina as a professor of journalism.

Dr. Allison Davis, professor of education and sociology, was the first Black to receive tenure at Chicago. One day when I chanced to meet him, he remarked that he thought I was the first Black doctoral candidate in the Department of Economics. It rather surprised me, since nobody else had previously mentioned it. In fact, racial topics rarely came up around the department. When the Supreme Court unanimously banned racial segregation in public schools in May 1954, I don't recall its being discussed by faculty, or even students. A similar silence greeted newspaper accounts of Rosa Parks's refusal to sit at the back of a bus, as well as Martin Luther King Jr.'s subsequent boycott in Montgomery, Alabama.

In retrospect, I imagine many of my teachers and classmates were well aware of the nation's slow awakening to racial intolerance. If they didn't talk about it, it wasn't necessarily because they disapproved or weren't interested. Two professors were beginning to track it on their econometric radar. Professor Margaret Reid, who had come from Iowa State with Theodore Schultz, was engaged in a pathbreaking empirical study of housing and income, part of which showed relationships between race and residential patterns that she considered demonstrably discriminatory. Professor Gary Becker wrote his doctoral dissertation on the economics of discrimination. He was the first to use economic theory to analyze the effects of prejudice on the earnings, employment, and occupations of minorities. He also established that discrimination is costly to the employer or corporation that engages in it. He won the Nobel Prize in economics in 1992.

. . . .

Dolores and I did get to know some local Negroes off campus. Among them were the Albrittons. Mrs. Frances Albritton was a schoolteacher, and Leon was the head of a local Democratic ward. They introduced us to a bright young high-school student, Donald M. Stewart, and some other younger couples. Stewart would become a high achiever in academe and philanthropy at the Ford Foundation and the Carnegie Corporation, as president of Spelman College, president of the College Board, and president of the Chicago Community Trust, and as a director of four corporations, including the *New York Times*, as well as a lifelong friend.

We rarely interacted with Chicago's Black elite. An exception was our accepting an invitation from Claude Barnett and his wife, Etta Moten, friends of my father's new wife Leonie, who had learned we were in Chicago. Barnett was the founder of the *Associated Negro Press*, and Moten was a concert singer and actress in movies and on Broadway. They invited us to a charity ball. It proved embarrassing when we learned that the occasion was a fund-raiser where guests were expected to make a substantial donation to the sponsor of the event. Spaghetti without meatballs was dinner fare for the three of us for two weeks following.

▪ The NPA Study

As research assistant to Theodore Schultz, my principal responsibility was to help with his National Planning Association–sponsored study. The goal was to help edit and prepare the studies of how U.S. organizations were assisting in improving agriculture, public administration, labor practices, and other sectors, mainly in rural Latin America.

Schultz had assembled a topnotch group of experts to work on the study. My old boss Jim Maddox was one. He was on leave from International Development Services to study the impact of U.S. missionaries and religious organizations. Others included Simon Rottenberg, a labor economist from the University of Massachusetts; George Blanksten, a political science professor from Northwestern; and Larry Witt, an agricultural economist from Michigan State.

I had begun my modest contribution to the project even before arriving at the university by writing a summary memo of my work with the AIA programs in New York.[26] Two other graduate students on the team were John Deaver, who was doing research on Chile, and a Spaniard, Marto Ballesteros, who was working on Argentina. We had an office on campus where we met regularly. We also issued a steady stream of outlines and briefing papers, often reviewing each other's work. Schultz, acting as overall coordinator, ran a very tight ship.

In late spring 1954, Schultz invited me to join the NPA group on a visit to Brazil. My academic schedule had precluded my going on earlier trips, but with my prior experience in both countries, Schultz thought my participation was appropriate.

We flew out of Idlewild on June 13, arriving in Rio the following day. It was a thrill to be back. The city was as vibrant as ever, a roiling brew of color, smells, sounds—all somehow intensely sexual. Our first stop was a courtesy call on the new U.S. ambassador, James S. Kemper. He was a former insurance mogul, one of a group of businessmen who had President Eisenhower's ear at the time.[27] Kemper received us brusquely. Although the State Department had formally requested his cooperation with our group, he claimed never to have heard of the National Planning Association. He also had a low opinion of the Ford Foundation. Though he was himself a Chicagoan, he acted as if Schultz had just landed from some alien, probably highly infectious, planet.

The National Planning Association Study of Latin American Technical Assistance Special Committee Meeting at the University of Chicago was chaired by (*left to right, 14th*) Laird Bell. The study leader was (*26th*) Professor Theodore W. Schultz. I (*behind Schultz to right, 27th*) served as his research assistant. This meeting included both committee members and study experts. Two other persons there were important in my life: (*13th*) Arthur T. Mosher, later head of Agricultural Development Council, and (*26th*) James G. Maddox, previously vice president of AIA.

Schultz got through the audience patiently, and at the end he asked Kemper to allow the team to meet with his key staff. The ambassador grudgingly agreed. But afterward we were appalled to learn that Kemper had directed his staff to keep notes on the conversation, temporize over questions, and submit any proposed responses to him in advance of delivery. Schultz was furious, a side of him I had never seen before. He cabled an immediate complaint to Secretary of State John Foster Dulles. In addition, he called Laird Bell, former chairman of the University of Chicago Board of Trustees, a powerful Illinois Republican, and himself a member of the National Planning Association.

Back in Rio, the reaction was electric. All the restrictions disappeared. Kemper never apologized, but everyone knew Theodore Schultz had made his point.

On June 16 I took off for Belo Horizonte in Minas Gerais, along with a new acquaintance,

Arthur T. Mosher. Mosher's father was Iowa's first agricultural extension agent. Subsequently, he worked in Illinois where he became the first person to systematically collect high-yielding corn seed from various farmers, which unintentionally became the base stock from which hybrid corn was developed by Henry Wallace. Arthur T. Mosher had done his undergraduate work at the University of Illinois in 1932, and received his MA in 1952. After five years as a Presbyterian missionary, working as an assistant agricultural engineer at India's Allahabad Agricultural Institute, he took a two-year leave of absence. One year he spent intensively reading up on Indian agriculture. The next he spent in Bhadan, a village about fifty miles east of Agra. Living there with his wife Alice Wynne and his first child, he learned to farm exactly as Indians did, with a pair of bullocks, a plow, and a sickle. For a teacher he hired the tenant who had previously cultivated the same fields.

In the midst of his farming, and with the help of five other evangelists, Mosher also collected information from 2,300 local farm families, around which he later built a doctoral dissertation at the University of Chicago in 1946. His supervisor was the recently arrived Theodore Schultz, who admired Mosher's combination of anthropological methods and rigorous economic analysis. In 1953, Schultz invited Mosher to join his NPA survey of Latin America. Although Art had no experience there, Schultz thought his talents and experience would make him an ideal collaborator to study the agricultural assistance programs.

"Unique" is an overused word, but in Mosher's case it fit. A diminutive five foot six, he smoked a pipe constantly and wore a French beret. If you wanted to find things out, he believed, you had to go to the roots. Rather than wasting time with ministerial "experts" in the big cities, he always headed straight for the countryside. His predilection matched my own habit since childhood of "casing the ship."

That was fine with me. For the next ten days we ranged across Minas Gerais, visiting ACAR programs in Curvelo, Sete Lagoas, Lavras, Varginha, Barbacena, and Viçosa. The roads were still just red laterite clay. Every time we crossed from one *municipio* to another we had to stop the jeep, open a gate, and walk around the cattle guard. By midmorning we were always covered head to toe in red dust.

As a rule you can quickly get tired or bored on field trips, especially with companions you don't know very well. But for Art and me there seemed to be an endless supply of topics mutually interesting. As the younger man, I was somewhat in awe of Art's experience and insights. But our temperaments and worldviews meshed seamlessly, and we deeply enjoyed each other's company. By the time we had been traveling for ten days in Brazil, we still hadn't run out of things to talk about.

Mosher hadn't a fiber of prejudice in his being. His Quaker great-grandparents, farming in Ohio in the 1830s, had maintained an "Underground Railway" station for Blacks fleeing slavery in the South.[28] Only after his death in 1992 did I learn this source of his quietly uncompromising opposition to racism and intolerance. His never mentioning this fact to me was typical of his sensitive character. Our relationship and friendship would be a major influence upon my life and career.

. . . .

In Minas Gerais, Ted Schultz joined Art and me on a visit to a farmer who was participating in an ACAR-supervised credit program. Climbing up into the farmer's wagon, Schultz picked up an ear of corn and shucked it. Holding it up, he said, "Wharton, how many rows?"

I hadn't a clue. "Seventeen?" I guessed.

Schultz guffawed, and when my answer was translated, so did the farmer.

"Wharton," Schultz chuckled, "the rows in an ear of corn are always even numbered. When it's hybrid corn from the U.S., there are eighteen."

I blushed. How was a charter member of the CBCBCRAEA supposed to know that?

During the trip, I informally discussed with Schultz my ideas about using ACAR and the farm data collected regularly from the farmers (using the forms that I had developed while at AIA) as a major aspect of a broader PhD thesis on technical assistance in Brazilian agriculture. Ted highly approved of it as a splendid idea.

Before returning to the United States, Art and I made two more field trips together—one with Ted Schultz to Campinas, Ipanema, and the second to Santa Rita and Matão. Separate from the team on our return to the United States, Mosher and I visited Venezuela and Costa Rica, observing the AIA programs in Valencia, El Tocuyo, Barquisimeto, and Turén, followed by a brief look around the agricultural center at Turrialba, Costa Rica.

Once back home, I continued working hard on the NPA project, editing books and articles and reading prepublication galleys. The material varied in quality and impact, but collectively it represented an impressive attempt to gauge the strengths and weaknesses of this new dimension of U.S. foreign policy.[29]

Of course, my highest priorities were completing my course work and planning my dissertation. The department saw to it that you were completely immersed in economic thought—not just in class, but also in a steady stream of seminars and workshops with distinguished guests from across the United States and abroad. One of the more memorable was W. Arthur Lewis, author of the *Theory of Economic Growth*, formerly principal economic adviser to England's Labour Party and now professor of political economy at the University of Manchester. After Lewis described Labour's commitment to providing subsidized housing for the working class, Milton Friedman came back with his usual line that it was tyranny to take people's money to buy things for them that they would not choose to buy for themselves. Arthur listened patiently, then said, "Milton, I'm not trying to *convince* you. I'm just *telling* you."

Friedman sat down, but he didn't give up. At the reception following Lewis's talk, he renewed the debate. Lewis must have been six foot five and easily weighed 250 pounds, and the sight of the massive West Indian scholar under pursuit by the much smaller Friedman was comical. Literally backed into a corner, Lewis looked at Friedman with a benign expression, "Milton," he countered, "your problem is that you believe in democracy. In England, no one does any longer."

. . . .

In the summer of 1956 Vanderbilt University professor Bill Nicholls, a protégé of Ted Schultz, invited me to lecture there on technical assistance—my first opportunity to be a professional academic lecturer. It was a six-week program with participants from all over the world. I worked hard, had some fun, and made several friends in the Department of Economics at Vanderbilt.

Back in Chicago, I worked on the prospectus for my thesis and took the final exam for my last course. A few days later I became so ill I had to be hospitalized. Dolores said it was exhaustion; the hospital said it was colitis. I thought I had better quit smoking, and finally did.

The core of my doctoral dissertation was an attempt to assess the impact of ACAR's supervised loan and technical assistance programs among a selected group of farmers, in the context of Brazil's overall economic agricultural growth.[30] In support fellowships were offered by the Social Science Research Council and the Doherty Foundation. I had to refuse the latter, since it required going to Brazil for an entire year. But the SSRC grant was sufficient. In the fall of 1956, moreover, Schultz promoted me to "research associate" in the department's Research Group on Economic Development.

My thesis committee included D. Gale Johnson (chair), Carl Christ, and Margaret Reid. Not surprisingly, the dissertation prospectus seminar was almost a mini-doctoral dissertation defense. The attendees included not only the economics faculty but also faculty from sociology, statistics, anthropology, geography, and history. Prominent among the participants were my fellow graduate students—who were often the most critical questioners.

After getting through the seminar without too much damage, I was surprised by a preliminary offer to join the economics department as an "instructor." I decided against it for a couple of reasons. For one thing, I suspected I would ultimately want a broader career canvas than a traditional academic position would promise. For another, a couple of my classmates had been offered assistant professorships. Maybe my work on economic assistance in the developing world wasn't "pure" enough, I sniffed. When I look back now, it's obvious that the others were better trained than I, with longer academic experience. My ego just wouldn't let me admit it.

The Development Economist 1: The ADC in Singapore, Kuala Lumpur, and Southeast Asia

I n spring 1957, as I began concentrating full time on my dissertation, Art Mosher called from Cornell, where he was a visiting professor leading a new three-year seminar on comparative agricultural extension for fifteen students—half foreign and half from the United States. At the same time, he was finishing two monographs dealing with his prior work in India.[1] Art had just agreed to take a new position as executive director of a relatively new Rockefeller organization, the Council on Economic and Cultural Affairs.[2] Art wanted me to join him in the venture. Unlike my previous work and study in Latin America, this would focus on agricultural development in Asia.

Even though outside my previous geographical experience, Asia was an intriguing region. Dolores and I discussed the offer at length. The idea of working again with Mosher appealed to me greatly. So did reentering the Rockefeller family orbit. But Dolores had a semester left to finish her undergraduate work, and my dissertation was just getting started. Another complication: Art needed me almost immediately, as an ally to offset two staffers he was inheriting with the job.[3]

In the end, Art promised to find a way to accommodate my finishing my dissertation, and though Dolores was disappointed over delaying the completion of her BA degree, we started packing for New York. (She would earn a BA in art history from Chicago State University after we returned to the United States.)

The Council on Economic and Cultural Affairs (CECA)[4] was a creation of Nelson Rockefeller's older brother, John D. Rockefeller 3rd. Tall, courtly, seeming diffident at times, "JDR 3rd," or "John" to his closer associates, was the more conservative, less mercurial of the two, but with a rock-firm determination in support of his beliefs. John was the full-time

philanthropist of the so-called brothers generation. He chaired the family's premier organization, the Rockefeller Foundation, and had created or helped create a number of independent
nonprofits in his particular fields of interest in Asia, culture, and population—the Japan
Society, the Asia Society, and the Population Council.

Although head of the board, John felt the foundation was giving insufficient attention to
the food production side of global race with population. He had been strongly influenced in
this direction by William I. Myers, dean of agriculture at Cornell and a Rockefeller Foundation trustee for several years. After John's urgings had been deflected repeatedly, he decided
to create a new organization, the CECA.

Art Mosher came to the Council through the offices of Donald McLean, a senior adviser to
JDR 3rd. Concerned about the extent to which Rockefeller might inject himself into program
management, Mosher had not exactly leaped at the opportunity. He was not, McLean later
commented, "one to wear any man's collar." But eventually Art relented—recognizing, I
suspect, that Rockefeller needed a strong agricultural economist to balance his own strong
interest in the population side of the global issue.

McLean and Rockefeller could have found no stronger hand to guide the work they
envisioned. From our short time together with the NPA Latin America project, I knew Mosher
was knowledgeable, creative, and energetic. He believed that countries and regions were sui
generis, rarely susceptible to preformed common strategies and solutions. He also thought
that in the long run trying to transfer institutions from outside was less likely to succeed than
developing local people's capacity to develop their own. His predilection to study an issue or
problem at the outset and at its basic or field level reinforced my own—his farm tours were
my childhood shipboard tours. Mosher was a living testimonial to the importance of effective
communication—thinking, speaking, and writing clearly in service of a vision. And he knew
the critical value of finding the best people for a job, then stepping back and allowing them
to use their own talents and judgment to get it done.

Unbeknownst to me, Art stirred up a debate by recommending me to the Council board
of trustees[6] as his first hire. Chief among those raising questions was Norm Efferson, chairman
of agricultural economics at Louisiana State University, a passing acquaintance when I was
still with AIA. His ostensible objection was to my lack of any specific training in agriculture,
particularly in farm management. At the time I was oblivious to the long-standing feud
between the farm-management "school," centered at Cornell, and the Iowa State production
economics "school," with its strongly statistical and econometric orientation. The respective
labels summed up both the nature of the conflict and its academic preciousness—"agricultural
economics" versus "economics of agriculture." As a student of Theodore Schultz, my presumed
allegiance fell squarely into the Iowa State group (though nobody had yet gotten around
to mentioning it to me), so Efferson might well have been unhappy even if my practical

agricultural experience had been extensive. In any event, Mosher insisted on my appointment and ultimately prevailed.

With the urgency of starting my new assignment with Art Mosher, identifying an immediate residence took us back to Riverton, the Metropolitan Life complex, where we promptly found a two-bedroom apartment. Dolores's mother wanted us to have a larger place. But there were positive points—the other Riverton tenants were notably successful persons, plus the rent allowed us to send five-year-old Clifton to Ethical Culture, one of the finest private schools in the city, and not as a scholarship student. Once again Clifton 3rd had to make a difficult shift in schools and learn to cope with the sharp divergence in culture and socialization. Nevertheless, with Dolores's motherly attention, he adjusted. As always Clifton's cheerful personality and incandescent smile enabled him to make friends.

. . . .

Dolores continued her crusade to bring my father and me back together. Dad admired Dolores for her style, high spirits, and intelligence, and she was fond of him, too. Their personalities just seemed to click. Eventually she invited Dad and his second wife, Leonie, for a visit from his post as U.S. consul general in Marseilles, France, much to the delight of Clifton 3rd. They seemed happy to see us, taking us out to their favorite Midtown French restaurants. It thawed the ice considerably.

Meanwhile my father kept up his steady stream of news clippings, photographs, and notes about what he was doing. I continued to think it self-serving. But I couldn't help a thrill of pride when in early February 1958 my father was appointed U.S. minister to Romania[7]—the first Negro foreign service career officer to be named chief of an overseas diplomatic mission. When initially offered the job, he bluntly told his longtime friend Loy Henderson, deputy under secretary, that he didn't want the appointment if it were being offered because he was Black. Henderson was happy to tell him that race had played no part in the decision.[8] He thereby became the first Negro to head a U.S. mission in Europe and behind the Iron Curtain. This achievement took him twenty one years serving in the so-called Negro circuit posts. Before this appointment when he met with an official from the department's personnel office, Dad characteristically and bluntly expressed his views, "You're not only discriminating against us [Negroes] in the Service, but you're exporting discrimination abroad in the Foreign Service."[9]

. . . .

Art Mosher's singular approach to staffing the Council was aimed at recruiting a cadre of U.S. professionals with strong academic credentials in the rural social sciences, who would provide hands-on program leadership in the field.[10] Stationed in one or more nations, typically on multiyear assignments, field associates would have relatively free rein to work with emerging Asian colleges, universities, and governments to identify and nurture indigenous scholars. They could consult, teach, conduct research, or make modest grants for libraries or research projects. Their brief also included identifying local professionals who might benefit from graduate study in the United States under Council fellowships.

Central to Art's method was recruiting superb associates. He canvassed academic leaders in agricultural economics, rural sociology, cultural anthropology, and agricultural extension to identify outstanding individuals who might fit the job as he envisaged it. His four early choices reflected this philosophy. John Provinse, a cultural anthropologist, had pioneered the first research on the Dyaks of Borneo in Southeast Asia and had served as assistant commissioner of Indian affairs (1932–49). One of the most respected cultural anthropologists in the United States, John was a wiry, bald Montanan, with twinkly blue eyes and a craggy wind-etched face full of wisdom and warm humor. He went to the Philippines. Abe Weisblat was lured from the Ford Foundation. Although a "city boy," he had studied for his doctorate in agricultural economics at the University of Wisconsin and was imbued with its institutional approach to economics. Abe came to the New York office as an executive associate and was given responsibility for India, Pakistan, and Bangladesh. Howard Beers, a rural sociologist with exceptional standing as a scholar, leader, and administrator, joined as associate in Indonesia, where his home, the University of Kentucky, had an AID contract to serve in the Faculty of Agriculture, University of Indonesia at Bogor. Milt Barnett was a professor of anthropology at Cornell University whom I had first met in 1952–53 when he was a researcher with AIA's CBR program in Venezuela. Fluent in Chinese, Milt had done work from Hopi and Mojave Native Americans in the Southwest to the Javanese in Indonesia, from Venezuelan Andean peasants to the Ifugao tribes in the mountain province in Luzon, Philippines. Milt became an associate in the Philippines in 1962, replacing Provinse.

A more strikingly diverse group of rural social scientists would be hard to imagine, except a shared fierce commitment to the human problems of rural development. We had been personally selected by Art. Consequently, the associates constituted a highly compatible group who enjoyed intellectual professional exchanges with each other and had the fullest mutual respect. We became the nucleus of a "faculty peers" in a unique, extended academic philanthropic enterprise for the next several years. We saw ourselves as pioneers who were given the freedom to apply and use our professional skills to create a totally new approach to agricultural development. This created among us a common excitement.

Art intended for me to go abroad as a field associate, but first I had to finish my dissertation. In the meantime, Art asked me to undertake a large-scale survey of how U.S. universities were approaching the training of Asian graduate students in agricultural economics. The Council's Asian graduate fellowship program had been experiencing serious problems that needed addressing. Over the course of several weeks I visited fifteen campuses across the country—Penn State; Cornell; Michigan State; Wisconsin; University of Chicago; Iowa State; University of Illinois; Ohio State; Purdue; Harvard; Minnesota; University of California, Berkeley; Yale; and Princeton. My contacts were with deans, department chairs, and faculty in economics and agricultural economics units. My interviews covered seventy-one faculty members and almost fifty Asian graduate students with whom the U.S. faculty had been working. Though I was generally well received, one Midwestern professor demanded to know why I was bothering with Asia rather than "helping your own folks," Negro farmers in the American South or Africa. The civil rights turmoil in the United States had begun to emerge dramatically. For example, the "Little Rock Nine" integration of Arkansas Central High School in September 25, 1957, was front-page news across the country. I agreed that the Negro south could use help, but since his name was Norwegian, I bluntly asked him whether he was working only with Scandinavians in Minnesota.

To complement my interviews in the United States, I planned my first trip to Asia, which I looked forward to eagerly. My first task was finishing my doctoral dissertation. Art Mosher offered a paid leave of absence for the first three months in 1958. Dropping everything else, I worked very hard, and by mid-March my thesis was done. All that remained was the formal conferring of my diploma.

· · · ·

In March 1958, I began the Asian leg of my survey where many of the nations to be visited were just throwing off the vestiges of colonialism. World War II and the Korean War were past, and the winds of change were rising. In some countries independence was at hand; in others, revolutions were stirring.

My fifty-day itinerary included Japan, Korea, the Philippines, Malaya and Singapore, Indonesia, Thailand, Burma, and India—a succession both kaleidoscopic and mesmerizing. The "East" was truly different from the "West." Although nearly a hundred people were interviewed, what was really dizzying was the chaotic profusion of people, languages, costumes, religions, foods, and customs. Yet almost everywhere, one thing was constant: the pervasive grinding ache of rural poverty. At the end of the trip I sat on a low wall outside the Imperial Hotel in New Delhi. It was just dawn, and the relentless Indian sun had not yet started to bake all beneath it. What I was thinking about was the most striking thing I had noticed throughout my stay. Everyone interested in rural development, it seemed to me, was studying one problem—theirs. No one seemed to be looking beyond a single issue in a single country. No one was looking at issues broadly, considering interrelations or points of convergence—much less pulling diverse facts together into a coherent theory of the economics of poverty.

Maybe this was the broad research topic I had been seeking.

I didn't know if I could pull it off. But it intrigued me more than anything had in a long time—maybe ever. My letter to Dolores about it tried to convey both the scope of the challenge and my surge of enthusiasm to undertake it.[11] Here was a canvas where I might make a worthwhile mark. Now, I told her, I had a clearer vision of what I could accomplish. No mention was made that during several stops in Asia there was a recurrence of my asthma.

The results of the survey were published in a Council monograph[12] presenting my findings, with recommendations for foreign students, US faculty, and interested colleges and universities. The report was widely distributed both in the United States and in Asia with positive reactions. Surprisingly, it was regularly listed in materials for foreign student counselors. Ten years later the report was judged "the classic study of professional training of foreign students . . . notable for its careful focus and marshaling of information. . . . Wharton's findings represent the most intensive analysis available of important substantive problems in the education of foreign graduate students."[13]

Personally and professionally the Asian visits dramatically boosted my knowledge about Asia and its problems while I became acquainted with the key academics in Asia and the United States. This outcome, I suspected, had been knowingly planned by Mosher in giving me the assignment.

Not long after my return to New York, Art Mosher offered me a position as a Council field associate in Southeast Asia, for at least ten years. My scope was to cover more than one country in the region and determine which nations might benefit from the Council approach.

Dolores and I discussed the pros and cons at great length. She was particularly concerned how going abroad for so long would affect my intellectual growth and future career prospects. Might it be a case of "out of sight, out of mind"? My just-completed survey had certainly turned up some evidence that it could happen. Very few younger professors were willing to spend time out of the country, believing it would hurt, not help, their promotion and tenure chances. How, for that matter, would Dolores fare, living abroad for the first time? How would it affect young Clifton, just six, to be thrown into an entirely unfamiliar culture?

In the end Dolores and I agreed that the opportunity was too good, the new adventure together too alluring, to pass up.

When my father heard the news about my working on Council programs in Southeast Asia, he was by no means pleased—especially since the job's time horizon would be so long. He had never stopped hoping I might yet reconsider the Foreign Service. A few months before, in fact, he had asked the State Department to send me application forms for a reserve officer position.

I reminded my father that he had been virtually the chief of mission at most of his own Foreign Service posts, with wide latitude to exercise independent judgment. In my opinion the same opportunities had now been dramatically reduced, especially as the State Department was concentrating personnel in capital-city embassies, with fewer outlying consulates and vice consulates to be staffed by younger people. In Southeast Asia, on the other hand, I would be building new programs from scratch for the Council. For better or worse both the leadership and the responsibility would be my own—plus hopefully I would acquire independent judgment abilities.

Although Dolores and I didn't discuss it, we also knew the impending change would ease the continuing friction between her and my mother. I realized that my mother's concept of an ideal wife for me was totally different from mine, and she blindly failed to see or appreciate the great qualities and special contributions that Dolores brought to our marriage. In large things and small ones, Mother continued to signal her disapproval of my wife. Right after we returned from Chicago to New York, Dolores had invited her to our apartment—some time alone together, she hoped, might improve things. Mother arrived from Boston with two uninvited guests, my cousin Marie Wharton and "Aunt" Ebba, one of our longtime family friends. Mother's excuse was "we are all family." Their presence meant no private tête-à-tête for Dolores and my mother—and in our small apartment, Dolores now faced the need to prepare extra meals for three guests. As if that weren't enough, as Mother departed she insultingly tossed behind her a check to Dolores "to cover the expenses for the visit!"

· · · · ·

My PhD was awarded on August 29, 1958, at the University of Chicago's Rockefeller Chapel. I was filled with joy and relief. My dissertation spawned the usual journal articles.[14] But the most significant fact was that I became the first Black to receive a PhD in economics from the University of Chicago.

Dolores and Clifton 3rd were there—Mother, too. Little Clifton, perhaps feeling he had earned a part of the degree, grabbed the diploma and playfully donned my mortar board. "Clifton!" my mother cried, snatching the diploma away. "Don't soil it!"

I took the degree from her grasp and placed it back in my son's hands.

· · · · ·

For my initial headquarters in Southeast Asia, I chose the city of Singapore.

At the time Singapore was still a British Crown colony, moving gradually toward independence. It had inherited all the virtues and efficiencies of the British colonial civil service. An oasis among the other less-developed countries in the region, mail was prompt, telephones were reliable, and if you had a problem, repair service was swift. You could even send cables from home via the phone—rare in the developing world. The environment was healthy, modern medical care was available, and you could drink the water without boiling it first! Finally, the University of Malaya had a department of economics, not one of agricultural economics. Since my own degree was in the former, I liked the idea of starting my overseas academic career from a position of strength.

In late August, not long before we were due to leave New York, Dolores and I interrupted our furious packing briefly to attend the annual meeting of the American Agricultural Economics Association in Winnipeg. There Dolores announced some wonderful news—she was pregnant! In Singapore we would have both a new home and a new baby.

▪ Singapore _____

I wanted Dolores to see firsthand the rural poverty that would lie at the heart of my work, so we decided not to travel through Tokyo and Bangkok—large, somewhat Westernized cities, atypical of Asia's impoverished "underside." Instead we flew east, on one of the earliest commercial jets. After a stopover in Rome, we went on to Pakistan. At the Karachi airport we were met by Kelly Roberts, who with his Nisei wife had been our next-door neighbor in Chicago's prefabs—his daughter Chi-chan had been little Clifton's favorite playmate. Kelly, in Pakistan for the Asia Foundation, drove us from the airport to our hotel. Dolores stared out the car window silently, gazing at the bedraggled people along the roadside—pulling carts, carrying water in buckets, or just shuffling dully forward. Having been jolted very much the same way on my first visit to South Asia, I knew exactly what was going through her mind.

The next day we flew on to New Delhi, where the contrast between the haves and have-nots was even more appalling. In the 1950s you could not visit any part of India without confronting the all-encompassing deprivation. From a luxurious old British Imperial Hotel, you had only to take a step or two outside to be thronged by the beggars, often horribly deformed, beseeching you for *baksheesh* (alms). Sacred cows lolled in the streets, placidly chewing their cud, while men and women threaded their way around them, bent with impossible burdens. Mingled with the dust of the streets, the smells of poverty rose to fill your nostrils—old grease, sweat, curry, hair oil, and burning dung. The teeming immensity of it all was like an assault, numbing the senses.

We stayed for seven days in New Delhi, where our hosts were Tom and Martha Keehn. Tom was the representative in India for AIA, my old employer, which was working with the Indian Cooperative League on programs of handicraft marketing, refugee welfare, and rural self-help. His wife Martha had helped launch the American International School and was doing volunteer work with refugees from the war that followed partition from Pakistan.

Tom and his colleague Dr. Allie C. Felder Jr.[15] took us to see a couple of typical villages. There we watched oxen plodding round great millstones, grinding wheat, and peeked into mud huts where people slept on rope stretched over wooden bed frames. Nothing we had yet seen prepared us for the dismal spectacle of people carrying pots of water two hundred yards to wash after relieving themselves in the fields at the edge of the village.

As so often in Asia, poverty butted up against lavish spectacle. On the country's Independence Day we sat in the stands of the New Delhi racecourse, watching the president of India arrive in an open limousine. Following him came the Indian cavalry, resplendent in red uniforms and turbans, their raised lances fluttering with pennants and regimental standards. The riders entertained the cheering crowd with their horsemanship, spurring their mounts through precision maneuvers, jumping hurdles, all under the blistering midday sun. It was as if we had traveled back in time to Kipling's day, with Gunga Din crouched somewhere just over our shoulders.

• • • •

A Westerner newly come to Singapore will be almost overwhelmed by marvels on every side, but by one thing above all: the all-pervasive heat. Sitting just one degree off the equator, the city's temperature ranges from 75 to 93 degrees Fahrenheit, while the relative humidity hovers between 75 and 80 percent   all year round. Outdoors, walking around feels like swimming in a heated pool while fully dressed. If invited to dinner, you carry your suit jacket in the car, put it on just before knocking at the door, then take it off as soon as you go inside. Dazed by the heat and a sumptuous meal, guests often doze off suddenly in the middle of a sentence, then jolt awake two or three minutes later. Conversation goes on as if nothing had happened.

All around us, Singapore was a riot of scents and color. Plants and flowers spilled over walls and climbed trellises on nearly every narrow street—white, sweet-scented gardenias, pulpy yellow and purple orchids growing free as weeds, red bougainvillea, brilliant orange flame trees, and white frangipani. Across the marketplace wafted the scents of bizarre, gleaming fruit: hairy red rambutans, yellow mangoes, purple mangosteens with their snow-white inner flesh, green and yellow star fruit, orange papaya, and spiky durian, queen of fruits, with its formidable stink of three-week-old garbage!

Singapore was also a paradise for gourmets or gluttons, with local and regional cuisines jostling for attention from a hundred rickety food stalls. The smells of cooking enveloped you like a drifting cloud—Shanghai whole carp, Mongolian hot-pot, Bangalore curries, Thai *krupuk*, Malay satays, sumptuous Indonesian rijsttafel—a savory dish for every conceivable taste. Food was not merely for nourishment, but also the base for extended social interaction. An entire evening would be spent leisurely eating eight- to ten-course Chinese meals while discussing anything from politics to the latest social gossip. It took us a year before our taste buds were able to differentiate the incredibly creative taste combinations of Chinese meals, arranged like a symphony orchestration. No wonder when a chef changed restaurants, faithful gourmets soon followed.

Nearly everyone in Singapore spoke English. The majority of its citizens are Chinese, but both Singapore and Malaya were multilingual societies of immense cultural diversity. The religious mix included Islam, Buddhism, Daoism, Hinduism, Christianity, Sikhism, and shamanism. Ethnically, there were Chinese, Malays, Indonesians, Arabs, Indians, Pakistanis, Afghans, Javanese, Minangkabaus, Bajaus, and Kadazans. Groups often subdivided linguistically, such as Chinese into Cantonese, Hokkien, Hakka, Hainanese, and Teochew. Indians, mostly from the south, spoke Tamil, Telugu, Malayalam, Gujerati, Punjabi, and Sindhi. There were a few other languages—Thai, Iban, and Kadazan, for example—thrown in for good measure.

Despite this pluralism, Singapore was dominated numerically by the Chinese. Since the British were leaving, the eventual independence and election of the brilliant Lee Kuan Yew and his People's Action Party were warily anticipated. "Harry" Lee, as he was affectionately called with a rare "double first" at Oxford, had surrounded himself with the brightest and the best of Singapore. Lee's party had a virtual monopoly on the city's future leaders.

Lee campaigned on an anticolonialist platform calling for social reforms and eventual union of Singapore with Malaya. Significant percentages of the electorate leaned toward the Socialist and Communist parties despite the civil war waged before independence by indigenous Communists on the peninsula. At the time Malaya still had some remaining pockets of guerilla Communists near the Thai-Malay border, and what was called the "Insurgency" had only recently abated.

Lee claimed that he was "not Communist, but not anti-Communist," and sought thereby to bring the Communists into the fold. This raised fears among the remaining British expatriates, especially the business community, and further heightened preelection tensions. Nevertheless, the election on May 29, 1959, was an overwhelming victory for Lee and his PAP—forty-three of the fifty-one seats.

During the first few months in office, Lee would receive no Europeans or Westerners, nor even accept the credentials of the Western diplomats assigned to Singapore. He refused to form a government until the British freed the jailed left-wing members of his party. During this period, JDR 3rd was planning a visit to Singapore and, as was his custom, wanted an appointment with the national leader. When the U.S. consul general and the Esso regional head failed, I was called upon to facilitate an audience. Through the close friendship of Dolores and Ina Gamba, wife of my colleague Professor Gamba, whom Lee was about to appoint chief justice of the Court of Arbitration, an appointment for a "secret private" meeting for JDR 3rd was negotiated. On the appointed day, I escorted him unceremoniously through the side door of the Istana (palace). Unaware of my stratagem, he had a puzzled look on his face.

Singapore politics proved to be an interesting feature of our residence.

. . . .

Soon after our arrival we found a two-story duplex at 33 Trevose Crescent near the University of Malaya along Bukit Timah Road. Upstairs were two bedrooms and a study; downstairs, a living room, dining room, kitchen, and servant quarters. We converted one bedroom to an office space. Out back there was a modest garden of orchids—growing in profusion. To help manage the home we hired a live-in Chinese *amah*, Ah Tai, who dressed like her peers in a white blouse and black pants. As was common then, Westernized homes such as ours lined one side of the street, with tin-roofed hovels on the other, downhill side.

The University of Malaya had been created in Singapore from the old colonial Raffles College. It was the only institution of higher education for the city-state and the entire country of Malaya. When I arrived in 1958, the Department of Economics was imbued with the British academic tradition. Instructors lectured to students, and students prepared tutorial essays. At the end of the year, a single examination determined each student's grade. For first-year students, the same exam decided whether they would continue or sit for an honors program   and not incidentally, what future careers might be open to them.

The "Professor" (or department chair) who ran the economics department was Thomas H. Silcock, a competent, rather Machiavellian Fabian Socialist whose parents had been missionaries in China. After graduating from Oxford, Silcock had lived in Singapore since the 1930s. During World War II he was interned by the Japanese in the city's notorious Changi Prison, then he survived a stint of hard labor building the infamous Burma-Siam railroad, dramatized in the movie *The Bridge on the River Kwai*. Other economics faculty included Lim Tay Boh, whose doctorate was from the London School of Economics; Yoh Poh Seng, who taught statistics; Siew Nim Chee, who in 1953 had been the first Malaysian to attend Cornell; and Charles Gamba, an Australian of Italian ancestry and labor economist who had written a book on the Malayan plantation labor movement.

The only Malay in the department was Ungku Abdul Aziz bin Ungku Abdul Hamid,[16] known to his friends as "Johnny." He had graduated from the university in 1951 with a first-class honors in economics. Movie-star handsome and charismatic, with a dramatic pointed beard, Aziz had a beautiful wife nicknamed Tita, a journalist and radio personality of Hadhrami Arab and Malay descent. They made a stunning and regal couple.

Early on Tom Silcock asked if I would teach the final-year economics course, perhaps providing the students with some exposure to Chicago-style "econometrics"—he used the word gingerly, as if it referred to some contagious disease studied only under strictly antiseptic conditions. I agreed, but said I would also like to teach the first-year course Principles of Economics. Silcock was surprised, thinking I would prefer more advanced students. My explanation was that the courses were equally important, hence my desire to teach both.

What I didn't explain was my belief that a sound foundation was a necessary condition for future success in studying economics. The older students had already been shaped by the university's heavy emphasis on Western and European economic content and ideas. Among the younger set there might be minds whose basic ideas about economics were as yet unformed. Most important, the freshman class would allow me a bit more flexibility in experimenting with course content and teaching methods.

In keeping with British practice my nominal title at the university was senior lecturer, not a visiting professor.

My first lecture section had about sixty students, mostly Chinese with some Malay and a few Indians. They seemed bright and eager, though they had some disconcerting habits. For one, they immediately sprang to their feet upon my entry to the classroom, which was hard to get used to. And though they listened attentively and took copious notes, they never asked questions. In my second week, I told the class my policy of leaving five minutes at the end of each lecture as they would ask about anything they had not understood. The first five-minute period passed in utter silence. Then, I alerted them, if they didn't have questions for me, I would spend the time putting questions to them. A stir went round the room—but at the next class, there were still no questions. Somewhat frustrated, I stressed that no questioner would be considered stupid for asking a question—the whole point was to help me understand whether I was getting the material across to them.

Eventually one student had the temerity to raise his hand—then a few others. The first student to do so was Augustine Tan Hui Heng, soon followed by other bright pupils, Francis Chan Kwong Wah, Wong Nang Jang, and Elizabeth Wee Kim Choo (all would later figure prominently in my academic role and have highly successful careers in government, business, and academe). When it became apparent that no "penalty" would be levied, the classes became more lively and more enjoyable for everyone—me included.

Weekly tutorial essays were required of each student, and when I looked over the file of topics assigned in previous years, they were dreadfully foreign and abstract. There was nothing in Walter Bagehot or Lombard Street or Bank of England interest rates that touched on the economic realities of Singapore and Southeast Asia, much less the students' own lives and experiences. So the traditional tutorial topics were replaced with some new ones I wrote:

> Since the supply of pineapples is inelastic, Malayan growers do not stand to gain by combining to restrict output and raise prices. True, false, or indeterminate? Discuss.
>
> Does the law of diminishing returns or variable proportions apply to agricultural production by (*a*) a padi [rice] farmer in Kelantan? (*b*) a Russian collective farm? (*c*) an Indian cooperative farm? (*d*) a Chinese commune? (*e*) a Vietnamese hill tribe? (*f*) a New Zealand sheep farm? Discuss.
>
> "Complaints have been made that there are far too many hawkers and taxis on the roads."— Mr. Ong Pang Boon, minister for home affairs reported in the *Straits Times*, August 1, 1959. Describe the different economic criteria which could be used to determine when there are "too many."
>
> Money change ... money change ... money change—ever the cry in Raffles Place. Explain as an international economic phenomenon.

No sooner had a dozen or so of my new topics been posted on the department board than Tom Silcock called me. "Dr. Wharton, these essays will not do," he told me heatedly in his office. "They will cause the students to think with their blood!"

Silcock and I had a vigorous debate. I pointed out that the topics I had assigned were the same things the students were reading about in newspapers and arguing over in coffee shops, so why not bring them into class for rigorous exchange? They would thus learn more about the tools of economic analysis and how to apply them to their own circumstances.

Clearly unconvinced, Silcock eventually relented. We would see how things unfolded, he sighed. But the students took on the unfamiliar work with gusto, and class time went by a lot faster as they listened to and debated each other's essays.

. . . .

Despite the Japanese wartime occupation, Singapore remained a beautiful city. The magnificent old colonial mansions still stood, occupied now by wealthy Singapore Chinese, a few Malays, and numerous foreigners. There were only two high-rise buildings in the entire city. Today's sea of Singapore skyscrapers brings me a pang. I remember the days when a favorite local pastime was to climb to the top of the old Cathy Hotel on Dhoby Ghaut (Road) and look out across all Singapore to the AIA (American Insurance Association) building in the heart of the downtown—the tallest multistory buildings in the entire city.

Along the roadsides the high grass was cut by teams of men with blades fixed to the end of long poles. At construction sites, most of the laborers were Chinese women, called "red tops" after the bandanas they wore over their hair. Carrying bricks and cement, they scrambled over the bamboo scaffoldings like antic worker ants. The few British yet on the scene wore their tropical khaki shorts and knee-high wool stockings—and *always* dressed for dinner.

As Dolores consumed the wonders of this new exotic life, her frequent guiding companion was Ina Gamba, the wife of my economics department colleague Charles. An experienced and wise older woman, Ina became Dolores's steadfast mentor, introducing her to the domestic, political, and cultural life of Singapore. In the process, they became lifelong friends, almost like a mother and daughter.

Dolores especially enjoyed the Singapore market, where items on offer ranged from rice sold by the hundredweight to live ducks to fresh python. Visiting the array of shops and stands, she endlessly bargained and quickly picked up fluency in "market Malay," the sturdy patois of daily use. Because my university colleague Ungku Aziz insisted I study "Rajah Malay," as old and stilted as Chaucer's English, my halting attempts to use it provoked great amusement among the villagers and farmers I visited on field trips.

As new arrivals we were continuously thrilled by local celebrations and festivals. During our first Chinese New Year, on February 18, 1959, long strings of firecrackers were hung throughout the city from second- and third-story windows almost down to the sidewalks, and lit from the bottom. All day and all night until dawn, the steady barrage of exploding firecrackers sounded almost like a war—close and distant, but constant. We could hear the noise even inside our air-conditioned bedroom. The next day, virtually every street of the city was at least a foot deep in spent red papers.

Another was the Indian *Thaipusam*, a day of devotion, thanksgiving, and atonement. After a month of cleansing and a full day of fasting, penitents pledged themselves to Lord Subramanian. As they paraded, they carried on their shoulders heavy *kavadis*, semicircular steel frames decorated with flowers and peacock feathers. Extruding from the frames were several two-foot needles, embedded in the penitents' flesh. In their trances, they sometimes pierced their cheeks and tongues or wore sandals embedded with nails, and a few even pulled large carts with multiple hooks embedded in the flesh of their backs. With no apparent pain or bleeding, the penitents paraded for miles to the Hindu temple downtown at Sri Mariamman, on South Bridge Road. There they twirled and danced feverishly outside before disappearing into the inner sanctum. The festival reminded me strongly of the *flagelantes* I had seen in the Canary Islands during my childhood.

Being exposed to so many sects and practices in Southeast Asia—Hinduism, Buddhism, animism, Islam, Confucianism, and all the rest—had an odd and lasting effect on me. While I could appreciate the similarity in the positive ethical cores that seemed to persist across most organized religions, I saw more clearly than ever the bitter negative excesses done in their names. So many doctrines and divinities, and all of them seemingly doomed to share the same frailties that finally corrupted their prophets, crusaders, clergy—and the faithful themselves. Sadly, most of the negatives were made by self-interested leaders to promote a differentiation of their faith from all other religions—the "other" is to be belittled or hated. Even in a relatively tolerant multicultural setting like Singapore, it wasn't hard to discern the underlying friction among the groups. Gradually my ruminations on God and religions focused on a sense of the divine as a creative force or collective spirit—a cosmological order more to be felt than understood. Both Dolores and I found our commitment to organized religion begin to weaken.

· · · ·

As one often does in new situations, I wondered about the issue of race and racism. While there was no question about our being U.S. Blacks, the subject rarely came up. Given the multiracial, multicolored host population, there was a virtual absence of any racial hostility toward U.S. Blacks. A couple of racist incidents, however, did occur. One involved a visiting white agricultural economist from the U.S. Department of Agriculture who is best unnamed. A local dignitary hosted a dinner in the visitor's honor. After dessert, the host, aware of the guest's reputation as a vocalist, asked him to sing. His choice of "Carry Me Back to Old Virginny" was unfortunate.[17] In a dialect mimicking an illiterate Black, he sang out after the first stanza the refrain "There's where this old darkey's heart am long'd to go." After each "darkey" refrain, Dolores and I looked at each other with the unspoken message—"we will have to leave." Protocol be damned. As soon as he finished, we thanked our hosts and departed, leaving in our wake buzzing consternation. I immediately thought of my father's outburst as a young foreign service officer that the Department of State was exporting American racial prejudice.

Other Negro professionals in the region—such as Harry Groves, dean of law at Texas Southern University, who helped to establish the new College of Law at the University of Malaya in Singapore,[18] and my Harvard classmate, Ernie Howell, who was stationed for the

Asia Foundation in Pakistan, Ceylon, then South Vietnam—probably had similar experiences. But the racial situation for Negroes in Southeast Asia was in dramatic contrast to that back in the United States, where tensions were rising around incidents like the Rosa Parks bus boycott in Montgomery, Alabama, and the attempted desegregation of the Little Rock Arkansas Central High School. The civil rights movement had shifted to sit-ins and "freedom rides" with growing violent attacks. Malayans were aware of these events, though not their full significance. Americans stationed in the area, while more aware, tended to reflect their political backgrounds and U.S. regional biases. U.S. Negro expatriates, however, were both aware and concerned.

Importantly, my race had no apparent impact on my interaction with my Southeast Asian colleagues and did not seem to be a consequential factor in my work in the region. One exception was on an early visit to Bangkok when an American-owned hotel refused me, even though I had reservations. I ended up in a small, comfortable Thai hotel frequented by Asians and Europeans.

· · · ·

After a hectic ride through the Singapore streets in a tropical downpour, Bruce Duncan Wharton was born at Seventh Day Adventist Youngberg Memorial Hospital on April 17, 1959. He was a beautiful baby—seven pounds, ten ounces, with a full head of black hair. His first birth certificate listed him as "Chinese." I quickly got it corrected, and the American embassy issued him a U.S. passport. To my dad's great amusement, Bruce was also a Singapore national and a British subject—his first grandchild or child born abroad who was not under his U.S. diplomatic umbrella. After Dolores came out of the hospital, we took him home and hired his *amah*, Yap Joon Foo, who slept in his bedroom and attended his every need.

· · · ·

As an ADC field associate, my role was a bit complex. Teaching at the University of Malaya was only part of my job. I had separate, independent Council activities and also undertook personal economic research with or without the university. ADC's ultimate goal was to develop and strengthen the rural social sciences. As a foundation official, my regional hat for this mission covered Singapore, Malaya, Thailand, Vietnam, and temporarily Indonesia. Art doubted that Laos and Cambodia had much potential for ADC. I concurred, but promised to look into future possibilities there.

In each country, I was authorized to recommend grants and to award study fellowships, mainly for graduate students who wanted to go to U.S. colleges and universities. This required identifying and supporting indigenous talent who could eventually step into the educational processes and institutions from which they emerged. Finally, I acted somewhat like the chairman of a dispersed faculty—overseeing American ADC visiting professors at universities in my region usually under two-year Council sponsorship.

Since I covered more than one country, unlike the other associates, that meant a great deal of traveling. A serious drawback was that I frequently had to leave Dolores behind with the boys. Fortunately, Art Mosher encouraged spouses to travel together with the associates, paid by the Council. So with the domestic support of Ah Tai and Joon, sometimes Dolores could join my peregrinations.

Mosher attached importance to developing intellectual and professional interaction among the NYC and field staff—associates and visiting professors. A key feature was regional staff conferences, usually held annually. Each of us prepared and distributed in advance a memorandum describing our work and our sense of how the ADC mission was proceeding in our country or region. Sometimes one or two were asked to cover a special topic. These sessions were both intense and rewarding. Spouses were invited to attend any of the sessions at their choice. The meetings developed a camaraderie and mutual respect that strengthened the Council.

In 1959, the first regional conference of ADC associates and visiting professors was held in Bandung, Indonesia.[19] Afterward, Dolores and Clifton 3rd went along with me to Bali. Bruce remained behind with his *amah* Joon. We visited the Tjokorda Gede Agung Soekawati[20] in his palace compound in the mountain village of Ubud, sleeping in one of his wives' unoccupied houses, with whispered chants and temple bells ringing softly outside our door. It was like a second honeymoon—with our son safely in a room of his own!

Throughout 1959 my travel was extensive—Cambodia once,[21] Thailand three times, Indonesia twice, and South Vietnam four times. My first-year trips were useful to learn about the status of the rural social sciences in these nations and to become acquainted with their key leaders and academics. One thing that took me aback was the shortage of Asian scholars with doctorates in economics or agricultural economics or the other rural social sciences. There were two economics PhDs in Singapore, one in Thailand, and none at all in Malaya, South Vietnam, Cambodia, or Laos. The colonial powers had deemed the social or policy sciences as sources of popular discontent, even revolution, so their teaching had been generally discouraged. Given the shortage of indigenous scholars, only a small body of research existed on the region's agricultural economies, economic development, and international trade. Even counting visitors sponsored by USAID and foreign foundations, the pool of expertise was tiny. Nonetheless, a handful of us shared the excitement of being there in the region, working at a turning point in its history.

In Thailand at Kasetsart University, the Council had Vince Plath, a visiting professor from Oregon State University, where we had strong relationships, and I was well received there at each visit. Also, I negotiated a visiting professor, Australian David Penny, for the new University of Medan in Indonesia.

Once I had made initial contacts throughout the region, subsequent visits let me pursue the Council's broader goals. One was identifying prospects for graduate study in the United States, a painstaking and difficult process. In countries like Thailand, where opportunities to

The ADC's first staff conference was held in Bandung, Indonesia, in 1959. (*Left to right, seated*) Horst Von Oppenfeld; Judy Von Oppenfeld; Abe Weisblat; Art Mosher; A. B. Lewis; Dolores Wharton; Clifton Wharton 3rd; Clifton Wharton Jr.; (*standing*) David Brown; Jeannie Brown; Howard Beers; Nancy Stevens; Robert Stevens; Janet Penny; John Provinse; David Penney; Gordon Sitton; Wells Allred.

study abroad were prized, government officials often tried to decide "whose turn had come," rather than allowing merit-based selection from a pool of candidates. Elsewhere, as in Malaya and Vietnam, there was little interest in or even hostility toward the United States, with candidates more likely to prefer universities in the former colonial power—that is, Britain or France. Moreover, given the acute shortage of individuals with any training at all in the rural social sciences, there was an understandable reluctance in officialdom to lose the ones they had, even for the purpose of strengthening their skills.

As the months went by I got a better sense of the development challenges facing the region. Paramount was the overwhelming predominance of agriculture. In most of Southeast Asia 60 to 80 percent of the population was engaged in farming or other poverty-level activities. Except for Singapore, most countries depended heavily on agricultural exports for foreign exchange. Often the principal export products, such as palm oil and rubber, had been introduced and exploited commercially by colonizers, receiving more attention and resources than food crops and thereby distorting the economies.

Several countries did have government policies that recognized agriculture's importance. Unlike in India, for example, which had chosen an "industrialization first" model, in Southeast

Asia "agriculture first" resonated among countries that found themselves importing foodstuffs rather than growing them at home.

If you cared about people in Southeast Asia, and if you wanted to help build a base for greater national prosperity and productivity, you had to start with agriculture. And to do that, you needed human capital—trained professionals, experts, and technicians to guide the process. That, of course, was the Council's own vision. Only time would tell if we would succeed.

• • • •

My first visit to South Vietnam was in early 1959, a time when the Communist infiltration was confined mainly to remote areas, or just starting to spread. The French had abandoned their fight for colonial rule after a military defeat at Dien Bien Phu in 1954, and Vietnam had been divided by the Geneva Agreement of July 21, 1954, which provided for a demilitarized zone north of Hue with Communist North Vietnam and a new regime led by Diem in South Vietnam. The Communist Vietminh government of Ho Chi Minh ruled in the North. When Ngo Dinh Diem returned from exile in the United States, he was appointed prime minister of South Vietnam by former emperor and then-current chief of state Bao Dai.

Five years after the French defeat, the United States had begun to play a role providing civilian advisers and limited military advisers to the Diem government forces to help them combat the growing Communist insurgency. The naïveté of the fledgling American efforts was the source of scorn among our knowledgeable friends in Southeast Asia. The wife of a British civil servant upbraided Dolores while I was away in Vietnam, "You Americans don't even know what's happening in Vietnam—it's going to blow to kingdom come!" We would soon learn that extended residence was a sine qua non for acquiring in-depth local Southeast Asian expertise. This philosophy ran counter to the policy of our State Department, which insisted on mandatory rotations that significantly reduced the ability of our diplomats to build long-term relationships.

South Vietnam was a marvelous brew of indigenous, French, and Chinese ingredients. The people themselves tended to be small, delicately boned. The women were stunning in their *ao dai* dresses, the long pastel panels worn over loose black or white silk trousers. Wearing the traditional Vietnamese leaf-covered conical hats (*nón lá*) while riding their bicycles or motorbikes, they filled the Saigon streets like a flock of lovely butterflies. Their local cuisine, a distinctive blend of French and Chinese, was based upon their balanced concept of five tastes and elements—spicy (metal), sour (wood), bitter (fire), salty (water), and sweet (Earth), invariably topped with the infamous fermented fish sauce, *nuoc mam*.

Like most of the region, South Vietnam's economy was dominated by agriculture, particularly rice. Before the North Vietnam guerillas began moving in, the country had been a significant exporter from the so-called Rice Bowl of the Mekong Delta. Under the stress of the insurgency, exports soon declined. At the same time, the government's sporadic attempts at land reform had largely floundered, with large landowners taking advantage of the failure to expand their holdings.

. . . .

During my visit I met key government and university officials to explore areas in which the Council might be helpful. Following French practice, Vietnamese universities taught economics within the school of law, and there were no departments of agriculture. The University of Saigon leaders were polite enough, but concerned mainly with the possibility of grants or study fellowships for their faculty. But the minister of agriculture was interested because of a new National College of Agriculture being established in the rural village of Bao Loc, and we eventually signed an agreement to bring an ADC visiting professor from the United States— Robert Stevens, who had just completed his PhD at Cornell and who brought his wife Nancy.

In Saigon contacts were made with some members of the Michigan State University Advisory Group,[22] which had been engaged by the U.S. International Cooperation Administration (the immediate predecessor to the U.S. Agency for International Development). The MSU program was to work with the Diem government in economics, public administration, and police administration. MSU professor of political science Wesley Fishel had a close relationship with Ngo Dinh Diem dating from before he became president, and he had translated Diem's trust into a contract for his group to help stabilize the country's economy, streamline the government bureaucracy, and help deal with the insurgency. Among other things, they had established a four-year training school, the National Institute of Administration. CIA involvement in the police administration program later became a major scandal in higher education.[23]

At the end of my trip a courtesy call was made on U.S. ambassador Elbridge Durbrow, who invited two others to sit in—the head of the USAID mission and the embassy's chief political officer. They wondered whether anything was learned during my tour that might be helpful to them. Given my father's position I had stringently avoided saying anything publicly about the burgeoning war, or for that matter any other foreign policy issue. But speaking up in private seemed unobjectionable.

My main point to them concerned the Vietnamese government's rice price policies. At the time the country was exporting a significant part of its rice crop production. At home, however, the government insisted on holding domestic prices below the product's export value, mainly to avoid discontent among urban consumers. In effect, the government was buying locally well below the world market, then reselling abroad for much more— in effect taxing its farmers to support itself. The Vietnamese who worked in the paddies understood perfectly well what was going on, and they didn't like it.

The ambassador and his colleagues didn't think it was all that serious a problem. After all, the farmers were illiterate. True enough, but my rejoinder was that the farmers weren't stupid. If unhappiness in the critical Mekong Delta spread and intensified, it could add fuel to the slow-burning insurrection.

My general feeling after the embassy visit was while the diplomats thought my ideas were interesting, they felt that the Vietnamese government had much bigger problems on its hands. But there was no point in arguing otherwise—no one was listening.

• • • •

Joining us in Singapore as a new Council visiting professor was David Brown, who had attracted Art Mosher's attention when he was working at the University of Tennessee. For two years Dave taught at the University of Malaya (later named the University of Singapore). His role was to introduce students to agricultural economics and farm management, and acquaint them with rural research activities. Later on I went with him on field trips to commercial rubber plantations and was impressed with his quick grasp of local issues. He did creative, valuable research at a coastal farm area of Johore, Malaya, as well as a study of small vegetable farms in Ama Keng, Singapore. But as he and his wife Jeannie neared the end of his first tour, he confided to me that he wouldn't seek to renew his contract, mainly because of his frustration with Ungku Aziz.

It was too bad. Brown had been making an impact on his students, showing them how to do research and analysis with hard field data. And that was probably the crux of Aziz's antipathy. He railed against foreign professors who did research in the developing world in order to build up their resumes back home—"white elephant hunters," he called them. In some cases, he had a point, but David Brown was not one of the hunters.[24]

Brown wasn't the only one to cross swords with Aziz. At a public symposium not long after my arrival, I had made a forceful argument for the ascendency of empiricism and economic analysis over classical or ideological economic theorizing.[25] Along with Tom Silcock,[26] Aziz took instant exception. Strongly influenced by Fabian socialism, Aziz believed that rural poverty in Malaya was caused entirely by capitalist exploitation, and that only a collectivist solution could bring progress. I tried to suggest that many of his ideas could be worked into a more rigorous analytical framework without altering his fundamental values, but he was having none of it. This was not helped by visiting economists who criticized Aziz's highly touted "Sarong poverty index," with which he attempted to explain normatively the causes of Malay rural poverty. Based on his studies, Aziz argued that by counting how many washed sarongs were hung out to dry per home you could determine each household's level of poverty. George Mehren, chairman of the Department of Agricultural Economics at the University of California, Berkeley, thought this idea clever but hardly solid econometric analysis. George and I conspired to find a way to encourage and finance a doctoral program for Aziz. We made a valiant effort to persuade Aziz, including funding, but our efforts came to naught. At the last minute Aziz declined. Eventually he went to Japan for his PhD from Waseda University.

Unhappily, the economics dispute spilled over into our personal relationship. Initially

Aziz and his wife Tita had been welcoming, but afterward things gradually became more distant between us, though always Malay polite.

Another unfortunate consequence of the debate was that it raised my profile within the local intellectual community in a rather perverse way. The rumor ran around that I was so clearly overqualified for my job that I couldn't possibly be just an "ordinary" visiting scholar. Maybe I was really a spy, using the Council as a cover for work on behalf of the CIA. It didn't help that the U.S. consul general in Singapore was Bill Maddox, who spoke freely of serving with my father in Lisbon. My father worked for the United States, so "like father, like son"—he too must be some sort of government agent. Suspicion of being a CIA operative caused me no small disquiet. After a while, luckily, the rumors ran out of steam. I decided to be more careful in my intellectual disputations with colleagues.

During home leave, I learned that the CIA actually had approached JDR 3rd seeking his permission to recruit me. According to Art Mosher, the U.S. government had told JDR 3rd their operatives in the region reported that I was a phenomenal source of information on the region, and they needed my extensive contacts and insights into the countries I was covering for the Council. He told them flatly, "No. Keep your hands off of him completely!" I was grateful to "Mr. John's" position because if the CIA approach had become known at the time, my effectiveness in the region would have been virtually nil.

Another related delicate issue during those years was the Asia Foundation. Although the Ford and Rockefeller foundations got more publicity, the low-key Asia Foundation was often larger and just as influential, with offices and staff in virtually every Asian capital (New Delhi excepted). When news broke in 1976 that the Asia Foundation had been funded primarily by the CIA—something long whispered among Asians themselves—it created a furor and touchy complications for other nonprofits operating in the area. (Ironically, Dolores became a trustee of the foundation in 1994.)

• Kuala Lumpur

In 1959, the University of Malaya was divided into two autonomous campuses—the University of Malaya in Singapore and the University of Malaya in Kuala Lumpur. In 1961 the governments of Singapore and Malaysia passed legislation making them national universities. On January 1, 1962, the University of Malaya in Kuala Lumpur was permanently located on 750 acres and kept the name, eventually becoming University of Malaya. At that time, the campus in Singapore became the University of Singapore (today the National University of Singapore). On June 16, 1962, the university celebrated the installation of its first chancellor, Tunku Abdul Rahman, Malaysia's first prime minister. The first vicechancellor was former dean Sir Alexander

Sponsored by the ADC, the first conference of the Southeast Asian Agricultural Economists was held at the University of Malaya in Kuala Lumpur, May 8–14, 1960. (*Left to right, front, 1st*) Floyd Underwood, USAID; (*2nd*) Francis Chan Kwong Wah, MA graduate student; (*4th*) Shanmugalingam, an undergraduate student; (*second row, 1st*) Chaiyong Chuchart, Department of Economics, Kasetsart University, Thailand; (*2nd*) Arb Nakajud, professor of agricultural economics, Kasetsart University; (*3rd*) Bachtiar Rifai, professor, Agricultural Institute, Indonesia; (*4th*) Udhis Narkswasdi, professor of agricultural economics, Kasetsart University; (*6th*) Pantum Thisyamondol, dean, College of Agriculture, Kasetsart University; (*third row, 1st*) John Mellor, professor of agricultural economics, Cornell University (India); (*4th*) Arthur T. Mosher, ADC executive director; (*fourth row, 1st*) Gordon Sitton, ADC visiting professor, Kasetsart University; (*2nd*) Clifton Wharton, ADC associate; (*2nd*) John Provinse, ADC associate (Philippines); (*3rd*) Abe Weisblat, ADC associate (New York); (*fifth row, 2nd*) David Penny, ADC visiting professor, University of Medan, Indonesia; (*3rd*) Eric Ojala, economist, ECAFE; (*4th*) Ungku Abdul Aziz, professor and chair, Department of Economics, University of Malaya (KL); (*5th*) Horst Von Oppenfeld, ADC visiting professor, University of the Philippines; (*sixth row, 2nd*) David Brown, ADC visiting professor, University of Malaya (Singapore); (*3rd*) Agoes Salim, MA graduate student.

Oppenheim, a world-renowned mathematician. I attended the installation, representing both Harvard and Johns Hopkins.

▪ ▪ ▪ ▪

The shortage of national rural social scientists in the region meant that little prior research had focused on agricultural economics, economic development, and international trade. Even including AID and foreign foundation personnel in the region, the number of U.S.

professionals in these disciplines was still small. In Malaya, for example, there were only a handful of Americans interested in such fields. Among them were Tom McHale, an economist consultant with Klcin and Saks who came to Kuala Lampur in 1959 with his wife Mary, and also taught part-time at the university; Norm Parmer, professor of history, University of Northern Illinois, whose first tour in Malaya began in 1952 and whom I met in 1960 with his wife Bess; Pete Gosling, geographer professor from the University of Michigan who came to KL in the summer of 1961 with his spouse Betty and their children; and later sociologist Gayl Ness, with a four-year grant from the Institute of Current World Affairs, who came to KL in February 1961 with his wife Jeannie and their children. We all shared an excitement over being in the region and working there at a major turning point in its history. Also, our close professional and social relationships with our fellow American adventurers and their children meant that we all became lifelong friends.

My extensive visits and contacts in the region convinced me that the few economists, sociologists, anthropologists, and extension agents would benefit from meeting at a regional conference. This led me to organize the first regional meeting of Southeast Asian rural social scientists, held at the newly opened Faculty of Agriculture at the University of Malaya (in Kuala Lumpur). Of historic significance as a first, the meeting was held May 8–14, 1960, with the opening session addressed by the Malayan foreign minister, Ismail bin Abdul Rahman, university vice chancellor (president) Oppenheim, and Art Mosher. A total of thirty-eight persons were invited, representing Thailand, Malaya, Singapore, the Philippines, Burma, South Vietnam, Indonesia, Cambodia, Ceylon, and the United States, plus sixteen observers. Several ADC colleagues also participated, along with representatives from ECAFE (U.N. Economic Commission for Asia and Far East), FAO (Food and Agriculture Organization), and the World Bank.

Each participant prepared a report on the teaching of agricultural economics in his respective country. Historical background, curriculum, courses, research projects, publications, and demand for agricultural economists were followed by recommendations on the adequacy of the training being offered, the suitability of training available abroad, and the priorities for agricultural research. National reports came from Burma, Ceylon, Indonesia, Malaya, the Philippines, and Thailand. Panel reports were made on selected topics, including some presented by ADC visiting professors. One result of the sessions was a new wealth of information for all participants—and for me. The conference also multiplied the effectiveness of education and training for stronger agricultural development in the region.

▪ Home Leave and Cornell University

Since the new campus in Kuala Lumpur included a Department (Faculty) of Agriculture, it was decided that the Agricultural Development Council's field associate should logically shift from Singapore to there. But first we were due for a break. Every two years, ADC field associates could spend up to four months back in the States, "recharging our batteries"—usually at a university campus. By the time my turn came, I had developed many ideas about research priorities in Southeast Asia. I wanted to pull them together into a broader context for my own work, as well as for assessing potential ADC grants. Getting ready for my mini-sabbatical at Cornell in the fall of 1960, I drafted a paper summarizing my thoughts.

Dolores, the boys, and I flew home, stopping over briefly in Hawaii. Rev. Shelton Hale Bishop, who had retired and moved from Manhattan to Honolulu, christened Bruce during our visit. Having baptized Dolores and her brother Jack, married us, and now christened both our sons, Rev. Bishop thus continued his tradition with the Duncan family and now the Whartons.

In Ithaca we rented Art and Alice Mosher's home[27]—characteristically, they even lent us their Hillman sedan. At Cornell the college of agriculture assigned me an office. Surrounded by outstanding agricultural economists, I was in a perfect position to observe the special Cornell approach to farm management, the fountainhead of the conflict among agricultural economists that had almost prevented my being hired by ADC.

A good part of my leave was spent working my earlier draft into a paper called "Economic and Non-economic Factors in the Economic Development of Southeast Asia."[28] It focused on several key factors I thought would influence the region as the basis for research priorities. The economic elements included the preponderance of perennial (tree) crops in local agriculture, and their dominance in the export trades; the coexistence of radically different models, such as plantation agriculture for exports and smallholder farming, mainly for food; the simultaneity of food deficits and surpluses; and the large sector of subsistence-level, noncommercial operations. Noneconomic factors ranged from climate and geography to explosive population growth to the adverse consequences of nationalism. Over a few weeks' time I read the paper at five different campuses—Cornell, Michigan State, Chicago, Wisconsin, and Minnesota. When I reached the University of Chicago, Ted Schultz asked me to speak at the famous "Friday Seminar"—usually reserved for leading national and international figures. I wasn't the only one who was shocked. Professor Gregg Lewis, who years before had guided my ill-prepared entry into Chicago's doctoral program, greeted me wryly. "I don't know any other graduate who has come back to this forum two years after getting his degree!" Ultimately the paper was published by ADC and distributed both in the United States and in Asia.

My U.S. campus presentations and the intellectual exchanges provided me with excellent preparation for the move to Kuala Lumpur and the next phase of my activities in Southeast Asia.

▪ Kuala Lumpur _____

Kuala Lumpur was very different from Singapore. Singapore was an entrepôt economy, flourishing because its central location was ideal for transshipments in the region. Its only natural resource was its people. Malaya was heavily dependent on exporting rubber (from smallholders as well as plantations), tin, oil palm, and rice. Although more easygoing and relaxed than bustling Singapore, Malaya's political and ethnic makeup was more complex. The Malays dominated the government through the United Malays National Organization, founded by nationalists led by Dato' Onn bin Jaafar, chief minister of Johore and Ungku Aziz's uncle. The economy, however, was controlled by the Chinese through the Malayan Chinese Association. Indians controlled the plantation labor market—their party was the Malayan Indian Congress. The prime minister, Tunku Abdul Rahman, was known fondly as Bapah Melayu, the father of Malaya, and much respected for his gentle promotion of harmony in the multiethnic nation.[29]

Before Malaya's independence, the local Communists had begun an insurgency based on their perception of being excluded from the nation's move toward acceptance into the British Commonwealth. From 1948 onward, British and Malayan forces fought a jungle war to combat the communist terror campaign. By the time we arrived in KL, however, the conflict was guttering, localized mainly around the northern border with Thailand.

. . . .

Dolores, the boys, and I moved into a spacious, well-designed new ranch-style house at 22 Jalan Damai, north of the city center, far from the university campus site. Chosen sight unseen, the house had been selected by Mary McHale, Tom's wife, whose taste Dolores trusted. We shipped some furniture from Singapore and had additional pieces made by local craftsmen for the living and dining rooms. A lovely Chinese folding screen divided the living and dining rooms, and in the rear we could eat breakfast on a portico. The bedrooms were air conditioned, and the crushed tile floors cooled our bare feet. There were also separate quarters for live-in help. Dolores hired a cook, Therese Chee, and a general housekeeper, Mary Chong. We no longer needed a baby *amah*—Bruce was two now, and Clifton 3rd was enrolled in the British Alice Smith School.

We had an enormous front yard, with a smaller garden in back, tended by an Indonesian immigrant named Rawat. Out front near the large culverts, Rawat rooted frangipani cuttings, which in the lush tropical climate soon grew into substantial trees. Bruce tagged behind Rawat, imitating everything he did.

Life in the tropics had its moments. One day the shiny terrazzo floors attracted a large cobra, which glided into a fold of our Chinese screen. When Dolores screamed, it reared high, hood fully spread. I rushed in and stood at a safe distance blurting, *Where is it?* Out of nowhere came Therese Chee with a hoe, and off went the cobra's head. Then she hurried down to the front gate and looked in the culvert under the bridge, where she found several baby cobras nesting. She dispatched them all.

· · · ·

The new Kuala Lumpur branch of the University of Malaya was seen by the nation's leadership as an important symbol of its new status and a recognition of the importance of higher education for its future. The branch or "satellite" designation was soon dropped, and the campus eventually became *the* University of Malaya. My offices there were in a new agriculture building that had been funded by a grant from the government of New Zealand, which also sent Max Davies as the new dean of agriculture. With a real office at last—two rooms, no less—the Council authorized me to hire a full-time secretary, Mrs. Pono Navarednam, whose sister Rasammah Bhupalan was the founder president of the Malaysian Teachers Union, and a younger clerk, Miss Somasundram.

Moving to Kuala Lumpur meant rearranging my schedule somewhat. Early on, travel and administrative responsibilities prevented my spending more than a quarter or so of my time on teaching and research. By 1960 the split was roughly even, and after we moved to Malaya, I spent between two-thirds and three-quarters of my time in academic work. Administrative duties and travel notwithstanding, I averaged between twelve and sixteen hours in the classroom each week, about the same "load" as a full-time U.S. professor.

My experience in Singapore had convinced me that the university's principles of economics courses needed to change, in terms of both content and pedagogy. I started with two basic assumptions. The first was that students should learn the major analytical methods of economics at the very outset of their studies. The second was that wherever possible, subject-matter applications should be local—that is, Malaysian or Southeast Asian—rather than Western. For example, in explaining the concept of "margin," I demonstrated its derivation from an actual production function based on a real Malayan farm. Only then did the students move on to the abstract concept of marginal utility. In one of my favorite lectures I challenged the class to explain the difference between the concepts of marginal product, marginal cost, and marginal revenue. I nicknamed that one "A Margin Is a Margin Is a Margin."

From the beginning, my emphasis was on the need to "think like an economist." I devoted considerable attention to conflict resolution, aggregate versus individual phenomena, independent versus dependent variables, and the difference between facts or data, analysis, and theory. We also surveyed the various schools and subdivisions of economic thought—empirical economics and philosophical or political economics, Western and non-Western economic thinking, collectivist versus free-market ideas—as well as the distinction between macro- and microeconomics.

When I learned that the agriculture curriculum made no place for rural sociology, cultural anthropology, or extension education, I decided to modify my introductory economics course to include at least an overview of those subjects. The proportions were about 40 percent principles of economics, 30 percent agricultural economics, 15 percent rural sociology and anthropology, 10 percent research methodology, and 5 percent government. My course became the only exposure that the agriculture students received in the rural social sciences in the entire curriculum.

Existing textbooks and materials were sometimes inadequate or off-point for students in the developing world. A case in point had to do with the economic concept of "monopsony," where there is only a single buyer for a product or service. In rural villages in Southeast Asia, Chinese merchants were often criticized because they were the sole sellers (monopolists) of farm input supplies and the sole buyers (monopsonists) of the crops and other farm outputs produced. The first time I tried to teach the theory of monopsony using the way the merchants operated, I was surprised to find that the first-year textbooks didn't mention it—only in advanced texts was it covered. So I wrote up and mimeographed a teaching paper that explained the basic idea, with some graphs illustrating its application to local products. The aim was to show the students how the predominant influence of the Chinese merchants could be understood strictly on economic grounds, without recourse to political partisanship or interethnic rancor. Eventually the paper appeared as "Marketing, Merchandising, and Moneylending: A Note on Middleman Monopsony in Malaya,"[30] To my surprise the "3Ms," as it was called, became a widely used reference in economics courses throughout the region.

This broad, intensive overview gave students a framework that they subsequently could use to delve more deeply into traditional micro- and macroeconomic analysis. With a good tool kit of analytical instruments and a template of the traditional areas of economics, the students reached a fuller understanding of what they were studying, and more quickly. Once they acquired proficiency in the basic analytical tools, economic analysis and theory became effortless.

▪ ▪ ▪ ▪

In this period, many U.S. universities had difficulties with entering foreign students. Not only were there language problems, but there were frequent questions about the content and adequacy of their undergraduate degrees. Consequently, the University of Colorado at Boulder established an Economics Institute for Foreign Students designed as a special orientation and preparation course for foreign students planning to enroll in graduate economics programs.[31] At the end of the 1960 program, my new ADC/Malayan fellowship students were tested. Imagine my delight when the program director, Professor Wyn F. Owen,

This picture shows the University of Malaya (Kuala Lumpur) Department of Agriculture's 1962 economics class. (*Left to right, front row, 4th*) Mokhtar Tamin; (*5th*) Lecturer John Bevan; (*7th*) me; (*second row, 6th*) Tan Bock Thiam. Both Mokhtar and Tan were sent to the United States on ADC graduate fellowships and returned to become professors in the university; Mokhtar later was appointed dean of the faculty of economics.

reported that one of my students had "topped" the entire class, even though he had only had two economics courses—my principles economics course and one senior-level course in agricultural economics.

My "experimental" course on the rural social sciences was taken initially by some thirty-five students. The racial and ethnic mix was similar to that in Singapore, with Chinese predominating, though there were now more Malays and Indians. (There was only one woman, because agriculture was not considered a womanly profession.) This multicultural mix prompted me to explore the significance of cultural values among the students.

During my sociology lectures, I regularly distributed a questionnaire, asking the students to rank the values that *they* thought were important to the three Malaysian ethnic groups from two perspectives—first, what each ethnic group thought were *its own* primary values, plus what they thought were those of *the other two groups*. The respondents were not identified by name, only their ethnic origin. Ten "values" listed included wealth, education, religion, family, personal success, morality, and so on. The answers from different classes changed little over the years, illustrating striking divergences among the Malays, Chinese, and Indians. For example, the Chinese students ranked wealth as of greatest weight to them, then family, and education third. But when the Chinese students assessed what they thought were the values of their Malay classmates, they attributed to Malays the greatest weight to religion, then personal success, and third wealth. (The latter turned out to be similar to how Malays ranked themselves.) I used these differences in values in my lectures to highlight the sociological basis for interethnic and religious frictions, disputes, and conflict in their country.[32]

Eventually five students from my classes for KL agricultural students received ADC scholarships for doctoral study in the United States. Two returned to teach at the University of Malaya—Tan Bock Thiam (Cornell, MS, 1967; North Carolina, PhD, 1973) and Mokhtar Tamin (University of Minnesota, MS, 1968; Stanford University, PhD, 1978). The other students who received ADC study fellowships were Tang Loon Boon, Yeoh Oon Lee, and Ti Teow Choo.

Ungku Aziz, who had moved from Singapore to Kuala Lumpur to become chairman of economics in the university's faculty of arts, asked me to take on two new courses, Economic Policy for final-year students and Economic Dynamics for honors students. "I know you Chicago economists can teach anything, so give us a hand," he remarked with a half smile. Still, I began to expand my research activities. Four of my Singapore economics students worked with me in Kuala Lumpur on their final year honors "theses." The students were Elizabeth Wee Kim Choo, Audry Chionh Chai Meng, Khor Tong Keng, and Lim Ban Choon. An

Taken March 1961 in Kuala Lumpur, this picture shows the student researchers who were writing honors theses for graduation from the University of Malaya in Singapore. (*Left to right*) Lim Bang Choon; me; Khor Tong Keng; Audry Chionh Chai Meng; Elizabeth Wee Kim Choo; and Francis Chan Kwong Wah.

ADC grant enabled them to use the Malayan statistics department for studies of selected aspects of the national economy such as household budgets and the income distribution of heads of households.

. . . .

In 1961 I was invited to be on a panel during the International Conference of Agricultural Economists in Cuernavaca, Mexico. En route I stopped over briefly at ADC headquarters in New York. The Council had funded the travel of several Asian agricultural economists to attend the conference. Art Mosher asked some grantees to prepare background papers on the status of agricultural economics in their respective countries used for a pre-meeting in New York, which was attended by JDR 3rd and some Council trustees and associates, including me.

I used the occasion of my New York visit to check on the recurring asthmatic attacks I had experienced in Singapore. None of the previous tests at the Boston Lahey Clinic had turned up anything definitive, an allergy to dust mites, maybe. I consulted with Dr. Hyman Zuckerman, physician to the Rockefeller family and their affiliates. He referred me to a specialist described as the best in New York. The physician didn't examine me at all, just asked a lot of questions, starting with my childhood in the Canary Islands. After I had answered all I could, he thought he knew the nature of the problem. He said that I suffered from dual allergies—first, to certain highly spiced foods, such as curries and peppers. I was secondly allergic to tropical pollens. "When you're in a temperate climate like the U.S.," he explained, "you can eat all the spices you want without difficulty. But when you're in a tropical zone, your susceptibility becomes asthma inflamed by the tropical pollens in the air."

I flew on to Mexico and the heady experience of speaking before seven hundred of my peers, from sixty-two countries around the globe. My assignment was to respond to D. G. Karve, from Poona University in India, whose paper was an encomium to the Ford Foundation's Intensive Agricultural Development Districts Program as the best road to sustained agricultural growth.

My comments were in the best take-no-prisoners tradition of Chicago-style debate. I pointed out the historic limitations of centralized planning for national agriculture. Farm products and practices were too heterogeneous, I said, and planners routinely failed to understand the needs and skills of small or subsistence farmers. Planners also overlooked the implications of wealth disparities that developed between districts initially included in the plan and those left out. Moreover, I concluded, there were inevitable obstacles that hindered the replication of intensive development programs beyond the original area. My contribution created quite a stir on the panel and in the audience. Unfortunately, it also brought heated objections from the Ford Foundation experts who had created the program, and my relationships with Ford officers in India were delicate for several years afterward. The program finally collapsed into the black hole of all failed development schemes.

When I returned to KL, I reported to Dolores my conversation with the New York

In August 1961 ADC Asian travel grantees attended the International Conference of Agricultural Economists in Mexico. The preliminary meeting was held in New York City with John D. Rockefeller 3rd, trustees, and officers. (*Left to right, seated, 1st*) Harold Loucks, president, China Medical Board; (*2nd*) Dean William Myers, ADC trustee, College of Agriculture, Cornell University; (*3rd*) John D. Rockefeller 3rd, chairman of the ADC Board; (*4th*) Lloyd "Shorty" Elliott, ADC trustee; (*5th*) J. Norman Efferson, chairman, Department of Agricultural Economics, Louisiana State University and ADC trustee; (*second row, 1st*) Arthur T. Mosher, president, ADC; (*2nd*) Professor Chihiro Nakajima, Japan; (*5th*) Dean Lee, Taiwan; (*6th*) Nat Tablante, College of Agriculture, University of Philippines Los Banos; (*8th*) Pantum Thisyamondol, dean, faculty of economics, Kasetsart University, Thailand; (*second row, 1st*) Donald H. McLean, adviser to John D. Rockefeller 3rd, secretary to the ADC Board; (*2nd*) Vernon Ruttan, professor of agricultural economics, College of Agriculture, University of Minnesota; (*3rd*) A. B. Lewis, ADC associate; (*4th*) John H. Provinse, ADC associate; (*6th*) me, ADC associate; (*7th*) Chaiyong Chuchart, professor of agricultural economics, Kasetsart University, Thailand; (*9th*) Abe Weisblat, ADC associate; (*10th*) J. Price Gittinger, ADC associate; (*12th*) John W. F. Neil, ADC treasurer.

specialist about my asthma. Interesting, she said. A couple of weeks later, she experimentally served a favorite of mine, hot chili con carne. I ate it all with great relish—and a few minutes later I was in the middle of a full-blown asthmatic attack. "The doctor was right!" Dolores exulted. From then on, I had no trouble keeping the problem at bay.

After Cuernavaca my professional reputation seemed to be growing, and I heard more often from colleagues in the United States, Southeast Asia, and beyond. But some of my relationships at the University of Malaya deteriorated further. Although Ungku Aziz continued to seek my help in teaching courses, he was increasingly distant. Given his antipathy, I went so far as to suggest to Art Mosher that he consider shifting me from Kuala Lumpur to a new base, perhaps in Bangkok or Los Baños, Philippines, to avoid things getting any worse. But Mosher thought it a bad idea, so I carried on as before.

. . . .

While I flourished professionally, every effort was made to ensure that Dolores joined with her own professional growth. For example, she expanded her art history studies by auditing several courses in the University of Malaya given by the historian of Chinese art Michael Sullivan. Some of her other activities included joining "dig" excavations in Malaya and observing researchers in the Philippines exploring ancient archaeological sites to recover ancient clay pots and other household items. She visited museums and important private collections wherever available; relished a two-day visit to an institute that trained classic Thai dancers in Bangkok (a school of movement that influenced the Martha Graham technique); and spent time with a Balinese guru in Jakarta, observing him teaching individual performers.

We believed that it was important that Dolores be able to learn and expand her own intellectual breadth and professional interests. We sought to learn and grow together in this new setting. This process was helped by Art Mosher's enlightened policy, which allowed wives to participate in Council activities. For example, Mosher funded the travel costs for the spouses of associates within a country or region. Wives were also included in regional conferences of the Council staff and were invited to attend the sessions. He believed that involving wives in the work of their husbands was beneficial to the professional activities of their spouses and to their personal lives. Thus a spouse became familiar with the work of a husband and met his colleagues. This practice allowed wives to continue to grow intellectually with husbands outside the traditional wife/mother/housekeeper roles.

Thanks in part to Dolores's involvement in my field associates' work, we became even more of a team. Visiting the hut of a *ketua kampong* (rural village head) outside Kuala Lumpur, for example, she would follow local custom and sit with the wives and other women in a back room. But with her fluency in "market Malay" she often learned far more about what was *really* going on than I did interviewing the village elders. In Malaya, South Vietnam, Thailand, and elsewhere, Dolores got to know the network of people and organizations I worked with, even the details of the programs I was involved with. In addition to supporting me and even pinch-hitting for me when I was away from Kuala Lumpur, she steadily broadened her own knowledge of the part of the world in which we had chosen to live. Our special bond of teamwork would be a hallmark in the future.

In Malaya as in Singapore, Dolores naturally gravitated to the cultural scene, given her background. Because the arts had been neglected during the colonial period, the new Malayan government now wanted to encourage them, and Malayan, Indian, and Chinese artists were

Taken October 23, 1963, this picture shows the University of Malaya Student Association, Persatuan Bahasa Melayu Universiti Malaya (PBMUM), who asked Dolores to choreograph special dances for a cultural festival.

now beginning to flourish. As Dolores's knowledge of and friendship with several painters blossomed, we began acquiring their work. Our first purchase was *Malay Kampong*, an ink and wash on rice paper by Cheong Soo Pieng. Later we bought *Peasant and Bullock* by Chuah Thean Teng, the first batik painter.[33] Over time our collection ran to twenty-six paintings. In 1999 we donated sixteen of the paintings to the Herbert F. Johnson Museum of Art at Cornell University.

In 1963 Dolores was approached by the Persekutuan Bahasa Melaya, the university student association. They wanted something dramatically new to present at several of the cultural festivals that were exploding throughout Southeast Asia. Instead of the traditional, ritualistically constrained Malay dance, they asked Dolores to develop something new and different. She responded with three choreographies: *Sepak Raga* was based on the popular Malay football game. *Tarian Teruna Dara* was a paean to youthful male and female exuberance. Last and most spectacular, *Wayang Kulit* retold part of the *Ramayana*, the epic Hindu story of Prince Rama and his beautiful wife Sita. In Dolores's experimental dramatization, the traditional shadow puppets took human form, cavorting first behind a screen before stepping out into full view to dance the story to life. The costumes and masks were stunning, and the students had trained tirelessly to learn the modern dance movements.

The audiences were appreciative, one critic applauding the works for their "dynamism, movement, colour, and excellent choreography."[34] But another review criticized them as an affront to the values of Islamic Malayans. The column was accompanied by a low-angle photo that showed the dancing girls' legs.[35]

Her visibility in the art scene led to related community arts activities. Dato Sambanthan, the leader of the Indian Congress (one of the wings of the UMNO ruling political coalition) had founded the *Malayan Times*, an independent national daily. In 1962, the paper decided to sponsor the country's first national children's art competition, largely at the instigation of the publisher's wife, Datin Uma Sambanthan, Dolores's close friend. Dolores was asked to serve as a judge.[36] The eventual winner was Dzulkifli Buyong, for a religiously provocative pastel drawing *Muslims at Prayer*.[37]

Dolores also served on the American Committee for the (Malaya) National Monument Fund organized by Bill Fleming, representative of the Asia Foundation. Being on this committee led in turn to an invitation for Dolores to be one of the judges for the decorative panels for the newly constructed Parliament House in Kuala Lumpur in August 1963.[38] The latter was part of the "Merdeka" celebrations when the new Federation of Malaysia was created on September 16, 1963, by merging the old Federation of Malaya with the British crown colonies of Singapore, North Borneo (renamed Sabah), and Sarawak.

Dolores's role was both a supportive spouse and an independent professional. Her ability to step into either part with equal skill was characteristic in all our subsequent life together. And through it all Dolores remained a devoted mother to Bruce and Clifton, now studying in the Alice Smith School. Run by the British military, the school enrolled British, American, and Malay children. The instruction was rigorous, and we were surprised at the intensity especially of the language instruction. Daily compositions were mandatory for all students, and Clifton's writing and speaking skills improved steadily. By the time the British-supported Alice Smith School was due to close, I had been elected president of the American Association. Larry Beemer, head of Esso, and I developed the basic plan for a new international school that was eventually built after we left.

Although Dolores had been the "Akela" for the school's Boy Scout troop, my own involvement had been peripheral until the fateful "Rally Day." After showing his classmates some of my track medals, young Clifton had entered me in the "fathers' race"—without bothering to tell me. So to live up to his bragging, I had to sign up for the event. I won—but could hardly walk for a week.

Both boys grew, and their differing personalities thrived. Clifton was happy-go-lucky and sometimes devilish—he liked dressing up and performing at parties. Bruce tended to be serious, sometimes stubborn—as with the fireman's hat he got as a Christmas present, and insisted on wearing backwards. All too often, attempts to correct him brought the same response—"I don't want to talk about it!" Bruce's insistence on doing things "his way" would become an adult characteristic of independence.

On family outings we often joined with other American families—the McHales, Nesses, and Goslings—going to the satay stalls on Batu Road for charcoal-grilled skewers of marinated chicken or beef, spicy with hot peanut sauce, and washing down the street food with green coconut drink. Or we visited a modest restaurant in Port Dickson for *beef rendang* (spiced beef with coconut), *sambal ikan bilis* (prawns), or a bowl of *laksa* (noodles in tangy fish soup). The only food that divided our household was durian, the odorous "queen" of fruit. Bruce, Dolores, and I loved it. Clifton 3rd hated it so much he once climbed on the roof to get away from the smell.

▪ ▪ ▪ ▪

One of my goals as a Council field associate was to create a program of fellowships for Asian students to pursue graduate work in the United States, but there were some formidable obstacles. For one thing, the gleam of the old colonial powers was slow to fade, and many Southeast Asians preferred British campuses to American ones. For another, in many countries foreign universities had to be approved for study abroad by one or another government ministry, and there were ludicrous inconsistencies in what universities were and were not "recognized." It was appalling to find "Podunk" junior colleges on the acceptable list, while the MITs and Stanfords were nowhere mentioned. Finally, amid the continuing exodus of British civil servants and professionals, there was an often valid reluctance throughout the region to encourage the brightest young academics and government employees to absent themselves from their positions, even temporarily—not to mention a fear that they might never return.

During my periodic talks with Tun Razak, Malaya's deputy prime minister, I pressed the case that visiting experts and professors from the West, no matter how talented and dedicated, would never be enough to meet Malaya's development challenges. The country needed its own cadre of trained PhDs. After three years of my sporadic wrangling, Razak finally relented.

The first Malayan doctoral fellow I selected was a bright young man named Agoes Salim, whose career I had been following at the government's Rural and Industrial Development Authority. As an honors undergrad, Agoes had been an effective student activist—a member of the student council, delegate to two international student conferences, and editor of three student newspapers. At the university in Kuala Lumpur I had supervised his master's degree work.

Agoes was a superb choice as the first Council fellow, and I thought he would set a strong standard for future candidates from Malaya and elsewhere. He attended the University of Wisconsin, where he worked with Professor Kenneth H. Parsons, a world authority on land tenure issues. With the Council's continuing support, he then came home to gather data for his dissertation. After getting his doctorate, he rejoined government service and was posted to

Agoes Salim, shown here receiving my congratulations in August 1961, was the first ADC doctoral fellow from Malaya. After completing his PhD at the University of Wisconsin, Agoes created a new research unit in the Ministry of National and Rural Development. He also served as secretary general of the Ministry of National Unity and chairman of the National Agricultural Bank, as well as on the oversight boards of the University of Malaysia, the National University, and the Agricultural University.

the Ministry of National and Rural Development, whose head was now the same Tun Razak who had previously "emancipated" him to study abroad.

Agoes was a perfect example of the ADC's "longitudinal" approach to fostering talent. Having detected his potential early on, the Council remained involved with him through several stages of his academic program and subsequent career—not just as a disburser of dollars, but also as a touchstone for continuing guidance and professional development. When tasked with setting up a new research unit in the Ministry of National and Rural Development, Agoes got a Council grant to visit similar installations in the Philippines. Over the years, the Council provided him more grants for travel to conferences of agricultural economists in Sidney and São Paulo. Over several decades, Agoes served as secretary-general of the Ministry of National

Unity and chairman of the National Agricultural Bank. While still in government he was a member of the oversight boards of the University of Malaysia, the National University, and the Agricultural University, having chaired the study that led to its creation. He even found time to teach part-time in the University of Malaysia's faculty of economics and administration. He was a perfect model of what the Council meant by investing in human capital.

· · · ·

By the end of 1962 I was working full throttle, and it was beginning to pay off. My teaching and research were going well, and my name was getting better known among agricultural economists in Asia as well as the United States.

I made a grant of $18,500 to the University of Malaya for a research project on rubber smallholders.[39] With the cooperation of the Rubber Research Institute, some forty students from the two departments conducted a survey covering farm yields, processing techniques, land-use patterns, and marketing. In addition the project sought to provide students with

Taken in January 1962, this picture shows the student field supervisors from the University of Malaya Rubber Research Project (ADC grant) examining a model rubber field station. (*Left to right*) Teoh Kim San, me, Wong Tang Ka, Mohktar bin Tamin, Chin Nyeok Yoon, and Ho Chai Yee. The research was conducted by forty University of Malaya students from my economics class in the Department of Agriculture and from the Department of Geography with assistance from the Rubber Research Institute of Malaysia.

experience in surveying and mapping, to test investigative techniques for securing information from smallholders, and to collect teaching materials

The same year I had three MA candidates to supervise—Augustine Tan and Francis Chan in economics (both two of the brightest students from my first class in Singapore) and Syed Husin Ali in sociology. With Council-funded "tutorships" I was prepping Augustine and Francis for doctoral programs in the United States. Their defense of their master's degree theses were high points for me, and I glowed with pride as two students to whom I had taught first-year economics now prepared to ascend to the highest tier of academic achievement.

Augustine Tan's MA thesis, "Natural Rubber: Problems and Techniques of Stabilization,"[40] was a skillful study of national and international commodity fluctuations with special reference to Malayan rubber, and the development or adaptation of appropriate stabilization measures. It presaged his future as an outstanding economist and politician. Tan was elected a member of Parliament (April 1970–1991), political secretary to the prime minister (1975), and professor and then provost at Singapore Management University.

Francis Chan's MA thesis was an expansion of his honors thesis study of the inelasticity of Malayan rubber supply.[41] I had been bothered for some time at frequent allusions by European economists to "lazy natives" who purportedly caused a backward-bending supply curve for rubber. The argument was usually related to the supply curve of labor, where instead of an increase in wages leading to an increase in labor—a forward-sloping supply curve—a level of wage-income does not lead to a greater supply of labor because laborers are paid enough to sustain their current lifestyle without having to work more hours, which creates a backward bend in the supply curve.[42] When applied to Malayan rubber smallholders, the "backward-bending supply curve" argument was that the Malays had limited wants—"the coconuts fall from the trees, and bananas grow anywhere. So, when the price of rubber goes up, they tap less to provide for their limited wants. They're sleeping on their porches in the afternoon, not working. " In the kampongs I had seen for myself that smallholders wisely tapped in the cooler predawn hours, not the hotter afternoon. But more was at stake than time of day for tapping. The critical question was whether Malaysian rubber smallholders were price responsive, a subject clearly a challenge to anyone from the Chicago school.[43] The argument was fundamentally an economic one that I was convinced required hard data.

Working with Francis, we launched a pathbreaking econometric study of the price responsiveness of rubber supply based upon large Malaysian rubber plantation. As far as I know, this was the first ever done anywhere. This work was delivered at a seminar (July 23–August 3, 1962) held at the Australian National University and was subsequently published.[44] The econometric analysis showed definitively that the supply curve of rubber was not backward bending but had a slight positive, inelastic slope.[45] The finding that rubber production increased when the price rose seemed to fly in the face of the fact that there were only so many mature producing trees—it takes seven years for a tree to reach suitable tapping age. At first our findings were disputed as physically impossible. Then we discovered from our village-level research that when prices rose, even smallholder farmers increased their yield by double cutting (that is, overtapping) existing trees. Our results disputed the "backward-bending supply curve" proponents and led to a brief seminar dispute with P. T. Bauer, the noted British development economist, during one of his visits to Malaysia.[46] We had successfully disproved the conventional wisdom about lazy Malays with hard data—a highly gratifying result.

My early work on the problems of monocultural crop export dominance in Southeast Asia and the need for greater agricultural diversification attracted the interest of the newly established Malayan Economic Planning Unit in the Prime Minister's Department. William T. "Bill" Phillips from the United States, who was the United Nations resident representative to Prime Minister Tunku Abdul Rahman, was interested in the development of his Economic Planning Unit. Bill asked me to help the EPU with the issue of greater diversification in Malayan dependence upon rubber.

▪ ▪ ▪ ▪

Traveling regularly throughout the region and occasionally beyond, I had gotten a thorough grounding in Southeast Asia's agricultural and other development issues. But except for the mini-sabbatical at Cornell in 1960, the Whartons had not had a real vacation in six years—all the way back to our days in Chicago. In April 1963, Dolores put her foot down—it was time, she insisted, for some extended recreation and recuperation. So we booked a six-week excursion aboard the eighty-six-passenger SS *Frankfurt*, a Hamburg-America liner steaming from Singapore to Japan and back again. We were joined by our good friends Stan and Dorie Priddle plus Ina Gamba. Stan was the labor attaché at the British high commissioner's office, but Charles Gamba, former professor in the economics department, could not join us because he had been made Singapore's chief justice of arbitration. We had regularly vacationed with the two couples at the government rest house in Malacca.

On board I fell immediately into a pleasant routine—breakfast, swim in the pool, nap, wake up for lunch, nap, afternoon swim, cocktails, dinner, bed by 8:00 P.M. Once again, being on the ocean worked its renewing magic. After a few days I started to feel like the string of a violin bow gradually going looser. The pace I had been keeping up had taken a toll I was just now recognizing. "Dolores," I said, "I must have been hard to live with the last few weeks."

"The last few *weeks*?" she exclaimed.

In the Philippines we debarked and were met by Lawrence "Lon" Howard, the husband of Dolores's cousin Betty. Lon was on leave from Brandeis University, serving as an associate director of the Peace Corps. We asked him to drive us to Los Baños to see the University of the Philippines College of Agriculture and its new International Rice Research Institute. When we pulled up to the gate to the institute grounds, I introduced myself to the guard and asked for permission to drive around. He took one look at three obviously Black Americans and arrogantly sent us on our way. I might have ignored the slight, but I had already heard complaints from Filipino friends about the high-fenced isolation of the institute from its surrounding community. "We invited them here," one acquaintance remarked, "but they don't even talk to the farmers right outside their own gates." I wrote to IRRI director Robert Chandler, who had visited Dolores and me several times in Singapore and who had consulted with me extensively about plans for the institute. After I finished my account, he apologized profusely and told me he would see that some changes were made.

But we had a lovely two weeks in Japan, with stays in Tokyo, Hakone, and Kyoto. At the Miyako Hotel we had asked to stay in the Japanese wing. Back on the ship in Yokohama for our return leg, I got a frantic call by ship's telephone from the U.S. embassy in Tokyo. The U.S. mission in South Vietnam now urgently needed my advice again on rice price policy. Could I leave the ship right away for a direct flight to Saigon? I said that I just couldn't leave my family in mid-trip, but I would definitely try to come after I returned to Kuala Lumpur. I did go after we got back and received pretty much the same reaction to my warning about rice price policy as the first time. I told myself I wouldn't ever revisit the issue, but as the old dictum says, "Never say never."

. . . .

During our years in Southeast Asia I was repeatedly impressed with the skill and subtlety of British and French diplomats. Among other things, they clearly understood the need for local contacts and long-term residence as the sine qua non for effective foreign relations. Our own State Department's penchant for rapid tour rotations suffered greatly by contrast. Time after time the British and French assessments of situations turned out to be accurate, even as our American representatives ignored them or waved them aside—often to their detriment.

In early 1963, at a Planned Parenthood conference on fertility, I was on the same program with the famous writer and physician Han Suyin.[47] A Eurasian with a Chinese father and Belgian mother, she had authored (among others) the semiautobiographical romance *Love Is a Many-Splendored Thing* and was then at the peak of her international celebrity. She was also an ardent admirer of China's Mao Zedong. After the conference ended, Dolores and I were invited along with Suyin and her husband to lunch with Viscount Anthony Head, the British high commissioner for Malaysia, and Lady Head. The venue was the commissioner's "Carcosa" residence, two nineteenth-century colonial mansions high on a hill overlooking the Lake Gardens in Kuala Lumpur. It was a treat to walk the grounds where the Malayan declaration of independence had been signed six years before. We spotted Colonel Vincent Ratnaswamy, the latest of Han Suyin's three husbands, swimming in the outdoor pool, and Dolores whispered to me that he had been the model for the Indian hero of Han Suyin's novel *The Mountain Is Young*. I didn't think he looked much like the demigod depicted in the book.

As lunch progressed it became clear that it was a socially convenient opportunity for Lord Head to pass on to Suyin some message for Chou En-lai, premier of the People's Republic. Despite Chou's harsh anti-Western rhetoric and his preeminence among the nonaligned leaders

This picture shows John D. Rockefeller 3rd, chairman of the ADC Board of Trustees, in discussion with me at the ADC staff conference in Bangkok, Thailand, on February 20, 1963.

of Asia, in private he was apparently more flexible and pragmatic. Since Great Britain still had limited official contact with Communist China, and since Suyin was about to make one of her regular visits to Peking (Beijing), lunch provided an occasion for indirect diplomatic exchange. Dolores and I were the "beards."

· · · ·

As the number of Thais studying in the United States for their doctorates increased, I began to notice a serious problem when they returned. The newly minted PhDs usually had learned the newest statistical and econometric techniques, which were a mystery to older Thai professors in their departments. The younger PhDs were soon frustrated in their attempts to employ these techniques and were discouraged from incorporating them into their grant applications. In typical Thai fashion, the ADC fellows did not criticize their superiors, but my suspicions were confirmed by Mel Wagner, the newest ADC visiting professor at Kasetsart. A subtle, indirect corrective was needed. I pointed out to Dr. Chaiyong Chuchart, chairman of the Department of Agricultural Economics, that several of his younger faculty who had not had the opportunity to go as yet to the United States might benefit from an intensive workshop on statistical analysis and econometrics. I would be prepared to organize the workshop and suggested that it would be preferable to have the group come to the University of Malaya in Kuala Lumpur under Council funding, away from the local demands in Bangkok. To "chaperone" the younger instructors, I indicated that he might include in the group some older professors, like himself.

The workshop ran for a month (May 20 to June 20, 1963), with five Thais from Kasetsart University's departments of Agricultural Economics, Business Accounting, and Statistics plus three senior professors. Some sixteen lectures were given by John Bevan (the British expatriate agricultural economist recently added to the University of Malaya agriculture faculty) and me, plus my two graduate students, Francis Chan and Augustine Tan. After the workshop, Chaiyong and the other senior faculty became generally knowledgeable about econometrics and more comfortable in encouraging younger faculty in their "modern" research efforts. Problem solved.

• • • •

We were by now having more and more visitors of our own. Briefings, receptions, dinners, field trips, press interviews—they were all part of the "Wharton visitors bureau service." In one three-week period in 1962[48] we had twelve guests, including professors from seven different universities. Some came to learn more about the region and its agricultural and economic development, while others were interested in Dolores's take on Malaysian art and culture. The visitors ranged from Chicago demographer Phil Hauser to José Limón and his dance group; from Bob Shaplen of the *New Yorker* to Frank Notestein, president of the Population Council. A few were old friends, such as Martha Dalrymple, who had helped me so much in my early days at the AIA, and Isabelle Savell, another Rockefeller aide. Most thrilling of all, perhaps, was a visit from Ted Schultz, my mentor at the University of Chicago. I had regularly sent him drafts and published articles about my work, and it was a delight to be able to show him what I was doing firsthand.

When the Alvin Ailey Dance Company visited from the United States in 1962, they took Kuala Lumpur by storm.[49] Dolores and I welcomed them to our home for a reception and buffet dinner. When the group arrived at Jalan Damai, they were greeted by several long strings of Chinese firecrackers that Dolores had hanging from a large tree in our front garden. As the firecrackers popped away, several of the Ailey troupe began dancing around the tree—to everyone's delight! We hosted a similar reception when the dancer José Limón and his company visited Kuala Lumpur during his twelve-week tour of the Far East in 1963 under sponsorship of the U.S. State Department.

Dolores's interests also were congenial with the cultural side of ADC's early activities. (ADC's original name was Council on Economic and Cultural Affairs.) We had begun a modest arts program, reflecting the "cultural affairs" in the Council's title, by offering touring fellowships to outstanding Asian artists. During the fellowships the artist visited their counterparts in other parts of Asia and then went to the United States for a period of work and exhibition. The first of these fellows was Krishen Khanna from India, who with his wife Renu visited us in Kuala Lumpur in June 1962 and even painted a portrait of Dolores that we bought. When the Council spun off its cultural activities into a new organization called the

JDR 3rd Fund, these fellowships continued, and we were delighted to recommend the artist Ibrahim Hussein as the first fellow from Malaya in 1966.

Occasionally visits led to fireworks. When Milton and Rose Friedman traveled to Malaysia in 1962, I arranged for him to speak at the university. As the fountainhead of "Chicago economics," he was viewed by many as Satan incarnate, and several of the locals were salivating at the prospect of baiting him. His lecture compared Japan's development in the early decades of the Meiji Restoration, when it was compelled by international agreement to practice free trade, with the development of India postindependence, under a regime of rigorous central economic planning. The contrast, Friedman left no doubt, was highly favorable to free trade.[50]

At the lecture's conclusion, Ungku Aziz, by then chairman of economics, could contain himself no longer. "Professor Friedman," he burst out furiously, "if we followed the policies you recommend, the Chinese would run our country. We Malays could not stand for it!" Friedman did not respond, merely smiled knowingly. Aziz subsequently became vice chancellor (head) of the University of Malaysia and then Professor Diraja (regius professor).

• • • •

Although my interest in poverty and the economics of subsistence never faltered during my years in Southeast Asia, the subject was not well received in the discipline. One problem was the difficulty of gathering numerical or statistical data from semiliterate or illiterate populations, especially given the trend in the profession toward quantitative analysis and econometrics. Early in my Southeast Asian tour, I learned the low esteem of subsistence agriculture. For my economics principles class I had developed a paper describing the conceptual and theoretical underpinnings of the "economics of subsistence." Several of my colleagues in the economics department encouraged me to have it published. Naively, I sent it off to two journals in the United States and received two rejection slips. Finally I published it in the *Malayan Economic Review*,[51] and it was subsequently included as a chapter in a book edited by the anthropologist George Dalton[52] that later became popular. Thirty years later, I received annual requests from a professor at Harvard for permission to assign my chapter on subsistence as reading in his course on economic development. He commented, "I do hope that something of mine will be read 30 years after I first published it."[53]

In 1964, I decided that one way to raise the relative priority and visibility given to the subject might be to sponsor a conference of leaders in economics, anthropology, sociology, and political science who had also done work on subsistence. Over the years I had made contact with several such scholars scattered around the globe. With permission from Art Mosher and encouragement from my ADC colleagues, I began putting together a conference to be held at the East-West Center in Honolulu, Hawaii, in 1965.

CHAPTER FIVE

The Development Economist 2: Back in the United States

By 1964, we had been in Southeast Asia for six years. We had made major progress toward the original goals for my ADC work. In addition to teaching and doing research, I had overseen the award of eighteen ADC graduate study fellowships in Thailand, eight to Singaporean and Malaysian students, and despite the widening war, even one in South Vietnam—all for doctoral study in the United States. A new ADC program had been built from the ground up, and my judgment and decision-making skills had been honed along the way. Most important, my work had helped expand the pool of human capital in an economically and agriculturally impoverished part of the world.

Based on the original commitment, my ADC tour had four more years to run. But once again, Art Mosher had other ideas.

The previous year, the Agricultural Development Council had received a grant from the Ford Foundation to increase the numbers of U.S. social scientists with professional experience in underdeveloped countries. As things then stood, younger scholars (or even older ones) who were interested in working overseas faced a catch-22. If they lacked prior foreign research experience, they couldn't get funding—but how could they get the experience without first getting financial support?

ADC proposed to cut the Gordian knot by setting up an entity called the American Universities Research Program (AURP), whose purpose would be to offer modest financial awards to attract new entrants and support their research on overseas agriculture and development. The researchers' universities continued their salaries, and AURP grants covered travel, living costs, and project expenses. An interesting feature of the grants was that they went directly to the academics, whose universities weren't allowed to deduct a portion for administrative "overhead," as was (and still is) common for most government and foundation research stipends.

Shortly after securing the grant from Ford, Mosher raised the possibility of my returning to the States as the AURP's first director. I loved my teaching and research, and felt something valuable was being accomplished in the region, and therefore I declined. Dolores, the boys, and I had made a life in Southeast Asia—friends and colleagues, a home, involvements in the community—and we loved it. Moreover the boys had become accustomed to the Asian/British lifestyle. Moreover, the idea of uprooting the family once again to move back to New York was unattractive. Until now we had never lived longer than four years in any one place, and in Kuala Lumpur we had just started to set down some roots.

But Art Mosher was his usual persuasive self. He insisted that my six years in Southeast Asia made me an ideal choice for the job. He reminded me of my extensive contacts developed within the U.S. academic community during my 1958–59 survey. And he promised to delay my start until after my sabbatical due at a U.S. university of my choice. This would enable me to finish several outstanding projects, decompress, and complete the planning for my proposed conference on subsistence agriculture the next year at the East-West Center in Honolulu, Hawaii.

In the middle of these developments came word about yet another opportunity from my father, who in 1961 had become the U.S. ambassador to Norway, attracting considerable press attention. During a brief consultation in Washington,[1] Dad had been called to the White House by Ralph Dungan, President Kennedy's special assistant and one of my colleagues at the founding of the NSA. My father wrote that Dungan asked him why I was not in the government.[2] I had previously turned down an inquiry from Secretary of the Interior Stewart Udall to be his special assistant for international affairs.[3]

It turned out that my friend Chuck Stone, at the time editor of the *Washington Afro-American*, had been pressing the Kennedy administration for more minority appointments generally, and pointing to me in particular. Chuck was unaware at the time of my prior friendship with Dungan from the founding of the National Student Association. In May 1963, news and television coverage of the civil rights movement in the United States was increasing back in Southeast Asia. The nonviolent civil rights movement, voter registration, the student Greensboro sit-ins, and the CORE Freedom Rides were reported across the globe. Even stronger spotlight was given to the horrific sights of Birmingham police chief "Bull" Connor urging his forces to turn fire hoses and vicious dogs on protesting Blacks, including children. The assassination of NAACP leader Medgar Evers in front of his home in Jackson, Mississippi, followed the next month. The White House was under growing civil rights pressure.[4]

My father thought a deputy assistant secretaryship, if offered, might be attractive—especially if it were with former ADC trustee Phillips Talbot, then assistant secretary for Near Eastern and South Asian affairs. On the whole, however, Phil counseled against accepting

Clifton R. Wharton Sr. met with President John F. Kennedy in the White House Oval Office after being appointed U.S. ambassador to Norway on March 22, 1961. This appointment was the capstone to my father's forty-year Foreign Service career.

anything just before the next presidential election. My dad was now thinking in terms beyond the Foreign Service, but the decision to take the AURP job had already been made.

. . . .

Several campuses invited me to spend my sabbatical with them, including the University of California, Berkeley; Purdue; and the University of Michigan. The most interesting was the Food Research Institute at Stanford University. Though small, it had a strong international reputation, especially in research. Led by William O. Jones, the institute had assembled a group of eminent economist scholars including Bruce Johnstone, Helen Farnsworth, and Roger Gray. They sent a cordial invitation.

On our 1964 return trip to the United States we stopped off first at the Canary Islands. My childhood friend Ignacio Rivero y Noble, whom I had not seen since 1936, and his wife Marisol met us at the airport when we landed in Las Palmas. Although it had been almost thirty years, I recognized Ignacio instantly. Many things had changed dramatically, but Paseo

Madrid looked just the same, with our old home on one side and the Rivero family still living right across the street. Both Ignacio's elderly parents greeted me with warm *abrazos*, and within minutes it was as though I had never left.

For the next several days Ignacio and I, with the two families, relived our island childhood days, with picnics on the beach, mountain tours, and endless local delicacies to keep up our strength. Ignacio, who had become a successful businessman and builder, organized a fiesta. He invited some of his siblings and their families, including his own eleven children. Although Clifton 3rd and Bruce spoke no Spanish, they seemed to have fun, especially whacking at a huge piñata the Riveros had hung in the garden. Ignacio's sister Pinito, my childhood crush, was now married with thirteen children of her own!

From Las Palmas we flew on to Oslo to see my father—a reunion looked forward to with some anxiety. Months earlier he had written to say that he intended to retire in the fall. On his government pension he could no longer afford to contribute to my mother's support, and he wanted me to be the one to tell her. His decision and his asking me to be his intermediary was unpleasant. I declined firmly since Mother was hoping to retire one day, too. After teaching for five years in the Boston public schools, my mother took a job as a principal supervisor in the Boston Department of Social Work, eventually earning a master's in social work from Simmons College. Although my father's contribution was modest, its termination would be no small matter. My brother Bill was now at John Marshall Law School in Chicago, and Richard, a new father, was in graduate school at Columbia. Any additional support would have to come from me. I told my father that he would have to write to my mother himself.

In any event our Norwegian stopover went well enough, with neither of us saying anything about the disagreement. Bruce, age five, had been eager to meet his grandfather for the first time. All he knew was that his grandfather was an ambassador like those he had seen in Kuala Lumpur, riding around in limousines with flags flying from the front fenders. When we arrived, my father was waiting at the foot of the boarding ramp, his official car and driver nearby. "If that's my grandfather," Bruce whispered, tugging at my jacket, "where are the flags?" When I repeated the question to my father, he explained that in Norway ambassadors flew flags only for state visits. In this case, though, he would make an exception. Bruce sat on the armrest in front between my father and his chauffeur as we barreled through the streets of Oslo, U.S. flags aflutter. "Am I your grandfather now?" Dad asked Bruce, who giggled merrily, "Oh yes!"

During the visit (as on almost all our meetings) Dad would invariably get around to the divorce and try to explain his actions. It was almost as though he was permanently haunted by a sense of guilt over what he had done to Mother and we children. He unburdened, and I mainly listened, but gave no absolution. He and Leonie would soon be retiring and moving to Phoenix, Arizona.

All in all, it was moving to see my father at the apex of his forty-year career. Despite both the personal trauma of divorce and hardships fighting racial discrimination, he had become the first Black chosen as a "career ambassador," that small, elite group of career Foreign Service officers. It had been a long road from the day he had not been allowed to attend the Foreign Service Institute.

But times were changing in the United States to which we were returning, and the civil rights turmoil was reaching fever pitch. In Kuala Lumpur, we viewed the news stories about the march on Washington for Martin Luther King Jr.'s "I Have a Dream" speech (August 28 1963) at a distance. We learned that Miss Marian Anderson had sung "He's Got the Whole World in His Hands" at the march, which brought the event especially close. However, nothing brought home the insanity of U.S. racism more than the bombing of the Birmingham's Sixteenth Baptist Church, which killed four little girls (September 15, 1963). The electrifying shock to the Christian values of most Americans spelled the ultimate doom of all that the Bull Connors of the South stood for. I was elated that changes were being made to topple centuries of degradation and suppression of our fundamental rights. The movement's nonviolence patterned after Gandhi's passive resistance was proving to be highly effective.

Back in the States, we spent six weeks at the MIT Center for International Studies in Cambridge, Massachusetts. Founded in 1962 the Center was led by Max F. Millikan, who had assembled a powerful group interested in foreign policy and development. The conference brought together forty-four economic development specialists from around the world to focus on the next steps in this field. As Art Mosher had predicted, the sessions gave me an invaluable reintroduction to the current status of the field and its leaders.[5]

· · · ·

The Wharton family then went on to Palo Alto, where we rented a house from a Stanford professor who was on leave. We lived near campus, and the boys enrolled in the local school. We got to know our neighbors, and at the encouragement of one—an orthopedic surgeon, no less—we all began taking ice-skating lessons. Dolores and I even learned to dance on ice. We also took trips up the Pacific coast and inland, including a visit to Yosemite National Park. There Bruce saw a bear rummaging at night through the refuse cans near our cabin. When peering down from the 1,430 foot top of Bridal Veil Falls, I had my first attack of acrophobia. (How could that happen to a brash pilot who had flown upside down in an open-cockpit airplane?)

Besides strengthening my professional contacts at Stanford, we had a delightful renewed friendship with Marc and Mary Ellen Nerlove, who had been with us at Chicago. Marc was now professor of economics. Their daughters Susan and Miriam became fast friends with Bruce. Also at the university as a doctoral student was Augustine Tan with his new wife Cecilia Yeoh under an ADC fellowship. Francis Chan's enrollment at Stanford had been delayed due to illness.

We also decided to have some family photographs taken, which was an unexpectedly revealing experience. A local professional came to the home but was unhappy with the results.

He told us, "You four are a very tight family, and you won't let me in to capture you. The only way I can take pictures of what you really are like is if you let me in." Dolores and I knew what he meant. The result were the best family photographs we ever had done—and we became more aware of our strong family bond.

At Stanford's Food Research Institute my title was "visiting scholar," and it soon became evident that my sabbatical was going to be anything but restful. Several academic departments pressed me to offer classes. The institute itself asked me to teach one, and the economics department wanted me to give the semester's regular Economics 216 course, Agricultural and Industrial Development, with case studies in Southeast Asia and Latin America. Next, Professor Paul R. Hanna asked me to teach a development-oriented class in the School of Education. But he wouldn't take no for an answer and asked if some of the education majors could instead enroll in the economics course I was already giving. Since his students lacked the economics prerequisites, my stipulation was that they attend an informal workshop I would create every Friday to get them up to speed on basic economic analysis. Amusingly, some of the regular students majoring in economics soon started to sit in, as well.

▪ The Subsistence Conference, Hawaii

At the end of February 1965 I flew to Honolulu for my long-anticipated conference on subsistence agriculture and economic development. Thirty-eight scholars and experts joined me, from the United States, Australia, India, England, France, Japan, the Philippines, Pakistan, Brazil, and Indonesia. Their disciplines included economics, sociology, psychology, anthropology, agricultural economics, rural sociology, and communications. Ted Schultz came from Chicago, and ADC was represented by John D. Rockefeller 3rd, Art Mosher, and three others. Bill Jones and Bruce Johnstone were there as well, from the Food Research Institute.

My remarks at the opening press conference tried to set the stage: "Covering roughly 40 per cent of the Earth's land surface . . . these [subsistence farmers] are the most backward, and have the greatest problems. . . . But they have been ignored."[6] The conference goal was to encourage interdisciplinary exchanges on the previously neglected issues of subsistence agriculture, and to work toward a consensus on priorities for future research aimed at developing subsistence agriculture.

JDR 3rd gave a warm and thoughtful welcome, pointing out that until world population growth leveled off, subsistence farming was what stood between much of the developing world and starvation. The challenge, he said, involved not only "the cold realities of economics but also the warm humanitarian impulses we feel toward these millions of farmers whose labors gain them hardly more than survival."[7]

For the next week the conference participants presented papers, reviewed case studies,

Arthur T. Mosher and I led the ADC Subsistence Conference at the East-West Center at the University of Hawaii from February 28 to March 6, 1965.

and sat on panels. Topics covered the values, attitudes, and motivations of subsistence farmers; the influence of social structures; theories of primitive economies and agrarian societies; and the transformation of traditional agriculture. There was even a paper based on ACAR, the AIA program in Brazil that had been the basis of my doctoral dissertation over seven years previously.

The most lasting impact of the meeting was putting many isolated individuals who had been working on particular aspects of subsistence agriculture and rural poverty into contact with each other. Now all had a "contact list" of colleagues around the globe with whom we could interact and exchange views.

The conference was a great success. But it took four years to finish editing all the papers for publication![8]

. . . .

Stanford had given me a taste of what life was going to be like as a "foreign economic development expert." When my sabbatical ended in June, my new job with AURP in New

The Wharton family, back in the United States after six years abroad in Southeast Asia, had a splendid sabbatical at Stanford University in the spring of 1965. (*Left to right*) Clifton 3rd; Bruce; Dolores; me.

York began. We rented an apartment on East Eighty-Eighth Street, in the Yorktown area near the Dalton School, where we enrolled both the boys. Dalton was just adding boys to its upper division, which probably helped Clifton's admission, given his checkered history in schooling. Clifton was thirteen and Bruce was six, but both had become international. Bruce at first disliked both the helter-skelter and noise of New York City children. I doubt that he encountered any racial animus, just a dramatic change in children's behavior from Asian courtesy to New York City brashness. His principal reported that during recess Bruce would sit on a nearby roof with his hands covering his ears. Eventually both boys adjusted and began to make friends.

In the ADC office, I moved into high gear, systematically publicizing the new AURP, restructuring the evaluation of grant proposals, and scheduling workshops across the country. My hope was for the organization to become a focal point for professional and financial support of rural agricultural research overseas by novices. In consequence, my frequent travel throughout the country fostered an ever-widening circle of U.S. academic contacts in the field, old hands and neophytes alike. Given my familiarity with their specializations and my own research in foreign settings, I became not only a source of potential financial support, but also a colleague and friend. However, I suffered substantial guilt over my frequent absences from Dolores, Clifton, and Bruce. In retrospect, my own father's extended absences during my youth may have muted my discernment. Nevertheless, despite the demands of the job, my writing and publishing continued.

The successful reception of my ADC monograph *Research on Agricultural Development in Southeast Asia* led me to propose that ADC commission a series covering different regions of the globe. Over the next five years, the organization published papers on North Africa, East Africa, the Middle East, Central America, West Africa, and Brazil by U.S. agricultural experts on each region.

In 1966, Art Mosher decided to take a one-year sabbatical, going to the University of Minnesota for an "update" on the latest agricultural economics research techniques. While he was away, I was appointed acting executive director.

▪ Mission to South Vietnam _____

In late January 1966, I made a trip to Laos on a U.N.-sponsored mission in connection with the Lower Mekong River Dam project. Since 1959, Dr. C. Hart Schaaf, previously deputy executive secretary of UN Economic Commission for Asia and the Far East (ECAFE), had been touting the benefits a huge dam would bring to Laos, Cambodia, Vietnam, and Thailand, the four nations watered by the Mekong River. Although the escalating war in Vietnam had clouded the prospects for successful cooperation among the nations, Schaaf had pressed for

U.S. DEPARTMENT OF AGRICULTURE PHOTOGRAPH.

The Presidential Agriculture Mission to Vietnam, headed by Secretary of Agriculture Orville Freeman, presented its report to President Lyndon Johnson at the White House on February 16, 1966. (*Left to right, seated*) Robert R. Nathan, president, Robert Nathan Associates; Secretary Orville Freeman; President Lyndon Johnson; Orville Bentley, dean of agriculture, University of Illinois; (*standing*) me, Agricultural Development Council; M. L. Peterson, dean of agriculture, University of California; Horace Holmes, rural programs adviser, Agency for International Development; Ken Naden, executive vice president, National Council of Farmer Co-ops; Eugene Olsen, special assistant to Secretary Freeman; Homer S. Swingle, professor of fisheries, Auburn University; Charles Brice Ratchford, vice president for extension, University of Missouri.

a team of experts to assess the project. My assignment was to look at organizing a village-level extension program for farms and villages that would be displaced by the dam's construction.

While I was in Laos, U.S. secretary of agriculture Orville L. Freeman telephoned our New York apartment; Dolores took the call and relayed his message that President Lyndon Johnson planned a special agriculture mission to Vietnam, and Freeman wanted my participation. In 1966 opposition was hardening to the U.S. involvement in Vietnam. Mike Mansfield, then Senate Democratic leader, had issued a report that touched off hot debate in Congress. In response President Johnson ordered a sudden review of all American programs in the country. He also orchestrated an unusual meeting in Honolulu between himself and South Vietnam's two top leaders, Prime Minister Nguyen Cao Ky and the ceremonial head of state, Nguyen Van Thieu. Along with President Johnson would be a delegation that included Secretary of State Dean Rusk; Secretary of Defense Robert McNamara; Secretary of Health, Education, and Welfare John Gardner; General Earle Wheeler, head of the Joint Chiefs of Staff; and Secretary of Agriculture Orville Freeman. Freeman and Gardner were there, Johnson explained, to underscore his attention to give broad attention to Vietnam's agricultural and educational needs, in the context of a hardheaded look at the war effort overall. The assassination of President Diem and his brother Nhu in November 1963 and the failure of the earlier program of "strategic hamlets" had made the agricultural problems even more critical.

The special presidential mission had ten agriculture specialists,[9] including me. Few of the team had any experience in Southeast Asia, even fewer in Vietnam. Moreover, every time the government representatives had previously asked me about Vietnamese agriculture, they had subsequently ignored my advice. Why would this time be different? Still, I thought I owed Secretary Freeman and the president one more try.

After a one-day briefing, we left Washington for Honolulu, landing around midnight, and checked into the Princess Kaiulani Hotel. The plan was for us to meet President Johnson the following day, after his private colloquy with Ky and Thieu, then depart immediately for Saigon—a highly visible, dramatic demonstration of the U.S. commitment to extramilitary aid and Johnson's own responsiveness to the two leaders.

The next day, while we waited to see the president, Secretary Freeman expostulated on his goal of making Vietnam again into a major regional agricultural producer and exporter. With Dave Bell of AID and Major General Nguyen Duc Thang, minister of rural reconstruction, Freeman predicted that with U.S. know-how, new seeds, and new farming techniques, Vietnam could double its rice crop and quadruple its corn within a few short years.

At the appointed time our mission drove to the Royal Hawaiian Hotel. As we waited in single file outside the president's suite, Averell Harriman, former governor of New York, came along. "What are you people doing here?" he asked Bob Nathan, who was standing next to me at the tail of the queue. When Nathan explained, Harriman grumbled, "I've been trying to see the president for the last two days."

"Get in line with us," Nathan suggested. Everyone deferred to the governor, who moved up to the head of the line. Just then the door opened, and Johnson spotted Harriman right away.

"Orville," he asked Freeman, "what's Ave Harriman doin' here?"

"Well, Mr. President," Freeman said with a sly smile, "the governor owns a lot of farmland in upstate New York."

"Yeah?" the president shot back. "Where I come from, we'd call ole Ave a real stud duck—always standin' round ready for service!"

I was aghast. Was *this* the president of the United States?

We departed for Vietnam on Air Force Two, giving me my first glimpse of "power travel." Freeman and his retinue took the plush seats at the front of the plane, while the rest of us made do further back. The seasoned pols and their aides changed into comfortable sweaters and slippers right after takeoff. Functionaries bustled up and down the aisle carrying stacks of manila folders, the distinctive White House seal emblazoned on the flaps.

In Saigon the team broke up into smaller units to look at different aspects of the

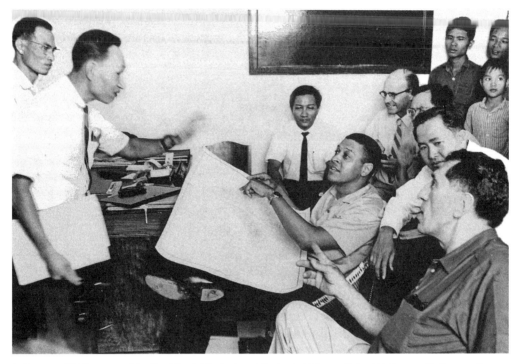

In February 1966, as part of the Presidential Agriculture Mission to Vietnam, Robert Nathan and I discussed strategy with Vietnamese technicians in the field at the Cai-San Resettlement, which housed refugees from the north, mainly from the Hua Hao religious sect.

"rice-roots" war. Most of the time I worked with my hotel roommate Bob Nathan, occasionally with Dean Bentley. We visited government agencies, markets, villages, and hamlets. When Nathan and I visited the Ministry of Agriculture, I was worried that friends there from my ADC days would now see me as an "envoy," or some other kind of representative of government officialdom. The warmth of their reception dispelled my anxiety like a breeze. Nonetheless the general atmosphere in Saigon was tense. The North Vietnamese had steadily escalated their guerilla offensive, and everywhere we went we had a close military escort. Just the year before, my classmate Ernie Howell, who was stationed in Saigon with the Asia Foundation, had lost an eye in a terrorist attack on the U.S. embassy. A car bomb parked outside virtually destroyed the building, killing nineteen Vietnamese, two Americans, and a Filipino, and injuring 183 others.

Cai-San was typical of the settlements we visited, a "strategic" rural hamlet that had been created to win the "hearts and minds" of the villagers.[10] Fifty-five thousand refugees from the North, mainly members of the Hua Hao religious sect, had settled there ten years before. When we stopped at the land reform office, school kids clustered around our jeep. Lined up along the road by their teacher, they cheered us dutifully. In front of the office there was a reception line of local dignitaries, headed by a venerable elder in the traditional black tunic and trousers. His face was lined, he had a wispy gray goatee, and when he stepped up for the usual brisk two-handed handshake, his palms were dry and gnarled.

When we asked what sort of problems they were encountering, not surprisingly most of the farmers mentioned the rice price squeeze. As before, the government fixed payments for their harvest low enough to keep Saigon consumers happy, while the costs of what the farmers needed to continue growing—fertilizer, seed, fuel, and tools—continued to go nowhere but up. It was the same problem seen on my first visit to the country in 1959. Now most of the farmers were more unhappy about the government's price ceiling than about Viet Cong "road taxes." Moreover, the insurgents were exploiting the situation with great acumen. Visiting the villages at night and expropriating as many bags of rice as they needed, they promised to return in a few days with payment calculated at the world market price. They then kept their promises—not only paying more than the government, but also building trust among the farmers. It was no wonder that the countryside was rife with Viet Cong sympathizers.

For our return flight to the United States, Air Force Two had disappeared, replaced by a troop carrier whose heaters didn't work—we nearly froze to death before we landed. A few days later, we met again with President Lyndon Johnson, national security adviser McGeorge Bundy, and Bill Moyers, a thirty-two-year-old special assistant and press secretary to the president. Johnson seemed interested in our findings, but his initial zeal had already begun to flag. Following our session at the White House, we talked with several people from AID and the State Department. One was Philip Habib,[11] to whom I mentioned how many times my recommendations on rice price policy had been sought, then ignored. With a PhD in agricultural economics from Berkeley, Habib understood what I was saying perfectly. But he candidly admitted that the United States was not prepared to recommend anything that might destabilize the Ky/Thieu administration in Saigon.

Despite my doubts about many of our other recommendations, I ended up writing most of the agriculture group's report to the president. "I appreciated . . . your comprehensive knowledge of the Vietnamese rural economy and land reform, but I would especially like to commend your leadership and organizational ability in compiling the whole report to the President."[12] I didn't bother to include in the report my view that further Viet Cong success, especially in the Mekong Delta, was almost inevitable.

▪ ▪ ▪ ▪

Within the broader foreign policy "establishment," nonetheless, concern was growing over the war in Vietnam, along with a sense that the nation's intellectual and academic resources could be better used to help resolve the conflict. Writers and editorialists pointed out the relative ignorance in the United States regarding Vietnamese history, culture, politics, and institutions. In November 1966, Secretary of State Dean Rusk set up a series of advisory committees for its regional bureaus. They invited me to join the Committee for East Asian and Pacific Affairs, under William Bundy, assistant secretary for the region.[13] His eighteen-member group included several outstanding "Asia hands," and altogether came to represent virtually a who's who of foreign policy expertise (see appendix 1).

Bill Bundy met with his group regularly, inviting key policymakers and their aides to sit in. With some of the country's most knowledgeable Asia experts on board, the committee had discussions that were often subtle and insightful, and in some instances it actually appeared to exert a degree of influence.

At one meeting we were talking about extrapolitical influences that impinged on foreign policy, and I gave a few off-the-cuff examples from Southeast Asia's agricultural sector. Bundy suggested elaborating my ideas for presentation to the committee later on. During a coffee break, I jotted down an outline, using as a framework the newly burgeoning "green revolution" in Asian rice and wheat farming. After I spoke, Bundy suggested my turning the presentation into an article for *Foreign Affairs*, which he had formerly edited.

Thus was born what would become my most widely read foreign affairs publication, "The Green Revolution: Cornucopia or Pandora's Box?" At bottom, it was a case study in the law of unintended consequences. It emphasized the need to be on the alert for unexpected problems in the miraculous, technology-based green revolution. The article pointed out, for one thing, that new seed and crop varieties were all very well, but they required well-irrigated acreage that was in short supply in many parts of Asia. Likewise, underdeveloped roads and storage facilities would make it difficult to use heavy new farm machinery, as well as to transport expanded farm output. With little margin for failure, subsistence farmers might well shun the risk of new varieties and methods, and difficult social and cultural adjustments would be needed for them and their families to take advantage of shorter growing seasons and multiple cropping opportunities.

My treatise concluded with several not-so-rhetorical questions: To what extent might the spread of new technologies accelerate rural displacement in Southeast Asia and speed migration to the cities? If agricultural innovation succeeded, would policymakers allow farmers to retain a fair share of the increased wealth, or just continue taxing them for nonagricultural development? Would more abundant foodstuffs lead to more productive specialization in the tropical and subtropical world, or would trade barriers and other nationalistic practices continue to undercut natural comparative advantage?

When it came out in *Foreign Affairs*,[14] the article sparked wide comment, both in the United States and abroad. Most was positive, though the experts at the Ford and Rockefeller foundations, architects and advocates of the green revolution, were livid. I thought they had missed the point. The piece wasn't criticizing Norman Borlaug, the plant geneticist considered the "father of the Green Revolution,"[15] and his scientist colleagues, nor denying the dramatic impact of their work. Rather it was pointing up the failure of their organizations to pay attention to the socioeconomic context and consequences of their work.

. . . .

In 1967 Art Mosher's title at ADC changed from executive director to president, and I was made vice president. The promotion was a nice vote of confidence by the Council board. And since Art had made it clear he planned to retire before age sixty-five, it implied a succession plan. Art was then fifty-seven, and I was forty-one. My sense of having "arrived" was reinforced when one day Dean Efferson, who had opposed my hiring, told me that he had been "pleasantly surprised" by my years of successful agricultural work in Asia.

By now my visibility had begun to spread beyond ADC and the programs of AURP, causing a variety of boards and organizations to invite me. My alma mater SAIS, now attached to Johns Hopkins University, asked me to join the school's advisory council. Kenneth Young, U.S. ambassador to Thailand during our Southeast Asia years and now president of the Asia Society, asked me to chair a new Malaysia Council, with Dolores as secretary—a nice recognition of our close partnership. Shortly afterward, JDR 3rd asked me to become a trustee of the Asia Society itself, and invited me to join the Rainbow Room luncheon club on the sixty-fifth floor of 30 Rockefeller Plaza. Pete Hudgens had taken me there in my earliest days at AIA—at the time, I didn't even dream of one day becoming a member.

Also in 1967, I became a founding member of the Agribusiness Council to encourage U.S. businesses to contribute to foreign economic development. Next, two nonprofit organizations asked me to serve as a trustee—the Education Development Center and the Franklin Book Programs. Then in 1968, the additions were the Board on Science and Technology in International Development of the National Academy of Sciences, the editorial board of the *American Agricultural Economics Association Journal*, and membership in the prestigious Council on Foreign Relations. Eventually it was necessary to limit my outside involvements to avoid becoming inattentive to my duties at ADC. My self-imposed rule was that for any new activity taken on, an existing one of equal time commitment would be given up. It forced me to be more selective, to set priorities, and to concentrate on things that meant the most to me personally and professionally.

. . . .

Despite the upward trajectory of my professional life, these were troubled times in the United States. The war in Vietnam seemed to have split the country in half, with mass sit-ins, teach-ins, be-ins, and other kinds of demonstrations on and off college campuses from coast to coast. On the civil rights front, voter registration drives and other kinds of peaceful resistance were being displaced by a different kind of activism, not always nonviolent. The week before my subsistence agriculture conference in Hawaii, Malcolm X had been assassinated in New York. Later the same year Watts had exploded into cataclysmic riots in Los Angeles, 350 miles south of where we had been in Stanford two months before. I worried that rage and violence might cost Blacks their moral high ground and the broad public support that had been building for their struggle. But the sight of Ralph Bunche locked arm-in-arm with Martin Luther King

Jn in their march from Selma, Alabama, to Montgomery was deeply moving. This prompted the hard question what my own part should be in the movement.

In April 1968, King's assassination shocked Dolores and me, and my anguish made me reassess my previous thinking. Dr. King and other civil rights leaders had made an incredible—all too often, an ultimate—sacrifice in the struggle for racial justice. Like most Blacks not personally on the front lines I felt keenly the expectations and judgments of my racial community. Was I my "brother's keeper"? Had I neglected marching in Mississippi or Alabama? What had I done for the cause?

Brooding over such questions led me to remember the title of Gordon Parks's autobiography, *A Choice of Weapons*.[16] Parks reminded that there were different important ways to contribute to Black advancement—alternative "weapons" in the battle for change. A multitalented person—photographer, musician, writer, and film director—Parks was himself the incarnation of many "weapons." I was no politician, and certainly no radical firebrand. But there had to be more to Black identity than clenched fists, dashiki robes, and Afro haircuts. Indeed, my working for economic development in the developing world represented no small activism for broader human and economic rights of all people—a majority nonwhite and dark skinned. Moreover, my deepening involvements in philanthropy and higher education were a kind of pioneering in themselves—clear and visible proof that a Black could succeed on innate talent and merit and in any area he or she chose. My personal "weapons" were being used where they could have special impact in achieving racial progress and integration.

Still my feeling was the need for a stronger direct activity that might be useful. In 1968, I submitted a proposal to the Rockefeller Foundation to create an organization that would attempt "to increase the involvement and the contribution of the Black American who is already wholly or partially integrated economically and socially . . . the professionals whose livelihood and daily contacts are with the white world, in government, business, education, industry . . . [such as] physicists, chemists, engineers, artists, economists, musicians, computer scientists, and mathematicians. Some would refer to these individuals as the middle class Black bourgeoisie."[17] My discussions with such individuals about what we might do in this broad area led me to the idea that one possible way of securing the greater involvement of such persons would be to utilize them to provide career awareness and guidance in schools in the Black inner city. The proposal rested on the belief, first, that such a group could increase awareness among minority youth about a wide range of opportunities that already existed for those who continued their education and would reduce the perceptions of limited opportunity so prevalent. Seeing and hearing Blacks who were already involved with varying degrees of success might help make the mainstream professional world more visible and concrete to the then alienated Black community. Second, the proposal would give "integrated black professionals" an opportunity to provide a useful service to their disadvantaged "soul brothers" based upon their special competencies—the professional would not only be able to tell about the opportunities, but what kinds of training and experience are required. Third, if carried out on a sustained basis over a number of years, the program would provide a much-needed basis for increased links and communication between the segregated ghetto community and the integrated Black American community on a positive basis—helping to strengthen the aspirations of disadvantaged youth and at the same time build up their competence to realize these aspirations.[18]

Although Ken Thompson, the Rockefeller Foundation vice president, declined any funding, my commitment remained undiminished to create an organization of like-minded young Black professionals in New York who might undertake such an effort. For an exploratory meeting, letters were sent to some twenty men and women on my list—business officers, lawyers, newspaper and television reporters, university professors (including two deans), bankers, nonprofit and foundation officials, and artists. When we met in the ADC offices, the attendees were unanimous about participating in such a program, even without outside funding. But the development of the activity fell entirely on me, and my constant travel meant that implementation was delayed. With critical events piling one upon the other, the "on hold" unfortunately became permanent.[19]

▪ ADC in Africa?

The possible extension of ADC operations into Africa resulted from frequent participants in the AURP/ADC workshops and seminars. Development economists who had experience in Africa regularly commented about the need for an ADC program in the region and the potential contributions that its unique approach could make. Art Mosher authorized me to take a seventeen-day fact-finding trip to Tanzania, Kenya, Ethiopia, and Uganda. Given the length of the trip, Art authorized travel to include Dolores and Bruce. Clifton 3rd joined us later, after attending summer camp in the Berkshires. The trip was from mid-June to mid-September in 1968, beginning with brief visits in Southeast Asia before East Africa and ending in England at a development conference at the University of Reading. The International Seminar on Change in Agriculture drew participants from all over the globe.

The visits in the four countries provided an opportunity to assess firsthand the prospects for graduate training in East Africa in the rural social sciences, especially those with a regional focus at a single center of excellence. This was a first, all too brief visit to East Africa that did not allow in-depth analysis of the situations. However, there were four general observations from the trip. First, while the nationals and expatriates were impressive, there was the predictable substantial shortage of high-level Black African talent in their universities and research institutes. Most Black Africans trained in agriculture or the rural social sciences entered government rather than the university. Second, the little training that had taken place tended to focus on technical disciplines rather than the social sciences. Third, the prospects for the emerging regional East African centers of excellence such as the University of East Africa were doubtful. Fourth, it was clear that a major contribution could be made by the ADC. Moreover, many professionals in the area were quite familiar with ADC's unique approach. They repeatedly asked whether we might bring the region into our program and thought that sustained professional contact and evolutionary program concepts would work extremely well in Africa.

This exploration was further complemented by my brief membership as a trustee of the Africa-America Institute. After one year, 1968–69, it was dropped due to my maximum policy. The institute's goal was to help Africans build human capacity through education and training programs, plus a portfolio of programs aimed at both educating Africans and educating Americans about Africa.[20]

In November 1968 I attended the first African-American Dialogues, held in Nairobi, where there were speeches by Kenya president Mzee Jomo Kenyatta and Dahomey president Dr. Emile-Derlin Zinsou. Thirty-one delegates attended the four-day meetings (see appendix 2). On the way home I stopped over in Lagos, Nigeria, where I met with academic and political leaders of the largest nation in West Africa.

After several months of traveling and investigation, I was convinced that ADC could do much to help in Africa. In fact, numerous leaders, academics, and professionals across the continent were familiar with the organization and eager to see its unique approach applied on their own soil. After reviewing my impressions, Art Mosher authorized me to undertake preliminary work for an ADC initiative in selected African nations.

▪ Graduate School of Foreign Agricultural Development _____

The AURP program focused attention on building more U.S. research professionals who could work on foreign agricultural development. During those three years, I became aware that improvement was also needed on the teaching of foreign economic development. The topic received limited attention in the courses on U.S. campuses due to an understandable focus upon domestic agriculture. Because students interested in foreign agriculture were a small fraction of enrollees, alterations in course content were seldom made. Even professors interested in the subject could not devote much time to agricultural economics and rural sociology dealing with foreign agriculture, and there was a continuing dearth of teaching materials. Probably the most neglected critical social science area was poverty in the developing world. Persons capable of training students interested in foreign agricultural development existed, but they were scattered at several institutions in the United States, Europe, and a growing number in the developing areas. Nowhere did they constitute a "critical mass" for pursuing their interests in the most effective manner.

. . . .

Two conferences were organized to explore my idea of a Graduate School of Foreign Agricultural Development. The first was held at Johns Hopkins University (March 30–April 2, 1969), and a second at the Rockefeller University (May 8–10, 1969). Participants came from Princeton, Cornell, Northwestern, Iowa State, Illinois, UCLA, Harvard, Wisconsin, Michigan State, Yale, Michigan, Vanderbilt, and Purdue, plus delegates from the World Bank, the Ford Foundation, the Rockefeller Foundation, Carnegie, and the East-West Center. We also had attendees from Argentina, Canada, Chile, Mexico, the Philippines, England, India, and Pakistan. All received an advance copy of a paper by Art Mosher and two background papers by me—one on the problems and possible solutions to the graduate training issue, and a second outlining a prototype graduate school of agricultural development. Afterward I followed up with a detailed confidential proposal for more formal exploration of the school's possible structure, funding, and location.

While there was considerable interest in this concept and approach, I detected two obstacles. First was the problem of choosing an institutional location and the question of a potential source of sustained, ongoing funding. Second, I had doubts about the ability to attract the level of persons required and the number needed to create a critical mass. A major effort would be necessary. Moreover, this proposal and the Africa initiative would clearly require my leadership, which fatefully would soon no longer be possible for me.

▪ The University Club

New York is a city of prestigious clubs, in which serious business often gets done on the social side. In May 1968, JDR 3rd asked me if I belonged to any. When I said I didn't, he continued, "Well, you're at a stage in your career when a club could be good for you, and I'd like to propose you for a membership."

John had an ulterior motive. He was a member of the city's renowned University Club, and he was unhappy that it was discriminatory—it had only a few Jews and no Blacks at all. His brother Nelson had recently resigned in protest.[21] John didn't want to follow his lead—he wanted to work from within. "Clif," he said, "I know this isn't something you generally do, but I would appreciate your giving it a try."

What could I say? With John's backing it might be an interesting experience, so I agreed. My application required a sponsor and four seconders, plus eight letters of recommendation. John was my sponsor, and for seconders he wanted "heavy hitters." My other sponsors were Harold H. Helm, chairman and CEO of Chemical Bank; James F. Oates, a Chicago lawyer who had become chairman and CEO of Equitable Life Assurance Society; Frank Pace Jr., former secretary of the army, now president of the International Executive Corporation and chairman of the Corporation for Public Broadcasting; and Eli Whitney Debevoise, a founding partner of the famous law firm Debevoise & Plimpton. Two, Helm and Debevoise, were former University Club presidents, which certainly put the nominating committee on notice. When the "establishment" decides to move, I was learning, it is usually with full flags flying. However, in this case my nomination was going to take longer than normal as the committee wrestled with its views on race.

One of my seconders opened for me a new door to corporate America. James Oates, chairman of the Equitable Life Assurance Society, had moved from Chicago to New York to try to improve the fortunes of the troubled life insurance firm. After a massive corporate cleanup, he and his second-in-command, J. Henry Smith, were on the verge of bringing the company back to vigorous health. One of their initiatives was to improve hiring and promotion of Blacks, and they did not have a Black on their board of directors.

In the fall of 1968, Oates and Smith asked me to join them for a meeting, and when I arrived, they unexpectedly "popped the question" of my joining the Equitable board. I was surprised and very flattered. It was clear that they were interested in my various academic credentials. Also significant was that I was Black, though they emphasized my appeal as an economist who had worked in economic development. The two men detailed the company's "directive 106," a farsighted commitment to equal opportunity.[22] In 1968 alone Equitable had hired one hundred Black agents, fifteen district managers, and two agency managers. By 1972 they intended to reach a total of six hundred Black "starters," one hundred district managers, and ten agency managers. I was particularly impressed when they shared with me a confidential timetable for promoting a number of Blacks in stages to regional vice presidencies, then corporate vice presidencies. They even told me the names of some of the people they had identified as candidates, such as Dar Davis, whom I had previously met.

Oates and Smith seemed genuinely committed to their goals, not just looking for a visible "token." Theirs was an invitation I was pleased to accept, and consequently I became a director of Equitable Life.

It was an unfamiliar role at a company I hardly knew, and I wanted to do as well as I could. I asked if I could spend my mornings for a week at the company headquarters, visiting its major divisions. No other director had ever asked such a thing, but Oates and Smith were happy to organize it for me (the new version of my "shipboard tours").

So for several days I walked a block over from my Fifth Avenue office to the Equitable building on Sixth Avenue for my daily briefings. My first board meeting, on March 20, 1969, was in the company's impressive grand room, where the directors sat in deep leather chairs at a well-polished oval table. When Jim Oates told the other directors about my orientation briefings, Henry Smith added with a smile that I probably knew more about the company now than anyone else on the board. This called for genuine modesty, so I gently opened my agenda, carefully placing aside the white envelope to be opened later with its crisp, brand-new currency—my first board attendance fees. So this is what it's like, I thought.

My Equitable appointment meant that I was the second Black to become a director of a major U.S. corporation. Actually I was tied for second. The first Black appointed to a Fortune 500 company had been Samuel Pierce, President Reagan's secretary of housing and urban development, as Prudential Life director in 1964. (Sam was the older brother of Chet Pierce, my childhood Atwater friend and a Harvard alum.) Five years later, William T. Coleman Jr., lawyer and later President Ford's secretary of transportation, and I were tied for "second place," both of us elected in February 1969 (Coleman to Penn Mutual Life). The fourth Black director was Robert C. Weaver, the secretary of housing and urban development in President Johnson's administration, at Metropolitan Life in June 1969. All four of us—interestingly elected by life insurance companies—were under scrutiny to see whether Blacks were up to the job.

. . . .

Soon after Richard Nixon's election as president in November 1968, a call came from his chief headhunter, Calvert Knudsen, who wanted to know about my possible interest in a position with the new administration. (Professor Milton Friedman had suggested my name.[23])

My initial reaction was that they probably wanted a Black candidate to showcase Republican "liberalism," but I agreed to go down to Washington for an interview. Originally the meeting was to have been with Alexis Johnson, the incoming under secretary of state for political affairs, whom I had known when he was ambassador to Thailand. When an emergency called Alexis Johnson away, I met instead with Elliot Richardson, the incoming under secretary of state—then the number two position in the department. We had a good talk. Richardson knew about my father's long Foreign Service career and was familiar with my work on the department's East Asia Advisory Committee. We discussed two possibilities: assistant secretary for Latin America and assistant secretary for Asia. Despite my fluency in Spanish I indicated a preference for the Asian slot, where my regional experience was more recent. Richardson, however, seemed to be leaning more toward the job in Latin America.

Art Mosher thought I should seriously consider any offer—either position would get me "out from under the shadow of Ted Schultz and Art Mosher," he smiled modestly. He also pointed out that a stint of government service would greatly enhance my future "marketability," perhaps for a leadership role with the Rockefeller Foundation. But Mosher also pointed out the likelihood of my becoming president of ADC within eighteen months, as he was planning an early retirement. In any event, he said, "There will be a job at ADC waiting whenever you want to return."

Several other people were consulted about the possible job. Ted Schultz thought I could make a real contribution, but he wasn't convinced the administration would be doing any fresh thinking about Latin America. "[They] may on Russia and Europe as well as the Middle East, but these are likely to dominate." On the other hand Ray Lamontagne, adviser to JDR 3rd and now a close friend, thought Latin America was no longer a dead end and might be at the heart of U.S. security policy. He believed that many people entering the Nixon administration were better than those who had worked under LBJ.

My father was pleased but warned me not to accept any position below assistant secretary. He sent along two pages from the February 1969 Department of State *Newsletter*, with an article on the new secretary, William Rogers. On the back of the clipping I happened to notice an interesting announcement—the appointment of John A. Hannah, president of Michigan State University, as the new Administrator of the Agency for International Development. As president of Michigan State, Hannah had led the response by public higher education to President Truman's "Point Four" initiatives. A splendid choice, I remember thinking at the time.

Probably the best advice I got was from Martha Dalrymple, my colleague from AIA. Washington, she told me, was a city of intrigue, filled with headaches and heartaches. "Everyone is looking for an inside pipeline to the Big Man. You'll have to be thick skinned, and you usually survive by hanging on by the skin of your teeth." The critical question, she added, was "What will *you* get out of it?"

After discussing everything with Dolores, I weighed the pros and cons. For one thing, I would be stepping from a specialized position as an "agriculture expert" onto a broader stage. For another, there was a nagging feeling that U.S. foundations were starting to lose interest in overseas commitments. While my future was secure at ADC, there were questions in my mind about the organization's overdependence on JDR 3rd, and the likelihood of attracting funding from elsewhere was a question mark. The Washington job might make a stressful change for both my family and me, and taking it might preclude some better alternatives in the long run. Moreover, I wasn't at all enamored with the "snake-pit" of partisan politics.

In the end the job went to Charles Meyer, vice president of Sears, Roebuck. There was a rumor that the first choice had been George Harrar, president of the Rockefeller Foundation, who had reportedly declined for personal reasons. My reaction to the outcome was strangely cheerful—maybe not so strange, actually. At least I had been in good company. But for the first time in a long while I began thinking seriously about the career choices that might lie ahead of me.

▪ Nelson Rockefeller Latin American Mission

Not long after the job offer that never materialized, Nelson Rockefeller invited me to join a presidential mission he was heading to Latin America.[24]

In spring 1969, several Latin American countries were in the midst of one of their cyclical spasms of anti-U.S. dissatisfaction. Some were languishing under authoritarian or dictatorial regimes. In others there was growing popular unrest, in certain instances (Argentina and

Venezuela) stoked by labor unions. For all of the region's geographic, economic, and political significance, U.S. policy toward it was famous for its vacillations. The one constant, American anticommunism, had deflected U.S. support toward right-wing despots and oligarchies, with democracy and human rights concerns decidedly secondary. The Cuban missile crisis exacerbated the U.S. anxiety about the spread of communism within the hemisphere, turning Latin America into a theater of the Cold War.

Rockefeller's extensive experience in Latin America persuaded him that other issues desperately needed attention. From his days as Roosevelt's wartime coordinator for Latin America, he had seen himself as a friend of the region. He was fervently concerned to reverse its deteriorating relations with the colossus to the North.

Rockefeller convinced President Nixon to let him head up a "blue ribbon" presidential commission, whose brief would be to visit nations throughout Latin America in preparation for a fundamental revision of U.S. policies toward the region. When he approached me about participating, I was pleased—in all his dealings Nelson was famous for calling on "the best and brightest" minds he could find. I couldn't help some reservations about the "presidential" nature of the mission—would Nixon really give the group a free hand to forge new directions? Nelson assured me that he alone was in charge, and we would have carte blanche. So I was on board, looking forward to revisiting countries not seen since my graduate work in Latin America some fifteen years before.

Nelson assembled an outstanding team. There was a core of around twenty-five people, with a dozen or so others who took part in some but not all of the mission's travel. The experts and specialists came from education, science, architecture, public health, cultural affairs, urban studies, and aid/assistance programming. Among the more prominent members were Arthur K. Watson, chairman of the IBM World Trade Corporation and son of the company's founder; George D. Woods, former president of the World Bank; Andrew McClellan, inter-American representative of the AFL-CIO; Thomas Hoving, director of the Metropolitan Museum of Art; Samuel B. Gould, chancellor of the State University of New York; David Bronheim, director of the Center for Inter-American Relations; George Beebe, senior managing editor of the *Miami Herald*; John Hightower, executive director of the New York State Council on the Arts; and Alan Miller, New York's commissioner of mental health. There was even a military adviser, which spoke volumes about the temper of the times.

The plan was for the mission to make four different trips. Between May 11 and 19 we would visit Mexico, Guatemala, Nicaragua, El Salvador, Honduras, Costa Rica, and Panama. From May 27 to June 2, we would see Columbia, Ecuador, Bolivia, Trinidad, and Tobago. June 16–21 would take us to Brazil, Paraguay, and Uruguay. Our last trip, June 27–July 6, would survey Argentina, Haiti, the Dominican Republic, Jamaica, Guyana, and Barbados. Unfortunately, Chile, Peru, and Venezuela had to be ruled out as unsafe—Rockefeller was particularly disappointed about Venezuela, where he had been personally involved for many years.

Governor Nelson Rockefeller, Mrs. Rockefeller, and mission members arrived at Mexico City airport on May 11, 1969, for the first stop on the presidential mission to Latin America. I am the third person from the right.

Nixon tasked Air Force Two to support the mission, with a commercial plane chartered for the press. A seasoned veteran on the Air Force Two plane, I took a pullover sweater and slippers in my briefcase. At our first stop in Mexico City, we were warmly greeted by an official delegation. Nelson addressed them in fluent Spanish from a platform that had been set up under the wing of Air Force Two. Local press coverage was extensive, including photographs. Happy Rockefeller was thronged by the spouses of the local leaders, and it all seemed a promising beginning.

That changed quickly in Guatemala, where the CIA warned the mission not to ride around or spend the night in Guatemala City. We had to use "safe houses" to meet our in-country counterparts. The next day in Honduras was even worse. A mob of five hundred or more had assembled to protest Rockefeller and his U.S. team, and the local police had killed a student who was part of the crowd. Characteristically courageous, Nelson was determined to speak directly to the furious Hondurans. The Secret Service tried to restrain him, but he shook off his minders and strode alone into the throng, reaching out and debating animatedly with some of the students.

Miraculously, he wasn't attacked and returned unharmed. Back on Air Force Two he remarked with a grin, "Nobody laid a hand on me, but somebody lifted my wallet."

The first trip was an augur of the disruptions that would dog the mission. In Uruguay, demonstrators set fire to the General Motors building in Montevideo, causing a million dollars in damage. In Argentina, rioting students fought with police, and seven of the country's sixteen Rockefeller-related supermarkets were firebombed. When Augusto Vandor, head of the metal workers union, refused to call out his 150,000 members in a general strike to protest our visit, he was assassinated in his office.

At times it was hard to know whether the protests were against the United States, the local government, or Rockefeller himself. A common complaint, expressed by Latin leaders and citizens alike, was that the visits were so short that they were both useless and insulting. Because the mission team worked in small, specialized groups, Nelson always said that each country visit added up to twenty-five days of consultation. Time and again we crowded into a van or bus and careened down narrow streets, where anyone with a rifle or grenade could have hidden on a rooftop above. I soon realized the virtual impossibility of protection from a single individual or small group that doesn't care about the consequences to themselves. After a while one became sanguine, almost fatalistic about the risks. I even got used to the local militias, who often rode ahead of us in an open truck, their rifles waving lackadaisically in every direction. Some of us wondered what might happen if the truck hit a pothole.

In Brazil, where we were received in the new capital of Brasília, things were superficially different. The government laid on intense police and military protection, also clamping down on media coverage of the demonstrations against us elsewhere. But the security was a mixed blessing, highlighting the regime's repressiveness and disregard of the civil and human rights of the citizens.

Controversies notwithstanding, the chance to revisit places where I had previously worked and studied was welcome, as well as countries not seen before. The contrast between Latin America and Southeast Asia was striking. Much of the former had been independent since the days of Simón Bolívar, while the latter was still sloughing off the dead skin of colonialism. Yet several Southeast Asian countries—notably Singapore, Malaysia, the Philippines, and perhaps Thailand—seemed to be building a better foundation for democratic politics and economic growth than most of Latin America.

With an entire plane full of reporters in our wake, press coverage of the mission was intense, and not always good. On the last trip, a photographer caught Nelson standing alongside Haiti's president Francois "Papa Doc" Duvalier on the portico of the National Palace. The photo sent an image of implicit support for the hated dictator, universally reviled for his corruption and brutality. It was just the opposite of the message the mission intended to convey. The next day Rockefeller visited the Dominican Republic, but the damage was done.

On one of the last legs of the trip, an attractive young woman named Gloria Steinem was along, writing an article for *New York* magazine. As representative for the entire press pool, she got a mid-flight interview with Rockefeller. Ever gallant with the ladies, Nelson beamed his high-wattage charm on her for an hour. Steinem took notes quietly, her long hair falling around her face, giving away nothing but an air of professionalism. Afterward Nelson clearly thought the interview had gone well—but when the article came out, Steinem focused squarely on some of the mission's failures and skewered Nelson himself.[25]

Back in the United States, Nelson asked me and Oscar Ruebhausen, a partner at Debevoise & Plimpton, to take charge of writing the final report. He particularly wanted to counter the negative press at home, which had concentrated on the demonstrations and dissent rather than what the mission was trying to accomplish. Many stories questioned the wisdom of the mission from its outset, especially headed by a Rockefeller. Lurid images of anti-American riots suggested that U.S. policy toward the region should focus on the hostility of the populace, rather than more fundamental issues of trade, development, and hemisphere security. A few more thoughtful journalists took on the complexities beneath the raucous surface, but not enough really to give our work a fair hearing.

Our report, "Quality of Life in the Americas," went to President Nixon on August 30, 1969. It focused on lowering tariffs though preferential trade treatment of Latin America, refinancing the region's public debt, and removing bureaucratic obstacles impeding the effectiveness of U.S. aid and technical assistance. Among other things, we called for suspending the Senator Hickenlooper 1962 amendment to the Foreign Assistance Act[26] that barred economic assistance to any country that expropriated U.S. property. We also proposed reorganizing the Latin American policy structure in Washington, as well as supplying more military aid.

Two months later Nixon gave a speech to the Inter-American Press Association. He praised the Rockefeller mission in passing, but mentioned only one of our recommendations—announcing that the U.S. would no longer require that 90 percent of AID funds for Latin America be spent on U.S. products.

As so often happens, our "blue ribbon" mission had virtually no impact. Even today, however, I remain convinced that it was a great pity that Nelson Rockefeller never achieved his presidential ambitions. From the day I first met him, he had always shown keen intelligence, determination, patience, and goodwill. Watching him stand firm in the midst of angry demonstrators gave proof of his poise and personal courage. He would have made a strong and effective leader at the summit of national and international affairs.

CHAPTER SIX

The President of MSU 1: The Start and Student Demonstrations

My career shift into university administration began unexpectedly and gradually. Soon after my return to the United States, I received several inquiries regarding academic nonpresidential jobs, among them the chairmanship of the agricultural economics department at the University of Massachusetts Amherst, in 1965. The following year came a preliminary inquiry from the search committee for the presidency of Colorado State University. Although I declined, it did cause Dolores and me to think about whether such a major career change made sense. A department chairmanship was logical because it was not too different from my role in Southeast Asia. But a presidency? That would be a major dramatic change—and challenge. I was very happy at ADC, with a clear shot at moving ahead within the organization. Still, the idea of a presidency was intriguing enough for me to decide to take a hard look if the right opportunity came along. I didn't have to wait long.

In late spring of 1968, I was contacted by Pete Gosling, professor of geography at the University of Michigan, whom Dolores and I had befriended in Kuala Lumpur. Pete and another friend from our Malaysia days, Gayl Ness, a U of M sociology professor,[1] had been talking about putting my name forward for the presidency of their university.

The prestigious U of M clearly was worth exploration. Gayl submitted a formal nomination of me on June 2, 1968. Ironically, this happened just four days before I was to give an address, "An Agrarian Strategy for U.S. Foreign Policy in Southeast Asia," on the Ann Arbor campus.[2] Pete wanted me to meet several key persons involved and sent bios as well as thumbnail sketches of all the regents, while I gathered similar information on selected members of the search committee. He also suggested that I research younger presidential appointments elsewhere in case my relative youth, forty-one, became an issue. I came up with a good list. James Conant became president of Harvard at forty. Meredith Wilson (Oregon) at forty-five, Kingman Brewster (Yale) at forty-four, Nate Pusey (Harvard) at forty-six, Bob Goheen (Princeton) at thirty-eight, and William Fulbright (Arkansas) at thirty-four.

On June 6 Dolores and I traveled to Ann Arbor and met Regent Eugene Power, founder of University Microfilms Inc., and his wife, Sayde, for dinner in Pete and Betty's home. It was a comfortable evening. Dolores's keen interest in contemporary art made a great impression—so much so that Gene insisted that we visit his home to see his collection of native Alaskan sculptures and Intuit carvings. Most of the next day I visited several key regents and search committee players.

Shortly after we returned home, Pete sent me a long letter assessing the reactions to my visit and proposing a detailed campaign strategy. Pete was soon off on an extended trip to Thailand and asked Gayl to follow up. On the whole, I doubted anything would come of the matter. At best it was a long shot, given U of M's self-image as a national leader in higher education, my limited experience in academic administration, and my relative youth. In addition, though a trained economist, my agricultural background was not a good "fit" for Michigan. Thus, I was not surprised by the subsequent selection of Robben W. Fleming, a leading labor economist,[3] as their president. Nevertheless, it was good to have tried my wings in a presidential search process. The practice might come in handy the next time.

Then came Michigan State University.

▪ The Search

Picking a university president sounds like a straightforward proposition, but all too often it isn't. My path to the presidency of Michigan State University led through a maze of politics and paranoia so Byzantine that writing about it even decades later leaves me in a state of near-disbelief. At the time, though, it was all too real.

In March 1969 John A. Hannah, MSU's legendary president,[4] announced that he was resigning to become director of the U.S. Agency for International Development. Hannah had been chair of the National Association of State Universities and Land-Grant Colleges when President Truman announced his Point Four plan for providing technical assistance to less developed countries. Hannah had responded to the president by offering the extensive intellectual resources of the land-grant institutions and forging them into a strong bloc of support. Subsequently he served for twelve years as the first chair of the U.S. Civil Rights Commission, under Presidents Eisenhower, Kennedy, Johnson, and Nixon. What he preached in Washington he practiced at home, launching an aggressive program to enroll minority students at Michigan State. In July 1967, after riots in Detroit during which at least forty died, Hannah pushed major funding increases for the university's equal opportunity and urban affairs programs. Hannah departed MSU on September 17, 1969, five months after his AID appointment and while the presidential search was under way.

President Hannah had headed the university for twenty-eight years, overseeing its transformation from a small agricultural college into the land-grant powerhouse of U.S. higher education. MSU styled itself the "pioneer land-grant university" under the Morrill Act of 1862, which provided land in each state to establish institutions devoted to industrial and agricultural education for the children of working families.[5] Once known throughout the state as "Moo-U," by the mid-1960s Michigan State had become a teaching and research colossus, and its international programs were among the best in the world. With over 40,000 students, it was the second largest single-campus institution in the country.[6]

Soon after Hannah's announcement, several friends called from MSU to ask whether I would be interested in being a candidate to replace him. Among my proposers were paradoxically Pete and Gayl, my two supporters in the earlier University of Michigan presidential search. Another person was William H. Sewell, professor at the University of Wisconsin and an ADC trustee (1963–72) who suggested my name to Ed Schuler, professor of sociology at Michigan State,[7] who relayed it to Dale Hathaway, chairman of the All University Search and Selection Committee (AUSSC).[8] Hathaway later said he had been getting the similar messages from several sources.

Dolores and I both sensed that here was a university we could really get excited about. Michigan State was a school with a strong tradition of extension and public service, plus a commitment to an international role that meshed smoothly with my background, experience, and values. MSU also was an early promoter of minority education, pushed by Hannah. I had visited its lovely sprawling campus in East Lansing several times, both as director of the American Universities Research Program and as vice president of ADC, as well as for the 1968 conference on the "Winds of Change" in Southeast Asia. I first met Ralph Smuckler, dean of international programs, in 1958, when he headed the MSU team in South Vietnam. I knew and liked many members of the Department of Agricultural Economics. Larry Boger, when he had been chairman before becoming dean of the College of Agriculture, was a contact for my Asian graduate student survey. Larry Witt had served briefly as a consultant to Ted Schultz and the Chicago/NPA survey in Latin America. Jim Bonnen and I first met when we were both graduate students at a meeting of the agriculture committee of the National Planning Association. Later we saw each other again at my first meeting of the Agricultural Economics Association, and thus began a lifelong friendship. Carl Eicher had participated in my 1965 conference on subsistence agriculture and contributed to the resulting book. Glenn Johnson had been a research contact because of his work in Thailand, and Bob Stevens had been an ADC visiting professor in South Vietnam.

At MSU the agricultural economics faculty were prominent and powerful. Dale Hathaway, the department head, also chaired the executive committee of the Academic Council—and he was now chair of the university's presidential search committee. This time, I thought, my stars just might be in the right configuration.

Nonetheless my feelings were mixed about such a dramatic career change. Although it had never been said in so many words, Art Mosher, along with John D. Rockefeller 3rd and his advisers Donald H. McLean and Raymond Lamontagne, made it clear that they expected me eventually to take over the presidency of ADC. Moreover, there were two special initiatives that had involved a lot of my time and effort preparing to launch—the new program for Africa and a proposed graduate school of agricultural development. I hated the idea of walking away from them before they even got off the ground.

ADC would continue to operate until 1985, when it merged with two other Rockefeller family-related organizations to become Winrock International. During its thirty-one years of operation, the ADC supported advanced degree studies of 588 men and women.[9]

As always, of course, I wondered what the change would mean for Dolores and the boys. Yet I could not deny that the new venture promised rich opportunities—to exercise leadership and take responsibility at an entirely new level, and to use my experience and abilities to help shape the next generation of scholars. If I had already been devoting myself to the development of human capital, what better next step than heading a major university?

Art Mosher was completely supportive. Michigan State, he said, was respected worldwide for its programs in agricultural development, and its presidency offered the chance of influence on both national and international stages. As my boss, mentor, and friend, Mosher told me it was a prospect not to be taken lightly. Years later he told me something he had left out at the time. After I had alerted my father about my candidacy, Dad called Art confidentially to urge him to talk me out of leaving ADC. He didn't want me to give up my security and long association with the Rockefeller philanthropies, and he worried that in uncharted waters I could run afoul of forces I had not previously encountered. Even if my father had spoken to me directly, he probably would have made me only more anxious to take on the new challenge.

My formal nomination for the presidency of Michigan State was by Nicolaas Luykx, an associate professor of agricultural economics. Nick had received an ADC grant when he was a doctoral student at Cornell. Later, he spent a year and a half in rural villages in Thailand and the Philippines. When he contracted hepatitis while visiting Hue, South Vietnam, I tried to be of assistance, and we remained in touch in the years that followed. Then relatively new to MSU and unencumbered by campus political baggage, he could make the nomination without drawing too much fire.

As chairman of MSU's search and selection committee, Dale Hathaway had two key goals.[10] First, he wanted to find candidates who, above all, were capable of *being* president of the institution. Second, he wanted candidates who would be *electable* to the position. Wisely, he had gotten an official resolution from the university's board that they would select no one as president who had not received the search committee's approval. The stipulation, on which

Hathaway insisted before agreeing to serve, would prove critical in dealing with factions and conflicting interests throughout the process.

In addition to Dale Hathaway, the AUSSC included four faculty from the East Lansing campus, one faculty member from the branch campus at Oakland, two undergraduates, one grad student, a representative from the Black students group, a Black faculty member, and one alumna (see appendix 3).

On July 30, 1969, I met the group in the United Airlines Red Carpet Room at the Detroit airport—the off-campus location to avoid premature public disclosure of candidates. Beforehand I had a long telephone conversation with Bill Sewell, the ADC trustee and outgoing chancellor at the University of Wisconsin. Bill's list of "dos" and "don'ts" was very helpful, and I thought the meeting went well.

By late August the committee had narrowed its list from three hundred possibilities to four: Stephen K. Bailey, dean and professor of political science at Syracuse University; Ed Pellegrino, vice president and dean of medicine at SUNY–Stony Brook; William Bevan, vice president and provost at Johns Hopkins; and myself.[11]

But three trustees had their own agenda and their own candidate: G. Mennen "Soapy" Williams, the state's former governor. Williams, heir to the Mennen family fortune and a lifelong Democrat, was a popular Michigan figure. After six terms as governor (1949–60), he had served as assistant secretary of state for African affairs. In 1966 he had lost a race for one of Michigan's seats in the U.S. Senate, and at the time of the search he was finishing up a stint as U.S. ambassador to the Philippines.

Mennen apparently saw the MSU presidency as a vehicle for returning to prominence within the state. He began a political-style campaign for the position, seeking support within MSU and among union leaders and other political factions. But he failed to appreciate how his heavy-handed lobbying and his lack of academic background would play on campus. Before long a group of faculty sent him an open letter criticizing his attempt to interject politics—and himself—into the search.[12] When he didn't make the committee's first cut, trustees Warren Huff, Clair White, and Frank Hartman demanded that he be reinterviewed. After he again failed to pass muster, the trustees retaliated by leaking to the press the names of the four finalists for the position, hoping that some or all would withdraw. Only Bill Bevan did. The premature disclosure presented no hazard in my relationships with Art Mosher and John D. Rockefeller 3rd, so I stayed in the race.

Complicating things still further, two "inside" candidates emerged. One was D. B. "Woody" Varner, president of Oakland University, a branch institution established under MSU's aegis in 1957 in suburban Detroit. Varner had served for years as vice president and head of MSU's Extension and Continuing Education unit, and though a decided long shot he was popular among many who saw him as a leader in John Hannah's old mold.[13]

The other insider was Walter Adams, an MSU economics professor. After taking his degree from and teaching at Yale, he had joined the MSU faculty in 1947. He was one of the university's most popular lecturers, styling himself an old-fashioned liberal and railing endlessly against big business, racial discrimination, and the military-industrial complex.

With his bow ties and ever-present cigars, Adams cut a distinctive figure on campus. In mid-October 1969, for example, he personally led a student anti–Vietnam War march from the campus to the state capitol, featured prominently in a photograph in the MSU *State News*.[14] This did not endear him to the Republican trustees.

Adams had been serving as the university's acting president since Hannah's departure. Working his liberal base of support, he courted student leaders as a fearless spokesman for their causes. For all of that, his critics usually missed that his quick wit and intellectual verve were highly effective in debunking the over-obstreperous student leaders. During one heated public meeting a student with an often-demonstrated penchant for obscenity let loose a string of four-letter words. Adams removed the cigar from his mouth and smiled. "Ah, Miss T———," he sighed. "Charming as ever, I see." Though Adams's judgment was often questioned, his critics missed the point that his crafty image as a pro-student and pro-antiwar leader enabled him to avoid and control possible student excesses during demonstrations.

For my own part, I thought it better to avoid lobbying, relying instead on those whose support was already on the record. But outside help came from an unexpected source. Ray Lamontagne, aide to JDR 3rd, was friendly with Michigan governor William Milliken. In 1968 Ray had been a deputy in Nelson Rockefeller's pursuit of the Republican presidential nomination, and he had been instrumental in persuading the then lieutenant governor Milliken to become chairman of Rockefeller's Michigan committee—breaking with his boss, George Romney. Although in Michigan the governor's preferences had no direct bearing on the university's presidential selection, he certainly had significant influence, especially with the Republican board members. Ray called Milliken directly and praised my virtues shamelessly.

An Equitable Life board meeting allowed me to speak confidentially with Coy Eklund, Equitable president, about my candidacy. As a student at Michigan State, Coy had been a protégé of John Hannah. Serendipitously, Fran Ferguson, president and CEO of Northwestern Mutual Life, was the alumnus member of the MSU search committee. Both men, loyal Spartans and working in the same industry, knew each other well. Coy contacted Ferguson immediately, endorsing me strongly for the job.

By summer's end in 1969 the scene was set, the actors all on stage, and the final act was under way. My supporters said I was the clear favorite among the outside candidates. Surprisingly, not once so far had anyone mentioned my race—much less that I might become the first Black to lead a predominantly white campus in the United States. But the symbolic charge of such an event was not lost on me, nor I was sure on many others.

I first met with the MSU Board of Trustees on September 3 at the Waldorf Astoria Hotel in New York. After accepting their invitation, I specifically asked for a second meeting so that they could meet Dolores as well. She had always been a strong partner to me, and I knew that she would add another dimension to my candidacy.

Dale Hathaway had given me an excellent advance précis of important recent events at the university, as well as a detailed profile of each trustee. Then as now, Michigan was unusual in its governance of higher education. In many states public colleges and community colleges are regulated by a state department of education, whose policies constrain individual campus boards and administrations—and, theoretically, buffer them from partisan state and local politics. But in Michigan the three major universities—MSU, the University of Michigan, and Wayne State—were constitutionally autonomous, exempt from the State Department of Education's oversight. Instead, each was governed by an eight-member independent board—"trustees" at MSU, "regents" at U of M, and "governors" at Wayne State.[15] While the state's annual funding allocation was recommended by the governor and approved (often in modified form) by the state legislature, the boards of the "Big Three" had wide latitude in setting tuition and managing other aspects of the institution's internal affairs.

John Hannah had been chairman of the higher education committee at Michigan's Constitutional Convention of 1961–62, when the system was established. While it may sound attractive to outsiders, the system has drawbacks. For one, even-numbered boards often impede decision-making. (Oddly, while the boards elect their own chairs, the three presidents are constitutionally empowered to preside at the meetings—but with no vote!) For another, board members serve staggered eight-year terms, with two positions open every two years. Such terms were a very long time to tolerate anyone who proves to be uninvolved, incompetent, or disruptive. Perhaps worst of all, university board members are elected in statewide elections.[16]

Every two years, the Republican and Democratic political conventions pick two candidates each for the three boards, who then run on statewide slates with candidates for other offices—for example, the governorship, the legislature, the attorney general, and secretary of state. When partisan politics determine board nominees, institutional values and needs often take a backseat to other priorities, such as the need to repay long-outstanding favors or to "balance" a ticket ethnically, geographically, or with respect to gender. Party loyalty usually comes into play, and financial contributions not infrequently. In day's end, moreover, board candidates often win or lose based on who is at the top of the ticket, rather than on the substance of their own platforms and records.

At the time of my nomination, the MSU board, then split between five Democrats and three Republicans, was widely regarded as one of the country's most difficult and politicized. Businessman Steve Nisbet, the highly respected "dean" of the Republicans, had been elected to the board in 1963. Tall and courtly, he had been a member of the state Board of Education from 1943 to 1961 and subsequently presided over Michigan's Constitutional Convention. He was a public-spirited citizen, whose calmness and good counsel made him an effective conciliator among a fractious group.

A second Republican was Frank Merriman, a dairy farmer from Deckerville whose principal support came from the state's powerful Farm Bureau. He saw his main job as protecting the College of Agriculture, the Cooperative Extension Service, and the Agricultural Research Station. He was a reserved man who spoke only when he had something to say.

Kenneth Thompson, vice president of Michigan Bell, was the only MSU alumnus among the Republicans. He was a Spartan first and political partisan only second, although he had a well-deserved reputation for a volcanic temper. His right index finger had been permanently crooked in a telephone installation accident when he was much younger, and when he pointed at some hapless object of his fury it looked like a small sharp hook.

The head of the board's Democratic contingent was Don Stevens, then education director for the state AFL-CIO. Chair of the MSU board since 1968, he was a person of great integrity—like so many Michiganders, he believed his word was his bond. He was a union man to the core, canny about the players and intricacies of the state's politics. He was also an avid collector of newspaper clippings, which often spilled from his briefcase onto the table in the boardroom.

Blanche Martin was a former MSU all-American fullback—a tall, good-looking Black with a deep chest and broad shoulders. After graduating, he attended dental school in Detroit, subsequently building a successful practice in East Lansing.

Warren Huff, who had just recaptured the seat he had lost in the previous election, was a local businessman, and the bête noire of Don Stevens, and there was no love lost between the two. Before losing his seat in 1966, Huff had been the board chair, and when he returned at the beginning of 1969, the friction between him and Stevens was sharp and undisguised. Huff was a hulking bear of a man, around six foot three, with thick glasses. It was widely rumored that Huff had once aspired to MSU's presidency himself and that he now hoped to become the state's next governor.

The board's other two Democrats usually allied with Huff, their previous chairman. Frank Hartman, a Flint native and former member of the State Board of Education, was a quiet man who somehow struck you as not a great figure in the scheme of things. In contrast Clair White, an assistant superintendent and economics teacher from Bay City, had no shortage of outlandish opinions, which he regularly expressed in flamboyant vitriol. For example, White refused to vote in favor of any faculty salary that exceeded his own as a high school teacher. He hated elites, Dale Hathaway said, especially people who had gone to Harvard—like me.

Such was the group I met for the first time during a four-hour interview at the Waldorf Astoria. As the session progressed I sensed congeniality and receptivity from Nisbet, Thompson, Stevens, and Martin. Frank Merriman seemed lukewarm, though pleasantly surprised by my background in agriculture. Huff and White, on the other hand, were blatantly hostile, firing questions implicitly disparaging my qualifications and often trying to trip me up. Several of the trustees were surprised by my teaching and research experience and professional publications, but Huff and White sought repeatedly to belittle both my ADC work and my academic credentials. One comment that baffled me was Clair White's complaint about "the intrusion of outside political forces" into my candidacy. At the time I had no idea what he meant, though eventually it would become clear.

Dolores made a strong impression—at least on the trustees with open minds. Huff, White, and Hartman seemed discomfited by the presence of an intelligent, independent spouse who might play a significant role on campus. Her poise, grace, and lively personality would make her a natural in reaching out to faculty, students, and alumni, and her activist involvement in the arts was a definite plus. Afterward, word came back that Steve Nisbet considered her as being ideal for the MSU students. He later told Dolores that the prospect of her as MSU's next First Lady tilted his vote toward me.

Soon after my interview, Warren Huff's prodding convinced the board to ask the presidential search committee to name additional candidates, even sending along twelve names of their own. Hathaway and the committee conceded only to the extent of adding Jim Dixon, president of Antioch College, but again declining Soapy Williams and refusing to bend further. This issue precipitated an emotional confrontation between Hathaway and Huff. (Huff, easily towering over the much shorter Hathaway, must have created a scene reminiscent of David and Goliath.) Pressure was brought to bear on the Democratic trustees, especially Chairman Stevens. But Stevens would not go back on his promise to consider only candidates recommended by the search committee.

Huff then issued a list of fourteen "criteria" for the next MSU president, commenting that none of the present candidates met more than 60 percent. Don Stevens wrote a seventeen-page rebuttal, challenging the criteria themselves while declaring that I and two other candidates no longer under consideration rated at least 90 percent—and that Walter Adams rated even higher.

That was enough to reenergize the Adams candidacy. John Henderson, a professor of economics, formed a "draft Adams" committee, and in its first fall-term issue the student-run *State News* published an editorial strongly endorsing Adams. Students organized a committee and promised to collect 20,000 signatures on his behalf. Black faculty and students were on the whole Adams supporters as well. Although Adams claimed to be a champion of civil rights, one of my MSU advocates recounted Adams's role in the floor fight over the Mississippi Freedom Democratic Party delegates at the 1964 National Democratic Convention. Serving as the convention's sergeant-at-arms, Adams had to enforce the "will of the convention" not to seat the all-Black group in place of the state's lily-white official delegation. When Adams said his personal predilection was for an "open society," a Black MFDP member demanded to know how many Negro sergeants-at-arms were on his staff. Characteristically, Adams quipped that he couldn't answer the question because he was color-blind.[17]

But Adams's real problem was getting the votes he needed on the board. All three

Republicans had voted against his selection as acting president, and they remained unyielding opponents. One who especially resented Adams's "noncandidacy" was quoted anonymously in a newspaper: "Walter Adams has been running—and running hard—for the MSU presidency ever since the day the five Democratic trustees decided to name him acting president."[18]

By the early weeks of October I thought my prospects might be doubtful. The student petition for Adams already had 17,000 signatures. Though I didn't know it at the time, the search committee had met secretly to debate adding Adams to the list of finalists. They had agreed in advance that a viable candidate would need eight out of twelve votes. Adams missed by one vote. And even though Woody Varner had early removed himself from the field, he had done so with a hint that he would reconsider if the board "found no one else."

On October 13 Ray Lamontagne telephoned to report that his contact in the governor's office thought that Adams was likely to get the nod. "Students are pushing hard . . . and [Adams] wants it very much," his public denials notwithstanding. Shortly afterward, however, I heard unexpectedly from John Hannah. The former MSU president said he hoped my nomination would prevail, and that if the presidency were offered I should accept it. Perhaps, I thought, he had some back channel to the search process whispering that things might go my way.

Meanwhile the Adams campaign had produced a counterreaction, and its tactics were being openly criticized. One professor complained Adams had turned the presidential search into "a popularity contest, with all the hoopla of a political campaign except the cheesecake."[19] John F. A. Taylor, an eminent professor of philosophy and chairman of the committee that drew up the search committee procedures, said that disregarding the search committee's judgment would "exchange . . . our community for an illusion of community, a failure of democracy." He publicly stated that the search committee was being "dealt with in contempt."[20] Charles Killingsworth, another distinguished professor, objected to the petition drives and the political pressures on the committee being brought by certain trustees. Powerfully the MSU academic elite were weighing into the process.

Under weight of the circumstances, trustee Don Stevens decided to clear the air. "What would you do," he wrote to Adams, "in case you were recommended for the permanent post by the All-University Search and Selection Committee, and in case the board were to extend a formal offer to you?"

Did Stevens want to give Adams one last chance to be considered? Or did he want to force his hand to pull out of the race once and for all? It was never clear. In the event, Adams held a press conference to announce that he would not under any circumstances take the job on a permanent basis. "Anyone thinking a man would accept [it] just for all the dazzling trappings of [the] post," he declared, "reflects a corrupt value system."[21]

The days remaining until the October board meeting were hectic and intense for the Whartons. All the questions and anxieties we had thought behind us came flooding back. Once again we reassessed our prospects and priorities. If it came to pass that I was offered the presidency, how would it affect us all? One potential problem was that Clifton 3rd was in the middle of his senior year at the Dalton School—should he perhaps stay in New York with family friends until he graduated in June? We went around all the old circles and trotted out all the pluses and minuses of our previous talks. And again we came to the same conclusion: MSU was the right choice for us . . . but were we the right choice for MSU?

In the final days before MSU's October 17 board meeting, the political pressure on several trustees was brutal, Don Stevens most of all. In his job with the state AFL-CIO he served at the pleasure of its president Gus Scholle, a longtime friend of Soapy Williams and his open supporter for the university presidency. Stevens was in a tough spot. If he voted for me he faced the wrath of the union and its boss—and probably the loss of his job. But if he capitulated to the board Democrats' clamor for Williams, he would break his promise to the university to support no one not approved by the presidential search committee. What price was he willing to pay to keep his word?

A few nights before MSU's October board meeting, Coy Eklund told me at an Equitable dinner that his brother Lowell, director of continuing education at MSU's Oakland University campus, had assured him my candidacy was alive and well. Almost as soon as I got home, I got an unexpected call from Ronald B. Lee, a former MSU assistant provost and director of equal opportunity programs,[22] who described his behind-the-scenes activities in support of me. At MSU he had been the first director of the new Center for Urban Affairs. Although he had left the university the previous May to become assistant U.S. postmaster general, he had been working closely with Don Stevens to line up Republican support for my candidacy. He said I should be ready for "favorable action."

On Lee's heels came another call. Dr. Robert L. Green, who had taken over Lee's portfolio at MSU, was anxious to tell me how excited he was about my likely selection. In retrospect it was the most telling contact of all, because at the beginning Green had been a strong supporter of Walter Adams, lukewarm at best toward me. His call suggested that Adams's noncandidacy was dead at last and that Green was anxious to back the winning team.

The meeting at which the issue was to be decided was scheduled for Friday, October 17. The night before the board met in executive session, during which Don Stevens called me. "We want to elect you as president," he said. "My guess is the vote will be five to three. But we want to be sure that if elected you'll accept."

Suppressing my excitement, I thanked Stevens profusely. "My one question," I said, "is whether the vote will be bipartisan?"

Stevens assured me it would. "The three Republicans will be for you—Nisbet, Thompson, and Merriman. There'll also be two Democrats, Blanche Martin and me." Huff, White, and Hartman would oppose. Stevens snorted, "At this stage they wouldn't even vote for the pope!"

Later that evening I heard unexpectedly from a peculiar source: Samuel Hayes, president of the Foreign Policy Association. I had met him during the founding of the Overseas

Development Council. Hayes said he had been contacted by Warren Huff, whom he had known years ago at the University of Michigan. Huff had told Hayes that he no longer wanted to oppose my election, but wanted to meet with me beforehand to resolve certain "issues" and clear the way for a unanimous vote. Would I ask the board to postpone its imminent action?

The more I listened the less I liked it. Either Huff wanted to cause delay in the hope of rebuilding support for Soapy Williams (or even himself), or else he hoped I might be willing to negotiate some quid pro quo: his vote in exchange for my appointing him to a top-tier job at MSU. Hayes tried to persuade me that Huff and I could reach an accommodation. But I thought negotiating on the side with an individual trustee would be highly improper— especially one like Warren Huff. I told Hayes that my contacts had all been with the board as a whole, and I preferred to keep it that way. Unanimity would be nice, but if the board's decision was split, so be it.

The next morning MSU's board of trustees was ready to take official action, but the shenanigans weren't over yet.

In executive session before the public meeting, Clair White opened by nominating Soapy Williams as president. Directly contravening the board's promise to consider only those approved by the search committee, the act aimed at forcing trustees Stevens and Martin to vote on the record against a popular Michigan Democrat. The proposal failed five votes to three.

Frank Hartman then nominated Jack Breslin, the board's own well-liked secretary. A former MSU football player, Breslin was a Republican with close ties to John Hannah. He was an effective administrator and lobbyist but had no academic or scholarly background. In nominating him, Hartman apparently hoped to break away at least one Republican supporter from me and throw the vote into a tie. Frank Merriman asked if Breslin's nomination was serious. Assured that it was, he said he would consider it if the search committee were given time to consider Breslin and approve him as a candidate.[23] The nomination failed in a four-four tie.

When the board went into official public session, chair Don Stevens made a motion to "add to the agenda" the appointment of a president. Hartman moved to table the motion, seconded by Clair White, who argued that it was "inappropriate for this board to elect a president having interviewed him only once." Hartman and White's motion failed, and after Don Steven's original motion passed he yielded the floor to Blanche Martin, who read a long resolution on behalf of my election.[24]

When the roll was called, I was approved, five to three. Two Democrats and three Republicans had just elected the first Black president of a predominantly white institution of higher learning in the United States in a century.

A minor controversial backstory was whether I was truly the first. In July 1874 the Jesuit priest Patrick Francis Healy had become president of Georgetown University. At the time, Healy and his light-skinned brothers, with a white father and Negro mother, were reputedly "passing" as white rather than "colored." Hence a dispute arose among later biographers over whether Healy was appropriately the first Negro president of a predominantly white university. In my public remarks I regularly corrected the press stories by citing Healy as the first and saying I was the first in one hundred years. Nevertheless, the overwhelming view of my pioneering status became fixed in the public mind.[25]

▪ The Launch

Back in New York, swarms of reporters and TV crews descended upon the ADC offices on Fifth Avenue—at one point the line backed up into the hallway outside. Journalists scrambled to cover the appointment—for Blacks a portent of change long overdue, for many whites an implicit vindication of their own progressivism. The next day the *New York Times* ran a front-page story with a photograph, headlined "Negro Economist Is Named Head of Michigan State U.: Clifton Wharton, Aide on Development Council, to Succeed Hannah."[26] The "Man in the News" sidebar on me caused a mini-flap. After the reporter repeatedly tried to solicit my admission that race had played a bigger part in my selection than my own qualifications, I finally said that I considered myself "a man first, an American second, and a Black man third." Some within the Black community reacted by muttering that I was disparaging my race, and that I hadn't been sufficiently scarred by prejudice (I knew I had). Most of those who complained chose to ignore the rest of what I had said, which was that "I do feel that my appointment is an important symbolic occasion."

My mother and siblings, of course, were thrilled by the news, as were Dolores's mother and stepfather. Letters poured in from friends and colleagues across the country and abroad. My father sent me slightly grudging congratulations, though when he later visited me on campus he was much more pleased.

Over the next several weeks, more than a dozen national newspapers and magazines did profiles and in-depth articles. One that particularly struck my fancy was a UPI wire story that began, "The year 1969, the year when man landed on the moon and the Mets won the World Series, has also become the year a Negro became president of a major American University." I was stunned—I had made history and become a national figure!

Oddly, none of the stories mentioned what I would have thought an inescapable backdrop—the Detroit riots of 1967 and the upheavals that had followed the assassination of Martin Luther King Jr. in 1968. Despite the journalists' silence, I knew what had to be in the minds of many of their white readers: After two years of racial turmoil both close to home and throughout the country, the MSU trustees had selected a Black president. *What could they be thinking?* This backstory reflected the complexity of the challenges I would face as a pioneer.

My appointment had a certain contrarian novelty. At a time when most news stories on

Blacks focused on discrimination, poverty, confrontation, and violence, my appointment offered tentative proof that a Black could succeed at a high level based on merit. But some stories, even if they acknowledged my qualifications, also questioned how at the age of forty-three I would deal with the stresses of running a major university in an era of student unrest. And that, I had to admit, was a reasonable question.

A prominent feature of the stories was descriptions of my role as a "quiet firster." This term referred to the contrast between my father and myself over one's Black pioneering achievements. "The father always shunned any publicity which focused on race; the son does not seek it, but does not avoid it. But both of them never accept a job or position if they feel that the offer was due to race and not their ability or competence."[27]

At least five or six profiles were devoted to Dolores as well. The article I liked best of all was the one that wrote, "When he talks about his wife, Wharton's face assumes an expression of pure affection."[28]

On the whole, the articles were positive, using phrases like "impressive credentials in education, foreign affairs, and as an administrator . . . a man who puts his full mental and physical energies into whatever project or projects he is committed to"[29]; "The smile is a bit toothy, the words diplomatic, and the comportment is definitely that of a high achiever"[30]; "quiet diplomacy and charm"[31]; "a man who is tempered by pressure, not bent by it"[32]; "his pedigree spells authentic black power—but not to the militants."[33]

On campus reaction to my appointment was mixed. Faculty and administrators were on the whole upbeat. Bob Green offered me the full support of the Black faculty, praising my "rare qualifications."[34] But C. Patrick "Lash" Larrowe, an economics professor and campus gadfly, raised concerns. Avowing pleasure at the appointment of a Black candidate, he worried nevertheless about my previous involvements overseas. "People who have spent a lot of time in Southeast Asia generally wind up as apologists for our policy [there]," he pronounced. Walter Adams, speaking perhaps from the sour grapes department, proclaimed, "I will always . . . regard Dr. Wharton as the great emancipator. He has liberated me from personal bondage."

Among students, many took a wait-and-see attitude, but some who had supported Adams were especially critical of my appointment. The local chapter of Students for a Democratic Society called me a "tool of the establishment."

Black students were conflicted. One Black senior said, "I'm pleased because he is a black man and I am a black man. It is encouraging to see a black man in a major office." But a member of the campus Black Liberation Front complained, "There's got to be something wrong with anybody the Republicans would vote for. . . . I'm not overjoyed about the whole thing." "The tokens," said another Black student, "are getting bigger all the time."

Jim Crate, editor of the *State News*, worried that I might be seen as an Uncle Tom. "I think Wharton is going to be in a bind, because black students are going to think they have a direct pipeline to him."[35]

On that score I didn't have long to wait. The evening after my appointment, several leaders of the Black Liberation Front called our New York apartment demanding to meet me. I asked them politely to contact my office for an appointment, to which they replied, "We're in town, and we want to see you *now*."

Annoyed but curious, I told them to come on up. I agreed to see them in part because I was aware of a campus incident that had recently occurred. Sam Riddle, head of the Black Liberation Front, had gotten into a scuffle with two white students when he attempted to enter a dormitory cafeteria through an exit door. The incident quickly escalated and took on racial overtones. The next day Riddle and 150 other Black students occupied the cafeteria, forcing white students to leave and closing the dining facility forty-five minutes early. One of the white students from the original altercation tried unsuccessfully to get the Ingham County prosecutor to press charges. In Lansing a state senator introduced legislation calling for the expulsion and criminal prosecution of "black hoodlums and black bums." It was soundly defeated, but the whole affair seemed an omen of what might be in store for me at MSU.

When they introduced themselves, I realized that one was Michael Hudson, a member of the presidential search committee. Sam Riddle, the most visible Black student leader on campus, wasn't part of the group. I listened attentively as the students set forth their concerns—most prominently, that Black students had little part in my selection. (They had, but their preference had been Walter Adams, not me, and now they were hurrying to recalibrate their stance.) When they expressed anxiety about how I would behave toward them and other Blacks, I told them gently but firmly that I intended to be president of the entire university, not a president of Blacks or a Black president. I could tell some of them were uncomfortable with the response—they hoped, they said, I wasn't the kind of Black who bent over backwards to avoid being partial to the brothers and sisters. I assured them that I would naturally be sensitive to Black issues, but that my major concern was fairness, regardless of a person's color.

Whether I got through to them I was unsure, though I had the impression that the bright, politically sophisticated Michael Hudson understood my position. What else, in any event, could I have said? How I handled "Black issues" might well make or break my presidency, but my best hope was to be entirely candid and to deal with students on the basis of my own values, if not necessarily theirs. After an hour or so the group left, with a promise to meet with me again once we moved to East Lansing.

Many congratulatory letters from the older Black generations differed from the current young campus militants. They saw my appointment as proof that the traditional goal of a fully integrated society was reachable. Perhaps the most touching letter came from the fifth Black male graduate of MSU, Delbert M. Prillerman (class of 1917), written on his seventy-fifth birthday (October 19, 1969). I learned from him that the fourth Black graduate from MSU was none other than Everett C. Yates (1916), my next-door neighbor on Walnut Ave. in Boston. (Only then did I learn that his middle name was Claudius.)

Unnoticed in all the coverage of my election was the predicted negative impact upon Don Stevens, who lost his job. Fortunately he got a position in the University of Minnesota's labor leadership education program. Later he joined the staff at Oakland University, by then independent of MSU. Despite the political wrangle over my election, Don was reelected to the MSU board in 1970 and remained a strong and supportive trustee throughout my tenure. I was always grateful for his steely integrity, which was the key to my election.[36]

• • • •

One entirely unexpected result of my election as president of MSU was that it brought to a head the long-simmering issue of my nomination to New York City's University Club. As so often with private clubs, the approval process had dragged on, undoubtedly slowed even more by internal filibustering. That summer Ray Lamontagne had reported gleefully that the membership committee was in a quandary. John D. Rockefeller 3rd, my sponsor, had lined up a powerful group of co-sponsors, and I clearly met the profile for acceptance—except that I was Black. But several committee members were angry, feeling that John had put me up intentionally to embarrass the organization.

Then came my appointment as president of Michigan State—now the delighted club officers had a way out. The by-laws allowed any college or university president to enjoy club privileges (after being proposed by a member who had graduated from the institution). Of course, I wouldn't be an actual member—just a temporary guest, and only so long as I was a university president. But surely that was good enough?

JDR 3rd was having none of it. After talking first with me, he refused to let the club off the hook with its hopeful nonsolution. My membership would be full and permanent, or not at all.[37] Faced with his strong stand, the officials finally capitulated. In 1970 I became the Club's first Black member. John's integrity made a great impression. Instead of a public confrontation, he had chosen to fight from within, because he believed that what the Club was doing was morally wrong.

• • • •

On October 23 Dolores and I flew from New York for our first postelection visit to Michigan State. My thoughts and emotions were at a high pitch, and I could tell Dolores was excited, too. As the plane banked high over East Lansing, I pointed out features of the 5,000-acre campus below. When we taxied to the gate, there were a couple of television crews on the tarmac, and in front of them were acting president Walter Adams and a number of other MSU representatives. Then as we stepped off the plane, the group surrounded us in welcome.

Our stay was a whirlwind. Our hosts took us directly from the airport to Cowles House, the on-campus presidential residence. The house was in the heart of the old campus, not far from the main entrance at Abbot Street and Grand River Avenue. Directly across West Circle Drive were several women's dorms. (At the time all the university residence halls were single-sex.) Landon Hall was nearest, and later that evening several of the "Landon Lovelies"

I held my first press conference as president-elect in the board room of the Hannah Administration Building on October 23, 1969. The announcement of my election triggered an avalanche of national press attention, and the East Lansing contingent was no exception.

came over with humorous gifts, including a "survival kit" for getting through student dem-onstrations—prophetic indeed!

The university had called a boardroom press conference in the Hannah Administration Building. Sitting at the head of the table, which would become my regular seat for board meetings, I was flanked by reporters from Michigan newspapers, with ten TV crews along the rear walls. I did my best to appear at ease, though until now my dealings with reporters had been exclusively one-on-one affairs. My comments acknowledged that my appointment had stirred unusual attention, and hence I planned to act somewhat cautiously and formally, at least until the novelty wore off. As the university's first Black president I supposed there might be extra pressures brought to bear on me, though as yet I could not anticipate what they would be. I refused to speculate on my plans for the university since I was not yet even in office. In answer to a question, I commended legitimate student activism as an expression of concern for society's ills. I thanked the public for its outpouring of support, and mentioned that I hoped the press would respect my family's private life, especially the boys.[19]

After the press conference came lunch with the university's vice presidents and deans. Except for Deans Boger and Smuckler, I had met none of them before.[39] My strong impression was of a fine group of academic administrators with whom it would be a pleasure to work. It was clear that they took great pride in the university and its accomplishments—not in a self-promotional way, but in their awareness of the institution's growing stature and rich record of

Dolores and I were welcomed by 77,533 fans in the MSU Spartan Stadium on November 1, 1969. The roar of the standing crowd as we walked along the fifty-yard line to the center of the field was awesome.

teaching, research, and public service. Later in the day there was a reception with student and faculty leaders, followed by dinner—I with the trustees and Dolores with the trustees' spouses.

Although the visit was brief and I had been to MSU before, this was the first time I began fully to grasp the size and scope of the campus, with its six hundred-plus structures covering more than seven square miles. In a room behind John Hannah's old office, I found a five-foot by five-foot map of a "Comprehensive Campus Plan" prepared by the university's planning and maintenance division. The map sat on a tilted stand, with a transparent acetate cover. On it were small-scaled roads, quads, parking lots, and playing fields, woven among little wood-block replicas of all the campus buildings. Those built from 1855 were dark brown; from 1939 to the present, green; under construction, beige; and in the planning stage, yellow. Looking at it was like looking down from the air at a midsized city.

The following weekend Dolores and I came back to campus for our first Big Ten football game, against Indiana. It was homecoming, and festivities began with a lunch at Kellogg Center hosted by acting president Walter Adams, who had also invited several prominent Michigan citizens and MSU alumni. After eating, we walked over to Spartan Stadium. There had been morning rain, but now it was a crisp, brilliant fall day. Throngs of people streamed toward the stadium decked out in green and white, the MSU colors. They carried green and white blankets and green and white pennants, and they wore green and white hats and green and white jackets—even green pants. Their excitement was infectious. In the distance we could hear the Spartan Marching Band, 180 students strong,

High above the playing field was the stadium's enclosed box for the president and special guests. From there we had a panoramic view of the emerald green field below, the two teams snapping off practice plays in their respective zones, and the waves of fans filling up the seating sections all around. As was his custom, Walter Adams excused himself (thoughtfully asking Bruce along) to join the band marching along the campus avenues prior to its entrance to the stadium. After that he took his regular seat in the stands, Bruce still in tow.

Just before the kickoff, Dolores and I were escorted down onto the field after the band had finished its warm-up numbers. "Please give a Spartan welcome," boomed out announcer Tim Skubick, "to the next president of Michigan State University, Clifton R. Wharton Jr., and Mrs. Wharton!" Holding hands, Dolores and I walked out the fifty-yard line to the middle of the field as 77,533 people stood up to cheer for us. The feeling is impossible to describe. MSU lost the game, 16-0, but nothing could dampen our excitement of this memorable moment.[40]

The weekend's embarrassing finale was that I got lost trying to drive our rental car off campus to the airport. Dolores suggested I ask for directions, but I had no taste for the risk of triggering a *State News* headline: "Lost on Campus, New President Needs Help." It was a useful reminder that I had a lot to learn.

. . . .

Although I had met John Hannah a few times over the years, we had done little more than exchange pleasantries. Soon after my election as president of Michigan State, I called to ask for any recommendations he could offer, and he responded with an invitation for Dolores and me to visit him and Mrs. Hannah at their Washington, D.C., apartment. Our November 7 meeting was cordial and relaxed. Hannah had what nowadays is often called a commanding presence, with a strong baritone voice. He also had great warmth, and he went out of his way to engage a listener. Dolores and Mrs. Hannah hit it off immediately, although their personalities were almost polar opposites—Mrs. Hannah was reserved and quiet, deferring in almost everything to her husband.

After congratulating me on being selected, Hannah spent some time recounting his own conflicts with the university's cranky board. When asked what advice he could give me, he shook his head. "I've looked into your background," he said, "and I'm sure you'll do fine."

"Surely," I persisted, "you must have some that might be helpful in the days ahead?"

"Well," Hannah said thoughtfully, "Always tell the truth to the legislature. You may not want to, but they're where your financial support comes from. Don't ever try to mislead them. They have long memories. With the legislature your most important asset is your integrity,

"Next, don't do anything to Cowles House. More college presidents have lost their jobs over building or remodeling their residences than ever got fired for poor management, budget overruns, or losing football teams."

"Third, keep up the campus. Michigan State is the most beautiful university in the country, deliberately developed as a giant arboretum. Its appearance is an important part of the spirit of the place."

"Finally," he said with a smile, "You don't have to read the *State News* unless you want to!"

These were the only words of advice John Hannah had to give me. Years later, after having lived the role, I concluded that he had given me the best advice he could have—particularly regarding the student newspaper.

· · · ·

Even before I attended my first monthly meeting of the MSU board, political mischief by the three dissident trustees ramped back up. Early in November Clair White issued a "press memorandum" setting forth a bizarre and convoluted conspiracy theory. He argued that my appointment had been "ram-rodded" by Governor Milliken to strengthen the Republican base in Detroit, boosting the mayoral election chances of the white Roman Gribbs against the Black Democratic candidate, Richard Austin. John Porter, another Black, had just been named acting state superintendent of public instruction, and according to White the governor was counting on the prospect of three Blacks in senior state positions as being too much for the electorate. White also claimed he had wanted to delay my appointment in order to scrutinize my work in Vietnam and the founding of the National Student Association, both of which he alleged involved CIA connections. "Based on our most painful recent experience"—i.e., attacks by *Ramparts* magazine and others on the university's programs in South Vietnam—he claimed he wanted "to exhaust every possible avenue of future trouble."[41]

Before the November 21 meeting I had asked all the trustees to meet with me individually to discuss the university's future. The talks went well—except for the dissident troika of Huff, White, and Hartman, who would only see me together. They also insisted on its being away from MSU, in a motel outside Flint.

At the appointed time, I began the meeting by urging that we all put the past behind us for the sake of the university's best interests. As for the civilities, that was it. For the next two hours, I stood accused of playing politics, using Nelson Rockefeller to run interference for me, conspiring with Bob Green, and being a hapless tool of John Hannah. Huff was especially vicious—"You'd better not unpack, Wharton," he said. "There'll be an election this fall."

"Mr. Huff," I responded, "I intend to do everything in my power for Michigan State University. If after November a new board no longer wants my services, I'll leave knowing I did my best."

I departed the motel room shaken and angry. Two aspects of the ordeal had been particularly unpleasant. One was the group's torrent of expletives and obscenities, at which I was flatly shocked—vile language was at the time by no means commonplace in polite company. The other was the sheer absurdity and paranoia of the group's charges—I felt like Alice in a nightmare Wonderland, with poison mushrooms sprouting on every hand. Their paranoid charges, allegations, and bullying gave me a surge of anger and energy that I had rarely before possessed. I vowed to go down fighting them tooth and nail—through my performance for the university.

Paradoxically in its way the confrontation had been invaluable—it put me on notice that as far as these three were concerned, I could never let down my guard. From now on every monthly board meeting would be a test. I would constantly have to watch myself—especially my back.

And indeed there seemed nothing too low for the troika to try. The evening before the upcoming board meeting, Walter Adams hosted a reception for us at Cowles House. After a while Dolores noticed our son Bruce was missing. Looking for him, she chanced to hear voices coming up from the basement room. When she investigated, she was furious to discover the three dissident trustees clustered around our ten-year-old son, pumping him for personal information about us and our family life.

At the board meeting the next day, the unsettled question of my salary was raised. Stevens said that the trustees would recommend $47,500. Clair White immediately demanded to know whether I would make my tax return public. Would I declare the imputed income value of our residence in Cowles House? Would I continue on the Equitable Board?

Since he was obviously trying to stir up yet another political storm, I thought it best to speak up. "I realize my actions will reflect on the university," I said. "The basic issue is whether or not I act in a manner by which I can maintain my integrity. . . . I realize fully my actions . . . will reflect on the university—including my salary, allowances, expenditures and income tax. And I want to make it clear that I will be operating in a public forum, and in a public manner. So from January 1 [1970] onward, I will make my income tax return fully public."[42]

Seeing that they had lost the PR edge, Huff and White piously congratulated me. Acting president Adams observed drily, "No matter what he's paid, it won't be enough." The board also made the symbolic gesture of naming Adams as the university's sitting (not acting) president for the three weeks remaining before I officially took office.[43]

Ironically, though I was quite ready to provide the information, no one ever asked for it again—trustee, reporter, student, parent, or state official.

At the MSU board's next meeting on December 12, the last before I would be assuming office, I reported my intention to resign from twelve outside committees and boards, while submitting for approval a list of six I proposed to continue, including my directorship at Equitable Life.[44] Because I considered the Equitable seat consistent with the university's interest, I stipulated that all my director's fees from Equitable would go directly to MSU. All my corporate director's fees eventually totaled nearly a quarter of a million dollars during my presidency. My decision to donate them was mainly to protect myself from conflict-of-interest and similar charges, but for the university it brought a substantial financial gain. (I eventually followed the same practice later when joining other corporate boards.)

As expected, Huff and White railed against my having any external activities at all, arguing that they were incompatible with the university's mission and that they were exploitative of its reputation. In a pleasant surprise Frank Hartman broke ranks with the other two and voted in favor of approving my outside commitments. With some further grumbling by the troika, the board also approved a presidential expense allowance, though Clair White voted against my being reimbursed for the expenses of moving the family from New York to East Lansing.

▪ The Start

On January 2, 1970, when I took office as president, Michigan State was an unusual if not unique place.

A newcomer was first struck by its enormity, and as John Hannah had emphasized, by the parklike beauty of its grounds. It had an almost idealized look, a "central casting" model of a college. Intersecting the campus's Abbot Road entry, Circle Drive curved around past mostly older buildings such as Agriculture Hall, the Student Union, several women's dorms, and the iconic Beaumont Tower, where the university carillonneur Wendell Wescott rang airs by hand on Sunday evenings. In the spring the botanical gardens flowered gloriously near the main library, and throughout the campus carefully tended trees and shrubs shaded winding paved walkways. South campus was home to academic buildings both old and new. Recently built high-rise dormitories flanked the east and west campus—"living-learning" complexes that combined student housing, classrooms, dining halls, and social and recreational facilities. Out beyond the Grand Trunk Rail tracks and Forest Road were thousands of acres used for the agricultural experiment station, university-run farms, research crops, large- and small-animal husbandry, dairying, and the Forest Akers Golf Course. It was all served by the university's own police force, food services, clinics, bus system, and power plants—virtually everything operated in house, not outsourced to commercial providers, as has become common today. Yet through careful siting and meticulous care of its facilities, the massive scale of things rarely intimidated—it wasn't so much disguised as muted.

Michigan State had experienced explosive growth in the 1950s and 1960s, not only in physical plant[45] and enrollment, but also as a center of academic excellence. Most observers invariably mention Hannah's pursuit of athletics, especially football, as key to building MSU's national image, but they fail to appreciate that while he never missed a football game at home and on the road during his twenty-eight years, he was also skillfully building an incredible center of academic excellence.

One of the most underappreciated aspects of Hannah's leadership had been his active recruitment of bright younger PhDs and other faculty, often recent graduates of the finest colleges and universities in the United States and abroad. His goal was to find and hire the best talents, nurture them, and give them the freedom to grow. If they stayed in East Lansing as their careers blossomed, fine—if after a few years they moved on, the university would have benefited richly while they were Spartans.

Though Hannah was sometimes caricatured by critics as a "chicken farmer with an edifice complex," his real legacy to MSU had been more than two decades of rapid growth in academic excellence, intellectual vigor, creativity, and administrative energy. He had transformed MSU from a little-known agricultural college into an educational powerhouse, with many programs and facilities rivaling or superior to those at top-rank schools across the country. The verification came in 1964 when Michigan State joined the prestigious Association of American Universities, whose members are the top sixty public and private campuses in the United States and Canada. At the same time, the university had staunchly maintained its commitment to its founding land-grant mission. Originally focused on the "agricultural and industrial classes,"[46] it had more recently been extending its reach to new audiences—military veterans and older students, minority students from Detroit and the state's other cities, and middle-class young people, often the first generation of their families to attend a college or university.

Two other things about MSU particularly impressed me. One was that although the majority of its students came from in-state, there was a very substantial enrollment from elsewhere—not only American out-of-staters, but also one of the largest groups of foreign students in the country. This complemented the university's extensive international programs, which reached from Africa to Latin America to Southeast Asia.

The other distinctive feature was Michigan State's commitment to undergraduate education. Even freshmen classes were typically taught by tenure-track instructors and professors, whereas at the University of Michigan and many other elite schools freshman, sophomore, and even some upper-division courses were usually handled by graduate teaching assistants. Little wonder that at the time MSU's enrollment of National Merit Scholars was the highest in the nation.

I was taking over this great university with all its challenges and with a unique "extra"—I was the first Black president of a major research university. My every word, action, and decision would be instantly seized upon, dissected, analyzed, and judged. The weeks and months to come would be daunting—of that I was sure. Survival would be the first prerequisite. Survival in turn would demand success, on several fronts simultaneously and under unusually intense public scrutiny. The customary "honeymoon" wouldn't be in the cards for me.

· · · ·

The board of trustees wanted a formal inauguration ceremony, but I was reluctant to start my job with needless pomp and pageantry—I also was concerned about the cost.[47] I suggested that something "inaugural-like" might be done during spring commencement or another regularly scheduled event. My eventual "inauguration" was at a subsequent board of trustees dinner, where there was a short ceremony of draping me with the MSU president's official bronze medallion on a fine silver chain. For that I got brownie points with the public and the press.

In mid-January I did give an "inaugural" address to the Faculty Club, intentionally avoiding specific proposals. Since it would have been premature at best to talk about my "vision" for the university after only three weeks on campus, I spoke about the personal values that would guide me in the days ahead: a belief in the centrality of individuals, in equal opportunity, in scholarly creativity as the heart of education, and in educational institutions as forces for positive change in the world.[48] Though the overflow audience in the Student Union ballroom gave me a nice ovation, the *State News* blasted the speech as "a rehash of old adages and clichés . . . at best a disappointment."

Well, as Hannah had counseled, I didn't have to read it unless I wanted to.

Even before taking the reins at MSU I had spent many hours talking with key senior people on campus to get a sense of the issues and problems I might have to confront, and the distillate of those interviews became the basis for the first board meeting over which I formally presided, on Friday, January 15.

My first concern was the board itself. Both on campus and in the community, its wrangling was seen almost unanimously as harmful to the university and its reputation. I promised to structure agendas so that trustees could focus on important matters facing the university, with minimum time devoted to nitpicking and bureaucratic procedure. I promised ample advance notice on topics that might be disputatious, and suggested opening certain parts of the board's Thursday evening executive session to the press.[49]

As a beginning I presented to the board the list of challenges put together from my interviews. At the top was student admissions—traditional standards versus "open" enrollment, numbers of out-of-state and minority students. I declared my intention to set up a university-wide commission to grapple with the issues. In the area of administration and personnel, I mentioned the need to energize private fund raising and my plans to create a vice presidency for university relations, to change the location and operation of the university's equal opportunity programs, to develop a full-time position for long-range planning and coordination, and to set up an assistant provost for undergraduate education. Other ideas included better prioritization of physical plant improvements and new buildings (in part to ease the already emerging conflict between plans for a new performing arts center and a new all-events building), as well as dormitory debt service needs and the inadequacy of the Olin Health Center, the student clinic. On the academic side of the ledger, I talked briefly about the improvement of faculty salaries, plans for a new college of osteopathic medicine, a proposed environmental center, the development of a more academic format for urban affairs and ethnic studies, the possibility of establishing a law school, the modernization of continuing education in an era of technology, and a new vision for MSU's international programs.

Student-life questions were high on my list of concerns, including the push for greater involvement in academic governance.[50] I also touched on student demonstrations and disruptions, the deficiencies in student leader elections due to low voting, residential option choice, dorm "open house" rules and women's hours, alcohol consumption in student housing on campus and off, the university's relation to fraternities and sororities, and the availability of the pill and other birth control devices through Olin Center.

I finished up with what I thought might be "hot button" issues in the near future—the status of ROTC on campus, whether campus police should carry arms, the push for a campus Black or African center, and the question of supporting fifth-year student athletes. Finally, I cited the issue of improved statewide coordination of higher education and the need to develop defensible criteria for university "productivity" and "benefit" to the state to offset the pressures from the state legislature on our cost/benefit ratio and funding.

I had covered a lot of bases, but from the trustees there was little overt reaction. In fact, I was confounded by their stony faces. I shouldn't have been—talking about their bickering had probably angered or annoyed them at the outset, and the rest left them numb. Lee Carr, the university attorney, told me later that I had captured everything the university needed to deal with—"and everything they'd prefer to ignore." I appreciated the comment, though at the time I little realized that I had just set forth much of the agenda that would occupy my presidency for years to come. Surprisingly, press coverage of the Board meeting mainly covered the controversy over proposals for an all-events building versus a performing arts center and the appointment of a new chancellor, Donald O'Dowd, at MSU's branch campus Oakland University.

My first two months were filled with meetings, get-acquainted sessions, and numerous off-campus speeches. The venues ranged from the Boy Scouts to the Michigan Press Association. One out of which Dolores and I got quite a charge was the Michigan Annual Agricultural Conference dinner, attended by about a thousand people, including the governor, 148 state legislators, and their spouses. Held at Kellogg Center, the event was nicknamed the "loot bag dinner"—at each place setting was piled a cornucopia of agricultural products—yogurt, cereals, grape juice, bacon, carrots, chicken franks, potato flakes, butter, dried cherries, apples, onions, sugar, asparagus, and more—all produced in Michigan.[51] Over the back of each chair hung a mesh potato bag with which to tote them away. The sight of these normally sober leaders hurriedly filling their bags before sitting down was unforgettable. It was great PR for the university!

· · · ·

I had been at Michigan State about six weeks when I had to face my first student demonstration.

On February 19 somewhere between five hundred and a thousand students collected to protest against the guilty verdicts in the "Chicago Seven" conspiracy trial.[52] After an evening rally at Beaumont Tower, the crowd flowed across Grand River and into East Lansing; soon glass was shattering loudly at City Hall. Five abreast in riot gear, police pushed the students back onto campus, but within minutes they flooded back, and the trashing spread to restaurants and retail stores up and down the street that divided town from gown.

The clashes continued intermittently until nearly midnight, when Dick Bernitt, head of the MSU campus police, came to Cowles House suggesting that I speak to the rioting students. It was a true "Who, me?" moment—what on earth was I supposed to say? But Bernitt was savvy enough to understand a basic law of crisis management: go, be seen, do *something*. Struggling into our winter coats, Dolores and I trudged across West Circle Drive to the Student Union, escorted by Bernitt and a couple of his officers. On the Union steps, pelted with sleet and snow, fumbling with an unfamiliar bullhorn above a yelling mob of students (and a few professors), I launched into my appeal: "Students of Michigan State, these activities are highly counterproductive!"

To my lame sally the student response was predictably scatological. Fortunately a massive young Black student (Ken Little, a former football player from Florida) shouted them down, telling them to shut up and listen. Once they quieted, I suggested that they go back to their dorms, reorganize, and consider buying television time to air their grievances with the outcome of the trial in Chicago. It was a hapless idea, and it drew only further hoots and jeers. Among the most vocal was a partially bald older man with a scraggly white mustache, who was egging the students on from the rear fringe of the crowd. Bernitt later identified him as Professor Lash Larrowe, the campus gadfly who had been so dubious about my years of involvement in Southeast Asia.

Before the night was over twenty people had been hurt by flying rocks and other missiles, including a police officer hit in the back of the head by a brick.

At least there had been a moment of bleak humor. Clifton 3rd, who had remained in New York to finish his senior year at the Dalton School, flew in that evening for his first visit. Because of the demonstration, neither Dolores nor I could meet his plane, so she told him by telephone to take a taxi to campus. When he arrived, the driver refused to turn into the campus melee, so Clifton got out to walk—in his long hair, jeans, granny glasses, and peace button, looking just like all the protestors. When he cut across West Circle toward Cowles House, a campus police officer intercepted him and demanded to know where he was going.

At six foot four and already a very assured lad, Clifton said, "I'm here to see my mother and father. He's the president of the university."

"Right," said the skeptical policeman. "Let's see your ID." Clifton complied, and the officer exclaimed, "Jeez, you really *are* his son!"

That night Clifton 3rd experienced the demonstration firsthand. Initially he quietly blended into the crowd, but the campus police made him join us on the building steps to ensure his safety. Years later he admitted his shock when he moved from the crowd, with which he identified as an activist student, to standing beside us facing a yelling, chanting mob. His changed perspective made a dramatic impact.

I had my own lesson. This first student demonstration convinced me that I quickly needed to develop major communication and outreach activities with the student body, as well as to prepare techniques for dealing with such confrontations in the future. The only problem was, I discovered, no one knew how to do it—there was no such presidential manual.

· · · ·

Although hardly as dramatic as coping with student unrest, one of my earliest and most important tasks was to review the senior administrators on whom I would be relying henceforth. My intuition was that they were a competent and effective team, but as an outsider I knew I would need time to get to know them, gauge their areas of strength and weakness, and earn their trust.

MSU's provost and vice president for academic affairs was John Cantlon, a nationally known plant ecologist. Previously a recipient of the university's distinguished faculty award, Cantlon was a first-class academic with an amiable disposition and snow-white sideburns. His personality and credentials made him a fine chief academic officer. He had been named provost only recently, on Walter Adams's recommendation. After probing gently but thoroughly to make sure there had been no quid pro quo, I was content that he would be very effective remaining in the position.

At thirty-five, Roger Wilkinson was young for his slot as acting vice president for business and finance, and he was working from a hot seat already. Well before my arrival, trustee Warren Huff had set his sights on the position, and given Roger's youth, it must have looked like low-hanging fruit. Of course, after Huff's behavior over the last several months, I would have assigned the post to Lucifer first. After observing Wilkinson for a few months, I thought he deserved the chance to show what he could do in a permanent capacity. He was bright, energetic, genial, and sophisticated beyond his years—also, I guessed he knew where all the proverbial fiscal "cookie jars" were buried. Anyway, I was only forty-three, myself—who was I to cast a stone?

Milton Muelder, vice president for research and graduate studies, was a political scientist, historian, and internationalist—he prided himself on speaking several foreign languages. He had been on the MSU faculty since 1935, eventually occupying several key administrative posts. A former chair of the Michigan Civil Service Commission, he was active in a number of state and national academic associations.

Gordon Sabine, vice president for special projects, had an eclectic set of responsibilities. Famous for having engineered MSU's astonishingly successful program of recruiting National Merit Scholars, he was known as an infighter and something of a prima donna.

Jack Breslin, secretary to the board of trustees, was the university's point man with the legislature. As an undergraduate he had been an MSU football star, and decades later he still "bled green and white," wearing his love of the institution on his sleeve. His new title of executive vice president entailed no substantial change in duties—it had been engineered among the trustees during the fight over my appointment as president—but in Jack himself I sensed no taste for subterfuge or intrigue.

Milt Dickerson, vice president for Student Affairs, was a subdued-seeming former professor of business, now an academic bureaucrat. He was also a former FBI agent—I wondered how many SDSers and campus Black Panthers had any idea!

I was bemused to learn that the university general counsel, Lee Carr, was a principal of the Lansing firm Anderson, Carr, Street & Hornbach. The son of a former chief justice of the Michigan Supreme Court, he was a shrewd lawyer and dedicated Spartan alumnus, even though his law degree was from University of Michigan. His work ethic was awesome—I never understood how he could handle the legal affairs of a megaversity essentially on a part-time basis.

I would soon come to realize that perhaps the most valuable member of my immediate office was Elliott G. "Al" Ballard, my executive assistant. Al had been the key budget staffer for the Michigan House of Representatives and later executive director of the Michigan Council of State College Presidents. John Hannah had recruited him, and he stayed on during the Adams interregnum. In an office adjoining mine, Ballard could invariably be depended upon to tell me what he really thought and was uncompromisingly honest. There is nothing more dangerous for a chief executive than having an inner circle of sycophants who tell you only what they think you want to hear, and who will not give you their genuine opinions. Al had a candid honesty all his own, and for candor he was in a class by himself. While Jack Breslin was my official political emissary, Al's intimate knowledge of state government made him a priceless second opinion on legislative strategy and politics.

I could have used a dozen Al Ballards. He loved smoking foul cigars, writing clever doggerel, playing golf, and Michigan State University. In a manner astringently direct, no-nonsense, yet nonpatronizing, he always got right to the heart of things. His gruff, occasionally sour humor somehow charmed almost everybody, even the most trenchant faculty cranks and bullheaded student radicals. Supplicants and critics alike often left his office not entirely mollified, but chuckling despite themselves.

Al made what turned out to be an excellent recommendation—to recruit James Spani-olo as another executive assistant. Spaniolo had just finished his BA at MSU, where he had been editor of the *State News*. Al argued he would bring a broad, up-to-the-minute student perspective to the office, something we sorely needed.

In addition to the old hands, there were some vacancies to be filled, for which Don Stevens suggested several candidates. I felt I owed Stevens, as a person critically involved in my election, the courtesy of at least interviewing any persons he suggested. Also, I suspected that, given the division among the trustees, Stevens had a vested interest in my succeeding and therefore would likely make useful recommendations.

One of his suggestions was Robert Perrin, then acting director of the federal Office of Economic Opportunity in Washington. A Democratic holdover uneasy in the Nixon administration, Perrin was a former *Detroit Free Press* reporter who had become senior aide to U.S. senator Pat McNamara, for whom he had worked ten years before taking the job at OEO. I was surprised to learn that Warren Huff had once approached Perrin about becoming MSU's vice president for business. Despite the tangential association with Huff, I thought he would be effective as vice president for university affairs and federal relations, a new position subsuming the university's information services, publications, and affirmative action. Although I could tell he wasn't overjoyed at the last duty, he agreed to take on that nettlesome area.

Another Stevens suggestion was Ira Polley, who had been Michigan's state comptroller under two administrations, then superintendent of education. Although a Democrat, Polley had sided with Governor Milliken in a recent attempt to abolish the State Board of Education. When the reform effort failed, he was forced out. I thought he would be a good director of admissions at Michigan State. When offered the post, I could sense that he had hoped for a higher one, but he accepted with good grace.

Stevens's final recommendation was Les Scott, whom I thought might be able to help get the university's private fund-raising program off the ground. Up to then, private dollars hadn't been a priority—John Hannah and others had felt that securing funds from private sources, especially in good economic times, would just give the state of Michigan an excuse to reduce its own annual appropriations. However, Hannah had been skilled at successfully cultivating high income individual donors whose names dotted buildings around the campus. But now we were entering a period of reduced support from public coffers, and I thought that Scott could help in jump-starting MSU's efforts in raising funds directly from nonpublic donors. A graduate of the university's School of Hotel, Restaurant, and Institutional manage-ment, Scott had worked for years in a variety of management jobs at MSU[53] before leaving to become president of Fred Harvey, Inc. When I got in touch with him, he was head of AMF, the national sporting goods manufacturer and franchiser. He was strongly interested in what I had in mind. But he wanted to complete his contractual commitment at AMF and protect his stock options and pension. I agreed to hold the job open, thinking he would eventually prove a solid member of the team.

When I brought my choices to the board of trustees, Huff and his cohorts vigorously opposed Perrin's appointment,[54] even though he had previously suggested that Bob throw his hat in the ring to be a university vice president. He objected to Bob's being also given tenure—a ploy to raise the hackles of the faculty by pointing out Bob had not undergone the traditional peer review of his scholarship. Huff claimed that he wanted to be certain that the appointment was not "political." He stated, "I am unalterably opposed to using the university for personal or political patronage." Howls of disbelief echoed across the campus.[55] At this point, I realized that he and the troika would oppose anything that I recommended, even hypocritically and inconsistently with their own previous positions. Could their disappointment or anger or hatred be so intense that they would completely reverse their prior positions?

• • • •

The internal administration needed to change. Hannah had called the weekly meeting of vice presidents the "Breakfast Group" because they met for an early breakfast at Kellogg Center. I felt the group needed greater formality and clarity, so I changed their name to the "Executive Group," who would now meet in my conference room at 9:00 A.M. on Mondays. The Group consisted principally of the university's senior vice presidents, plus direct-report executive staff such as Al Ballard. Similarly, I set up regular meetings of the deans, called the "Administrative Group," to provide me with a channel for direct communication with the chief academic administrators of the sixteen colleges. These governance structures were designed to increase my regular interaction with key nonacademic and academic administrators, as well as strengthen my ability to tap their knowledge and competence in running the university.

Although new to Michigan State—new to running any university, for that matter—I was fortunate in the support offered from the outset by many of the school's leading scholars. In the early days in particular, great help came from my friend Professor Jim Bonnen. The son of a distinguished professor at Texas A&M, Jim had an easygoing, down-home manner that belied a keen and probing intelligence. He also had the rare ability to combine meticulous empirical analysis with a focus on policy, honed during a tour as senior staff economist with the president's Council of Economic Advisers (1963–65). By 1970 Bonnen had become a nationally respected agricultural economist, specializing in public policy, information systems theory, and statistically based decision systems. When I arrived at MSU he was involved in directing a major study called "The Role of the University," cosponsored by the Carnegie Corporation and the National Association of State Universities and Land-Grant Colleges. The areas he was exploring were acutely relevant for my own new undertaking, and we began an extended dialogue on the future of Michigan State. Working with Jim helped me think through and express more clearly what I wanted to accomplish at MSU—to develop a philosophical framework for the initiatives I would pursue in the years ahead.

In 1970 I created an MSU Executive Group to strengthen internal governance. (*Left to right*) me, president; Milt Dickerson, vice president for Student Affairs; Robert Perrin, Vice President for University Affairs and Federal Relations; John Cantlon, provost; Elliott G. "Al" Ballard, assistant to the president; James Spaniolo, assistant to the president; Roger Wilkinson, vice president for business and finance; Leland W. Carr, university attorney; Milton Muelder, vice president for research and graduate studies; Jack Breslin, newly titled executive vice president and secretary to the board.

It didn't take long to find out the difference between being a foundation administrator and being a university president. The range of situations and issues a president faces is extraordinarily broad. A campus is a small, tight, complex community—in Michigan State's case, not all that small! You are, as they say, where the buck stops—the visionary leader, the disciplinarian, cheerleader, fund-raiser, and crisis manager. Your constituencies include students, faculty, families, staff, alumni, sports boosters, business and labor leaders, government officials, accreditation agencies, athletic conferences, education associations, donors, and more. Each group, of course, considers itself paramount.

. . . .

Dolores and I quickly realized we were living in a fish bowl. It is hard for most people to understand the intense level and scope of scrutiny involved, and how it covers the entire immediate family. In Michigan, four public officeholders were automatically conferred celebrity:

the governor, the mayor of Detroit, and the presidents of Michigan and Michigan State. Wherever Dolores and I went, whatever we did, we were the objects of constant scrutiny—in those early days, moreover, intensified by race. Nothing seemed too trivial to publicize. When we needed a replacement for Cowles House's retiring chef, the student union manager whose office oversaw operations for the residence asked Dolores if she had any particular preferences. She mentioned in passing that it would be nice if the new chef could do Asian food, a cuisine we had come to love. The manager played it to the hilt, giving the press a headline reading, "She Wants a Chinese Cook." Dolores soon shifted responsibility for Cowles House operations, food, and entertainment to Bob Emerson, director of the Kellogg Center, who was perfect.

On another occasion, the principal of Central Elementary School, where our ten-year-old son Bruce had been enrolled, called Dolores about a local reporter who had shown up at the school. The principal asked if we had given permission for him to follow Bruce around the school and to observe how his classmates accepted him. An aghast Dolores told the principal she had not, and the school escorted the reporter out of the building. Even our young son had no privacy.

Then there was the *State News* reporter who interviewed Dolores for an hour, talking about our years in Southeast Asia, her professional field of art history, and her forthcoming book on contemporary artists of Malaysia, among other matters. Near the end of the session the budding journalist asked what Dolores thought of graffiti in the New York subways. (At the time there were debates in the press between those who considered graffiti a new frontier of artistic expression and those who thought it just ugly vandalism.) Dolores said she thought the jury was out, but any kind of human expression deserved a fair hearing. After the story came out in the *State News*, the *Detroit Free Press* picked it up under the headline, "MSU's First Lady a Graffiti Lover."[56]

By the end of my first month in office I began to duck interviews—big mistake. After I turned down a request from a reporter for the *Lansing State Journal*, the publisher, Louis Weil, insisted on coming to see me in person. He was a longtime friend of John Hannah. Common hearsay was that the two men, with Howard J. Stoddard, founder of Michigan National Bank, were the three most powerful leaders in the state. Weil wanted me to understand why press contacts were important, even when we knew we sometimes wouldn't like the stories that came out of them. The press, Weil insisted, could be an important resource for me, especially if I were always open and evenhanded. "Even if you don't want to answer a question," he said, "always call back to say so. Eventually mutual trust would develop, even when the two sides disagree."

Weil was absolutely right. Eventually I got to know a number of journalists who were fair, accurate, and—within the constraints of reportorial independence—supportive. In addition to Weil, there were Frank Angelo, publisher of the *Detroit Free Press*; Helen Clegg of the *Lansing State Journal*; Jeanne Whittaker of the *Detroit News*; and Tom Jones, the editorial writer for

Lansing radio station WJIM. But I also learned two cardinal rules for press relations: there's no such thing as off the record, and you can't be crucified in print for something you didn't say.

· · · ·

Learning how to be a university president was mostly on-the-job training. The American Council on Education had a yearly program for new presidents, but the timing didn't fit my crisis schedule. Early on President Robben Fleming invited me to Ann Arbor to talk with him about administration at the University of Michigan. John Hannah had previously done the same when Fleming was new at the University of Michigan. My visit to our rival campus provided useful insights. A bit later Father Ted Hesburgh of Notre Dame made a similar offer, though circumstances prevented my taking him up on it.

A different hands-on sort of training came from Dick Bernitt, head of campus public safety. Every morning he called at 7:30 sharp with his incident report on the past twenty-four hours. I got to hear all about the students who had passed out behind the library from too much booze (or something) . . . spouse abuse in the Cherry Lane apartments for married students . . . athletes spraying dorm hallways with fire hoses . . . attempted suicides by students on the verge of flunking out . . . faculty members arrested in drag in downtown Lansing at midnight. Then there was the day Al Ballard told me about the power plant that was spewing heavy coal particulates into the air all over campus. "Well," I told him, "we've got plenty of good scientists around here. Let's get them together, have them do a study, then recommend the best way to proceed." Al looked at me whimsically. "Boss," he said, "the state environment department wants an answer in two days."

It wasn't exactly what I had expected as an academic administrator, but eventually I began to get used to it. I relied a lot on intuition. One habit became asking myself what I thought John Hannah would have done in a given situation. Hannah had run the university incredibly well during his years, and no one could have denied his skills and wisdom. Although Hannah had run Michigan State for twenty-eight years, he never second-guessed my leadership there. In fact, he didn't visit the campus at all for five years after my election. On his first visit after his self-imposed moratorium, he telephoned in advance to let me know he was coming. He didn't need to do that, I protested. "Listen," he replied, "I know that campus. Ten minutes after I set foot there, somebody's going to let you know, and you'll wonder what the dickens I'm up to." And the call came.

Of course, Hannah and I were different people, with different personalities and attitudes. More important, the times were different. John (like many of his peers in the Big Ten) was not greatly enamored of participatory governance. While command and control had worked well during his decades of building the university, nowadays students were pressing for more say in their own education, and faculty were demanding a greater role in institutional governance. Alumni and the public at large wanted their voices to be heard, too.

In the emerging era of multiple "stakeholders," another style of leadership was needed.

As I came to see, Michigan State University almost was a municipality in itself. Like any municipality, we had our own police force and grounds and maintenance staff, as well as the largest university housing complex in the world, with twenty-seven residence halls (including three-times-a-day food service for the 17,800 residents), married student apartments for 2,200 (not including children), two power plants, a medical clinic, a radio station, and a daily newspaper (student run)—in fact everything except our own fire department. And I was the "mayor."

But the university campus was also a unique *kind* of municipality—what I called a "city of youth."[57] The vast majority of its "citizens" were between eighteen and twenty-three, and their interaction with older adults was confined on campus to classrooms and laboratories. Far more of their day-to-day contacts were with their own age group, whose ideas and values could transcend differences in background, income, race, and even intelligence. And at that moment, young Americans' ideas and values were in a maelstrom. An unprecedented clamor was rising among students for personal "liberation"—the right to do what they wanted, say what they wanted, be what they wanted. With all the self-righteousness of youth, they attacked their elders' complacency and materialism, as well as what they saw as the shibboleths and failures of society. With the demise of in loco parentis, little more than self-discipline was left to regulate student behavior. And all too often "freedom" translated as unbounded license, with no responsibility or liability. One important step in April was my creating a Student Advisory Group, drawing upon heads of key student organizations: Associated Students of Michigan State University (ASMSU), the *State News*, the women's interresidence council, the men's hall association, the interfraternity group and Pan-Hellenic association, the Black Liberation Front, and the council of graduate students. They would meet with me regularly and become a useful sounding board where I could interact with student leaders.

Initially the older citizens of the university municipality, its faculty and administrators, viewed the new rebellion a bit indulgently, considering it just the latest manifestation of the age-old revolt of every generation against its predecessor. But before long it became obvious that it was something quite different from swallowing goldfish, chugging too much beer, and panty raids on shrieking sorority houses.

• • • •

Saturday, April 25, was a glorious spring day, and the sap was rising after a long Michigan winter. Case Hall residence was celebrating a "festival of life," and at some point a few of the of frolicking students decided to "liberate" the grassy lawn in front of the dorm. Pulling up several metal posts and a chain fence, the students declared the space a "People's Park"—though not with any social message like its University of California, Berkeley, namesake. The students pitched three tents and fetched sleeping bags, vowing to spend the night.

The tents violated a university ordinance, and the students knew it. The campers waited to see what the "grown-ups" would do, while their dorm-mates watched out the windows from inside.

When the matter reached official ears, the VP for student affairs chuckled. "It's just spring fever. Let them alone and they'll be back in their rooms by tomorrow."

The next day thirty tents dotted the Case Hall lawn. As the area got more and more crowded, the students decided to liberate additional space, between Erickson Hall, the International Center, and Wells Hall, next to the Red Cedar River. It was a spot I could see from my office window.

By the time more than a hundred tents had been pitched, the *State News* and a couple of TV stations were on the scene, and the rest of the student body was enjoying the drama. Although the tent people claimed to be a "communal alternative" with no leaders, two campers privately promised that if we let them continue to sleep outside, the area would be kept orderly and students would use lavatory facilities in the nearby buildings. Trying to arrest or forcibly clear them out was problematic and could have led to ugliness, so with some misgivings I decided to see whether time alone would resolve the problem.

▪ Student Demonstrations

On Friday, May 1, President Nixon announced his decision to send U.S. troops into Cambodia. Among students, reaction to Nixon's move was nearly instantaneous and spread rapidly. Across the country campuses exploded in protest—not only at places like Berkeley and the University of Wisconsin–Madison, but even at small campuses such as Union College and Hobart, in upstate New York. Nixon was burned in effigy, demonstrators pelted police with rocks and brickbats, and ROTC offices were firebombed.

Michigan State was no exception.[58] An MSU committee against ROTC held a peaceful rally that afternoon. ROTC was a visible reminder of the military on campus and an easy target for those who detested the U.S. war in Vietnam. Earlier in the week the group had presented demands on abolishing ROTC at MSU and canceling all university contracts with the military. Since I was in Flint giving a speech, Bob Perrin read a statement to the crowd from the Administration Building steps. When told that two faculty committees and a majority of students had already voted to keep ROTC on campus, the protesters jeered. Four hundred or so broke away and headed for the International Center. There they staged a sit-in, with rowdy, obscenity-laced tirades against Nixon, the war, imperialism, and "the pigs."

After the speeches started to run down, the protesters voted to stay in the building, barricading themselves in with furniture. When campus police made no attempt to dislodge them, many slowly drifted away. About 250 split off to try to take over Demonstration Hall, where ROTC offices were housed.

Back from Flint, I had, on advice from Dick Bernitt and others, requested outside help, and 265 police from five different law enforcement agencies had joined our own campus police to confront the demonstrators. Dick Bernitt wisely insisted that every outside officer be paired with one of his own men. Since many of our police officers were themselves either former or current MSU students, they were familiar with the student body and the activist leaders. The practice gave Bernitt greater control over the off-campus police and helped avoid blunders and overreactions due to their unfamiliarity with the university community.

With a double line of blue-helmeted officers blocking their way, the Demonstration Hall (coincidentally the building's real name) protestors hurled taunts and obscenities—then bricks and bottles. When a Molotov cocktail shattered a window and set a fire inside, the police responded with tear gas. Coughing and cursing, the mob broke up. But smaller bands now took off about the campus on rounds of trashing—spraying paint, breaking windows, blocking intersections to traffic. Fast and dispersed, the guerilla marauding was difficult for the police to suppress, and the pillage flared intermittently into the early morning hours.

By time things settled down, the property damage was extensive. Besides seven campus police cars, it involved Olin Health Center, the main Library, South Kedzie and Linton dorms, Ag and Olds halls, and the home economics building. The worst, about $35,000 worth, was at the Hannah Administration Building, where demonstrators hurled heavy concrete benches through the floor-to-ceiling plate-glass windows of the main lobby. Five campus police were injured. Two eighteen-year-old men, one a student and the other not, were arrested, and a third student was subsequently charged with arson in connection with the firebombing at Demonstration Hall.

I got back to Cowles House around two in the morning, exhausted. Worse, I was stunned at the uprising's intensity and its obviously calculated destruction. How could such wanton violence break out at a great university?

No one had instructions on how to deal with student protests of this magnitude. So I needed to develop my own guidelines to follow in handling this and any future demonstrations. I developed four unwavering policies:

1. Never compromise the university's core principles such as academic freedom and defending the right of divergent views to be heard. Broken windows could be replaced, but once the core values of academe were abandoned the damage would be irreparable. Otherwise the university would lose its central role as a place where conflicting ideas could contend in civilized discourse in the search for truth.

2. Emphasize the difference between acceptable forms of dissent or protest and the illegal ones. This policy was responding to a gradual shift that was taking place in the patterns of social protest in the United States from civil to uncivil. There was a move away from Gandhian nonviolent, passive resistance such as the civil rights movement into

the more extreme forms of protest against the Vietnam War, generating illegal, even violent acts.

3. Base my actions upon unquestioned integrity and, hopefully, fairness. Even those who might disagree with my decisions or statements should recognize and accept that I had listened and seriously considered their views before arriving at my decisions.

4. Conduct myself with calmness and dignity whatever the circumstances. The chants, screams, and epithets were the tactical currency of demonstrators, usually designed to intimidate and to produce either reactive anger or capitulation. When met with calm response and without fear, this tactical ploy failed. Most important, the office of the president should be respected regardless of the occupant, and in my case it was especially important that I do nothing to demean the reputation handed down to me by Hannah.

▪ ▪ ▪ ▪

Within a few days, student protests over the Cambodia invasion reached a level of intensity never before seen on a nationwide basis. Though I had too much on my hands to think about U.S. policies at the time, I was angry and frustrated by our ongoing missteps in a region about which I had extensive personal knowledge and to which I had formed a strong attachment. Ho Chi Minh, I thought, was a nationalist through and through, hardly a Russian client, and with a long-standing antipathy toward China shared by most Vietnamese. The United States' famed "domino theory" seemed to me mistakenly based on mostly unreal ideological affinities, rather than on actual national histories and cultures. And it totally discounted the failure of postcolonial regimes to address mass poverty and disenfranchisement in Southeast Asia. But, as president of MSU, I maintained a public posture against the war without becoming a spokesman for the protesters.

Demonstrations and strikes, sometimes with violence, were sweeping across the country. National television news was filled with pictures of angry students burning their draft cards or the U.S. flag, taunting police in riot gear, and chanting for an end to the Vietnam War. It was as if the nation had exploded into a civil war—sparked by college students. National Guard troops were used to quell demonstrations at the University of Wisconsin and Ohio State, and the governors of Maryland, Oklahoma, and New Mexico ordered their Guards to an alert or standby status. There was an ongoing general strike at Stanford, and there were conflicts with police at the University of California, Berkeley, and fire bombings at the Universities of Utah, Illinois, and Kentucky. Brown, Tufts, and Boston University announced termination of classes for the rest of the academic year. The "Groves of Academe" were in turmoil as never seen before—and Michigan State was part of it.

As if all that weren't enough, on May 4 a contingent of National Guardsmen, called in to a campus demonstration, shot four students a Kent State University in Ohio. Jeffrey Miller, one of those killed, had transferred there only four months before from Michigan State. The violence the students decried in Vietnam and Cambodia had now come to their own doorsteps, and the resulting dismay and revulsion energized many who had previously been on the sidelines.

At MSU the escalating disruptions exacerbated our concern over "People's Park," potentially a safe haven for violent protestors. On Sunday, May 3, Assistant Dean of Students Louis Hekhuis visited the scene and asked the occupants to leave. But despite lengthy negotiations between the administration and student leaders,[59] the campers refused to disperse.

▪ ▪ ▪ ▪

Throughout the tumult, there was still a university to maintain. The incongruity came home vividly one afternoon in campus police headquarters, where I was listening to radio reports on demonstrators marching along Farm Lane. Looking out a window at the same time, I could also see hundreds of MSU students, quite absorbed in football and baseball games on the intramural playing fields. The student demonstrators at MSU never exceeded 10 percent (or four thousand), though the number of student sympathizers who were against the war was much larger. Still four thousand is a large number of people.

On May 4 a national student strike committee convened at George Washington University with the aim of closing down colleges and universities to protest the Cambodia incursion. That evening a newly formed MSU strike committee rallied five hundred students, who afterward began canvassing the dorms with leaflets that called for picketing classrooms the next day. In addition to abolishing ROTC, the group's demands now included withdrawing the U.S. from Indochina and freeing the Black leader Bobby Seale, then in jail for kidnapping and murder. Constantly adding more demands, it seemed, was a classic way for the protestors to attempt broadening their base of support. And though most MSU students seemed not overly exercised over ROTC and Bobby Seale, they were increasingly upset and irate over Cambodia and the killings at Kent State.

Monday class attendance was normal, and the protest leaders called for another demonstration at noon Tuesday at Beaumont Tower, their favorite rallying point. The central campus landmark was a stone's throw from Cowles House, so Dolores and I could gauge the crowd's numbers from our windows.

I deliberately chose the noon hour to appear on the university's closed-circuit TV network. In the broadcast I told the campus that I supported the right to protest, but without violence, and I asked students to find peaceful outlets to voice their concerns. I suggested a petition drive to gauge student sentiment comprehensively, whose results could be presented to Michigan's congressional delegation. I condemned the previous Friday's on-campus destruction—rather than attacking the university, I thought the students should focus their attention on Washington, D.C. And I added that I personally thought that expanding the war in Indochina was a great error and miscalculation.

That afternoon about four thousand demonstrators converged on the Administration Building, where I reread the statement. Though the line about Cambodia being a serious miscalculation drew scattered applause, it was clear nothing would satisfy the leaders but closing down the school—which I had no intention of doing. The demonstrators then left for a "death march" about the campus, their already large numbers continuing to grow.

In the evening my Executive Group met from nine until almost midnight to thrash out strategies and options. In the middle of the session we got word that the board of the ASMSU had voted fourteen to nothing in favor of shutting down classes and furloughing university staff "until such time as all American troops are withdrawn from Cambodia." They also wanted the university to sever all ties with ROTC and (a new demand) campus police to cease carrying firearms.

However satisfying it might have been to the protestors, canceling classes wasn't in the cards—it would have put the university in breach of contract, in effect, with the large majority of tuition-paying students who expected their education to go on uninterrupted. We put out a statement to that effect. Provost John Cantlon reported that the previous day's class attendance had been down slightly but not alarmingly.

On Wednesday, May 6, picketing began at 8:00 A.M. at five classroom buildings. Throughout the day protestors sporadically sat-in or formed human chains to block campus entrances and streets, including Bogue, Abbot, Beal, and West Circle Drive. When campus police arrived at Bessey Hall to roust the sitters from Farm Lane, the strikers jumped back to the curbs. After police started taking pictures, the strikers ran back and forth across the street until a passing motorist accidentally hit one, causing minor injuries.

I spent almost the entire day using a police Quonset hut as a command post. I talked with Governor Milliken several times. "If you need me to call in the Guard, let me know," he said, "but I won't without your approval." Subsequently he said the same to the press. The governor's strong support while depending upon my command post judgment was a great gift.

In the afternoon some seven thousand students (including those from many other Michigan universities), the most to date, rallied at Beaumont Tower to honor the four slain Kent State students. Despite chants of "Pig U" and "Close it down," the crowd was peaceful. There were music and speeches, and Jackie Vaughn, a Black state representative, urged the students to continue their memorial. Then a column "eight to ten deep and stretching six blocks long"[60] marched to the MSU Chapel for a brief service. Afterward a thousand or so continued on to Demonstration Hall, ROTC headquarters, on whose parade ground they planted four white crosses bearing the names of the Kent State students.

Although it got little notice at the time, that night campus police arrested Michael Pierce, a former student, carrying two two-inch metal pipes filled with gunpowder and wicks. When Dick Bernitt told me about it the next morning, I took a deep breath and said a silent prayer of thanks. With even one explosion or death, the situation might have spiraled irrecoverably out of control.

The demonstrators were well organized, and I soon learned the importance of knowing who was in charge. There were essentially two factions: those who wanted to keep the protests peaceful, and those who would stop at nothing, including violence, to make their point. Luckily the former predominated at MSU, although an additional complication was the presence of non-students attracted from elsewhere by the escalating agitation.

Time after time I had to confront a crowd of hostile students (and often a sprinkling of faculty), but I had learned from my time with Nelson Rockefeller in Latin America that if someone really wants to harm you and doesn't care what subsequently happens to himself, there is virtually no way to protect yourself. Often with Dolores at my side, I stood face to face in front of a jeering mob, answering challenges and presenting views without showing any intimidation. I could usually deal rationally with the young people who really cared about the war. The hard ones to talk with tended to be smug, self-righteous, and inflexible, with a whole grab bag of often unrelated demands. Not surprisingly, their intractability gradually undercut their influence among more sophisticated students.

By the time the demonstrations had gone on for a week, public pressure began to mount on government officials. State legislators pointed out that there was little they could do—Michigan's three biggest universities, where protests were widest spread and most intense, were constitutionally autonomous. Moreover, lawmakers were reluctant to cut university budgets because of the harm it would do to the student majority not involved in sit-ins, marches, and strikes. With Lee Carr's help we discouraged Ingham County prosecutor Raymond Scodeller from calling in the National Guard, which had already demonstrated its capacity to precipitate violence. Nonetheless one Republican state representative, Philip O. Pittenger, submitted a resolution calling for the resignation of the Big Three presidents, including me. The resolution accused us of blaming President Nixon for our own failure to cope with mob rule, and even of sympathizing with the rampagers.

Governor Milliken called Pittenger's blast "asinine and irresponsible,"[61] but the representative had gotten fifteen fellow legislators to endorse his proposal, which accurately reflected the views of many Michiganders. People were understandably upset, even outraged, by TV news broadcasts showing students overrunning the campus and the surrounding community. Half a dozen alumni sent back their diplomas, claiming to be ashamed to be MSU graduates, and others wrote to say they would no longer contribute to the university.

Yet the students were the citizens' own children, and keeping them safe in the midst of the turmoil often meant having to bend without breaking. After a long evening meeting of the Executive Group, we decided to suspend classes on Friday in favor of a "teach-in" to address the war and other issues that concerned the demonstrating students. It would be a joint effort between the administration and students, including several leaders of the strike. Workshop topics included "External Pressures on the University," "Race Issues," "The Campus Police," "The War in Indochina," and "Tools of Effective Protest." Each workshop would be run by a student, with faculty assigned as resource persons. MSU's Black faculty and students announced their own teach-in for Friday as well, which focused on racial justice in the United States and in the academic community.

I attended some of the Friday teach-in sessions, most of them well organized and effectively run. The next morning, Saturday, the Executive Group met for three hours to draft a "Report from the President" to be distributed on campus and off, clarifying the university's position on the strike and related issues. John Cantlon reported that Friday's class attendance had been down by about 25 percent. More serious was the news that several academic units were proposing to shut down for the duration, including the Department of Social Work, Justin Morrill College, and some parts of Psychology and Sociology. For Cantlon it was a delicate situation. On one hand, he didn't want to intrude into the internal management of academic units. On the other, he couldn't allow faculty to shirk their teaching duties. (A faculty–graduate assistants strike committee soon recognized the dilemma and added to their list a demand that amnesty go to any faculty member who joined the strike.) Working with the University's Academic Council, John eventually crafted a compromise: anyone who for reasons of conscience did not want to continue teaching would be required to submit final grades for all students in his or her classes.

Student reporters from the *State News* criticized me for not meeting with the strikers—and from their perspective they were probably right, but I felt that any contact should be limited. The strikers' principal tactic was the "nonnegotiable" demand—and acceding to three or four out of five wasn't enough. The expectation was all or nothing, total capitulation. "The real world doesn't work that way," I commented, to no avail. But whatever I negotiated was something I might have to live with for a long time. Even in the heat of the moment, I couldn't let myself be pressured into an agreement that in the cold light of later day might prove unworkable, even disastrous.

On-campus reaction to my "Report from the President" was mixed, depending on whether you were for or against the proposed strike. Among other things, the document declared that the university couldn't endorse a strike that would close its classrooms, especially given the practical ramifications—an extended school year, the disruption of campus services, the interruption of student financial assistance, grants and fellowships, veterans benefits, and more. We declined to disarm campus police, adding that the university had no authority to interfere with city, county, and state law enforcement officers performing their duties. We reported on steps to bring the ROTC question before the Academic Council. On Black enrollment, we pointed out that it had increased threefold since 1967, based on providing adequate financial aid and support services rather than proclaiming destined-to-fail quotas. I also mentioned a newly created commission on admissions and student body composition, to which students and others could submit their views.

Now there was no doubt where the university stood on the issues.

At 1:00 P.M. on Monday, May 11, another Beaumont Tower rally drew three thousand students, who heard reports from the strike leaders, plus pleas for lodging for students from other campuses who would be converging on MSU for marches on the state capitol planned for Wednesday and Thursday. A few lines from one of the speeches offer a glimpse of the thinking, which by now had clearly slipped poet John Magee's "surly bonds of earth"[62]:

> We are striking to demonstrate our outrage at this society. Not only that, but striking is a peaceful way to withhold goods and services from those in power. We are the goods, and the instructors are withholding their services.
>
> When we say "shut it down," we only mean it's time to stop filling our heads with knowledge that is useless at best and address ourselves instead to those issues and institutions that make it impossible to live a normal life in this country.[63]

At 2:00 P.M. I was supposed to meet a group from my Student Advisory Group and five representatives from the strike committee. At the actual event some two hundred people, including members of the Radical Caucus and student mobilization committee, crowded into the Administration Building boardroom. When I politely suggested a smaller group would be more practical, student leader Rick Kibbey and Professor Lash Larrowe said that they could not ask anyone to leave.

Thereafter followed four solid hours of shouts, expletives, and vituperation. The first demand was for open admissions, the next for curricular reform, and after that for disarming the campus police—all issues that had come up before and been addressed in public statements.

When leaders criticized my commission on admissions plan as too slow, they were silenced by Rodney Watts, a Black junior and member of the Student Advisory Group. "This is a Black problem; let us solve it." And he explained steps already taken by the Black Liberation Front, the Office of Black Affairs, the Equal Opportunity Program, the Center for Urban Affairs, and the Black Faculty.[64]

Time after time, nevertheless, I reiterated university positions and answered the same charges and challenges. Although many of the questioners were obviously sincere, they were often so emotional as to be incoherent. Professor Larrowe didn't hesitate to join the fray with an ominous proclamation: "I have a feeling there are enough of us to cause a problem for the university, and we will remain on strike until something is done."

I came away musing on the Children's Crusades, about which I had read as a boy—hordes of thirteenth-century youth marching off to conquer the Holy Land from the Muslims by love instead of force. Like their crusading predecessors, our modern protestors had no reservations, no uncertainties, no disbeliefs—their cause and methods were right, pure, and just. They could admit no slightest error, no tiniest margin for doubt. Worse, they were utterly lacking in humor. It was as if they were wrapped in a damp gray blanket of spleen.

Not all student contacts were confrontational. Some were decidedly amusing, such as

LANSING STATE JOURNAL, MAY 12, 1970. PHOTOCOPY OF NEWSPAPER BY MANFRED WEIDEMANN, COOPERSTOWN NEW YORK.

Two hundred MSU demonstrators swamped the Hannah Administration Building Board Room to engage me in a give-and-take dialogue for four tense hours. On my left are Provost John Cantlon and Vice President Milton Muelder.

the time when a Black student leader, Stan McClintock, began his speech to the Academic Council by addressing me as "Honorable Brother Doctor President Wharton"! Of course, I gave him quick recognition.

An interesting angle on the demonstrations, then and later, was how few Black students participated. Many seemed to consider the protests a "white thing." The white student leaders did everything they could to attract minority support, and their lists of demands usually featured items aimed at trying to draw Black students into the confrontations. Perhaps they thought including Black students would make it harder for me to negotiate with them. But for the most part MSU's minority students saw through the gambit and declined rising to the bait.

That night the Lansing City Council, at the request of the student mobilization committee, approved permits for back-to-back marches on the state capitol for Wednesday and Thursday. The students assured the council that there would be no violence, and that Lansing police and student marshals would supervise the marchers. Each day there would be a noon rally at Beaumont Tower, followed by a four-and-a-half mile march to downtown. About 20,000 strikers and sympathizers were expected.

· · · ·

The big event of May 12 was the regular monthly meeting of the University Academic Council, which consisted of deans, department heads, and distinguished faculty members. I regularly chaired the Academic Council, which Hannah had rarely done, in order to demonstrate personally my commitment to academic and faculty values. The Council meeting had been moved from its regular site to the campus auditorium, where the balcony could accommodate 1,700 boisterous student observers. After prolonged debate over faculty bylaws and a recent report on academic freedom, the council suspended its rules to allow two student representatives, who had voice but no vote, to submit a resolution. Teresa Sullivan, a junior enrolled in the university's James Madison College, began by asking a series of sharp questions—Would a dedicated student fee help improve the university's ability to enroll more minority students? Could trustees order the campus police disarmed, or keep state and local police off campus? Were there orders on file to terminate nontenured faculty who were on strike? Dave Snyder, the other student representative, proposed a resolution affirming the right of faculty to teach classes without interference, as well as the right of every student to satisfactory fulfillment of the teaching contracts they'd entered into with the university. The resolution also recognized the right of faculty to dissent without jeopardizing their livelihoods, and that of students to dissent without endangering their degrees.

I was proud of Sullivan and Snyder. The two students had represented their constituencies effectively, working within the "system" so loathed by their more radical peers. They had drafted their position judiciously, and their resolution passed the Academic Council unanimously. Moreover, most of the students in attendance had never before been exposed to the council or any other mechanism of academic governance. I hoped that they had found the new experience interesting and worthwhile.

Rain usually spelled smaller rallies and demonstrations, so we prayed for it almost every day. On May 13, the day of the first of two marches planned that week on the state capitol, our prayers were answered—of the 4,000 who converged on Beaumont Tower, only about half set out for downtown Lansing. Under a sea of jostling umbrellas, the dripping, bedraggled students shuffled along one lane of Michigan Avenue, escorted by two hundred student marshals and a police car. There was some dispute over whether the marchers had properly received a permit, so Lansing police were waiting at the border with East Lansing, ready to arrest the first student to cross. But MSU police lieutenant Haywood Julian worked his way to the front of the column and blithely led the group over the line, knowing his friends on the Lansing force would have no appetite for arresting him. With a puckish spirit, Julian was popular among students, whom he often managed to cajole or humor out of improper or illegal antics.[65]

The next day the university trustees and I were having lunch at Kellogg Center with the development board of the MSU Alumni Association. As the meal ended, we heard a ruckus outside. Looking out the window, the trustees and I could see a long line of chanting students, apparently heading our way. As the group came closer, I looked around to find that the trustees had vanished, leaving only me and a couple of the alumni staffers. Though the trustees apparently thought the mob was headed for Kellogg Center, they were actually only passing by, a second day's march on the capitol in Lansing.

It was raining softly again, and the temperature was a chilly fifty degrees, but with around ten thousand people, the crowd, including students from other Michigan universities, was larger than before. Carrying an American flag and the yellow and blue banner of Kent State, the marchers were orderly and peaceful, intoning "Peace now!" all the way to the capitol. Once there they were greeted by representative Jackie Vaughn, who had just introduced a bill to allow Michigan servicemen to decline to fight in undeclared wars. "Pass Vaughn's bill," the protestors roared. Other speakers included state senators Coleman Young, Roger Craig, and Sander Levin, as well as Representatives Dale Kildee and Daniel Cooper. Governor Milliken also came out to address the marchers, but he was repeatedly heckled and drowned out by chants of "One two three four, we don't want your f——ing war!"

The only untoward incident came when an intoxicated elderly man lost control of his car and plowed into the marchers, injuring nine of them and a police sergeant. When the crowd broke the car's windows, student marshals and the police rushed the stunned driver away.

When I got back to Cowles House that night, after two full weeks of unrelieved stress—I was visibly dragging. "I've got a surprise for you," Dolores said after a welcome-home kiss. Then she dropped into my lap a wiggling ball of gray fur—a miniature schnauzer puppy. She had bought it to be Bruce's dog, but when the puppy jumped up and started licking my face, all my cares vanished. We registered his name as "Wharton of Michigan," but we never called him anything but "Mich."

I ended the month weighing 153 pounds, down from 178.

• • • •

Eleven-year-old Bruce had to stand up to grade-school classmates, who sometimes echoed their parents' angry complaints: "Why doesn't your father *do* something?" Although he rarely complained, one day he came home with news that the son of a professor who had been a leading instigator of the protests had joined in the gibes. I was angry, but Dolores was furious—the professor, she said, was "a senile hippie in a tie-dyed shirt!"

Dolores and I were both uncomfortably aware of the pressures Bruce had to cope with. Cowles House was steps from Beaumont Tower and the Student Union, epicenters for the protests, and the routine noise, chants, and breaking glass must have been frightening for our young son. During the early demonstrations Bruce's Cowles House sitters for protection were occasionally campus police, hardly routine companions at his age. We wanted Bruce to be allowed to grow up and go to school in a normal setting, like other children. For one thing, being the son of MSU's president inevitably shaped his interactions with his friends. On the whole Bruce held his ground, eventually developed solid friendships, and got on with the business of learning the local ropes. For another, the on-campus tensions of the period meant constant questions and challenges from acquaintances of his own age and older. And I worried greatly about spending too little fatherly time with him during the years before his onset of puberty.

Throughout the entire period Dolores was a rock for both Bruce and me. She was frequently by my side facing groups of protesting students. When dealing with demonstrations or other circumstances kept me from honoring prior commitments, she stood in and pinch-hit for me. In New York, for example, she accepted on my behalf an Amistad Award for my "special concern for the impoverished people of the world." The society was named for the famous slave ship whose cargo of fifty-three Africans, en route from Cuba in 1839, revolted and took over the ship. They were eventually freed by the U.S. Supreme Court, persuaded by the arguments of former president John Quincy Adams.

One evening a group came to Cowles House to solicit our participation in a peace march they were organizing. I was in bed—I had been averaging about four hours' sleep a night, and Dolores had finally put her foot down. When the candle-carrying students arrived, she and visiting son Clifton 3rd met them on the front steps. "President Wharton cares deeply for the cause of peace," she told them, "but he's exhausted. Would you accept me instead?" The crowd roared approval, so Dolores and Clifton each lit a candle and led the march through the campus, everyone singing "Give Peace a Chance."

Although the attacks were rarely upon me personally, there was one incident when a female demonstrator spat at me while I was walking on campus with Carl Taylor, a Black undergraduate and presidential fellow. When Carl started to go after her, I stopped him saying, "She can spit on me, but I will do nothing in reaction to tarnish the dignity and reputation of the presidency. That would be worse than her spit."[66]

. . . .

At the monthly board meeting on May 15, the MSU trustees stunned me by passing a unanimous resolution commending my handling of the campus upheavals: "We believe [Wharton] has been sympathetic to the legitimate concerns of students and faculty, demonstrating a willingness to move as rapidly as possible toward objectives which can be attained, while maintaining the integrity of Michigan State."

In the afternoon the University Academic Council reconvened, while another anti-ROTC occupation of Demonstration Hall was under way. Later that evening the Demonstration Hall occupation started to turn ugly. The protestors were breaking out all the small windowpanes, and we were worried about the possibility of fire or bombs. I ordered the building cleared, and the campus police used tear gas. The broken windows were repaired with square tin covers that remained for the next four decades. It became an unintended visible memorial to the 1970 demonstrations.

On Saturday, May 16, came news of the deaths of two students at Jackson State University, in Mississippi, closely followed by a similar tragedy in Georgia. This was especially shocking because one of our students was the brilliant daughter of John Peoples, president of Jackson State University, and a National Merit Scholar at MSU. The deaths provoked further protests throughout the country, and to help forestall escalation at MSU, I ordered all campus flags to fly at half-mast for five days. Nevertheless it was a window of opportunity for the student strike leaders, who hoped it would draw more Black students into their ranks. True to form, six delegates from a new "Action Group to Combat Racism" showed up in my office on Monday, May 18. They demanded that the university be shut down the following day to "focus attention on the causes and implications of these crimes and to take concrete action to combat racism." I think virtually all the delegates were white.

I told the six students I had no plans to close the university, and said the same thing later in the day when fifty to seventy-five more came to the Administration Building to reiterate their demands. Instead, there was a public announcement establishing a campus Black Cultural Center, based on lengthy discussions with MSU's Black community. I wanted more than a token day off from classes—I wanted something permanent and constructive.

The "action group" returned to the Student Union, angry that their move to co-opt Black students had been stalemated. By dark their numbers grew to around two hundred, and groups of three to five were slipping furtively from the building and ranging across campus, throwing rocks, breaking windows, and crying havoc. When campus police gave chase, the bands would scatter, each individual fleeing in a different direction. Avoiding arrest easily, they then slipped back into the Union to rejoin their comrades' "discussion" of racism, while yet more groups would sidle outside to continue the trashing.

At one point during the evening a group left the Union and came to Cowles House. Wearing a long red, white, and blue gingham skirt, Dolores fearlessly greeted them at the front steps. One leader, a woman, demanded that Dolores and I should allow the students to stay in the Union beyond the closing hour. "We're talking about racism," she proclaimed. "As a Black, racism ought to be important to Wharton, and we're committed to its solution for him and Blacks everywhere!"

Provoked, but with her usual humor, Dolores pulled from her skirt pocket a large matching kerchief. Whipping it over her head and holding the ends tight under her chin, she drawled in mock southern, "Lawzy me. After two hunnert yairs, you young folks is he'ping my people. Today is mah big day!"

The young woman fell back, stunned for once to silence, and the crowd returned to the Student Union. Who was that supposed to be, I later asked Dolores, Hattie McDaniel or Louise Beavers? "Aunt Jemima!" she burst out laughing. There was a sequel later that evening. A smaller group of prelaw students came over and asked Dolores to intercede with me not to arrest the students. When she asked them why they weren't over in the Union with their friends, they said, "Oh, we don't want to run the risk. If we are arrested, we might not get admitted to law school!"

The Union was supposed to close at 11:00 P.M., but it was obvious that the group had no plans to leave. Up to then, we had made a practice of giving illegal occupiers of buildings three warnings—one from the facility manager, one from the dean of students, and finally one from Dick Bernitt, just before his officers would go in to clear out the protestors—only then did students begin to leave. This evening I asked Barnitt and student dean Eldon Nonnamaker how many warnings the law required. Just one, they said.

At midnight the students were still using the Union as refuge, so with additional manpower from the Ingham County sheriff I had the campus police surround the building. Then an assistant building manager gave the students their first warning. As usual, the militants declined to disperse. Now our new strategy began to unfold. After the students ignored the second warning, directly from the campus police, the officers immediately closed all the exits. Instead of charging into the building to chase the demonstrators away, they locked the doors, put guards on the windows, and then moved in quietly to arrest every illegal occupant.

In all some 130 adults and two juveniles were arrested without incident.[67] The first bus started loading at 1:37 A.M. Two more buses were needed, with all the offenders in the Ingham County Jail by 4:00 A.M. Early the next morning we found a bullet hole in a window of the Cowles House solarium. I had campus maintenance replace the glass immediately and asked that the entire incident be kept quiet. If the shooting became public, some copycat might try again.

Damage from the night of pillage had been significant, especially at Eppley Center, the International Center, and the Administration Building. A predictable consequence of the riots was that university insurance rates soared, from $150,000 annually almost doubling to $280,000. Worse, our deductible went from $100 to $100,000.

Individually and collectively, demonstrations and public disturbances often follow a discernible sequence, like a fever on a hospital chart. While the temperature is going up and the fever stays high, there's little to be done. Recognizing the peak—the point at which treatment can start to work—is crucial. So it was at Michigan State University, where the Student Union demonstrations and arrests represented a peak. Although the protests and trashing continued for several more days, their intensity began to ebb—the fever had broken.

The morning afterward, the Union arrests were the main topic at my administrators group meeting—some students already out on bail appeared, asking that charges against them be dropped. In the afternoon my Student Advisory Group heard more discussion on the matter, including whether the local prosecutor or judge could dismiss the charges and turn the offenders over to the university for appropriate discipline. The student advisers suggested that their group be routinely consulted before any future police actions—a position I appreciated but thought impractical in the extreme.

. . . .

Fortunately, there were occasional moments of delight that distracted me from the intensity of the marches, confrontations, and random violence. One came on May 26 when a fourth-grade class from the Garfield School in Flint came to visit me. The students had written in advance, stating, "We have been studying Michigan and we are coming to visit Lansing next week. We are also going to visit Michigan State. We would like to meet you and your family." The letter was on a large two- by four-foot sheet of paper with a picture of the entire class of twenty-nine. I told the press that the letter made my day—no demands, no complaints, no problems.[68]

Another was an unforgettable evening when Wendell J. Westcott, the university caril-lonneur, climbed the seventy-three steps of Beaumont Tower to play a special rendition of "Nobody Knows The Trouble I Seen" on the forty-seven-bell manual carillon. The Tower, site of so many predemonstration gatherings of students, was only 300 yards from Cowles House. Dolores, Bruce, and I listened with reverence to his wonderfully empathetic performance. That great Negro spiritual was welcome balm for our strained nerves.

Although the number of protests and protesters gradually dwindled, it wasn't yet time to "declare victory." Resentment of the demonstrations was running high among taxpayers, perhaps especially those who hadn't themselves been able to attend a college or university. Even some of the university's own employees were disgusted. Around four hundred sent a petition to state senator Robert Huber, calling for the restoration of order, the end of property destruction, and the enforcement of an ordinance prohibiting camping on university property. I was annoyed, but anyone could see their point. Built and maintained at public expense, MSU was one of the loveliest, most admired campuses in the country—and here it was being wrecked by the very youngsters for whom it had been created.

・・・・

After a campus-wide referendum showed strong support for ROTC, the Academic Council vote on its status was anticlimactic. Two deans and five professors moved to remove academic credit for military and aerospace programs, but they were defeated overwhelmingly. The council then reaffirmed that "academic credit [for ROTC] shall be based on academic content in the same manner as for any other course in the university."

During the trial of the Union trespassers six weeks later, two students insisted on serving me personally with a subpoena to appear. Since subpoenas weren't exactly rare at the university, the standard procedure was that the legal office accepted service. This time the students demanded that I be served in person. When I accepted the document with some nonchalance, I could tell they were disappointed that I wasn't trembling with fear. So I explained the situation. When I added that this was the first time I had ever been served directly, the students smiled with obvious satisfaction. The event was captured by the *State News* front page photo.[69] (Several months later, eight defendants in the trespassing trial were acquitted in U.S. district court, but Judge Noel Fox held that the university had acted in good faith in enforcing its rules.)

・・・・

Although the student protestors had cried out continually for an end to "business as usual," the truth was that I had a university to run. While all hell was breaking loose that spring, I had simultaneously to learn and manage the tangled ropes of institutional administration—chairing MSU board meetings, reviewing personnel actions, presenting budget requests to the state legislature and attending awards banquets—to participate in an alumni weekend including the Patriarch's Luncheon and to give my only out-of-state speech, at the Johns Hopkins University commencement, where I received my second honorary doctorate. I had previously given commencement addresses at the University of Michigan, where I had received my first honorary degree, but I left the U of M stage right after my speech to rush back to the MSU campus turmoil. The most personal recognition that year was to be awarded the Boston Latin School "Man of the Year," which historically recognizes their celebrated alumni.[70] Throughout May, I still chaired the internal executive and management groups and attended the regular meeting of the Michigan Council of State College Presidents—not quite business as usual, but different.

Despite the disorder and occasional violence, the university came through without loss of life and I hoped without compromising its basic values. A bit later I was gratified by a "report card" compiled by MSU's urban survey research unit on campus attitudes toward the demonstrations and the administration's handling of the turmoil. Some 4,250 questionnaires went out, about 60 percent of which were completed and returned. On "President Wharton's handling of crisis events," some 89 percent of administrators, 82 percent of faculty, 70 percent of graduate students, and 60 percent of undergraduates approved to a "great" or to "some" extent. Only 15 percent of undergraduates completely disapproved. More than 50 percent of all groups "approved of protest if it does not interfere with the rights of others."[71] This opinion accorded with the intuitive assumptions that I had followed in dealing with the campus unrest. Dealing with student demonstrations had not been included in my job description, but I now had firsthand experience.

Finally came the problem of "People's Park," which we had reluctantly tolerated since late April. Any move by the university to tear it down could reignite the guttering flames of student ire. When a local weather bureau issued a tornado warning one day, university relations vice president Bob Perrin asked the campus police to use the "need to protect the students" as a pretext for striking the tent city. But by that time most of the real students had deserted the park, and the nonstudent campers unfortunately refused to be persuaded to leave.

Understanding our apparently hands-off attitude was difficult for many people—at one point we had to head off a vigilante group of local citizens, armed with baseball bats and heading for the tent enclave. Meanwhile sanitary conditions deteriorated, and the area began to smell. Worse, it had become a magnet not only for nonstudent protestors, but also for drifters, high-school truants, and runaways. Then the *State News* published a photograph of two "tent citizens," a male and female, frolicking in the Red Cedar River. The picture was hazy, but one detail looked to many state legislators suspiciously like a bare breast. It's a knee, we insisted—just a knee!

The end finally came in the early morning hours of June 8, a date Dick Bernitt and I had chosen with care. It was the beginning of final exam week, and the *State News* was in abeyance—at no other time would students be less likely to erupt anew into protests. About a dozen MSU police moved in, evicting forty kids. They tore down the tents, many already empty, and the grounds crew filled four trucks with trash and debris.

The long, dreary episode of People's Park was over, and with it the last phase of MSU's student uprisings of 1970. Perhaps, I mused, I should have taken the risk of moving sooner. But in the future, I vowed, I would never assume anything was "just spring fever."

• • • •

My first tumultuous months in office generated several press articles and editorials.[72] One by Bob Berg received the widest national coverage with headlines about how I had behaved under pressure. "His trials and tribulations have been many, but in his first six months as president of Michigan State University Clifton Wharton Jr. has managed to keep his cool."[73] Another piece that caught my attention had a quote from a Black student about my "Blackness" and administrative style: "A few who worked hardest for his [Wharton's] election now say they have second thoughts. Wharton's polish, moderation, and step-by-step progressiveness unsettled them. 'He's not an Uncle Tom,' says one undergraduate, 'but he ain't a nigger either.'" The author aptly pointed out, "The quote could not be better from Wharton himself."[74]

The *State News* commented, "If there was a 'winner' during the strike, it had to be Clifton Wharton. Despite whether one agreed with Wharton, he was impressive. He proved that he was articulate, thorough, intelligent, cunning, quick and witty. And he showed that he knew all the administrative moves—he was both evasive and ambiguous at times or hard and concise when he had to be."[75] I wish that I had felt as confident and knowledgeable as they believed.

Over the first six months, I had to deal with and overcome each problem and challenge with every skill that I possessed. I had to do so with equanimity, mastery, dignity, and, above all, without compromising my basic values. There were times when I felt as if I were hanging by my fingernails over a wide chasm. At other times, I felt like St. Sebastian pierced with multiple arrows and stretched on a cross being pulled in multiple directions by all the various constituents trying to pull me apart, limb from limb. Little wonder that my all-time favorite MSU *State News* cartoon[76] showed me as though on a cross with my arms outstretched while being tugged at by students on my right arm, by legislators on my left, and by two trustees gnawing on my ankles. I just hoped that I would not end up like St. Sebastian, surviving the arrows, only to be stoned to death. Any misstep would have meant almost instant disaster and loss of my presidency. Nevertheless, I was determined to do more than survive—I was determined to succeed.

One result of my successfully handling the demonstrations was that criticism of my performance abated, leaving few malcontents. Best of all my organizing the university to cope with the demonstrations, avoid major violence, and enable the university to continue operating gave me an elevated stature of leadership. Oddly enough there was one exceptional disparaging remark made by a midlevel Black administrator. A few days after the comment appeared in the *State News*, he was confronted by Dolores, who told him that his critical

STUDENTS

MSU

APPROPRIATIONS

LEGISLATORS

TRUSTEES

The new MSU President as "St. Sebastian" cartoon, by Doug Huston, is a pictorially accurate depiction of my new role.

remarks about me reminded her of crabs in a basket: "When one of us climbs up the side to get to the top, there is always another ready to pull him down." She concluded, "And you actually expect Clif to help you climb up that slippery slope!" In response he stared back at her with a shamed expression.

The fitting coda to my first six months was the undergraduate commencement Sunday afternoon, June 14. The ceremonies were held in the Spartan football stadium, with some 16,000 parents and friends attending for 3,763 baccalaureates. Personally gratifying one of the honorary doctorate recipients was legendary contralto Miss Marian Anderson, at whose Danbury estate Dolores and I had been married twenty years before. She stayed at Cowles House while Dolores briefly attended Clifton 3rd's Dalton graduation in New York City the exact same day! I was dismayed by this unavoidable conflict preventing me from attending our son's event. However, this was my very first MSU commencement, and I dared not miss it, though I deeply wanted to be with Clifton. I would learn that such painful sacrifices are too often the cost of leadership.

The weather captured the tenor of the year. The two-hour ceremony began under cloudless skies and a hot sun. Officiating on the stage in the middle of the football field, I noticed an enormous black thunderhead in the distance. Gradually it came closer and closer, though unobserved by most in the stadium, who were facing the stage. I began to speed up my speech trying to beat the oncoming storm. As the bottom of the cloud began to curl over the top of the stands, I ended the ceremony, and we hurried to leave the field. Suddenly, a thunderous downpour drenched us all. We got wet, but we finished the ceremony and granted the degrees—symbolic of my first six months. I got wet, but I did what had to be done—and survived.

This picture shows Dolores and me at the president's residence, Cowles House, on September 23, 1970.

CHAPTER SEVEN

The President of MSU 2: Developing a Pluralistic University

At the end of the spring quarter the majority of MSU students went home for the summer. With "only" 17,000 or so taking classes, the campus somehow managed to seem empty, almost forlorn. During the summer Dolores and I eagerly looked forward to their return.

After Clifton 3rd graduated from the Dalton School and came out to Michigan for the summer, Bruce left for the Becket summer camp in the Berkshire Mountains of Massachusetts. Bruce's greatest challenge still lay in developing a "normal" social life in East Lansing. When he invited friends to Cowles House, a few of them referred affectionately to him as "Prince Bruce." Ever courteous, well mannered, and proper, Bruce drew raves from all our adult friends.

Clifton 3rd stayed a few months at Cowles House before heading off to his freshman year at St. Lawrence University, a small campus in upstate New York. He also took a couple of courses on campus to get a step ahead for college. It was at this point that Dolores and I realized something we had suspected for some time: that our two sons felt the pressure of high-achieving parents and even that of their grandfather. The boys suffered the awesome weight of living up to the expectations that they should be equally successful—a serious challenge to their self-esteem and performance. Dolores and I tried to offset the problem by regularly praising their accomplishments and providing genuine love, but we knew it was a serious difficulty for them to overcome.

. . . .

Although the student protestors had cried out continually for an end to "business as usual," the truth was that I had a university to run.

It didn't take long to realize that being president of a major university would be an occupation like no other. I found myself on call twenty-four hours a day, seven days a week, and the responsibilities demanded total concentration. Issues and problems varied from minor to hair-tearing—a series of dustups punctuated with crises, plus the occasional cataclysm. Everything seemed to require my personal attention—impossible of course. But if I stood down or delegated too much I would be seen as an "absentee" president, an aloof and uncaring bureaucrat. Time management was critical, and I had to be able to juggle all sorts of matters simultaneously. Some could be dealt with in hours or a few days; others would need months or even years to reach any sort of resolution. Especially in the early days, I often felt as if I were running in several gears at once—low, drive, and overdrive. It was a feeling that never entirely went away.

In 1972, I decided to do a systematic study of what had been my time allocations over a three-year period.[1] The initial data was collected for 1970 through 1973 and was then averaged to represent a typical year in order to smooth out the atypical impact of the student demonstrations of 1970 and 1972. Using calendars and datebooks, I developed a system to classify activities into nine generic areas, broken down into percentage allocations of time for each.

I was surprised to learn that even before the year began, some 35 percent of my time was already allotted to fixed commitments: trustee meetings, academic governance activities, and higher education or presidential association meetings (state, national, and Big Ten). (Another nonnegotiable area was "crisis management.") My work week averaged sixty-five hours, six ten-hour-plus days per week for fifty-one weeks (I took a one-week vacation). In a typical year, I spent 12.8 percent of my time in general administration; campus officers, personnel, and employee relations took another 13.8 percent; and correspondence, 14.9 percent. Academic governance, such as the Academic Council and Faculty Council, required 17.7 percent, while student contacts (individuals, student orientation, campus dialogues, dorm visits) took 13.9 percent. A catchall category of university relations—speeches, alumni functions, fund-raising, and the media—consumed 13.9 percent; general public interactions took 7.4 percent. Finally, relations with other universities and businesses required 2.8 percent, while service on corporate boards I had joined was another 2.8 percent. As I told a *Newsweek* reporter,[2] the demanding pace was more "due to the nature of the job of a university president, *not* due to outside non-academic activities." Despite my admonition that the vast majority of my time was devoted to the university, the final article, though quite positive, concentrated on the heavy external involvement of Dolores and myself—dubbing us the "flying Whartons who only met in airports."[3]

. . . .

Dolores had adjustments of her own to make. We were a team, and there were extensive expectations for Michigan State's new First Lady—traditional activities such as acting as hostess at campus social events and accompanying me to dinners, speeches, and sporting

PRESIDENT WHARTON TIME ALLOCATION (TYPICAL YEAR)		
ACTIVITY	TOTAL HOURS	PERCENT
General and board of trustees	465.0	13.8
Administrative	430.5	12.8
Correspondence	500.0	14.9
Academic governance and faculty	594.0	17.7
Students	466.5	13.9
University relations	468.5	13.9
General public	250.0	7.4
Interinstitutional relations and general higher education	93.0	2.8
Foundations and corporate	93.0	2.8
Total	*3,360.5*	*100.0*

events. On the other hand, atypically of university spouses at the time, she was involved in numerous professional activities on her own, independent of her activities at MSU. Dolores thrived in both roles—although not without occasional rough spots. When Faculty Folk, the leading campus women's group, offered her a "temporary provisional membership," she politely declined, thinking (though not saying) it was a slight to her position if not herself. When the same group later wanted to take over Cowles House for their annual reception, she gently explained that it was our home, not a campus facility. Gradually, the group began to realize that Dolores was not an ordinary hausfrau, but would be a new version of the traditional president's spouse.

In the traditional "First Lady role," Dolores organized luncheons and dinners for university staff, met students and new deans, and entertained visiting dignitaries. During a typical year, between three thousand and four thousand persons passed through the Cowles House doors—faculty, staff, students, alumni, local and state officials, and visiting dignitaries that ranged from celebrities to heads of state. Whether hosting Henry Ford II or receptions for the Mortar Board student honor society, she set a marvelous standard to complement my academic goals. Dolores transformed Cowles House into an elegant, comfortable residence warm and welcoming to guests of every background. She brought to Cowles House a style and sophistication in social and academic entertainment that soon gave our residence an image of elegance and refinement.

Dolores pushed vigorously to build stronger relationships with the local and greater Lansing community—a critical area of town-gown relationships. She set about developing a systematic activity where the leaders of the local community would be involved and recognized

Dolores developed a new annual program hosting the widows of MSU faculty and staff. These receptions were held at the Cowles House, as shown in this picture taken June 19, 1973. This activity enhanced the sense of academic unity among previously neglected long-time members of the MSU "family."

as part of MSU. Visiting dignitaries or celebrities to the campus were promptly honored with invitations for receptions and dinners at Cowles House at which the greater Lansing community would also be included. These events supplemented our entertaining guests in the president's box during home football games. Such efforts would pay important dividends later.

On the other hand, Dolores's greatest initial impact upon the university came by drawing on her extensive art background and taste: she championed the university's commitment to the fine arts. With the cooperation of Erling Brauner, chair of the Department of Art, and Paul Love, director of the campus Kresge Art Gallery, she organized highly publicized exhibitions of faculty art on the walls of Cowles House. "I was [told] . . . that this is a college less gifted in the arts than it really is," she commented to a reporter. "To find it so excellent is extraordinary."[4]

Dolores's program was an instant hit. There was even a 1971 special television show devoted to it titled "Cowles House: Art in Residence."[5] The premiere film showing at our home was attended by selected faculty and several community arts advocates.[6] Rotating the art of MSU professors made an enormous impact not only on the morale of the faculty painters and sculptors, but also on the awareness within the MSU community that there was more to MSU than just "aggie" football. Students were invited to drop by—often unannounced—and encouraged to see the works. If we were not available our housekeeper, Mrs. Virginia Blair, was always pleased to give the student callers a tour of the artwork. Spartans began to realize it had a fine arts dimension of which they could be proud.

· · · ·

From the outset I worked hard to communicate extensively across the university community and beyond. In my first year I gave over twenty speeches, plus numerous short remarks, welcomes, and so on.[7] Certainly the most important from my vantage were three presentations in a series that would be devoted to what I called "the pluralistic university"—a new incarnation of the land-grant institution, developing in response to increasing social diversity, economic change, and technological progress.[8] The speeches were greatly influenced by Jim Bonnen's study, "The Role of the University in Public Affairs."[9] My vision focused on five priority areas: (1) promoting greater access and diversity in the student body (minorities, women, older students) while enhancing MSU's academic excellence, (2) broadening the university's land-grant mission to include lifelong learning initiatives and a stronger focus on urban issues, (3) contributing to the international programs through my own professional base of experience and contacts, (4) promoting research and graduate activities in our areas of academic strength, and finally, (5) launching MSU's first major private fund-raising effort, with special emphasis on building up the cultural dimension of the university. The pluralistic university speeches would become not only my philosophical template, but also an action agenda for my tenure at Michigan State.

Soon after our arrival, I unexpectedly discovered that I was seen as singularly equipped to

First Lady Dolores Wharton's rotating MSU Faculty Art Program display at the Cowles House featured high-quality faculty art and was captured in a special television film, "Cowles House: Art in Residence." Taken on September 3, 1970, this picture shows First Lady Dolores Wharton and Erling Brauner, chairman of the art department.

pursue the first three initiatives. One day, when I chaired a regular meeting of the Academic Council, I had resolved a contentious issue. Sociology professor Ruth Useem came up and said to me, "President Wharton, you are truly a 'third culture kid'!"—her new field of sociological research. She defined a third-culture kid (TCK, or "transculture kid") as someone who during childhood spent a significant time in one or more culture(s) other than his or her own. She coined the term after her 1958 research on Americans living in India, with her MSU sociologist/anthropologist husband, Dr. John Useem.[10] TCKs are often children of U.S. missionaries, diplomats, business officers, or agents of nonprofit organizations working abroad. Their children integrate elements of the foreign cultures and their own birth culture, creating a third culture. As a result TCKs tend to have special characteristics. Useem said that they are often multilingual and highly accepting of other cultures. TCKs grow up in a genuinely crosscultural world and have incorporated different cultures into their thought processes and behavior. They are really multicultural individuals or world citizens. For example, research showed that TCKs understand other cultures and peoples better than the average American, and they overwhelmingly believe they can get along with anybody.[11] "That's your behavior," she exulted.

· · · ·

To get acquainted with the university's far-flung constituencies, agriculture dean Larry Boger suggested that Dolores and I hold a series of "listening posts" around the state—an approach the college's extension service had found helpful in their outreach to farm communities. At each listening post, the fifty or so attendees included local and regional business leaders, alumni, donors, government officials, and the media. Over time the posts took place in Grand Rapids, Jackson, Flint, Ann Arbor, Inkster, Saginaw, Grand Haven, Mt. Pleasant, Antrim-Kalkaska, Traverse City, Holland, Bay City, Clare, Gaylord, Battle Creek, Rochester, Kalamazoo, Detroit, and greater Lansing. Both Dolores and I spoke at each meeting, and her presence reinforced the public awareness of our partnership at the university. Eventually, I developed a sizable mailing list of statewide contacts I called "influentials" to whom I regularly mailed all my major speeches. This program proved effective in giving them an understanding of my goals, policies, and actions.

· · · ·

Ample communication was especially critical on campus, where rumors always seemed to spread faster and be more readily accepted than fact—especially when any nuance was involved. Communicating with faculty and staff was relatively straightforward—existing channels included the *Faculty News* and the minutes of the Academic Council and Senate. I also systematically visited each of the university's seventeen colleges for faculty "dialogues," while my executive and administrative group meetings were the main vehicle for administrative and academic policy communications.

Reaching the students was harder. For one thing, there were a lot of them—around 42,000 at the time. For another, because their turnover was so high, the student body lacked a cohesive collective memory. Every time you thought a question settled once and for all, the students went home on break—and when the next quarter began, you had lots of new voices raising the same issues all over again.

Soon after our arrival at MSU and at Jim Spaniolo's suggestion, Dolores and I launched a series of dormitory visits (always contingent on an invitation from the residents).[12] Usually we ate with the students in their dining hall, then adjourned to a lounge or auditorium form questions and answers. Initially we were a conspicuous novelty, but as the visits became more commonplace the students began to prepare in advance, leading to some interestingly argumentative, though almost always congenial, back-and-forth. The students were usually a joy—curious, fun-loving, working hard toward their degrees—and Dolores and I invariably

I visited an MSU dormitory for an evening dialogue with the students in 1970. Dolores and I averaged two to three such evenings at student residences every week during each of the eight academic years of my tenure.

got a charge out of interacting with them. (We quickly learned never to call them "kids," which most took as a paternalistic "put down.") We also visited students who lived off campus, ranging from fraternities and sororities to co-ops to individual apartment complexes. In 1970 we made thirty-nine visits to student housing on and off campus. Over all our years at MSU we averaged two to three visits to student dorms and housing per week.

From 1970 to 1972 I wrote a regular column, "A President's Perspective," in the *State News*, which gave me a direct voice to students. I could respond quickly to issues or problems whether picked up during our regular dorm visits or covered in the media. In March 1972, however, the newly elected editor of the *State News* summarily terminated the column. I also tried to develop a regular public television show that was well received, but I discovered that to produce each show took an inordinate amount of time, and we discontinued it after a few months.

Dolores's successes included extended stays in the campus dorms. She spent the week of April 19, 1971, in McDonel Hall as guest in residence for their "Week of Arts," with a reciprocal visit by the students to see the art in Cowles House. She also visited Snyder-Phillips dorm, which housed the residential Justin Morrill College (January 29–31, 1972), gaining a very different perspective on a place that had been a focal point of student unrest in 1970. She came away with excellent insights into student life—and wonderful kudos across the campus.

Over time, the visits seemed to reduce complaints that "the President's too busy for ordinary students"—although no sooner did we finish one cycle than we had to start all over again. Once we accepted an invitation from what turned out to be a spaced-out group of longhairs, who clearly hadn't expected us to show up. When they asked us about the then-hot topic of coed living, Dolores replied, "Clif and I have been living together coeducationally for twenty-four years." The group's next mimeographed newsletter, aptly named *The Toke Weekly*, concluded that "she's a hip lady!"

During the week of April 19, 1971, Dolores visited students in McDonel Hall dormitory as a guest in residence for several days and nights. Such extended visits gave her splendid insights into student thought and life.

▪ Orientation Programs ─────────────────────────────

Another important communications venue was the university's orientation program for incoming students. I realized that this was an opportunity to reach the students *before* they arrived, when they might be especially impressionable. When Milt Dickerson, vice president for student affairs, agreed to my unusual proposal, I told him that I would like to go beyond offering a quick welcome to MSU. Because of the size of the entering classes, there were between eighteen and twenty-two sessions every summer, each a two-day affair for both students and their parents.[13] First I spent an hour with each group of students, followed later by an hour with the parents. In each session we talked about the dos and don'ts of campus life—rules and regulations, dorm hours, and drinking on and off campus. I touched on the differences among the student body by income, ethnicity, race, and religion, stressing the importance of understanding and mutual respect. I urged their involvement in extracurricular activities and underscored the importance of learning how to use university channels to deal with concerns and complaints.

With the spring demonstrations and protests fresh in mind, I told the students to think about the difference between legal and illegal dissent. They needed to know the real meaning of academic freedom and freedom of speech. "If you get arrested for blocking traffic on Grand River Avenue," I said, "don't tell me afterwards you didn't know it was against the law."

Two issues of great concern among parents were drinking and coed residence halls. The trustees had just relaxed the long-standing ordinance against alcohol in campus housing, subject to state law, and at the same meeting (in April 1970) they approved coed living. Until then the university had offered single-gender dorms, single-gender wings within the same dorm, and alternating-gender floors. The new arrangement provided for "apartment style" living, with male and female suites adjacent on the same floor—though in no case with men and women sharing the same room. Coed living required parental consent for freshmen, which led one irate father to upbraid me for having introduced the option. When I explained that the decision was between him and his student, he retorted, "My daughter will hound me until I give in!"

At orientation I liked to tell parents that I would always know when their sons or daughters made their first trip back home from MSU. "You'll call me," I said, complaining that "your sons and daughters are using words you never heard before. They'll be drinking beer or smoking cigarettes, and you'll be upset that the university has corrupted your children. Just remember two things. First, I can't undo in three weeks what you did while raising them for eighteen years. Second, have a little faith that the eighteen years you spent with them will have the more lasting effect—not the passing impulses of their first few months at college."

Probably my favorite "parent story" was about the father who was furious that we seemed to have omitted his son's name from his graduation program. The boy had not, it turned out, enrolled for his senior year. When I explained to the man that his son was a junior in good standing, the father objected—the boy had crossed the stage at commencement, and he'd even gotten his (token) diploma.

"When your son was living off campus last year," I asked, "did you send his tuition and rent checks to him, or to the university directly?"

The line was silent for a long time. Then, "You mean he hasn't even been . . . ?"

Perhaps, I suggested gently, he and his son might want to modify their financial arrangements. Parents in the audience at orientation roared with laughter.

At each orientation, I wound up by asking the new students to go to "Smile School." During the early years of student unrest, far too many students, often unshaven with long, unkempt hair, would amble grudgingly across the stage for their diplomas, shooting horrific looks at me or more likely at their parents for being forced into observing the traditional ceremony. For me a commencement should be a joyous occasion, so whenever I noticed another unhappy graduate reaching for his diploma, I would quietly whisper "smile." Startled, they usually did, before immediately recapturing their mask of disdain. When I recounted such incidents to the incoming class orientations, I suggested that they practice smiles to prepare for graduation. I proposed that whenever they chanced to see Dolores and me walking around campus with our miniature schnauzer, Mich, they should wave, smile, and say "Hi." From then on, Dolores and I could always tell freshmen, many of whom would wave, smile, and say with a grin, "I'm practicing." Imagine my shock years later in New York City, as I was walking near Saks Fifth Avenue, when a well-dressed young man—a successful Spartan lawyer on Wall Street—approached me, waved, and said with a smile, "I'm practicing!"

I participated in these orientations every summer for my entire tenure. Any loss of personal summer vacation time was more than offset by my chance to build strong base relationships with students and their parents.

• Governance

As much as I admired and respected John Hannah, one thing that I thought needed to change at MSU was the cult of personality he had forged. In the 1940s Hannah had taken over an institution small enough to be run personally. Soon he knew everyone—not just the one vice president and five or six deans of the period, but most of the staff and faculty. He rose by five every morning, and promised that any memo on his desk by the close of business would get an answer by 8:00 A.M. the next day.

But Hannah, like so many other Big Ten presidents of the day, had been formed in an imperial mold. Like his peers, he spent decades shaping not only his campus, but also the surrounding community and even the state at large. As postwar demands for higher education exploded under GI Bill financing, his managerial style evolved from the need for decisive, entrepreneurial management. Savvy and politically connected, by the 1960s he was known throughout Michigan as "Mr. Republican," and had he wanted it, the governorship would have been his for the taking. Even trustee Clair White, a dogged critic, claimed that when Hannah retired, the campus cement mixers churned for two days in his memory.

Yet in 1970 the general tolerance for benign autocracy was definitely on the wane, undermined by changes in society, politics, and the university itself. Newer, stronger faculty were restive, losing no chance to remind anyone who would listen of Hannah's origins as a chicken farmer. For their part, students were pressing not only for the demise of in loco parentis and single-sex dorms but also for a bigger role in institutional governance—seats and votes in curricular and disciplinary committees, even in academic senates and on university boards.

As far back as my peripatetic days heading ADC's American University Research Program, I had become convinced that higher education was entering a period of much more participatory governance. But at MSU as elsewhere, the transition would be rocky, in large part because many of those pushing for reform were seen, rightly or not, as campus radicals. Their disruptive tactics and occasional tolerance for violence made them suspect among the traditional campus community, not to mention the largely conservative trustees.

A pivotal question was how to nourish more participatory decision-making without undermining my own influence. Then as now, few realized how limited a college president's authority really is (or that of most other executives, for that matter). Aside from a few basic, clear-cut prerogatives, "moral suasion" and the bully pulpit are a president's principal tools. In laying the foundations for my tenure, I had to support more faculty and student involvement in campus affairs without giving away the power needed to discharge my own responsibilities. It was a delicate balance, not least because change could be a one-way street. Once shared or delegated, power could be difficult to recapture—even in hard fiscal times, when control traditionally recentralizes to ensure institutional survival.

At MSU as elsewhere, the faculty had always taken the leading part in setting the curriculum, determining course content, and maintaining academic standards. Deans, provosts, and presidents might get involved in creating new programs, but in general senior administrators deferred to the faculty on administrative matters. Early on I surprised the University Academic Council by attending and chairing its regular monthly meetings—Hannah had ordinarily left the job to his provosts, except when highly controversial issues might be on the agenda. At my first session I told the members that I felt that faculty were the heart of the educational enterprise, and that they held the key to the fundamental purpose of the university. I also stressed that reforming academic governance would be one of my highest priorities, including expanding faculty participation in budget development and sharing information on political, fiscal, and other nonacademic developments of interest. As expected, this new policy won plaudits.

On the student side, sociology professor James B. McKee had already chaired a study group whose report had recommended creating a number of nonvoting seats in the Academic Council for student representatives. Although resistance to the idea was substantial among council members, I managed to get passed an interim proposal to allow two students to speak, though not vote, at the meetings.

When time came to push for formal voting representation, a thorny issue arose. The Associated Students of Michigan State University (ASMSU), the all-campus student governing body, tended to be dominated by near-professional student operators, whose views and attitudes often diverged from those of the majority of people they represented. Most of the leaders came from the social and political science departments, as well as Justin Morrill College.[14] As a student politician myself during my National Student Association days, I understood that it wasn't an unusual situation, but I wanted to see broader participation across the campus. As a result, I proposed allocating student seats in the Academic Council across the university's seventeen colleges, weighted by enrollment, with a number of "at large" slots aimed mainly at encouraging minority participation. I also shifted the dates of voting to be at the time of registration, thereby increasing the total vote dramatically. Having each college elect its own student representatives had an immediate effect of significantly increasing the diversity of views on issues. After February's demonstrations I had previously created an informal student advisory group to improve communications with students. Its role was to replace conventional "student" issues like dorm hours and drinking on campus in favor of a broader agenda, including university budgeting, tuition and fees, and long-term planning.

The plan caused an uproar in ASMSU, where some insisted that they were the elected student leaders. But arguing against what was clearly a move toward greater campus democracy and diversity put them in a manifestly weak position, especially because the plan would channel participation toward meaningful educational issues rather than narrow campus politics. I had learned well the lessons from the NSA founding that broad-scale representative democracy is powerful.

▪ Presidential Fellows _____

Recalling the help I had received from mentors as a young trainee at AIA, I wanted to do something similar at Michigan State. With an initial grant of $60,000 from the Rockefeller Foundation, I developed an internship plan based loosely on the White House Fellowships,[15] modified for a higher education environment. Each year, three presidential fellows would be selected from a pool of applications and nominations—an undergraduate, a grad student, and an instructor or assistant professor. Working in my suite of offices, they would have the chance to observe and learn about academic administration from the top down. I usually

The first MSU presidential fellows program was modeled after the White House Fellowships. Taken September 1970, this picture includes: (*left to right*) Dale E. Work, PhD candidate in chemistry; Ronald W. Richards, assistant professor in the College of Human Medicine; Teresa Sullivan, undergraduate in James Madison College and student member of Academic Council; Carl S. Taylor, undergraduate student from Detroit in the MSU "Project Ethyl"; me. Thirteen persons would be MSU presidential fellows.

had them begin their two-semester assignments by drafting responses to the office's heavy volume of mail—a choice designed to disabuse them of any idea that senior management was a "glamour" job. After a few weeks of drudgery, they worked up individual projects, the completion of which would henceforth be their main responsibility. Fellows also went with me to most meetings of the board of trustees, the Academic Council, the Michigan Council of State College Presidents, and elsewhere. Every other week we took time for a private workshop—just them, Al Ballard, and me—where they could ask me anything they wished. I promised them candid, truthful answers, the only condition being that they hold my comments in confidence.

In fall 1970 the initial group included two undergraduates, not one. Teresa Sullivan was a campus leader and student member of the academic council. Carl S. Taylor was a Black undergraduate from Detroit who had been one of the first students from Detroit to enroll under the "Project Ethyl" program. Dale E. Work was a doctoral candidate in chemistry. Ronald W. Richards was an assistant professor in the College of Human Medicine. After the first two groups of fellows, it was clear that a full academic year would be better, even though for the undergraduate fellows it would mean a delay in finishing their studies. We mitigated the problem by arranging for them to receive academic credit for their work.

Twenty-five years later, a reunion of the former fellows took place on the MSU campus. The subsequent careers of the fellows far surpassed my expectations, ranging from college or university president to foundation officer to corporate executive (see appendix 4).

▪ Admissions Commission _____

At the beginning of the 1970s, college admissions policies had become a litmus test for liberalism nationwide, with "open admissions" a linchpin of reform.[16] Because of the Detroit Project (initially called "Project Ethyl")—a special recruitment effort John Hannah had started in the early 1960s—by the fall before my arrival, MSU had the most minority undergraduates of any nonurban campus in the country. But its success came with problems. Some saw the Detroit Project as a kind of enrollment ghetto, separate from (and less demanding than) the regular admissions process. Whites often regarded it as a "benevolent work" on behalf of disadvantaged inner-city youth, while many Blacks saw it as "reparations" owed for past (and present) racism. Neither view was an adequate basis for a strong, sustainable effort that would deserve the respect and support of the university at large.

We needed a more objective basis for special admissions—one that was academically as well as morally defensible, and not incidentally, one that wouldn't appear dependent upon presidential or administrative magnanimity, especially mine. (I later learned Trustees Huff, White, and Hartman were promoting the rumor that I intended to use my position to push for the admission of hordes of unqualified, semiliterate Blacks.)

In our initial meeting before my taking office, Gordon Sabine suggested the idea of a special commission to look into Michigan State's entire admissions process. It sounded like a great plan—to look at admissions issues globally, against the broad backdrop of the university's mission and its future, not just in terms of numbers and quotas. Moreover, Sabine's recommendation was consistent with the trend toward broader participation in university policy formulation. I put it among the "front burner" items on my action agenda.

The first meeting of the Commission on Admissions and Student Body Composition was on June 1, 1970. It had thirty members drawn from the university's faculty, students, alumni, campus at-large, and the general public (see appendix 5). MSU's eight trustees served ex officio. I chaired and designated provost John Cantlon as vice chair with Ira Polley, the new director of admissions, as executive director. By chairing the group myself I attempted to signal the importance I attached to the commission, as well as to give myself an opportunity to influence the directions taken in its efforts.

The commission's immediate charge related directly to broader issues—the present and future size of the university itself; the student body's changing composition as to ethnic, gender, geographic, and family backgrounds; and MSU's educational role in the state, as well as its relationship to other Michigan colleges. Five subcommittees were appointed to study (1) the mission of Michigan State University; (2) enrollment mix; (3) special programs; (4) high-risk, minority and disadvantaged students; and (5) admissions procedures and standards. Starting early in the fall, the commission and its five subcommittees took their work to the people, holding six public hearings in Detroit, Marquette, Grand Rapids, and East Lansing. With considerable coverage by local and major metropolitan papers and TV stations, the meetings brought valuable citizen input and helped generate a base of support for the commission's eventual recommendations.

After more than a year's work, the panel issued its report on July 23, 1971, with seventy-nine recommendations ranging from financial aid and advising to instructional models and interinstitutional transfer rules. Rejecting the then-popular numerical goals or quotas for minority applicants, the commission set forth a plan for increasing minority enrollment under criteria no different from those applied to all other students. It distinguished carefully between *educationally* and *economically* disadvantaged students. The former were defined as those students with academic potential who, because of their economic, cultural, or educational background or environment, were unable to succeed without special support services. The latter were defined as "those individuals who possess acceptable academic credentials but who, because of financial disability, are inadequately represented in institutions of higher learning."[17] This artful but careful distinction was very important, since in the minds of many the two groups were the same—the former were those students whose personal circumstances and inadequate prior schooling left them unlikely to succeed on campus without remediation, and the latter were those with sound academic backgrounds who simply couldn't afford to attend college.

The commission also recommended that "over the next five to ten years the university should recruit and admit economically disadvantaged students . . . in sufficient numbers to achieve a more heterogeneous student body and to provide wider access to education, but the number of economically disadvantaged students to be admitted should be dependent upon the resources available to the university for their adequate support."[18] (The latter was particularly important given the "revolving door" that had developed for minority students at many other universities, where they were admitted only to fail within a semester or two. I was determined that the MSU minority students admitted would succeed and graduate.) The commission called as well for better academic advising, centralized financial aid, and enhanced financial counseling.

Campus reaction to the Admissions Commission report was broadly positive, save for some grumbling by some who had hoped for more extreme proposals. I was particularly happy that the group had sidestepped the political "third rail" of quotas, while outlining a comprehensive, practicable, forward-looking plan. The MSU Board of Trustees went along—given the enthusiasm the commission had generated on campus and throughout the state, even the adversarial troika found it difficult to make mischief.

One of the great strengths of the Admissions Commission's work was that it anticipated what would become future university initiatives, such as action on behalf of handicapped students. MSU had a small but highly effective group of handicapped student activists, with whom we were able to work rather well on issues ranging from housing and transportation to facilities accessibility and building alterations. Eventually we created an office of handicapper programs, headed by Judy Taylor, a paraplegic student.

The Admissions Commission also pointed out that although women were about 40 percent of MSU's student body (at a time when the Big Ten averaged 25 percent or less[19]), we still had rules that worked against them.[20] One of my first acts at MSU had been to make our residency rules consistent for men and women—that is, after living in the state for six continuous months, both males and females who had enrolled as out-of-staters could apply for in-state tuition.[21]

In March 1972 I appointed a seventeen-member steering committee to study women on campus, which recommended a number of steps to improve their campus experience. Actions included expanding child-care facilities, defining a policy on women in intercollegiate athletics, and providing fringe benefits for temporary and part-time employees, the majority of whom were women.[22] The most important was correcting the pay inequities for women, allowing me to earmark for the purpose part of the university's anticipated 1972–73 state appropriations. Allocations specifically to correct inequities in women's compensation were made ahead of other departmental budget items, which enabled eliminating most of the disparities in less than three years. By 1973 we had established a new Women's Advisory Council and created new posts of an assistant director for minority programs and an assistant director for women's programs in the Department of Human Relations. All this activity helped us get a quick start in meeting the requirements of the Federal Title IX Education Amendments of 1972.

▪ Issues of Race

From the moment I arrived in East Lansing, it was clear my success would depend in very large part on how I dealt with the "race problem." Lots of people were watching for any misstep—the university's Black faculty and students, nonminority members of the campus community, state officials, alumni, and the public at large. Almost everybody had an opinion, a perspective, a pet (and pat) solution. Would I live up to their best hopes, or confirm their worst fears?

Now for the first time I had to deal personally with the imperatives of collective Black activism. I hadn't marched in Alabama or Mississippi—did that mean I hadn't "paid my dues"? Certainly some of the more militant Black students thought so, criticizing me behind my back as an "Oreo cookie"—Black on the outside, white on the inside. The view they shared was that you were one of two things: either an old, shuffling, hat-in-hand Negro, or a proudly militant Black, relentlessly confronting the white oppressors.

To some—Black and white alike—I appeared unencumbered by any personal baggage of racism, "dressed for success" in white society. Others saw my election as president of Michigan State as no more than an enemy's slick ruse in the fight for true equality. My challenge was to make clear my personal commitment to equal opportunity, without appearing willing to sacrifice high standards of academic excellence. As a corollary, I had to underscore that my upbringing, education, and career had by no means protected me from the afflictions of racial prejudice. Finally, I needed to stress that my agenda was based on "integration," not "separatism."

With Black faculty and administrators I had to walk a fine line. Many were uninterested in public political action. Although they strongly supported increased Black enrollment and hiring, they stuck mainly to their own jobs. On the other hand, the most prominent leader was the decidedly activist Robert L. Green, who never tired of alluding to his long association with Rev. Martin Luther King Jr. With his colleagues Joseph H. McMillan, Don Coleman, and Thomas Gunnings, Green stood at the epicenter of minority affairs at MSU, and my arrival presented a conundrum. As a Black president, I was in a powerful position to advance his causes—but by the same token, my visibility and authority could undermine his own influence. Green was clearly an issue for me, too, if only because the university had allowed so much responsibility for minority affairs to collect in his hands. After student demonstrations following the assassination of Martin Luther King Jr. in 1968, a special $1.5 million fund had been created and turned over to Green. Subsequently he had assumed sole leadership over three functions: affirmative action, special minority programs, and the university's Center for Urban Affairs.

The concentration of power was problematic, and I thought that for maximum effectiveness each area needed a full-time administrator of its own. To his credit, Green acceded to the need for change. Keeping him as director of the Center for Urban Affairs, I appointed Joe McMillan as director of equal opportunity, reporting to Bob Perrin. For a new position as assistant provost for special programs, I named Dr. James B. Hamilton, an assistant professor of chemistry, who had attracted attention for his successful efforts to encourage more Black students to major in chemistry. Jim's quiet, scholarly determination seemed just what the doctor ordered to strengthen academic and support services for minority students. He and his wife Ruth, a sociologist who pioneered research on the Black Diaspora, were Black intellectual leaders.[23] Jim created a pre-enrollment summer intensive tutoring for entering minority students that was an outstanding success. This activity was complemented by the university's regular program for entering freshmen to determine their weaknesses or strengths for their studies. From the 1950s to at least 1980, the Office of Evaluation Services gave MSU tests to all incoming undergraduates to help evaluate their preparation for college. The test results provided for several uses, including for student placement in courses, or remedial work if needed, and to provide faculty teaching introductory courses a sense of the preparation level of students. The data also helped provide for changes to course content.[24]

By 1976, Hamilton's minority student program could point to an impressive record of accomplishment. The persistence and graduation rate for the students in his program was 63.5 percent—almost identical to the 65 percent rate of MSU undergraduates overall.

▪ ▪ ▪ ▪

Soon after Hamilton's appointment, Bob Green suggested that I hire Nolen Ellison, an associate director of the Urban Center, as an executive assistant in my own office. A former basketball star at the University of Kansas, Ellison was finishing his doctoral dissertation and interested in university administration. When interviewed, he freely admitted his debt to Green, but he promised not to allow it to interfere with his responsibilities to me. I thought him capable and trustworthy and soon added him to my roster of assistants.

The other important move in minority personnel brought Dr. Lloyd M. Cofer into my office from his post with Vice President Gordon Sabine. Cofer was an elder Black statesman in Michigan education, with thirty-four years of experience as a counselor and principal in Detroit public schools and a stint as dean of men at Fisk University. He also was a trustee of Central Michigan University. He was heavy-set and invariably cheerful, part of the older Black establishment. Since he had overseen the first two waves of MSU's special recruits from Detroit's inner city, Cofer understood the students and the challenges they faced when they arrived on campus. His knowledge, reputation, and personality would be invaluable in helping strengthen relations between the university and Black communities in Detroit, Flint, Grand Rapids, and Lansing, among others.

Reaching out to Black students was another matter. The Black student leadership was internally contentious and (particularly within the Black Liberation Front) confrontational. The most visible of the leaders was Sam Riddle—bright, articulate, with a huge bristling Afro. Although he had been in a few scrapes before I met him, he had a basically clean record. Because any arrest could have jeopardized his plans to go to law school, his activism had an odd push-me, pull-you aspect to it. Riddle had taken over the minority resident assistants program, funded out of Bob Green's special fund. It didn't take long to discover that many of the minority RAs had become Riddle's "troops," parroting his views and sometimes intimidating moderate Black students from speaking out in opposition.

In truth, many Black students were conflicted about even being at MSU. They were often filled with hostility and smoldering anger toward the university—while at the same time arguing vehemently for expanded admissions and hiring efforts to increase the Black presence on campus. It wasn't exactly a paradox, but it could be confusing. In the meantime, the differences between whites and Blacks went beyond color, to speech, dress, food, music, and behavior standards. Classrooms were integrated, but social life was less so. Racism in the larger society had hypersensitized many Blacks to the slightest affront, real or perceived. White students brought their own sensitivities and insensitivities, which in most cases weren't much different from those of their parents and families back home. With some notable exceptions, the two groups generally avoided each other, and any visit to a student dining facility would find many if not most Black students sitting apart in a self-segregated area.

There was undoubtedly some racism at MSU. But you didn't have to be there long to discern that there was also a great reservoir of goodwill and widespread hope that the society's racial dilemma could be resolved—at home in Michigan if not everywhere else. Many faculty and administrators were anxious for the university to provide more opportunities for disadvantaged students. They thought that "urban education" should be added to the classic land-grant mission of teaching, research, and service to the "industrial and rural classes."

During his presidency, John Hannah's approach to race issues, while gradualist, laid a strong base of positive racial sentiment within the campus. His twelve-year service as chairman of the Civil Rights Commission had given him valuable insights into the evils of racism. Father Ted Hesburgh, an original member who in 1969 succeeded Hannah, later told me that despite their political differences, he and Hannah's mutual respect and desire to achieve racial equality made for a strong early leadership for the commission.

Before I arrived at MSU, acting president Walter Adams had created an ad hoc committee to develop antidiscrimination policies and procedures. Chaired by sociology professor Wilbur Brookover, the committee proposed to set up two permanent bodies: a standing, nine-member committee against discrimination and a ten-member antidiscrimination judicial board. The former would review campus policies and operations, recommend changes when appropriate, and investigate possible infractions of policies. The latter would be a quasi-judicial panel that would rule on specific complaints from members of the university community.

In February 1970 I took the Brookover report to the monthly board meeting—my second, and the day after the year's first student disruptions on campus. Several Black faculty and students made well-reasoned presentations in its support, and pointed note was taken that Black students had taken little or no part in the previous night's demonstrations. "I didn't see one Black student throw a brick," insisted Bob Green, perhaps over-indignantly. "In fact, I didn't see any Black students out there at all."

White kids breaking windows, Black kids working through legal channels—it was a pretty irony. But the board was divided. The Republicans hesitated to adopt bold and untried measures, especially any that had originated under Walter Adams. Don Stevens and Blanche Martin did their best to stand up for the new initiative. While trying to sound supportive, Huff and his Democratic allies cagily exploited the situation with scare tactics aimed at the other party. When passage looked doubtful, I stepped into the argument, pointing out that in my fifty days as president, not one week had passed without one or more complaints of discrimination at the university. The board then accepted the Brookover recommendations "in principle," postponing final action for a week. After a five-hour special meeting on Saturday, the trustees gave their final assent, and MSU became the first university in the United States to adopt a formal antidiscrimination policy and procedures. I made the first appointments to the committee and judicial board on May 13, just in time to deal with a flurry of charges and countercharges flying between some Black students and the white director of the MSU cheerleading squad.

There were incidents, of course, for which no committee, disciplinary group, or policy would be adequate. On February 27 the boxer Muhammad Ali spoke on campus to a heavily Black audience of 2,500. His main theme was that integration was not the answer to the problems of Black Americans, and that the races should be segregated—"Preachers of integration are either helpless or dead." His only good advice, I thought, was his rejection of violence as an alternative. When a student disagreed, he snorted. "Violence with white America wouldn't be violence, it would be slaughter. . . . You're trying to get me killed."[25]

My own experience had been that, while voluntary separation is comforting and occasionally benefits some minorities, it was a tactic that too often led to misunderstandings and conflict. Moreover, Black students who self-segregated were denying themselves the chance to teach and learn from people different from themselves, and to become part of those networks and elites they so often decried. Self-isolation rarely solved problems, and usually made them worse. But saying so was contentious, so Dolores and I tried to avoid preaching in favor of setting what we hoped was a persuasive personal example. While we often gave special attention to MSU's Black students and their needs, we did not behave in an exclusive manner.

MSU was hardly the only campus with racial tensions. At Northern Michigan University, in the state's Upper Peninsula, several Black students recruited from Detroit had been harassed with "nigger hunting licenses" posted on dorm doors and campus trees. When their car was shot at one day crossing a bridge, several of the Black students decided they had had enough. A group of the leaders came down to East Lansing and called on me personally for help. NMU president John Jamrich, deeply shocked at what had happened, promised an investigation, anxious to do everything he could to protect the students. We also worked out an agreement under which students who wanted to leave Northern could transfer to MSU with full credit for their previous studies (several did so).

⁑ ⁑

In fall 1971, I talked dean of students Eldon Nonnamaker into hiring Carl Taylor, one of my first presidential fellows, to take over the minority student residential aide program in the dorms.[26] Carl came from a strong inner-city Detroit family that treasured education. During his fellowship he had seen how "the system" worked, and I had watched him develop a low-key but forceful leadership style. He knew Black students had legitimate problems and complaints, but instead of turning to conflict and intimidation, he helped them learn to use appropriate channels of redress. Once at the head of the minority aide program, Carl set up a more formal application and hiring process, insisting that credentials be assessed and applicants interviewed by a review committee. Despite consternation from Sam Riddle and some other Black activists, Carl's changes had the therapeutic effect of identifying candidates not entangled in extremist political machinations and more representative of typical Black students at MSU.

Once Carl's first group of minority aides were in place, Dolores and I invited them to an informal dinner at Cowles House. After I welcomed them and said a few words about their role, one new aide asked about my hairstyle—why didn't I wear it in an Afro? Well, I said, I had always worn it very short, and I still liked it that way. If I took up the current faddish look, wouldn't he think I was just pandering to his expectations? The aide gave me a nod and a grudging smile.

As Carl's leadership took hold, Black problems in the dorms and elsewhere declined significantly. The aides helped Black students deal with unfamiliar challenges and gave them a channel of communication other than protest and confrontation. Through Carl, they could also let me know about potential problems and flashpoints, so that when warranted I could act quickly or preemptively.

• • • •

Not everyone saw collective participation in university governance in the same light. In 1972, a substantial number of faculty undertook a unionization drive at MSU. Faculty unions had sprung up at a number of campuses nationwide, where they were promoted as an alternative to overbearing or exclusionary administrations. At Michigan State two groups were contending for control: the MSU Faculty Associates (affiliated with the Michigan Education Association), and the American Association of University Professors. Although I hoped the governance reforms already put in place at MSU would be sufficient to derail unionization, I made a public statement of my willingness to abide by the faculty vote. I stressed, in fact, that everyone on the faculty *should* vote, so that the outcome would be determined by a legitimate majority of the university's 2,450 faculty, not just a minority of activists.

A pivotal influence in the mix was a Committee of Concerned Faculty, led by Professor Gerald Miller, Dean Paul Varg, and Professor Jim Bonnen (at the time, also chair of the Academic Council Steering Committee). The committee launched a campus-wide campaign

I chaired the Academic Council Meeting with Professor Jim Bonnen, head of the Council Steering Committee.

that systematically and objectively set forth the pros and cons of unionization. Bonnen, Miller, and Varg divided up the colleges and persuaded one or two people in each department to call their colleagues to impress upon them the importance of voting. Meanwhile, although the AAUP was actually *against* the unionization effort, it got onto the ballot in order to present an alternative to the MSU Faculty Associates in case the unionization vote succeeded. Agricultural economics professor Les Manderscheid was president of the AAUP, and although independent of the Committee of Concerned Faculty, the two groups made a powerful one-two punch.

For the vote more than 80 percent of faculty turned out, and unionization was defeated by 72 percent.[27] The pro-union forces were stunned, having previously gotten the required

50 percent of faculty to sign their petition in favor of putting unionization to a vote. What they hadn't realized was that many of the signers had wanted to vote as a chance to express their opposition to collective bargaining as the faculty's principal voice at MSU. From my standpoint the rejection was evidence that my approach of reforming the existing governance structure and adding meaningful advisory groups (especially including the critical issue of budgets) was seen as a valid alternative. Another unionization attempt was made in 1978, soon after I left East Lansing, and was similarly defeated.

· · · ·

A problem that continued to plague me was the MSU Board of Trustees. Prior to my taking office, Don Stevens and Frank Merriman asked university counsel Lee Carr for an interpretation of article 7 of the bylaws, which covered communications between the university faculty as well as officers and the board. Lee's reading made it clear that everything had to go through the president's office, but it had little or no effect on Warren Huff, Clair White, and Frank Hartman, who regularly roamed the campus in search of disgruntled employees and unfulfilled expectations.

A favorite venue for mischief was the informal dinner held the night before each regular monthly meeting. Though it was a tradition of long standing, Huff, Hartman, and White now decried the dinners as "secret sessions," where university work was improperly being done beyond the view of the taxpaying public. It was true that the dinner meetings sometimes allowed for discussion of sensitive topics scheduled for public airing the next day. But in most cases, private or executive sessions usually dealt only with bids, contracts, and personnel items, which state law sheltered from disclosure requirements. My solution was to add an after-dinner session to the evening meetings where public comments or presentations could be made.

Every board meeting was a challenge, largely because the Huff troika used most sessions as possible occasions for my defeat and ousting. Even before convening, I usually had to count noses to myself, and if I thought there might be a problem I often postponed acting until I could round up a majority of votes. After a while, in fact, it got to be assumed that if I brought an item up for action, I had the support I needed for its passage.

Although I tried to limit occasions for grandstanding, individual trustees had a hard time resisting playing to their favorite constituencies—and not incidentally, the media. Official meetings were often thronged by TV crews, with a backbench of local and wire-service reporters. It was often the best show in town, but trying to conduct business on a "live" feed was often disconcerting—it could distort not only the debate but also how the votes went.

Some trustees encouraged students, faculty, alumni, and others to approach them individually with their causes and complaints. One example was a group of women in the university's married housing, who came to the board directly to demand help with day care (something the administration was already working on at the time). Another was Sol de Aztlan, an off-campus group, which brought in seventy hand-clapping Mexican Americans in an unscheduled effort to show how hard it was for Chicanos to get a hearing from the university.[28] (Prior to the meeting the group had refused to meet with us for a private dialogue.[29]) The mother of a student also spoke in Spanish about her difficulty in fulfilling her dream for her son to go to college and demanded an accounting of where her tax dollars to the university had gone.[30] My response to her in fluent Spanish, agreeing with her pleas, caught the group off guard. Most of their concerns could have been handled administratively without board action, though I suspect they wanted a more dramatic public demonstration of their activism. In both cases (and many others), it was a tactic that undercut ordinary university governance, and sometimes it resulted in mandates that could be awkward if not impossible to carry out.

▪ ▪ ▪ ▪

Conflict erupted among the five Democratic trustees once again at their party convention in August 1970. Standing for his own reelection, Don Stevens also nominated alumna Pat Carrigan for the slot that had been vacated by the retirement of Republican Steve Nisbet. In opposition, Huff, Hartman, and White put forward a former trustee, C. Allen Harlan, who traipsed around behind White for most of the convention, seeking delegate votes. White declared Stevens had to be defeated "because he and Blanche Martin always vote with the Republicans." If Stevens were reelected, he vowed, "I'll quit the Board."

In fact, Stevens and Carrigan both prevailed, thanks to a UAW endorsement and the efforts of fifty or so MSU students, led by Harold Buckner, the young Black president of ASMSU. I was tempted to remind White of his promise, but reluctantly decided against it.

The Democrats' internecine animosity ran so high that for a while in early 1971 the board couldn't even elect a chair. At one point Don Stevens tried to defuse the situation by arranging a meeting between former governor Soapy Williams and me. By then Williams had been elected to the Michigan Supreme Court, and we got along quite well. It had no effect, however, on the troika, and the debacles continued. In July 1971 Warren Huff tried to amend the bylaws so that "any action affecting the policy of governance of the university must be approved by the board of trustees before becoming effective." I objected immediately that Huff's motion was a serious infringement on the administration's ability to manage the institution, and I pointed out that under the existing bylaws the president was executing previous policy decisions of the board so that his actions already reflected board policies. After some parliamentary maneuvering, the measure failed six to two, with only Huff and Clair White supporting it. The *State News* headlined "Board Clash Ends in Triumph for Wharton."[31] The outraged campus and public reaction was gratifyingly supportive, belatedly recognizing the lengths to which Huff and White seemed willing to go in their efforts to neutralize me or drive me from office.

The two never gave up. At a public meeting a few months later, in October, White nonchalantly passed to the press in attendance his copy of the entire MSU faculty salary list—notwithstanding that doing so violated the board's own long-standing policy of confidentiality. As employees of a state university, faculty were technically "public employees," subject to state salary disclosure rules—most of which, to be sure, were originally intended to cover elected officials and high-level administrative bureaucrats. Many faculty were furious, especially when Bob Repas, a professor of labor and industrial relations and Clair White's confederate, distributed copies broadly across the campus. The Academic Council censured them both for their action, especially because they knew that the council had been about to issue its own recommendations on salary disclosure. Meanwhile the *Lansing State Journal* devoted a full two and a half pages to listing academic salaries with names, stirring campus outrage further yet. The tempest began to die down only after the board of trustees voted formally in favor of full disclosure in January 1972.

The same month, Warren Huff wrote to the other trustees and the state legislature, claiming despite all evidence that I was against a board-approved plan to add a law school to Michigan State—an idea even his own cronies found hard to swallow. Later in the fall, he tried to block Joe McMillan's appointment as director of human relations, alleging that a discrimination grievance had been filed against him in the past. Although there was no evidence of any such complaint, Huff persisted in his accusations, withholding any information about the nature of the complaint, who had filed it, or when and where the supposed infraction had occurred.

At the board meeting in October, charges of "McCarthyism" flew around, and counter-charges of "cover-up." With many Black faculty and students in the audience, the atmosphere was tense. I began by pointing out to Huff that on three separate occasions I had asked for information supporting his allegations, and that he had indicated that he could not provide it.

"I didn't say I couldn't," Huff retorted. "I told you I wouldn't."

"All right," I replied, "you wouldn't. But it is quite obvious that you could have provided it before the meeting, and I submit that you did not do so . . . to make use of it at this particular moment."

When Huff finally gave the trustees and me the information privately, after the meeting, we cleared the matter up in ten minutes. No grievance had been filed against McMillan—just an anecdotal complaint of discrimination, which had been handled properly by his deputy and submitted to the university's antidiscrimination judicial board. By a four-to-three vote McMillan got the human relations job, and Warren Huff was blistered in the press. Bizarrely, it turned out that Huff himself had previously been a witness for the complainant in an earlier hearing. His unsupported charges and obvious conflict of interest in the case led to a *Lansing State Journal* editorial: "Mr. Huff . . . is a man who has never seemed to accept proper limits on the role of trustees in running a university. . . . [He] has confused the trustee's job with that of the president, trying to poach on what is President Wharton's proper sphere of responsibility."[32]

Eventually Huff's brazen, sometimes surreal harassment led to calls for state action. Two powerful Black legislators, Coleman Young and Jackie Vaughn, introduced resolutions in both chambers calling for an investigation of Huff's "contemptuous action and negativism . . . toward Wharton and other blacks." Huff blustered that the charges were "political," and Clair White had the temerity to ask me to repudiate the "blackmailing" of an MSU trustee by Michigan lawmakers. (I declined.) But no resolution or even investigation would make any difference as long as Huff and White held their seats on the board.

White and Frank Hartman failed to be reelected in November 1972, largely thanks to Don Stevens's engineering of rule changes at the Michigan Democratic state nominating convention, where candidates for the Big Three boards were selected. Better late than never, as Hartman left the board he privately told me that Huff's and White's behavior had literally sickened him. "I couldn't always vote in your favor," he confessed, "but I am pleased that you are still president."

Al Ballard, ever a fount of ironic perspective, dug up an excerpt from a Michigan legislative document of 1840:

> A new board of trustees, like a legislature of new members, not knowing what to do, generally begins by undoing and disorganizing all that has been done before. At first they dig up the seed a few times, to see that it is going to come up; and after it appears above the surface, they must pull it up, to see that the roots are sound; and they pull it up again, to see if there is sufficient room to support so vigorous branches; then lop off the branches, for fear that they will exhaust the root; and then pull it up again, to see why it looks so sickly and pining, and finally to see if they can discover what made it die. And, as all these several operations are performed by successive hands, no one can be charged with the guilt of destroying the valuable tree.[33]

If university trustees had been acting like that for 130 years, who was I to complain?

▪ ▪ ▪ ▪

The storied rivalry between the University of Michigan and Michigan State made for exciting if not always relaxing autumn Saturdays. In my first year at MSU, when the Spartans were hosts, I had called University of Michigan president Robben Fleming to invite him and his wife Sally to join Dolores and me in our enclosed president's box at Spartan Stadium. After a long pause (possibly from shock), he accepted cordially. But when I mentioned it to my executive group the week of the game, the response was neither silent nor cordial.

"You're from the Ivy League," cried one vice president, wrestling visibly with outrage. "You don't get it. This is the Big Ten!"

"So?" I asked.

"Dammit, U of M is the *enemy*!"

The Flemings came to our box without incident, and thereafter we alternated invitations to the annual event.

▪ Athletics _____

My first real sense of the potential explosiveness of big-time sports had to wait until early 1972. On February 10, with no advance warning, Bob Green, Joe McMillan, and Tom Gunnings (a psychologist assistant director of the MSU Counseling Center) held a press conference to release an open letter to Wayne Duke, commissioner of the Big Ten, demanding that more Blacks be hired as game officials and conference administrators. Pointing out that the Big Ten had at the time only one Black official (in basketball), they proposed that a group of Black athletes attend the next conference meeting to discuss minority underrepresentation. "This is not Green against Michigan State University or Green against the Big Ten," he was quoted.[34] "The entire sports system must change." Organized sports, he added, were among "the most racist institutions in America."

The issues were real, and I sympathized with Green's position if not particularly with his tactics. I suggested a special meeting of Big Ten presidents on the subject, and I asked Professor John Fuzak, MSU's faculty representative to the conference, to raise the subject at its next meeting.[35] But Green and his allies were unsatisfied. "We don't want just a reaction from Dr. Wharton," he said. "I hope [Commissioner] Duke invites us to attend [the conference meeting]. If he doesn't, we'll go anyway."

Public anger toward Green and the others was widespread, and I was caught somewhat unprepared by its intensity. Hotheaded calls and unsigned hate letters poured into my office. Ironically, MSU and Duffy Daugherty had pioneered in recruiting Black football players and confronting discriminatory scheduling for Black athletes. The university had also refused to play certain teams in the segregated South, and its Black superstars (Bubba Smith, Gene Washington, George Webster, and Jimmy Raye, to name a few) had blazed the trail for integrating many other college and university teams across the nation.

In the early 1960s, Coach Daugherty made a recruiting push into the segregated South. As a result, Michigan State won national championships in 1965 and 1966 with some of the most racially and geographically integrated teams in all of college football. The 1965 roster included eighteen black players, nine from southern states. The 1966 roster featured seventeen black players, ten from the South, including Jimmy Raye, who quarterbacked Michigan State to an undefeated season.

But basketball was another matter, and just before the start of the 1972 Michigan State–Iowa basketball game, Black Liberation Front leader Sam Riddle led around a hundred Black students onto center court during the playing of the national anthem.[36] Refusing to leave, they delayed the game's start for forty-five minutes, until Jack Breslin allowed Riddle to use the PA system to read a statement supporting Green's charges of racism in the Big Ten. The statement was roundly booed by the impatient spectators in the bleachers. The campus police had called me to defuse the situation, but by the time Dolores and I got to Jenison Field House the game had started, and the damage was already done.

In the hope of preventing further escalation, I subsequently issued a public statement deploring the flagrant abuse of freedom of speech. The university, I added, would not tolerate any repetition of the incident, and future violators of MSU rules should expect to face consequences.[37]

As soon as the statement came out in the *State News*, Sam Riddle appeared in my office. "You've drawn a line in the sand!" he blustered.

I told him I wanted to be sure he understood what he and his colleagues could expect if they tried to stage another disruption. Public protest was one thing, but forcibly interrupting an official university function was another. Riddle wanted to go to law school, so the prospect of an arrest on his record was no small threat.

Bob Green helped by calling on Black students to exercise restraint and refrain from "overt action." Toward the end of the week Riddle announced that the administration was moving "in a positive manner." Even so, public safety director Dick Bernitt and I planned to be ready. On Saturday afternoon at game time, the court was ringed by campus police, Dolores and I were in our usual seats, and the student spectators were watching intently to see what would happen. Just before the tip, Riddle came striding into the field house, with his formidable Afro and glinting granny glasses, escorted by two supporters. All eyes moved back and forth between the Riddle entourage and us in our seats. But they sat down quietly and the game got under way.

At the half, Riddle and his companions jumped up and dashed to a balcony, where they unfurled a large banner—"The Big Ten, Open It Up or Close It Down." They then ran for another balcony with a second banner, with the campus police now in hot pursuit. Dolores and I hurriedly left our seats and stopped the officers. "It's okay," I said, pointing at the first banner. "That's free speech."

Then Riddle and his friends unfurled the other banner "MSU Uncle Clif's Cabin." The fans roared, and Dolores and I laughed along. The tension eased, and the game continued without further interruption. Riddle had made his points, including his attack on me, playing by the rules. And the university in turn had accommodated his protest without compromising its values or the integrity of its functions.[38] Best of all, MSU beat Michigan 96 to 92.

The Big Ten did take up the issue, but progress moved very slowly. There were a couple of new minority hires on a few campuses, but nothing dramatic. At MSU, I made my first affirmation by appointing Clarence Underwood as MSU assistant athletic director for student athletic services in August 1972[39] and setting up the choice of the first woman faculty representative to the Big Ten, Professor Gwen Norrell, in 1979.

▪ College of Urban Development

Student and faculty activism were all very well, but the university's student recruiting and other affirmative action efforts needed to be complemented with a corresponding stronger focus on the academic side of diversity. The Center for Urban Affairs, with its "special" fund under Bob Green's control, was supporting urban and race-focused initiatives in various academic departments, but the dollars provided were temporary, not part of an established, ongoing line of appropriation. Even the word "special" connoted a sense of separation, disconnection from everyday educational activity—a sort of "goodie bag" for campus Blacks and other minorities. The not-so-subtle implication was that "special" programs wouldn't stand up to regular standards.

Against the backdrop of my blueprint for a "pluralistic university," I wanted to institutionalize the university's programs on race and urban culture in a new, cohesive, academically rigorous degree-granting college. I was convinced that solving the emerging problems of U.S. cities warranted the same sound intellectual basis that the land-grant universities had previously developed for agriculture and rural America. My idea was that a college would bring greater understanding and respect to the field, while fostering research on urban problems and training career professionals to grapple with them. It would also have full membership standing in the university's Academic Council and Senate, rather than the "special" or provisional status accorded to the Center for Urban Affairs.

Once unveiled, the College of Urban Development initiative immediately drew the expected resistance. Although denying that their objections had any relation to Bob Green's challenge to Big Ten athletics, trustees Warren Huff and Clair White pulled out every stop. They argued that the proposed college would be "a political base for attacks on racism," rather than a vehicle to promote black education.[40] In a letter to me, they raised a series of canards: Was there an actual body of knowledge sufficient to justify the proposed college? Would the study of race be a meaningful basis for solving urban problems? Would the new college be primarily for Blacks? What employment opportunities would there be for its graduates? Particularly nasty was the unspoken suggestion that the college would be a mechanism for providing college degrees to unqualified students. Throughout, there was an undertone of pure bigotry under the guise of "impartial" analysis. In the background was the emerging issue on U.S. campuses of South Africa's apartheid policy. The Congressional Black Caucus in 1972 introduced the first bill proposing steps to dismantle the apartheid. Proposals for economic sanctions were coupled with pressure on U.S. corporations operating in South Africa to cease operations (disinvest) and on U.S. universities to remove from their investment portfolios' stocks of companies doing business there.

If the College of Urban Development were to have any chance of being accepted on campus, I knew it had to be blessed by the regular academic establishment. Professor Les

Manderscheid, chair of the Educational Policies Committee, skillfully developed two alternatives for this new urban initiative, a "college" and an "office," which the committee submitted to me for consideration without an expressed preference. At its meeting in May 1972, over the objections of Huff and White, the board approved the College of Urban Development, MSU's seventeenth college[41] and the first such college in the United States. At the outset it was composed of two departments—Urban and Metropolitan Development Affairs and Racial and Ethnic Studies. (A proposal for an urban extension service was tabled pending adequate state funding.) Bob Green was named interim dean, and steps began toward developing a curriculum.

The college was dismantled in 1980 in the wake of low enrollment and massive state budget cuts that also required eliminating or modifying the university's Justin Morrill, James Madison, and Lyman Briggs residential colleges. I have often wondered what might have happened if the urban development college had survived long enough to establish a real academic and fiscal foothold. Perhaps some of the later economic and fiscal ills of Detroit might have been avoided.

· · · ·

While MSU struggled to reach out more effectively to inner-city youngsters, it had compiled a remarkable record in attracting gifted students, both in Michigan and nationwide. A separate "Achievement Scholars" program had been developed for high-achieving Black students, whose enrollments regularly put MSU among the top ten nationally. Much of the credit went to Vice President for Special Projects Gordon Sabine, who had designed and overseen a multiyear recruiting program aimed at National Merit Scholarship semifinalists. Early every year, his office sent individually addressed and signed letters to some 13,000 high school juniors and seniors across the country, along with a thick packet of promotional materials and, for finalists, an invitation to visit the university. Those who accepted toured the lovely campus; visited the libraries, classrooms, and athletic facilities; and stayed over a weekend in the dorms. They also took a highly competitive examination for MSU's own Alumni Distinguished Scholarships, ten winners of which got a full four-year financial award—tuition, residential and dining charges, fees, and costs of books included.

Thanks to Sabine's recruitment machine, at my arrival Michigan State had for several years enrolled more National Merit Scholars than any other college or university in the United States—from 1965 to 1972, for example, an average of 628 per year, compared to 492 at Harvard, 335 at Yale, 300 at MIT, and 358 at Stanford.[42] (The number of semifinalists who enrolled at MSU was large as well, although no count was kept that I know of.) At the end of their freshman years, those with 3.5 or better GPAs (the majority) were admitted to the university's Honors College, which allowed more flexibility in designing degree programs, as well as use of a dedicated lounge and library in Marshall Hall.

I chafed at what seemed like a general public ignorance of the caliber of MSU students and graduates. While some lag in public perception was natural, MSU's image as a "cow college," "jock" campus, and "party school" told far too little of the real story. One thing that especially surprised me was that no MSU student had won a Rhodes Scholarship since 1952. Having seen how assiduously other universities worked to nurture potential Rhodes applicants, I asked Honors College director Frank Blackington to lead an effort to identify strong candidates and help prepare them for the rigorous competition. It was a telling gauge of the university's reservoir of student intellectual excellence that in 1972, just two years later, our first modern-era Rhodes winner was named (Alan Ver Planck). Over the next five years four more Spartans would win Rhodes awards, including Mary C. Norton in 1977, the first year of women's eligibility.

▪ Lifelong Education

Another offshoot of my concept of a "pluralistic university" was the recognition that MSU could not meet its full potential so long as it remained a place almost exclusively for "traditional" students—that is, eighteen- to twenty-four-year-olds pursuing conventional undergraduate and graduate degrees, mostly if not always on a full-time basis. Scientists, psychologists, economists, and other commentators had long talked about the explosion of knowledge that had been taking place in the nineteenth and twentieth centuries, with its corrosive impact on the nature of the American workplace and the skills people needed to sustain themselves in their jobs and professions. Agriculture provided the prototype—between 1900 and 1970 those engaged in farming had dropped from 38 percent of the U.S. labor force to 4.6 percent, even as output and productivity had skyrocketed. Similarly, after subsequent generations of migrations into industrial employment, Daniel Bell and other sociologists were now beginning to talk about yet another shift toward *postindustrialism*, where more and more new jobs would be created in services and the "knowledge" sector.

The subtext of all the changes was that few skills were immune to change and obsolescence, and that higher education needed to reinvent itself as a lifelong, rather than youth-focused, process. No longer could our clients be almost entirely adolescents and young adults. Increasingly we would have to accommodate older adults, with a far broader set of backgrounds and a much more diverse group of needs. To do so effectively, of course, colleges and universities would have to change all sorts of things, ranging from admissions and financial aid policies to course requirements and class scheduling.

In the early seventies the concept of lifelong education was regarded as novel at best, radical and impractical at worst. My awareness of the issues had been sharpened by my participation in a commission on nontraditional study, which looked at (among other programs) the University Without Walls, SUNY's Empire State College, and the New York Regents' external degree program, later Excelsior College. Launched in 1971, the twenty-six member commission was chaired by Samuel B. Gould, chancellor of the State University of New York.

Many faculty liked the *idea* well enough, just not its implications—having to teach students as old as (or older than) themselves, often in courses that met at night or on weekends, perhaps in formats that didn't award academic credit or lead to formal degrees, maybe even using telecommunications and other technologies to reach beyond ordinary classrooms into unfamiliar learning environments. Probably more than a few of them weren't thrilled at the implication that their own skills might need updating, too.

To overcome foot-dragging among the too-well settled, in 1971 I applied for and subsequently got from the Kellogg Foundation a grant to support a university-wide task force on lifelong education.[43] The group's charge was to analyze how MSU would have to change—its organization and curriculum, practices and procedures, service areas and constituencies, and its relationships with other institutions—to apply its resources effectively to the society's emerging needs. The traditional model of adult and continuing education had served a limited audience—primarily mobile, middle-class professional groups. But if MSU were to maintain its heritage of service to a broad spectrum of people, it needed to extend its reach and expand its vision.

Taking the university's pathbreaking Admissions Commission as a model, the task force had a large and broadly representative membership—three deans, three teaching faculty, three students, two alumni, an assistant provost, and the directors of the university libraries, continuing education, and cooperative extension service. The chair was Bill Wilkie, a young assistant professor of administration and higher education, a staff member of the Admissions Commission, and a recent appointee as one of my special assistants. James Harkness was hired to write the report and later became my speechwriter.

The task force worked for more than a year, at the end of which its final report defined what it would take for MSU to become *The Lifelong University*.[44] Among other things, it recommended that the university work toward establishing a number of degree programs, aimed at working adults, that could be completed entirely though night and/or weekend classes. The group also called for more robust support services, more flexible financial aid criteria, and modified or eliminated campus housing requirements for mature students.

Not entirely surprisingly, the task force's most difficult decision was over how and where the university's future lifelong education programs should be administered. Although the majority favored establishing a dedicated associate provost's office, a minority were convinced that only a new vice president would have the clout and visibility the initiative needed to succeed. Ultimately I recommended and the board approved the new post of dean of lifelong education programs, reporting directly to me. I also appointed Armand L. Hunter, a task force member who was then director of continuing education, on an interim basis.

Another "lifelong" education activity was an MBA degree program for current corporate officers serving in Michigan companies. Five years before I arrived, MSU had been operating an advanced management program in the greater Detroit area in rented space. The courses were taught by regular MSU business faculty, and the curriculum was intentionally designed for current business executives. Classes were given on evenings and weekends to facilitate the work schedules of the executive students. By 1973, the program had granted MBA degrees to 381 executives from 171 companies in southeastern Michigan.

Les Scott, as a former director of continuing education and a former corporate CEO, recognized the program's need for a permanent physical base. Building plans were developed. Les, business dean Richard Lewis, and I persuaded Edward N. Cole, president of General Motors, to lead a private fund-raising drive. Chrysler donated twenty acres of land. GM supplied the engineering and design, and Ford made a cash donation along with BorgWarner and IBM. The new Advanced Management Education Center building in Troy was completed in 1974. It was later called the "Executive MBA Program." Few initiatives during my tenure had more impact on the corporate profiles of Michigan companies. Many hundreds of executives received additional training and their MBAs leading to greater upward mobility within their corporations. For example, in November 1993, I voted to elect Alex Trotman chairman and CEO of Ford Motor. Alex reminded me that he had completed the Troy program and received his MBA from my hand on June 10, 1972.

. . . .

For most of my tenure, commencements were my favorite university activities—though not so much at first. During the era of student unrest, an event that should have been bright and jubilant all too often turned drab and hostile, clouded with surliness and confrontation. Some students refused to wear their academic robes; others wore them with little or nothing underneath. All too many cloaked themselves in palpable disdain for the pomp and ceremony that made commencement something more, after all, than just another day. When the days of rage waned, the bleak mood lifted, to the relief of just about everybody.

MSU had three commencements a year—the biggest in June, usually at Spartan Stadium. Graduate and professional school degrees were handed out at a morning ceremony independent of the undergraduate commencement. Occasionally we talked about breaking them out by college, which wasn't a bad idea given the numbers of graduates involved. But I resisted, considering it important for students and their families to think of the university as a whole. Since I had virtually sole discretion over the choice of commencement speakers, I made an effort to look for exceptional role models, especially for the steadily growing number of women and minority graduates. Among those recognized were Kenneth B. Clark, the psychologist whose work underlay the NAACP successful *Brown v. Board of Education* battle against "separate but equal" in 1954; Bayard Rustin, the civil rights activist who orchestrated the famous Black march on Washington in 1963; Percy Julian, the distinguished Black research chemist and inventor; Esther Peterson, consumer advocate and women's rights leader; Sarah Caldwell,

LLD honoree Senator Edward Brooke attended the MSU commencement in the spring of 1974. I knew Brooke from when he lived in Washington, D.C., during my SAIS years, before he moved to Massachusetts.

a year after she became the first woman conductor at the Metropolitan Opera House; Edward Brooke, the first Black U.S. senator since the Reconstruction in the 1870s; Vernon Jordan, then head of the National Urban League and a fellow trustee of the Rockefeller Foundation; and Nancy Hanks, chairman of the National Endowment for the Arts, with whom Dolores worked as a member of the National Council on the Arts.

The Hanks commencement had a tragic backdrop. The night before, I was called to the Sparrow hospital because a student, Martin V. Brown, had been knifed and died. During the next day's commencement, I announced a memorial scholarship in between several intermissions to consult with the campus police behind the stage curtains. Despite the tragedy, the ceremonies were conducted with proper dignity. The campus police were reasonably certain that two Black youths had committed this random act of violence, though they were not able to prove it. The police knew that the two belonged to a secret and bizarre organization called the Topographical Institute that would only accept members who had killed a white person. Unable to prove their case for many years, the police eventually made arrests thirty-two years later.[45]

. . . .

After a few commencements had passed, it became obvious that the university board was getting annoyed with the faculty honorary degree committee, whose idea of suitable candidates diverged considerably from the trustees' own. The committee tended to look with favor on distinguished scholars, authors of weightier literature, and public intellectuals. The trustees leaned more toward political figures, successful businesspersons, and notably public-spirited citizens, with considerable emphasis on those home-grown in Michigan.[46] While not inclined to infringe on the prerogatives of the faculty committee, I could see the trustees' point as well. As a result, Bob Perrin suggested to me the creation of a Michigan Distinguished Citizen Award,[47] to be presented at MSU commencements in conjunction with the honorary degrees. Recipients of the award were selected by a trustee committee, which could use different criteria than the traditional academic ones. Over time, the Distinguished Citizen Awards went to such leaders as billionaire philanthropist and founding partner of General Motors C. S. Mott; U.S. district judge Damon Keith; Michigan secretary of state Richard Austin; retail giant S. S. Kresge; and State Supreme Court justice Mary Coleman.

The university had a long-standing practice of recognizing at commencement four graduating seniors—two men and two women—with the highest and second-highest GPAs in their class. Before the ceremony the winners came by my office for congratulations and modest checks, with photographs taken for their hometown papers. Once the group included an older woman who had dropped out of MSU many years earlier to marry a fellow student. When her children were in college themselves, they and her husband urged her to go back to finish her degree. After so long a time away, she was nervous. Finally she took the plunge. But when she arrived at her first registration, with literally thousands of bright young students milling around the controlled chaos in the Men's Intramural Building, she froze on the steps. She couldn't go in—but how could she go home to face her family's disappointment? Just then she saw me—I had started dropping in on registration at random moments, walking the lines and stations to buck up both the fatigued students and harried registrars. Not knowing who I was, the woman later said she told herself: "Good grief. If that old guy can do it, so can I." She finished her degree with a perfect 4.0.

The most interesting, and apprehensive, commencement was in December 1974, when I had invited Van Cliburn to either speak or play—hoping that he would choose the latter, which I thought might be a great national photo opportunity. The week before the commencement, I still had not heard his travel plans. His office did not know his whereabouts, nor did the Waldorf in New York City, where he maintained a suite. I even called his mother with no answer. At breakfast two days before the event, I read in a Detroit newspaper that

Walter Cronkite was the MSU commencement speaker and honoree in the spring of 1973. Cronkite's son Chip was a classmate of our son Bruce at Deerfield Academy.

Imelda Marcos from the Philippines was visiting Henry and Cristina Ford, accompanied by Van, who had a crush on both women.[48] I immediately called Henry at his home, who cheerily confirmed that Van was there! Van promised to arrive as planned by Ford Motor helicopter. That Saturday was one of the worst ice storms in Michigan history. Dolores, who served with Van on the National Council on the Arts, went to the airport at noon and waited, while I hosted the official luncheon at the Kellogg Center. Still no Van Cliburn. Ken Beachler, MSU's performing arts director, and I ate our chicken lunch at a table with eight empty seats, maintaining an air of assured nonchalance.

Half an hour before robing, I told Dolores to give up and come back and asked Dean Gordon Rohman to repeat his morning commencement speech in Van Cliburn's place. (The campus police had to drive Gordon home to get the text!) During the ceremonies, I temporized by rearranging the program to delay the commencement address by awarding the student diplomas first.

Then, just before I called upon Dean Gordon Rohman, onto the stage swooped a gracefully robed crane-like Van Cliburn! He gave a splendid speech without notes. (He used an acronym, PROFIT, to outline his points.[49]) I was disappointed that he did not play instead—we had kept a piano at the ready backstage, just in case. I also wished that someone had told me that he is always late for his own concerts. When we all returned to Cowles House, Dolores asked Van Cliburn if he would like some lunch (she also had missed it), and Van said yes. In typical MSU fashion, they had already prepared two boxes of the chicken lunch!

Probably the most entertaining commencement speaker was Walter Cronkite. When we entered the stadium on a beautiful, sunny June day, the crowd of 25,000 burst out in a roar of welcome. "Wave," I told him, "they're cheering for you." Somewhat hesitantly he did so, and the roar redoubled. I waved too, with a similar result. "This could really get to you," Cronkite beamed. The students greeted his speech equally warmly, and several youngsters came down out of the stands and sat directly under the speaker's podium, just as if they were watching "Uncle Walter" on the *CBS Evening News*.

▪ Finances

During the "golden years" of Michigan State's explosive growth, state and federal funding had been more than ample. But not long after the beginning of my tenure (and for the most part throughout the rest of it), both the national and state economy were slowing, with a substantial impact on the university's budget. The old adage was that when the U.S. economy got a cold, Michigan caught pneumonia. Thus, in much of the 1970s during my tenure, the Michigan economy, and hence its tax revenues upon which the university depended, suffered.

Although the automotive industry was still strong, its competitiveness was starting to erode under the rising costs for unionized labor and benefits. The early danger signs of the Japanese car "invasion" were not fully appreciated. As a director of the Ford Motor Company, I personally witnessed the beginnings of this process and was involved in its attempted responses.

The developments in Michigan were also influenced by the adverse economic events at the national level. The U.S. balance of trade, heavily positive since the end of World War II, was starting to shift, if only slightly thus far, under the pressure of competition from abroad. The 1970s were also a period of "stagflation" when inflation and unemployment increased causing double-digit interest rates. The economic effects of the growing costs of the Vietnam War also played a negative role. President Nixon's gutting of the Bretton Woods currency mechanism further contributed to the nation's economic malaise. Thus the 1970s were a period during which many of the country's economic pigeons were coming home to roost.

In the 1970s student tuition covered about a third of the cost of running the university—the rest came largely from state appropriations, plus smaller amounts from federal sources, foundation grants, and private donations. Since allocating funds was the prerogative of the state legislature, approving them that of the governor, and overseeing their use that of MSU's autonomous board, putting together a budget was a three-way porcupine mating dance that took up a good part of every academic year. My first exposure to the process came early, with the news that Governor Milliken was proposing a 1970–71 appropriation for MSU (including Oakland University) of $78.4 million—about $10 million above 1969–70. Although it was below the university's request, we responded with muted appreciation—there was a long road ahead before we would know the final figure.

My experience in testifying before government bodies had been at the federal level, and never in search of public funding. But legislative relations had been in Jack Breslin's portfolio for some time, and he excelled at it. He knew the state appropriations apparatus top to bottom, and whatever unhappiness he might have felt at my being elected as president instead of himself, his love for MSU was unquestioned and energizing. In addition, my executive assistant Al Ballard had previously been a member of the legislature's budget staff—so I was in the fortunate position of being able to learn from two masters of the process.

In budget hearings Breslin and I regularly had to field pointed questions from the legislators, and the fact that the campus was just four miles from the state capitol didn't necessarily help the cause. The committee chairman, Charles Zollar, said he would not allow "other influences" to affect his judgment, mentioning "campus incidents and hysteria." But the day of one hearing in May, the *Lansing State Journal* front page headline was "Police Arrest 132 on MSU Campus"—with a story on "Decrease in Michigan State Appropriation Expected" immediately below.[50]

The state's fiscal austerity complicated more than budget requests and appropriations. It also led at times to midyear reductions in funds that had already been allocated. Virtually every year was a struggle to absorb reductions without laying off employees or raising tuition too steeply. One year the cuts came in the fourth quarter, which was especially painful on regular operations—courses were planned, faculty assigned, and instructors or graduate assistants hired. Business and finance vice president Roger Wilkinson and his staff developed creative coping mechanisms. For example, they market-timed coal purchases for the university's two power plants, building up huge surplus coal piles when prices were low, then drawing them down when prices went up or state dollars faltered. In another case, the state insisted on capping enrollment in our college of education. They believed—mistakenly—that an oversupply of schoolteachers was developing in Michigan and the Midwestern United States. We avoided budget-cut firings by developing part-time appointments for education faculty in the colleges of medicine and osteopathy. When demand for K–12 teachers turned around, the university had retained its capacity to respond smoothly and effectively.

One less visible, but important, step to maintain morale during the stress was my action in 1973 to broaden the availability of the TIAA-CREF retirement program beyond the faculty to include all university employees. The contributory pension replaced the state noncontributory fixed pension plan.

A few years into the era of austerity, when I had become chairman of the Michigan Council for State College Presidents in 1975, Al Ballard and I pushed for agreement among the member institutions on a formula approach to state funding for all the state colleges and universities. The goal was to reduce behind-the-scenes warfare among the campuses over public dollars. We worked with Tom Freeman, associate director in MSU's Institutional Research unit, to develop a nuanced plan that recognized individual institutional missions, enrollment levels, undergraduate versus graduate and professional education commitments, and special circumstances such as medical schools and hospitals.

We shared the draft privately with key legislators, who seemed to think it worth pursuing. Then we sent the proposal to the other fifteen council members, and everyone acceded to it—except the University of Michigan. Even though the funding formula deliberately put U of M ahead of everyone else, their veto was enough to kill the idea for good. So much for rationality and logic in higher education finance.

· · · ·

Although I had planned on strengthening the university's private fund-raising all along, the state's declining fortunes made it even more critically important. In a more affluent era, John Hannah could count on steady or growing revenue from both state and federal sources. He also cultivated a relatively small number of wealthy friends of the university, often large farmers or landowners. But he had not been enthusiastic about pursuing private funds from many individual donors, suspecting that Michigan politicians would use such gifts as an "offset" for cutting state appropriations.

During most of his regime it was undoubtedly a fair way of looking at things, but at the beginning of the 1970s many big public universities had pushed past similar fears and developed substantial private fund-raising programs without being punished for it by their states. At MSU, in contrast, I was surprised to learn there were only sixty-one members of the "President's Club," in which membership required a contribution to the university of at least $10,000. Also, after their gifts, they were virtually ignored. To encourage more supporters and alumni to join, Dolores and I began inviting Club members to daylong annual events, where they could see for themselves the strengths and resources the university needed help to maintain. Each of the one-day programs always ended with a reception at Cowles House, where we tried to practice the old adage, "Raise friends before you raise funds." On this front, Dolores's role in building wider local and statewide relationships with potential private donors was exceptional.

When Les Scott came on board in May 1972 as vice president for development, we were ready to take MSU fund-raising to another level. A few months after his appointment, Les established the Michigan State University Foundation. He knew that cultivating prospective donors was almost always a long-term process, with many years between an initial contact and the actual gift. He also made it clear that a president's fund-raising responsibilities were personal, not something that could be delegated to "the pros" in the development office. Potential donors expected to meet and work with the person at the top, and successful appeals often depended on the strength of the personal bond I could develop with them. For example, MSU alumnus Eli Broad was a builder in California, and later founder of a successful insurance and real estate business. Les and I visited him often. For years he promised to make a major gift, but not until he could correct his "cash-flow situation." Years later, he made a donation that resulted in the university's school of business being named for him. Then in 2007 he and his wife, Edythe, gave $26 million to build a new university art museum, named for the two of them and designed by Zaha Hadid, the first woman to win the Pritzker Architecture Prize.

Another key to better fund-raising results was strengthening the university's alumni relations, with which there were two problems. The first was that MSU's database of contact information was poor. It would take time to build one that was comprehensive and reliable, but Les Scott correctly insisted that it was an indispensable tool.

The other problem was tougher. Jack Kinney, executive director of the Alumni Association, had for years made no secret of his wish to separate his office entirely from the university. On several occasions he came to Scott and me to argue that complete independence for the alumni office would help the university, not hurt it. He insisted that the organization would be more effective politically, particularly in influencing the nominating process for MSU trustees. A former MSU tennis star, Kinney had a strong affection for intercollegiate athletics, and he put a lot of effort into filling the coffers of the Ralph Young Fund for athletic scholarships. An independent alumni office, he claimed, would also make for greater flexibility in directing private funds toward the varsity sports programs.

Kinney had substantial control over his board of alumni trustees, who eventually approved an independence proposal. Les Scott and I had serious doubts about Kinney's views, but chose not to confront him directly. Les modified the proposal so that he could veto any decision or action he considered ill-advised. The final plan gave the appearance of an independent alumni association, but without ceding power to it in any fundamental way. Problems with the "independent" alumni association came to a head not long after I left Michigan State. Kinney departed, and the organization reverted to its previous standing as a regular unit of the university.

Our fund-raising efforts had some lighter moments. At one state appropriations committee meeting, a legislator asked how much the state had contributed to the university's new Faculty Club. Prior to its construction, John Hannah had gotten the local powers-that-be to shift the plot on which it was sited from East Lansing (which was dry) into Lansing (which wasn't) so the club could serve liquor. One consequence, however, was that the grounds, swimming pool, tennis courts, and the beautiful facility itself were highly visible from the state highway, and it became the subject of public aggravation over "faculty who spend all their time [playing] . . . when they should be teaching."

When I explained to the legislator that the Faculty Club had been built entirely with private funds, no state money involved, he came back with "Yeah? What about the rocks?"

"Rocks?" I raised my brows at Jack Breslin, who groaned softly, "Damn."

It seemed that when certain state highways had been built, numerous large rocks and boulders had been used to anchor the steeply verged sides, often near overpasses. But hoodlums often dropped the rocks onto cars passing below, so the state highway department had removed them and offered them free to MSU for landscaping accents. In turn, MSU used the rocks to decorate portions of the Faculty Club grounds—technically, stirring state-owned property into what we had thought an entirely private funding recipe.

Money wasn't the only thing I got to talk about with state legislators. There were also "The Doctor's Bag" and the Beal Film Cooperative. "The Doctor's Bag" was a column that appeared regularly in the *State News*, written by Arnold Werner, an assistant professor of psychiatry who also worked as a physician at Olin Health Center. The column discussed questions purportedly submitted by MSU students, and almost every issue included one or two frank, even graphic disquisitions on sexual acts, organs, or functions. For example, one student asked the doctor to settle an argument he was having with a roommate. The roommate said that humans had first contacted venereal disease from sheep, which sailors on long voyages used as sexual substitutes for women. "I refuse to believe," the student wrote, "that anyone could get that horny."

The column amused most students and many adults, and sometimes it even passed on useful information. But it sent many conservative readers around the bend—particularly legislators. One lawmaker telephoned me regularly. Each time the *State News* hit his desk, he would be on the line, reading the column aloud with detailed attention to the most objectionable items. "Don't give me any crap about freedom of the press," he always ended. "It's a student paper at a state university paid for by Michigan taxpayers!" Eventually, in fact, the column was syndicated, appearing in campus papers across the country.

Legislators were even more fraught about the Beal film group, which had been founded by an enterprising student, Michael Sunshine. In those innocent days before HBO and on-demand adult movies on TV, Sunshine and his group rented and showed pornographic films, using the ticket revenue to rent a "collective" house where they all lived. As a duly registered student organization, the Beal group was entitled to use university facilities to screen the films. Actually, student attendance was never very large—at least at the time, porn movies would have been an embarrassing thing to see on a date. But they were advertised in the *State News* and elsewhere, and many legislators were scandalized and furious. There was not much I could do—if we had turned the group off campus, there would have been an instant outcry about censorship and freedom of expression. But that was never an acceptable answer to the lawmakers, who believed that since campus facilities were owned by the state, the state should be in a position to prohibit the "filth" that Sunshine and his cohorts relied on for rent and pocket money.[51]

. . . .

In May 1972 there was another multiday student demonstration. Initially a few hundred students took over and blocked traffic on Grand River Avenue, to protest paying their telephone bills because the tax contributed to the support of the Vietnam War. Since Grand River was a state highway, the Michigan State Police eventually showed up with riot gear and tear gas. Although I had advised the East Lansing City Council not to disturb the students—just let them sit—the council was unable to control the state police reaction when pelted with a few cans. Their overreaction was to use tear gas, and the student numbers exploded. In support of the original protestors, thousands more students soon flooded East Lansing, and what had started as a relatively small protest blossomed into a full-scale riot. My information sources learned that the students had conflicting leaders, so I initially resisted negotiating with them. However, the East Lansing City Council did so, acceding to their demands (among other things) that the city stop doing business with firms that directly or indirectly supported the war in Vietnam. Though the city council eventually passed their demanded ordinance, the demonstration continued unabated. Today, some forty years later, the law is still on the books.

Having learned from our baptism two years before, my colleagues and I kept the university largely on the sidelines until true leaders emerged—and once again the university survived. But in the disruption's aftermath, Dolores and I decided we needed to spare Bruce the impact of campus politics and unrest on his life at home and in school. That fall, after we had looked at five private schools, Bruce enrolled in Deerfield Academy, in the beautiful hill country of northwest Massachusetts, near the border with Vermont. Founded in 1797, Deerfield had a reputation for emphasizing individual responsibility and intellectual growth. We hoped Bruce would prosper in a calmer setting, and without the peculiar pressure of being everywhere recognized as "the president's son." In fact, we were soon disconcerted to learn that Bruce was being pressured to join the school's Black Coalition, and that Deerfield had tried to assign Bruce a "special faculty advisor" for disadvantaged Black students, irrespective of his own preferences and wishes. Although he graduated in 1977, Bruce later told us that his years at Deerfield were the worst time of his life. So much for good parental intentions.

Meanwhile, Clifton 3rd had not done well in his freshman year at St. Lawrence, and the school recommended he try to improve his academic performance at another college for a while. Our search for an alternative led to Metropolitan Junior College in Kansas City, Missouri, where my onetime assistant Nolen Ellison had become an aide to the chancellor. Clifton enrolled at its Penn Valley campus, and he soon flourished. From there he transferred to Oakland University, majoring in philosophy and working part-time in the campus bookstore.

On June 12, 1972, the art department hosted a reception celebrating the publication of Dolores's *Contemporary Artists of Malaysia: A Biographic Survey* (Malaya Publishing for Asia Society, 1971), which was the first book on modern Malaysian art. This picture includes: (*left to right*) Toni DeBlasi, professor of art; Irving Taran, professor of art; and Dolores, the First Lady of MSU.

▪ ▪ ▪ ▪

In 1971 Governor Milliken appointed Dolores to the Michigan Council for the Arts, and in 1972 the Asia Society published her book *Contemporary Artists of Malaysia*, based on her experiences there and based on surveys she had conducted in 1966 and 1968. As the first book ever written on modern Malaysian art, her work became famous in the region. Later the governor named her to his Special Commission on Architecture and finally as vice chair of the Michigan Bicentennial Commission under the National Commission for the Bicentennial Era. All this and her rotating faculty art in Cowles House program increased her credentials in this area.

Dolores also called upon her arts background and contacts to help secure a National Endowment for the Arts matching grant for a sculpture in downtown Lansing. The selection committee's first choice as sculptor was one of pop art's reigning aristocrats, Claes Oldenburg. Unfortunately the press described his proposal—erroneously—as a giant baseball mitt, jokingly rendering Michigan's glove-like shape. This caused Oldenburg to withdraw his proposal. Instead, Lansing ended up with a lovely kinetic piece by Jose de Rivera.

In April 1971 the Cowles House hosted a reception for pianist Van Cliburn. Both Van and Dolores were appointed as members of the National Council on the Arts by President Gerald Ford and served from 1974 to 1980.

Although she had no "official" university standing, Dolores was my active and supportive partner. In addition to her more traditional duties as MSU's "First Lady," she met the press, gave speeches, and launched programs on her own, such as creating an annual reception for the widows of former faculty and staff. Universities often have difficulty avoiding the impression of elitism, or at least distance from their surrounding communities, so Dolores pushed hard for stronger ties with East Lansing, greater Lansing, and other towns and cities of mid-Michigan. Before long, Cowles House became a town-gown crossroads where Dolores and I entertained visitors from business, music, dance, politics, and academe. Visiting dignitaries such as pianist Van Cliburn, economist John Kenneth Galbraith, newspaper publisher Kay Graham, and others often found themselves pressed into temporary service as acting university ambassadors, helping build a statewide appreciation for MSU's breadth and depth of academic and cultural excellence.

One memorable highlight, which I missed, was the overnight visit in Cowles House by First Lady Betty Ford on September 15, 1976, while President Ford was launching his election bid at his alma mater, the University of Michigan. The next morning when the MSU Marching

First Lady Betty Ford visited MSU campus with Dolores on September 16, 1976. Mrs. Ford honored us by staying overnight in the Cowles House.

Band awoke the First Lady, she graciously went outside and greeted them. Dolores used the occasion to highlight the university's art faculty and Folk Art Museum, greeted by curators Kurt Dewhurst and Marsha MacDowell. Included in the tour was Helen Milliken, wife of the Michigan governor. It was quite a sight to have three first ladies on the tour—Betty Ford, Helen Milliken, and Dolores.[52]

CHAPTER EIGHT

The President of MSU 3: Enrichment, Athletics, and Politics

J ust before coming to Michigan State, I had been invited to join the Rockefeller Foundation board of trustees, taking the seat being vacated by Ralph Bunche, deputy secretary-general of the United Nations (see appendix 6). Before accepting I asked the MSU board for its approval, which passed on the usual five-to-three vote. A few months later, the trustees agreed on my becoming a trustee of the Museum of Modern Art in New York, the Agricultural Economics Association, and shortly thereafter the first board of the Public Broadcasting Service. The later votes were unanimous, so we seemed to be making progress.

Other board invitations—this time corporate—soon followed, including General Motors, Federated Department Stores, Consumers Power, and AT&T, all of which I turned down. Ken Thompson, Steve Nisbet, Blanche Martin, and Don Stevens were vexed with me, believing that such appointments reflected well on the university. But at that point my joining for-profit boards would have provided the dissident trustees with ammunition to paint me as either self-seeking or a tool of the corporate establishment, so I was careful which opportunities I considered. I could probably have gotten General Motors and some of the others approved on split votes by the MSU board, but I had plenty on my plate getting to know the university and my responsibilities there.

Over the next few years I did join several other boards, including the Carnegie Foundation for the Advancement of Teaching, the Carnegie Council on Policy Studies, and my old employer, the Agricultural Development Council. Throughout, I kept a strict ceiling on the number of outside organizations I worked with and the hours per month that I devoted to them. Of course, many people, even when entirely well-meaning, had a hard time understanding why, much less how, someone with the all-consuming job of a university chief executive would take on the additional burdens of outside corporate and nonprofit governance bodies. The cynical answer was "for the money"—that is, the fees the for-profit boards paid their directors to prepare for and attend meetings. But that was facile, and in my case irrelevant—I was already on record as donating my outside fees to the university.

The real answer was more complex. As some of the MSU trustees themselves argued, a president's board memberships could add a bit of luster to the university's public image, and occasionally more tangible benefits as well. Networking came into it, too—it was through serving on nonprofit boards that I met and became friends with William Friday, president of the University of North Carolina; Jim Perkins, president of Cornell; Sam Gould, chancellor of the State University of New York; and Felix Rohatyn of Lazard Frères, among many others. Most often my personal motives grew out of long-standing professional ties—the Rockefeller Foundation and the Agricultural Economics Association, for example. In other cases they included a sense of civic or cultural commitment, or just the desire for continuing intellectual growth. Another little-known dimension of these relationships were those boards where the directors flew together to meetings on corporate jets. These long flights, where everything from economics and politics to CEO stock options and director legal liabilities were informally discussed, were like a postdoctoral class on current events and management. The most subtle value for me was the opportunity to observe and learn about the qualities of successful leadership (and its pitfalls). Most boards, especially the corporate, had members who epitomized the qualities of leadership from which I could benefit. And finally, of course, I couldn't help realizing that by serving effectively as a trustee or corporate director myself, I might help empower Blacks and other minorities who could follow me.

Having already taken a seat on the Equitable and Rockefeller boards, I was something of a known quality, thus an attractive candidate for others. In late 1972 I got inquiries from two major Michigan corporations, the Ford Motor Company and the Burroughs computer company. Both, where I would be the first Black director, put me on new learning curves, especially Ford. Henry Ford II, who visited East Lansing personally to deliver his company's invitation, considered the Ford board to be "his people," reflecting the corporate autocracy prevalent at the time. It was Henry—"The Deuce" as he was called around Detroit—who began the practice of combining the positions of board chair and corporate CEO. He was a temperamental man, alternately charming and irascible. (When I arrived in Dearborn for my first board meeting, he met me in the company's basement garage and personally escorted me upstairs by elevator to my assigned room.) He could be brilliant in his assessments of people, or at other times a terrible judge of character. In the 1970s his knowledge of the automobile industry was encyclopedic, although his slowness to adapt to change made it hard to dispute those who later blamed him for Ford's inconstant fortunes. During most of the period when I knew him, he could stay up until three in the morning drinking wine with a few favorite trustees, then be ready for a breakfast meeting not visibly the worse for wear.

For reasons that I never understood, Henry treated me with great respect, and we always got along extremely well.

The Ford directors were among the "movers and shakers" of the country, such as Roberto Goizueta (Coca-Cola—the first Hispanic corporate CEO); Kenneth H. Olsen (founder of Digital Equipment); Joseph F. Cullman 3rd (CEO, Philip Morris); Colby H. Chandler (CEO, Kodak); Franklin D. Murphy (CEO, Times Mirror and former chancellor, UCLA); Marian S. Heiskell (founding family of the *New York Times*); Michael Dingman (CEO, Wheelabrator, later the Henley Group); Carl E. Reichardt (CEO, Wells Fargo); George F. Bennett (CEO, State Street Investment); Secretary of Transportation Drew Lewis; and Secretary of the Treasury and Texas governor John Connally. Many had served in multiple areas, such as Carter L. Burgess, who was secretary of the general staff of General Eisenhower's Supreme Headquarters in Europe during World War II, organized the administrative side of the San Francisco founding conference of the United Nations, became CEO of two major corporations (TWA; American Machine & Foundry), and was appointed U.S. ambassador to Argentina. Each director brought a highly diverse base of experiences and competencies on leadership in a wide array of fields. A director's quiet comments weighted with years of experience revealed a perceptiveness and insight that was often deceptively powerful. A seemingly simple ten-word question could dramatically shift the discussion or final action. Observing and learning this skill at the board level was far superior to any Harvard Business School corporate case studies!

The structure of Ford board meetings always began with a superb overview of the U.S. economy followed by its relevance for the automotive industry. To my delight, the regular economics presenters were my University of Chicago classmates, John Deaver, who had previously been an economist with Chase Bank in New York, and William Niskanen, who later became chairman of the Cato Institute in Washington, D.C. My twenty-four-year service with Ford would prove to be a valuable experience working with one of the largest multinational companies in the world.

• • • •

Dolores's breakthrough into the corporate sector came in January 1974, when she was elected to the Michigan Bell Telephone Company board. She had acquired a statewide reputation for dealing with student unrest and for her highly effective speeches around the state. Her knowledge of what was happening with students and her fluency on contemporary issues made her extremely attractive to a state based business like Michigan Bell, where she became the first woman and first Black on the board.

Two years later (February 1976) she joined the multinational Kellogg Company of Battle Creek, again as the first woman and first Black. That same year, a major class action suit against the Phillips Petroleum Company, another multinational, led to an agreement to appoint new outside directors acceptable both to the company and to the litigants. The front-page story in the *New York Times*[1] listed those selected—Melvin Laird, former congressman and secretary of defense; Harold M. Williams, then dean of the Graduate School of Management at UCLA, who would soon become chairman and CEO of Securities and Exchange Commission; Victor Palmieri, the venture capitalist savior of the Pennsylvania Railroad; David Meeker, CEO of Hobart, an Ohio kitchen equipment manufacturer; attorney Francis M. Wheat of Gibson, Dunn & Crutcher in Los Angeles and former SEC commissioner; and Dolores. She thereby became the first woman and first Black on the Phillips board.

Dolores thus had forged ahead on both the arts front and the corporate front. I was extremely proud of this independent role that Dolores was pioneering as one of the earliest Black women to serve on U.S. corporate boards.

Some questioned Dolores's qualifications for corporate board service—often not so subtly. The simple truth was that each time she was selected by a board, her solid performance proved that she brought a new and different set of experiences and awareness of relevance to the corporation's bottom line. The steady stream of invitations to serve on other boards validated her reputation as an effective director.

Somewhat irksome at times, however, were the veiled criticisms that Dolores encountered from other women because she was not exclusively following the path of the traditional campus president's wife. In the late 1960s and early 1970s, women in the United States were going through major changes—names like Gloria Steinem and Betty Friedan were gaining the headlines. Dolores was not cast in the mold of a typical "women's libber," but she was a highly intelligent, articulate person. She could stand on her own with men without engaging in excessive or hostile aggressiveness. She fought for the rights of minorities and women but never lost sight of the fact that she was a director representing all the shareholders, not just one constituency. Twice she initiated and chaired board corporate social responsibility committees.

· · · ·

As a university president, I participated in a number of outside education associations, such as the American Council on Education, the American Association of Universities, and the National Association of State Universities and Land-Grant Colleges (chairman 1981–82). I also joined the visiting committees of the international centers at Harvard and MIT, which kept me current on trends in foreign policy and reinforced my ability to support international programs at MSU.

In 1974 I was named the first chairman of the Food Advisory Committee of the Office of Technology Assessment, a new agency created by Congress in the wake of the global food crises of 1972 and 1974. Later the same year I joined a U.S.-Latin American Commission, chaired by Sol Linowitz, previous CEO of Xerox and U.S. representative to the Organization of American States, and reporting to President Gerald Ford.[2] The twenty-one commission members included former U.S. cabinet officers, corporate CEOs, university presidents, professors, foundation officials, and specialists in Latin America (see appendix 7). Funded by grants from the Ford and Edna McConnell Clark foundations and the Rockefeller Brothers Fund, the commission focused on trade and investment policies, and particularly on Cuba.[3]

Our most controversial recommendation was a call for an "immediate and unconditional end" to America's twelve-year-old embargo of the island nation. The commission's work continued through 1976, and its second report (to President Jimmy Carter) contained even sharper recommendations[4]—not only for more dialogue with Cuba, but also on promoting human rights in Latin America, restricting arms trafficking, and concluding a new Panama Canal treaty that would eventually lead to Panamanian sovereignty over the waterway. "This is no call for a resuscitated Alliance for Progress," the *New York Times* editorialized, "but an identification of tough problems that demand priority attention."[5]

The following year Carter appointed Sol Linowitz as co-negotiator with Ambassador Ellsworth Bunker for negotiating the Canal issue. Several commissioners were supporters of the incoming president, including Mike Blumenthal, who had already been tapped to be Carter's secretary of the treasury. There was speculation on seven other commissioners who were likely to be tapped for the new administration—including me. One amusing sidelight on the Carter cabinet search is that I was chairman of the Rockefeller Foundation nominating committee and ten RF trustees were also being considered, which led me to jokingly plead that they all not go to Washington thereby creating a major crisis in any search for their successors.

· · · ·

In 1976 I took on what would become a decade-long commitment, when President Ford named me to chair a new Board for International Food and Agricultural Development, advisory to the Agency for International Development. BIFAD, as it was universally called, had been created largely through the efforts of Representative Paul Findley and Senator Hubert Humphrey, under the "Famine Prevention and Freedom from Hunger" Title XII amendment to the U.S. Foreign Assistance Act. I had testified in Congress on the proposed amendment (bill H.R. 9005) and worked for its passage with key legislators.[6]

At a time when land-grant and other universities' participation in assistance programs seemed to be waning, its aim was to revitalize their involvement in overseas agricultural teaching, research, and service. BIFAD, which was composed of seven members appointed by the president, was charged with helping AID plan and implement all its food and nutrition programs. Joining me initially on the board were Gerald W. Thomas, president, New Mexico State University; Orville Bentley, dean of agriculture, University of Illinois; Anson R. Bertrand, dean of agriculture, Texas Technical University; Charles Krause, president, Krause Milling Company (Milwaukee); James O'Connor, a private consultant (Houston); and Peter McPherson, former special assistant to President Ford and managing partner with Vorys, Sater, Seymour and Pease (later elected president of Michigan State, 1993).

While the agency had long called on U.S. university and college expertise—in 1976 it had contracts with 143 campuses—the new authorization aimed at more systematic and longer-term relationships. Among other things, it would put a high priority on famine prevention, signaling to the world that the United States considered freedom from hunger a fundamental foreign policy goal.

Among the board's duties were helping to formulate policies and procedures for selecting projects; recommending which nations and regions could most benefit from them; advising AID on how to allocate project support; and assessing the impact of Title XII programs while and after they were carried out.

The three executive directors whom I chose and who built the strong base of BIFAD were founding director Dr. D. Woods Thomas, professor of agricultural economics, Purdue University with extensive experience in Brazil; Elmer Kiehl, dean of the College of Agriculture, University of Missouri; and Dr. Fred E. Hutchinson, vice president of research and public service, University of Maine—later its president, 1992.

Although BIFAD was (and is) an advisory body, it had considerable power because it was required to comment on relevant sections of AID's annual budget request, and to submit to Congress an annual report on its own and AID's activities. I deliberately negotiated for the BIFAD offices to be placed in the Department of State to symbolically provide "location status," a move that I had to defend vigorously on occasion. Also, I insisted that AID's administrator attend each of its monthly meetings. This frequency of meetings was my deliberate device to give regular impetus to its role and activities. I also insisted that only the administrator or his immediate deputy be eligible to stand in. Once, when neither expected to be "available," I threatened to cancel the meeting and report the matter to Congress—the administrator, it turned out, was available after all. This action gave BIFAD considerable clout and respect in its early years.

▪ Campus Enrichment Campaign and a Center for Performing Arts —

During the middle years of my presidency at MSU, one of the things that was closest to my heart and Dolores's was the university's effort to build a new performing arts center. The idea had been around a while. For decades most large-scale campus cultural events had taken place in the old university auditorium, a gloomy cavern of a building built with WPA funds back in 1939, when the student body numbered around 6,800. A later addition called Fairchild Theatre shared the same stage as the main building, which meant that only one side or the other could be used at a time. The auditorium also lacked permanent seating, so risers had to be pulled out and folding chairs set up for every performance. In 1967 a university committee on undergraduate education had reported that the building had become a "major hindrance" to the further development of the university's programs in the fine and performing arts, recommending a new facility "at the earliest possible time." At my first Board of Trustees meeting,

January 15, 1970, the major controversy was the issue of a proposed all-events building, which would replace the ancient Demonstration Hall and be used for larger campus activities. Faculty objected to the proposal and stated their preference for a fine arts center. The controversy led Provost Cantlon to ask for all departments to review their construction needs so that a campus-wide priorities list could be presented to the Board.[7]

Then in November 1971 the board of trustees approved plans for three capital projects, including the performing arts center. The other two projects were a new ice arena and, contingent on financing, an all-events (read: basketball) building. The ice arena opened in 1974, named for Biggie Munn, the university's former football coach and athletic director, who had died a year earlier. The all-events building took a lot longer. It was eventually built and dedicated in 1989, and appropriately named the Jack Breslin Student Events Center.

Dolores and I were delighted at the priority given to the performing arts, though we knew that the road ahead would be long and turning. Aside from painting and music, the fine arts had for years played Cinderella to MSU's pampered stepsisters—football and basketball. Since our two largest athletic programs generated sizable income, it was easier to justify capital spending to the state. (It was probably also the case that lawmakers generally liked football and basketball more than symphonies and theater productions.) Under the circumstances, funding for the new performing arts center would have to come from private sources. At the time, some suspected (and said as much) that I was trying to correct what I saw as an "overemphasis" on athletics, but that was off the mark. I considered the arts a unifying force in the world, bringing people together across the many fissures that divided them. Any university worthy of being called great needed a rich foundation in the arts—physical no less than intellectual. At MSU the former was long overdue.

In November 1972 Bob Perrin produced *A Place to Grow*, a film in which Dolores and I made the case for a new performing arts center on campus, comparing the old, out-of-date auditorium with mock-ups of the proposed new one. The tape, which also included shots of the proposed facilities and a mock-up, was designed for use among potential contributors, alumni, and other groups around the country. Several MSU alumni with strong commitment to the arts played key roles in energizing the drive. Phyllis and Bud Maner, alumni who met and married at MSU, were in the forefront throughout the campaign. Phyllis was a highly talented puppeteer who performed regularly at MSU and around the state. Bud was a successful public accountant. They became two of our closest lifelong friends.

A few months later, in March 1973, I appointed a special "architecture visiting committee" under Provost John Cantlon and university development vice president Les Scott. The committee's charge was to make extended visits to major performing arts complexes throughout the United States—auditoriums, recital halls, and theaters—to analyze their strengths and weaknesses, and to develop a "master plan" to guide those who would actually draw up the specifications and blueprints for MSU's facility. The members included Ken Beachler, director

The MSU First Lady led the pledge of allegiance with the MSU Band and Director Ken Bloomquist in Spartan Stadium on November 3, 1973.

of the auditorium and the university's "Lecture-Concert" series; James Niblock, chair of the Department of Music; Anne Garrison, professor of business law and chair of the University Committee on Buildings; and Frank Rutledge, chair of the Department of Theatre.

Dolores was a member, too. She was already known on campus and across mid-Michigan as a vigorous arts advocate,[8] and she was ecstatic to have the chance to play a part. Among other things, she organized large receptions at Cowles House to build support among faculty, alumni, and friends. Participants met such visiting artists as Alvin Ailey, Vladimir Horowitz, Isaac Stern, Rudolf Nureyev, Joan Sutherland, Daniel Barenboim, Jacqueline du Pré, and Van Cliburn. When we hosted Bobby Short at a Cowles House reception in his honor, he turned the tables and played for our twenty-fourth wedding anniversary.

Then there was the time when Duke Ellington visited Cowles House, after he had dedicated a performance of "Satin Doll" to Dolores. Ellington was already ill at the time of his visit. When he later died, I asked Wendell Westcott, the university carillonneur, if he would play an Ellington composition in memorial. Westcott's widow, Iris, told me years later that after my call, her husband "went over to Marshall Music and bought every [Ellington] composition.... [He] came home, sat down at a table, and started to arrange each ... for the carillon. He only stopped to eat and sleep.... He was still arranging the music right up to the time of the concert; as we left he said, 'Well, I didn't have time to put in any of the measure bars, but that's okay. I can play without them.' This ... is like saying, 'I can read an entire book without any spaces between any of the words and without any punctuation at all.'"[9]

In 1974 Dolores was appointed by President Ford to the National Council on the Arts, and slightly later she joined the board of the Museum of Modern Art,[10] both of which underscored her increasingly pivotal credentials in developing MSU's proposed center. Yet even with this growing national recognition and her pivotal role in pushing the center, she never stepped over the proper bounds of being MSU's first lady or behaved as its "second president."

Collectively and as individuals, she and other members of the planning committee visited sixteen performing arts centers and thirty theaters around the United States—including the University of Illinois's Krannert Center; Indiana University Auditorium; Iowa State's Stephens Auditorium; the University of Akron's Thomas Hall; the University of Iowa Hancher Auditorium; Manhattan's Lincoln Center (Alice Tully Hall); and metropolitan complexes in Milwaukee and Midland, Michigan.

After a preliminary report in August 1973, their second report provided specifications to a special architecture panel that would develop detailed recommendations. A few months later, in May 1974, MSU trustees selected a lead architectural firm, Caudill, Rowlett and Scott (CRS), of Houston, Texas, along with Michigan architects Harley Ellington Pierce Yee Associates; subsequently Bonner Associates signed on as consultants in acoustics.

Led by CRS's Tiny Lawrence, the architects designed a magnificent facility, to be sited south of Owen Hall between Shaw Lane and Wilson Road. It consisted of a 2,500-seat main hall and a more intimate 600-seat theater with a thrust proscenium stage, as well as a spectacular great foyer entry and a second-floor lounge. Tiny Lawrence's innovations included a continental seating plan that allowed guests to move sideways when taking their seats, and fourteen giant pillars to enhance sound projection.

▪ ▪ ▪ ▪

Although in the mid-1970s it wasn't rare for major private universities to set fund-raising targets in the hundreds of millions of dollars, such campaigns were then less common at public campuses, and accordingly less ambitious—Minnesota had conducted a $25 million drive, and the University of Michigan had raised $72 million. We placed MSU's goal quite low, at $17 million, because of our inexperience—the university had never held a major fund-raising effort, and neither had Les Scott or I.

The MSU "Campus Enrichment Campaign" had four major components: (1) $1.75 million for endowed faculty chairs, including the John Hannah endowed professorships, (2) $1.5 million for library enrichment, (3) $2.75 million for a major expansion of the physical facility of the University Museum, and (4) $11 million for the construction of a center for performing arts.

Along with its 2,500-seat auditorium and smaller theater with a thrust stage, the arts center proposal included an academic facility for the Department of Theatre offices, classrooms, and a small workshop theater.

Perhaps the most interesting reaction to the drive was reported to me by Lloyd Cofer. Some of the Black MSU faculty, all of whom were quite supportive, were bemused by the fact that it took a Black couple to raise the level of arts and culture at a Big Ten university that was formerly regarded as a glorified agricultural college and football factory. Lloyd told me that this in-joke circulated among the group, giving rise to proud laughter.

At my invitation, John Hannah became our national campaign chairman, establishing a bridge between old and new. George Brakeley interviewed potential major donors, while his colleague Ted Alexander prepared the traditional campaign "casebook." Surprisingly, it turned out that several individuals we had long cultivated could have funded the entire drive on their own, though they manifested few if any signs of great affluence. Brakeley said it wasn't unusual—successful people often went out of their way to maintain friendships and relationships forged long before they achieved wealth.

Since it was our first capital drive, it was important that the public see the strong support it had from the university community itself. Dolores and I, jointly and apart, held meetings all over Michigan State University campus, shamelessly promoting the need for the MSU family to make a statement by contributing first. We met with faculty groups, student organizations, and staff, and to each audience my plea was, "I want to be able to tell outside donors how handsomely the MSU community has already committed its support." The campaign committee sold dedicated bricks and named seats, among other special recognition devices. Contributors also got a lapel pin with a rather cryptic logo, designed to prompt others to ask its significance and thus learn more about the capital drive. I thought the idea a bit forced, but it actually seemed to work. Les Scott and I set a goal of $500,000 from university sources. By mid-November 1977 we were happily surprised to discover that campus contributions topped a million dollars, more than double our goal.

Oddly, our efforts got a lukewarm reception from a couple of unexpected quarters. One was Frank Rutledge, then chairman of the theater department. With his office and classrooms in the dreary basement of the old auditorium, his lack of enthusiasm was hard to understand, and it surprised his colleagues. There was also opposition at first from some leaders of the Lansing Symphony, who wanted to build their own facility in downtown Lansing. Even Les Scott's repeated references to the new "State Center for the Performing Arts" seemed to fall on deaf ears, at least until the very late stages, when symphony officials finally signed on to the campaign.

The drive made for an exhilarating if occasionally fatiguing round of fund-raising events, many of them at Cowles House, where we had set up a small preliminary model for the proposed center. One evening a potential donor, Catherine Herrick Cobb, saw the maquette and looked at Dolores with a sparkle in her eye. "What are you waiting for?" she demanded. "Let's get going!" The Cobb family exemplified the value of historic relations for fund-raising. Catherine Herrick Cobb was a lover of music and the performing arts from her MSU undergraduate days. Her father, Ray Herrick, the founder and chairman of Tecumseh Products Company, had in 1965 donated building funds for MSU's Hidden Lake Gardens, a famous arboretum. When the university offered him at age eighty an honorary degree, he was unable to travel to East Lansing for the ceremony, because of his frailty and a fear that he might break down in public because his late wife had not lived long enough to attend. At my request the trustees authorized a special presentation in his own home. Jack Breslin and I flew with our wives to Tecumseh, where in traditional academic robes we read the words of conferral to Herrick, daughter Catherine, son-in-law Donald Cobb, and the family minister and his wife.[11] Catherine Herrick Cobb eventually donated one million dollars to MSU's capital campaign, which led to the center's Great Hall being named in her honor.

The public phase over the next few years saw a massive effort to "shake the money trees." On April 26, 1974, I had sought to lay the groundwork for a lead gift by inviting Henry Ford II to visit MSU. He had been tremendously impressed by an all-day tour of the campus. As hoped, the first big hit for the campaign came from the Ford Motor Company with a gift of $1.5 million in October 1977.[12] Later that year, I received an unusual invitation to make a personal presentation directly to the board of trustees of the Charles Stewart Mott Foundation, which eventually gave $1 million.[13] Again, this action had been preceded by regular cultivation of the Mott family. The patriarch was C. S. Mott, a legendary cofounder of General Motors, who looked like a twin of the late British actor C. Aubrey Smith. He and his wife Ruth were regularly invited to our fall football weekends, and at times we had visited them in their home in Flint. When C. S. Mott was awarded the first MSU Distinguished Citizen Award (May 24,

1972),[14] he and Ruth arrived at the Kellogg Center luncheon an hour ahead of time. When Dolores and I arrived, C. S. was seated holding a beautiful bird of paradise in his hand, which he then presented Dolores. Ruth explained that he was very fond of Dolores and had held the flower in the car all the way from Flint. To top it off, C. S. then removed from a pocket another gift for her . . . a bottle of Chanel perfume! Our relationship with them, their son Harding and daughter-in-law Isabel, as well as their granddaughter Claire and her husband Bill White, would several years later prove invaluable to the university. Such were the early activities that laid the groundwork for the major MSU capital drive. Other successful approaches were made to the Kresge Foundation and several Michigan corporations.

As a personal boost to the drive we commissioned a sculpture to be placed in front of the proposed center. *Orpheus*, a thirty-foot-high, six-ton sculpture was to be created by MSU professor Mel Leiserowitz. Les Scott proposed that its $30,000 costs be paid from the corporate director fees that I had donated to the university.

▪ MSU and the NCAA

I enjoyed intercollegiate athletics, especially when we won. But there was more to varsity athletics than wins and losses. Hence I frequently met and spoke to the incoming athletes. From the outset I believed it was crucial to emphasize the importance of players' finishing their university degrees. Many dreamed that they would catch the brass ring of professional stardom, but the statistics said otherwise. As the Black sociology professor (and former athlete) Harry Edwards put it, "You can work out the odds with a pencil and paper, and they're 20,000 to one or worse. Statistically, you've got a better chance in the next ten years of getting hit by a meteorite." I could never tell how well my remarks were received.

A lot of sports-loving students and alumni saw me as an Ivy League academic who didn't understand or support big-time sports. For example, on the season's opening football game in 1972, Georgia Tech returned the first kickoff for a touchdown. A fan sitting just below the open windows of the president's box cried out, "Damn it, another Wharton academic year!"[15] And we lost 21–16.

This opinion improved somewhat in October 1972 when I ruptured my Achilles tendon while giving thirteen-year-old Bruce pointers on how to run track. The *State News* ran photographs of me hobbling along on crutches with my right leg in a full cast, and highlighted that I was a former college track star.[16] My reputation among Spartan "jocks" rose even higher when I hinted that I might paint the cast green and white!

Still the image persisted with the removal of Duffy Daugherty, the school's storied football coach. Though popular on campus and throughout the state, Duffy's last several years had been abysmal. (Following Duffy's banner teams in 1965 and 1966, he never did better than 6–5–1, in 1971.) Jack Breslin, to whom athletic programs reported, felt strongly that Duffy's time had passed. I concurred, but accepting Jack's recommendation was awkward for me because Duffy had been a national pioneer in recruiting Black players, and I admired him for it.

When I commiserated with John Hannah, he confided, "I should have fired Duffy and saved you the trouble. I only kept him on out of sentimentality." Nonetheless Duffy himself accused me in his autobiography of being unsupportive of athletics and implied that I was indirectly responsible for the poor record that led to his retirement as head coach of the football program.

Finding Duffy's replacement was educational. The finalists were Lee Corso, Johnny Majors, and Barry Switzer, rising stars all and highly competent coaches. Switzer was the favorite of athletic director Burt Smith, who had moved into the job after Biggie Munn had a stroke in October 1971. But I found Switzer arrogant, too lenient with off-field discipline, and clearly spoiled by Oklahoma's high-stakes standards. When we met, his main question was, "How many recruiting planes do I get? Oklahoma has three." In my book the top outsider was Lee Corso. But in the end I decided that Denny Stolz, an MSU assistant coach, deserved a chance to step out of Duffy's shadow. Breslin agreed. Stolz got the job, and by 1974 he had been named Big Ten coach of the year.

· · · ·

My first inkling something was amiss in the university's football program came in early 1975. Clarence Underwood, assistant director of athletics, alerted me that David Berst, an NCAA junior official, was investigating possible recruiting violations by MSU coaches and boosters. Underwood, a young Black graduate of MSU, was a man of integrity, devoted to the university.[17] Especially bothersome was his report that one of the "boosters" in Berst's sights was a man named T. Michael Doyle. Doyle lived across the street from Jack Breslin, whose son (also an MSU football player) regularly did Doyle's yard work.[18]

I was both angry and apprehensive. Under NCAA rules, university presidents have to submit an annual statement that they have reviewed NCAA regulations and that their schools are in full compliance. Before signing, I had always asked Breslin, Burt Smith, and John Fuzak (the MSU faculty representative to the Big Ten and NCAA) if they knew of any violations or improprieties, and they had assured me there were none. Now I faced the possibility that either my administrative team had been misled, or that I had. I was upset by the prospect that my oversight of the athletic program might be found deficient. Worse, I feared that any corruption might reach higher and further than was yet apparent.

Official confirmation of the investigation came on April 15, 1975—a three-page letter with a thirty-one-page attachment that hit like a single-spaced atom bomb. Warren S. Brown, the NCAA's assistant executive director, listed fifty alleged infractions,[19] not omitting my own putatively erroneous certification of university compliance with the rules. They fell into six different categories, including recruiting violations, improper gifts to prospective student athletes, improper cash payments and credit card subsidies to MSU athletes, and unethical and improper actions by coaches and boosters. The allegations targeted four coaches, twelve student athletes, four non-MSU athletes, eleven other people not affiliated with the university, and eleven stores, restaurants, and shopping malls.

The NCAA directed me to look into the charges and report back to the commission's Committee on Infractions at its June 12–17 meeting—a tight two-month deadline. I informed the MSU board on April 18, then issued a press release the next day. Since the NCAA had admonished us not to reveal specifics, the tight strictures on confidentiality in my release led to accusations of a "gag order," which would persist throughout the investigation. The media coverage far exceeded that of any other MSU activity of my entire tenure—speaking volumes about sports and societal priorities.

Bob Reynolds, a longtime announcer with WJR and strong Spartan partisan, seemed to have some, but not all, inside information on a few of the charges, and WJIM's Tim Staudt claimed to have an independent source in Cincinnati. Both were incorrect in reporting that 90 percent of the charges were against a single assistant coach. Lacking hard facts, media stories were generally filled with errors, distortions, and speculation. We had announced the probe early on to avoid charges of a cover-up, but if we had released details and unproven allegations, reporters would have contacted all involved, inevitably smearing the innocent along with any who might be guilty, and increasing the odds of legal action against the leaker and MSU.

I held a meeting with the entire athletic department staff. At the meeting Lee Carr explained the legal reasons for our decision to ban any public discussions of the allegations. We pointed out that we had no way of knowing in advance which of the allegations were true and that any premature release of information that later proved to be false might lead to litigation on libel or defamation of character against anyone responsible for leaking the information. This proved to be a powerful deterrent on any leaks, much to the annoyance of the media.

At some universities the president personally handles any investigation into possible NCAA rules violations; at others, it falls to an athletic faculty representative, the university general counsel, or an outside law firm. In our case there were so many land mines I decided to take the reins myself. Jack Breslin and Burt Smith held athletic department duties, so they needed to stand aside. So did John Fuzak, the MSU faculty representative to the Big Ten and NCAA, because he was at the time serving as the NCAA conference president. In their stead I convened and chaired a special investigating committee. It included John Bruff, a lawyer, alumnus, and newly elected MSU trustee, as well as two professors who were current members of the university athletic council and one who was a former member. In addition to Bruff, the members were Jacob A. Hoefer, acting dean of the College of Agriculture and Natural Resources; Charles Scarborough, associate professor of natural science; and Frederick

Williams, professor of history and chair of the University Faculty Affairs Committee. Lee Carr, our general counsel, would advise us at every step, and I also commandeered as staff Robert Wenner, director of internal audit, whose persistence and accounting skills I thought would be invaluable. Al Ballard and Bob Perrin would be on the sidelines but fully apprised.

At the outset none of us fully appreciated the bizarre high-handedness of NCAA practices. When we contacted several other campuses that had faced similar investigations in the recent past, we found them all quite critical of the process. We wondered whether such comments were just rationalizations for guilty behavior, but we soon learned otherwise.

From the beginning and thereafter, the committee had one overriding problem: we had to try to confirm or disprove the NCAA's charges *without knowing their source*. All we knew were the names of the accused and the nature of the alleged infraction. We were never told who had made the accusations, nor on what basis. We were at the mercy of unknown informants. And in the process of protecting its "sources" the NCAA had no compunction whatsoever about trampling every rudiment of due process for those upon whom the organization had brought its sights to bear.

Given the tight deadline for responding, the committee moved on several fronts at once. We wrote to everyone mentioned in the allegations, asking for copies of bills, invoices, credit card slips, telephone records, store receipts, tickets, and travel vouchers. The answers from over one hundred persons filled a three-inch binder, and we used them to decide whether to conduct personal interviews with the individuals mentioned in the charges. Some people we interviewed more than once, in the presence of counsel for those who requested it. All interviews by the committee were tape-recorded. Most interviews were transcribed by court reporters. I wanted an actual, vocal record of their responses to our questions. While we had no legal authority to compel anyone to participate in the interviews, virtually all did so voluntarily. They allowed those accused to respond and provided strong evidence for our final decisions.[20]

A rare lighter moment came when my son Bruce, then sixteen, surreptitiously pasted on my green 1975 Mustang back bumper a green and white sticker, "No Comment." The *Lansing State Journal* printed a photo of the bumper sticker and quoted Dolores saying, "Bruce had the foresight to make the sticker a couple of years ago and save it for just the right moment. He knew his Dad."[21] I rode around several days without noticing it, much to the amusement of all.

Meanwhile, on May 12 we got another letter from the NCAA's Warren Brown, which mentioned in passing that the investigation was now broader than previously described. Naively, we thought this might be an example of the organization's declared "cooperative principles of enforcement." We wrote back, asking for further details. In its first letter the NCAA had directed that the university not limit its inquiries to the fifty specific charges, and our select committee took the requirement seriously. At the same time, we thought it only reasonable to know if there were allegations that the NCAA's own ongoing investigation had already proved unfounded.

When the NCAA responded on June 5, we got our first clear look at what "cooperative principles" really meant—and what the university was in for. The investigative staff, we were informed, would provide information on sources only at the actual meeting of the infractions committee in June.

> This procedure provides more than adequate opportunity for the institutional representatives involved to debate any of the information presented for the first time to the Committee . . . and to be advised of the sources of information upon which the allegation is based. . . . [T]he NCAA enforcement procedure is not a legal proceeding. . . . Contrary to the belief of the MSU Select Committee that [NCAA] procedures might be contrary to "generally accepted pre-trial discovery procedures," the NCAA Committee on Infractions and the Association's legal counsel believe that these administrative procedures provide the basic elements of due process *to the institution* and are not contrary to generally accepted pre-trial discovery procedures. . . . The NCAA procedures do not provide . . . for the NCAA investigative staff or University *to produce at the hearing the individuals who have reported information concerning allegations.*[22]

Shortly afterward, Brown rescheduled our deadline for responding to July 1, with the infractions committee hearing on July 11–14. On June 26 he telephoned again to say the hearing was being postponed once more so the NCAA could prepare to submit additional allegations that had previously not warranted investigation because of lack of evidence. We had asked informally about the "additional" charges some time before, thinking they might help us with our own inquiries. Now, simply because we had asked to see them, the NCAA had converted them into formal accusations!

Brown indicated no new evidence had surfaced, and it was difficult for me to believe that a simple request to expedite a "cooperative" investigation could metastasize into a whole new set of charges. Unperturbed by our dismay, he mailed a second set of twenty-four new allegations on July 17. For the first time Jack Breslin was named, charged with knowing about a "slush fund" and with prepping booster Mike Doyle and assistant coach Howard Weyers for their hearings. Another claim was that Duffy Daugherty had once helped an Ohio vice principal with an auto purchase in return for his help in recruiting.

Still another charge concerned Charlie Baggett, then MSU's star quarterback, and it was a clear example of the Draconian technicalities the NCAA lived by. During an early April snowstorm, Baggett had wrecked his car beyond repair. Assistant coach Jimmy Raye, who had known Baggett since childhood in North Carolina, gave him the names of several local automobile dealers, though he contacted none of them on the player's behalf. Baggett bought a new car, which he financed through the Michigan National Bank under a deferred payment plan available to any other student, athlete or not, on identical terms. The dealer Russ Kelly,

"Wharton Place" was built by John Wharton 3rd, my great-great-great-great-grandfather, in 1798, in Mappsville, Accomack County, Virginia. The Federal style home is on the National Register of Historic Places. Wharton was a wealthy maritime merchant who could see his ships enter and leave the nearby Assawaman Creek. The house and gardens on 100 acres have been handsomely restored by the current owner.

My paternal great-grandmother, Maria Wharton (b. 1850, d. June 20, 1917), was the granddaughter of Peter Wharton, a Free Negro, son of John Wharton 3rd. At age twenty-three, Maria bought two acres of Accomack land as a homestead, which is still owned by the family today.

My father, Clifton Reginald Wharton Sr. (b. May 11, 1899, d. April 23, 1990), received two law degrees from Boston University (LLB 1920; LLM 1923). This picture was taken in December 1924, just before his appointment as a Foreign Service officer in the Department of State on March 25, 1925.

The U.S. postage stamp honoring Clifton R. Wharton Sr. was issued on May 30, 2006. He was one of six career Foreign Service officers honored in the U.S. Postal Service "Distinguished American Diplomats" commemorative series.

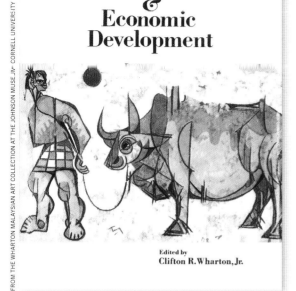

The cover of *Subsistence Agriculture and Economic Development* (Aldine Publishing Co., 1969) features the batik painting *Peasant and Bullock*, by Chuah Thean Teng, Penang, Malaysia, 1962.

The cover of the March 27, 1988, *New York Times Magazine*, *The Business World Magazine* featured tho ctory "Procious Cargo: Tho $60 Billion Challenge" and me crossing Wall Street on a high wire holding an open safe of money.

President Jimmy Carter greeted me at a luncheon at the White House on February 29, 1980. This was a private meeting with a small group of national minority leaders.

OPPOSITE: The TIAA-CREF Future Agenda meeting was held in the summer of 1987. This group, along with key senior TIAA-CREF officers, produced a report leading to unprecedented change in the corporation. (*Left to right*) Andrew Brimmer, former Federal Reserve Board member; Frederick R. Ford, executive vice president, Purdue University; Nancy L. Jacob, dean and professor, Finance School and Graduate School of Business Administration, University of Washington; Clifton Wharton Jr., chairman and CEO, TIAA-CREF; Leonard S. Simon, chairman and CEO, Rochester Community Savings Bank; Marcus Alexis, dean, College of Business Administration, University of Illinois, Chicago; Phyllis A. Wallace, professor of management, Sloan School of Management, Massachusetts Institute of Technology. (*Four members missing from photo*: Robert Roosa, partner, Brown Brothers Harriman & Co.; William A. Waltrip, president and COO, IU International; Dave H. Williams, chairman of Board, Alliance Capital Management; and John Biggs, chairman, president, and CEO, Centerre Trust Co.)

Dolores Wharton was the first woman and first Black director of the Phillips Petroleum Board of Directors. Among the directors were well-known corporate and national figures. This July 1991 portrait taken in Bartlesville, Oklahoma, includes: *(left to right, seated, 1st)* Dolores Wharton; *(2nd)* Pete Silas, chairman and CEO, Phillips; *(4th)* Congressman and former Secretary of Defense Melvin Laird; *(standing middle row, 5th)* Governor of South Carolina and former Secretary of Energy James Edwards; *(standing back row, 1st)* Robert Froehlke, chairman of the Equitable Life Assurance Society; *(2nd)* Norman Augustine, chairman CEO of Martin Marietta; *(4th)* George "Spike" Beitzel, senior vice president, IBM; *(5th)* Doug Kenna, chairman CEO, Carrier Corp.

The third presidential debate was held at the MSU Clifton and Dolores Wharton Center for Performing Arts. The Democratic nominee Governor Bill Clinton, the Republican nominee President George Bush, and independent candidate Ross Perot contended on October 19, 1992. Dolores and I proudly stood in front of the Center before attending the event. Clinton won the election and nominated me to be U.S. deputy secretary of state, the second position in the Department of State.

Dolores and I danced at the New Year's Eve Black-tie Gala, held at the MSU Wharton Center on December 31, 1987.

who had been an MSU football player in the 1950s, had been selling cars to MSU students for many years, and there was no evidence that he was a "booster" as defined by the NCAA.

The problem was that on his own initiative Baggett had asked a local manufacturer, John Demmer, to cosign the loan. Because Demmer had employed Baggett for two summers, he did meet the NCAA definition of a booster, so his cosigning was technically a violation. Before even taking out the loan, Baggett had asked the university athletic department for clearance, and Clarence Underwood had spoken to the Big Ten office about the propriety of the loan. Unfortunately, the conversation revolved around the deferred payment arrangement, which the conference said was not a problem. The issue of the cosigner had not come up.

Discovering the situation two weeks after the fact, the select committee notified both the NCAA and the Big Ten. Baggett turned the car back in, despite losing his down payment. The infraction was obviously inadvertent on all sides, and the university had taken immediate steps to correct it. But the NCAA considered what we had self-disclosed worthy of further investigation, and it became allegation number fifty-one. The sequel was even worse. After the NCAA Committee on Infractions ruled that its allegation of "improper benefit" had not been mitigated by the corrective actions taken by the university and Baggett himself, it accused MSU of allowing him to play in five games that fall when he should have been ineligible. Yet two weeks previously, the NCAA's own eligibility committee had ruled in favor of reinstating Baggett. They concluded that the case was essentially one of "no harm, no foul," using arguments virtually identical to our own. On behalf of the eligibility committee, the letter was signed by the same Warren Brown who was signing other letters indicating that Baggett had been in substantial violation of the rules.

Another similar example of NCAA arbitrariness focused on Ted Bell, a high school athlete whose older brother had accompanied him on a recruiting visit to MSU. Bell's parents had eight children, and in the ninth grade Bell had moved in with his brother and sister-in-law. They became his surrogate parents, providing food, clothing, financial support, and guidance during his high-school years. But because the brother had not secured a court order making him Bell's legal guardian, the NCAA found him in violation of the rule specifying who could accompany a student prospect on a campus recruiting tour. The well-recognized practice of in loco parentis by extended families within the Black community was not considered valid by the NCAA. I found the NCAA's willful blindness to an unfortunate sociological phenomenon among economically disadvantaged Black families particularly offensive.

Sometimes the application of their travel rules fastidiously ignored common sense. Another booster was found guilty of a violation because he traveled with three prospects on only one leg of a recruiting flight—if he had made the round-trip, there would have been no infraction. That the booster in question was Mike Doyle probably didn't help.

Some in the press had concluded very early that Woody Hayes, the Ohio State football coach, was at least one if not the main instigator of the allegations against Michigan State.

Hayes was notoriously irascible (some said troubled), and his acute dislike of MSU was a secret to no one. Worse, MSU had the previous year defeated Ohio State in a 16–13 cliffhanger, when the referees ruled that time had run out before the Buckeyes' last play.[23] The ruling was officially confirmed only when Big Ten Commissioner Wayne Duke intervened, some forty-five minutes after the game ended. Cheering MSU students flooded the field, and a few followed Hayes, taunting him as he headed for the locker room. When one student grabbed at his hat, Hayes exploded, smashing the student on the jaw with his forearm—Dolores and I had seen it quite clearly from our box above the stands.[24]

The entire campus saw it soon enough. A student photographer captured the incident, and the picture appeared in the *State News* on page one (November 11, 1974). But not one national media outlet used the photo, clear evidence of their regard for (or perhaps fear of) the Buckeye head coach. Hayes never denied his role in the NCAA investigation of MSU, though it was some time before he confirmed it. When he finally confessed, he angrily tried to choke the *State News* reporter who had put the question to him directly. This event led to a fact-finding series on possible Ohio State violations that eventually led to a Big Ten investigation and an NCAA public reprimand.

. . . .

As the select committee went about its work, rumors kept circulating that Ohio State football players were the source of many of the allegations, and that the NCAA had given them immunity from being investigated or punished themselves. (The NCAA denied it categorically.) With the voluntary cooperation of Harold Enarson, OSU's president, we arranged interviews with three players, all of whom had been unsuccessfully recruited by MSU. We met them in a conference room in Fawcett Center, on the Columbus campus. Afterwards we found out that Woody Hayes had gotten a room directly above ours, and that each player went from Hayes's room to ours, then back again after his session with us was over.

The OSU players' testimony was inconclusive, and the facelessness of most of the allegations continued to plague our self-investigation. Wayne Duke, the Big Ten commissioner, conducted his own interviews with four Ohio State athletes in the presence of Lee Carr, the MSU attorney, and he interviewed various coaches and individuals investigated by us as well. Duke's conclusions matched our committee's.

For a few charges we could find corroborating evidence, and a few others we could refute definitively. But most cases were extremely difficult to prove or disprove, because we had no access to the accusers. Anyone with an axe to grind could make an allegation, knowing he would never be challenged, much less cross-examined in a public proceeding. Yet when we complained about the anonymous sources or tried to defend the rights of the accused, the NCAA complained that we were fighting with or stonewalling its investigators.

That fall our opening football game was against Ohio State. MSU's athletic department put out a highly undiplomatic press release, mentioning that Woody Hayes had never denied the rumors that he was behind the NCAA probe, as well as the controversy around MSU's defeat of Ohio State the previous year. The situation was so tense that even the *New York Times* covered it,[25] and Walter Byers, executive director of the NCAA, called for calm, taking the unprecedented step of issuing a formal statement that Hayes and his program were not among MSU's accusers. (Hayes's own admissions later called Byers's claim into question.) OSU president Enarson and I issued a joint statement that if tempers got out of hand on the field, the athletic departments would suffer for it at both schools.[26]

By coincidence the big game was on September 13, my birthday. My secretary, Bea Mott, and agriculture dean Larry Boger talked me into presenting an "honorary alumnus" award to president emeritus John Hannah at halftime. But when Hannah and I started to walk back from the fifty-yard line, a huge banner reading "Happy Birthday, Clif" unfurled along the sideline and the stadium announcer asked the 76,000 in the stands to sing "Happy Birthday" accompanied by the Spartan Marching Band. The whole subterfuge had been orchestrated by my colleagues, recognizing the stress I was under in dealing with the NCAA. It was a carefree moment, and it gave my spirits a much-appreciated temporary boost. Unfortunately, we lost the game 21-0.

In the course of its investigation, the select committee inevitably turned up a lot of shocking information about recruiting and coaching practices at many otherwise respectable campuses, some of whose tactics made MSU's alleged infractions pale by comparison. Yet it gradually became clear that there were indeed problems within our program, and that many of them had begun years before my arrival. A fairly egregious case was that of booster Mike Doyle, who had among other things made a practice of letting MSU athletes use his credit card. Two players bought clothes and records at five different stores, totaling about $500. Doyle denied responsibility, telling the press he had loaned the card to assistant coach Howard Weyers, but was unaware of the purchases because the MasterCard in question was actually his wife's. Weyers gave Doyle an affidavit in which he stipulated having been loaned the card, but claiming to know nothing about improper uses by himself or anyone else.

All interviews of persons named by the NCAA charges were tape-recorded by the select committee. But their stories changed repeatedly, and what had been said to the select committee wasn't necessarily what would later be said to the press or even to the NCAA.[27] That was true in several cases, including that of student athlete Joe Hunt, who told the press he had used Doyle's card but not how he got it. Then in testimony to the select committee, with his mother and lawyer present, he confessed that he had stolen the card from the glove compartment of Weyers's car, which Hunt had borrowed to go to a medical appointment. At first this sounded on a par with "The dog ate my homework," but Weyers swore it was true. Of course, that raised the question of why Weyers kept his credit card in a glove box, not to mention why he would lend his car to an athlete at all—an NCAA violation in itself.

Growing unease on the select committee fed in part on secondhand hearsay from other

Big Ten coaches. Especially troubling was a letter from Lee Corso, by now head coach at Indiana, who wrote at the request of Denny Stolz. "At our first Rose Bowl game together," Corso wrote, "I stated [to Stolz] . . . Howard Weyers was not beneficial for his staff and that he would eventually get Stolz in trouble . . . I mentioned . . . that [prospective recruit] Robert Roberson had told me that Howard Weyers had given him money in his shirt pocket." Stolz maintained that the rumors were "payback" for his successful recruiting in the previous year, and he cited several such acts by Woody Hayes in the past.[28]

Eventually we asked two assistant coaches to take voluntary lie-detector tests. Weyers was one, and the other was Charlie Butler. Weyers was the focus of the largest number of serious allegations. All of the charges regarding Butler came from just two sources. One, a student, claimed Butler had promised cash payments while recruiting him. The other was an MSU booster named Peter Knezevich, who was angry at the university for not recruiting his son. Knezevich changed his story every time he told it, but he admitted that he had coached (later, "suggested") the first student to ask Butler for an illegal inducement.

On the recommendation of the Michigan State Police, lie-detector tests were administered by an expert with twenty years' experience. Both coaches passed without difficulty. Even so, the select committee continued to be concerned regarding Weyers, principally because of the frequency of similar charges and the repeating patterns of improper behavior. We suspected some action against him might be warranted, though the most serious charges were doubtful. On the other hand, while Butler had admitted to making a few gifts of athletic apparel, he strongly denied the more serious charges, including those of cash payments. When we talked to seven prospects whom Butler had tried unsuccessfully to recruit, all said he had been above reproach. To the committee it seemed unlikely that Butler would have offered special promises to a subpar player, but not to others much more highly regarded.

In its written response to the NCAA, our select committee divided the allegations against MSU into two groups—"technicals" and misdemeanors, versus major and substantive. Though resisting in instances where corroboration was weak, we acceded to NCAA findings regarding most of the credit card misuses and improper gifts of athletic clothing and equipment. We disagreed on most of the irregularities charged in campus recruiting visits. The areas of the greatest remaining contention were the alleged recruiting violations and illegal inducements, the majority allegedly by Weyers. We protested the allegations against Charlie Baggett and Ted Bell as unduly technical.

. . . .

On October 13th the MSU committee and I flew to Denver to meet with the NCAA panel on infractions. Also attending were university counsel Lee Carr; Big Ten commissioner Wayne Duke; and MSU coaches Stolz, Weyers, Butler, and Raye. John Fuzak, the university's faculty representative, was not present because as president of the NCAA he was in possible conflict of interest. After checking in at the Brown Palace Hotel, we were taken aback to learn that the same staff who had conducted the field investigation and prepared the allegations would now act as prosecutors during the hearing, and that afterward they would be available during the infraction group's private deliberations.

The first day's meeting went from 9:00 A.M. until 10:00 P.M., with short breaks for lunch and dinner, and from 8:00 A.M. until 11:00 A.M. the next day—far longer than even the NCAA committee members expected. The discussions were given substantially over to a one-by-one review of the accusations and the university's written responses. Individual members of the NCAA committee asked occasional questions. They seemed not to have expected the university's spirited and detailed defense, and the NCAA investigative staff were obviously nettled by our positions on due process and the rights of the accused. Representatives of the University of Kentucky, whose hearing was scheduled to follow ours, waited outside the hearing room with ever-increasing impatience. A little before lunchtime the hearing concluded. The infractions committee took what it had heard under advisement, and the MSU participants and I headed back to East Lansing.

Ten days later a whole new episode began to unfold. A booster named Kenneth R. Erickson called Pat Carrigan, vice chair of the MSU board, claiming to have facts not previously available to the select committee. Carrigan, a longtime fan of Spartan athletics and a close friend of Duffy Daugherty, told Erickson to call me directly. She then wrote to me,[29] explaining Erickson's long history with the MSU program and his more recent disaffection with Daugherty. Among other things, Erickson was chairman of the Ralph Young Scholarship Fund, a source of financial aid for MSU sports programs. The fund-raised contributions from large numbers of MSU alumni and friends were used to provide full and partial scholarships to athletes, especially in football, basketball, and hockey. Since the fund was independent and I had never attended any of its events or officers meetings, I had not previously met him.

Upon investigation, Erickson turned out to be the son-in-law of Burt Smith, who six weeks previously I had moved from director of athletics to another position outside the sports program. Before seeing Erickson on October 23, Lee Carr and I tried to persuade him to meet with the select committee, but he adamantly refused. In the privacy of my office Erickson outlined his prior involvement with MSU athletics. Though not named in any of the NCAA allegations, he admitted that he had collected funds improperly for the football program, going back to the days of Duffy Daugherty. In coming forward, Erickson said, he had two motives. The first was to tell "what was really going on." The second was to trade his information for immunity for his father-in-law, so that Burt Smith could tell his own tales in turn before returning to his old job. Burt would also agree not to sue the university for removing him as director of athletics.

I told Erickson that we weren't in the immunity business, and that in any event Smith's removal had been unrelated to the NCAA investigation. We then pressed him again to meet with the university's select committee, and when it was clear we had called his bluff, he reluctantly agreed. His testimony that afternoon was a rambling travelogue of illegal alleys and channels, mostly concerning the football program though touching at times on basketball and three less prominent sports. Much of what he said concerned a series of short-term, non-university bank accounts he used to handle large sums for eventual distribution in cash, as well as the improper diversion of unaudited contributions collected at the annual football bust. Erickson agreed to tell us how much he had raised over the years. He refused to give the names of the donors, but he did identify recipients, including Duffy Daugherty, Burt Smith, and Denny Stolz.

One rather damning piece of evidence was a letter Erickson had written to Duffy Daugherty in 1971. In it he criticized the coach for a poor work ethic (lazy recruiting, snubbing boosters, weak spring training) and questioned his use of "extracurricular budget monies" Erickson had raised on his behalf. Unless Daugherty made changes, the letter continued, Erickson would withdraw his support. In addition to sending the letter to Duffy, Erickson copied twelve other people, including Jack Breslin, John Fuzak, and Biggie Munn, then the athletic director. I had no recollection of its ever having been mentioned to me, and I wondered why not.

The next day the select committee interviewed Smith and Stolz. Stolz denied taking any money from Erickson. He admitted knowing about Duffy's gambling and liquor debts and said he had canceled the former coach's permanent party rooms at two local motels. In his turn, Burt Smith said Erickson had told him that money had been given to Stolz (who again denied it emphatically). He also said that in 1974 he had given the proceeds of the football bust to Stolz. Stolz conceded it, but he claimed he had not known what the money was for, had done nothing with it, and had ultimately given it back to Smith.

A few days later Erickson began to have second thoughts about what he might have unleashed. His lawyer demanded that we surrender or destroy all records of our meeting with him, which we politely declined to do.

Now, in the meantime, we had a dilemma. We didn't want to hide Erickson's claims from the NCAA, but neither did we want to pass them along without verifying that there was at least something to them. On the other hand, if we notified the NCAA immediately, the infractions committee might delay their decision, leaving the original accusations in limbo.

When the NCAA opened its investigation, the Big Ten had been obliged to follow suit, although the conference had been a model of courtesy and collaborativeness compared to the NCAA. After talking with John Fuzak, I called Wayne Duke, who agreed to look into the Erickson charges and include them in his final report to the NCAA. He also notified the association directly about the new inquiry, and I wrote directly to Walter Byers on January 30,[30] also disclosing the matter. I could just imagine the field day the media would have over a "cover-up," if we had not notified them while we tried to verify Erickson's truthfulness.

. . . .

On November 24 the Committee on Infractions disclosed its findings and proposed penalties, and they were far worse than expected. The committee disallowed all the arguments and evidence we had presented, including the lie-detector results. In certain cases they used the evidence we had presented to punch up their weaker allegations, reintroducing them as new ones now "proven." The proposed redress was severe: three years' probation, with no television appearances or postseason games during the period, plus a cut of ten football scholarships in 1976–77 and five in 1977–78. Coach Weyers was to be permanently dissociated from the football program, Coach Raye was to be admonished. Boosters Mike Doyle and Peter Knezevich were to be banned from all contact with MSU athletics.

Probably the coldest of all the penalties fell on Coach Charlie Butler. Disregarding his lie-detector test and an unblemished record of fourteen years, the NCAA accepted at face value the charges of one player. Butler was to be banned from off-campus recruiting for a year; far more seriously, his reputation and career prospects stood now indelibly stained. Soon after the first NCAA hearing, I heard privately from infractions committee member Charles Alan Wright, a constitutional law professor at the University of Texas. Wright said his personal impression was that Butler was innocent of any serious offense, and he hoped I could be lenient with him. Two years later Wright accidentally revealed why Butler's lie-detector test had been discounted. "I never had any doubt that our findings were soundly based in the case of Coach Weyers," he was quoted in a news story. But since both Butler and Weyers passed the polygraph test, he couldn't differentiate between the two men on their guilt—either both were innocent or both guilty.[31]

The harshness of the NCAA's proposed penalties put the university in a difficult position. Although it was clear that some serious violations had taken place, the committee and I disagreed with 70 percent of the findings, and many of the ones we did accede to were minor or technical. Even the serious accusations rested on major conflicts in testimony and evidence, as well as witnesses never identified nor challenged.

It would have been a relief simply to bow our heads and accept the inevitable, but not at the expense of trampling the rights of many who were innocent of any wrongdoing. Though not optimistic, the committee and I believed that fairness and due process mandated that we appeal the infractions committee's recommendations to the eighteen-member council that governed the NCAA itself. The MSU Board of Trustees unanimously concurred. We drew up a formal statement, which said in part:

> It would have been far easier to have ended further prolongation of the burdensome and detrimental impact of continued indecision. But a review . . . convinced us that failure to appeal would be far more damaging of individual rights as well as institutional integrity. Admittedly, it may prove a fruitless cry of frustration and anguish, but our . . . commitment to individual

rights and the underlying principles of our national commitment to constitutional rights made our decision inescapable.

The infractions committee answered with a blast of its own.[32] Among other things, it criticized the select committee and others for relying "primarily upon information [from] individuals associated with the athletic interests of the university." (Since the NCAA would not reveal its sources, what choice did we have?) We were depicted as engaging in "an uninterrupted attack on the NCAA enforcement procedures" and attempting to "dictate" policies and procedures rather than accepting them unquestioningly. (Why would we agree to flawed procedures and the abrogation of due process just because the goal of finding and punishing the guilty was a worthy end?) Worst of all, though our objection to anonymous witnesses and sources were "not relevant since the basis for each . . . had been fully reported to the university" (not true), *we* were charged with failing to provide *them* with our arguments and evidence in advance of the committee hearing.

The NCAA council meeting was in St. Louis on January 18, 1976. We made as strong a plea as we could, but it was easy to see that it fell largely on deaf ears. We went back to East Lansing with a sense of impending doom, but glad we had taken what we considered the path of principle.

The council released its decision a week later. Its statement reaffirmed most of what the infractions committee had maintained and left the proposed penalties almost entirely in place. Interestingly, the university was no longer required to fire Howard Weyers, only to ban him from recruiting for three years. Charlie Butler's one-year recruitment suspension and Jimmy Raye's admonishment stood unchanged.

Bob Perrin scheduled a press conference at Kellogg Center, where a standing-room-only group of spectators crowded in. With his usual good judgment, Perrin warned that the press would consider any attempt to explain our position on the charges as defensiveness, de facto evidence of guilt. He also cautioned against complaining about anonymous sources and unexamined evidence, since skeptical reporters and TV commentators would simply think, "Where's there's smoke, there must be a fire."

The press conference lasted two hours, and I was on my feet for all but twenty minutes, when Denny Stolz took questions. John Bruff, the trustee member of the select committee, told a reporter that as an attorney he was "very disturbed . . . as to the complete absence of due process . . . that rules of evidence weren't followed and hearsay was admitted. . . . [He] was disappointed with and disagree with the conclusions" reached by the NCAA.

One consolation was that in response to our appeal the NCAA council dismissed allegations against three coaches, eight student athletes, five parents, one university employee, and six people not connected to the university. In my public statement I made a point that had the detailed allegations been published at the outset of the investigation, at least twenty-three individuals would have been unfairly and indiscriminately tarred by the brush of public opinion. So our "gag order" against premature disclosure had been worth it, and I made no apologies for it. Of course the press still criticized my having done it.

▪ ▪ ▪ ▪

The ordeal wasn't over yet—there remained the Erickson controversy, as well as the as-yet unfinished inquiry that the Big Ten had been required to undertake once the NCAA had brought its own charges. This two-stage process was not fully understood by the press or the general public.

It might have seemed like double jeopardy, but in fact the Big Ten investigation stood in stark contrast to the NCAA experience. When Commissioner Wayne Duke asked to interview students and coaches, for example, he stipulated that they were entitled to have counsel present, as well as anyone else cited in the allegation. They could cross-examine accusers and witnesses, directly or through counsel, and bring witnesses on their own behalf. The university could send a representative to the interviews, which would be taped, transcribed, and made available to anyone with a valid reason for asking. The NCAA had offered no such niceties. (Our position may have caused the NCAA to begin the process of changing its practices. Beginning in 1977, accused coaches and boosters could have legal counsel in any appeal before the NCAA Council and could even make presentations.) Because Commissioner Duke and his staff avoided rushing to judgment and worked with us collaboratively, we were able to nail down several of the more serious infractions, while still protecting the rights of the accused.

As the investigation proceeded, the select committee recommended that I take supervision of athletic programs back into the president's office, where it had been under John Hannah. Jack Breslin had been found guilty of no violations, but the NCAA made clear they thought him suspect. He was the only university official who had been deeply involved with athletics back to the early 1950s. The NCAA remained unjustly suspicious of him, we thought, and there was a good possibility it would go harder for us—and him—unless we put some distance between him and the sports programs.[33] At the end of January, Breslin himself asked that athletics be moved in the best interests of the university. It was a bitter pill for him to swallow, but in typical fashion he did it because of his love of the university; and I was genuinely sorry for its necessity.

On the Erickson front, the most serious charge was that money had improperly been channeled to Duffy Daugherty, Burt Smith, and Denny Stolz. How had it worked? Erickson would open a bank account in the name "MSU Football Bust." Into it he deposited contributions from MSU alumni or from local and regional corporations that they had made payable to "MSU Football Bust" but which the university never received. Later he would close the account, distribute the proceeds, and start all over again. Seeing the actual copies of the checks that had been misdirected into the bogus accounts was appalling. They convinced the select committee that there was a strong likelihood that serious corruption had existed in the

MSU football program for some time, so we dug even harder. Internal auditor Bob Wenner contacted thirteen firms Erickson had solicited for contributions; all but one provided copies of their records. Wenner found that from 1968 through 1976, some $13,300 out of $16,800 in corporate gifts had been diverted through the "football bust" accounts from these firms.[34] Digging further, he next determined that Erickson had opened at least four bank accounts, in which the majority of transactions took place just after the legitimate annual MSU football busts. This time some $67,200 had been deposited from November 1971 through February 1976.[35] He also found major discrepancies in the records of bar and raffle proceeds at the events.

Oddly, the outside funds seemed to have reached very few athletes. In an attempt to gather data that might bear at least indirectly on the likelihood of illegal payments to MSU athletes, I asked Al Ballard to conduct a "snap" survey with a questionnaire given to seventy-one MSU football players, aimed at uncovering any unusual patterns of expenditure on automobiles, luxury apartments, and similar items. We found that football players owned cars that on average were very similar to that of regular nonathletic students—an average age of seven years. Two-thirds of the players lived on campus, with only one paying an off-campus monthly rent higher than $100. Nothing unusual was found with their summer employment. We took a special look at "top recruiting prospects" (ten freshmen, seven sophomores, and three juniors) and found that only one did not live in the residence halls or married student housing, and only three owned cars.

· · · ·

The seedy drama dated back to the Duffy Daugherty years, and its key actors had been Daugherty, Burt Smith, Denny Stolz, and Erickson himself. Others alleged to be on the periphery were Assistant Coach Gordon Serr and Frank Palamara, director of the Ralph Young Scholarship Fund, who had died in 1973.

There was damaging evidence against head coach Stolz. In 1973 and 1974, just before the each year's final game, Erickson had withdrawn $10,000 from his secret accounts, alleging that in both instances he had given the money to Stolz for recruiting and coaching expenses. Wayne Duke got confirming evidence on the withdrawals, as well a statement from a cosigner on the accounts and another witness that the funds had been transferred to Stolz. The coach vehemently denied both to the university and to the Big Ten that he had ever taken the money. But he did admit to accepting a $2,300 fee for speaking at a fund-raising event, and the select committee was alarmed by his increasingly conflicting versions of the events, which in turn led to a Big Ten allegation of his having given false testimony.[36] The Big Ten finding of guilt on top of the NCAA's was the clincher.

Burt Smith was a sad culprit. As the evidence piled up, he eventually confessed to having received or collected funds improperly, initially insisting he did it because Jack Breslin expected him to. Like Stolz to some degree, he had inherited a nasty situation, and his major failing lay in not acting decisively to correct it. What made things worse in his case was that the committee believed that, through his son-in-law Erickson, he had a clear and detailed understanding of the full scope of the illegal bank accounts problem.

In Commissioner Wayne Duke's official report[37] on the investigation conducted jointly by Michigan State and the Big Ten, the most serious findings documented collections and transfers of substantial funds outside the university's control. They included $7,800 given to the retiring Duffy Daugherty to reimburse him for expenses incurred in what may have been improper recruiting of student athletes; $10,000 transfers from Erickson to Stolz in both 1973 and 1974; improper diversion of proceeds from football bust events to "representatives or members" of the athletic department between 1967 and 1974; and Stolz's acceptance of a $2,300 "speaker's fee" at a fund-raising affair.

Many of the infractions dated back nearly a decade—again during the Daugherty era. On the other hand, the number of athletes involved was a small fraction of the team rosters, and many were no longer students at the university. In several cases Stolz had apparently felt he had to honor improper promises made by his predecessor (for example, providing aid to a former player's child and unwed mother). And there was evidence that as head coach he had been trying to rectify the situation, such as his refusal to pay for Daugherty's perennial party rooms at two local motels.

But in the end there was just too much evidence, both circumstantial and from witness testimony. The Select Committee agreed I had no choice but to ask for Stoltz's resignation,[38] and on March 19 the university board approved his removal as head coach.[39] Stolz went on to coach football at Bowling Green State University (1976–85), then at San Diego State (1986–90). Although as far as I know Stolz was never aware of it, Bowling Green president Hollis A. Moore asked me about him and his role in the recruiting scandal. I told Moore that I had liked Stolz and thought the situation was largely one that he had inherited from Daugherty. I believed he had been slowly trying to extricate himself and his program from the mess, and that I seriously doubted he would allow violations in any program he headed in the future. I recommended him to Moore. On several occasions Stolz blamed me for the NCAA investigations results. "Michigan State never had to change the coaching staff, and they shouldn't have. Had there been strong leadership, there wouldn't have been a change."[40]

Burt Smith had been detached from the athletic department and assigned other duties in October, even before Erickson came forward.[41] Based on the latest findings, we started proceedings to separate him from the university entirely. In December 1977 Smith sued the university for $3.5 million, plus reinstatement to his old job. A token settlement was made, though the details were not made public.[42] Coach Weyers was already on a six-month terminal contract, and Charlie Butler had a one-year contract. Letters of dissociation went to the boosters Doyle and Knezevich, and seven football players involved in the various violations were declared ineligible, pending appeal.

During the committee's nine months, we met eighteen times and spent 110 hours on its work, including interviews of our football coaching staff, football players, director Burt Smith, Executive Vice President Jack Breslin, and several alumni and boosters. We estimated spending an additional one hundred hours in specific investigative tasks, plus another thirty relating to the Big Ten.

Football was not the only problem while the NCAA investigation was under way. Earlier in 1975, there had been an unfortunate incident involving ten Black MSU basketball players. For the January 4 game with Indiana, Coach Gus Ganakas had insisted upon using a freshman white player against a top Indiana senior.[43] The Black players objected to his using such an inexperienced player in such a crucial game. When Ganakas made clear that it was his decision, the ten players walked out. When they didn't apologize for their behavior, Ganakas suspended them and used mostly junior varsity players in the game, which MSU lost 107 to 55.

Although Ganakas had received Jack Breslin's okay for his action, Jack was extremely unhappy at Ganakas's inability to impose proper discipline on the players. He already had serious reservations about Ganakas's coaching ability, though he waited four months before taking action to avoid possible criticism of unfairness. He then asked Burt Smith's assessment of the varsity basketball program under Ganakas's leadership, which Smith in turn characterized as "ineffective and disorganized."[44] Breslin, Smith, and Clarence Underwood decided to extend Ganakas for one more year, anticipating his removal or change in assignment after the 1975–76 season. The decision was not made public at the time because Ganakas insisted upon a clearer description of his future job. He was finally removed and reassigned to an administrative position in the athletic department, effective March 16, 1976.[45] When the news became public, Ganakas expressed "surprise" at the development followed by the predictable press outcry.[46] We didn't need an additional distraction during the NCAA crisis, but it had to be dealt with as expeditiously and humanely as possible. (A popular figure, Ganakas later became a successful popular radio commentator.)

Over time it became commonplace on campus to blame me for the severity of our treatment by the NCAA. Instead of pleading guilty and throwing the university on the mercy of the infractions committee, our "defiance" was supposed to have inflamed the association's wrath and brought down harsher penalties than otherwise might have been levied. Duffy Daugherty himself was quoted in the *Lansing State Journal*: "You put your hat in your hand . . . then maybe you get one year probation, not three."[47]

The NCAA staff was certainly self-righteous, insisting on the sanctity of practices and procedures that most outsiders would be hard put to defend. Did our insistence on due process and the rights of the accused antagonize them into intensifying their punitiveness? I don't really know—though I certainly doubt that anyone on the infractions committee or staff would ever admit it. But what I do know is that running roughshod over the rights of many innocent individuals in pursuit of greater leniency toward the institution would have been a terrible miscarriage of justice, an ethical price far too high to pay.

Shortly after the press conference announcing the sanctions, I launched a search for a new athletic director, ultimately hiring Dr. Joseph Kearney, then athletic director at the University of Washington. The forty-eight-year-old Kearney, a former World War II navy fighter pilot, seemed undaunted by the prospect of taking over in a time of crisis. By early April he had brought in a new head football coach, Darryl Rogers, as well as a new basketball coach, Jud Heathcote from the University of Montana.

I knew we were back on our feet when Rogers attended his first Big Ten kickoff luncheon, where Woody Hayes was boasting that he had "finked on Michigan State and was proud of it."[48] Unfazed, Rogers facetiously thanked Hayes for paving the way for his own appointment at MSU. Before he arrived, he added musingly, he had reserved judgment on all the bad things he had heard about Ohio State and Woody Hayes. Now that he had seen them firsthand, he added, he "didn't like either Hayes or Ohio State."

. . . .

The epilogue to the NCAA inquisition came in February 1978, after I had left Michigan State. The U.S. House Subcommittee on Oversight and Investigations of the Committee on Interstate and Foreign Commerce held hearings on NCAA enforcement practices and invited me to testify.[49] In my testimony I described the MSU experience in detail and the problems we had encountered—presumption of guilt, rejection of valid polygraph tests, and the catch-22 nature of NCAA regulations. I stressed that I did not

> challenge the personal integrity of the members of the Infractions Committee nor do I suggest malicious intent. Quite the contrary since their objective to control, if not eliminate, violations is one which I passionately share. . . . While one should not expect a voluntary, professional organization such as the NCAA to conduct itself with the strict legalistic formality of the courtroom, one does expect at least the basic protections enumerated in the U.S. Constitution, and particularly its fifth and sixth amendments.
>
> I would point out the lack of due process, the free admission and consideration of hearsay evidence, reliance upon an investigator's handwritten notes of interviews, the inability of those charged to face their accusers or even know their identity and, at least until recently, the refusal to permit those accused or witnesses to have legal counsel present. We were never informed where many of the accusations had originated except for the admission, incredibly enough, that some were based on newspaper articles.[50]

Acting committee chairman Representative James Santini commented, "I have never witnessed anything like this. They [NCAA] break down the essence of fair play."[51] The press coverage on my testimony was extensive,[52] ranging from the *New York Times* and the *Los Angeles Times* to the *Chronicle of Higher Education* and *Sports Illustrated*. The latter stated,[53] "The most impressive witness was Dr. Clifton Wharton, Jr., former president of Michigan

State and new chancellor of the State University of New York, who, though defending the need for effective police work, decried . . . a process that allows for 'hearsay evidence' and presumes guilt."

Two weeks later, President Peter Magrath of the University of Minnesota presented similar examples to the congressional committee of what he called the NCAA's use of "monopolistic powers [making a] . . . sham of their due process rights." I was amused by the irony of NCAA's reaction to the hearings when they complained that the congressional panel was unfair because critics were allowed to present their side of investigations out of context and without a chance for an immediate public response by the NCAA.[54]

The NCAA eventually changed their rules.

The best description I ever read of the NCAA's "Bizarre-World" procedures came from one of their own, Brent Clark, a former field investigator. At the congressional hearing in 1978, he testified that the Committee on Infractions hearings were deceptive and unduly influenced by the intimate relationship between the panel and its investigators. "By the time of a hearing," he said, "the committee has very likely been informally briefed by staffers on the nature of the case . . . [it] may have been asked to grant immunity to a prospective informant . . . and told in the process what evidence is likely to be forthcoming. Finally, just before the hearing actually begins, the committee is prepped by enforcement staff about the nature of the evidence and what to expect from the other side"—all without the knowledge of "the other side." Clark also charged that the NCAA abused its investigative and enforcement powers and failed to provide institutions under scrutiny with "the tools to defend themselves against unfounded charges."[55]

. . . .

Like the student demonstrations before them, the NCAA and Big Ten investigations consumed a disproportionate amount of time. The intensity of feelings and clamor of the media were constant preoccupations. But there were still many nonathletics issues, from mundane to critical, that demanded attention—though when I turned to ordinary matters their very normality gave them a surreal cast, like things fragmented and seen at a distant remove. The MSU Board of Trustees still had to meet regularly, as did my Executive Cabinet and administrators groups, the Academic Council, Student Advisory Group, and others. The university budget had to be prepared and presented to the legislature, and I had a number of continuing outside commitments—corporate and nonprofit board meetings, legislative and congressional testimony, and public speaking—though far less of the latter than in previous years.

Dolores and I also hosted the usual social (and semisocial) events, as well. My father and stepmother came for visits, as did John D. Rockefeller 3rd and his wife Blanchette, and even my old AIA mentor, Martha Dalrymple. We met students, faculty, and alumni. We attended commencements and receptions, including a *satay* party for the Malaysian students at MSU. A high point of the entire year was the graduation of Clifton 3rd from Oakland University.

His journey had been long and not always easy, and Dolores and I were thrilled and proud when he finally received his BA in philosophy.

▪ A Law School? _____

For some time pressure had been building to establish a law school at Michigan State. The existing two at University of Michigan and Wayne State couldn't accommodate all the qualified applicants, and there was also a push by younger state legislators for a program where they could earn their LLBs near the capitol. The earliest proposals for a law school at MSU had been in 1966, but the university had quietly held off until its new medical schools were well on their feet.

My preference was to develop a law school that would emphasize special legal programs related to state government, taking advantage of our location near the state capitol, with executive, legislative, and judicial branches of state government. Our plan also proposed that the curriculum focus on public service, in keeping with our land-grant philosophy.

Governor Milliken believed the state needed a third law school, and for some time had favored Michigan State as the best choice among institutions that were interested in establishing one. His 1973–74 budget supported the MSU bid, but it was rejected by the state senate. Given the governor's endorsement, the university's 1974–75 budget request included start-up funding for a law school.[56] Milliken agreed, adding $500,000 for an entering class of seventy-five. Charley Zollar, chairman of the Senate Appropriations Committee initially spoke in its favor.[57]

But Milliken's action set off a melee over the university's own priorities and the ambitions of other schools. Some legislators argued that any newly available money should go to the new MSU medical schools. Others linked the law school proposal to Michigan State's College of Urban Development, for which the governor's budget had recommended a first-year appropriation of $700,000—a tactic apparently aimed at getting lawmakers who opposed a college built around urban issues to help reject both new colleges. This appealed to those who still opposed the urban college seen as dedicated to inner-city Black issues and who did not like its dean, Bob Green. Conflating the College of Urban Development with the proposed College of Law was a devious maneuver. Still others wanted to move the recommended law school funds to other state campuses. William Copeland, chairman of the House Appropriations Committee, had originally seemed to support MSU, but after a couple of weeks announced that he preferred Western Michigan University. "Other schools need some prestige," he said. "It would be a fine thing for WMU."

We argued that Michigan State was more suitable, in part because of its proximity to the state government headquarters in Lansing. Moreover, we had strong complementary programs in criminal justice, social science, education, and labor and industrial relations. We also planned on concentrating on new fields such as environmental law and public service law, consistent with the university's land-grant mission.

Our strongest argument was that some two thousand qualified Michigan residents had been turned away by the law schools at University of Michigan and Wayne State.[58] What I didn't mention, in public at any rate, was that unlike medical schools and hospitals, which are huge financial millstones around university budgets everywhere they exist, law schools can actually be campus "profit centers." They need no laboratories, expensive equipment, clinics, or extensive support personnel—just a faculty, classrooms, and a good library. Just as important, a college of law at MSU would eventually mean more university alumni in the state legislature, expanding our support base there.

Nevertheless the conflicts escalated, with counterproposals coming forward in support of both Western and even Grand Valley State College. A strange twist along the way was a rumor that Jack Breslin had negotiated a deal for Bill Copeland, chairman of the House Appropriations Committee, not to oppose the law school in exchange for Breslin's support for a new optometry school at MSU. Though Jack angrily denied it, some of the MSU trustees were annoyed. Then came a second rumor that Breslin was a finalist for the presidency of Western Michigan. He swore it wasn't true, and I had confidence in him, but it was enough to raise questions about conflict of interest while we were contesting with Western over the law school.

Things came to a head at a senate appropriations hearing on March 15.[59] The legislators first asked our assurances that funding for the law school wouldn't come at the expense of our medical schools. We said that it wouldn't, even committing to honor the legislature's proposed "ennoblement" funding goal for the med schools rather than the governor's lower amount. The next question was whether the university could still open the law school if state funding was below our original request (we said we could). Addressing the perception that the university had started its College of Urban Development without prior legislative approval, I pointed out that it was an outgrowth of the Center for Urban Affairs, which had existed since 1969. When the optometry college red herring came up, I told the lawmakers that it wasn't an either-or situation. "The trustees are not rejecting optometry, but the board felt a law school should have top priority."[60]

Soon Grand Valley was out of the running, and the contest boiled down to MSU versus Western. By now a publicized but continuing problem was a clandestine campaign by the University of Michigan to prevent the new school from going to its in-state rival—attacks reminiscent of when Michigan State was working toward its first medical school. I was tempted to call Robben Fleming, but Al Ballard talked me out of it. The main troublemakers were Michigan law alumni in the legislature, he pointed out, and that President Fleming was probably unaware of what they were up to.

Meanwhile the state house leadership was clearly in favor of putting the law school at Western, while the senate and the governor supported Michigan State, and it began to look as if the final appropriations bill might not pass by its July 1 deadline. That meant not only further delay in our own plans, but also more time for the competition to snipe away. By the end of June a new stratagem was in the air called "language only," which would authorize the law school at MSU without providing funding for it.[61] That was the course the senate took on July 2, voting twenty-nine to six in favor.[62] (Shockingly, the appropriation refused to recognize and provide funds for the College of Urban Development.[63])

Now the battle shifted to the house. As expected, the appropriation committee supported the Western proposal, also on a "language only" basis. But in the full house the amendment substituting WMU for Michigan State failed fifty-two to forty-six, and the house then passed fifty-seven to thirty-one a new amendment deleting the MSU law school from the appropriations bill entirely. After the senate rejected the house action and the issue went to a senate-house conference committee for resolution, Jack Breslin shook his head. "The law school is gone," he said. "It looked good for a while, but there's no chance we'll get it now."[64]

And as it turned out, he was right. It was one of the biggest disappointments of my tenure at Michigan State. The university offered an immense range of resources that would have added scope and depth to legal education in the state, while our adversaries had seemed concerned primarily with prestige, regional balance, and the intricacies of legislative prerogatives. The only consolation was that in spite of the sorry tactics of our opponents, we had given our best efforts and fallen short only in the eleventh hour.[65]

▪ Tony Bennett and Lena Horne Gala

On April 19, 1975, we launched the public part of the Enrichment Campaign fund drive with a gala benefit concert by Tony Bennett and Lena Horne—yes, in the old auditorium. (The choice of artists was skillfully engineered by Ken Beachler, director of the MSU Lecture Concert Series and the auditorium.) The benefit was specifically aimed at the proposed performing arts center. Predictably, there were negative comments, but Richard Sullivan, dean of the College of Arts and Sciences, and I published counterarguments.[66]

The idea for the gala was Les Scott's and Dolores's, and she talked the MSU Faculty Folk into acting as its sponsor. Lil Smuckler, the group's president and wife of the dean of international programs, asked Lotta Hunt and Frankie Boger to be cochairs of the black-tie-optional benefit. Together the Faculty Folk easily sold all the tickets, even though $100 apiece for the best seats was fairly extravagant for the time and place.[67] The women also arranged special preperformance dinners for most ticket-holders in private homes around Lansing and East Lansing, including at Cowles House.

The afternoon before the concert, I went over to the auditorium while the legendary Lena Horne and her music director were trying out the building's acoustics. Ms. Horne had tried to fly into Lansing on Friday but, prevented by major rainstorms, returned to Detroit. Ken Beachler sent a limo to drive her up to the University Inn despite the floods. After running through a few trills and arpeggios from different areas of the stage, Horne remarked drily that she could understand why we wanted to build a new facility.

But it had been raining hard for several days, and now the downpour became so torrential that the Red Cedar River reached flood stage. Overflowing its banks, the water inundated the lower-lying sections of campus—including the basement of the auditorium, where the building's mechanical utilities were located. The power in the building went out. Communities throughout mid-Michigan were in the same straits, and portable generators were in short supply. By late afternoon we were getting desperate. Then someone suggested moving the program to the just-finished Munn Ice Arena. Horne's music director joined Roger Wilkinson and me in a quick trip across campus, where we found the rink still iced over. If we could cover it, we thought it might work to set up a stage on the arena floor on top of the ice. We called the university grounds and maintenance departments, and by the time we were leaving the crews were already coming in to get started. Ken Beachler brought his team of ushers and ticket-takers, who created a new seating plan around the makeshift stage. Meanwhile, we designated new parking areas and arranged bus transportation for those unaware of the gala's change of location. The Spartan "can-do" spirit was in charge.

Miraculously, the show started exactly on time. It was a spectacular success. As Dave Easlick, head of Michigan Bell, quipped, "Some evening! Dinner at Cowles House with Lena Horne and Tony Bennett for afters!"[68] The gala was a dramatic demonstration of why the university needed a new performing arts center so urgently.

All the costs of the gala were covered by my corporate fees given to the university, which Bob Perrin pointed out would mean that all profits from the benefit could be used for the building fund campaign.[69]

. . . .

In September 1975, I recommended to the board a number of changes in senior administrative personnel. The previous summer Milt Muelder announced his plan to retire as vice president for research and graduate studies, which triggered several shifts on my leadership team. After considerable reflection I asked provost John Cantlon to move to Muelder's old job. Cantlon had been an effective and successful head academic officer, and I worried that he might see the change as a demotion. But the university needed a strong leader to strengthen its graduate education and research capabilities, and Cantlon's own outstanding scholarly career made him the right man at the right time. A loyal Spartan and great team player, Cantlon agreed without protest, and as expected he proved a perfect choice for the job.

In the same management realignment, Larry Boger became acting provost, then (after

Lena Horne and Tony Bennett's spectacular performance at the MSU Campaign Gala for a Performing Arts Center, held on April 19, 1975, gave MSU's first fund-raising campaign a huge boost. (*Left to right*) Clifton Wharton Jr., Lena Horne, Dolores Wharton, and Tony Bennett.

a national search) was confirmed in the position permanently. (Two years later he became president of Oklahoma State University.) Bob Perrin's title was changed to vice president for university and federal relations, recognizing the political dimensions of the university's growing interest in federal support. Executive Vice President Jack Breslin added the title of vice president for administration and state relations to his job description, reflecting his effectiveness as liaison to Michigan state government. His duties as secretary to the board moved to Al Ballard, who also continued as my lead assistant. Jack Shingleton, head of MSU's student placement bureau and a former tennis star, was named interim director of athletics until Joe Kearney arrived.

Most if not all the personnel shifts aimed at improving the university's ability to handle ongoing fiscal stress. One year after another of recessionary state and national economies gave rise to tight budgets and cutbacks. No matter how hard we worked to keep our state funding requests reasonable, appropriations often came back well below what we asked. The state's 1976–77 allocation was a good example, requiring departmental cutbacks totaling $3 million —the equivalent, I noted at the time, of eliminating the university's College of Veterinary Medicine.[70] Worse, Jack Breslin expected more midyear executive-order reductions–give-backs from approved appropriations that were particularly disruptive.

⁙

Once in a rare while a president has the opportunity to have administrative "fun." Such was the occasion in September 1976 when I needed to fill the position of faculty grievance officer. The faculty grievance policy of 1972 provided for the creation of an FGO responsible for receiving and seeking to resolve grievances brought by full- or part-time faculty members. When I thought about someone who would be seen by the faculty as impartial and not a "tool" of the administration, the person who came to mind immediately was Professor "Lash" Larrowe! An economist whose fame rested upon his pro-union research and books on Harry Bridges and the International Longshoremen's Union, Lash saw himself at the champion of the underdog and the voice of the antiestablishment (read facing off against the administration), especially the MSU presidents. For the prior six years, Lash had been a frequent critic, writing columns in the *State News* targeting me seemingly almost every other week.

I somewhat whimsically (but seriously) called him to my office and asked him, "How can you refuse my offer when you are the persistent champion of the underdogs on campus?" He accepted and justified my choice by doing a fine job—though he still wrote the occasional column blasting me, if only to reassure his public that he had not joined "the establishment." But I didn't mind. It was quite a change since my first glimpse of him on February 19, 1970, egging on the demonstrating students I was addressing from the steps of the Student Union.

Years later when I made a return visit to MSU, I was walking through the Kellogg Center parking building when a vintage Rolls Royce pulled up, blocking my path. Out jumped Lash Larrowe, older and retired, still in his tie-dyed shirt, but unfazed at the contrast of the wealthy car with his corporate gadfly image. "President Wharton," he cried out, coming around toward me. "So glad to catch you. We miss you at MSU." Then shaking my hand: "Want you to know I think you were a great president!"

▪ Finances ──────────────────────────────────

By early 1977 the years of austerity were starting to take their toll. To make the most of ever-scarcer resources, MSU needed to take a hard look at its academic and budgetary priorities. Clearly, changes had to take place, but they couldn't be determined and imposed by top-down administrative fiat. Not only for the sake of good decisions, but also for that of university morale, I wanted to take a broadly participatory approach, making full use of existing management and governance structures. In February, consequently, I circulated a "Plan and Procedures for Reassessing University Priorities in a Long-Range Context." Its premise was obvious: our total resources were limited. In order to maintain quality, support the expansion of some programs, and develop important new initiatives, we would have to increase efficiency, consolidate or eliminate some efforts, and "redistribute the wealth" in ways consistent with the university's evolving mission as well as the hard realities of its political and economic milieu.

The operational result was the creation of a new University Long-Range Planning Council.[71] The council's approach was based upon the five guidelines in my report. The first guideline was to use "existing governance and administrative structures . . . [to avoid] creating an array of new ad hoc committees or task forces. . . . In all instances, the role and assignment of responsibility should be in conformance with the existing by-laws for academic governance, and the Board of Trustees." The second guideline stipulated the "involvement of faculty, students, and administrators." The third emphasized that the review should be "meshed with regular evaluation and budgeting procedures." These two guidelines were vital in assuring the university constituencies that their voices would be heard and that the recommendations would be an integral part of the regular processes, not some ad hoc unilateral act. The statement's fourth guideline reaffirmed the value of decentralized dependence upon the appropriate levels within the organization and their close knowledge of its role. An example was the use of the Academic Council's University Committee on Curriculum for any elimination of course duplication. The fifth guideline restated that the ultimate decisions rested with the MSU Board of Trustees.

The guidelines were to be used to evaluate every program and unit on campus, both academic and nonacademic, setting forth their long-term goals in priority. As part of the evaluation process each department reviewed itself and prepared related budget materials. After the reports were completed, they were to be examined by the twenty-six-member Long Range Planning Council and then referred to the proper university body for action. Existing governance bodies would prepare final proposals, which ultimately would be acted upon by the president and then the MSU Board of Trustees.

While there was some predictable initial concern and resistance, especially over the emphasis upon what critics called "Priorityism," which was seen as "a visionary dream forced . . . by bureaucratic pragmatism."[72] Nevertheless, the process proceeded and was built upon the input of the entire university.

One development in particular showed innovation could succeed even in the face of budgetary austerity—the establishment at MSU of the world's first heavy-ion superconducting cyclotron.

Cyclotrons are circular channels lined with electro-magnets controlled by a central computer bank. In the late 1970s they could hurl atoms or atomic particles together at speeds approaching 100,000 miles a second (today's cyclotrons can achieve even greater velocities). The resulting collisions generate rare isotopes, quantum particles, and antimatter, many of which exist for tiny fractions of a second and which can be studied in no other environment.

The small cyclotrons developed earlier in the decade had proved spectacularly successful in probing lighter-weight atomic nuclei, which in turn spawned cut-throat competition among leading research universities to build the first superconducting cyclotron. A number of young scientists at Michigan State, led by professor Henry Blosser, were determined that MSU should enter the fray. These leaders were both brilliant scientists and adept technologists; equally important, they were politically savvy. Blosser followed the novel approach of requesting funds to construct magnets that would be *movable*, theoretically suitable for being configured within a cyclotron in any given location. His "movable magnets" concept made it possible to organize a cluster of laboratories and universities supporting the project, and a grant to construct them was awarded to Michigan State.

Winning the National Science Foundation's $13.2 million contract to construct the cyclotron itself took a bit of last-minute administrative agility. A few days before the deadline for applying, Blosser found out that several competing universities were offering housing for visiting scientists in their submissions. To stay in the competition, MSU needed to do the same. Business vice president Roger Wilkinson worked quickly with his colleagues in campus housing to designate dorm rooms near the proposed facility that could be described in our application. In due course, the contract went to Michigan State, and the superconducting cyclotron came on line in May 1977, directly across from the site earmarked for the university's new performing arts center. This was a juxtaposition I thought epitomized my sense of a truly great university.

▪ Recruiting Magic Johnson

The year 1977 also brought a couple of "déjà vu all over again" episodes—one involving athletic recruiting, and the other a student protest.

Joe Kearney had hired Jud Heathcote as MSU's head basketball coach, and one of Heathcote's first challenges was to try to sign up the local Lansing superstar Earvin Johnson, already known to all as "Magic." Johnson had attended Michigan State basketball games from the age of ten. While playing at Lansing's Everett High School, he developed a bond with Gus Ganakas, the coach Heathcote replaced. Johnson had also become friends with Jay Vincent, a player at Lansing Eastern High. Despite the intracity rivalry, they wanted to play together in college. When Ganakas left and Heathcote came on the scene, Johnson's interest in MSU waned somewhat. But despite being frantically recruited by such basketball powerhouses as Maryland, North Carolina, and North Carolina State, Johnson's main choice remained between Michigan and Michigan State.

All we needed, of course, was another recruiting scandal, this time in basketball. In March I met briefly with Joe Kearney and Jud Heathcote, stressing the importance of a "squeaky clean" effort. Kearney assured me he had a close eye on the situation.

In April, Lloyd Cofer, one of my special assistants, told me about Dr. Charles Tucker, a former professional basketball player now working part time in the university counseling center, who might be involving himself in Johnson's recruitment. On April 5, Cofer and I had lunch with Tucker at the Faculty Club, where I repeated my insistence that there be no recruiting infractions. Tucker claimed to be an old and close friend of the Johnson family and Magic himself. He said he was angry about rumors circulating on campus that Johnson's father, Earvin Sr., had refused an invitation to visit Cowles House, insisting that I come to his home instead. Tucker stressed that the Johnsons were hardworking and honest, and that Earvin Sr. would under no circumstances have expected, much less demanded, that I come to his home. As for himself, he was faithfully observing all NCAA and Big Ten recruiting regulations. Magic had not made up his mind between the University of Michigan and MSU, he said, and his choice would depend largely on his feelings about the university basketball program and in particular his view of Jud Heathcote.

Tucker's comments confirmed something I had already heard. A local Black businessman who claimed influence with the Johnson family had suggested to Heathcote that I should visit them at their home. Later Heathcote was allegedly overheard laughing with football coach Darryl Rogers about the bind that would put me in. If I got involved and Magic didn't sign with MSU, I would be blamed by students, alumni, and the media for letting him get away. If I didn't step in, critics would rake up all the old complaints about my being aloof and "antisports."

I thought I had better clear the air. Kearney and Heathcote were invited to my office, and I repeated the rumor, telling them that if it was true, I didn't appreciate being manipulated or characterized in this fashion. I didn't imagine Robben Fleming would be visiting the Johnson home, I said to Heathcote. "Why would I?" I asked. "Just because the Johnsons were Black, and so was I?" Heathcote claimed ignorance, sputtering that all he knew was that I had previously offered to see the Johnson family on campus, as I would have with other athlete recruits. I told both the coach and the athletic director that I didn't care about rumors, but that I wanted no hint of impropriety in their recruiting, and that I would hold them both personally responsible if anything untoward came about. Finally, I said that as far as I was concerned, the only person responsible for recruiting Magic Johnson was Jud Heathcote.

Jay Vincent had signed with MSU in mid-March, which gave us an edge, and Heathcote promised Magic he would play as point guard, not center. But the clincher was actually Vernon Payne, a Black assistant coach who was about to become the head coach at Wayne State. Payne visited Earvin at Everett High on April 21, and in an act of selfless generosity urged Earvin to sign with MSU. Payne told Magic that Jud Heathcote was an excellent teacher who could enhance further Magic's already wonderful skills. The same day Johnson decided to sign a letter of intent with Michigan State. He called his parents, who had preferred MSU but insisted on their son making his own decision. Then Johnson met privately with the MSU coaching staff, his Everett coach George Fox, and Charles Tucker to plan a press conference to announce his decision.

Tucker phoned to tell me in confidence that Johnson would be going to Michigan State. He assured me that whenever Magic asked his advice, he told him to consider his own best interests, then decide for himself. I crossed my fingers and hoped it was the truth.

After the press conference the next day, I called the Johnson home and spoke to Mrs. Johnson. When I told her how pleased I was that Magic would be joining the MSU basketball team, her response was rather muted. Then I said, "I don't know how long Earvin will be with us, but as long as he's here we'll do everything we can to see he gets a fine education." With feeling, Mrs. Johnson replied, "Now *that's* important."

The combination of Johnson and Coach Heathcote resulted in an MSU national championship in the Michigan State defeat of Indiana State 75–64 in 1979.

A sequel to the football and basketball controversies came in 1984. I strongly endorsed Coach Rogers to William Ford, owner of the NFL's Detroit Lions, who eventually selected him as head football coach—something I doubt Rogers ever knew. I chose to ignore the pettiness of Rogers's prior negative comments about me: "I once asked the president [Wharton] if he 'supported athletics'. . . . He said, 'yes.' He lied. He thought supporting athletics was going to the game and waving a pennant."[73]

▪ ▪ ▪ ▪

Another déjà vu moment came at the end of the spring quarter 1977, when controversy erupted on campus over a proposed grant from the government of Iran. Professor Ali Issari, an Iranian naturalized American citizen, taught cinematography in the College of Communications Arts. Issari had been offered a grant from the Iranian government to produce a series of historical films on the Persian Empire. MSU had a sizable enrollment of Iranian students, and many of them were infected with the anti-Pahlavi, pro-Khomeini fervor festering back in Teheran. They saw Issari's proposed films as designed to glorify Shah Reza Pahlavi, who liked to stress the links between his modernizing land and ancient Persia.

On May 25 about 150 Iranian students rallied against Issari's project at Beaumont Tower. The next evening a smaller group, wearing brown paper grocery bags over their heads with holes cut for their eyes and mouths, disrupted the MSU board meeting for twenty minutes, insisting that the university refuse to accept funds from a repressive and corrupt regime.[74]

Given the nature of the controversy and the students' vehemence, the board postponed action to allow a campus debate. Both those in favor and those against would have the chance to argue their views, with university officials and selected trustees among the audience. I thought it was an ideal opportunity for the university to provide a neutral forum for contending ideas. On Friday night, June 3, some five hundred people crowded into Anthony Hall, including the protesting students still in their brown-bag masks. For almost four hours the speakers pressed their opposed positions. Soon it became indisputable that the subject matter of the planned films was indeed ancient Persia—specifically the sixth and fifth centuries B.C.—and not the glory of the shah; moreover, each film would be subject to review by a panel of Middle East scholars from major U.S. universities. An encouraging number of faculty well known for their liberal views nonetheless defended the grant. Though clearly pained by the shah's regime, they recognized that academic freedom was at stake, their own no less than Ali Issari's. At the end of the debate one student commented to me, "That was the best lecture I've ever had at MSU."

At the next board meeting the trustees approved Issari's grant five to three. As expected, the Iranian students were inflamed. Eight hundred or so occupied the International Programs building, chaining the front doors closed.[75] The takeover lasted three days, at the end of which a smaller group marched to Cowles House to tape a list of "demands" to the front door. As I recall, most of the demands were either outside the university's purview or had already been answered by the board's action. All this took place while I made a hurried one-day round-trip to Deerfield Academy to give the commencement speech at Bruce's graduation. Ironically, the university dropped the project in the following year because its funding was inadequate to its scope. Two years later the shah of Iran was forced out of office, and Ayatollah Khomeini triumphantly returned to the capital, Tehran, on February 1, 1979, to be followed in November by the ill-fated student takeover of the U.S. embassy and its personnel as hostages in what became a 444-day crisis for President Carter. In an interesting twist of fate, one of the hostages was Richard Morefield, who had served with my father in Oslo.

▪ ▪ ▪ ▪

Most foreign students during my tenure at MSU were invariably positive. They enriched the diversity of campus life and provided the university with a large global alumni present for the future. Our ongoing programs in Latin America and Africa were especially significant, and their students regular embarked on careers of leadership thereafter. Because of my foreign experience, there was often a touching personal unexpected dimension. I was regularly surprised when my former students in Malaysia enrolled at MSU without my prior knowledge. Pee Teck Yew, who also had been my research assistant in Kuala Lumpur, turned up to earn his PhD in 1973,[76] as did Kwong-Yuan Chong, who had been a member of my Admissions Commission, to earn his PhD in 1977—both in agricultural economics. Equally surprising was the arrival of Abdul Yahya Samad and his wife, formerly Marina Merican, who had been the lead dancer in Dolores's special program—she went on to earn an MA in communications (1972) and he an MBA in business (1973). The unpredictable historic interweaving of mentor or teacher with the lives of their students and pupils is a distinctive reward.

CHAPTER NINE

The Chancellor of SUNY 1: Building a Higher Education System

As my eighth year began at Michigan State, I felt at ease as president. True, budgets were tighter than ever. But we had developed methods for coping with austerity, and the university was running smoothly. A variety of academic and research initiatives were under way, and our first capital drive was moving into high gear. The days as a curiosity, "MSU's Black president," were largely past; usually I was just "the president"—respected as such, I believed. Dolores had been accepted similarly.[1]

Even my relationship with the trustees had improved. Clair White and Frank Hartman had not been renominated in 1972, and they had been replaced by two new Republicans, Dr. Jack Stack and Aubrey Radcliffe. (Stack was a family planning and infant health psychiatrist from Alma, while Radcliffe was a Black vocational counselor in the Lansing public schools.) Two new Democrats had come on board in 1974, both lawyers. John Bruff (who had served on the select committee investigating the NCAA charges) and Ray Krolikowski. Warren Huff failed to secure renomination and left in 1975.

The trustees weren't entirely bereft of eccentricity. Both Radcliffe and Stack had a tendency to inject their personal agendas into university business, an irritant that by now no longer particularly surprised me. In addition, Michael Smydra, a graduate student who had joined the board in 1977, was more than happy to carry on the board's tradition of grandstanding and self-dealing. (Eventually Smydra's antics crossed so far over the line of propriety that he became the only trustee ever forced off the board in midterm.) But in general, changes over time brought more balance to the board's deliberations and reduced the personal and political conflicts that had used so much energy in the years before. Moreover, I had the strong support of Patricia Carrigan,[2] who had become the board chair after Don Stevens stepped down.

Almost from the day of my arrival, rumors had been rampant that I wouldn't be at MSU for long—most implying that I was using the university only as a stepping-stone to some higher post. Yet in January 1978 I would begin my ninth year at Michigan State—longer than the five-year average presidential tenure nationwide, and longer than almost any other MSU president except John Hannah. Yes, my name at times surfaced in newspaper articles about other presidential searches—usually though not always entirely speculative. (For example, Harvard University in 1970,[3] where I was reputed to be one of 23 semifinalists, and the University of California in 1975,[4] where the 239 names under consideration had been reduced to 6.) The most annoying instances were when a university would leak the names of people being considered, including my own, without ever having contacted me—possibly trying to lend a public "coloration" of diversity to a selection process. But there were legitimate inquiries over the years, too. Among them had been New York University in 1974, the University of Chicago in 1975, and the University of Wisconsin system in 1977. The only one about which I felt somewhat torn was University of Chicago, for which I had great admiration and, as an alumnus, affection.

There had also been rumors from time to time about my taking a government or presidential cabinet post. For example, a *New York Times* article in November 1976 said I was under consideration for secretary of agriculture.[5] In fact, I had declined an invitation from a Carter confidante to meet the president-elect in Plains, Georgia, with other potential nominees to avoid jeopardizing my political neutrality in the eyes of Governor Milliken and the Michigan legislature. Continuing leaks about other Carter positions led me to issue a press statement.[6]

But early in 1977 came an unusually intriguing inquiry. The caller was Donald M. Blinken, a board member of the State University of New York system and chairman of the search committee for its next chancellor. Ernest Boyer, the prior chancellor, had left after seven years to become the U.S. commissioner of education. Blinken said that the search committee wanted to explore my interest in becoming a candidate for the vacant position. As the nation's largest institution of higher education, the sixty-four-campus SUNY system certainly presented interesting challenges, not least because it represented the major legacy of Nelson Rockefeller, who had taken a deep personal interest in its expansion and enrichment while he was governor of New York (1959–73). But having seen the pitfalls common to so many presidential searches, I wasn't about to leap blindly into the fray. I thanked Blinken and told him that if my name reached the committee's short list, it might then be worthwhile to talk further, but not now.

Though the position was a long shot, Dolores and I discussed it just the same. On the whole the idea of leaving MSU was unsettling. Professionally we were extremely comfortable, benefiting from strong positions on virtually all fronts. Too, there were several unfinished items on our agenda. The most urgent were the university's first capital campaign and the planned performing arts center, which couldn't be allowed to falter. Others included the fledgling College of Urban Development, which needed nurturing and support, as well as the university's ongoing quest for a law school, which I still harbored hopes of reenergizing. Most important of all, Dolores and I had come to identify personally with Michigan State. We loved the beauty of the campus and the fresh-faced intensity of the students. We loved the intellectual rigor of the faculty and the cultural richness of the campus. But we knew that the fractiousness of the board might erupt at any time, so an attractive new challenge was a lingering possibility.

As for SUNY, there was no shortage of negatives. Times had changed dramatically since its "days of wine and roses," when Governor Rockefeller had lavished money to forge a motley scatter of public and private campuses into a comprehensive system of higher education. Established in 1948 under then-governor Thomas Dewey, SUNY initially consolidated twenty-nine previously unaffiliated institutions, including eleven teachers colleges. By the late 1970s, the system included graduate-research campuses, liberal arts colleges, community colleges, agricultural and technical colleges, and a number of special-purpose institutions, including five so-called statutory colleges associated with Cornell University and Alfred University.

In 1968, then-chancellor Sam Gould, a colleague with me on Nelson Rockefeller's mission to Latin America in 1969, had appeared on the cover of *Time* magazine, and SUNY was being compared favorably to its model in California. In reality public higher education in California consisted of three separate systems: the University of California system, the California state college system, and the California community college system. By contrast, SUNY incorporated all institutional types. In addition, SUNY operated largely (though not entirely) outside New York City, where the City University of New York (CUNY) largely predominated.

But by the early 1970s the state coffers had dwindled. Gould's successor, Ernie Boyer, faced a series of cutbacks as the national economic malaise hit New York State with a body blow (it was in 1975 when President Gerald Ford refused financial aid to New York City, prompting the famous *Daily News* headline "Ford to City: Drop Dead"). In addition to the prospect of unrelieved belt-tightening, SUNY existed in a state of perpetual cold war with the New York board of regents, who claimed an authority over the system that its own trustees strenuously disputed. Other problems included unrelenting political attacks by the state's powerful private colleges and universities, which contended for public support for their own financial needs. Finally, there was the possibility of the state's taking over the City of University of New York system (CUNY), aggravating still further the chronic competition for a slice of the ever-shrinking state fiscal pie.

In the summer came news that I had been included on the SUNY search committee short list, and that a subcommittee wanted to visit me at MSU. The group included Don Blinken, James Warren, and Dr. John Holloman. Blinken, an investment banker with E.M. Warburg, Pincus & Co., had been a classmate at Harvard, though neither of us could recall having met there. Warren, who was vice chair of the board, was a successful plumbing contractor who was a pillar of the Albany community. John "Mike" Holloman, a Black physician, was an acquaintance from our days in New York's Riverton apartments. He had spent several tumultuous years as head of the city's health and hospitals corporation and had been a SUNY trustee since 1966.

Although the committee came shrouded in secrecy, I gave an extensive tour of the campus, whose stunning grounds and facilities made an obviously favorable impression. The subcommittee was told about major academic initiatives, showed some planned construction, and described many of the campus and community activities in which Dolores and I were involved. As usual, the group was much taken with Dolores, both as MSU's First Lady and as an independent professional with ever-growing responsibilities on corporate and nonprofit governing boards.

After the group left, I called outgoing chancellor Ernie Boyer for a confidential assessment. Boyer was frankly surprised that I would consider the job, given the stress the system was under. When probed about other candidates, Boyer said that the only one he knew about, Executive Vice Chancellor and Acting Chancellor Jim Kelly, had recently had a heart attack and probably wasn't a likely choice. Later I learned that another finalist had been Willard Boyd, president of the University of Iowa, who withdrew after a visit to Albany.

After the subcommittee's visit I had a strong intuition that the chancellorship might be offered, which forced me to think about it more seriously. Blinken said that the search committee wanted someone who could raise the system's intellectual profile, improve its management, and forge better relations with the governor's office and the state legislature. As I saw it, the critical questions were whether a system as huge and complex as SUNY was in fact manageable as an entity, and whether it could develop a genuine, coherent sense of identity. For decades SUNY installations had sprouted around the state like mushrooms, paid for by Governor Rockefeller's creative use of a new bonding mechanism.[7] When Nelson Rockefeller took office, the system enrolled 38,000 students; when he left fourteen years later, enrollment stood at 325,000. The SUNY campuses had multiplied to include four university centers (undergraduate and graduate research institutions) in Buffalo, Albany, Binghamton, and Stony Brook. There were also fifteen four-year arts-and-sciences campuses; six two-year agricultural/technical colleges; thirty community colleges; and two stand-alone medical schools upstate (Syracuse) and downstate (Brooklyn). In addition to several specialized schools (e.g., the College of Optometry in Manhattan and the Maritime College in the Bronx, New York[8]), there were five "statutory" colleges financed by the state but located at and run by private colleges—four of them at Cornell University (agriculture, veterinary medicine, human ecology, and labor and industrial relations) and one at Alfred University (ceramics). (The statutory colleges did not see themselves as really part of SUNY—in fact, they saw the arrangement as a barely tolerable legal technicality.) The largest category of system campuses was the thirty community colleges.

On a professional level, was there a creative role I could play in such a gigantic operation? As president of a megaversity, I knew how to deal with operations on a very large scale. But did I really want to trade the immediate, day-to-day give-and-take with faculty, students, and alumni for the distanced, mainly administrative work of a managerial bureaucracy? Both East Lansing and Albany were in the middle of winter snowbelts, but at SUNY my role would clearly be a lot "colder" than at MSU.

Moreover, Dolores reminded me, we would once again have to rise above the inevitable low expectations so often encountered by Blacks moving into prominent positions. It always seemed to take several years to bat away the preconceptions. Together Dolores and I had built a strong, mutually respectful partnership with MSU and the state of Michigan. In Albany we would have to start all over again. Among other things, Dolores would have to give up some corporate and nonprofit boards that required Michigan residence, such as Michigan Bell, Michigan National Bank, and the Detroit Institute of Arts. On the other hand, she would be able to continue with Phillips Petroleum, Kellogg Corporation, the National Endowment for the Arts, and the Museum of Modern Art.

Was a new challenge worth giving up everything we had accomplished so far, and the prospect of even greater gains yet to come?

On September 7 Henry Ford II hosted a dinner at his Grosse Point home for the U.S. Governors Conference, then meeting in Detroit. Since the Ford Company directors were meeting at the same time, we were all invited as well. At my request Ted Mecke, Ford's top public relations officer, arranged for Dolores and me to sit at the same table as New York's governor, Hugh Carey. Although the governor of New York didn't appoint the chancellor of the university, he did appoint the board of trustees, so his indirect influence was significant— second only to his control of the state budget. Before dinner, without mentioning my own candidacy for the job at SUNY, I was able to talk with Carey about the critical importance of public universities. Ever the politician, Carey made only a few neutral comments. Later, Dolores, sitting next to the governor, chatted with him about Michigan State and her own work in the university, in the state, and on corporate boards.

In the middle of the SUNY search I unexpectedly heard from William Bundy, on whose advisory committee I had served when he was assistant secretary of state. Bundy was chairing a search committee to find a successor for Yale University's President Kingman Brewster. Because I had become fairly prominent in higher education, he was interested in any "suggestions" I might have regarding potential candidates. In mid-September we met for breakfast in New York at the University Club. After we talked a while, Bundy admitted delicately that the committee already had a short list . . . and that I was on it!

I was taken aback and pleased, but the SUNY process was already too far along to give Yale's feeler serious consideration. Privately, moreover, I thought the likelihood of Yale's selecting a Harvard man quite low—both universities tended to select their own alumni as presidents. Perhaps the Yale committee wanted to be able to point to at least one minority on its list of finalists, a position to which I decidedly didn't aspire.

Although I thanked Bundy sincerely for his interest, one thing that I didn't mention was that Dolores and I were meeting with the SUNY Board of Trustees that very afternoon. At the women's Cosmopolitan Club we were introduced to the board chair, Elisabeth Luce Moore, sister of Henry Luce, the famous founder of *Time* magazine. Also present were John Roosevelt, the former U.S. president's son; Robert Douglass, Governor Rockefeller's former chief of staff; and five other trustees. (Subsequently we met separately with two other trustees who hadn't made it to the group session.) Trustee Manly Fleischmann, a lawyer who was one of my fellow directors at Equitable, was initially surprised that I was seriously considering the SUNY job, but he quickly began to campaign on my behalf.

I was impressed with the trustees and their commitment to the SUNY system, regardless of party affiliation. Dolores, on the other hand, reacted with considerable reserve. Later she contrasted the meeting with our first session with the MSU trustees, who evidenced high esteem for the concept of MSU's First Lady, except for the usual three. The SUNY trustees, on the other hand, seemed impersonal and coolly businesslike, focusing on the challenges of leading an entire university system rather than a single campus. No one mentioned any role for the chancellor's spouse. *This*, Dolores thought, *is going to be quite a switch*.

By the end of the meeting my sense was that SUNY's trustees wanted me to become their next chancellor. (The possible exception was Jim Warren, who had worked closely with the acting chancellor Jim Kelly, liked him, and thought he deserved a shot at the top job.)

Two weeks later, word of my candidacy leaked to the Albany press and was immediately picked up by the MSU *State News*.[9] Bob Perrin put out a bland statement neither affirming nor denying the rumor. When Don Blinken subsequently let me know that the board would like to move forward with my selection, I took a deep breath and told him I was ready to proceed. On October 25, 1977, Blinken and the other trustees formally elected me as chancellor of the State University of New York.

At SUNY, as at MSU, I never had an employment contract. My philosophy was that I was serving at the pleasure of the board of trustees, who should be free to remove me at will. I could also leave them and the university at will, if I were dissatisfied. I also believed that too often university presidents, through the presidential search firms, developed complex arrangements for special compensation, delayed bonuses, and permanent retirement support at the expense of the institution. I refused to "play that game"—sometimes to my financial detriment.

. . . .

Our departure was a bittersweet moment, at a time when both Dolores and I felt a strong sense of dedication, gratification, and huge affection toward Michigan State. We had faced a lot of trials, and shed no few tears, and we had some happy triumphs to show for it. At a hastily arranged press conference in the MSU boardroom the next day, I had a hard time even with Dolores at my side. It was one of the few moments in my life when I struggled to control my emotions in public.[10] Restraining a lump in my throat, I tried to say how much our time at MSU had meant to both of us. The excitement of taking on a new challenge, I added, was tempered by the deep regret we felt at leaving this university community. For the rest of our lives, Dolores and I would be Spartans at heart.

As eight years before, the news of my selection brought extensive press coverage. The *New York Times* published a picture of Dolores and me on the front page above the fold,[11] the main story accompanied by another "Man in the News" sidebar.[12] Much of the coverage sounded the familiar theme of racial pioneering—"the first Black to head the largest university system in the country."

Coverage in the Black press was quite supportive, though I was bemused by one commentator who felt that my appointment "isn't a plus for Blacks and poor people of this state . . . we can expect the present racist policy [in the state university] to continue. . . . Any man who places his race third when defining himself . . . is a splendid example of the de-culturized man."[13] I couldn't help reflecting on why, for some, wearing their version of a badge of "blackness" was mandatory above everything else. Previously I had been able to overcome barriers in part because I had not constantly waved the flag of racism or the banner of blackness—either as a dominant reality or an excuse to justify special treatment. Instead I had committed myself to superior performance to overcome any racism and stereotyping. Why weren't achievements sufficient evidence of what I—and our people—could achieve if given the opportunity? In counterpoint to the critics, the Black politician Louis Martin noted, "The question of [Wharton's] racial identity seems not to have entered the trustees' minds. They were looking for the best qualified person to fill a complex and highly demanding post."[14]

On campus and around the state, there was a stretch of public uproar in reaction to our impending departure. Resolutions of praise were passed by the state legislature, MSU's Academic Council, the Minority Advisory Council, and other campus organizations. The *Lansing State Journal* headlined "'The Wharton Years,' Progress . . . and Holding MSU Together: New Colleges, New Buildings, Rhodes Scholars."[15] Frank Angelo, editor of the *Detroit Free Press*, wrote, "Wharton has helped mightily to lift MSU several notches on the academic scale. . . . One might say that more than a little of the touch of class that Clifton and Dolores Wharton brought to East Lansing has rubbed off on the institution they have served."[16] Several other papers and media outlets published generous editorials, and trustee Don Stevens credited me with "bringing the university into the twentieth century."

In retrospect what stands out were mostly private moments. One was when Eric Gentile and Judy Taylor, two student advocates for the handicapped who had recently married, came buzzing into my office in their electric wheelchairs to present a plaque of an open door, symbolizing my commitment to greater accessibility throughout the university. On another occasion art professor Mel Leiserowitz presented Dolores and me with the maquette of *Orpheus*, the sculpture he had designed to stand outside the university's planned performing arts center. The $30,000 cost for the sculpture was funded by my corporate fees, which I sent to the university. Dolores was presented with a beautifully printed brochure of photographs that summarized her various activities and contributions to the university, both on and off campus, during her eight years. And yet another was a surprise serenade in front of Cowles House by the Spartan Marching Band, who had regularly practiced outside our windows for eight years. When director Ken Bloomquist led a slow rendition of "MSU Shadows" in our honor, the moment inspired tearful reverence that pulled at our heartstrings.

The most insightful summary of my tenure was by Dean Richard E. Sullivan, College of Arts and Letters. With the sharp eye of a historian, Dick stepped back from the emotion of the immediate moment and offered a superb longer-term objective assessment of my tenure.

> Wharton was an innocent when he assumed the presidency of Michigan State University. He was an innocent in an almost forgotten sense of that word: lacking in consciousness of the nature of the moment which he had been charged to manage.
>
> How could he have known the complacency and self-righteousness of a crucial segment of the University community which he had been selected to direct, complacency and self-righteousness generated by two decades of remarkable growth that had vaulted Michigan State University into institutional greatness?
>
> How could he have anticipated the intensity of the rage harbored by another segment of the University angered by what was perceived to be the moral bankruptcy of an entire society?
>
> How could he have anticipated that the University would be mandated to provide instant answer for a bewildering array of social problems emerging from decades of American history?
>
> How could we have dreamed of the end of the love affair between the American public and American higher education, a breach that would inflict on universities bitter criticism, increasing interference and reduced resources?
>
> How could even an economist have predicted the terrible toll that would be exacted from universities by the errant vagaries of the economy of the 70s?
>
> In short, how could Clifton R. Wharton, so exquisitely qualified to preside over the university of the 60s, dare assume command of a university about to enter the 70s?
>
> It was because he was innocent.[17]

At the time, I confess taking mild issue with his characterization of me as an "innocent." Over the intervening years my own objectivity grew so that eventually I came to agree wholeheartedly and fully with every word Dick Sullivan wrote. He perfectly captured my eight years. So, from my perspective he was a great historian!

This 1978 picture shows the SUNY Plaza, the system administration headquarters. Behind me is the central tower, and to my left is the South Tower (formerly the headquarters for the *Albany Evening Journal* newspaper). The top three floors were redesigned to create a new chancellor residence. We later learned that the building's original owner, Billie Barnes, Republican leader and *Journal* publisher, had a home on the same floors.

▪ State University Plaza

When I arrived at SUNY in January 1978, its system administrative offices had been in a variety of buildings scattered around Albany, the state capital. But plans were under way to consolidate everything in a spectacular old building downtown, at the foot of State Street near the Hudson River. Though built early in the twentieth century, the building had been designed by the architect Marcus T. Reynolds and was supposedly an exact copy of the thirteenth-century Cloth Guild Hall in Ypres, Belgium. It was composed of two flanking wings, constructed separately and later joined. The first wing, built in 1913–14, had housed the headquarters of the Delaware and Hudson Railroad; even now it was popularly known as the "D&H building." The second building, on the south, dated from 1916 and had housed the offices and presses of the *Albany Evening Journal*, owned by William A. "Billie" Barnes, a friend of the architect and a backroom Republican power in the town from 1899 to 1921.

The building had been virtually abandoned and was in severe disrepair in 1973, when Governor Rockefeller and Albany mayor Erastus Corning persuaded Chancellor Boyer to centralize SUNY's administrative units there."[¹] A massive remodeling began the same year, which would eventually cost about $15 million. (In 1977 the state acquired a third building nearby, which had previously housed federal offices and courts, adding it to the complex now dubbed State University Plaza.) The main building was 660 feet long and only 48 feet at its widest point. There were a thirteen-floor spire where the wings met and a nine-floor tower at the south end. The top floor of the larger tower was to house the boardroom. At the top of the center tower was placed a weathervane replica of the *Half Moon*, the ship that Henry Hudson sailed to Albany in 1609. According to the Smithsonian Institution, it is the largest working weathervane in the United States, at six feet, nine inches in length and eight feet, ten inches high, and weighing approximately four hundred pounds.

Since construction was still winding up in early 1978, I suggested that my office be immediately below the boardroom. Although the system's several vice chancellors would report directly to me, their offices were situated near their own staff units rather than adjacent to mine.

Despite a record snowstorm that virtually shut down the city for several days in February 1978, moving the university administration to SUNY Plaza went smoothly enough. Not so easy, however, was the Whartons' move into our own new home. During a visit to Albany before my election, Dolores and I got a look at the chancellor's official residence, a fourteen-room, eight-bath house at 40 Marion Avenue. It had been originally bought for Sam Gould in 1962, a few blocks from the SUNY–Albany university campus but several miles from the system offices downtown. A sagging, faux-Tudor pile, it was the dreariest place we had seen since our married-housing days at the University of Chicago. Musty and ramshackle, the house had only a few slits for windows, allowing slivers of sunlight only in the early morning. There was no shortage of furniture—all donated, none matching, the sofas and chairs clad in slipcovers that had lost whatever shape they had ever had. Most of the light fixtures were broken, and a thermostat hung from a nail on a bare wall, attached to nothing at all. None of the several bedrooms were large enough for more than a cot-sized bed and nightstand. The living room was on the second floor. Near its entry stood a gift from the SUNY Maritime College—a huge five-foot ship's bell!

Even worse than its lack of charm and comfort, the house's weird floor plan and shortage of amenities made it highly unsuitable for entertaining large groups, which we knew would be as important in Albany as it had been in East Lansing. Visitor parking was almost nonexistent—during any event, cars would fill up all the on-street spaces, block neighbors' driveways, and create general havoc. My predecessor, Ernie Boyer, had refused for years to live in the residence, preferring his own home in nearby Slingerlands.

The trustees understood the problem, and as part of my employment they authorized a search for a more suitable residence, meanwhile suggesting we use the house on a temporary basis. Unfortunately, word of our concern about the old house leaked out. Nothing makes reporters salivate more than attacking the presumed "perk" of any kind of official tax-supported housing, and at my first press conference a reporter asked what was wrong with 40 Marion Avenue.[19] Even after trustee Jim Warren explained that SUNY had been looking for a replacement residence for several years, the resulting stories and editorials were censorious, and the mini-flap continued until the house was finally sold. I was forcibly reminded of John Hannah's sage counsel—never rebuild or remodel a president's house!

James Lyng, deputy for central administrative services, canvassed greater Albany for possible replacements, ranging from a palatial mansion first built for the Roman Catholic bishop of Albany to a fourteen-acre suburban estate. Cost aside, the main difficulty was that any house with only the few bedrooms we needed for ourselves lacked sufficient space for public entertainment—and vice versa. Just when we were about to despair of ever finding the right house, Dolores happened to be exploring the as-yet unoccupied south tower of the main University Plaza building. With her sharp eye, she saw the potential for the top three floors to be transformed into an apartment with just the right combination of private and public space. Oscar Lanford, vice chancellor for capital facilities and head of the SUNY Construction Fund, agreed that the idea was feasible. We later learned from Norman Rice, the head of the Albany Institute of History and Art, that Billie Barnes had built an apartment for himself on the exact same floors. The result was a wonderfully livable space on three floors with modern angular interiors folded around the hexagonal shape of the building. The two elevators in the center of the building, which served the lower floors, required a key to reach the top residential areas.

Dolores's selection of modern furnishings and large paintings combined wondrously with the crenulated edges, buttressed piers, gabled dormers, and gargoyles of the building's facade. The seventh floor included a foyer, living room, large dining room, and kitchen—it was mainly for meeting with guests of the university. The eighth floor was our private area, with a family room, master bedroom and bath, small kitchen, and dining area. The ninth floor had a second bedroom and bath (originally for son Bruce, later for guests when he was away at college). Below our residence, the sixth floor was essentially left as office space for Dolores and her secretary, with an adjoining large library that also served as an informal conference room.

When we began developing our South Tower apartment, board chair Beth Moore asked Dolores if another trustee, Jeanne Thayer (a former actress and wife of the publisher of the *International Herald Tribune*) might take charge of the decorating.

"Jeanne is *special*," Moore gushed, "and she's so accomplished in her tastes."

"Beth," Dolores responded in glacial tones, "I'm special, too." And it was Dolores, not Jeanne Thayer, who presided over the finishing of our triplex residence.

As soon as the project got under way the public furor reignited, even though the $145,000 price tag was well within the budget that had been set for a new chancellor's residence (one story listed the retail prices of every item of furniture installed, from sofas to credenzas).[20] But when reporters found out that those costs were being paid from corporate board fees I

The dedication of the new SUNY system headquarters took place on June 5, 1978. (*Left to right*) Governor Hugh Carey, Chancellor Wharton, Lt. Governor Mary Anne Krupsak.

had turned over to SUNY,[21] the media and legislative criticism gradually faded. The tide of opinion eventually stopped when our tower residence became a source of community pride, with a two-page spread of photographs running in the *Albany Times Union*.[22]

The new SUNY Plaza was dedicated on June 5, 1978,[23] attended by former governor Nelson Rockefeller, Governor Hugh Carey, Lt. Governor Mary Anne Krupsak, and SUNY chair Beth Moore, plus other trustees and luminaries. During the session, Governor Carey announced the appointment of Don Blinken to succeed Beth Moore as board chairman.

• • • •

Moving from East Lansing to Albany had involved more for both of us than traveling six hundred miles. Dolores soon became the mainstay of our presence in the community. Invitations from local organizations proliferated and our own entertainment in the Tower became a social cachet. Early on she became a trustee of the Albany Law School and Albany

Institute of History and Art, which helped her establish a local foothold. Later she joined the boards of Key Bank National Association and the Golub Inc., owner of the Price Chopper regional grocery chain. These commitments were added to her existing roles on multinational corporation boards. It was interesting, if sometimes irritating, to observe the attitudes toward Dolores in our new venue. As in the past, many expected her to conform to the traditional role of executive spouse, joining ladies' lunches and book clubs, dispensing smiles in receiving lines, exhorting the locals to good works. A *New York Times* feature article on Dolores set forth her multiple nontraditional roles and captured her image at the outset as a "forthright wife" who "never gets around to pouring tea."[24]

As an attractive, intelligent woman—a Black woman at that—she wasn't supposed to be an independent professional, and reactions to her professional involvements were often perplexed if not resentful—especially among women who didn't see her life as a mirror of their own. "My dear, how did *you* get to be a corporate director?" was a frequent question. It never seemed to occur to people that Dolores had proved her competence one board at a time, and that corporations and nonprofits continued to seek her out based on a record of past successful contributions. In addition to continuing with the Kellogg and Phillips Petroleum boards, where she was the first woman and first Black, she added New York Telephone, based on her experience at Michigan Bell. Subsequently she joined the media giant Gannett, again the first woman and first Black director. She also became a member of the board of visitors of Tulane University and the board of governors of Massachusetts Institute of Technology.

But women corporate directors were rare at the time, and some people had a hard time with the idea. Soon after my appointment, SUNY chair Beth Moore hosted a dinner attended by Nelson and Happy Rockefeller. Dolores sat next to Maurice "Tex" Moore, Beth's husband and a founder of the law firm Cravath, Swaine, and Moore. After he and Dolores exchanged views on some topics of corporate conduct, Moore commented, "You certainly have a lot to say." He then remarked, "You shouldn't be on all those boards. You should be home helping your husband!" Dolores deflected the remark with aplomb, but it was quite hypocritical. Moore's own wife Beth was no shrinking violet when it came to interests outside the home.

As for Dolores's "helping her husband," in that year alone she accompanied me on visits to twelve SUNY campuses and six SUNY-wide conferences. She also gave the commencement address at Schenectady Community College, plus talks to the Albany Rotary and Chamber of Commerce and hosted the city's annual prayer breakfast. And since the state provided no reimbursement for many SUNY-related expenses such as official entertaining, she was also using some of her corporate board fees to defray these costs.

A more positive aspect of moving from MSU to SUNY was that I had a board of trustees that had elected me unanimously. They were a committed, hardworking group who took seriously their accountability for the university system's well-being. Though they had been appointed by both Republican and Democratic governors, they rarely displayed ideological divisiveness. They were never rubber stamps, even if they had to disagree with a governor who had appointed them. They understood their fiduciary responsibility, and they always approached issues from the standpoint of the system's needs. Consequently my early days were far easier than they had been at Michigan State.

There were other differences. The most obvious, of course, were size and scope: MSU was big, but with sixty-four campuses and 345,000 students, SUNY was truly gargantuan. At Michigan State, I often had the satisfaction of making a decision or taking an initiative and seeing fairly immediate results. Now I had to work at a remove, far from the day-to-day flux of campus life. There would be little contact with students and faculty, teaching and research. While there was an academic dimension to managing the system, it tended to involve review and approval, not initiative, which was the prerogative of campus officers and faculty. The chancellor's main tools were budgetary and oversight authority, not intellectual energy or soaring rhetoric. Even if I tried to advance new ideas, execution was dependent on campus intermediaries, whose dispersal around the state often made regular interaction problematic.

There was also a centrifugal tendency within the system, as disparate campuses resisted central management in order to "do it their way" and differentiate themselves from both one another and the overarching system administration. The competitiveness was natural enough, though it often undermined the collective interest. Nowhere was it more evident than in the struggle of several campuses to distance themselves from the SUNY name. The university center at Buffalo, for example, wanted to be known as the "University of Buffalo," not "State University of New York Center at Buffalo." In New York City, the "Fashion Institute of Technology" didn't answer to the "SUNY Fashion Institute." Worst of all were the so-called statutory colleges, whose diplomas such as Cornell's were regular degree certificates with no acknowledgment of the SUNY connection at all.

One thing I hadn't counted on was the widespread disdain in New York toward public higher education—SUNY most decidedly included. It was shocking how many people saw the public campuses as second- or third-rate, inferior to private colleges and universities. At Michigan State and around the Big Ten, public campuses had been the face of higher education, and set the highest standards of excellence. But in the Northeast private higher education was the model, and the fact that by far the majority of private schools fell far short of the Ivy League ideal was rarely acknowledged. It was an attitude that took some getting used to, and I never entirely did. Although all my higher education had been at private universities, I had visited a large number of public and private universities for ADC. Thus, I thought I had a good sense of the comparative strengths and weaknesses of both sectors.

I had learned the ropes of dealing with legislators and the governor in Michigan, but in New York the attitudes and balance of power were different. In New York the governor wields enormous power through the state Division of the Budget—more, some said, than in any other state. The governor, state senate majority leader, and speaker of the house controlled all fiscal policies and decisions. In both chambers the higher education committees operated similarly to those in Michigan, though there was less of the Midwestern straight-from-the-shoulder style. In Michigan you knew where most lawmakers stood, and they stood by their word. Here, Mayor Erastus Corning, then legendary boss of the Albany political machine, warned me in a candid moment, "New York politicians can throw their arm around your shoulder, stab you in the back, and then arrest you for carrying a concealed weapon."

Nevertheless, I soon found that the state's political leaders were reasonable partners when it came to the university system. My work was particularly helped by two Black legislators, Arthur Eve, deputy speaker of the assembly, and Carl H. McCall, state senator and later New York State comptroller, U.S. ambassador to the United Nations, and chair of the SUNY Board. Eve had been the driving force creating funding for the SUNY equal opportunity centers. McCall had been raised in Roxbury, Massachusetts, and had been a childhood friend of my three siblings.

There was a SUNY campus within fifty miles or so of every citizen in the state—voting citizens, and the politicians knew it. The campuses were also major employers in towns or regions. Of course, local political support didn't necessarily translate into clout for the university system as a whole. I knew that would happen only if campus trustees, administrators, faculty, and supporters came to understand that collective, coordinated action could be in their best interests—an idea that would take time and skill for me to put across.

I needed to reach out to the general public, and particularly to the university's broad political constituency. My first opportunity came in mid-February, when I was invited to give the keynote address at the annual dinner of the New York State Black and Puerto Rican Caucus. Held in downtown Albany's huge Empire State Plaza convention center, the event was a confab of power brokers from both parties. Throughout the evening much of the crowd mixed restlessly, meeting and greeting one another, exchanging arcane in-jokes, and negotiating deals across the tables (and hopping among them). The noise was deafening, the list of speakers preceding me was long, and for the most part the audience was paying little attention—except for the governor. By 10:45 P.M. I still had not been introduced, and it seemed unlikely that I would be able to connect effectively with the audience. I also suspected that my rather academic-type presentation—"Education and Black Americans: Yesterday, Today and Tomorrow"[25]—would probably fall flat.

Just before it was my turn, a Hispanic politician from Buffalo began berating the caucus, speaking in Spanish about its neglect of Hispanics. His litany of complaints got only perfunctory applause, mostly from Hispanics themselves, but I thought I saw an opening. After being introduced to the unruly throng, I stood at the podium and turned to the prior speaker. I declared to him in Spanish that I fully agreed with his points! As I spoke heads swiveled in confusion, and the audience lapsed into puzzled silence. A SUNY chancellor speaking fluent Spanish? Nobody had seen *that* on the program. *La lengua es el alma del pueblo* ("Language io the ooul of the people"), I reminded the Hispanic members with a grin. After an outburst of applause died down, I gave the rest of my speech in English to a most attentive group.

▪ Visiting Sixty-Four Campuses

What would be the best way to get my mind around the SUNY conglomerate? In discussing this with Murray Block, deputy to the chancellor for campus liaison, we concluded that the best way was to visit the campuses in person—like my childhood shipboard tours. While a daunting task, it offered a sense of how the institutions differed and what their most pressing needs were. Bob Spencer, Murray's deputy, prepared briefing books on each campus to be visited. These contained basic facts about enrollment, curricula, recent issues or problems, and the names of key campus administrators, faculty notables, campus council members, top alumni, and local political figures. The books enhanced my ability to ask probing questions, propelling me up the "learning curve" of the SUNY system.

My plan was to listen and learn. There would be no predetermined agenda or format, though I asked for the chance to speak with faculty and students as well as with administrators, alumni, and members of the local campus councils. How the presidents handled the visits would say something about their self-confidence and leadership styles.

Murray Block went with me on most of the visits. Sometimes Dolores came along. Usually we traveled by car, except to the westernmost locations. Soon after the tours began, local and statewide media began to cover them. Calling me "the peripatetic chancellor," the *New York Times* ran a long feature with photos and a map showing the campuses and indicating those already visited.[26]

My first trip was to the university center at Buffalo, on February 1; my last was to the two-year College of Agriculture and Technology at Cobleskill, on November 6. In the intervening ten months all the rest were completed. Several reported that my visit was the campus's first visit by a SUNY chancellor. The great benefit for a new chancellor was that I then knew and could recall each and every campus in the entire system—an important feat when it came to dealing with state legislators, county executives, and local mayors.

Among other things, the visits revealed a lot about SUNY's public image problems—particularly (I thought) inaccurate perceptions that it was overbuilt, bloated, a burden on taxpayers, and inferior in academic quality. In New York State and the northeast generally, a private college education was almost by definition better than education at a public college. Although the product of private universities myself, I knew there were great schools in both sectors. Education at many SUNY campuses was demonstrably superior to private campuses in the same region. But too often students and their families were spending their hard-earned savings not on a top-notch academic experience, but on the hoped-for prestige of a "private" label. The problem was further exacerbated by a well-organized, continuing campaign against SUNY and CUNY by the Commission of Independent Colleges and Universities (CICU), a private campuses' lobbying organization.

CICU insisted upon calling its members "independent" in contradistinction to SUNY and CUNY, which they pejoratively labeled either as "state-subsidized" or as "dependent." In fact, the state's private higher education campuses had generous state support through New York's Tuition Assistance Program (TAP), paid directly to students, and Bundy Aid, an unrestricted "bounty" paid to each institution for each graduate.[27]

The level of TAP for individual students depended on whether the student was enrolled in a public or private institution. A complex formula related aid assistance to estimated family income compared with the institutional tuition cost. The minimum and maximum levels were determined by the state legislature. Thus a student who attended a private university with a tuition level higher than SUNY might receive a higher TAP award (up to that year's maximum) than if he or she attended a SUNY campus. The goal was to offset the tuition differentials and to promote choice among campuses and diversity for students.

Because the so-called independent campuses enrolled nearly half of the state's students, they had over the years laid claim to an elsewhere unheard-of amount of public funding. Competition over state appropriations had made for less-than-friendly relations between public and private institutions well before I took over at SUNY. In the late seventies, the state's tight budgets were making things steadily worse.

Led by Hank Paley, CICU's top lobbyist, the independent campuses' strategy for boosting state funding was based upon the core argument that state tax dollars went further when directed to the private sector, arguing that the cost per student to the state was lower. Pointedly ignored was the original reason why SUNY was created—the failure of private institutions to increase their enrollment levels for GI Bill students as well as the historical discrimination against Jewish students.[28] The CICU attacks were not only distasteful, but harmful.

I believed that both higher education sectors needed to stress the advantages that greater diversity offered New York. We needed to respect, if not support, each other, instead of resorting to internecine academic warfare. In speeches around the state I soon began to promote these views while including refutations of CICU's attacks.

Another SUNY problem was its relationship with the state board of regents. The regents are unique to New York—no other state has a similar entity. The regents comprise seventeen members elected by the state legislature for five-year terms: one from each of the state's thirteen judicial districts and four members who serve at large. Their mandate is to oversee all education in New York State—public and private, K–12 through graduate and professional school. The state education department and its commissioner serve as the regents' administrative and enforcement agent. They have broad power over both public and private education at all levels, ranging from setting K–12 academic standards to approving curricula in colleges and universities. They also select a commissioner of education, who heads the state education department and serves as president of the University of the State of New York (often confused with the State University of New York). Among other things, the regents also issue a master plan for the "development and expansion" of higher education in New York every four years.

The regents historically had exhibited a strong bias toward the private colleges—they had in fact opposed the system's creation in 1948. Just before my arrival the regents had attempted to close graduate programs in English and history at SUNY's university center at Albany, arguing that their right to register new academic programs throughout the state also conferred the right to "deregister" programs already in existence—especially when the state was experiencing hard times. Ernie Boyer, my predecessor, had resisted, arguing that English and history were core disciplines in any university. SUNY took its case to court, lost, appealed, and lost again.[29] But the battle sowed the seeds of future victory, because the court stipulated that henceforth the regents should cease their attempts to interfere in the routine operations of the state university system.

While still getting my campus tours under way, I met with all the senior staff at SUNY central and created an executive cabinet of my direct reports. I wanted a strong, open, and collegial team, and was happy that nearly all the existing managers were willing to stay on. (Three who did leave were Executive Vice Chancellor Jim Kelly, who had been passed over for the chancellorship; General Counsel Walter Relihan, who took a partnership in a law firm; and Provost Loren Baritz, who became president of the University of Maine at Orono.) Among the top officers remaining were Murray Block; Oscar E. Lanford, who soon retired and was replaced by Irving Freedman, who had extensive experience in SUNY central and in state government; James Perdue, vice chancellor for academic programs, policy, and planning; Harry Spindler, senior vice chancellor for finance and business; James Smoot, vice chancellor for educational services; Neal Robbins, vice chancellor for community colleges; and Herb Gordon, deputy to the chancellor for state relations.

An area demanding new leadership in my judgment was the health sciences. SUNY was building medical schools at the university centers at Buffalo and Stony Brook. It was also trying to energize its Upstate and Downstate Medical Centers, the College of Optometry in Manhattan, and nursing and health science curricula at several four-year campuses. These high-cost programs needed full-time advocacy and oversight. Our search turned up the ideal candidate, Norman Haffner, who had been the founding president of the College of Optometry. Appointed to a new position as vice chancellor for health sciences, Haffner knew the medical field broadly but carried none of the baggage of the dominant specializations. His political skills were well honed, and he soon proved an all-purpose administrative guru as well. He was later joined by Dr. Ruth E. Baines, an outstanding nursing specialist, as assistant chancellor of health sciences.

Over the next year and a half I also reached out to some of my most valued colleagues at Michigan State. Bob Perrin would come to Albany as vice chancellor for university affairs and development, with a portfolio that included public relations, federal relations, alumni affairs, and fund-raising. His choice was important for me personally because of his ever-present advice on handling contentious issues involving the media. Don O'Dowd, president of Oakland University (once part of MSU), accepted an offer to become executive vice chancellor, bringing his keen administrative skills and experience in team-building. Tom Freeman was persuaded to come from MSU to be associate vice chancellor for policy and analysis to address SUNY central's relative weakness in planning and institutional research. Finally, Al Ballard said a sad farewell to Forest Akers Golf Course and took a spot at SUNY Plaza as my executive assistant. With his dry style and acute nuts-and-bolts understanding of university management, he proved as invaluable as ever. All these Spartans from East Lansing were jokingly referred to in Albany as "MSU East."

• Rockefeller Foundation

In January 1979 John H. Knowles passed away unexpectedly after seven years as president of the Rockefeller Foundation. Although I didn't know it at the time, his death would present me with a painful dilemma.

Many of the Rockefeller Foundation's trustees had been discomfited by what they judged an opaque process by which my Harvard classmate Knowles had been appointed. Foundation chair Father Theodore M. Hesburgh, president of Notre Dame, was determined not to repeat the mistake, especially because the Rockefeller family had been rocked by the recent deaths of John D. Rockefeller 3rd on July 10, 1978, and Nelson on January 26, 1979. (I had been an usher at Nelson's funeral at Riverside Church.) Hesburgh chaired the search for Knowles's replacement personally, and I was one of five others on the committee. The others were Robert Roosa, a senior managing partner at Brown Brothers Harriman; Paul Volcker, president of the New York Stock Exchange; Jay Rockefeller, governor of West Virginia; and Jane Pfeiffer, senior vice president of IBM.

We adopted strict rules of confidentiality, though we took pains to keep the other trustees briefed on our progress. After months of wading through a pool of literally hundreds of candidates, on September 12 the committee presented nine finalists to the full board. Among the newer members of the board were Henry Schacht, chairman and CEO of Cummins Engine; James Fletcher, former president of the University of Utah and administrator of NASA; James P. Grant, founding director of the Overseas Development Council (soon to be executive director of UNICEF); Kenneth Dayton, CEO of Dayton Hudson; Richard Lyman, president of Stanford University; Vernon Jordan, president of the United Negro College Fund (about to head the National Urban League); Eleanor Sheldon, president of the Social Science Research Council; and Billy Taylor, composer and jazz pianist.

The plan was for the trustees to choose three "outside" candidates and three "inside" ones (i.e., sitting trustees or foundation executives), ranked by preference. From the shorter list a first choice and alternate would be selected, whom Chairman Hesburgh would approach (in sequence) to offer the job.

But Father Ted had something else in mind. After unveiling the finalists, he unexpectedly asked three trustees to leave the room: Dick Lyman, Jane Pfeiffer, and me. Guessing what was up, both Pfeiffer and I objected immediately. She had just taken over as president of NBC, and I had made it clear from the beginning that my commitment to SUNY was too recent for me to consider leaving. Lyman, president of Stanford, did not comment. But Father Ted was immovable, so the three of us withdrew. In what seemed like only moments, we were recalled, and Hesburgh announced that I was the trustees' unanimous choice as the next president. I began to protest again, but Father Ted interrupted. "Don't say anything," he commanded, "until you've thought it all the way through." Vernon Jordan later told me he had noticed that Dick Lyman was visibly shaken by the board's action. Vernon called him outside and said, "Now Dick, I know you must be disappointed by losing twice to a Black—to Franklin Thomas at Ford and now to Clif at the RF—but each was the best choice. Because of it I don't want you to go around hating Blacks!"[30] Not to be outdone, trustee Bill Moyers reported his disquiet when he confidentially gave the news to his wife Judith, who was vice chair of the SUNY Board of Trustees, over their possible loss of the new chancellor.

So began several days of soul-searching, one of the most difficult decisions in my life. Though it came out of nowhere, the opportunity would mean the culmination of my association with the Rockefeller philanthropies. The foundation was an organization I knew minutely, from top to bottom—better, probably and immodestly, than any other candidate. It offered the prospect of making a lasting impact in the areas about which I cared most deeply—global poverty, discrimination, and economic development. I could imagine exactly the steps I would take, the new directions I would mark out. Though not uppermost in my mind, the financial incentive was considerable: almost double what SUNY paid, for a very secure position with a ten-year horizon or more. And it certainly didn't help when I got a call from the widow of JDR 3rd, Blanchette Rockefeller, who had been confidentially told of the offer by her son Jay. The foundation needed my familiarity with the family's hopes and ways of thinking, she said. And the heart-tugging clincher: "I know Johnny would have been terribly proud and pleased if you accepted."

But I had been out of the Rockefeller orbit for almost a decade, tasting the freedom of answering only to the boards to which I reported and my own conscience. Just as important, what would be the impact on Dolores, who had hardly begun to adjust to her new role in Albany? How happy would she be as the partner to a foundation president? True, Blanchette

PHOTOGRAPHER MARY ELLEN KNOPP, RANDALL PHOTOGRAPHY, PHOENIX, ARIZONA.

Father Theodore Hesburgh and I attended the Business-Higher Education Forum meeting in Scottsdale, Arizona, in January 1987. Father Ted and I served together on several boards and commissions. I succeeded him as chairman of the Rockefeller Foundation in 1981.

Rockefeller was one of her all-time role models (the other two were Eleanor Roosevelt and Marian Anderson), but with a newly rising generation of younger Rockefellers, would there be a comfortable niche for her within the organization's evolving hierarchy? Dolores was her own person, but she was devoted to our marriage, and I had to ask myself if the move would be fair to her.

Then there was the very distressing prospect of leaving several colleagues who had come with me from Michigan to SUNY—two in particular. Bob Perrin and his wife had just closed on a 140-year-old farmhouse in New Scotland, New York—they arrived in Albany literally in the midst of my quandary. Don O'Dowd had accepted SUNY's number two position as executive vice chancellor, and though not due to start until the beginning of 1980, he had sold his home and announced his departure from the presidency of Oakland University. Before making his decision, O'Dowd had actually asked how long I planned to stay at SUNY, and I had assured him I would be there for a long haul!

Dolores and I consulted with our old friend Art Mosher, who was elated at the prospect of my taking the helm at Rockefeller. Mosher dismissed my guilt over the prospect of walking away from my friends—they would be fine, he assured me. When we took Bob Perrin into our confidences, he told us not to worry. He and Barbara were willing to take their chances at SUNY even if I left.

Undecided, I left on a long-scheduled trip to China. Perrin prepared a press release in case news of the Rockefeller offer leaked while I was away, but it wasn't needed.[31] I spent two weeks negotiating an umbrella agreement to govern future contracts between Chinese universities and individual SUNY campuses. The process was difficult, tedious, often confounding—and a partial break from my torment.

After my return I continued to agonize for another week, but the more I thought about it the more dishonorable it felt. I had never been so indecisive, and Dolores finally forced the issue. "You can't keep the board waiting any longer," she insisted. "I'll support whatever you decide."

That did it. I called Father Ted Hesburgh and told him I couldn't take the job—abandoning SUNY so soon after being appointed would have been too much of a betrayal of trust. Father Ted and several other trustees pushed me to reconsider, and Art Mosher asked Dolores, "What more could Clif want out of his life and career?" But the time for second thoughts was past, and the story soon got out.[32]

Dick Lyman was chosen president,[33] and in 1981 I was elected chairman of the foundation. Both Mosher and Father Ted acknowledged that things had turned out even better than if I had accepted the presidency.[34]

▪ SUNY as a System

At SUNY my overriding goal was to fuse the hodgepodge of sixty-four campuses into a more functional system. From talks with Clark Kerr, among others, I knew how powerful the University of California had become as a system—not just in political clout, but also in its reputation for academic excellence. SUNY was far more heterogeneous than the California system, which embraced only the state's eight graduate-research campuses. But I thought greater integration and cohesion would be of considerable benefit to the SUNY campuses, individually as well as collectively.

Not everyone agreed—in fact, quite a few didn't. Many campuses operated as independent fiefdoms, especially in the political arena. The state-operated campuses—that is, the university centers and four-year arts-and-sciences schools—worked their representatives in the state legislature assiduously for greater support, often regardless of what central administration and the SUNY trustees might have recommended. Campuses with friends on high got better treatment—for example, state senate majority leader Warren Anderson invariably protected and went out of his way to nurture the university center in Binghamton, his district. (A campus represented by a freshman assemblyman was usually on its own.) Moreover, years of infighting over funding and enrollments had subverted any campus impulses to pull together, and an invidious hierarchy had developed among them. University centers looked down on four-year colleges, which in turn sneered at the community colleges and agricultural/technical schools. There was snobbery even among the "peer" institutions. Because the university center at Buffalo had begun as a private university, for example, it played up its heritage as "more prestigious" than the others, while the center at Stony Brook never tired of beating its drum as the "Berkeley of the East."

Nonetheless, there was an incredible range of talent throughout the system, and a spectrum of programs and resources that I thought were collectively unmatched anywhere in the country. They needed to be brought into greater visibility and relief, and they needed to be marshaled in ways that would extend their reach and efficiency. While touring the campuses I had seen a wealth of opportunity for collaboration. For example, at Erie Community College there was a course on offset lithography—plate preparation, paper handling, inking, and bindery operations. It was a key component of Erie's program in graphic arts and communication—but couldn't it also be of great benefit to art majors at nearby Buffalo State? From the cutting-edge Fashion Institute of Technology to the nationally renowned statutory School of Ceramic Engineering and Materials Science at Alfred University, the system abounded with academic riches. I was convinced its potential synergies, harnessed and made more evident to citizens and policymakers, could help SUNY realize its latent potential.

Although a unified front would boost SUNY's academic and political clout, there seemed to have been no significant prior attempt to build one. The challenge was to convince, persuade, and cajole campus leaders and their constituents to see that sustained cooperation and mutual support were in their own best interests. The key was to engage them in a dialogue, respecting their perspectives even as I hoped to change them. As chancellor, I couldn't dictate a plan ex cathedra. No matter what directions were proposed, the campuses would have to implement them, and they would need to see their own fingerprints anywhere they looked.

Constant communication was vital for getting buy-in to the system vision. During my first year at SUNY I gave some thirty speeches. Again I was able to rely on Jim Harkness who had just completed his graduate work at University of Massachusetts and rejoined me at SUNY. My speech topics ranged from university public service to the diminishing returns of excessive state oversight (the latter didn't sit well at all with the Albany budget department bureaucrats). My speeches were distributed to my statewide list of contacts and leaders. I also began the practice of annual briefings with the editorial boards of key newspapers in New York City, Long Island, Albany, Buffalo, Syracuse, Binghamton, and Rochester. Whether it was the *New York Times* editorial board lunches on Forty-Second Street or a soup-and-sandwich press room meeting at the *Buffalo News* or the *Rochester Democrat and Chronicle*, these were opportunities to set out my ideas while putting a human face on SUNY—not in a crisis setting. Also, I met mayors, county executives, and business leaders, again trying to put a human face on the huge SUNY aggregation. In the South Tower Dolores arranged for me to host quiet luncheons for individual legislators and state officials. Quiet and off the record, the one-on-ones helped head off misunderstandings and confrontations in more public settings. In addition, I developed an annual dinner for key state legislators hosted by the SUNY board, held in the first-floor conference room of the South Tower.

To reach grassroots leaders beyond Albany, Bob Perrin and Jim Van Houten, his assistant for alumni relations, organized Chancellor's Regional Report dinners around the state. At the dinners, I would begin extolling the SUNY system's resources and contributions to New York, followed by comments from Dolores and then a general Q and A for both of us. Our invariable theme was the excellence of both SUNY's individual campuses and the system as a whole. I wanted New Yorkers not just to appreciate the university more highly, but to become outspoken in the pride they felt in it. The program exceeded our expectations. In all, we held nine meetings and attracted more than five thousand guests—who even paid for their own meals! Buoyed by the success, we went national with dinners in Washington, Boston, Miami, and Los Angeles—the SUNY campuses identified key alumni in each of the areas.

Not all the steps we took were so sweeping, and some were a little corny. For example, neckties with SUNY's gold and blue logo were distributed to officers in SUNY central administration, as well as to campus presidents and trustees, with matching scarves for women. I thought them a bit contrived, but it was surprising how often people wore them.

In 1981, the *New York Times* published a five-part series on SUNY.[35] We compiled the articles into a booklet and distributed it widely, even though they contained a few comments neither flattering nor accurate—at least we were "getting ink." When we realized that the spring 1985 commencements would include SUNY's one-millionth graduate, Bob Perrin's office launched a system-wide "You're One in a Million" celebration that culminated in a festive evening at New York City's South Street Seaport.

SUNY's improving quality image was reflected by my election as chair of the Council of Presidents of the National Association of State Universities and Land-Grant Colleges (1981–82). Also, I appeared on the CBS's *Face the Nation* as a guest along with Steve Muller, president of Johns Hopkins (September 12, 1982), where we discussed the critical problems facing higher education in the new academic year.

▪ Presidential Selection _____

Although most SUNY campus presidents saw their own institutions as their first responsibility, the presidents were one of the keys to building the university system. Presidents rarely wield the power outsiders imagine; nevertheless their leadership can change a college or university in ways both small and, occasionally, quite large. SUNY needed to attract and retain the best ones it could. Most I met during my sixty-four-campus tour were energetic and well qualified, differing mainly in temperaments and approaches. But given the sheer numbers, there was bound to be steady turnover in the ranks due to the average tenure of college and university presidents nationwide, which then was between five and six years. This offered an opportunity to shape a cadre of leaders with a more expansive view of SUNY and their role within it.

In practice, presidents of the state-operated campuses were nominated by governing councils, whose members were themselves named by the governor from local business and civic leaders. The councils created presidential search committees, from whose recommendations they selected a candidate to submit to the SUNY chancellor and board of trustees. In the past approval had generally been pro forma. But since council members were politically appointed, with close ties to local businesses and government, I thought more oversight might be warranted. I also wanted to do what I could to make sure my own relationship with new presidents got off on the proper foot. With help from Murray Block, the deputy who was my liaison to campus presidential searches, I worked out a practice of meeting with local councils at the outset, discussing the process that lay ahead and stressing the importance of reviewing or revising the institution's existing mission statement. The new practice also required my meeting personally with finalists before any formal recommendation was made to SUNY central. Without indicating a preference, I could then informally convey to the campus council any questions or reservations I might have about a particular candidate. It was a way to avoid putting any council in the awkward position of backing a candidate I might ultimately have to turn down.

The entire new process stemmed in large part from problems with a search at the university center at Stony Brook, which in April 1979 was my first as chancellor. Stony Brook's then-president John Toll had spent thirteen years skillfully building the campus virtually from scratch. Shortly after I arrived, Toll left to assume the presidency of the University of Maryland system, strongly pushing for the appointment of the campus provost as his successor. But when the search committee turned over its list of finalists to the campus council, the provost's name wasn't on it. I wasn't particularly unhappy—Stony Brook routinely circumvented SUNY central in seeking special treatment through Long Island's state legislators, and I was hoping the new president wouldn't come from the old mold. But the campus council disregarded the search committee's recommendations and submitted the provost as its nomination.

Based upon my experience, I knew that not being accepted by students and especially faculty members was a very ill omen regarding a president's future viability—especially if the person was from the inside.

On the day the SUNY board would vote, trustee Don Blinken and I met the provost beforehand and explained that we couldn't approve him without his being supported by the search committee. We urged him to withdraw, which would leave his reputation and future prospects undimmed. After making a few private telephone calls, the provost declined to step back. When we took his name to the board, the trustees voted him down.

The outcry from Long Island was clamorous, and to vent its resentment the Stony Brook council submitted the provost's name a second time, with a similar result. I was accused of all manner of calumny—the gist was that I was trying to destroy Stony Brook. I countered that a weaker university center was in no one's interest, but the integrity of the search committee couldn't be undermined. I recommended appointing an acting president while a new search was undertaken. Still seething with anger, the council finally agreed. Richard Schmidt, the president of SUNY's Upstate Medical Center at Syracuse, took the interim job. Although I had stipulated that the acting president could not be a candidate for the permanent position, only two months later the college council was so enthralled with him that they asked if he could be appointed as president. I chuckled inwardly but stuck to my guns. Eventually John H. Marburger 3rd was selected and served for fourteen years before becoming the science adviser to President Bush in 2001.

The episode might seem to have contravened my belief that campuses couldn't be forced to embrace a vision from on high, but it was important that campus councils realize that the SUNY board and I were fully prepared to exercise our authority when circumstances warranted. After all the furor died down, so did objections to "outside" involvement in presidential searches, and the caliber of future candidates at other SUNY campuses grew steadily. Overall during my chancellorship I was involved in selecting fifty-seven presidents, which averaged ten or more searches a year.

Once appointed, presidents were subject to periodic evaluation developed by my predecessors. Not surprisingly these yearlong evaluations had morphed into campus-wide "gripe" sessions for dissidents or else into little more than popularity contests. Even worse, such long-lasting evaluation periods could immobilize campus governance and could be debilitating for the president and everyone else. In June 1979, I secured SUNY board approval of a new evaluative procedure. My solution was to create a three-day campus visit by a group composed primarily of college or university presidents from outside the SUNY system. I believed that another respected president was far better able to judge the effectiveness of a fellow president than any ad hoc group. Their campus visits always involved in-depth, extensive interaction with all the "stakeholders," from students, faculty, and staff to council members, alumni, donors, local leaders, and elected officials. This new system produced sound evaluations and uncovered problem areas where they existed. Equally significant, the reports were disseminated widely to the different campus constituencies who had provided the information.

I thought it was important to allow an underperforming president to step down with full dignity. Fortunately, in most cases I was able to work with such presidents privately, allowing them to take the initiative to exit for whatever reason they chose to give. To this day, only the individuals and I knew the circumstances.

Another component of my formula for strengthening campus leadership was to improve the existing program of presidential "study leaves" by converting them into "mini-sabbaticals." There is no other academic position that has a similar all-consuming requirement. Presidents, just like faculty, need a "break." Faculty have regular sabbatical programs, usually for an academic year, but as a rule presidents do not. They cannot be away from their presidential duties too long, so I developed a three-month mini-sabbatical. During the sabbatical they engaged in preapproved activities that related to some aspect of higher education or to their role as campus leaders or even to their previous professional disciplines. Afterward, they had to prepare a report that they then presented to the SUNY trustees and often to their campus council. Determining when a president needed to take a break was one of my most important tasks. Having been a campus president myself, I could often spot the symptoms of excessive stress.

Finally, with approval of the SUNY trustees, I introduced a new practice where any president who retired would be offered a professorship at any state-operated campus in the system, with the host campus concurrence. A new campus often proved to be an optimal choice so that the president was not encumbered by remaining at an institution headed by his or her successor, and most important where a history of actions and decisions affected his or her now-peers. This policy applied to all presidents stepping down, the good and the underperforming. This gesture was welcomed because most of them had at one point been professors.

A persistent problem with attracting top presidential candidates was compensation. When I accepted my own job as chancellor of the SUNY system, I had gotten an unexpected jolt—at $56,650, my salary would be 15 percent below what I had been paid at Michigan State, to run an enormously larger operation. The SUNY board had promised to fix the problem but soon found its hands were tied. It was never quite explained why no one seemed to have known it beforehand, but all state employees' salaries were legally capped below the governor's salary, and it would take an act of the legislature to change the rule. (Only a few senior medical positions were exempt.) Presidential compensation was similarly constrained. Even though salaries could have been boosted without much budgetary impact, the governor and the legislature were obdurate. In consequence SUNY's embarrassed trustees decided that I should keep my corporate director's fees, which added up to a lot more than my compensation as chancellor. But the system-wide problem remained unresolved, and more than one talented presidential candidate took a look at the pay package on offer and said thanks, but no thanks.

After the first year or so at SUNY, the subject of my race rarely came up. An exception was with the problem of South Africa, which reared its head in several contexts during my tenure. When I started as chancellor all sixty-four presidents were white males. Although I didn't stress it overtly, I wanted to advance minority issues and to recruit more minorities and women as campus presidents. I needed to diversify presidential leadership throughout the system. The goal wasn't to create a veneer of affirmative action, but to demonstrate that it was possible to recruit outstanding candidates who were neither white nor male. The first woman I approved as president was Virginia L. Radley, at the SUNY college at Oswego. Radley had been Oswego's executive vice president and provost, and in 1978 she was serving as acting president. She was not merely an academic administrator, but also a well-respected teaching professor and scholar of English literature. Respect for Radley ran high among faculty, and confirming her as the permanent president was an easy decision to make. By the time I left SUNY, there were three Black presidents, one Hispanic, and five women.

I subsequently adopted an informal policy against allowing acting presidents to become permanent ones. Problems regularly arose when an internal individual obviously wasn't likely to be chosen. The thinking seemed to be that "Dean Jones" had been a hardworking loyalist who had "earned" the honor of an interim appointment. But instead of being flattered and stepping down amiably when a permanent choice was named, all too often the disgruntled person considered it a slap and eventually felt the need to leave the campus where he or she had been "rejected." My alternative was a policy to assign acting presidents whose ambitions lay elsewhere and who were not to be candidates for the position. My policy did allow a campus council to include the acting president in the final list at the very end of the search if the committee felt strongly in favor of his or her candidacy. Sometimes I assigned someone from SUNY headquarters (occasionally a woman or minority to gain experience for the future); other times, a president who was about to retire from another campus. Even more frequently I brought in someone who had already retired. Unfettered by the baggage of being potential candidates themselves, they could be responsible caretakers without being tempted to curry favor with campus constituencies and search committees. Among the SUNY central administrators who served as acting presidents were Sherry Penney, who eventually became chancellor of University of Massachusetts, Boston (1988–2000); Frank Pogue who served as president of Edinboro University of Pennsylvania (1996–2007); and Murray Block, who served as acting president at eighteen community colleges.

Although I met often with individual campus presidents, it was also important that they get to know each other, share experiences, and become more comfortable with being part of the SUNY system. One approach was my holding semiannual retreats at the Otesaga Hotel in Cooperstown and the Gideon Putnam Hotel in Saratoga Springs. The inclusion of the community colleges had the benefit of reducing the sense of "second-class" citizenship and made the state-operated campuses and statutory colleges aware of their shared contributions and problems. SUNY trustees attended one of the Cooperstown meetings each year, bringing them also into the process. My goal was to get everyone to "think system." The sessions also allowed presidents to explore issues candidly with peers without the constraints imposed by their visibility on campus. They, and especially their spouses, often developed lasting friendships.

At the early meetings in 1978 and 1979, Dolores organized luncheons for the spouses with presentations describing different parts of the SUNY central administration. But she soon expanded the sessions and invited the presidents to attend. For the larger Cooperstown sessions, she organized a regular "invitation-only" luncheons funded by my corporate fees and held in the SUNY Research Foundation. Prominent speakers included former First Lady Rosalynn Carter; sociologist Kenneth Clark; pollster Lou Harris; New York Telephone's chief financial officer Grace Fippinger; chairman of the National Endowment for the Arts Michael Straight; and business entrepreneur Victor Palmieri. The prominence of the speakers brought a certain flair and glamour to the meetings and proved a counterweight to more traditional "spouses" activities.

Dolores also developed a brochure called *The Partners* with photos of the presidents' spouses because they were interested in having their campus roles brought to light. The booklet showcased the spouses' activities among their peers and, more important, elevated the level of recognition of the critical role of spouses.

Another system "image building" activity was my work to establish authority for the state-operated SUNY campuses to grant honorary degrees. In June 1979, after a lengthy effort, we succeed in securing legislative permission to grant honorary degrees at the individual campus level and also to award a system-wide honorary degree by the SUNY Board of Trustees. The degrees were vetted by a system-wide faculty committee (as on individual campuses), then awarded on the campus that had nominated the individual.

To confer the annual system-wide honorary degree, we organized a formal, robed ceremony at the central administration SUNY Plaza. In addition to the campus presidents, I invited distinguished professors from all the campuses to participate. It was a colorful occasion, unique in downtown Albany. Led by the SUNY system provost carrying the university's mace, the procession marched to taped music across the open SUNY Plaza (with SUNY employees waving or leaning out of office windows) to the former federal court building, where ceremonies were conducted in the largest chamber. This bit of academic pomp and circumstance in a bureaucratic space at the foot of State Street was a subtle public reminder that we were, after all, an academic institution.

There was a third, different set of SUNY awards. Because even system-wide honorary degree candidates were vetted by a faculty committee, I recognized that there might be cases where SUNY board trustees were interested in candidates who would not fit the typical academic profile. Therefore, I designed and the board established annual awards for meritorious citizenship in the state. The Trustees Distinguished Service Award was a practice I had developed at

Michigan State as a supplement to awarding honorary degrees. Among those recognized was Mstislav Rostropovich, the acclaimed cellist. Although given during the Otesaga presidential retreats in Cooperstown, without the pomp and circumstance of academic robes, the awards provided recipients an opportunity to describe their lives and careers.

▪ Carey Budget Veto

Early 1980 brought the chronic fiscal problems for the SUNY system to a head. Governor Carey's budget proposed $861.9 million for the state-operated courses—up $23.3 million over the previous year, but almost entirely for nondiscretionary costs such as utilities. Moreover, the increase had been achieved by cutting $26 million from academic programs and personnel, which would require eliminating more than two thousand full-time positions. The proposed budget, I told the board's executive committee, confronted SUNY with a grave crisis, raising serious questions about the system's ability to sustain quality and academic integrity. Moreover, shortages in the capital fund would require delaying $34 million in construction for a long-sought new campus for the College of Technology in Utica/Rome.

As in previous years we lobbied the state legislature for relief. The lawmakers agreed with our position, passing an appropriations bill that restored some $22 million above the governor's recommendation. When the bill reached Carey, he vetoed the legislative increase, undoubtedly assuming that would end the dispute. But as things stood the governor's veto put SUNY in a precarious fiscal condition, and the developments we had undertaken to strengthen the university system would be undercut. Building centers of academic excellence takes years, and tentative gains can be wiped out by one year of draconian cuts. SUNY was on the way up, but protecting and extending the gains we had made was critical.

With the unanimous concurrence of the SUNY board, I took an unprecedented step, beginning a statewide "crusade" to get the legislature to override Carey's veto. Herb Gordon, the astute deputy for governmental relations, said no gubernatorial veto had been overturned in New York in a quarter-century—but he was game to try. With SUNY central administration I developed the playbook, and then campus presidents were persuaded to work with the campus councils, alumni, media, and local leaders. Each could use his or her own situation as an example of the potential budget crisis, but always in the context of why the entire system needed and deserved greater support. Success would hinge on university constituents from every region of the state, conveying back to the legislature a groundswell of support.

Would the strategy work? I didn't know, but I was prepared to go down fighting. Fortunately, the system's response was galvanic. Campus councils spoke up forcefully. The faculty union brought its considerable influence to bear. Even the system-wide student organization chimed in. Editorials supporting SUNY appeared from Long Island to Buffalo, and Albany

ALBANY TIMES UNION, FEBRUARY 7, 1980. PHOTOCOPY OF ORIGINAL CARTOON BY MANFRED WEIDEMANN, COOPERSTOWN, NEW YORK.

The "Hot Foot" for Governor Carey from Chancellor Wharton cartoon, by Hy Rosen, captured the override of the governor's veto of the SUNY budget increase by the state legislature.

to Binghamton. (My regular meetings with their editorial boards helped.) The *Albany Times Union* editorial cartoonist Hy Rosen published a sketch of Carey and me on a race track, with me giving the governor a hot foot (February 7, 1980). (Our track uniforms reflected that it was the year of the Olympics held in Moscow.)

On April 30, the State Assembly and Senate voted unanimously to restore the additional $22 million to SUNY's appropriation, trumping the governor's veto—the first in twenty-five years.

The action was little short of stunning—even I had a hard time believing we had pulled it off. Carey was decidedly unhappy, and our relationship would be distant and formal for some time. Thereafter, however, his budget division treated SUNY with a bit more respect and caution—they had found out that when cornered, we could and would fight back. Even more important, from my perspective, campus presidents and others throughout the system had discovered for themselves the power of collective action. "As a system, we could win," President Radley of SUNY–Oswego told me. "You proved it to us all."

▪ Multiphase Rolling Plan

Annoying the governor was a big risk to have taken, so I hoped the victory wouldn't prove pyrrhic. In the meantime, it was increasingly clear that SUNY needed a better way to manage its finances. The austerity the university system was experiencing was unlikely to abate. The standard year-at-a-time appropriations process was inadequate for even a single campus, much less for the system as a whole. We needed a process to deal with both ongoing stringency and immediate, usually unanticipated crises. During budget hearings for 1980–81, Governor Carey and legislative leaders had asked for a five-year plan to align SUNY services and priorities with public needs and resources. The directive was consistent with my own leanings, but it didn't go far enough. The result would still be a fixed snapshot—but what would happen after the five years were over?

What we really needed was a way to project needs and resources over a *rolling* period of years—a self-renewing cycle in which the year elapsing at the near term was perennially replaced by another year at the far end. We gave the concept the catchy name of the "multiphase rolling plan," introducing it at a SUNY administrators' retreat in Sarasota Springs in early October 1980. To enhance its reception across the system, a committee was appointed to work out details, chaired by Associate Chancellor Tom Freeman and Clifford Clark, president of SUNY–Binghamton. The other members were SUNY presidents Walton A. Brown, Clifford J. Craven, D. Bruce Johnstone, and James H. Young; vice presidents Edward W. Doty and Jerome Supple; dean Jerome Ziegler; and professor Harry E. Pence. Two community college presidents were observers, Donald J. Donato and Robert McLaughlin. Central administration staffers Bill Anslow and Mike Reynolds documented the formal plan.

Major changes were entailed in both budgeting and academic planning, requiring campuses to prepare in advance not only their next year's budget request, but also a five-year projection of programs and capital outlays. For the fiscal 1983–84 request, for example, campuses would take updated mission statements and resource allocation plans to a budget hearing in July 1982. Then in the August–September period, they would submit a final appropriation request, including an estimate of their five-year academic and operating needs. The immediate fiscal-year plan then became the basis for the years to come, rolling progressively forward and evolving as circumstances dictated.

The great advantage of multiyear planning, or "MuRP" as Al Ballard wryly dubbed it, was that it offered substantial foreknowledge of individual campus needs while allowing the system's total fiscal requirements to be projected far in advance. Well-thought-out plans meant that annual budget requests were unlikely to diverge dramatically from prior years. They also encouraged dialogues among and across campuses and helped create a stronger sense of interinstitutional fairness.

Additional major goals were to reduce redundancy among programs and increase the efficient, collaborative use of resources. MuRP called for consolidation of programs and activities on individual campuses as well as among campuses. We wanted to encourage those campuses that maintained identical or similar programs to strengthen them though trading and affiliation with others. Hard times made for a conducive environment, and some presidents, such as John Van de Wetering, president at Brockport, pursued them diligently. Elsewhere, resistance could be fierce. A proposal to transfer a nursing program from Utica to Oswego, which would have benefited both by creating a single larger, more viable school, failed because of strenuous objections at both campuses. On the other hand, SUNY–Oneonta successfully moved its acclaimed art restoration program to the State College at Buffalo. The program had begun as a stand-alone effort in Cooperstown, twenty-five miles north of Oneonta, under the leadership of Dr. Sheldon Keck and his wife Caroline, using scientific methods to convert a centuries-old craft to modern technology. After initially suggesting that the unit move to his own campus, President Clifford Craven recommended transferring it to the State College at Buffalo. The program in Cooperstown was nationally recognized, and its graduates worked for major art museums throughout the country, but Craven realized that at Buffalo it could affiliate with a stronger art department, with access as well to the outstanding Albert-Knox Art Gallery. Mrs. Keck, who lived in Cooperstown until she died at age ninety-nine, never forgave me for being the architect of her program's relocation—and she didn't move to Buffalo.

Shortly after the university trustees formally adopted MuRP, I asked the state director of budget to consider incentives to encourage campuses to make hard decisions. I proposed that any campus that cut back or eliminated a program should be permitted to keep half the amount saved and allowed to shift it to other efforts. The redirected funds would then become part of the campus's permanent base of appropriations. An early test of the idea centered on the K–12 schools many SUNY campuses ran as part of their teacher-training curricula. The schools had long been contentious because they were seen as providing affluent families around the campus community with better free education than available through most public schools. (Anything that smacked of state support for elites was a hot-button issue in New York State.) Applying MuRP, I recommended to the trustees that educating elementary and secondary school students should not be a SUNY priority unless it served purposes directly related to local campus missions. There was a great public melee, and the state legislature passed a resolution requiring that the campus schools continue in operation. But Governor Carey wisely vetoed the bill, noting that it would "override the decisions of the university central administration and . . . [constitute] a disruption of the university's ability to allocate resources . . . and in general plan for the future."

The plan worked the first year, but as I had been warned by some campus presidents, the Division of the Budget in the second year reneged on their promise and removed the K–12 savings from the base budgets. It was no consolation that we had made an intelligent attempt at improved fiscal policy.

In some cases our multiphase rolling plan led us to consider changing campus missions and even reconfiguring the system itself. But even given the state's money problems, the idea of program closings (never mind campus closings) was anathema. There were a few abortive attempts at mergers, including a secret feeler from the private Hartwick College, then experiencing its own severe fiscal straits, but they got no further than boosting cross-registration for courses between the two campuses.

One particularly thorny attempt involved the SUNY College of Technology at Utica/Rome. The college, which operated in sites scattered around downtown Utica, wanted to move to a completely new facility to be built on land it owned in Rome. Campus underground infrastructure was in place and roads had been cut, but state funding for building construction was not in the cards. A possible solution lay in merging the SUNY college and the private Utica College, then affiliated with Syracuse University. Ed Duffy, chair of the Utica College board, was also chair and CEO of Marine Midland Bank, and his business experience made him a persuasive advocate. Don Blinken (who had succeeded Beth Moore as board chair) and I were literally about to leave Albany for final negotiations in Utica when we got a call from the governor, informing us that he couldn't support the merger. Although Carey gave no reason for his position, he was probably concerned that it would bring more demands for funding that the state could ill afford.

Another proposal involved the so-called colocating of the SUNY College of Technology on the campus of Mohawk Valley Community College. It made sense because MVCC's was a two-year associate degree curriculum, while the college of technology offered an "upper division" curriculum leading to a bachelor of science degree. Moreover, their curriculums were a highly complementary "fit." The two presidents—Bill Kunsela at SUNY Tech and Michael Schafer at MVCC—were wary but agreed to discussions. (Kunsela, who had worked hard for the site in Rome, was understandably reluctant to give up his dream.) We had a meeting in March 1981, where a sizable group of demonstrators objected to the proposal, clearly favoring development of the site in Rome. Jerome Komisar, the new provost at SUNY central, and I defended the proposal. State senator James Donovan was present, and while he was courteous and understanding of the university system's goals, he made it clear that his opposition would be unyielding—as he saw it, the new campus must eventually be built as planned. Little wonder that the colocation idea went down to defeat. Despite our hope to increase efficiency while strengthening both the campuses involved, politics, ego, and parochial loyalties won the day.

Later that year groundbreaking ceremonies took place for the new College of Technology campus in Rome. Some time afterward, I learned that local speculators had already purchased most of the land around the planned site—we hadn't really realized what we were up against.

. . . .

A disadvantage (most of the time) of heading a university system was that I hadn't much contact with students. At Michigan State I saw and talked with students almost every day. In contrast, SUNY's far-flung student body cared sincerely enough about their own campuses— central administration, not so much.

There were two system-wide student organizations: the Student Association of the State University (SASU), an activist-led body, and the student assembly. The assembly, with representatives chosen by each campus, was supposed to be a forum for communications between students, the chancellor, and trustees. But since few students had much interest in system issues, the assembly was virtually a creature of SASU, whose leaders dictated its composition. This held the potential for interesting consequences, because by law the president of the student assembly each year was a voting member of the SUNY board. But despite the SASU influence, most student trustees proved bright, responsible, and actively engaged with the university's affairs.

During my first couple of years I went to the student assembly's annual meetings, but I soon gave it up. The hearings were usually disorganized "gripe sessions," and my presence too often occasioned wandering ideological rants against SUNY leadership with little meaningful dialogue. Those students who attended appeared to be SASU cat's-paws. In any event, only a few campuses actually sent delegates, usually not elected by popular vote.

Few real campus leaders had much use for SASU, and they often ignored it completely. The organization's strength derived from a handful of campuses, particularly the university centers at Albany and Binghamton and the State College at New Paltz. When SASU leaders wanted bodies for a demonstration at the state capitol or SUNY Plaza, they could rarely round up more than a few hundred—a few more if joined by their colleagues from CUNY.

In early 1982 SASU called for a protest against higher dorm rent, and two hundred or so students showed up at SUNY Plaza. There they set up two tents, their presumed "future housing" now that they were being priced out of their dormitories. "Wharton Village" a large sign proclaimed for all to see. Remembering "People's Park" and the days of rage and tear gas on Grand River Avenue in East Lansing, I was curious about how things would turn out. I needn't have worried. When the protesters wanted to burn a symbolic housing contract in effigy, they actually asked us for permission! Go ahead, we said—but be *careful*. The students burned the document for the local press, but only after locating a metal wastebasket to catch the ashes.

When the burning was over, one protest leader climbed onto a large concrete planter on the Plaza lawn and used a bullhorn to harangue against the heartless chancellor who was hiding up in his office tower. He mistakenly pointed to the South Tower where we lived, not the main central tower, but his intent was clear. Bob Perrin had been milling unobtrusively with the crowd, reporting its mood to me by walkie-talkie. At his signal, I went down, walked quietly up behind the speaker, and tapped him gently on the back. "Would you like me to say something?" I asked politely. "Uh, yeah," he mumbled, and after a moment's confusion he handed over the bullhorn. I took it and spent several minutes outlining to the students why the university had little choice about raising dorm rates. When finished, I asked if there were any questions. Hearing none, I handed back the bullhorn and took the elevator back to my office.

The tents were supposed to be removed no later than 5:00 P.M., but in an act of radical disobedience the group left them up until 5:10. Perrin and I agreed that the SASU demonstrators couldn't hold a candle to those in the bad old days at Michigan State.

. . . .

If anything could catalyze SUNY students' wrath, it was a tuition hike. Nominally setting tuition rates was the sole responsibility of the SUNY Board of Trustees. In reality both the governor and the legislature played key roles, but neither wanted to take public responsibility for the never-popular act of raising tuition. For my first several years at SUNY the process was almost like a Japanese Noh play, with masked actors playing their assigned parts in a ritualistic, well-orchestrated dance. First, SUNY central would review budget requests by the state-operated and statutory colleges. The trustees would submit a collective request to the State Division of Budget, almost invariably asking an increase in state funding but no tuition increase. After discussions between ourselves and the DOB, usually including its formidable director Howard "Red" Miller, the department would predictably deny or substantially reduce our requested increase—almost invariably cutting budget lines they knew we considered vital. Miraculously, the cost of restoring our top priorities would almost exactly match that of a specific, though always unstated, increase in student tuition.

Once incorporated into the governor's budget recommendations, our request then went to the legislature predicated on "expected" system revenues that could not, in reality, be realized at current tuition levels. Of course, everyone knew what it would take to fill the gap. At committee hearings in the assembly and senate, higher tuition levels were rarely mentioned, and then almost always in private sidebar conversations. Often the legislature would vote to increase our appropriation above the governor's, but still without endorsing any specific tuition target.

When at the end of the day SUNY's final appropriation was determined, the trustees of course had little choice but to raise tuition to provide the funding needed to meet the system's needs. The governor and the legislature knew the predictable outcome very well—but if criticized, they could blandly declare that the trustees were "solely responsible" for the university's tuition. Some would even cynically and disingenuously protest that if it had been left up to them there would be no tuition hikes! The trustees took the heat (I usually got singed as well), but the politicians' fingerprints were nowhere to be seen.

▪ Private Fund Raising _____

The state's budget problems made one particular SUNY deficiency more glaring—the lack of significant private fund-raising by the campuses. Fund-raising efforts came late to Michigan State because in Hannah's era it had been largely unneeded, plus the worry that private gifts might lead to offsetting reductions in state appropriations. There was a similar concern around the SUNY system; historical/demographical factors were also salient. Many of the original campuses had begun as normal (teachers) colleges and vocational-technical schools, whose middle-income alumni weren't likely to become significant donors. (An exception was the university center at Buffalo, which had been private from its founding in 1846 until it joined SUNY in 1962. Likewise, SUNY–Binghamton had been created from the private Harpur College.) The statutory colleges attached to Cornell, Alfred, and Syracuse universities could piggyback on their host campuses' funding drives, and a few of the statutory colleges had small foundations and cultivated a few donors, but everything was offhand and very low key. There had been work by SUNYCUAD (SUNY Council for University Advancement), which offered a vehicle for the administration and campuses to develop programs.[36] But there was a lack of proper recognition of private fund-raising as an appropriate and critical role in a state university.

As at MSU, getting SUNY up to speed in fund-raising was imperative for me, and encouraging campuses to test the waters was one of the assignments undertaken by Bob Perrin as vice chancellor for university affairs and development. From Michigan State Bob recruited Charles "Chuck" Webb, a Spartan with hands-on experience in shaking the money trees, as assistant vice chancellor for alumni relations and development. The two of them soon found that inexperience wasn't the only thing that was holding the campuses back. They really did fear, as had Hannah, that any substantial private funds they raised would be "taken out of their hide" during the following state appropriations cycle. This would not only defeat the whole purpose of the effort, it might well discourage or even offend alumni and others who had made gifts or donations.

Interestingly, another reservation was that SUNY central administration would claim a share of the spoils, a suspicion Bob and Chuck managed largely to allay. But given the well-known Machiavellian tactics of the Division of Budget, the possibility couldn't be entirely discounted that the state would indeed "absorb" private contributions by corresponding reductions in the university's operating fund.

I tried to convince the Carey administration that public universities elsewhere were reaping millions of private dollars to strengthen their missions. On one occasion I put together a chart for budget director Red Miller. It showed public and private dollars received by the ten largest universities in the country in 1980—but without displaying the schools' names. I challenged Miller to identify which were public and which were private universities. It turned out that five of the ten largest recipients of federal dollars were private (Johns Hopkins was number one) and that three of the ten largest recipients of private contributions were public (Minnesota was number five). Miller got even testier than usual but otherwise remained unmoved, and didn't budge on his pro-private-college bias.

Only when the state approved positions specifically designated as fund-raising jobs would the campuses feel that their efforts wouldn't be contravened by the bureaucracy. It took a lot of time and lobbying, but Bob Perrin, Chuck Webb, Herb Gordon, and Harry Spindler finally managed to make the university's case. In the end, legislation authorized a substantial number of campus positions, and the campuses were assured that any dollars they raised privately would be theirs to spend. Strangely, lawmakers also approved five fund-raising staff for Cornell's statutory colleges, even though SUNY hadn't asked for them.

Of course, it was widely understood that private fund-raising was indispensable to the state's "independent" campuses (whose lobbying arm CICU exhibited unrelenting hostility and disdain for SUNY's efforts to get up to speed). What wasn't so well known was the private campuses' appetite for public funds. One source was Bundy Aid, which had been called for by a select committee on the future of private and independent higher education chaired by McGeorge Bundy.[37] For example, in 1980–81 eighty-nine private colleges and universities got a total of $92.4 million in Bundy payments directly from New York State—a "bounty" of $450 for each associate degree awarded, $1,200 for each bachelor's, $900 for each master's, and $4,500 for each doctoral degree. In addition, the state's tuition assistance program (TAP) offered financial aid to eligible students regardless of where they matriculated (inside New York). In 1980–81 the maximum TAP award was $1,800. By 1984–85 it was $2,200. Within upper and lower limits set by the legislature, awards were calculated according to a complex formula based on family income and institutional tuition. A student who attended a private campus might get much more TAP aid than one who attended SUNY or CUNY—even if their economic backgrounds were identical. The goal of both TAP and Bundy Aid was to mitigate tuition differences between public and private campuses, and to give students a wider range of choice in where they went to college.

With ever-increasing inflation and skyrocketing operating costs, SUNY, CUNY, and the state's private colleges and universities found themselves competing in a zero-sum game—one side's gains usually came at the other's expense. The resulting struggle was rarely elevating and often quite nasty. Leading the charge for the private campuses was Hank Paley, a hard-boiled former union organizer who headed the hundred-plus-member CICU. CICU's playbook for boosting its state funding consisted mainly in depicting SUNY and CUNY as "overgrown," "wasteful," "duplicative," and of lower academic quality and reputation compared to private campuses.

It would have been far better for both sectors to respect, if not support, our respective missions, and I found the CICU line both specious and distasteful. In speeches around the state I began to refute Paley's claims. Our system was hardly overbuilt, I pointed out—many states spent far more on their public campuses, especially on a per capita basis. Similarly, no one argued that English and math programs at the private Hartwick and Hamilton colleges were "duplicative," so why claim they were when offered at various SUNY university centers and arts-and-sciences campuses? In a memo to all sixty-four SUNY campus presidents, I noted that private institutions were free to charge whatever the market would bear and practice any degree of elitism they liked. In contrast, public colleges and universities had a responsibility to provide quality education at the lowest possible cost, and to reach out not only to the highly gifted but also to students of many different backgrounds and levels of ability.

My counteroffensive stirred up a hornets' nest in CICU and among some private campus presidents. When I showed that CICU's had skewed upward its estimate of SUNY's average cost for an undergraduate student by incorrectly including graduate and medical program costs, Paley accused me of "nitpicking." And because I had the temerity to point out Paley's inaccuracies publicly, Fordham president Rev. James C. Finlay jumped into the fray, accusing me of trying to destroy the two sector's long-standing "irenic" relationship. On another occasion, when I showed that New York's level of spending on SUNY and CUNY ranked the state disgracefully low on a nationwide scale, a member of the board of regents took me aside for a private talk. The prestigious private campuses (read: Columbia, Cornell, Rochester, Syracuse, and NYU) deserved to be "first at the table," he argued, because they were older, more venerable, and added greater luster to the state's reputation. CICU's attacks were justified to maintain their lofty position.

▪ Engineering Programs

Two case studies in the private sector's reflexive opposition revolved around SUNY's attempts to address the state's (and nation's) growing demand for engineers. The campuses involved were the university center at Binghamton and the state-operated campus at New Paltz.

SUNY–Binghamton wanted to expand an existing program. At President Clifford Clark's request, a team from the National Center for Higher Education Management Systems (NCHEMS) had analyzed engineering education across the region in early 1980. They found a clear need for more engineering curricula at both undergraduate and graduate levels, with particular shortages in electrical and mechanical engineering and materials science. SUNY–Binghamton had already generated broad local support for converting its existing school of advanced technology into a full-scale college of engineering, which would offer bachelor's and graduate degrees in a wide range of specializations. At the same time, Syracuse University was operating an extension program nearby, at IBM Endicott. Syracuse University chancellor Mel Eggers geared up to fight the Binghamton proposal, and there was concern that other private campuses would lend their support to a fight before the state board of regents. But IBM, led by the director of the Endicott installation, made it clear that it wasn't happy with the Syracuse program, a segment of which required commuting to Syracuse. A great many IBM employees were already enrolled in Binghamton's School of Advanced Technology, and they strongly supported the proposed change. In the end Syracuse backed down, and SUNY–Binghamton's plan was approved by the New York regents in May 1982. IBM had begun in Binghamton, and it seemed fitting to name the school for its founder. Since I had become friendly with Arthur K. "Dick" Watson, the founder's son, during the 1969 Rockefeller to Latin America mission, I contacted him for permission. He graciously agreed, and in 1983 the new college was named the Thomas J. Watson School of Engineering and Applied Sciences.

At New Paltz, the plan to develop an engineering program began as a response to the need for expanded technological education in the mid-Hudson region. It wasn't a particularly new idea—as far back as 1968, a study commissioned by then-chancellor Sam Gould found that no part of the state needed such a program more. Soon after she was appointed in 1979, President Alice Chandler sponsored a survey that found that while the region ranked second in computer employment in New York, it could claim not one school offering a bachelor's degree in computer engineering.[38] SUNY–New Paltz had a fine physics department and a strong mathematics department that was already moving into computer science, so there was a good foundation in place. Thanks to emerging trends in miniaturization, moreover, the electrical engineering and computer science concentrations that New Paltz planned would require only minimal investments in equipment and facilities.

In June 1982 the New Paltz engineering proposal was approved by the SUNY board. From there it had to go to the state education department and board of regents, into whose "master plan" it would have to be incorporated before getting under way. Included in the documentation were detailed analyses of regional economic needs, along with a five-year enrollment projection. The cost over the same period was estimated at $3.6 million.

The outcry from the private universities was immediate and near-deafening. Like clowns piling out of a tiny circus fire truck, critics stood forth from Columbia, Syracuse, Hofstra, the University of Rochester, Union College, Clarkson, Manhattan College, Pratt Institute, the New York Institute of Technology, and Rensselaer Polytechnic Institute. To the regents they appealed piteously that any new public dollars for engineering should go to their own "underfunded" programs. (Fifteen of the state's twenty-four BA programs in engineering were at private campuses.) There was already a shortage of engineering faculty, they argued, and still another program at SUNY, with its low tuition, would reduce the attractiveness of private curricula to prospective students.

After a pro forma canvass of opinion, state education department head Gordon Ambach asked SUNY to withdraw the proposal.[39] When we refused, Ambach recommended against it at a meeting of the regents. Without addressing its merits or suitability to regional needs, he merely repeated the private colleges' canards that an engineering curriculum at New Paltz would have a "deleterious" effect on their own programs.

The battle intensified when RPI and the Polytechnic Institute of New York wrote to the regents, offering to create new engineering programs in collaboration with Marist College. Not coincidentally, Marist was in Poughkeepsie, on the other side of the Hudson River—due East from New Paltz! The same voices that denied the need for any new SUNY engineering program between New York City and Albany were now proposing their own, in exactly the same region, almost the identical location. Even so, regent Emlyn Griffiths suggested postponing a decision on the New Paltz plan for four months so that the new players could have time to prepare their counterproposal.[40]

In November 1983 the regents voted down the New Paltz proposal ten to six, but the fight was hardly over. New Paltz launched a lobbying campaign to change the regents' vote, while thirty-eight private college presidents signed a letter calling the proposal "wasteful and inappropriate." Local businesses such as Key Bank and IBM weighed in supporting New Paltz, along with many county executives and concerned citizens. Stanley Fink, speaker of the state assembly, wrote a blistering letter of support, and the *Albany Times Union* published a sarcastic editorial, "Are the Regents in New York's Best Interest?"

In early December Alice Chandler met with Mario Cuomo, who had recently succeeded Hugh Carey as governor. There had always been a degree of tension between New York's governors and the regents, who although appointed by the legislature viewed themselves as politically independent—almost a fourth branch of state government. After his meeting with Chandler, the governor made clear his own independence, endorsing the New Paltz plan and asking the regents to reconsider their previous rejection.[41] A few weeks later, Cuomo followed up with a calculated bit of fiscal prestidigitation. In his executive budget, he proposed $2 million for SUNY engineering programs, including $400,000 to start up the New Paltz program—conditioned, as was legally required, on the regents' approval.[42] At the same time, he cut $465,000 from the state education department budget—curiously, very nearly the same amount earmarked for New Paltz.

Gordon Ambach and the regents were livid. How dare the governor provide funding for a program that couldn't exist without their approval? And add further insult by implicitly taking it from their own budget! Nevertheless, it was clear by now which way the winds were blowing. In February 1984 SUNY submitted to Ambach a "new" proposal (there were only a few insignificant changes), accompanied by supportive letters from U.S. senator Al

D'Amato, Speaker Fink, Representative Matthew F. McHugh, the state Black and Puerto Rican caucus, and others. In mid-April, Ambach reversed course and recommended that the regents approve the plan.

CICU fired several more salvos. First, it issued a formal statement: "The Regents must stand firm and disapprove this second request by SUNY New Paltz if they are to reaffirm their position as the non-partisan guardians of [higher education] in New York."[43] Then Hank Paley distributed a notice at the regents' regular April meeting, even though the topic was not on the agenda, blasting: "Through 15 years of experience in New York State higher education public policy, all working within the legislative process, I have never witnessed a more blatant attempt to politicize the decision making process of the Board of Regents."

Trying to calm the waters, Governor Cuomo invited the regents to a meeting in New York City. The battle of wills dragged on a bit, with one regent, the distinguished sociologist Kenneth D. Clark, proclaiming that "the self-respect and integrity of the board is at stake." But in the end the support SUNY had marshaled was overwhelming, and CICU knew that it had lost. On May 25, the regents approved the plan for engineering education at New Paltz—ten in favor, five opposed, one abstention.[44]

I was never certain why the New Paltz episode inflamed the private sector so much more than did Binghamton's effort. Maybe it was because Binghamton was a university center and simply expanding an existing program, while New Paltz's ambitions looked like a case of mission creep that might spread to other state-operated campuses. Or it may have been that CICU and its members perceived state senator Warren Anderson, always Binghamton's white knight, as too formidable to take on. Or was gender part of the issue? Engineering was then (and to some degree even now) seen as a male occupation. At the time Alice Chandler was one of SUNY's two women presidents, and her prominence as New Paltz's advocate may have agitated traditionalists. She later told me about a male university president who began a lecture during the imbroglio by saying, "Alice, you're a smart girl."

Almost thirty years later, at any rate, the New Paltz School of Science and Engineering is fully accredited and thriving, offering both undergraduate and master's degrees. Full-time enrollments are higher than original projections; part-time enrollment is lower, probably because of the decline in IBM jobs over the years. So far as can be determined, the school's nine engineering faculty have not decimated private campus programs in the mid-Hudson region.

CHAPTER TEN

The Chancellor of SUNY 2: Excellence, Flexibility, and Independence

The head of a university system has few opportunities to launch major academic initiatives, which for the most part (and properly) originate at the campus level. But at a strategic level I thought it reasonable to lay out some initiatives, setting broad priorities and wielding budget authority judiciously. Even then, however, lasting results were often elusive.

It surprised no one that I hoped to expand the system's international role. SUNY was ripe for a broader and more vigorous outreach. It had already established a position of associate vice chancellor for international programs, and in September 1979 I hired Thomas D. Scott, whom I had known through the Asia Foundation. Two years later Scott was succeeded by Wilbert LeMelle, a former director of the Ford Foundation's development programs in East and North Africa and President Carter's ambassador to Kenya and the Seychelles (1977–80). A Black who spoke seven languages, LeMelle brought sophistication and broad international experience to the university's initiatives.[1]

. . . .

Communist China was just beginning to emerge from its isolationist cocoon, and many SUNY campuses—especially the technical and community colleges—seemed tailor made to address some of its probable needs. Working through a variety of contacts, I organized a two-week educational "mission" to China, with the principal goal of establishing a partnership between SUNY and the nation's educational leadership. My leader for the China visit was Dr. Frederick F. Kao, a professor at SUNY's downstate medical center. Kao was a founder of the *American Journal of Chinese Medicine*, a leader in integrating Western medicine with traditional Chinese treatments such as herbalism and acupuncture. Dolores was included in the trip because she was then a trustee of the China Medical Board. The board had operated in China, especially with the Peking Union Medical College Hospital, from 1914 to 1951.

The trip was both exhilarating and exhausting. My idea had been to negotiate an umbrella contract with the Chinese Ministry of Education, under which individual SUNY campuses could develop subcontracts with Chinese schools and institutions for specific purposes. That proved difficult, because our Chinese hosts had only a vague idea of what was involved in the SUNY "system." I pushed hard for emphasizing the resources of our agricultural and technical campuses to help modernize and strengthen China's vast rural sector—site of the dominant population activity. But the Chinese themselves were interested primarily in our graduate-research university centers, linkages they thought would lend greater prestige to their own universities. They were especially enthusiastic about SUNY–Stony Brook, whose faculty included Chen Ning Yang, a Chinese scientist who had won the Nobel Prize in physics in 1957.

Professor Kao was invaluable throughout the trip, a recognized medical scholar wherever we went in China. Dolores was also extremely well received. She was able to visit the old China Medical School and Hospital, the first China Medical Board trustee to do so since the Communist regime had broken off contact in 1950.[2] (The board had continued to operate elsewhere in Asia, biding its time in the hope of eventually restoring the relationship—in philanthropy as elsewhere, patience will win out.)

After the trip a few SUNY campuses actually developed ties in China—not many, alas, in the mold I had hoped. In 1983, however, the university won a contract with Indonesia for fifteen SUNY campuses to provide graduate teacher education to Indonesian students over four years. As then-associate chancellor Wilbert LeMelle observed, the World Bank's $15 million backing made the program "one of the largest ever negotiated for development assistance between an American university and a foreign government."[3]

■ The Nelson Rockefeller Institute

Nelson Rockefeller considered SUNY the greatest achievement of his governorship, and at the June 1978 dedication of its new University Plaza headquarters, trustee Jim Warren called Nelson "the godfather of the State University." Consequently Rockefeller's sudden death on January 26, 1979, triggered immediate talk of an appropriate memorial. Although recommendations were solicited from the campuses, I already had something in mind. SUNY owned a building at 411 State Street, where some university offices had once been housed. Built in 1903, it was a townhouse that had been fashionable in its day, with a cobblestone porte cochere; now it was in a state of sad disrepair. I had met with Rockefeller three months before his death, and after reminiscing a bit I told him about the structure. With the advantage of being close to the capitol building as well as state offices, I told him, the building would be an ideal location for a new SUNY institute dedicated to research on state government. The topic was dear to Rockefeller's heart, and the possibilities excited him. No costs were discussed, nor any Rockefeller contributions. He surely knew I would return to him and the family if the idea developed, but his death precluded any further discussions.

After reviewing a number of the campus ideas, the trustees narrowed the memorial proposals to two. One was a Nelson A. Rockefeller College of Public Affairs and Policy at the university center at Albany, urged by its president Vince O'Leary. This new college was planned as an umbrella over the SUNY–Albany Department of Public Administration and Policy and the Department of Political Science. The other was a Nelson A. Rockefeller Institute of Government, to be housed at 411 State Street, as the former governor and I had discussed.[4] Using the Rockefeller name would require the family's approval, so I met with Nelson's brother Laurance and followed up with a detailed letter,[5] explaining that the university was prepared to move forward with the college, the institute, or both. Laurance said the family would happily defer to the trustees,[6] who subsequently decided to approve both initiatives.

There was one snag. While the college could be established under the aegis of SUNY–Central Administration, the institute would require modest start-up funds from the state legislature. Unhappily, Frank Mauro, a senior aide to the speaker of the assembly, refused to fund it, dismissing our claim that the institute could enhance nonpartisan policy development in New York. In the end we got around the problem by putting both units under a single head, "provost of the Rockefeller college and director of the Rockefeller institute," whose salary was paid by the SUNY–Albany campus. Ironically, years later Mauro joined the institute, which he praised in nearly the exact words I had used at the outset.

Warren Ilchman, a political scientist with a doctorate from Cambridge, moved into the dual post from his prior job as SUNY–Albany's vice president for research. Hank Dullea, who had just stepped down as the governor's director of state operations, became the institute's first senior fellow. Ilchman's initial goal was to establish the institute as a neutral site, where nonpartisan dialogue could occur among representatives from academia and the state's executive and legislative offices. A board of overseers was set up, with a large contingent of state leaders included to give the nascent organization some weight. The institute also began a private fund-raising drive, with initial gifts from SUNY board chair Don Blinken and T. Norman Hurd, a former director of the State Division of Budget. David and Laurance Rockefeller gave $575,000 to the original endowment fund, and other family members later contributed another $700,000.

Simultaneously we began restoring the building at 411 State Street to house the institute. The restoration was initiated when Dolores discovered that the age-darkened wall murals in a small third-floor room were the work of Will H. Low, a famous Hudson River School painter. (Low had also painted ceiling murals in the Waldorf Astoria Hotel and the state education department building in Albany.) Dolores urged that the State Street murals be restored, for which we called on the art restoration program at the SUNY College at Oneonta. In mid-process Norman Rice, director of the Albany Institute of History and Art, revealed that the room in which the murals had been painted was originally a two-and-a-half story music room, boasting a dramatic arch with a stained glass skylight.

The project was headed by an all-star team that included John Mesick, whose architectural firm had recently restored Blair House in Washington, D.C. With Rice's help, original plans and photographs were unearthed from his organization's archives, and the architects even interviewed Margaret Farrell Lynch, who had frequently visited as a child when her grandfather Anthony Brady, a railway magnate, had lived there. Her memories of the layout and even wallpaper designs were invaluable in restoring the mansion to its original and spectacular 1903 condition. In the process the architects discovered false floors, removed temporary partitions, and discovered startlingly beautiful structures such as a vaulted carriageway and side entrance with green marble columns.

Along with the restored building, the Nelson A. Rockefeller Institute of Government was officially dedicated on October 6, 1982. In the audience were David and Laurance Rockefeller, along with Nelson's widow, Happy. Also in attendance were Governor Hugh Carey, senate majority leader Warren Anderson, and the SUNY trustees and senior officers. The fledgling institute was a particularly apt memorial, reflecting Rockefeller's characteristic "best minds" philosophy of policy formation in government. I couldn't help remembering his think-tank style from my own days with AIA, his Rockefeller Brothers Special Studies project, his Critical Choices National Commission, and his presidential mission to Latin America.

Particularly under the leadership (1989–2009) of Richard P. Nathan, the institute exceeded my initial vision. Nathan was a former Princeton professor who had also served as assistant director of the Federal Office of Management and Budget, as well as director of domestic policy for the National Advisory Commission on Civil Disorders (Kerner Commission). Today the institute conducts independent policy research and sponsors major conferences on American federalism, public management and finance, welfare, jobs, and health. It also publishes the *New York State Statistical Yearbook* and periodic reports on other issues.

For several years the institute also sponsored an annual fund-raising dinner where an award was given to "recognize extraordinary public servants whose accomplishments in the public arena met the high standards and ideas of Nelson Rockefeller." The black-tie event was regularly attended by Governors Carey and Cuomo, Nelson's widow Happy Rockefeller, and other family members—it became a popular, bipartisan "reunion" of those involved in the Rockefeller years in Albany. Awardees included Senator and Ambassador Mike Mansfield, Secretary George Shultz, former Federal Reserve chairman Paul Volcker, Secretary Henry Kissinger, Governor Hugh Carey, and me. Despite their popularity the dinners ended after six years.

Eventually the institute physically expanded by adding two handsome restored Dutch Renaissance Revival townhouses and an adjoining carriage house. After twenty years it had become a preeminent national center for the study of state government.[7] When Nathan retired in 2009, the new SUNY system chancellor transferred the administration of the institute to the SUNY at Albany university center.[8] Although the move was inconsistent with the institute's original system-wide mission and the intent of the institute's private donors,[9] the fiscal strains upon SUNY headquarters prevailed. Nevertheless, the institute continues to thrive.

▪ Public Service and Small Business Development _____

Virtually all U.S. state universities provide expertise to the broader community through their public service dimension—continuing education, faculty consulting, agricultural and urban extension, and resource sharing. This activity is considered a natural complement to their teaching and research functions. There had been a recent New York panel on "Examples of the Effect of Public Service Activities on Campuses of the University." But unfortunately, public service was somewhat of a new concept to SUNY. When I toured the sixty-four campuses, it was easy to see that most had not developed any very significant grasp of the public service concept. Yet public service not only would be politically appealing and responsive to statewide needs, it also would delineate SUNY sharply from private colleges and universities, in turn dissolving the old image of the university as a conglomerate of second-rate undergraduate teaching campuses. I realized that SUNY campuses could become a major force for economic development across the entire state.

Hence public service was added to my agenda of university-wide initiatives,[10] and I appointed John Mather, previously head of SUNY central administrative services, as associate vice chancellor for continuing education and public service. Mather worked on several fronts, probably the most ambitious of which was an effort to develop small business development centers throughout the state. At the heart of the program would be a computer database of business-relevant skills across the university's participating campuses, a network with a central "node" in Albany connected to regional nodes around the state. Any small business needing assistance could approach the nearest SUNY installation. If local capacities were found wanting, the contact campus could use the network to identify appropriate resources elsewhere.

Later on, when Mather learned that federal funds were available, we quickly put together a proposal built around expanding the network to embrace both public and private colleges. In preliminary contacts, the Small Business Administration called our approach visionary, a model that might be replicated elsewhere in the country. But reactions by the New York "independent" sector were unhappy, which (somehow) I still found shocking. Though we had proposed a joint public-private board to develop policies and monitor operations, many private college leaders complained that SUNY was trying to "usurp" their skills and make them "subservient" to the university system. Worse yet, they enlisted the state education department's commissioner, Gordon Ambach, in their cause. What SUNY sought was not an empire but a structure for harnessing a full range of educational resources—a win-win for all concerned. But Ambach submitted a formal objection in Washington and managed temporarily to block the SBA grant.

Enthusiasm remained high at SUNY campuses, so we moved ahead without the federal dollars. Mather put together an advisory board of prominent figures in business and local government who might eventually help persuade the state to support the program with new appropriations. Luckily, the SBA eventually did come through with a $300,000 grant, seed money to set up the centers and begin operations. The first opened in Albany, Binghamton, Buffalo, Niagara, and Plattsburgh, and others soon followed.[11]

The program thrives today, with twenty-four regional centers and twenty-six outreach stations offering a variety of consulting and training services. Since its founding it has worked directly with more than 287,000 firms, helping them invest over $2.3 billion in the state's economy. In addition to SUNY, participants now include CUNY, a host of private colleges, the Empire State Development Corporation, New York Business Development Corporation, and the U.S. Department of Labor.

Another dust-up with Ambach and the state education department had been over SUNY enrollment projections. Using the old "pig-in-the-python" demographics, the department believed that the aging of "Baby Boomers" would lead to fewer high school graduates, hence fewer college applicants—an argument justifying funding cuts for SUNY and CUNY. But their analysis concentrated on the traditional, eighteen- to twenty-year-olds in the pipeline and ignored the growing importance of older, "nontraditional" students. When we broke down recent New York enrollments by age cohorts, our data showed exactly what could have been expected—a steady increase in older students as a percentage of total enrollments. When I presented these findings at an informal meeting with the regents, one regent was particularly angry. How dare we take a stand that differed so dramatically from that of the state education department experts? Eventually the department itself conceded that SUNY's view might have some merit, though it didn't change its own estimates until years later.

▪ MSU Performing Arts Center Dedication ——————————————

Even though SUNY was a full-time job and Dolores had a full plate of her own, part of our hearts never left Michigan State. From Albany (with occasional trips back to East Lansing) we stayed in close touch with plans for MSU's new performing arts center. Unhappily, problems had developed almost immediately after we left. The university asked the state for $6 million for an "education" wing to house the Department of Theatre, but acting president Edgar Harden felt that the appropriation was unlikely. (One state legislator reportedly said he wasn't about to support "young men dancing around a stage in tutus.") Although the Academic Council urged completion of the center as originally designed, Harden opted for a revised plan without the education wing. The university trustees backed him up, promising to look for another home for the theater department at a later date. The sleekly modern concept by Caudill Rowlett Scott was dropped in favor of a more conventional one by a Michigan firm.

The incident slowed the capital campaign, though Les Scott and Ken Beachler continued to be optimistic that it would succeed. Especially with Scott's imminent retirement, though, fund-raising momentum flagged. One of our Lansing friends told us that at a downtown business luncheon Ed Harden expressed doubts that the center would ever be built at all.

But in August 1978 John Hannah stepped back into the picture. Harden and Les Scott had convened a meeting of several key players—in addition to Hannah, senior administrators Jack Breslin, Roger Wilkinson, and Al Ballard. One by one they reviewed the situation from their respective areas of responsibility, and before long it began to sound as if the new building could not be successfully financed. Then Hannah spoke up. "Gentlemen," he said, "you start from where you're at. . . . If the university doesn't proceed [with the project], it will set itself back in fund-raising . . . [for] many decades in the future."

Hannah proposed that he take over leadership, concentrating on major donors, and asked that Jack Shingleton, director of student placement and an aggressive MSU advocate, be assigned to help with legwork. Hannah's forceful personality reenergized the team, while finance vice president Roger Wilkinson and his staff (especially Steve Terry and Nancy Craig) creatively restructured the funding blueprint. Now a third of the money would come from new gifts, another third from unrestricted gifts already on hand, and the rest from refinancing MSU's outstanding debt. The debt balance had previously been lowered, allowing a new increase through refinancing without any increase in the tuition committed to its coverage. In June 1979, Hannah even got the board of trustees to agree to a public groundbreaking, both as a fund-raising event and as a symbolic promise that the center would indeed be built.

At the July 20 ceremonies, President Harden said, "By having the groundbreaking, we are giving the project impetus so no letdown will occur with the changes in administration."[12] At the same occasion former president Hannah's prophetic remarks struck the central theme.

This is a significant day in the history of this university. . . . What takes place in the Performing Arts Center has the potential for not only providing better training and better opportunities for students . . . it will provide an opportunity for this university to achieve what it has not been able to do until now. . . . It will make available opportunities for all students, and all townspeople, and all the people in middle Michigan and elsewhere to better appreciate why the performing arts are of first importance. This new impetus will have great meaning and significance for this university.[13]

He clearly recognized my vision and urged that "the project be completed as rapidly as possible."

Naming issues came with some drama. The publisher John McGoff pledged a $1 million on the condition that either the center's recital hall or the festival stage be named after his wife Margaret. Instantly, Blacks on campus and in the community objected because of McGoff's alleged ties to South Africa and apartheid.[14] Harden ignored the controversy and recommended to the trustees that they name the festival stage after Margaret McGoff, and the great hall after Catherine Herrick Cobb, whose major contribution Dolores and I had previously developed. A few years later McGoff withdrew his pledge when it emerged that without registering as a foreign agent he had taken $12 million from the South African government to purchase American publications in order to influence U.S. public opinion of apartheid.[15] The festival theater space was then eventually named for major donor Athanase "Tony" Passant and his wife Shirley, both MSU alumni.

Equally important in the recovery was the strong support of MSU arts advocates and friends like Phyllis and Bud Maner—Phyllis took over as MSU mid-Michigan campaign chair. Other strong sponsors and friends stepped forward—Evie Machtel had the Green Room named for her father Jack Wolfram, and Jennie Stoddard, who was a close personal friend and confidante of Hannah and ours, named the Grand Tier Lounge in memory of her husband Howard, founder of Michigan National Bank.

In August 1979, the university's incoming president, Cecil Mackey, pledged his support for the future center. In October a construction contract was awarded to the Christman Company, a Lansing, Michigan, construction firm. The amount was $17.5 million. Eleven million would come from private donations and the balance from university sources, including liquidating four existing endowments. Incredibly, the state's auditor general criticized the university for not considering alternatives such as renovating the auditorium and better use of Jenison Field House, Demonstration Hall, the Munn Ice Arena, or even the horse judging pavilion. The thought of Van Cliburn playing in a horse pavilion boggled the mind.[16]

Another controversy broke out in mid-1981 over a proposal to pay for the center's planned $4.2 million parking facility by charging higher parking fees to students. Facing a phalanx of students and faculty who felt that parking wasn't an "academic priority," and unwilling to increase university debt, trustees put the facility on hold, later going forward with a smaller structure. (Years later, predictably, it had to be enlarged, at a greater cost than that of the original plan.)

In the end MSU's performing arts center rose above all obstacles, its 850,000 bricks and 2,450 tons of steel a monument to all who had contributed and worked on its behalf.

On April 2, 1982, five months before opening night, the MSU board voted to name the facility the "Clifton and Dolores Wharton Center for Performing Arts." Among others, Black trustee Blanche Martin had lobbied President Mackey and other university leaders

The Clifton and Dolores Wharton Center for Performing Arts was dedicated on September 25, 1982. (*Left to right*) me, Dolores Wharton, and Ken Beachler. As the first executive director, Beachler laid the foundation for what would eventually become a major performing arts facility in Michigan and the Midwest.

with continuing determination. Our friend Phyllis Maner, chair of the capital campaign for mid-Michigan, asked business executives, arts supporters, and mutual friends to write Mackey with the same request. State senator Jackie Vaughn weighed in. So did Aubrey Radcliffe, the other Black trustee, who wrote a supportive letter to Mackey and copied it to John Hannah and the MSU Black Faculty. Then at the board meeting when the matter came up for a vote, Radcliffe eagerly put our names into nomination, peremptorily eclipsing Blanche Martin's attempt to offer what would have been a lovely coda to his having nominated me for president more than a decade ago.

Dolores and I were deeply touched by the board's action.[17] We loved Michigan State and the performing arts. Now the two strands of our affection were permanently entwined, and the university would have a cultural showcase that could stand proudly with its other centers of excellence.

On Saturday afternoon, September 25, Dolores and I drove quietly onto the campus to see the building for the first time. That evening there would be a black-tie dedication, featuring the Chicago Symphony Orchestra and the famous soprano Birgit Nilsson. The 2,500-seat Great

President Emeritus and Mrs. John Hannah rejoice with Dolores over the opening of the Wharton Center on September 25, 1982. The Hannahs, MSU's revered elders, played a critical leadership role in the completion of the Wharton Center. They shared an exceptional friendship with us based upon mutual respect and love of MSU.

Hall would be filled to capacity, with four other MSU presidents and their wives among the audience (Mackey, Harden, Adams, and Hannah). At intermission Dolores and I would be presented with a "Crystal Clef" award of recognition from the Bell Telephone Company, one of the new center's corporate contributors, and we would both somehow struggle to put our churning emotions into words.

For the moment, though, we just parked across from the building. We didn't get out of the car. We admired *Orpheus*, Mel Leiserowitz's thirty-foot high, six-ton sculpture, which we had commissioned long before construction had begun. We were delighted with the black-and-silver geometric work and could understand why the students used it for sunbathing, calling it "The Sizzler." Some even skateboarded inside the twelve-foot diameter oval, in keeping with frolicsome campus traditions.[18] Mostly we just sat staring at the large chrome capital letters blazoned over the door: *CLIFTON AND DOLORES WHARTON CENTER FOR PERFORMING ARTS*. How were we supposed to feel, seeing our names etched for posterity on that pristine new building, its interior dim and silent now, but soon to blaze with light and song? Overwhelmed.

Afterward in the Stoddard Grand Tier Lounge, we were welcomed by a crush of people who came to congratulate us. One of our favorite faculty members, Professor Bea Paolucci, who had been challenged for years from childhood polio and was in failing health due to cancer, had sent word that she was too weak to attend. We were saddened but understood. At the reception the crowd around us suddenly seemed to part magically, opening a path from the elevator—and there she was!—Bea Paolucci struggling out of the elevator and coming toward us valiantly. As she reached us she said, "Thank you both for what you did for MSU. I had to come—if only for a few minutes."

Tears filled my eyes at her words, but even more at her coming to show, once again, her support—a great human being and typical Spartan academic.

• Corporations, Commissions, and BIFAD _____

My SUNY responsibilities allowed modest leeway for outside activities. At the outset I had dropped my Burroughs directorship but stayed on the boards of Ford Motor Company and Equitable Life Assurance. Subsequently I stepped down from four more boards,[19] while joining Time, Inc., and the Federal Reserve Bank of New York, both with the concurrence of the SUNY trustees. On the nonprofit side, I remained a trustee of the Rockefeller Foundation (chairman in 1982) and joined several others.[20]

In 1978 I joined the Business-Higher Education Forum, created by a group of university presidents and corporate CEOs. The idea came from Jack Peltason, then president of the American Council on Education, who wanted an organization to promote discourse and action on issues of mutual concern. Peltason asked several presidents and chancellors to suggest one or two prominent corporate leaders who might be interested in joining (I identified Phil Caldwell, then chairman and CEO of Ford Motor Company). Meetings of what grew into a ninety-member group took place twice a year, usually at a resort or retreat. At first the corporate CEOs were reserved, but gradually a strong and collegial bond formed between the two sides. We worked hard to develop a useful agenda, gradually focusing on government regulation, health and safety standards, and trade policies.

An influential Forum publication was *America's Competitive Challenge: A Report to the President of the United States* (April 1983), which eventually led to the creation of the Council on Competitiveness. Forum members involved in preparing it presented the publication to President Reagan personally at the White House, where we shook hands with him and explained how pleased we were to have worked on so critical a topic. Reagan greeted each of us with a nod, a smile, and a mumble, but made no comment on the report itself. Finally he said, "This reminds me of the summer when I was digging ditches, and the noon whistle blew. I dropped my pickaxe in midair, and it accidentally hit the foot of the supervisor standing right behind me. The great lesson I learned was, always follow through with what you're doing." After being escorted outside, we all stood around the oval driveway, baffled. "What was that about?" asked someone. "They probably forgot his cue cards," answered somebody else.

. . . .

Also in 1978, Ambassador Sol Linowitz, then President Carter's special envoy to the Middle East, asked me to chair the administration's proposed Commission on World Hunger. Because I was so new to the chancellorship of SUNY, I preferred to participate only as a regular member of the fourteen participants (see appendix 8).[21] The major recommendation was that "the U.S. government should make the elimination of hunger the primary focus of its relationship with the developing countries." To this was added that the "Commission's concern for the hungry of the world is matched by its corresponding commitment to meet the human need of those who still remain malnourished in the United States." We presented both short-term and long-term policies based upon a broad plan of action calling for a major reordering of U.S. national priorities. The two-hundred-page report described the challenges and opportunities for the U.S. role, the problem of world hunger, the special role of U.S. exports, the U.S. efforts to combat hunger through development assistance, overcoming hunger at home, and the need for public education.

After our final report came out,[22] member and economist Wally Falcon wrote a perceptive review in the *American Journal of Agricultural Economics*: "Much of [its] extensive and often moving description of hunger can be captured in five words: Asia, children, calories, chronic, and poverty."[23] But as was so often the case, the short-term public furor over the commission's efforts failed to translate into substantial longer-term impact. While the report was extremely well done, setting out useful prescriptions, the follow-up leadership failed to overcome the dominance of other international problems and issues. Another attempt to reorder U.S. priorities for international development assistance would have to wait twenty-three years.

• Board for International Food and Agricultural Development ⎯⎯⎯

Much more significant and rewarding was my six years working with BIFAD, the Board for International Food and Agricultural Development. President Carter had reappointed me as chair in 1979. The goal was to strengthen ties between the U.S. universities and the state department's Agency for International Development, reenergizing higher education's efforts in the global war on hunger while increasing access by the less developed nations and AID missions to U.S. institutional resources.

Over time we identified more than a hundred agricultural colleges and universities as

The Hunger Symposium honoring Senator Hubert Humphrey, Washington, D.C., was held on December 19, 1977. (*Left to right*) Clifton Wharton, president, Michigan State University; President Gerald Ford; Senator Hubert Humphrey; and Representative Paul Findley. Humphrey and Findley coauthored the legislation creating the Board for International Food and Agricultural Development (BIFAD). Humphrey died a month after this event, on January 13, 1978.

"eligible" to participate in Title XII programs. We also developed a computerized registry of some five hundred academic departments and three thousand individuals qualified to work in development assistance. "Strengthening program grants," designed to enhance the capability to contribute effectively to Title XII overseas assistance, went to fifty-four institutions, including nine predominantly Black universities (the so-called 1890 public campuses). By the time I left in late 1983, BIFAD had significantly rejuvenated the commitment by American universities to agricultural development abroad, broadly increasing access to U.S. institutional resources to AID missions in less developed nations.[24] The program had produced an impressive portfolio of statistics that documented the extent of university commitment and access.[25] Our report listed large numbers of new university courses, or offerings modified to include international development content; increased faculty participation and student enrollment in international programs; encouraged active interest by graduate students in international development and thesis research; proposed seminars in the United States and abroad on such topics as women in development; and significantly enhanced direct research and technical transfer work by

Three Wharton male generations celebrated Thanksgiving dinner in Albany, New York, on November 27, 1980. (*Left to right*) Bruce, Clifton Sr., Clifton 3rd, and Clifton Jr.

university personnel in almost every part of the developing world. (The incredible durability of BIFAD is that it is still functioning and thriving today!)

Another of my international activities in the early eighties was serving on a Commission on Security and Economic Assistance, created by then secretary of state George Shultz and chaired by Frank Carlucci, former deputy secretary of defense. I cochaired the group, along with Lane Kirkland, president of the AFL-CIO, and Larry Silberman, former U.S. ambassador to Yugoslavia and former deputy attorney general. Consisting of almost forty members, including nine U.S. senators and fourteen representatives, the commission was a rather unwieldy group. Its charge was to examine the relationship between U.S. foreign economic and military assistance—tacitly, to combat the common view that "foreign aid" was an unwarranted waste of public funds. My own hope had been to highlight some of the differences between military assistance and genuine overseas development spending, perhaps even encourage some modest shift in Washington's priorities. But when we submitted our final report in November 1983, military issues predominated. It didn't especially matter. After a brief flurry in the media, the commission's work vanished down Washington's black hole of forgotten studies and reports. It made me wonder why people kept on trying—"hope springs eternal," I supposed.

. . . .

Dolores's own public visibility increased steadily during our years in Albany, both in corporate governance and civic leadership. She spoke frequently in public, usually drawing on her board experiences, to audiences that ranged from the New York Cosmopolitan Club to the American Association of University Women, the Financial Executives Institute, and the New York state senate higher education committee. (She also gave talks on nonbusiness topics, including three college commencement addresses.) At Kellogg and Phillips Petroleum, she pushed for creating board committees on social responsibility, becoming the committee chair at both firms. Then a rarity in the world of commerce, such committees championed ethical behavior as an important gauge of corporate success, with a particular emphasis on employee and officer diversity.

Our mutual involvement on corporate boards occasionally created challenges. At one point Dolores's board at Gannett and my own at Time, Inc., were engaged in secret merger talks. I was asked to serve as a back channel between Gannett's Al Neuharth and Time's Dick Munro, the companies' CEOs. When the senior executives from the two media firms met for preliminary discussions, both Dolores and I knew exactly what was going on, but we couldn't discuss it at all with each other—even mentioning it would have been a serious breach of confidentiality. The negotiations broke down, but when Time much later merged with Warner Communications, *USA Today* reported on the earlier situation: "Their lips were practically glued shut."[26]

Being the husband of a woman on a corporate board brought some funny moments. At Phillips Petroleum I was at first the only male spouse and always joined the "ladies" while the directors met privately. Their initial consternation soon dissipated—once I even went with the other spouses on a bus tour of Norway, while Dolores and her colleagues were flying around the Ekofisk oil platforms in the North Sea. At a lunch stop, they insisted on a group photograph, which they later mailed me with the legend "Clif and his harem." Some years later, when U.S. ambassador Carol Laise joined the board, we were joined by her husband Ellsworth Bunker. Former U.S. ambassador to Vietnam (1967–73) Bunker later worked with Linowitz to negotiate the treaty that turned the Panama Canal over to Panama. He was known in diplomatic circles as the "Refrigerator" because of his ability to deal with trying circumstances without showing emotion. This tall, white-haired, polished former ambassador became the second male "spouse." At his wife's first annual stockholders meeting, he and I met in the Bartlesville, Oklahoma, arena where the Phillips 66 basketball team used to play. Five hundred or so folding chairs had been set up on the court for seating stockholders, the first row reserved for directors and the second for spouses.

When Bunker and I sat down in the second row, an usher hurried right over. "I'm sorry," he said, "but this row is reserved for the wives of directors."

"But we *are* wives of the directors," I said, struggling to keep a straight face. To which Bunker added in his crisp semi-British accent, "We certainly are!"

Fund for Corporate Initiatives, Inc.

Dolores and I always tried to encourage other minorities and women in business, seeing in them the next generation of leadership. Dolores went a step further. At Hewlett-Packard in 1979, Katherine Lawrence and Marianne Schreiber described how while paths to promotion for women looked clear on the surface, in actuality they always seemed to hit a point beyond which their progress stalled.[27] Dolores had observed the same thing in her boardrooms: though corporate executives seemed sincerely committed to greater diversity, minorities and women more often than not stalled somewhere between middle and senior management. To find out why, she personally surveyed a number of corporate CEOs, as well as her fellow board members. From their responses a common thread emerged: despite good educations and strong performance on the job, for both minorities and women there were key areas where training had been deficient—among them written and oral communications, interpersonal skills, and interacting in corporate social settings.

From that finding grew the Fund for Corporate Initiatives, Inc., which Dolores set up in 1980 as a private operating foundation aimed at preparing young minorities and women for greater success in the corporate world. Primarily funded by Dolores's corporate fees, FCI's initial target audience was college juniors and seniors, preferably business majors, selected from public and private campuses in the Albany region. The vehicle was ten-week summer internships, offered in partnership with several local and regional companies. During the six years of its existence, each program enrolled seven to ten students[28] who were assigned to such corporations as NY Blue Cross, Key Bank, General Electric, Albany International, the *Saratogian* (Gannett newspaper), Golub (Price Chopper), and the State Bank of Albany. The employers agreed to pay the interns' wages and assign them substantive, meaningful tasks, working with regular employees, supervisors, and upper managers. On weekends, the interns were bused to the Rensselaerville Institute, an upstate conference center, where they attended workshops on key aspects of business leadership: writing and public speaking, team-building, and how to understand and get along in a corporate culture. Dolores had enlisted the help of several key resource people. Dr. Harvey Kahalas, dean of business at SUNY–Albany, and Tom Anderson, professor at SUNY–Albany, conducted special seminars on leadership and team-building. Jim Harkness, a colleague from SUNY central administration, gave hands-on sessions in business writing, while Joseph Balfiore, of the New York State Theatre Institute, taught public speaking. At an end-of-summer graduation, interns spoke about the experience, displaying some of the skills they had honed, often with their supervisors and corporate sponsors in the audience.

At various times, the FCI Board of Trustees included Ambassador Ulric Haynes, former vice president of Cummins Engine and corporate director; Professor Ruth Hamilton, MSU and corporate director; Bruce Pulling, vice president of NYNEX; Don Miller, vice president of

Dow Jones & Co. and corporate director; Isabelle K. Savell, historian and author; Dr. Eleanor Sheldon, former president of Social Science Research Council and corporate director; Dr. James Smoot, vice chancellor of SUNY; Chuck Stone, columnist at *Philadelphia Daily News*; J. Vanderbilt Straub of Hinman, Straub, Pigors & Manning; and Anne Viglione, vice president of Blue Cross, as well as FCI's key resource persons, Dean Kahalas and Jim Harkness. Later some of the FCI alumni were elected.

After the internships had been in place a few years, Dolores described the program to Joe Slater, president of Aspen Institute, who then urged her to launch a similar program in cooperation with Aspen, but this time aimed at corporate professionals. From his suggestion grew FCI's second initiative—the Young Executive Program begun in 1984. With her same core team, Dolores developed the framework for a series of annual, weeklong seminars for under-forty, high-potential middle managers, mostly though not exclusively women and minorities. The programs took place at the Aspen Institute's facility in Wye, Maryland, on the Delmarva Peninsula. Each participant was nominated by the employing corporation, which paid a fee to Aspen. Dolores's Fund for Corporate Initiatives paid for incidental expenses, including per diem reimbursement for resource guests.

Over time the guest list began to read like a who's who. Among corporate CEOs were Dick Munro and Nick Nicholas from Time, Inc.; Phil Caldwell and Harold Poling from Ford; Charles Brown from AT&T; Coy Eklund from Equitable Life; and William LaMothe from Kellogg. From politics, the roster included U.S. Representative Amo Houghton and former EEOC chair Eleanor Holmes Norton (later U.S. representative for the District of Columbia). Celebrities abounded, such as pianists Billy Taylor and Bobby Short, tennis great Arthur Ashe, and power-broker Vernon Jordan, executive director National Urban League.

An interesting aspect of the Young Executive Program was that each group of participants always included a few white males. Afterward a number of them remarked that it was their own first time as a "minority" in a professional group, and that they had found it a remarkable experience.

In 1992 Dolores decided that the program, while still meeting a need, no longer required her leadership, as several universities and even corporations had developed similar activities. By the time she officially turned the program over to the Aspen Institute, over two hundred younger executives had participated, representing Exxon, Ford Motor Company, General Electric, Time, Inc., Verizon, Kellogg, AT&T, NBC, Showtime, the Federal Reserve Bank of New York, and dozens of other Fortune 500 corporations. Today many are in senior vice presidential positions, and at least one is a chief executive officer of a major multinational.

▪ South Africa: Divest or Disinvest or Stay?

South Africa and apartheid were continuing issues during my early SUNY tenure. As SUNY chancellor, a corporate director, and a Black in a highly visible position, I attracted predictable attention on the subject, as had happened at MSU.

South Africa's white rule with its vicious apartheid system of segregation was a contentious, thorny issue. Civil rights activists demanded that U.S. companies doing business in South Africa pull out or be boycotted. Universities and pension companies were targeted when they held shares in such companies and faced demands that they divest themselves of such investments. The counterargument was that the United States actually could help the native Black population by staying and using fair employment practices to battle the pernicious apartheid effect, but this usually was drowned out by the symbolism of divestment and disinvestment. (The former solution involved the sale of the corporate shares if a company operated in South Africa; the latter was the cessation of a company's operations in South Africa—or removing their investment in the country.)

In March 1977, Rev. Leon H. Sullivan, a prominent Black civil rights activist whose successful training programs in Philadelphia had been replicated across the country, developed six principles that U.S. corporations should adopt in order to justify their continued operations. He became a corporate leader on the issue after he joined the board of General Motors in 1971. His principles included nonsegregation of the races in work facilities; equal employment practices for all employees; equal pay for equal or comparable work; training programs to prepare Blacks and other nonwhite minorities for supervisory, administrative, clerical, and technical jobs; increasing the number of Blacks and other nonwhites in management and supervisory positions; and improving their lives outside of work in such areas as housing, transportation, school, recreation, and health facilities. A seventh principle, added in 1984, was to work toward eliminating laws and customs that impeded "social, economic, and political justice."

Sullivan was trying to use the economic leverage of U.S. corporations to force change and the removal of apartheid, and within a year more than one hundred corporations had signed up to his principles. Because both Dolores and I were directors of corporations that operated in South Africa (Ford Motor, Kellogg, Phillips Petroleum, and Burroughs), we had already faced the issue at Michigan State. At SUNY, we continued to move with great care and deliberation to respect both roles. CEOs and fellow directors looked to us for counsel on policies in this sensitive area, and the campus community looked to us to provide leadership. I strongly disapproved of apartheid, but this was troublesome because, as with the Vietnam War, I needed to maintain academic neutrality by not becoming a spokesman for any particular university view.

By the time we moved to SUNY, activism on South Africa had reached a new level of intensity due to the killing of the African National Congress leader Steve Biko while in police custody and the Soweto riots. The U.N. Security Council declared an arms-trade embargo on South Africa, while President Jimmy Carter administratively banned the export of materials that might be used by the military or police in South Africa. I concluded that I had to voice my own views, so in 1978 I wrote an op-ed piece for *Newsday*[29] condemning the government of South Africa for "pressing their odious policies to the brink of genocide." I applauded the Sullivan principles and agreed with the judgment that "withdrawal would set back precisely the group of South African Blacks who represent the cutting edge of economic change and progress" by wiping out the few gains they had made through the progressive influence of U.S. firms.

In my judgment, divestment or sale of a university's shares was a far weaker instrument than economic sanctions, and I therefore urged greater pressure on the "Federal government—the president, Congress, and the State Department—[for] South African sanctions … [as] far more likely to lead to stronger, all-encompassing action than firm-by-firm withdrawal or piecemeal divestiture by individual institutions." I concluded with a plea for using the "collective weight of world opinion and action . . . that stands the best chance of achieving the goal we desire—the ultimate liberation and equality of all the people of South Africa. . . . However humane our own intentions, we must recognize that it is the collective will of the nations of the world that will shape the future we seek." The article received considerable attention and triggered several responses from Black colleagues who said that my courageous position merited serious consideration.

Several years later, however, pivotal events reversed my thinking. In 1979 the Rockefeller Foundation created a Commission on U. S. Policy Toward South Africa, headed by Franklin Thomas, the president of the Ford Foundation. At my suggestion, Professor Ruth Hamilton from Michigan State was included in the commission and became a key member. Its 1981 report provided the first comprehensive look at the effects of U.S. policy and recommended actions. Then three years later, the Ford Foundation conducted a review of a series of follow-up studies of what changes, if any, had taken place in South Africa since the publication of the earlier report. I was stunned by the results. For example, the number of Black South Africans below the minimum living standard had *increased*, almost doubling from 4.9 million to 8.9 million between 1960 and 1980. Despite the improvement in the living standards of the few Blacks aided by U.S. corporations, the Black majority, constituting 73 percent of the country's population, had moved backward, not forward. I, therefore, reversed my South African position 180 degrees. In a second *Newsday* op-ed in November 1984, I said that "U.S. firms and corporations should withdraw all personnel and investments from South Africa. . . . In commerce and foreign policy, we must treat the South African government as the pariah it long ago chose to become."[30] The reaction among my corporate colleagues was understanding, even among those who disagreed. But the response to my complete reversal of my position by Blacks in the corporate sector was electric. As one Black corporate director said, "Clif, as one of the deans among Black corporate directors, your views are bound to carry a great deal of weight among your colleagues."

I followed the article up with testimony before the House Subcommittee on Africa of the Committee on Foreign Affairs on January 31, 1985, further explaining my views and position. At Ford Motor, I continued my practice of abstaining from any votes on our operations in South Africa, while expressing my dissenting views on their continuing operation. The company finally sold its plant and operations to an automotive subsidiary of the Oppenheimer family's conglomerate, Anglo American, creating SAMCOR, the South African Motor Corporation.

The SUNY Board of Trustees continued to wrestle with the issue of South African divestment, undoubtedly influenced by my change in position. In April 1985, the board voted to sell holdings in four companies that were not complying with the Sullivan principles, while keeping the stock in thirteen companies "which they said had been active in helping Blacks . . . in the belief that, through them, more leverage could be exerted on the South African government." Then five months later, the board changed its position once again, this time voting nine to four to sell its stock worth $11.5 million in all companies doing business in South Africa.[31]

Meanwhile, Dolores questioned my position, especially as it related to one of her corporations, Kellogg, which had operations in South Africa. Before voting on a Kellogg board resolution to remain there, she asked chairman and CEO William LaMothe if she might make an onsite visit to explore all aspects of the troubling issue. This was in June 1988, when South Africa still clung fiercely to its apartheid policies. It was uncertain how the authorities would treat her once in the country. She wanted to see the conditions firsthand, to ask questions in person, and to speak with as many leaders and thoughtful people as possible.

With no apparent hesitation Kellogg prepared an extensive itinerary for her visit. In a private plane, she flew from Johannesburg to Cape Town, with several stops in between. Accompanied by another Kellogg director and the Kellogg general counsel, plus the company's head of security, Dolores visited Black South African workers and union leaders at the Kellogg Plains plant. She found not only that Kellogg met the Sullivan principles, but also that it was making a significant difference in the hiring and promoting of Blacks, in housing owned by workers, in improved schooling, in wages and salaries of minority employees, and in the development of Black labor leaders, especially Chris Dlamini, the Black heading Kellogg's labor union and one of the earliest labor leaders in the country. The late Wayne Fredericks, former deputy assistant secretary of state for Africa and a leading South African expert, facilitated special meetings for her with several Black South African leaders, including Zulu chief Mangosuthu Gatsha Buthelezi, and a secret nighttime visit in Soweto to Mrs. Albertina Sisulu, who was under house arrest.

During her visits with thirty-four persons, Dolores asked several questions: "How did

Black South Africans feel about the role of U.S. and other foreign corporations? Did they favor or oppose their continued presence and why? Did they consider disinvestment an effective strategy to force the government to dismantle apartheid? Even if disinvestment undercut the South African economy, would the government respond by eliminating its racist apartheid policies? What alternative means would South Africans propose that U.S. and other foreign corporations use to bring about progress in South Africa? Educational programs for youth? Housing for company employees? Job training? Or did the majority of Black South Africans believe that nothing short of revolutionary restructuring would bring about the human and political rights so long denied?"[32]

When Dolores returned, she prepared a thoughtful, confidential report for her fellow directors and CEO LaMothe. It was a masterful summary of what she had learned from her interviews with Blacks and whites alike. She had conducted research like an investigative reporter and written it up with objectivity and balance. The report was filled with direct quotes, even colorful comments. For example, one highly revered Black woman considered disinvestment a "droplet in the bucket" when measured against the magnitude of the struggle. Many Black South Africans pointed out that, once disinvested, a corporation could easily wash its hands of the whole problem. When asked about alternatives, education was universally identified as the place where corporations could make a significant contribution. Positive references were often made about Kellogg's well-known support for Black labor unions against the early opposition by the South African government. Opinions on the effectiveness of economic sanctions were mixed, though there was considerable evidence that the U.S. 1986 ban on new investments[33] was having an impact. But unlike the broad international efforts against white rule in Rhodesia (Zimbabwe), the failure of other nations to join the United States reduced the impact.

Dolores concluded that "as long as Kellogg's business was economically viable and its presence continued to be constructive for its employees and families, as well as others in the schools and business enterprises and those fighting the apartheid system (i.e., the labor leaders), then Kellogg should remain."

The Kellogg board and management complimented her on the thoroughness and insights of her report—and I could fully appreciate how she reached her strong conclusion opposite to mine. Within the male-dominated corporate world, Dolores's contrarian position surprised many people. But our friends who knew us well realized that throughout our marriage she always held and articulated her own independent views. Her position rested upon her own explorations on the "front lines of apartheid." Our honest intellectual differences and mutual respect on those rare occasions where Dolores and I differed strengthened our marriage, making it all the richer.

With the release of Nelson Mandela on February 18, 1990, the all-race elections of April 1994, and the triumph of the African National Congress, the government policy of apartheid came to an end. Dealing with the South African issue forcefully brought home to me the extent to which symbolic action in a just cause can have a tangible impact. If the cause is principled and just, and if public awareness and conscience are galvanized, the effect can contribute to the final goal. But my reservations remained about the need for university presidents to maintain the neutrality of academe. They should speak out when moved, but they should be careful that their advocacy of a position not be interpreted within the academy as a gag upon dissent. Free speech and the right to personal opinions are even more than constitutional foundations of our nation; they are the precondition for the search for truth. Many people might contend that academic "neutrality" was, even in the 1970s, a casualty of the culture wars. For me the fundamental issue is the role of a university in the search for "truth" and new knowledge that must be protected. I would not argue that the external forces (such as the "culture wars") impacted academe, as long as they did not bias or distort the integrity of its pursuit of knowledge. In this the president or chancellor plays a pivotal role.

• Independent Commission on the Future of the State University of New York

In an era when using resources efficiently was paramount, one of SUNY's greatest difficulties was the incredible weight of state bureaucratic oversight that encumbered it. Fighting off regents and the state education department was bad enough, but there were also the state attorney general, the comptroller, the Department of Audit and Control, the Department of Environmental Conservation, and more. All the rest put together were nothing, however, compared to the steely grip of the state Division of Budget, whose director reported to the governor, his own conscience, and God, in exactly that order. The tentacles of DOB, as it was not at all affectionately known, seemed to reach into every aspect of SUNY's administration, from the university's annual appropriation request to audits, postaudits, and post-postaudits long after the fact. There were independent "lines" for the most minute items, and every expenditure required specific preauthorization—even though already approved in budgets passed by the legislature and signed by the governor. There was also an ironclad rule that funds on hand for one line couldn't be transferred to any other purpose, even in emergencies.

A clear example of how things worked was a travel "freeze" DOB imposed in 1980–81. All campus and SUNY central personnel were required to secure state approval of individual travel vouchers, and other restrictions were imposed across the board, including a ban on out-of-state travel. Thus a physics professor from SUNY–Stony Brook could attend a conference at SUNY–Buffalo, 430 miles distant, but not at Yale (Connecticut) or Rutgers (New Jersey)—both about one hundred miles away. After a couple months of wrangling I finally got permission for the university itself to approve travel under certain circumstances, but DOB retained authority over each and every out-of-state trip. Requests were reviewed *personally* by the deputy director of the department, and during a visit to the director I saw a foot-high stack of vouchers on his desk, waiting to be signed. Not surprisingly, decisions were often arbitrary. For example, a faculty member could go to a professional conference if he or she was giving a paper—but not for the equally important purpose of recruiting outstanding graduate students as teaching assistants.

With SUNY's 23,000 faculty and professional employees, the travel restrictions were a serious hardship, not to mention a monumental waste of time and money. Each campus had to write up special travel summaries and submit them quarterly to DOB. Since the whole idea was to put a lid on expense reimbursements, I audaciously asked why didn't DOB just cut travel budgets outright, then leave it up to campus and system managers to oversee the proper disbursement of whatever was left? But it took a year and a half for DOB to change its policy.

The red tape was no recent development. As far back as 1960, Governor Rockefeller had appointed a committee chaired by Henry Heald, president of the Ford Foundation, to look at growing demand and funding needs for higher education. The Heald panel remarked that SUNY was subject to extremely tight controls by state agencies, and that "as a whole [it] appears to have less administrative and management freedom of operation than any other publicly supported institution or group of institutions in the United States."[34] Four years later, another group led by Herman B Wells,[35] then chancellor of Indiana University, found SUNY still swaddled in excess bureaucracy and recommended that it be given "the power to use its funds more effectively" as well as "increased powers of self-determination, easing . . . restrictions on administrative flexibility."[36] But both committees' recommendations were ignored, and fifteen years later the situation was considerably worse.

Nine months into my tenure at SUNY, I made a speech that attempted to lay the groundwork for future reform. I had been invited to address a regional conference of the American Society for Public Administration—a group composed heavily of the malefactors themselves. *An ideal opportunity!* I thought. I set out to work on a speech eventually titled "Administrative Flexibility: Accountability's Point of Diminishing Returns." A few weeks later, I got up before the assembly and blithely aired my views.[37] A basic problem of management arose, I said, from the tendency to make rules and impose restrictions in reaction to specific abuses; such rules made it harder for the 1 percent of problem cases, but unreasonably hampered the effectiveness of the remaining 99 percent. Moreover, the next time an abuse occurred, the bureaucratic response was too often not to apply the existing rule, but to write a second . . . a third . . . a fourth. One after another, rules piled on rules, with oversight agencies necessarily growing and multiplying apace. To cope, subjects of the oversight regimes inevitably had to add their own new personnel, offices, and so on—not to carry out their basic public purposes, but simply to meet their mandates for "accountability." In the end, I said, what we needed to realize was that "accountability, like investment, has a point of diminishing returns. At that point, over-regulation undermines rather than enhances organizational effectiveness and efficiency."

I was pleased by the applause—until I noticed it was coming mostly from the spouses in the audience. After the speech, Paul Veillette, the chief budget officer for higher education, warned me, "Chancellor, you need to realize that New York isn't Michigan." I told Veillette that I was speaking about effective management, not a lessening of accountability. But I knew I would have to bide my time until the right conditions emerged.

Five years later, I felt that the moment had come. In January 1983, board chair Don Blinken and I met with Governor Mario Cuomo, who had just been elected to succeed Hugh Carey. Cuomo had talked about flexibility in government during his campaign, so we were hopeful. The meeting was pleasant, but Cuomo's sense of urgency didn't appear to match ours. Given sure resistance from DOB and other "apparatchiks," dramatic action was unlikely. Any proposal from the governor might well run into objections from the legislature, and vice versa. For that matter, if either side took the initiative for an investigation, if they didn't like the conclusions they could easily ignore them.

New York State had a tradition of looking to commissions for reforms in education and government, and they were certainly a mechanism that had worked well in my own experience. After talking at length with Blinken and SUNY trustees, I decided to convene a blue-ribbon Independent Commission on the Future of the State University of New York. I wanted a body that would be in no way beholden to state government, but also with enough distance from SUNY to make its findings and recommendations credible. To support the first goal I secured operating support from outside sources: the Carnegie Corporation of New York, the Ford Motor Company, the Rockefeller Foundation, and the Rockefeller Brothers Fund. For the second I approached a group of respected leaders inside and outside the state, representing business, labor, finance, and government, as well as public and private higher education. Ralph P. Davidson, chairman of the board at Time, Inc., joined Harold K. Enarson, president emeritus of Ohio State, as cochairs (see appendix 9). Acting as my liaisons to the group were my longtime assistant Al Ballard and Tom Freeman, associate vice chancellor for institutional research and planning. Ed Palmer and Richard P. Schmidt, two recently retired SUNY presidents, served as staff directors, providing personal perspectives and quick access to local campus information. Nevertheless, the commission's cochairs set agendas and ran meetings entirely on their own.

My only suggestion, made at the first meeting, was that members of the group try to tour at least two SUNY campuses on their own, with no escort from SUNY central administration before their second meeting. I had an idea that once they saw the facts on the ground, their subsequent recommendations would be astute. And so things proved: Commission members returned from their visits replete with vivid tales of bureaucratic overreach. They were dumbstruck, for example, by an incident at SUNY's Upstate Medical Center, where the State

Department of Audit and Control had held up a $5,000 kidney transplant because the hospital hadn't gotten competitive bids from other donors! Elsewhere, at the Alfred Agricultural and Technical College, a request to replace the roof of the student center went unanswered so long that janitors had to hang plastic sheeting to prevent rainwater from dousing athletic events in the gymnasium below. By the time DOB had approved $152,000 for repairs, the leaks had caused an additional $86,000 in damage. The list went on, like an endless Laurel and Hardy series script written by Franz Kafka.

I knew beforehand that this is what they would discover, but had strenuously kept my own counsel. Anything different would have looked manipulative—it not only wouldn't have worked, it would have been counterproductive.

Over the course of 1984 the commission held six daylong meetings, interviewing state legislators and staffs, officials from state agencies, SUNY presidents and faculty leaders, private campus heads, and representatives of higher education associations. It held public hearings in Albany and New York City. It heard a litany of complaints, horror stories, and no shortage of flimsy excuses. Tracing the tangle of red tape within which SUNY was ensnared, more than a few members professed themselves baffled that the university system managed to function at all.

The commission issued its report, *The Challenge and the Choice*, on January 16, 1985. Media coverage, which ranged from the front page of the *New York Times* and *Time* magazine to *Newsday* and the *Binghamton Press*, focused on the report's blistering overview.[38] "No great university, and no very good one, has been built or can be built under the state rules that presently govern the administration of SUNY. . . . New York State has become an extreme example of what *not* to do in the management of public higher education." Compared with ten other states, the report found, SUNY had the least administrative flexibility. It was, in cochair Ralph Davidson's words, the victim of "a tradition of over-regulation originating from [its] initial conception . . . as just another state agency." Commissioner W. Clarke Wescoe added morosely, "New York State runs its university like it runs its prisons."[39]

The commission's twenty-nine recommendations aimed at unshackling the university system from excessive and redundant bureaucracy. For example, it proposed replacing the Division of Budget's line-by-line expenditure approval procedure with "lump-sum" budgeting, allowing the SUNY trustees and administrators authority to divide the state's total appropriation among the various campuses. Prior spending review would be removed, with standard postaudits retained to prevent abuses. The report also pointed out ways to enhance SUNY's contributions to New York State, from increasing minority recruitment to building stronger graduate-research programs. Perhaps a bit anticlimatically, the commission did not call for major structural changes or downsizing, that is, closing campuses, although it did take note of high costs of and partial overlap among medical programs.

Undoubtedly the most controversial recommendation was a proposal to convert SUNY to a "public benefit corporation." Unique to New York State, public benefit corporations operate as quasi-private entities, though with boards of directors appointed by elected officials. They exist to serve public ends and share certain characteristics of state agencies, but they are largely exempt from state and local regulations. Well-known examples included the State Thruway Authority, State Bridge Authority, and Port Authority of New York and New Jersey, but by the mid-1980s there were literally scores of them, often operating well below the horizon of public visibility.

Because public benefit corporations were exempt from constitutionally imposed state debt limits, they had become popular mechanisms for financing public works—so popular, in fact, that their off-the-books, so-called moral authority bonds constituted more than 90 percent of the state's financial obligations. Nevertheless, the commission believed that converting SUNY to a properly structured public benefit corporation would be a workable solution. As a semiautonomous organization, the university system would be sheltered from excess bureaucracy. Both central administration and the campuses would enjoy greater latitude in planning programs, setting salaries, and moving funds as necessary to meet the dictates of circumstance.

Before the report came out, cochairs Davidson and Enarson, SUNY chairman Blinken, and several other commissioners briefed Governor Cuomo, key state political leaders, and senior legislative staffs. Publicly, Cuomo was cautiously receptive, in a letter to Davidson calling the public benefit corporation idea "intriguing." Privately he was hesitant. Despite the report's prestigious provenance, he probably realized he could accept or reject it, but in any event he wanted a firm grip on reforms. Senate majority leader Warren Anderson and Assembly speaker Stanley Fink came out in favor of most recommendations. The heads of the two higher education committees, Mark Siegel in the assembly and Ken LaValle in the senate, held joint public hearings in Albany, Binghamton, Buffalo, and Farmington, lending the issues greater visibility as well as their personal support. Not surprisingly, DOB and the State Comptroller's Office made it clear they had no use for any changes with the potential to erode their own authority.

Many warned me it would take years to accomplish our goals, but I was determined to bring matters to closure in the current legislative session. Delay would likely mean defeat, so we had to capitalize on present momentum. The legislative session had six more months to run when we began translating the commission's recommendations into draft legislation. Vital to the process were Sanford Levine, university counsel, and Herb Gordon, head of state relations. As usual, they saw things differently from one another. Levine wanted to work primarily through the governor, while Gordon preferred the legislative route. But they worked together without too much friction to complete a working draft.

No sooner had SUNY's trustees endorsed our proposed bill at their February 1985 meeting, however, than Cuomo yanked the rug away.[40] Dismissing the public benefit corporation recommendation, he announced that he would propose his own SUNY flexibility bill, to be based on a two-year study by a special task force on SUNY and CUNY.[41] It was the first time any of us had heard about such a group. (Herb Gordon guessed that Cuomo hadn't at first believed our bill would have a chance in the legislature, and now he was belatedly working to preempt our efforts.) The governor's alternative plan reproduced some but not all the commission's recommendations. Within limits, it would allow the university trustees to transfer funds between campuses, determine salaries and benefits for presidents and top administrators, and enjoy greater latitude in appointing and assigning employees. It exempted endowment and outside financial support (e.g., fund drives) from state appropriations oversight and preaudit. It also allowed campus managers to purchase supplies, equipment, and consulting and print services on a multiyear basis, subject to no review other than the state comptroller. But the governor did not eliminate preaudits and (as noted) made no mention of the public benefit corporation proposal.[42]

Now we had two plans, partly overlapping and partly divergent. Sanford Levine argued in favor of accepting the governor's plan, while Herb Gordon pointed out that if we backed off after our extended work with the legislature, we would lose all credibility with the state senate and assembly. I appreciated the political pragmatism of Levine's position, but my own view was the same as Gordon's. Sanford, ever the loyal team player, agreed to the legislative approach.

For the next three months my legal, finance, and state relations team negotiated furiously with lawmakers and their staffs, doing their best to line up the votes we would need not only to pass our bill but also to discourage the governor from vetoing it. In mid-March, meanwhile, to maintain public pressure I held a press conference backed by all four former SUNY chancellors still alive—Alvin C. Eurich (1949–51), William S. Carlson (1952–58), Samuel B. Gould (1964–70), and Ernest L. Boyer (1970–77). Their collective support underscored the critical importance of our draft legislation to the future of both the university and New York State.

The main stumbling block was the public benefit corporation idea, and all of us were convinced SUNY needed the greater autonomy it promised. Why not, we then wondered, draft a bill that provided essentially the same powers and protections, without actually *calling* it a public benefit corporation? Dick Rohstedt, associate general counsel, and Bill Anslow, vice chancellor for finance and budget, worked alongside Herb Gordon during several weeks of fevered effort to craft a bill that would be acceptable to the governor without raising the hackles of legislators who had already lined up behind the original plan.

It seemed to work. On June 29, 1985, the legislature passed our second bill virtually intact, with a governor's signing ceremony a month later. However, one last-minute disappointment concerned the deficient salaries paid to campus presidents. Although both the senate and the assembly approved giving the SUNY trustees authority to determine presidents' salaries, CICU introduced a companion bill in the senate to give the same authority to the New York Board of Regents. The assembly was unwilling to agree, so both the SUNY and CICU

On March 20, 1985, the five living SUNY chancellors, the SUNY Board chair, and the vice chair gathered as a public demonstration of unity, testifying that the passage of the proposed flexibility legislation was critical to the university system's future. (*Left to right*) Donald M. Blinken, chair, SUNY Board (1978 to present); Samuel B. Gould (1964–70); William S. Carlson (1952–58); Clifton Wharton (1989 to present); Alvin C. Eurich (1949–51); Ernest L. Boyer (1970–77); and Judith Davidson Moyers, vice chair, SUNY Board (1983 to present).

provisions failed to pass. Nevertheless, the SUNY flexibility proposal became law under the New York Code, to enthusiastic applause from throughout SUNY and around the state.

We had gained important ground—significantly more managerial flexibility for the university—and we had done it in less than six months. Carrying out the legislation required careful planning. Jerry Komisar, newly appointed as executive vice chancellor, held meetings of special committees on SUNY campuses to develop detailed recommendations on the administrative and budgeting details, which then became the basis of proposals to the SUNY board.

The new system was approved by the board on March 27, 1986.[43] Now campus presidents could set salaries for professional staff when making appointments. The chain of authority for making purchases of different sizes was simplified, circumscribing where competitive bidding was required. Campuses could contract for goods and services up to $2,500 without central administration approval; the state attorney general approval would only occur for transactions above $20,000. The chancellor now had authority to designate central administration staff

SUNY Independent Commission Legislation was signed by Governor Mario Cuomo on July 28, 1985. (*Left to right, standing front, 3rd*) Chancellor Wharton; (*4th*) Assembly Higher Education Committee Chair Mark Siegel; (*5th*) Senate Higher Education Committee chair Kenneth LaValle; (*6th*) Ralph Davidson, cochair of the Commission. In the background behind my left shoulder is SUNY Chairman Blinken. (Cochair Harold Enarson, president emeritus of the Ohio State University, was unable to attend.)

and campus officers who could execute specific types of contracts. Perhaps the most important changes empowered SUNY trustees to transfer funds among SUNY units and to shift to campuses the authority to reallocate financial resources to areas of local need. The official changes were the final step in giving SUNY its freedom by providing greater flexibility in its operations to meet the educational needs of its constituents and the state of New York.

The new flexibility legislation energized me to refresh leadership at SUNY Plaza.[44] Executive Vice Chancellor O'Dowd was resigning to become chancellor of University of Alaska in October, and Jerry Komisar was selected as his replacement.[45] I persuaded Joe Burke, president of SUNY Plattsburgh, to become provost. Sherry H. Penney, vice chancellor for academic programs, policy, and planning, moved temporarily to serve as acting president at Plattsburgh.[46] Alden N. Haffner, vice chancellor for research, graduate studies, and professional programs, moved to Penney's slot as acting vice chancellor.[47] Frank G. Pogue, vice president for student affairs at SUNY–Albany, became acting vice chancellor for student services and special programs, pending a search for a permanent person. Thomas Law, a temporary deputy chancellor for community colleges, was named associate vice chancellor for contracts and purchasing (coordinating efforts to improve use of women and minority owned businesses).

· · · ·

With the flexibility legislation approved, our attention turned to two other areas highlighted in the Independent Commission report: increasing community college funding and strengthening SUNY graduate-research programs.

SUNY's community colleges were distinctive from the other campuses not only in their close community ties but also in their funding—towns and/or counties contributed on average about 33 percent of their operating funds. For example, in 1980–81, the state share was 35 percent and student share 32 percent. But these colleges too had suffered from underfunding, and sometimes from interference by local political figures. The Independent Commission had also called for measures to improve their effectiveness, so in early 1986 I named a special task force to identify major issues and recommend ways to address them. Chaired by Stuart Steiner, president of Genesee Community College, the group focused on better funding, greater independence from local sponsors, easier transfer of student credits to four-year campuses, and better centralization of student and graduate information. The report went to the SUNY system board on December 16, 1986, seeking $5 million in competitive grants to improve teaching on community college campuses.[48]

But the report was problematic for a number of reasons. For one thing, community college faculty and staff were legally employees of their sponsoring towns and/or counties, and to transfer employer status to the college boards would have taken a major push in the legislature. So would the recommendation that county funding be on a "lump sum" basis—most county sponsors would probably have fought bitterly on both counts. As for easing transfer difficulties between the two- and four-year colleges, admissions standards varied significantly among and across institutional types. What credits a given program would or wouldn't accept was generally the purview of local deans and department chairs, regardless of the philosophical preferences of the college presidents—or even the chancellor.

Nevertheless, the report Steiner and his committee put together had several positive if provocative ideas. Unfortunately the report failed to generate the needed momentum for change. As Steiner himself observed in the report, "SUNY cannot address many of the recommendations in this Report without taking a more proactive role in all of the areas addressed." I had always maintained a sympathetic view of the unique role of community colleges within SUNY and New York State. Helping them realize more of their special potential might well have been worth an uphill fight, but it was going to take time and a sustained effort.

· · · ·

Graduate programs had long been undernourished in SUNY, even at the four university centers, where they should have flourished. The question wasn't whether they needed more attention, but when and how to go about providing it. Avoiding or at least mitigating internal conflict was critical. Any significant inflow of new research dollars would automatically sharpen disputes over fiscal priorities and allocations. Compounding the challenge was the serious drain on system resources represented by the SUNY medical schools and teaching hospitals. Particularly on the four-year campuses, medical education was commonly thought of as a fiscal millstone around the university's neck.

The Independent Commission had recommended building the university centers at Buffalo and Stony Brook into comprehensive research institutions, with the centers at Albany and Binghamton to be developed in "selective" academic areas. At a subsequent meeting with the four presidents, I raised the possibility of a new graduate-research initiative that would commit $75 million over five years. It would take a determined effort to overcome the competition from other campuses, to work with the City University as a partner, and to sell the plan to the state. But New York had been underinvesting in the area for years, and a catch-up strategy would be indispensable to success.

Vince O'Leary, president of the university center at Albany, agreed to coordinate plans among the university centers, damping one-upmanship and ensuring that they spoke with a single voice.[49] His political skills were proven, and, based in Albany, he knew many key legislators and committee chairs, often personally as well as professionally. I would take the lead with the SUNY board, the legislature, the Department of Budget, and the press. Along with Herb Gordon, deputy for state relations, O'Leary and I became a mini-subcommittee to move the initiative forward.

Competition among the campuses was a given, of course, and a certain amount of it might even be healthy, but it couldn't be allowed to get out of hand. Moreover, the university center presidents needed to avoid at all costs the tempting label of "flagship" campus. The press would just trot out their old argument that the state couldn't afford four flagships, so which one was it really going to be? Whenever I reminded them that California, for example, had more than four "flagships," the inevitable (and inaccurate) retort was that California didn't have as many great private universities as New York State. Using AAU membership as the criterion for "flagship" status, California had at the time three public campuses (Berkeley, UCLA, and UC–San Diego) and three private ones (Stanford, USC, and Cal Tech). New York had four private colleges on the roster (Columbia, Rochester, NYU, and Syracuse) and one "mixed" (Cornell). Ignoring my refutation, we would then be back facing the spurious old argument that the state's education dollars could be more effectively "leveraged" by funding new programs at private universities rather than at SUNY or CUNY.

Working together, the four presidents crafted a plan to raise the quality (and public profile) of each of the university centers. On October 21 the SUNY board of trustees approved an $84.5 million plan to improve graduate research over five years. The proposal included a $16.9 million increase in their annual base operating budgets in each of the next five years. Over time it worked out to $4.3 million for SUNY Buffalo; $19.5 million for Stony Brook; $13 million for Albany; and $12 million for Binghamton. Substantial new dollars also would go to the SUNY College of Environmental Science and Forestry ($2.9 million); the Health Science Center at Brooklyn ($3.2 million); Upstate Medical Center ($2.4 million); the College of Optometry in Manhattan ($500,000); and other state-operated colleges ($2 million). The amounts were driven by local needs, from capital projects to new faculty positions, new doctoral programs, and more graduate assistantships. As SUNY provost Joe Burke remarked at the time, "We didn't put together a program just for the sake of building up the university and its reputation. . . . [W]e started by asking ourselves what we could do to fulfill the needs of the state."

O'Leary and his colleagues did a fine job developing a balanced and equitable budget. The SUNY board approved it at their October 1986 meeting. In his budget recommendation to the legislature for fiscal 1987–88, Governor Cuomo asked for $10 million for SUNY graduate-research initiatives. It was nearly $7 million less than we had asked, but it looked like a reasonable beginning. However, SUNY's hopes to enhance graduate-research funding would eventually fall victim to the state's own ever-deeper fiscal problems.

The excitement of the legislative victory on greater flexibility masked what proved to be a serious negative action with long-run implications—a change in who was the final decider of SUNY tuition. Assembly speaker Fink was a New York City legislator who remembered the good old days when CUNY was tuition-free. He was highly supportive of both university systems, but he also fiercely believed in low tuition. On one occasion when the SUNY board was considering a tuition increase, Herb Gordon had called me out of the meeting to take a telephone call from Fink. He asked me to prevent the board from acting on the recommended tuition hike. I explained that the trustees were staunchly convinced of their fiduciary duty to meet the needs of the system. Fink's frustration finally led him in July 1985 to amend the State of New York Education Law, which stated: "The trustees shall not adopt changes affecting tuition charges prior to the enactment of the annual budget." The amendment, one month after our flexibility triumph, formally established the legislature's stronger role and effectively ended the SUNY and CUNY "tuition dance" with the governor and key legislators.

But this action also had unintended consequences that proved disastrous for the university and the students over the next two decades, creating dramatic swings from feast to famine. Under the old system there had been three tuition increases during my first six years, averaging 11 percent a year. After Fink's amendment a new pattern began in which tuition would remain constant for several years, then spike upward dramatically. Tuition remained unchanged from 1984–85 until 1990–91, followed by three years of increases aggregating $1,300—a 96 percent jump. Two years later, there was a $750 hike, then a seven-year drought to 2003–4, when the SUNY trustees proposed the largest dollar increase in SUNY's history—$1,400, or 41 percent.

This had an especially adverse effect on the enrollment of students from low- and middle-income families.[50] Uncertainty over when tuition would rise dramatically adversely affected enrollment. Sudden dramatic higher tuition and costs meant larger loans. Spikes in the middle of a student's study program led to unplanned higher debt burdens for borrowing students—a powerful disincentive to continued attendance. Instead of a state policy promoting investment in the human capital critical for the development of New York, the state was short-changing the very generation that could drive future economic growth.

The final irony was that Fink's amendment was added to our vaunted flexibility legislative package of 1985.[11] We got the legislation, largely due to the legislature's support, but at the same time the SUNY board's authority and flexibility in setting tuition was undermined. So much for tuition and politics—the students who had objected to modest periodic tuition increases were now subjected to course-offering disruptions, more and higher fees, and a more unpredictable setting for planning their college attendance. This outcome confirmed Al Ballard's wonderfully apt dictum about legislation: "The large print giveth while the small print taketh away."

CHAPTER ELEVEN

The Chair and CEO of TIAA-CREF: Promoting a Future Agenda

Both Dolores and I found our life in Albany extremely comfortable and rewarding. The situation overall was captured by a profile on Dolores and me in the *Albany Times Union*, "Clifton Wharton: Life at the Top, Reaping the Rewards of Pride and Prodigy."[1] The author's 2,300-word essay sounded the theme that we were part of a little-known story of "the generations of [Black] achievers for whom education was the key to success and aspiration was the hand that turned the key."

Then suddenly, an unexpected telephone call threw me once again into a quandary. The Teachers Insurance and Annuity Association and College Retirement Equities Fund—usually called TIAA-CREF—was the dominant provider of pensions and annuities to U.S. higher education. Would I be interested, the caller asked, in being considered for the chairmanship and chief executive officer position of the organization?

I was familiar enough with TIAA-CREF—I had been a client (or "participant," as the company preferred) since 1957. A substantial part of my retirement savings was invested there, as were those of many people I knew in higher education. But outside the fold, it was a different story. TIAA-*What*? was the most common reaction when you mentioned the firm—even though as the nonprofit pension carrier for higher education employees nationwide, it was in fact one of the largest institutional investors in the world. Founded in 1918 by Andrew Carnegie, its original purpose had been to encourage professional mobility and retirement security for college teachers. During nearly all the intervening decades it had mostly stuck with the original mission, as both its clientele and its assets increased steadily. By the late 1980s TIAA-CREF managed pension plans covering around a million people, working at 3,700 colleges and universities across the United States. It also served education associations, research organizations, some private (but not public) it is schools, and a variety of other nonprofit employers. With more than $50 billion under management, it was one of the richest firms you had never heard of.[2]

It was Andrew Brimmer who first called me about TIAA-CREF. When Brimmer, a former governor of the Federal Reserve, was working on his doctoral dissertation at Harvard in the mid-1950s writing about TIAA-CREF, chairman William Greenough invited him to work at the headquarters, provided work space, opened archives, and introduced him to operating and investment officers, who in turn described the firm's inner workings. Brimmer, who also served with me on the Equitable Life board, explained that Jim MacDonald, the company's current CEO, had decided to retire, and a search was under way to replace him. Cochaired by trustees David Alexander, president of Pomona College, and John Biggs, chairman, president, and CEO of Centerre Trust Company in St. Louis, the committee had hired Russell Reynolds, but the search firm's eventual roster of candidates generated less than full enthusiasm—in part because no minorities had made the list. Brimmer said that when he raised my name with the board there was considerable interest, particularly among those trustees who came from higher education. Another academic trustee was Harry Spindler, SUNY's vice chancellor for finance. Coincidentally, a couple of years previously Jim MacDonald had approached me about joining the TIAA-CREF board. I had declined and recommended as a substitute Harry Spindler, who accepted.

Prominent Blacks routinely work to help fellow Blacks reach leadership positions—as Vernon Jordan and Andrew Brimmer did for me. Dolores and I also tried to "pass it forward" for others. In 1980 Dolores played a similar role for Brimmer himself, strongly supporting his appointment to the Gannett board. Though rarely mentioned in the press, such efforts have been key in building a deeper reservoir of Black talent at the middle and high echelons of the corporate world. This practice is the same as that in the white-dominated world.

As always, Dolores and I discussed the job's likely pros and cons. After nine years as chancellor, the longest serving in SUNY's history, I was a fixture in the state. I had marvelously supportive, hardworking trustees. The board was committed to my vision of SUNY as a system. Almost invariably they could be counted upon to meet their fiduciary responsibility to serve the best interests of the university. No academic leader could have asked for a better board. They had made serving as SUNY's chancellor a pleasure. My professional relationships throughout the system's sixty-four campuses were also quite satisfying—with presidents, administrators, campus councils, and alumni. I was even getting along fairly well with the state political leadership and the bureaucracy. I had developed sound relationships with both Democrats and Republicans in the state legislature. My relationship with Governor Cuomo, though distant at times, was workable, as were my interactions with the executive branch bureaucracy. In the aftermath of the recent flexibility legislation, the SUNY campuses were far better able to capitalize on their resources and competencies. And with a broad initiative imminent in graduate education, the university system was poised for a reenergized climb up the ladder of academic excellence.

Yet as experience had taught, in every job some business is always unfinished, and there is never an ideal time to move on. If I chose to, I would be far more comfortable leaving SUNY now, in a position of strength, than I would have been a few years before. Our two sons were "out of the nest"—Bruce was in Detroit, managing the Summit restaurant at the Renaissance Center, and Clifton was a reference librarian at the Enoch Pratt Free Library in Baltimore, about to start his master's in library science at the University of Maryland. Dolores's corporate directorships were independent of where she lived. Although her FCI internship program would have to find a new local sponsor, the new Young Executive Program could be run from New York as easily as from Albany. Dolores admitted she would miss her "Tower" home on the Hudson, but there were other "Manhattan Towers" that beckoned, with the fast pace and cultural whirl of New York City.

For myself, I had so far worked mostly in foundations and public higher education administration, with government commissions, education associations, and corporate boards on the side. I had enjoyed a good deal of personal freedom, intellectual stimulation, and a sense of contributing to the public good. Throughout, I had the satisfaction of helping to build human capital, a touchstone of my personal values.

At TIAA-CREF my imperatives would be almost wholly corporate, and the bottom line would be paramount, no matter how you looked at it. But the corporate world was one where I was hardly a stranger. Over nearly twenty years I had been a director of five Fortune 500 companies and three semigovernmental organizations—nearly always as the first Black. I had seen how businesses rose and fell, from auto manufacturing to publishing, department stores to computers to banking. I had met power brokers, selected (and fired) CEOs, and developed a sense of what made for successful corporate leadership. I had had an intimate education in management styles, mergers, lawsuits, compensation issues, and executive hiring and firing. More than once, not surprisingly, my corporate experiences had kindled thoughts of trying my wings outside academia, and there had even been a couple of near-misses. At Equitable Life, fellow director Herb Longenecker, president of Tulane University, had once suggested to CEO Coy Eklund that I become chairman of the board, a position with primary responsibility for federal and regulatory affairs. (John Carter, Eklund's successor, didn't like the idea and let it drop.) In the early 1980s Phil Caldwell, CEO of Ford Motor Company, toyed with my joining the company as senior vice president for public affairs, personnel, and Washington relations. In that case I was the one who demurred—given the balance of power at Ford, I would have taken the position only if it came with the vice-chairmanship of the board, something Caldwell hadn't felt able to offer.[3]

The TIAA-CREF opportunity warranted serious thought. For one thing, a small but highly vocal group of critics had begun attacking the company as inflexible and paternalistic; it would be an enticing challenge to help restructure and modernize its business and investment practices. For another, the compensation package was extremely attractive—a base salary of $425,000, plus an annual performance bonus. Compensation had never before been a deciding factor in whether I took a job, but after nine years at SUNY the prospect of actually being well paid wasn't to be brushed aside. Even though SUNY was the largest university system in the country, its executive compensation was among the lowest. In 1986 my annual salary was $89,000, compared with the average of $115,000 for state university system presidents and chancellors. In systems similar in size and scope to SUNY, the average was $163,000.

Most important of all, I was deeply impressed by TIAA-CREF's current and past trustees, many of them longtime colleagues and friends. Several were economics "celebrities"—Paul Samuelson, Ken Boulding, and Jim Tobin, and my former Chicago professors Milton Friedman and Allen Wallis. My two predecessors at SUNY, Sam Gould and Ernie Boyer, had been on the board, as well as Vivian Henderson, Luther Foster, Polly Bunting-Smith, Juanita Kreps, Jill Ker Conway, and other education luminaries. There were also a host of my regular comrades in arms: Father Ted Hesburgh, Bill Friday, Clifford Hardin, Herman Wells, Bob Roosa, and Jim Perkins. Taken together they were a virtual who's who of my professional world.[4]

Was TIAA-CREF the sort of challenge I wanted to take on? It would certainly be intellectually novel—though from my thirteen years at Equitable Life I knew a good bit about insurance and the financial services. At MSU and SUNY I had learned to manage large-scale operations. Did I have reservations about my ability to move successfully from a major public university to a major private corporation? Not really—and the compensation was *very* attractive.

Was this challenge one that I wanted to take on? Perhaps, though it meant that Dolores and I would face another wholesale change in our lives. Was it interesting and challenging enough? Definitely. Did I have any reservations about my ability to do it? The answer to that was a definite no.

I called Andrew Brimmer thanking him for his confidence and told him that I would be happy to be considered.

· · · ·

TIAA-CREF was actually two companies, more or less fused at the hip. TIAA was the Teachers Insurance and Annuity Association, an insurance company; CREF was the College Retirement Equities Fund, a registered investment company. Together, TIAA-CREF provided "defined-contribution" rather than "defined-benefit" pensions—that is, income varied based on individual contributions and investment performance over time, rather than on some formula based on years of service and final salary. The company charter defined its "market" principally as higher education and research, and its "product" was overwhelmingly retirement and supplemental tax-deferred annuities—though in its rather insular culture such commercial terms were uncommonly heard. The company also enjoyed a double tax advantage—customer contributions were made on a pretax basis, while as a "charitable" organization the company itself was exempt from federal and state income taxes.

Although few of its participants realized it, TIAA had been, in its low-profile way, a consistent innovator in retirement investing. From its earliest days, many decades before IRAs and 401(k) plans became available to the working public at large, it had offered individually owned accounts that were fully portable—that is, they could be taken, without loss or interruption, from one eligible employer to any other. I was a typical example: my policy began with ADC and then went with me to MSU, to SUNY, and later to TIAA-CREF. I had owned and carried the policy for thirty years.

For much of its history the company's sole investment choice had been a fixed-income account based on bond and real estate holdings. In 1952, however, TIAA CEO Bill Greenough created and introduced CREF, the pioneering concept of a "variable" annuity, based on a broadly diversified portfolio of U.S. common stocks as a second vehicle for retirement investing. Simply put, a variable annuity is rather like a mutual fund account, though with important differences—such as the ability to compute income payments on the collective lifespan of a group rather than a single individual. The underlying rationale came from research showing that over extended periods returns on a broad portfolio of common stocks exceeded all other types of investment. Interestingly, most of the numerical analysis on the topic was done by TIAA associate actuary Robert J. Randall, the first Black to become a fellow of the Society of Actuaries and the first Black to become an officer of a major U.S. insurance company. Finally, although TIAA-CREF was legally a "stock" company (with all shares "owned" by a seven-member board of overseers), its nonprofit status enabled it to function more like a mutual company. Operating and investment expenses were extremely low, and instead of distributing a portion of revenues as profits to shareholders, virtually all gains were passed on to participants themselves.

At the time TIAA-CREF was the dominant pension carrier for much of higher education's private sector. At public colleges and universities, it was more commonly offered as an optional plan, in addition to state employee and/or teacher retirement systems. But in part because of its quasi-monopoly status in higher education, TIAA-CREF had in some ways failed to keep up with its customers' evolving expectations. Unlike investment companies such as Fidelity and Vanguard, where available fund choices could run into the hundreds, TIAA-CREF still offered just the fixed account through TIAA and the stock account through CREF—there was not even a money market fund. Participants had little access to their own accounts. They could not withdraw funds at all except as an annuity. At retirement a participant converted from an "accumulating" to a "pay-out" annuity account. (In 1972 a "retirement transition benefit" was introduced allowing up to 10 percent withdrawal of accumulation funds.) Transfers were allowed, but only from CREF to TIAA—not the other way, and only once every six months. Transfers or moving to other retirement carriers were entirely disallowed.

A pension was the only way you received any payment from your accumulations. The final straw was that a participant's individual premiums and benefits were reported to them once a year. What difference did it make? The company seemed to wonder. The participants couldn't get their money out anyway.

In the face of growing customer disgruntlement, TIAA-CREF had been slow to change. When it did acknowledge the restrictiveness of its policies, it justified them as in its participants' best interests. Retirement investing, TIAA-CREF officials pointed out, wasn't like investing discretionary funds—the consequences of bad choices were much graver. Moreover, most of its clients were college teachers, administrators, and support staff, not professional or even experienced investors. With increased options would come the questionable tactics of inexperienced investors: chasing returns, attempting to time the market, and both over- and underdiversifying of portfolios. In addition, the company argued, restricting participants' access to their accounts brought higher returns through longer-term investing, while limiting options made it possible to keep expenses lower than at competing financial service firms. Clearly there were valid arguments on both sides, and healing the rift would call for a broad range of management skills—diplomacy, communication, and vision.

• • • •

A few days after the Brimmer conversation I got a call from the Russell Reynolds firm, and we set a date for me to meet with the TIAA-CREF search committee on August 25. In an unusual move, the current CEO, Jim MacDonald, was acting as secretary to the committee. It developed that MacDonald was taking early retirement for an unexpected reason. Although in the corporate world incumbent CEOs often recommend their successors, MacDonald was convinced that an "inside" candidate would be unlikely to champion the changes needed to modernize the organization and to satisfy its critics. The inside heir apparent was Walt Ehlers, the president, who had come up through the investment side of the firm. But most board members felt that Ehlers wasn't right for the job. Jim Martin, head of CREF investments, was well respected but not seen as a true manager of the kind now needed. The only other inside possibility was John McCormack, who headed the institutional sales area. But though bright and able, he was thought too young and lacking adequate management experience.

McDonald's views, though unconventional, were selfless and farsighted, and he played a pivotal part in the search process. The TIAA-CREF trustees drawn from higher education seemed to like my record at Michigan State and SUNY, while those from business and finance were reassured by my experience as a corporate director. And it certainly couldn't have hurt that SUNY was the pension firm's largest institutional customer, with MSU not very far behind.

At around two-thirty in the afternoon on September 27, 1986, David Alexander, John Biggs, and Jim MacDonald formally invited me to become chairman and CEO of TIAA-CREF.

The appointment was prematurely leaked to the *New York Times*,[5] apparently by trustee Donna Shalala, then president of Hunter College. The story actually came out before the board's final approval of the hiring, much less a press conference or release. Perhaps because of the reporter's haste to make a deadline, the news was treated like any other prominent corporate personnel change, without mentioning that I had just become the first Black to be named head of a Fortune 500 service company. When I called Max Frankel, the *Times* executive editor, to chide him for missing the symbolic import of the moment, he gave me an explanation both disconcerting and refreshing. "You're well known here at the newspaper, Clif," he said, "and I must confess that we don't think of you as primarily a Negro. We know you are, of course, but it's a secondary or tertiary thing. The reporter should have picked up on the significance of the event, and I'll see what we can do to correct it." Frankel was true to his word, and the correction came in the final sentence of a second *Times* story: "Today, Dr. Wharton is the first black chairman of the Rockefeller Foundation and, with his latest appointment, he becomes the first black chief executive officer of a Fortune 500 service company." TIAA did not become a member of the regular 500 until 1995, based solely on its insurance assets. Nowadays everyone appropriately sees TIAA on the Fortune 500 list.

▪ Leaving SUNY

Our imminent departure from SUNY brought the usual spate of kudos from friends, colleagues, and the press.

The accomplishments most frequently mentioned were winning management flexibility during difficult financial times, strengthening the university's research capability, and "changing the image of the university by . . . bringing greater cohesion to the system." At the press conference when my move was announced, Chairman Blinken stated that my most enduring achievement was the Independent Commission and the flexibility legislation. "Without his unique vision, there would have been no Independent Commission on the Future of the State University and the commission's alarming finding that (the university) was 'the most over-regulated university in the nation' would never have come to light."[6]

President Vince O'Leary of SUNY–Albany said that I would be a great fit for TIAA-CREF with my dual background in economics and academe,[7] adding that I had brought the state university through the crises of the 1970s unscarred. For example, between 1975 and 1976, the SUNY system lost 3,600 staff positions, 12 percent of its workforce, but the system's quality improved. Jerry Komisar, who would take over as acting chancellor upon my departure, pointed out that during my tenure the sponsored research received by the university had more than doubled.

Irv Freedman, vice chancellor for capital facilities, said I had helped make the university more visible throughout the state, and made New Yorkers more aware that SUNY was a system of distinction.[8] An editorial in the *Albany Times Union* reviewed my accomplishments and concluded that "all this made Mr. Wharton one of the most revered men in New York education."[9] Not overly original, but admittedly still nice to hear.

Dolores was similarly hailed. An article, "SUNY's First Lady Looks Back,"[10] reviewed her major activities during our tenure, ranging from her involvements in the greater Albany community and her extensive service on major corporate boards to her creation of the Fund for Corporate Initiatives.

Albany Mayor Tom Whalen hosted a reception where he presented us with a large framed photograph of the State University Plaza buildings, viewed from the eastern side of the Hudson River, taken by Kodak for their exhibition in NYC Grand Central Station. The photograph plaque was signed by all the Albany City Council members, thanking us for our pioneering in establishing a residence in downtown Albany. I thought this was a fitting coda—being praised as we left over our highly successful South Tower chancellor housing, obliterating the inaccurate negative criticism over our housing when we first arrived.

Another event at the Albany Hilton was attended by more than nine hundred persons.[11] Chairman Don Blinken commended me for my "directness, intellectual honesty and a willingness to communicate forthrightly and honestly."[12] Vice Chair Judith Moyers noted Dolores's role in both university and community affairs, praising her creation of the Fund for Corporate Initiatives. There was a surprise announcement by Blinken that the trustees had approved naming the building of the SUNY Nelson A. Rockefeller Institute of Government at 411 State Street as the "Clifton and Dolores Wharton Research Center."[13]

All this was balm for bittersweet feelings about our departure.

· TIAA-CREF Launch

My new job created some stir in the business community. Not surprisingly, a salvo came from an Equitable Life officer, where I had previously been a director. The Life Insurance Council of New York (LICONY) was hosting its annual black-tie dinner at the Plaza Hotel, February 4, 1987. At the reception, my first, I went up to greet John Carter, Equitable's new president and CEO. His first shot at me was, "Clif, I hope you can wake up that dinosaur!" My polite response, "Oh, I think we'll give it a good shot," belied my inner resentment at his offensive attempt to disparage the company I now headed. Even more contemptible, Carter's tone implied that he didn't think I was up to turning around a company in crisis, besieged by mutual funds and other insurance companies, Equitable included. All were salivating at the prospects of making inroads into TIAA's large higher education pension market.[14] "Well, Mr. Carter," I thought, "not if I can help it." Carter's sneering jibe was galling since he had been the key person blocking my candidacy to be chairman of Equitable in 1982. Years later, Darwin Davis, a senior Black officer in Equitable, confided that Carter feared me because of my strong participation on the board. Dar divulged that "Carter thought you were smarter and stronger than he was and would upstage him as chairman."

One of my fellow directors at Ford Motor, a liberal southerner, confided that many of his associates assumed I lacked real experience and that my hiring was a publicity-seeking affirmative-action stunt. I couldn't help wondering why the experience of managing two major universities was somehow irrelevant. It also struck me as odd that similar criticism wasn't typically heard when white university presidents took on corporate roles—such as Clarke Wescoe, the former University of Kansas chancellor who became CEO of Sterling Drug, or Franklin D. Murphy, chancellor of the University of California at Los Angeles, who became chairman and CEO of the Times Mirror Company. But over the years I had become well accustomed to racial stereotyping.

Within TIAA-CREF, oddly enough, no one mentioned (at least to me) any awareness that I had become the first (and thus far sole) Black CEO among the nation's largest and most influential firms. But as I took my first tour of the company's offices, I noticed that a Black employee had prominently displayed on her bulletin board a clipping about me from *Ebony* magazine—and when I greeted Hispanic staff in Spanish, they invariably beamed. Though it was probably my imagination, I had an impression that many minority employees seemed to hold their heads a little higher and step a little more briskly when I passed by.

A crowning moment of satisfaction came at the November board meeting, after I had been elected, but before I had formally taken the reins, when I learned from the minutes of the TIAA mortgage committee that it had made a large loan to the venerable Willard Hotel. It was the same Washington, D.C., hotel where, as a young Black graduate student at the School of Advanced International Studies, I had been virtually thrown out while waiting for two friends who were guests there. In August 1986 the Willard was reopening after a $90 million makeover. The funds underwriting the restoration of its faded splendor had come from TIAA-CREF, which was—delicious!—about to have as its next chairman and CEO the same Black male who had had the effrontery to invade the exclusive white hotel's lobby nearly forty years before! The incident was a dramatic personal example of Black progress over time.

• • • •

My first official act as chair and CEO was to meet with the company's top officers. In addition to the president, Walt Ehlers, there were six executive vice presidents: James S. Martin, CREF Investments; J. Daniel Lee, TIAA Investments; John J. McCormack, College Services; Francis P. Gunning, general counsel; Russell E. Bone, Administration; and John A. Putney, Office and Information Systems. I asked their views on the challenges the company faced from outside, as well as on problems they faced internally. Serious deficiencies weren't hard to spot. Although several executives acknowledged the validity of external complaints, they rarely had specific suggestions for change. Also surprising was the general failure to recognize what I considered the company's internal insularity. The corporate structure was more suitable for the 1940s of 1950s, a bundle of administrative "silos" where decisions and actions too often took place in a vacuum. On the other hand, almost everyone seemed to be aware that TIAA-CREF's computer infrastructure was hopelessly antiquated. For two years the company had been struggling to develop a system for valuing individual customer holdings on a daily basis, a precondition for adding a money market account to its roster of only two investment vehicles. The effort required a total reconfiguration of central computing, and no one seemed to have any idea when it might be finished.

But probably the most surprising thing was what I *didn't* find—any real sense of the crisis the company was facing, or any urgency about addressing it. In fact there was if anything a feeling of near-serenity about the place. Wasn't TIAA-CREF the premier pension plan carrier for higher education in the United States? Why *wouldn't* it be able to go on doing business as it always had? Surely the disturbances were temporary, soon to fade away. Meanwhile, whenever I asked why something was done in a particular way, the answer was almost always the same: "It's how we've always done it." It reminded me of John Kenneth Galbraith's well-known maxim: "In any great organization it is far, far safer to be wrong with the majority than right alone."[15]

On the plus side, the two major investment arms, CREF Investments (equities) and TIAA Investments (fixed-income) were in excellent shape and well managed (though both Jim Martin and Dan Lee grumbled that company compensation levels were below industry standard, making it hard to attract and retain top talent). Indeed, the entire group of senior officers struck me as professionally quite competent and notable in their commitment to the company and its participants. One thing I didn't like, however, was the obvious cultural "separatism" among the CREF staff. Personnel assigned to CREF saw themselves as a group apart even though all its employees were technically TIAA. They might as well have gone around in T-shirts emblazoned "Elite Equity Investment Managers." (Among other things, they were the only TIAA-CREF employees, save the CEO and president, who were eligible for performance bonuses.) Even their business cards identified them as representatives of CREF, not *TIAA*-CREF. I could appreciate the team spirit, if that was what it was, but I knew that it was bad for the company as a whole and would eventually have to be dealt with.

A troubling discovery was that for the most part senior officers met with one another only to make recommendations at the annual meeting on TIAA dividends. Even then the president chaired the meeting, while the chairman/CEO sat in but didn't conduct the meeting. (When I asked why, I was told that the group was "advisory" to the CEO, so there was no need for him to chair the meeting.) What other opportunities did officers use to collaborate with one another on the broader issues faced by the company? Well, they said, we have lunch together sometimes. Since all the executive offices at the time were grouped on the same floor, they spoke to each other casually. But it was astonishing that there were no regular, formal sessions for systematic, collective discussion of corporate-wide planning and policymaking.

To remedy the peculiar situation I set up a three-tier internal management structure. At the top was my "Executive Cabinet," composed of all executive vice presidents and my executive staff; it met every Monday morning. Next was an "Executive Council," which included both the cabinet members and the next tier of officers—initially about sixty-five individuals—who would meet once a month. A final group, including both the cabinet, the executive group, and all corporate officers, numbered around seven hundred. This "Officers Group" met on a quarterly basis.

Some of the Executive Cabinet members were dubious about what we would deal with—especially once a week. But once under way it didn't take long for the team to begin to get the point. The cabinet was, in fact, my principal leadership fulcrum. In an organization of any substantial scale, no leader can be intimately involved in each and every major operation—it is impossible for the leader, counterproductive for best results, and demoralizing to everyone concerned. The Executive Cabinet served as a forum for prioritizing, delegating, and monitoring, allowing me to hand off responsibility without losing touch with the progress of key issues.

Because the second-level Executive Council was a manageable size and met only monthly, it soon became my vehicle for ensuring prompt, clear communication throughout the company. The meeting format was usually a series of presentations by council members (and sometimes their staff), focusing on developments of general interest, particularly recent or pending actions before the boards of trustees. TIAA and CREF each had its own twenty-member board of trustees.

The goal of the Officer Group was to increase cross-contact throughout the organization, which had previously been startlingly weak. It wasn't unusual to find that individuals with twenty years' service in one area had never actually interacted with those in the next division over—worse, they sometimes didn't even know what each other actually did. In addition to scheduling a series of programs in which divisional representatives explained their functions to the larger group, I also made time on each agenda for question-and-answer sessions. That might not work too well, some old hands advised. When one of my predecessors had tried it, he had been so upset by some pointed questions that he had abandoned the practice immediately, leaving most officers gun-shy about the whole idea. We got round their nervousness by having questions submitted ahead of the meeting in writing, signature optional.

All three groups served an ongoing effort to broaden company-wide understanding of the changing imperatives TIAA-CREF was facing, both in the marketplace and in the regulatory arena. It also gave officers a chance to air their concerns directly, but without stepping outside established channels of authority. I hoped that with a better understanding of the steps being taken by management and the board, there would be greater buy-in and cooperation throughout the hierarchy. If people understood how the work immediately before them fit into the bigger picture, they were more likely to identify with their jobs and thrive in their assignments rather than just going through the motions.

* * * *

At the time of my arrival TIAA-CREF was housed in three Midtown buildings, 730 and 750 Third Avenue, plus 485 Lexington—the 750 and 485 buildings sat back to back in a single block. Early on I took two days to walk through the complex, floor by floor. This was again my "shipboard tour." Like the apocryphal Chinese proverb: "Footsteps of owner on shop floor equals one hundred supervisors." The main reason for the tour was to get an idea of the physical layout in which employees worked. It also enabled me to see, be seen, and say hello to as many of the company's 2,850 employees as practicable. My prior research had revealed the startling fact that the company's annual turnover rate was around 26 percent—on average, like changing the whole workforce every four years! The turnover was most acute among lower-level employees responsible for much of the back-office or "grunt" work, and replacing, training, and integrating a quarter of its employees every year had become a substantial if somewhat hidden cost of doing business.

Walking around floor by floor, you could begin to guess why. In several areas the density of occupation was astonishing, while in others the floors, walls, and furnishings hadn't been renovated since the building's initial occupation. Years before the company had been small enough to need only the lower six floors of one building. But as it had grown the workforce had increased and moved higher and higher, spilling from the 730 building into the other two. In the process, little thought had apparently gone into colocating units that worked closely with one another, much less into the importance of a pleasant working environment. Colors were dark, carpets were stained and fraying, boxes of supplies and sundry blocked walkways and even stairwells. Open space was at a premium—and with smoking still permitted in the workplace, so was fresh air. From the standpoint of employee psychology, things could hardly have been worse.

After finishing the two-day tour, I asked for board approval to refurbish the three buildings over two years, promising to do it without significantly increasing the regular capital budget. In addition to reducing density and colocating related units, I wanted the TIAA-CREF workplace to be a place where workers would enjoy their environment and not dread spending time there. A more attractive setting would boost morale, and that in turn would translate into friendlier and more satisfactory service for our customers. By the time the two-year project was complete, employee turnover had dropped to less than 5 percent per year, although obviously there were other factors besides the remodeling. At the same time, I created a new boardroom on the twenty-seventh floor and moved the office of the chairman and CEO to the twenty-sixth floor, including offices for the president and chief operating officer, the secretary to the board, and the executive vice president for external affairs. My immediate office staff of five was led by Ms. Nancy Cutrone and included Kathryn Sartori in the new position of corporate travel and special functions.

. . . .

Both Dolores and I were thrilled to be back in New York City. Marian Heiskell, a fellow director at Ford Motor, suggested we look for an apartment at 870 United Nations Plaza, at First Avenue and Forty-Ninth Street, where she and her husband Andrew, former head of Time, Inc., also lived. Coincidentally, I had considered buying into the building in 1965, when we were just back from Southeast Asia, but the asking prices were too steep for our budget. Designed by the architects Harrison and Abramovitz, the cooperative apartment building visually complemented the nearby U.N. and had become something of a "prestige" residence, with occupants ranging from author Truman Capote and politician Bobby Kennedy to media mogul S. I. Newhouse and builder Sheldon Solow. As we looked at available units, I couldn't help asking the realtor what the current price was for the apartment I had passed up in 1965. Some economist! The apartment I could once have had for $42,000 was now worth $700,000. We sighed, signed, and settled into 21B.

Dolores and I also wanted a second home to get away from the cacophony of New York. We looked at several places north of the city and even in Connecticut without finding exactly what we wanted. Help came from our friend Norman Rice, director of the Albany Institute, who was acting as one of the executors for the estate of the late Don Curran. Dolores had served with Curran on the Albany Law School Board and the Albany Institute Board. He also had been a successful trust officer at Merrill Lynch and had built his "dream home" on twenty-two acres of hillside overlooking Otsego Lake, just outside Cooperstown in upstate New York. Dolores and I had actually visited the home when we still lived in Albany, but considered it far too large. Now we were looking for a property that would, among other things, accommodate our burgeoning archive of personal and professional records, and Norm Rice urged us to take a second look at the Curran estate. The semimodern, single-floor ranch-style house had been cut into the shale hillside. It had a huge room designed specifically for Curran's palace-sized Persian rug, with an entire wall of floor-to-ceiling windows opening onto a panoramic eastward vista of Otsego Lake. Except for one north bedroom and bath, every room had a spectacular view. The minute we walked in we knew it was what we wanted—the clincher was that the cavernous finished basement was more than large enough for our large archives.

Owning a second home near Cooperstown, a village with a permanent population of 2,500, was a new experience. Though small, Cooperstown is home to the famous National Baseball Hall of Fame and the Glimmerglass Festival (then Glimmerglass Opera), which draws many thousands of visitors annually. The other main employment base was Bassett Healthcare Network, which covered eight upstate counties. (I would become a member of its board of trustees.) The founding Cooper family and the Clark family (Singer Sewing Machines) dominated the social and economic life of the area.

A few months after we bought the house in 1987, Bruce decided to leave his job with

Westin Hotel, to enroll in a business and human resources degree program at SUNY's College of Technology in Utica. He wanted to store most of his furniture and personal effects at our new home, which by now we had dubbed "DOECLIF." The day before his shipment was due, there was a heavy snowstorm. Our long, steep driveway was plowed during the evening, but in the early morning more snow and ice built up, making it impossible for movers to reach the house. My regular plowing contractor said it would be a couple of hours before he could get back, so I decided to get rock salt to spread on the icy drive. At the local Agway I met a pleasant, slightly grizzled oldster whose name I later learned was Ralph Pink.

"How many bags ya want?" he asked.

Oh, three, I guessed. Pink looked at me quizzically. "Didn't you buy the house up on the hill?" That was us, I confirmed. "Well," said Pink, "you're gonna need six!"

An unexpected surprise about owning property in Cooperstown was the discovery that a Caucasian Wharton ancestor had once owned a large portion of Otsego County. In 1770, Thomas Wharton, a merchant in Philadelphia (and a relative of my John Wharton 3rd), received a huge tract of land by a letter of patent from King George III. Wharton Creek near Edmeston is a remaining vestige. I was bemused that one of my extended family ancestors had operated there at the time of the legendary Cooper and Clark families, but I never mentioned it to them. Somehow it was enough to become a friend of Jane Forbes Clark, Henry Cooper, and Katherine Cooper Cary without becoming pretentious. Why bother seeming to appear lofty about ancient history? We were well accepted in the community on our own merit, joining the boards of Glimmerglass Opera, the New York State Historical Association (Fenimore Art and Farmers' Museums), the Clark Foundation, and the Bassett Healthcare Network. However, there was an occasion when I was tempted to reveal my ancestral ties to the region. One day our son Bruce was visiting Cooperstown, and we all went to a local outdoor event where we encountered Kent and June Barwick from nearby Cherry Valley. As we walked toward the party, Bruce, in typical Deerfield School–style, escorted June with social chitchat. She suddenly stopped and exclaimed, "My goodness . . . you're a preppie . . . you're one of us!" But I resisted the opportunity to recount Wharton history, which might cause shocking disbelief.

Our initial social interactions in the community were limited but would gradually increase to friendship with both locals and summer residents—such as the Ahearnes, Evans, Dusenberys, Tadgells, McCoys, Severuds, Smiths, Paula DiPerna, and our Glimmerglen Road neighbors, plus several Bassett physicians. The local service providers such as Mark Schoellig, Matthew Kane, Rob Mulligan, and Wayne Granger were especially welcoming.

Whether in New York or Cooperstown, Dolores and I saw little change in the level of our outside involvements. Dolores remained immersed in working with her Fund for Corporate Initiatives (FCI), while sitting on the boards of Phillips, Gannett, Kellogg, Asia Society, MIT, and the Museum of Modern Art. I continued to serve on the boards of Ford and Federated Department Stores. I added the New York Stock Exchange, while dropping Time, Inc. and the Federal Reserve Bank of New York, whose rules precluded my staying on after joining TIAA-CREF.

· · · ·

Sustained success combined with market dominance are sometimes the harbingers of corporate failure. I am not sure if I heard that somewhere or thought it up myself, but it certainly applied to TIAA-CREF. The company had dominated the academic retirement landscape for almost seventy years, giving yeoman's service to both institutional customers (i.e., the colleges and universities that offered its plans) and individual participants. Thus it was easy to discount the early rumblings of unhappiness. After all, its customer satisfaction survey results were the envy of its competitors. And in fact the company's alleged restrictiveness and paternalism were things many university presidents and benefits administrators actually endorsed, though not always publicly. "Our literature and philosophy professors don't know the first thing about investing. All we need is for them to start playing the market, lose every cent of their retirement funds, and end up on our front door, crying poverty and looking for us to bail them out!"

In 1978, revisions to the federal Employee Retirement Income Security Act (ERISA) had opened up the college pension business to commercial carriers such as Fidelity, Vanguard, and T. Rowe Price—all companies with long menus of investment choices and many fewer restrictions on fund withdrawals and transfers. Within a few years, TIAA-CREF's position in the market began to come under pressure—though at first the potential competitors were fairly few. In academia itself some gadflies emerged, such as Roy A. Schotland, professor of law at Georgetown, whose purplish sallies drew regular attention in the *Chronicle of Higher Education* and other education media. Schotland even launched an attempt to elect new TIAA-CREF trustees who would promote change. One of his successful candidates was Marcus Alexis, then dean of the College of Business Administration of the University of Illinois at Chicago. Ironically, Alexis soon became one of my staunch supporters.

More substantively, in 1983 the Carnegie Corporation created a special commission on college retirement, chaired by Oscar M. Ruebhausen,[16] to review pension programs in higher education and recommend improvements. The gist of the three Carnegie reports was a proposal to reestablish TIAA-CREF as a "trust" from which beneficiaries could remove their accumulations. But this work by my former Rockefeller Latin American colleague was ignored. At about the same time the National Association of College and University Business Officers created an ad hoc committee on TIAA-CREF, while TIAA-CREF itself set up an ad hoc trustee committee on goals and objectives. Despite its stentorian title, the "Report of the TIAA-CREF Ad Hoc Committee on Goals and Objectives to the Joint Boards of Trustees of TIAA-CREF" satisfied few critics.

Complicating the broader issues of the marketplace was TIAA-CREF's long-overdue push to create a money market fund, which the company had proposed early in 1983 as a safe haven for participants in times of market turbulence. Putting in the money market fund required

CREF to become a registered investment company with the U.S. Securities and Exchange Commission. (Previously CREF had been governed by New York State insurance law.) Given its unique history, when it applied for registration in September 1986 CREF sought certain exemptions from the federal Investment Company Act, most of whose provisions aimed at commercial firms managing largely discretionary investments. The registration process included a public comment period, which predictably enough turned into open season for the company's critics and competitors. Stanford University led the charge, demanding a full-dress hearing before an SEC administrative law judge. John J. Schwartz, Stanford's general counsel, accused CREF of trying to manipulate the registration to keep all the old rules intact. "In this country," he said, "we've long passed the point where private entities like TIAA-CREF can assert total control over the assets of individuals." Ten individuals and eighteen organizations joined the fray—even Equitable Life! Also involved was the Investment Company Institute, which though a self-proclaimed protector of small investors was actually a foil of the larger commercial mutual fund companies, that is, our potential competitors. CREF was in for a bitter battle.

CREF's application precipitated consternation within the SEC itself because it was the largest enterprise ever to register de novo. (Because CREF had been created by a special act of Congress, the SEC had never asserted jurisdiction over its affairs.) The SEC rules insisted on redeemability and transferability of funds, from which CREF sought exemption, arguing that such liquidity would undermine the basic design of TIAA-CREF's long-term, portable pension plans.

CREF also asked to be exempted from the SEC's requirement that trustees be elected directly by participants. TIAA-CREF had a byzantine procedure reserving four slots on each board for candidates selected from a slate chosen by an independent policyholder nominating committee. Each year one policyholder-nominated trustee was chosen for each board. The rest were nominated by an internal trustee committee. In reality, however, the policyholder votes were purely advisory, and the actual election was controlled by TIAA-CREF's "top board," whose members were (and are) a self-perpetuating panel whose main purpose is to elect members of the two operating boards and to ensure that the two boards adhere to the company's original mission. The top board was also the sole "owner" of TIAA-CREF stock, a gambit designed to preclude any takeover of the organization by competitors or outside groups.

Facing a full SEC hearing and a Pandora's box of likely attacks and objections, TIAA-CREF tried to negotiate. Since I knew Donald Kennedy, Stanford's president, I offered to visit him and his general counsel, a leading voice of dissent. I flew to California to meet the two. Kennedy was courteous, but Schwartz bristled with hostility. The only thing that would satisfy him was full capitulation on all demands. It was almost like being back at Michigan State, facing a student antiwar protestor.

Schwartz notwithstanding, I came from academia myself and hoped to reach across the gap that separated TIAA-CREF from its critics in higher education. In April 1987 I attended a conference on faculty retirement sponsored by the Consortium on Financing Higher Education, which proved a splendid opportunity for candid exchange. In Washington I met with a secretariat committee on pensions formed by Bob Atwell, head of the American Council on Education. The cochairs, Ernie Benjamin (general secretary of AAUP) and John Chandler (president of Association of American Colleges and Universities), probed strongly but were gracious. Not long afterward I visited the National Education Association's college retirement service committee, a session arranged by Georgetown's Roy Schotland. From one organization to the next, I didn't hear much I hadn't already learned, but I hoped that listening personally and attentively to their views might at least demonstrate the company's willingness to compromise. Unfortunately, TIAA-CREF's past intransigence had underscored the critics' suspicions and stoked their anger. After all the stonewalling, they were unwilling to offer much benefit of doubt.

The meetings did turn up a long-standing residual issue concerning the treatment of women annuitants. Because of their greater longevity, women's income payments had to continue over a longer period, on average, than men's. Assuming the same retirement accumulation at retirement, a woman's monthly income would be somewhat less than a male retiree's of the same age. Although the actuarial rationale was unchallengeable, a number of women's groups considered the practice unfair and discriminatory. The problem had been resolved by the U.S. Supreme Court in July 1983, which in the Norris case ruled against the company's position. But the dispute was just another lingering dollop of controversy in the boiling pot of the company's troubles.

The changes TIAA-CREF needed to make were so numerous that the biggest initial question was what to tackle first. Internally, a major problem was the company's central computing system. Until that point CREF's unit value—that is, the price of a share in the stock account—had been calculated monthly. Putting in a money market fund meant registering with the SEC, which required that all equity fund values (and individual accumulations) be calculated following the end of each business day. TIAA-CREF relied on huge mainframes capable of fast mass transactions (e.g., cutting 150,000 benefit checks once a month) but not configured to value both unit prices and individual accounts on a daily basis. TIAA-CREF had also been slow to climb on the personal computer bandwagon—at the time of my arrival, the majority of staff still used workstations networked into the mainframe system. A concomitant problem was that TIAA-CREF could send only annual statements to its policyholders, even though they and their employers were making contributions as often as biweekly. Thus, converting the systems and their numerous operating programs and subroutines was a monumental task, and it provided plenty of opportunities for foot-dragging. Again and again the launch of the money market fund had to be postponed, and it was hard not to detect a strong corporate cultural aversion to the whole idea.

Even leaving systems work aside, there were a broad range of challenges that had to be prioritized and systematically addressed—all while keeping the company running smoothly. It was a little like trying to change a car's fan belt while the engine was running—a good way for a mechanic to lose fingers. At the same time, I wanted to avoid, if possible, significant human disruption. I had always abhorred the "Chainsaw" Al Dunlap approach to corporate reform,[17] decimating management and firing large numbers of employees just to prove "there's a new sheriff in town." Market analysts and some shareholders may be impressed with what seems like dramatic evidence of change, but the more lasting effects are typically a precipitous drop in employee morale and a severe attenuation of the collective memory so critical to the ongoing functioning of almost any large organization.

Over the years, I had seen more than one new CEO fall prey to an irresistible urge to achieve overnight results—to put a distinctive stamp on an organization at the very outset of his or her tenure. My own experience had taught me otherwise, and my personal practice was to try to lead largely from within, relying on knowledgeable insiders, stakeholder groups, commissions, and task forces not only to determine new directions but also to build a broad base of consensus for change. At TIAA-CREF, however, I was forced to modify my approach by the breadth of what had to be done and the time available to do it. For one thing, I felt it would be helpful to bring in a management consulting firm. I was not particularly a fan of outside consultants, who usually swoop through a company with a great beating of wings, snatching up one bit of information and dropping another, spending more than a little time trying to find cozy future nests for their own fledglings—at the end of the day, laying only a few speckled eggs of preformatted squawk. But consultants do have the tenuous advantage of perceived independence and objectivity, and their imprimatur can help inoculate recommended strategies, reforms, and initiatives from the internal stigmas of whim and arbitrariness.

At TIAA-CREF, I thought a good deal of change could be pursued internally, but for reforms in organizational structure and major improvements in technology the company could benefit from outside expertise. After reviewing the candidates, I chose the firm of Booz Allen. I also realized I would have to involve myself directly in the development of new programs and products—particularly sensitive areas because they represented the front lines in the battle between the company's old guard and its critics in academia.

▪ One Hundred Days

One hundred days into office, I prepared a report to the two boards and the TIAA stock board on how I planned to proceed. The TIAA stock board was key because it was comprised of the "owners" of the TIAA stock and had general oversight responsibility to ensure that the company adhered to its original mandate. My presentation noted that Booz Allen would lead a reorganization study, as well as a special review of our computing systems. Most important, I recommended that the board itself name a special committee to review major issues confronting the company, an idea that the outgoing CEO, Jim MacDonald, had suggested to me.

Finally, I recommended changes aimed at enhancing the board's own practices and procedures. A joint meeting of the operating boards involved some forty people and typically ran from early morning to mid-afternoon—six hours, if each outside director spoke only ten minutes. To harness the trustees' talents more effectively, I proposed pushing more of the boards' work down to smaller committees, which could complete a great deal of work on any given issue in advance of a board meeting. When the full boards met afterward, they could focus their attention on broad policy questions rather than minutiae. There was no board committee on products and services, so I proposed that one be established to deal with this critical area. I transformed the board's ad hoc Committee on Social Responsibility to a permanent Committee on Corporate Governance and Social Responsibility and renamed the old Nomination and Compensation Committee as the Board Committee on Compensation and Personnel Policy. And I restructured the boards' and committees' meeting schedules to reduce the time and travel commitments required of outside board members.

Following my report to the board, I worked closely with Booz Allen to reorganize the company's management structure. Previously there had been myriad departments reporting to one of seven vice presidents, whose areas tended toward independent "chimneys." Now there would be four major operating units, two old (TIAA Investments and CREF Investments) and two new (Pension and Annuity Services and Insurance Services). The heads of all four would report directly to me. The executive presidents of the four operating units were moved from the old cluster together on the sixth floor to the areas of their respective responsibility. The remaining staff areas—human resources, finance and planning, operations support (information and computer systems)—would report to President Walt Ehlers, as would the internal auditor and chief ombudsman.

Making so many plans and changes so quickly was a big change from the ponderous deliberative processes I was accustomed to in academia. But there was a real pleasure in seeing things happen that you knew needed to be done. I told Dolores I hadn't had so much fun since my days in Southeast Asia, experimenting with nontraditional economics courses. And as things unfolded, I could feel a new energy buzzing through the company buildings. Morale seemed good and getting better. While there was plenty of uncertainty about how things would turn out, everybody from the trustees to the mailroom messengers seemed upbeat and engaged. TIAA-CREF was finally getting out of its rut.

▪ The Future Agenda

Shortly after I had been selected as CEO, I created the special committee suggested by outgoing leader Jim MacDonald to develop a long-term, high-level agenda for corporate reform. The previous trustees' ad hoc committee on goals and objectives had fallen flat, mainly by restricting involvement to board members with only limited management participation. This time I proposed creating a special committee with representatives from both operating boards, plus the "top" board, with myself as chair. The members were TIAA trustees Marcus Alexis, Frederick R. Ford, Leonard S. Simon, and William H. Waltrip; CREF trustees Andrew F. Brimmer, Nancy L. Jacob, and Dave H. Williams; and TIAA Stock trustees Robert V. Roosa and Phyllis A. Wallace. The key difference from earlier studies was that the fundamental fact-finding and analysis would be done by working groups of senior TIAA-CREF officers, who would prepare four "white papers" as the basis for the special committee policy discussions.[18] The officers would also be present and take part in the deliberations, which I hoped would yield the support of both trustees and senior management.

By the end of summer 1987 the special committee had completed its report, titled *The Future Agenda*, and I thought it definitively disproved the widespread idea that TIAA-CREF was impervious to change. For a start, it recommended creating five new CREF investment funds: an actively managed stock fund, an indexed or "passive" stock fund, a bond fund, a balanced fund, and a global stock fund. In addition, the committee called for an "alternative" TIAA account that would permit transfers to CREF, as well as increased flexibility in managing funds and enhancements to customer service. The most dramatic proposal, of course, was that CREF allow "cashability" (withdrawal) of participants' retirement accumulations, subject to approval by employing institutions. The committee did not recommend cashability of TIAA funds held within retirement annuity contracts for reasons both technical (for example, to avoid disintermediation) and probably emotional. TIAA-CREF's other principal offering, its individually purchased, tax-deferred "supplemental retirement annuities," had always allowed withdrawals of up to the full account value.

The Future Agenda, in a format labeled "draft for comment," was deliberately distributed to key college and university presidents and other academic leaders at the beginning of October. Some trustees worried about what seemed a risky step, since it increased the chances our plans would fall into the hands of competitors. But I thought it a convincing way to underscore TIAA-CREF's unique relationship with the education community, showing our willingness to hear comments from those most likely to be directly affected by the changes we were proposing. Senior TIAA-CREF officers visited the heads of major education associations, including American Council on Education, American Association of University Professors, American Association of State Colleges and Universities, National Association of Independent Colleges and Universities, and Association of American Colleges and Universities. Our field associates visited numerous campuses with the draft, reporting largely positive reactions. I also circulated the report to former company chairs Bill Greenough, Tom Edwards, and Jim MacDonald, who were generally supportive—though Greenough was deeply concerned over the cashability recommendation. Regular critics Oscar Ruebhausen and Dave Robinson, executive vice president of the Carnegie Corporation (and my Harvard classmate), offered detailed commentaries on the plan. Stanford's John J. Schwartz sent a furious letter declaring that since CREF was now registered with the SEC, the federal Investment Company Act took precedence over New York State insurance law—therefore TIAA-CREF should adopt full cashability at once.

On October 19, 1987, I was set to deliver a speech at a meeting of the member presidents of the Association of American Universities—fifty-six institutions, half public and half private, representing the most powerful and prestigious of the nation's research universities. As president of Michigan State University, I had been the first and only minority member in AAU.[19] Because I was a former member, I had wrangled an unusual invitation to speak on *The Future Agenda*, as well as TIAA-CREF's imminent launch of its money market fund. Only a few minutes before entering the ornate ballroom of the Westgate Hotel in San Diego I heard about the tumult back in New York: The stock market had just dropped by more than 170 points, and it was still in free fall. By day's end the Dow Jones Industrial Average was down more than 500 points, and the value of securities traded on the New York Stock Exchange had shrunk by more than $500 billion. Since my audience was already buzzing about the day's events, I began my remarks by pointing out that TIAA-CREF followed a long-term investment model and didn't attempt to time the market, so I was sure our participants would suffer no permanent losses. (I couldn't resist pointing out, somewhat inconsistently, that participants who might have wished for a safe haven had been denied access to a money market fund by the company critics' campaign of objection and dissent.) From there I went on to the draft of *The Future Agenda*, which I summarized for the group.

After that I took questions and comments from the presidents. Steve Muller, a friend and president of Johns Hopkins University, kept pressing me to give a deadline for implementing all the recommendations—six months? a year? I refused to specify a date, promising only to move as fast as possible. But most comments were constructive, if not effusive. "I was surprised at how polite everyone was," commented Robert M. Rosenzweig, the group's president. "But Wharton has always known his way around a lion's den."

This AAU meeting was memorialized by the *New York Times Magazine*'s "The Business World" with a cartoon cover drawing of me trying to walk a tightrope from the top of two buildings over Wall Street carrying an open safe spilling dollar bills—the legend was "Precious Cargo: The $60 Billion Challenge; Clifton Wharton Struggles to Preserve a Pension Fund" by L. J. Davis.[20]

With no stockholders or owners in the ordinary sense, TIAA-CREF existed solely for its participants, and everything we did needed to reflect that. Soon after the release of *The Future Agenda*,[21] we launched a new "At Your Service" campaign, aiming for the highest possible levels of customer satisfaction. The campaign ranged from the contrived ("At Your Service" buttons, which many considered juvenile) to the sophisticated (calculating the average number of rings before customer calls were answered). Despite initial resistance (some women employees disliked answering calls "TIAA-CREF . . . at your service!" because of perceived sexual undertones), the campaign soon caught fire. It became a company-wide exercise in consciousness-raising, reaffirming the staff's commitment to courtesy, accuracy, thoroughness, and integrity—internally as well as externally. As part of the campaign, we began presenting monthly Star awards and a quarterly Chairman's Award for outstanding service. Winners' photos were prominently displayed in the employee dining room, and the Chairman's Award was accompanied by a check for $1,000. Before long our already-strong customer satisfaction ratings soared higher yet.

In December 1988 TIAA-CREF's settlement with the SEC finally opened the door for the new money market account, but it also required that CREF trustees now be elected directly by policyholders instead of by the company's "top board." It was a good time to make some additional changes in corporate governance. Given the persistent confusion over using "trustee" to refer to members of the two operating boards and the top board, I decided to change the name of the latter to the TIAA-CREF Board of Overseers which I thought would reflect more clearly their oversight role and authority. The overseers didn't run the company, but they were responsible for ensuring that it was well managed by the two operating boards who did. Their duty was much more than perfunctory, and it put the overseers in the position to challenge any significant policy or action they judged inconsistent with the company's fundamental mission. Though rarely used, the overseers' power to question or even countermand the actions of either or both operating boards was a unique check-and-balance mechanism, unlike anything existing elsewhere in the world of corporate governance.

The process for nominating new trustees to the operating boards needed to be changed as well, not least because it didn't yield a broad spectrum of candidates. The independent policyholder nominating committee, which was used only for four slots on each board, tended to operate without much insight into the skills and competencies required for successful trusteeship. If there was a vacancy, it might nominate two candidates—a professor of communications at a small liberal arts college, say, and a professor of business from the University of Chicago. Or the vice president of a community college might be matched up against the dean of a prestigious law school. The outcome of the popularity (or prestigious) contest was seldom in doubt—policyholders voted for the candidates with the more impressive jobs and resumes. After the 1988 trustee elections, we ended up with four trustees from Harvard! Of course, they brought valuable abilities as individuals, but the boards ended up "packed" in a way that didn't reflect the full spectrum of higher education, as well as deficient in terms of geography, ethnicity, and gender. To change things, we eliminated the policyholder nominating committee, and we offered policyholders the opportunity to submit nominations directly during the proxy process to be reviewed and discussed by the nominating committees of the operating boards. As a result we eventually began to add trustees from different sectors of the company's constituency, including private secondary schools and community colleges.

. . . .

Major organizational change often entails changes in senior management, and TIAA-CREF was no exception. When the senior external affairs officer left two months after my arrival, I talked Bob Perrin, my close aide at both Michigan State and SUNY, into coming out of early retirement in Michigan and joining me in New York. I tried hard to lure my other aide, Al Ballard, but the attraction of good golf courses ten minutes from SUNY Plaza was too strong to overcome. In keeping with my habit of giving people inside an organization every opportunity to realize their potential, I moved several old TIAA-CREF hands into new slots. Tom Walsh, previously the company's chief actuary, became executive vice president for financial planning. Jack Putney became executive vice president for operations support; John McCormack, executive vice president for pension and annuity services; and Russell Bone, executive vice president for insurance services. My policy was to promote from within, especially minorities and women. Sometimes it worked out well, other times less so. The good results usually outnumbered the poor ones.

CEO in-boxes are always full of complaints from customers, who often seem to expect you to resolve each one personally. On college and university campuses it had long been common for ombudsmen to act as "customer advocates," with the power to cut through red tape and take on individual cases on their specific merit. Thinking that such a position would give our policyholders a sense that we genuinely cared about them, I appointed Lou Garcia, who had been an affable secretary to the boards, as TIAA-CREF's first ombudsman. He fit the role perfectly, and in short order he installed assistant ombudsmen (and ombudswomen) in some of the company's branch offices.

Moving Garcia made way for the appointment of Albert J. Wilson as a new vice president and secretary to the boards. Wilson, a tall, courtly Black graduate of Indiana University and Georgetown Law, was a respected associate general counsel in the company's legal department. He had pioneered TIAA-CREF's involvement in corporate social responsibility, especially on the South Africa issue. Over time I hoped that he could expand and elevate the secretary's prominence, developing close relationships with trustees and bringing issues to the boards, their committees, and my three internal management groups. In this highly confidential role, Wilson was the only officer, besides myself, who regularly to attended "executive sessions" with trustees.

In June 1988, soon after the corporate reorganization went into effect, President Walt Ehlers retired, opening up the opportunity to find a chief operating officer whose skills complemented my own. A highly attractive possibility was a prominent TIAA-CREF trustee, John H. Biggs. That he had cochaired the search committee that selected me as CEO didn't enter into my consideration. More germane was his varied academic and professional background. He received a BA degree in classics from Harvard University and a PhD in economics from Washington University in St. Louis. Beginning as an actuary with the General American Life Insurance Company, he rose to the position of vice president and controller, after which he became vice chancellor for finance and administration at Washington University. Subsequently he was appointed chairman, president, and chief executive officer of Centerre Trust Company in St. Louis. He had also been a member of the Carnegie Commission on College Retirement. With a background in insurance, higher education, investments, and banking, Biggs was a natural to step into the vacancy left by Walt Ehlers. He did have a tendency to be brusque and a bit intimidating to lesser intellects. Nevertheless, when Centerre Trust Company was taken over by Boatmen's Bancshares, I thought I could tempt him to move from his lame-duck job as chairman to become my second-in-command at TIAA-CREF. He accepted the offer and was appointed president and chief operating officer on February 1, 1989.

Biggs's arrival coincided roughly with some further shuffling of senior managers. Frank Gunning, general counsel, took early retirement and was replaced by Charles Stamm, formerly senior vice president and deputy general counsel at the insurance company Cigna. After Russ Bone left on a medical disability, Tom Walsh took over as head of Insurance Services, which meant searching for a new executive vice president for finance and planning and a chief financial officer. When I asked friends in the insurance business who was the best chief financial officer in the field, one name kept coming up—Thomas W. Jones. I didn't know him, but soon learned that he was the number two financial officer at John Hancock Mutual Life, in line for the top job within a few years. I also found out that he was Black.

Alan Monroe—my friend, Boston Latin classmate, and manager of the track team—was an officer at Hancock, and he gave Jones a glowing evaluation. So without prior introduction I called Jones up at work, explaining that TIAA-CREF needed a chief financial officer—could we talk? "I get calls from headhunters all the time, and I never respond," Jones told me. "But you're the first CEO ever to call me directly."

A few days later we met, and Jones was extremely impressive. Toward the end of the interview, when I had already decided to offer him the job, he looked at me quizzically and asked, "You know who I am, don't you?" He then explained that in April 1969 he had been a leader of the armed takeover by Black students of Willard Straight Hall at Cornell University. My mind flashed back to the dramatic *New York Times* photographs of Black activists with bandoliers strapped across their chests, waving loaded rifles from the building's first steps.[22]

Did that change my mind? Jones wanted to know. I thought about it for a brief second and replied, "No."

In October 1989 Tom Jones became TIAA-CREF's first Black chief financial officer. After Jones agreed to join TIAA-CREF, I called Jim Perkins, who had lost his job as president of Cornell as a result of the Straight Hall takeover. Jim, a former TIAA-CREF trustee, was a good friend who had served with me on several boards and commissions. When I told him I was about to bring Jones to TIAA-CREF as our next CFO, his reply was immediate and typical: "I think that's marvelous!" Both men, who hadn't spoken since the demonstration, wanted to meet again, so I organized a private lunch for them at the company. It was a memorable reunion—the sensitive university intellectual, steeped in his humanitarian Quaker faith, and the former Black firebrand, now a respected member of the corporate business establishment. Their conversation ranged back to the days of 1969, their recollections offering sharply differing angles on what had been a searing experience for both. In 1995, after Jones became a member of the Cornell Board of Trustees, he personally endowed a James A. Perkins Prize for Interracial Understanding and Harmony at the university. Jim Perkins died three years later, on August 18, 1998.

Jones had an immediate impact, particularly in developing the company's first long-range incentive compensation plan. Before this I had made two other changes—I linked together annual personnel evaluations and salary changes (previously done at separate times) and began a process of annual one-on-one evaluations with my direct reports. The latter proved most interesting since in them I would share (without attribution) their evaluation by their peers, as well as ask them to evaluate my performance. The latter took some time to become reasonably candid and honest. On the whole, these moves created a more unified sense of team.

Jones also guided TIAA to its first "triple-triple"—that is, triple-A ratings from Moody's, Standard & Poor's, and A.M. Best, the big-three independent ratings agencies for the insurance industry—confirming that TIAA-CREF's balance sheet and business prospects were among the best in the industry. Even more important, he visibly embodied the intersection of diversity and excellence. His performance was so first-rate that not a single individual in the company could call Jones an "affirmative action" appointment. The only real drawback was that his prodigious abilities had a tendency to cow subordinates, some of whom saw him as a threat to their own ambitions.

When I arrived at TIAA, annual incentive bonuses were limited to the Investment area, the CEO, and the chief operating officer. I thought that such a system should be used far more broadly across the company and at lower levels as a critical step to link each employee to the company's performance and their role in it. As a beginning and in anticipation of such a change, I deliberately refused to allow the boards of trustees to raise my base salary. Then I asked Tom Jones to develop a creative, multiyear compensation plan.

Tom developed a plan that had two components, annual individual and long-term. The latter was intended to provide a payment similar to a stock option in the private sector. Since we were not a profit-making company where such plans are customary, it was necessary to develop a substitute approach that would measure the contribution that an individual and a unit made to the "profitability" of TIAA-CREF as a whole. Tom created a "pseudo stock" unit using a complex process.[23]

The long-term bonus was especially creative. This bonus was based upon a rolling three-year performance measure where the bonus was paid in the third year. The long-term "awards" were made each year; thus there were sequential overlapping allocations. What was especially different was the creation of summary performance measures for each unit and division so that the performance of peers and those who made the company successful as a whole would benefit. This collective responsibility for success and dependency upon your colleagues made it clear both conceptually and practically that all persons were part of the TIAA-CREF "team" and we were mutually responsible to each other for the total outcome.

Two months after Jones came on board, I hired Matina Horner, former president of Radcliffe, as executive vice president for human resources. A psychologist by training specializing in women and human development, Horner had extensive academic and corporate board experience, which made her a good choice to take over TIAA-CREF's large and complex personnel department.

▪ A Final Reunion

Christmas 1989 brought a poignant moment in my life. My father's second wife Leonie had died two years before, and Dolores was determined to orchestrate a holiday reunion between my parents at our New York apartment. The two had not seen one another since my mother's anguished visit to the Azores in the summer of 1947. I agreed to the plan with trepidation, remembering my vain wishes of forty years past, when I had hoped my parents' differences might be resolved. Dolores first contacted my father, who reluctantly consented, and then asked my mother, and she agreed.

At the event my anxiety proved groundless. The meeting went off without incident, virtually an anticlimax. On video I captured both my parents walking with canes, my mother leaning on the arm of my sister Mary. Mother had been living with Mary in Montclair, New Jersey—where my sister had been a highly respected public schoolteacher—for several years. Grandmother Nana had died in October 1968 at the age of eighty-six.

My parents sat down side by side. My father, now ninety and almost completely blind, mumbled a few halfhearted attempts to explain his actions of so long ago, while my mother, eighty-nine, was quiet but relaxed. They were timeworn souls, almost strangers now, yet they seemed to look around with quiet cheer at the offspring of a union that had collapsed decades before. Our sons Bruce and Clifton 3rd were there, along with Mary, her husband Lowell Sampson, and their two children Matthew and Lydia. The younger grandchildren were curious without fully appreciating the weight of the event, but soon turned their attention to the Christmas decorations and meal.

During the return trip to her home in New Jersey, my mother's only remark to Mary was "You know, I discovered that your father was not the man I married. All these years I have been in love with a man who no longer existed. He was a stranger." Four months later, on April 23, 1990, my father died in a Phoenix, Arizona, care facility, just before his ninety-first birthday.[24] When I had reluctantly checked him in, he had been in a wheelchair, wearing his ever-present homburg. His wit and charm were undimmed. As I pushed him past a nurse, he smiled brilliantly at her and joked, "My son has kidnapped me!"

At the memorial service, grandson Bruce's eulogy movingly captured Dad's life and character, "loyalty and dedication combined with a cosmopolitan sophistication . . . a formidable perseverance, combined with common sense and good humor . . . most important of all, unwavering integrity, tempered by a compassionate humanity."[25]

My mother died in Montclair, New Jersey, on October 5, 1991, from an undiagnosed cancer, soon after her ninety-first birthday.

On May 30, 2006, my father was honored by a thirty-nine-cent U.S. commemorative postage stamp, along with five other "Distinguished American Diplomats." At the unveiling ceremony, all Dad's children and their spouses, plus five of six living grandchildren, attended, along with a large number of other Whartons, including the two eldest—Edgar Wharton and his sister Elaine Wharton Weatherly, my father's first cousins. I spoke.[26]

. . . .

During the TIAA-CREF period, I averaged eleven speeches per year and continued to receive honorary degrees, with or without a commencement speech. On one occasion, in the robing room, a faculty member came up, delighted to meet me, "because I use your father's book in my course on economic development." I politely countered that my father was a diplomat and had not written a book. My respondent was puzzled, "You know, the book *Subsistence Agriculture and Economic Development*?" When I told him that it was my book, he blurted, "You mean there are two of you?" Clearly, he meant to refer to my two different careers. This was not the only time my father and I were confused.

The most touching occasion involved an invitation to speak at the University of Chicago Graduate School of Business in 1991. I decided to go out early in order to visit my mentor, Professor Ted Schultz. My purpose was to tell him, while he was still alive, how much I appreciated all his help and how much he had meant to me. Too often one waits until a funeral eulogy to express such thoughts, and I wanted to tell him personally. He was still erect in his bearing and mentally sharp, but his office library shelves were almost empty since, now retired, he had given many books away. Ted was his usual diffident self, but afterward typically turned my compliments back at me. "Our conversation while you were here is a gem," he wrote. "It gives me much joy. I shall be rereading [your letter] again and again to recapture what it means to have known a very special student."[27] Dolores and I saw him once again in 1992 before his death in 1998. I was honored to speak at his memorial service at the University of Chicago.[28]

. . . .

At TIAA-CREF as at Michigan State, I tried to nurture the next generation of leaders, launching a program of rotating special assistants for mid-level corporate officers. The assistants spent about five months "shadowing" me as I went about my job—handling correspondence, accompanying me to regular meetings, sitting in on board and trustee committee deliberations. Among other things, we got together roughly once a week for private meetings, when they could ask anything they liked. Why did I follow one strategy, not another? What was I getting at or trying to accomplish with a particular comment at the officers group meeting? How seriously had I taken a critical remark by a trustee? As long as the special assistants honored the confidentiality caveat, I answered as fully and candidly as possible.

Participants were selected from a pool of candidates nominated by area managers, usually two at a time, with special effort to ensure women and minorities were fully represented. (The first special assistants were Ed Van Dolsen, a white male assistant advisory officer in the individual counseling unit, and Rema Smith, a Black female assistant vice president in human resources; they served from September 1987 to January 1988.) In addition to day-to-day observing, each special assistant had to complete a substantive project on a subject outside his or her regular sphere of work. The projects were by no means theoretical or make-work exercises; one, "Toward an Equity Real Estate Fund," by TIAA Investments officer Joan Fallon, eventually became the impetus for the Real Estate Account, TIAA's first and only variable annuity offering. Introduced in 1995, the account's portfolio consists principally of actual properties (office buildings, retail centers, multifamily residential complexes, and other kinds of commercial realty), rather than Real Estate Investment Trusts and/or other "bundled" derivatives. So far as I know, it is unique in the investment market.

At the end of the tour, each assistant presented a report to the operating boards. Not only did it give them a sense of having accomplished something substantial, it gave the trustees a chance to meet some of the company's rising younger leaders. All the special assistants also attended Dolores's FCI Young Executive Program at the Aspen Institute, where they had the opportunity to get to know upwardly mobile, mid-level executives from other major corporations. The assistants came away from the experience with a greater appreciation of how management worked at the top of the corporate pyramid. It made them better at the jobs to which they returned, and in many instances it pointed them toward personal and professional choices they might not otherwise have considered. Moreover, they frequently became informal emissaries to their friends and colleagues back in "the ranks," helping communicate what senior management was trying to accomplish and why. The program seemed very well received, and two executive vice presidents set up duplicates of it in their own areas.

During my tenure some twenty persons served as special assistants. Ed Van Dolsen rose highest at TIAA-CREF, becoming the company's chief operating officer in 2010, then president of Retirement and Individual Financial Services in 2011.

An unanticipated outcome of the program was that substantial interest developed among nonofficer staff in having a similar experience. In 1989 I initiated a shorter summer program for supervisory-level employees. Unlike the special assistants, the supervisors continued in their ordinary jobs, while spending three days a week in a modified schedule that included systematic visits to corporate divisions with which they were previously unfamiliar.

▪ Corporate Governance and Social Responsibility _____

TIAA-CREF was one of the earliest companies to become an advocate of corporate social responsibility, including governance reform.[29] When I arrived in 1987, governance was the province of CREF staff, and social responsibility issues were under an ad hoc board committee on social responsibility. The latter had come into being largely in response to various controversies, notably the hot topic of whether businesses and pension funds should disinvest in companies operating in South Africa or encourage the companies themselves to cease operations there. As an institutional investor, CREF has a substantial partial ownership of a large number of public corporations and is thus entitled to cast proxy votes (how many depending on how many shares it holds) in corporate trustee elections, as well as for or against resolutions proposed by shareholders, management, and/or trustees.

Based on extensive staff work done largely by Al Wilson, then an associate general counsel in investment law, the ad hoc committee had begun to look carefully at other areas where TIAA-CREF's proxy votes might shape the behavior of portfolio companies in a positive way. In addition to South Africa and apartheid, some of the issues under review included nuclear power, particularly waste disposal; strife in Northern Ireland and the role of U.S. companies operating there; the marketing of infant formula (including products made with contaminated water) in poor nations as an alternative to breast-feeding; and the marketing abroad of medical products not government approved for use in the United States. Sometimes issues seemed picayune—how much did a given company pay in legal fees to the firm of a sitting director? Did external auditors sign off on corporate travel regulations? In other cases they went to the heart of corporate ethics—should the company stop buying products made by child labor in sweatshops? Was the electric utility pumping coal particulates into the atmosphere?

In the larger corporate world, trustees, CEOs, and other managers tended to see governance and social responsibility advocates as buzzing gadflies—coldly tolerated at corporate annual meetings, sneered at in private conversation. But the TIAA-CREF trustees and I were convinced that despite a widespread attitude that maximizing shareholder value was all that mattered, corporate policies and decisions also needed to be measured against more than the holy "bottom line." With the board's concurrence I decided to convert the ad hoc committee on social responsibility into a permanent one on corporate governance and social responsibility, reflecting a broader mandate and greater importance. Initially the CREF investment committee and staff were discomfited by the shift in responsibility for proxy voting. Like most of their peers, Jim Martin and his investment officers tended to see the new committee's work as "do-goodism," not relevant to their investment practices. Later their attitudes would come into sharper focus when CREF's new Social Choice fund required applying social responsibility "screens" to investment decisions while still maximizing financial performance.

Meanwhile the new committee soon became one of the hardest-working of all the board groups, especially during proxy season. In time it began developing its own proxy resolutions for portfolio companies, often making use of the independent assessments carried out by the Investor Responsibility Research Center (IRRC). Al Wilson, who had been a member of the IRRC board since 1979, brought sharp insight to the process, and when TIAA-CREF submitted a resolution at a company's annual stockholders meeting, he often was the lead presenter. In one interesting instance, a proxy presentation was scheduled for a firm where I was currently on the board. Wilson conceded some unease at the situation, but I told him just to act as if I weren't there. After Al's thorough, incisive remarks, one of my fellow directors leaned over and whispered, "That man of yours is extremely good. I hope you pay him enough!"

For a while TIAA-CREF had a reputation as an "institutional" gadfly for its stances on things like board diversity, independent audit committees, shareholder votes on stock options, and poison pills. We were treated courteously enough, but clearly considered on the fringe. With time the attitudes began to change, though grudgingly.

Having served on corporate boards myself, I felt that there were often alternatives to direct confrontations. Before submitting an official proxy or response we sometimes invited the CEO or other corporate representative to meet personally with our board social responsibility committee (without me). My stratagem served two purposes: it made clear that our stance wasn't just a whim of TIAA-CREF management, but rather a carefully considered position of the trustee committee, and it made clear the depth of the group's understanding of the relevant issues. More than one visiting CEO walked out of the boardroom shaking his or her head and vowing to do a lot more homework before coming back. From 1992 to 1996 TIAA-CREF privately negotiated compliance with corporate governance guidelines with forty-two out of forty-three firms, and in only eight cases did it have to put an issue to shareholder vote. Today many of the reforms we championed have become part of the fabric of enlightened corporate policy. In the wake of Enron and WorldCom, not to mention the financial, banking, and mortgage crises of the Great Recession, the subject has undoubtedly become one of much greater concern among the general public.

▪ Business-Higher Education Forum_____

One continuing "extracurricular" corporate commitment was the Business-Higher Education Forum, where I now had moved over from the academic side to the corporate side. The leadership had become increasingly concerned over the problems of minorities, which affected both corporations and universities.

The Forum decided to undertake a study on the status of minorities in the United States and asked me to cochair the group with Steve Mason, president and COO of Mead Corporation. Our report,[30] *Three Realities: Minority Life in the United States*, issued in June 1990, focused on a candid appraisal of racial problems in our society. The three central realities that we found were different than the conventional wisdom of that time.

The first reality was that many minorities were succeeding, that is, roughly one-third of all Blacks (36 percent) were middle class with incomes of $25,000 or more. The Black middle class had tripled in a generation due to working-class Blacks joining the middle class. More than 40 percent of working-age Blacks were middle class. Although this compared with about 60 percent of white families, the Black middle class had tripled in size in a generation. Nearly half owned their own homes. Three years before, about two out of five Black and Hispanic families had incomes over $25,000.

Second, another third of U.S. minorities (34 percent), who earned incomes from $10,000 to $25,000, were surviving on the margin due to limited skills and poor education. We stated that this group was "falling behind economically and seem[s] to be virtually invisible to our policymakers." Most of these families did not qualify for public aid, had no health insurance, and did not qualify for Medicaid. Food stamps and unemployment programs rarely reached them.

The reality for those who earned below $10,000 was the persistence of poverty; this affected three out of ten minorities, many of whom were trapped by drugs, delinquency, and broken families.[31] We warned that the proportion of minorities in persistent poverty was escalating rapidly. The poverty rate among Black families was nearly three times that of whites in 1986. From 1970 until 1980 the number of poor people in the country's five largest cities rose 161 percent. We stressed that minorities were held back by racism, poor education, limited business opportunities, and "the stranglehold of the inner city" that stifles expectations. "Severe minority poverty in the U.S. remains a paradox in a just and compassionate society."

Our eighty-five-page report described the situation starkly, pointing out that in the time
it would take to read our report an estimated 250 people would become Americans—220
born here and 30 immigrants.

> In that same 30 minutes, more than 160 young people in the United States will make personal
> decisions that will affect them for the rest of their lives. Their families, their communities, and
> the entire nation will also live with the consequences.
>
> Nearly 50 will drop out of school; 85 will commit a violent crime against another human
> being; 27 teenage girls will give birth, 16 of them out of wedlock.

Our report recommendations called for full teenage employment by the year 2000;
inflation-indexing of public employment and training programs to their 1980 budget levels; a
redesign of public assistance to avoid discouraging work and education; increasing programs
to discourage teenage pregnancy and dropping out of school; full funding of Head Start and
Chapter I programs so that by the seventh grade students would achieve a level such that their
college education costs would be guaranteed; restructuring of student-assistance programs with
grants instead of loans for low-income students in the first two years of college; and strengthening affirmative action and outreach programs onto campuses and into career-track jobs.

During the press conference release of the report, I pointed out that "Over the next 10
years, over 40% of the new entrants into the work force will be immigrants and minorities.
Unless they come fully into the economic and civic mainstream, U.S. business and industry
won't have the men and women needed for an energetic and productive economy."

Steve and I made a presentation at the National Press Club in Washington, D.C., and I
made a special presentation to the U.S. secretary of Health and Human Services, Dr. Louis
Sullivan. Despite this, our study had limited visibility and little traction in policy circles.
Columnist David Broder observed, "The report . . . drew less attention than it deserved when
published earlier this month."[32] Two and half decades later I am deeply saddened that the
problems of minority life in our nation we described still require virtually the same recommendations. Nevertheless, I felt our effort was worthwhile in having prominent academic
and corporate leaders show their commitment to the problem. I remained a member of
the Business-Higher Education Forum. An occasional guest there was a young governor of
Arkansas named William Jefferson Clinton. At one meeting I saw him sitting alone, a rare
event, and sat down for a chat. We didn't talk very long, but after we parted I couldn't help
thinking, "He's certainly smart."

· · · ·

In January 1990 TIAA-CREF entered a new decade with restored energy and confidence. We
introduced long-term care insurance to help educators and their families cover the costs of

extended custodial care in nursing homes, adult day health centers, and at home. On March 1 we opened two new participant investment options, the CREF bond market and social choice accounts. Though the bond fund invested mainly in fixed-income securities, it was actually a "marked-to-market," that is, variable-return account—an interesting complement to TIAA's traditional fixed-income annuity.

TIAA was regularly pelted by demands that our CREF stock fund divest certain holdings for some social, political, or religious reason. We created a new social choice account that applied "social screens" so as to invest only in companies that met certain standards of corporate conduct—that they did not, for example, have economic ties to South Africa, or produce and market tobacco and alcoholic beverages. By creating this new fund I was able to mute these complaints, even though some participants still wanted their views to affect others who did not share their concerns. The social choice account was also a "balanced" fund, aiming at a mix of roughly 60 percent stocks and 40 percent bonds. Its balanced aspect seemed to make it as attractive to certain participants as its ethical criteria did to others. Contrary to public expectations, this fund's performance was outstanding for several of its initial years.

Concurrent with the new funds, TIAA-CREF crossed the Rubicon and began offering transferability and cash withdrawals in 1990. For the first time, participants could not only withdraw funds from their retirement plans, but also move them to other carriers. There were, however, conditions. The cash and transfer options were limited to money held in CREF's variable annuity accounts; funds in TIAA remained illiquid. Moreover, both options were available only subject to the approval of employers, who had to adopt them as part of their retirement plan documents. In 1991 the company created a "transfer payout annuity" that allowed funds to be withdrawn or transferred from TIAA's traditional annuity over roughly nine years.

Received enthusiastically by employers and participants alike, the new funds and options paved the way for other changes to come, many of them mapped in advance in *The Future Agenda*. By now I had a sense that higher education as a whole was regaining confidence in TIAA-CREF. Changing perceptions translated into solid asset growth, more new participants, and better retention of existing ones. Survey research confirmed that customer satisfaction was strong. By the end of 1991 TIAA-CREF assets under management topped the $100 billion mark, roughly double what it had been at my arrival. The participant base was approaching a million and a half, and our retirement and tax-deferred annuity plans had spread to some 4,500 education, research, and related institutions. Even our press coverage improved—rarely a strong suit in the company's reclusive past—as the company's image as a stodgy, rule-bound behemoth gave way to one of nimble, responsive innovation. A feature story in *USA Today*[33] quoted Bob Atwell, TIAA-CREF trustee and president of the American Council on Education, saying that changes at the company had been made "with dizzying speed. . . . I have probably never seen a more spectacular performance." While personally gratifying, the greater significance was that the reality of change at 730 Third Avenue was finally getting through. The image of TIAA-CREF as an antiquated, tradition-bound institution was being reversed.

Almost as satisfying was the upbeat mood among the company's own employees, who seemed pleased to be part of a more vibrant organization—though one of my more deliberate, if less noticed strategies had been to keep a close eye on total staff numbers. In previous positions I had seen that too-rapid personnel increases could lead to the need for sudden, sometimes draconian retrenchments when business conditions changed. Abrupt cutbacks inevitably demoralized the employees who remained, particularly those who had to pick up the workloads of the ones who had left. It was a cycle that needed to be avoided—sometimes by keeping a margin of authorized positions, other times by allowing position attrition in operational areas of lower corporate priorities. I didn't talk about such things or involve senior management directly, to avoid spreading the mistaken belief that I was expecting trouble. Undoubtedly a few of my direct reports knew what I was doing, but none of them brought it up with me. Total personnel growth was slower during my tenure than in the ten years before I arrived.

Even with my monitoring, however, the workforce did grow. As it approached four thousand it was clear that we needed more space for our New York headquarters. There was considerable discussion about building a subsidiary office complex outside the city or even in another state, where personnel costs might be lower. After consulting with trustees and key managers, I decided against it. Moving major units could be seriously disruptive and cost high-performing employees who might be unwilling to relocate—it could also lead to less diversity in our workforce. I also suspected that it would undercut the employee bonding that came from daily, face-to-face contact—an important though often ignored intangible in the formula for successful operations. (Digital networking and teleconferencing, then in their infancy, didn't really figure in the mix.) In the end the solution was to expand our existing footprint by making use of a lot we owned on Forty-Fifth Street, adjacent to the 730 Third Avenue building. The twenty-story addition added 160,000 square feet, including a lobby renovation aimed at bringing the building up to an "A" real-estate appraisal. We also added a much-needed auditorium[34] and took advantage of the opportunity to combine some "dispersed" units into unified spaces. Eventually, TIAA-CREF opened a "regional" headquarters in Denver, followed by much larger "back-office" installations first in Charlotte, then in Dallas.

· · · · ·

In 1991 I was due to turn sixty-five, the normal retirement age for corporate executives, but the trustees passed a resolution exempting me from the rule and extending my contract for another three years. Later that year I decided that while the "At Your Service" campaign had served its purposes, a further corporate tune-up was in order. I set up a "Needs Working Group" to develop recommendations for improved practices and technology, calling on Jim Wolf (senior vice president, Corporate Systems) and Kirk Dorn (vice president, Pension and Annuity Services) as cochairs. With a small staff headed by Susan Young (vice president, Finance and

Planning), Wolf and Dorn arranged to interview over a hundred people on the company's "front lines" of participant service, including thirty-five middle and senior managers. In their report, they listed over five hundred separate challenges, which they divided into major categories and prioritized for an action plan. Afterward I joined Wolf and Dorn in meeting with two groups, including all the employees they had interviewed, aiming to assure them that we had heard their concerns. It was encouraging and gratifying to find confirmation of my belief that answers to so many of the company's questions lay close at hand. Best of all, the group would be the major players in executing their own recommendations.

TIAA-CREF was now running quite smoothly. I was reminded that Michigan State business professor Eugene Jennings had once predicted: "Clifton is a superb intellectual leader. He assumes that reasonable people will agree with the reasonable goals he articulates so well. The point of danger at TIAA-CREF will come when he becomes bored, always a problem with a gifted mind."[35] My amused response was, "I've never been bored with a job in my life." But though I wasn't yet ready to set the cruise control, I thought the time was approaching to begin succession planning. At least once a year I had discussed three topics with the operating boards: the most likely candidate to replace me; my direct reports and their own possible successors; and the top ten mid-level and/or junior officers who showed greatest potential as future leaders. Early in 1992 I began to meet individually with each of the company's thirty-five "outside" trustees[36] to get their perspectives on what qualities they were looking for in my successor, as well as their evaluations of inside candidates. For the most part, their views were congruent with my own. Aside from one trustee, an investment manager who strongly championed Tom Jones, the overwhelming choice to follow me was John Biggs with Jones as his chief operating officer. One accomplishment in which I took much pride was increasing the diversity of the TIAA-CREF trustees and overseers. By 1992 the two operating boards had seven women, five Blacks, two Asians, and one Hispanic. Two of the five overseers were women.

▪ When the President Calls

June 4, 1992, Harvard University awarded me an honorary doctorate.

> Unbroken success in difficult assignments has made one observer say, "This man can lead anything." . . . He has a history of holding several jobs at once and doing them all so well that his entry in "Who's Who" might make us wonder if he were three men with the same name.

I barely heard the university marshal through my surging emotions. I had received honorary degrees before, but as an alumnus this one was exceptional because my own Harvard class of 1947 was celebrating its forty fifth reunion. If my classmates had told me at our own commencement in the same outdoor Tercentenary Theater[37] that I would stand before them almost half a century later to be honored, I would have said, "Inconceivable."

How had I come to this point? I had pursued three different careers—in philanthropy and foreign economic development, in higher education, and in business. I had become the first Black to head a major U.S. university in this century, the first to chair a major philanthropic foundation, and the first to lead a Fortune 500 company. As always at such events, my eyes searched and found Dolores, my lifetime partner, smiling proudly in the reserved section, and silently I thanked her for all that she had contributed to this journey.

I was wearing my favorite academic robe from my Johns Hopkins honorary doctorate, its brilliant yellow standing out in the sea of Harvard crimson robes of the faculty on the stage. Seated behind the front row honorees were the Harvard Fellows and Overseers in business dress with their traditional top hats, among them my longtime friend, Notre Dame's Father Ted Hesburgh, and Charlie Slichter, a fellow student on the Crimson Radio Network, now a Harvard Fellow.

My swirling thoughts abruptly dissolved—President Neil Rudenstine was reading my citation: "[As] one of the commanding leaders of our time, yours is the great talent to transform organizations into communities of purpose working devotedly together to serve the common good of all people from all backgrounds."

Yes, I thought, I had "transformed organizations into communities of purpose" wherever I had become the leader. Yes, I had tried "to serve all people from all backgrounds" throughout my life. But as I looked out at my classmates, I asked myself: Was I any more deserving than many of them? Why not honor other '47 classmates like the legendary movie actor Jack Lemmon, or Arthur Hartman, U.S. ambassador to France and Russia, or witty songwriter and performer Tom Lehrer? In keeping with tradition, the honor had been kept secret until that moment, and I knew my classmates were as surprised as I had been when previously notified. I never discovered who had nominated me, though I always suspected Father Hesburgh.

Standing there with the other honorees including Pulitzer Prize–winning author John Updike, legendary violinist Isaac Stern, Harvard president emeritus Derek Bok, and Nobel laureate economist Robert Solow was seductively overpowering.[38] My life and my careers had brought me pridefully to this platform in Harvard Yard on this day. I mused at the coincidence—my forty-seventh doctorate in front of the class of '47 reunion. My mind flashed back over the challenges and the rewards of my life at this fitting capstone. What more could possibly happen next?

· · · ·

Over the years, my good friend Chuck Stone had suggested in his news columns that I should be considered for the U.S. secretary of state position. While flattering, I gave little thought to such a possibility until the 1992 presidential contest when another friend and serendipity intervened.

The third debate in the 1992 presidential campaign was held on October 19 at the Wharton Center at Michigan State. MSU was between presidents at the time, but acting president Gordon Guyer invited Dolores and me to attend. I was reluctant, but Dolores insisted that it was a momentous event for MSU (and "our named Center") and that we should attend. That morning, as the two of us walked up to the building draped with the presidential debate banner, there was a flurry among the television crews, who turned their cameras onto us. A few students stopped to watch, wondering who the "celebrities" were. A couple came over and pointed to our names above the building's doors. "Are you . . . ?" When I confirmed that indeed we were, one student blurted out, "Oh, I thought you were dead!"

During the debate, Bill Clinton was notably more impressive than either George Bush or Ross Perot. Clinton's stage presence and performance had improved dramatically since the days when he had attended Business-Higher Education Forum meetings. Clinton also had participated in the 1967 National Student Association some twenty years after my involvement in its founding. After the debate Dolores and I avoided the crush of well-wishers seeking to shake the candidate's hand, not wanting to do anything that might be seen as self-promotion. A few days later, though, I got a gracious letter from Clinton, expressing regret that he had missed us and congratulating Dolores and me on the Wharton Center at MSU.

On October 26, a week before the election, I was scheduled to attend a meeting in Washington of the Knight Commission on Intercollegiate Athletics. A premeeting dinner had been laid on for the night before, but my flight from New York was delayed and I arrived late. When I got to the restaurant and asked the maître d' for the Knight Commission, he pointed me toward a smaller private room in back. As I threaded past a series of small dining alcoves, I saw my good friend Vernon Jordan sitting with a colleague. Jordan had left the National Urban League and was now a senior partner at Akin, Gump, Hauer and Feld, one of the city's largest legal and lobbying firms. We greeted each other warmly and chatted for a minute. Just before I had to move on, Vernon said, "You ought to give some serious thought to helping Bill Clinton out. He's going to need all the assistance he can get."

"Well, that's an interesting thought," I countered, and proceeded on to the Knight Commission dinner.

After saying hello to my colleagues and sitting down to a belated meal, my mind wandered back to Jordan's remark. Vernon was close to Clinton—TV news clips often showed them playing golf together, riding in the same cart between holes. Jordan was also rumored to be a possible head of his transition team if Clinton won the election. On my way out, I found Vernon again and asked him quietly if he had been serious. "Definitely," he replied. "Clinton is inexperienced in many areas and needs seasoned people to back him up." Smiling, he added, "Gray heads like us."

What did he have in mind? I asked, the Department of Education? No, that was already committed to Richard W. Riley, former governor of South Carolina and coincidentally our TIAA-CREF legal representative in the state. Although Warren Christopher was rumored to be running for the secretary of state spot, I raised that as a possibility as well. Vernon merely asked that I send him my curriculum vitae, and we left it at that.

Afterward I wondered whether such a development was either possible or desirable. I had deflected previous inquiries from Presidents Carter and Reagan, but what about this time? When Dolores and I talked briefly about it, we both thought it a remote possibility. Cabinet and near-Cabinet-level jobs usually went to figures who had made major campaign contributions, played active parts in the election, or both. I had done neither, so I would have no special standing with the candidate. Still, maybe it was worth a shot. I sent Vernon my CV. His return letter came back with a handwritten note: "This is obviously a form letter, but you are not in the form file."

On November 3, election night, Ambassador Bill and Melinda Vanden Heuvel invited us to watch the returns with them at their Park Avenue apartment. By evening's end it was clear Clinton had won, and Jordan's "casual" inquiry took on greater weight.

Soon afterward I ran into Jordan again, and we sat together on the air shuttle from New York to Washington. By now he was cochairing the transition team with Warren Christopher, playing a pivotal role in selecting President-elect Clinton's Cabinet and other top-level nominees. Vernon and I chatted most of the flight, but neither of us raised the question of my joining the administration-to-be. We both knew the steps in the "dance," and further conversation at this point would have been thought gauche by both of us.

As I thought about it, it was clear to me that there were several logical candidates for secretary of state. One was U.S. Representative Lee Hamilton. A Midwesterner, Hamilton was chairman of the House Foreign Affairs Committee, a strong, knowledgeable statesman. Another possibility was Senator Sam Nunn, from Georgia, though I doubted he would leave his powerful Senate seat—and even if he did, it would be more likely for the Department of Defense.

The most likely candidate was of course Warren Christopher himself. He had been deputy secretary of state in the Carter administration and had been the lead negotiator in securing the return of the American hostages in Iran, along with our friend Ric Haynes, then U.S. ambassador to Algeria. Christopher had never forgotten that Carter had selected Senator Ed Muskie, not him, to take over as secretary of state when Cy Vance resigned. Moreover, he had helped sway the California vote to Clinton, so the president-elect owed him a debt.

Warren Christopher and I had been trustees together at the Council on Foreign Relations, where he seemed a reserved, somewhat phlegmatic figure. He clearly knew what he was talking about when he spoke, but he rarely engaged in the usual banter before and after meetings. Some newspaper stories claimed he preferred not to return to Washington, but I suspected that it was misdirection, just in case he didn't get the position he had coveted so long. (Christopher had also served two years, 1967–69, as deputy attorney general, so there was also the possibility he might be appointed Clinton's attorney general.)

Despite the long odds, I thought it worth doing what I could to make sure my name got a serious look. Learning that Clinton would be meeting with Senator Jay Rockefeller, I called Ray Lamontagne, who contacted one of Rockefeller's top aides to ask him to bring my name into the conversation. Don Harrell, who had replaced Bob Perrin as TIAA-CREF's vice president for external affairs, was from Arkansas,[39] and he talked about my candidacy with Clinton's childhood friend, Mack McLarty. Peter McGrath, president of the National Association of State Universities and Land-Grant Colleges, put in a call on my behalf to Joe Duffey, president of American University, and his wife Anne Wexler. Both Duffey and Wexler were former Carter administration officials, and they knew the Clintons well. (Anne was supportive but reluctant to inject herself into the process because she was engaged in "other activities" with Hillary.) I also enlisted Franklin Murphy, who knew Christopher well and, though a Republican, he promised his support if contacted by Christopher or Clinton.

That, I decided, was going far enough—anyway, Vernon Jordan was my best ace in the hole. Still, I decided to cancel a planned trip scheduled for December 26 to January 8 to Kuala Lumpur, where I was to give a speech at the Malaysian Institute of Economic Research. When Washington is playing musical chairs, it is wise to stick close to home.

Not long after the election I got a "hurry-up" invitation to attend President-elect Clinton's economic summit in Little Rock. I looked forward to the two-day event (December 14–15), which would give me an opportunity to observe Clinton more closely and perhaps to make some useful contribution to the proceedings. Red Poling, chair and CEO of Ford, offered me a seat with him in the Ford corporate jet. Arriving in Little Rock, I learned that I was scheduled to make a "response presentation" on a panel on international affairs. I would have preferred to sit on the domestic economy panel, talking about human capital investment and the role of pension funds. But the organizers insisted, so I agreed to stick with their assignment.

The summit brought together a highly diverse group of 330 "movers and shakers," political leaders, academics, and representatives of innumerable special interests. Economists were prominent in the mix—MIT's Nobel winner Bob Solow, as well as Laura Tyson, Alan Blinder, Paul Krugman, Alice Rivlin, and Michael Porter. Labor figures included Owen Bieber from the UAW, Rod Carey from the Teamsters, Tom Donahue from AFL-CIO, and Al Shanker from the American Federation of Teachers. Encouragingly, the presence of the U.S. Black establishment was substantial, including Earl Graves, founder-publisher of *Black Enterprise*; banker Richard Parsons; Ford Foundation president Franklin Thomas; *Ebony* publisher Linda Johnson Rice; economist and TIAA-CREF trustee Andrew Brimmer; and Marian Wright Edelman, of the Children's Defense Fund. Business leaders were well represented, even though the majority might have been Republicans—Coca-Cola CEO Roberto Goizueta; Alcoa CEO

Paul O'Neill; Xerox CEO Paul Allaire, AT&T CEO Bob Allen, and Apple's John Sculley. Most surprising of all was my fellow Ford director Drew Lewis, now head of Union Pacific, once President Reagan's secretary of labor. Appointees-in-waiting included Goldman Sachs co-chairman Robert Rubin, selected to head the new National Economic Council; Senator Lloyd Bentsen, secretary designee of labor; and Donna Shalala, president of the University of Wisconsin–Madison and former TIAA-CREF trustee, now slated to become secretary of health and human services. All told, it was a most impressive group.

During a break I ran into Warren Christopher in a hallway. Atypically, he was pleasant and garrulous—he said more to me in that brief moment than he had in all our previous conversations combined.

The first evening of the summit, Vernon Jordan hosted a small dinner party. Attendees included Bob Crandall, CEO of American Airlines; John Reed from Citibank; Ford's Red Poling; and Zoë Baird, general counsel at Aetna Life. Later on Mack McLarty, soon to be White House chief of staff, made an appearance, as did several other higher-ups in the emerging Clinton organization. I told Dolores that my being on the guest list might be a good omen, though there had still been no further discussion of what might be in the offing for me.

During the international panel on the afternoon of the summit's second day, I commented first on the importance of investing in human capital, primarily in colleges, universities, and graduate schools, which was central not only to the U.S. domestic economy but also our competitiveness in the global market.[40] I pointed out that "we are not paying attention to protecting what is one of our greatest international comparative advantages." Instead of strengthening this vital infrastructure, we have had massive reductions in the level of financial support of institutions of higher education across the United States, particularly in our public universities. These reductions were threatening to wipe out our capacity to create human capital that took many, many years to create and build.

My second issue was my perspective on an amazing confluence between the faces of poverty in the United States and those abroad. I commended President-elect Clinton's proposals with regard to how to address positively on the domestic front. But I urged that the new administration take a harder look at the importance of economic development assistance, security assistance, and the totality of foreign aid.

Finally, I argued that ethnic and religious conflict have major economic consequences, and how we in the United States handle it domestically influences how we are perceived internationally. I argued there is a tremendous price paid by such conflicts within our boundaries and within the boundaries of most foreign countries. And I added that the issue of ethnic conflict is where leadership and symbolism are very important.

I ended by commenting that the summit itself represented a fine example of excellence in diversity, and that Clinton deserved commendation for putting it together. That brought spontaneous applause for the first time during the meeting.

Throughout the summit, Clinton made a strong and positive impression. For one thing, he really listened to the dialogue—something reporters and others remarked as unusual in a political figure and a key element in the meeting's success. For another thing, Clinton had a stunning command of virtually every subject that came up—and not just because of the thick briefing books on his desktop. Again and again he engaged with the experts in different fields, his knowledge ability seeming as keen as their own. His performance was a tour de force of brilliance, displaying not only his intellectual acumen but also his commitment to crucial issues on the national stage. I came away persuaded that the United States was about to enter a new period. The atmosphere that permeated the two days reminded me of the early days of John F. Kennedy's administration. In a new national era, I thought, I might be able to make a useful contribution to the public good.

Three days later I got a telephone call from Vernon Jordan, who said I would soon receive an offer from Clinton to be his ambassador to the United Nations with Cabinet-level status.

It was an interesting idea, but not one I was sure I wanted to consider. Almost immediately I heard from Warren Christopher, who had been tapped to become secretary of state. Would I be willing to come to Little Rock to discuss the U.N. job with Clinton? I told him I would be happy to, but I was unsure that the post would appeal to me. Although I didn't mention it to Christopher, I had read that Clinton had previously offered the U.N. ambassadorship to Ron Brown, the chair of the Democratic National Committee, a Black who had turned it down. Was Clinton "bean-counting" the U.N. job as a "Black" position? Vernon Jordan had assured me it was going to be at Cabinet level, but I had my doubts about the offer. Never in my career had I ever taken a "token" job, and I wasn't about to start.

Out of courtesy to the president-elect, however, I flew down to Little Rock on the morning of December 20. Clinton greeted me with a mug of coffee in hand, apparently just risen. After a bit of inconsequential chat, I got to the heart of things—that is, that the position on offer wasn't one I was especially interested in. Clinton responded that there was another possibility—deputy secretary of state. That was more in keeping, I conceded, with my administrative and managerial background. As we talked further, I confessed that the job that would genuinely excite me was the presidency of the World Bank, but I knew that Lou Preston was still in the middle of his term. Clinton said that he had spoken the day before with Preston, and that the slot would not soon open. At the end of the meeting I promised to get back to Clinton as soon as possible, since he was under considerable pressure to meet his self-imposed timetable for appointments.

Afterward I visited the transition team's temporary headquarters and had a short talk with Warren Christopher about the deputy secretaryship. "You know, Clif," Christopher said offhandedly, "you could just as easily have been sitting in my chair as secretary." Taken aback by his candor, I made some polite protest, then told him I wanted to think further about the offer. We then had lunch with Richard Riley, soon to be secretary of education. Both Riley and Christopher were cordial and seemed to hope I would respond favorably to the offer from the president-elect.

Back in New York I sought advice from two wise heads, Phil Talbot and Sol Linowitz. Linowitz was a true Washington insider, with whom I had joined forces on several Latin American committees and commissions, and more recently when he chaired the presidential commission on world hunger. My friendship with Talbot dated from his days as a trustee of ADC. After four years as ambassador and assistant secretary of state in the Kennedy administration, he had become president of the Asia Society, where I was a trustee. Linowitz and Talbot agreed that the deputy secretary of state position was far more substantial than the U.N. slot, even given the latter's Cabinet status. Sol emphasized that two critical, long-neglected problems at the State Department were its budget and organizational structure, which he thought I had the experience and competence to address. Both concurred that there was a sea change imminent on the international scene that would require significant shifts under the new administration. Given my background, Linowitz and Talbot thought I would be a strong asset to Clinton's foreign policy team.

Dolores and I agonized about whether to accept the offer. Dolores had been unenthusiastic about previous feelers from Washington, and she had deep misgivings about this one. We both had reservations about D.C.'s intense partisan "culture," as well as the financial cost of forgoing my last year at TIAA-CREF. It was the only time in my life when Dolores seriously resisted one of my career moves, but in the end she said the decision was mine, and she would abide by it.

As for myself, I thought I could make a useful contribution as deputy secretary of state. I wasn't going to Washington to make a name for myself or to get ready for a lucrative later role as a lobbyist or political fixer. I had twenty-two years of foreign development and foundation experience, with sustained involvement in U.S. foreign policy under five presidents stretching back some thirty years. I had ample reason to consider myself qualified and to assume I was wanted for the skills I could bring to the job. In retrospect I have often wondered if another factor in my decision, probably buried deep in my subconscious, was my father. Was I trying to climb higher up the diplomat's pinnacle than he had ever reached?

Once I accepted the offer, there was a great and hasty flurry of activity. Dolores and I had to race down to Little Rock for a public announcement. I was surprised at the disorder of the occasion but attributed it to the after-effects of the hard-fought election. A few hours before we were to speak, I had been given a hastily prepared text that made no mention of my relevant background in international affairs. I should have taken it as a warning, but at the time I just rewrote the text to make it more suitable.

Designees for the key foreign policy and defense appointments stood in an arc on a stage: James Woolsey, director of the CIA; Madeline Albright, U.S. ambassador to the United Nations; me, deputy secretary of state; President Clinton and Vice President Gore; Warren Christopher, secretary of state; Les Aspin, secretary of defense; Anthony Lake, national security adviser; and Sandy Berger, deputy national security adviser. After the nominees were introduced and made their remarks,[41] the press Q and A that followed quickly ran off the track, focusing almost entirely on gays in the military—a hot issue at the time, on which the reporters wanted to pin Clinton down. When the press conference was over, Clinton came immediately over to Dolores and took her by the hand. In a voice still raspy from a long campaign, he looked sincerely into her eyes and croaked, "I want you to know how pleased I am that Clif is going to join me. He will add greatly to my team."

Dolores looked back and beamed, completely charmed.

CHAPTER TWELVE

The Secretary: Department of State

My acceptance of President Clinton's offer meant that I left TIAA-CREF before completing my new extended term. Although I departed rather quickly, the choice of John Biggs as my successor and Tom Jones as president and chief operating officer[1] was smooth due to my practice of systematic succession planning. When their appointments were announced on January 7, 1993, Russell Reynolds, head of an executive search firm, called to complain that his company had not been engaged for the selection process. When I explained my systematic succession planning at TIAA over the years, which made the choices easy, Reynolds not so jokingly muttered his hope that other CEOs would not emulate me or he might be out of business.

Customary exit press interviews and farewell dinners were similarly abrupt or delayed. Nevertheless, my departure from TIAA-CREF received extensive press coverage.

A *Newsweek* article outlined my six years' accomplishment in converting a "stodgy professors' pension fund" into an "eye-popping $113 billion . . . Wall Street 2000 pound gorilla."[2] My turnaround of TIAA-CREF was later summarized by Professor Michael Useem's book on leadership,[3] which included a case study on my tenure.

I had succeeded as a corporate CEO and pioneered another first.

. . . .

My welcome to our nation's capital was a *Washington Post* headline, "Wharton Is Well-Established in Foreign Policy, Education, Business." Clifford Alexander Jr. was quoted saying that my selection was "nice and creative, except it would have been even more creative if [Clinton had] named [me] secretary of state."[4] However, as might be expected, there were a few negative echoes that ignored my prior foreign experience or suggested my appointment was merely racial window dressing.⁵ These negative articles produced strong objections from my former colleagues.⁶

My launch into the Washington scene was both hectic and different from all my previous moves. First, though candidates are nominated with a public pronouncement, they are not officially appointed. Candidates for high office in any administration are fully investigated before their names are revealed. In my case the vetting was mostly after my nomination became public. After submitting a sheaf of questionnaires and forms, I was interviewed in the law offices of O'Melveny & Myers. Though the interview was friendly, it wasn't at all perfunctory; they asked some very probing questions to make sure there were no buried "land mines" that might embarrass the new administration. My FBI interview was on January 14, a few days later. Because of a mix-up between two Bureau offices, several of my friends and neighbors got double visits, prompting a few to call asking what kind of crime I was accused of.

As with any presidential appointee, I had to resign from all my corporate boards and transfer my stock holdings into a "blind trust"—which meant sizable financial losses. Then when Dolores and I met with James Thessin, the State Department's deputy legal adviser and designated agency ethics officer, he dropped a bombshell: Dolores should resign from all her boards as well! Why, we asked, would her board service represent a conflict of interest for me? Because she was a compensated director, Thessin argued, I might make a decision that would affect one or more of her companies favorably, translating into joint financial gain.

"I resent the implication of your views," Dolores snapped. "I thought wives gave up being our husbands' property years ago!"

Frustrated, we asked Thessin whether Dolores would have to resign her directorships if she and I were merely living together, not married? Probably not, he reluctantly admitted. Wasn't that an interesting commentary on family values, we retorted—a wife constitutes a conflict of interest, but not a mistress? After further tense discussion, Thessin agreed that Dolores could continue with Gannett and Kellogg but would have to leave Phillips Petroleum. "Big Oil" issues were so globally pervasive that many decisions I might be involved in could affect Phillips's interests. Ironically, Dolores's replacement on the Phillips Petroleum board was Larry Eagleburger, my immediate predecessor as deputy secretary of state. Thessin's ethical sensitivities even prevented my attending a Ford Motor Company board dinner in Washington, D.C., when my fellow directors had planned to recognize my years of service.

. . . .

President Clinton was sworn in on January 20, 1993. It was a cold day, but the sun was bright and warming on the west front of the Capitol. Dolores and I sat in a back row of the special stands, and it was like a winter sunbath. The inauguration itself was somewhat moving, especially Maya Angelou's reading. President Clinton's best speech line was, "Today we pledge that the era of deadlock and drift is over . . . a new season of American renewal has begun."

Afterward Senator Pat Moynihan and his wife, Liz, invited us to their apartment overlooking Pennsylvania Avenue for a perfect view of the Clinton and Gore inaugural parade. We had occasionally entertained the Moynihans in Cooperstown when they had had a farm near Oneonta in upstate New York. That evening Dolores and I went to several celebrations, escorted by two military attachés. We ended up at the main black-tie event at Capital Center, in Landover, Maryland. The entertainment included Michael Jackson singing "Gone Too Soon" and Barbra Streisand singing "Evergreen," Bill Clinton's favorite song.

Until formally confirmed by the U.S. Senate, Warren Christopher and I took unused offices in the State Department basement, following the unwritten protocol of not seeming to presume our approval in advance. At one point I was pulled into a hastily called meeting to discuss the deteriorating situation in Haiti, from where increasing numbers of people were seeking U.S. asylum. Eventually Tony Lake got around to asking my opinion. Having visited Haiti just once in my life, I was taken aback. Nevertheless, I pointed out the inconsistency of treatment between Cuban and Haitian refugees, suggesting that we consult my cousin Congressman Charles Rangel (great-grandson of Frazier Wharton), who had previously been outspoken on the issue. Under the Cuban Refugee Adjustment Act of 1966, Cubans could enter the United States and seek asylum even if picked up at sea. Haitians stopped at sea were turned back, and those who reached our shores were held in detention and often returned.

On January 22 my confirmation hearing at the Senate Foreign Relations Committee proved relatively easy. Speaking on my behalf were Senator Pat Moynihan (D-NY), my cousin Representative Charles Rangel, and Eleanor Holmes Norton, delegate representative for the District of Columbia, whom I had once recruited as a trustee of the Rockefeller Foundation. After I spoke there was a light moment when Senator Paul Simon (D-IL), who had taken part in the founding of the National Student Association, asked me, "Can you still do the 'lion hunt' game you did at the NSA convention?" Senator Jesse Helms (R-NC) asked Dolores to stand, saying, "Dr. Wharton, you have outdone yourself!"

On January 26 I was unanimously confirmed. I wanted to avoid a formal swearing-in, which ordinarily involved a crowd of family and friends. (At MSU and SUNY I also did not have a formal investiture.) Instead, there was a brief ceremony in my office with Warren Christopher, Dolores, and the acting chief of protocol, Richard J. Gookin. British ambassador Robin Renwick, who had made an appointment to pay his respects, was invited to join the small audience. He had previously been stationed in South Africa, where he was key in obtaining Nelson Mandela's release from prison.

On January 30 there was a gathering of the new Clinton team at Camp David, including Clinton, Gore, the Cabinet secretaries and deputies, and top White House aides. The president and vice president welcomed us, followed by a general discussion on the theme "Toward a Shared Vision." Campaign advisers Stan Greenberg, Paul Begala, and Mandy Grunwald lectured us on the obvious, i.e., that the election had been a "mandate for change" and a demand by voters that Washington "do public business in the public's interest." George

Stephanopoulos warned us not to become "captives of the Beltway." (Most of the people present were Beltway captives of long standing, so the caution was probably as pointless as it was predictable.) Later in the day there were sessions on "Priorities: 100 Days" and "U.S. Economic Context: Budget." Hillary Clinton made a very impressive speech without notes, mesmerizing everyone.

After dinner the group sat around a fireplace, where we were supposed to share something that wouldn't have been on our resumes or public biographies—Clinton himself talked about being taunted by other children at age six for being fat. It was interesting enough but too much like encounter-group therapy for my taste. The idea was to build friendships and foster trust among the team—a laudable goal, though I wondered how it would work in real life. At least it was a chance to renew acquaintance with some in attendance whom I already knew (such as Leon Panetta and Bob Rubin).

After the Camp David confab came the usual tedium of settling into a new job. Local lodging was one issue. Most Washingtonians preferred houses to apartments, but with our properties in Cooperstown and New York, we didn't want to take on a third home. In the end we found a rental in the famous Watergate Hotel—a small kitchenette, twice-a-day maid service, room service on call, and minimal personal furnishings required. Dolores rented an office downtown on Fifteenth Street NW, where she could conduct her FCI Foundation work and corporate and other business.

For office staff I initially kept three people I had inherited, though for my executive secretary I eventually hired "Bunny" Kelly, who came recommended by Marc Grossman, executive assistant to the secretary of state. I also persuaded Kathryn Sartori to take a leave from TIAA-CREF to join the larger secretarial/administrative assistant pool. After a while Bob Perrin agreed to come east from his retirement in Michigan as an occasional consultant.

Getting approval for the car and driver that had been assigned to my predecessor entailed a tortured review that ended up in the White House, along with a similar request by U.N. ambassador Madeleine Albright. The web of rules and restrictions and procedures all seemed to be aimed at preventing anyone from using bad judgment or attempting to game the system. Every time someone made a misstep, somebody else wrote a new rule. It reminded me of the New York State Division of Budget back in my SUNY days. I began to think the nickname "Foggy Bottom" ought to be changed to "Swampy Bottom," with a prominent warning of "Quicksand—Beware!"

The two-room office assigned to the deputy secretary took some getting used to. Its former occupant, Larry Eagleburger, had somehow managed to set the inside temperature permanently to a chilly forty degrees, and having it changed back to normal required almost a month. Eagleburger had some unspecified illness that made this necessary. He was hugely overweight, and he chainsmoked cigarettes, sometimes with an aspirator to ease chronic asthma.

Even worse, my office computer was a nonfunctioning Wang—as were all the other computers throughout the department! If the whole Department of State had a broken, outmoded computer network, I asked, how could it possibly work efficiently on a global basis? Well, I was told, changing over to a new system had regularly been disapproved in the appropriations bill actions. Since one of my duties was supposed to be taking charge of the department's budgeting process, I could see that my work would be cut out for me.

Inadequate computer resources played a part in one of the first crises to be faced by the new administration. On February 26, a group of Islamic terrorists set off a car bomb in the underground garage of New York's World Trade Center. The blast was felt all over the city's financial district. Five persons died, 650 were injured, and hundreds were trapped in stairwells and elevators. Suspicion fell immediately on a blind radical cleric, Omar Abdel-Rahman, who had close ties to the Egyptian Islamic Jihad and the Al-Gama'a al-Islamiyya.[7] Abdel-Rahman's fatwa was thought to have led to the assassination of Anwar Sadat in 1981, though the cleric had been acquitted in court. He was also thought to have been involved in the murder of Rabbi Meir Kahane, founder of the Jewish Defense League.

At the time of the 1993 Twin Towers bombing, the blind sheik had been preaching in mosques in Brooklyn and New Jersey. Our problem at State was that even though he had been on the terrorist watch list maintained by the Immigration and Naturalization Service (INS), he had received a visa to enter the United States in July 1990. When I tried to find out how and why, I discovered that he had actually been traveling in and out of the United States even after his visa had been revoked. In December 1990 he had gone to Denmark and returned without being stopped. In April 1991 he went to Saudi Arabia and was even identified when he returned—but was admitted anyway. In August 1991 he once again tried to reenter from another trip abroad, which started a procedure to revoke his permanent residency status. But he was readmitted pending an appeal!

How had it all happened? When the sheik first applied for a visa at the U.S. embassy in Khartoum, Sudan, the terrorist watch list was kept on individual two-by-four inch cards in a box. Why paper cards? Because Immigration and Naturalization Service requests for computers had been turned down by Congress, along with numerous other State Department funding requests. Not only were the department's Washington offices handicapped by their antiquated and collapsing Wangs, our overseas posts were incapacitated as well. This was an early example of the customary Washington "blame game." Failure to stop the frequent entries of the terrorist Blind Sheik was laid at the door of INS and the Department of State, led by the U.S. Congress, whose prior failure to fund the computer replacements was a major cause. But the politician "fingerprints" as original culprits were not to be found.

In April 1993, Egyptian president Hosni Mubarak claimed he had warned the United States in advance of a pending terrorist attack. Several weeks later he muddied the waters still further, alleging that the sheik had been able to enter and leave the United States so frequently because he was a CIA agent. "The sheik has been a CIA agent since his days in Afghanistan....

he still earns a salary. . . . The visa he got was not issued by mistake. It is because of the services he did." Mubarak's government issued a statement refuting the story the next day. Three years later, the sheik was sentenced to life in prison for the bombing.[8]

The ultimate irony—and tragedy—was that the visa system was not reformed in time to prevent the disastrous September 11, 2001, attack on the World Trade Center. However, by December 1999 the Wangs had been replaced and improved.

Acting as deputy secretary was a big change for me. For almost twenty-five years I had been number one, the leader at the top of the ladder. Now I was to be a second in command. In previous jobs I had always had a number-two person—a provost, an executive vice chancellor, a president, and/or a chief operating officer—so I knew both the importance and the difficulties of the position. That didn't necessarily make it easy to slip comfortably into the role. But I wanted to be a team player and make whatever contribution I could as best as possible.

Before I accepted the job Dolores and I had spent an evening with John Whitehead, who had been deputy secretary of state under President George H. W. Bush. John and his media-savvy wife Nancy were both most helpful. Some time into my term of office, Dolores also paid a courtesy call on Gay Vance to ask about her experience as spouse when her husband Cy had been secretary of state. A basic point that emerged from both conversations was that a deputy secretary's role varied greatly from one administration to the next, depending largely on the secretary of state. My delicate task was thus to develop a set of responsibilities satisfactory to Warren Christopher while building a relationship that was compatible and complementary in nature. That Christopher himself had previously been in the number-two job might or might not make things easier—only time would tell. I was determined to do my best, particularly because at that point I had become the highest-ranking Black ever in the Department of State.

The key agencies responsible for U.S. foreign policy are the Department of State and the White House National Security Council, strongly influenced by the Department of Defense. From the beginning Warren Christopher and national security adviser Anthony Lake wanted to avoid the conflicts they had experienced during the Carter administration. Along with defense secretary Les Aspin, they had regular weekly lunch meetings to ensure harmony and cooperation among the three organizations.

In January President Clinton approved a decision-making protocol that increased the membership of the National Security Council, stipulating greater emphasis on economic issues related to security policy. The president, vice president, secretary of state, and secretary of defense were members as prescribed by statute. The director of the Central Intelligence Agency and chairman of the Joint Chiefs of Staff, statutory advisers to the NSC, were also on the roster. New members included the secretary of treasury; the U.S. ambassador to the U.N.[9]; and the president's assistants for economic policy and national security affairs, as well as his chief of staff. Though not a member, the attorney general was invited to attend meetings.

The enlarged NSC was designed to broaden the scope and sharpen the focus of U.S. foreign policy deliberations. The key support mechanism was the so-called Deputies Committee, which would perform the lion's share of interdepartmental work. Under the reorganization, I soon discovered, the State Department representative on the Deputies Committee was not me, the actual deputy, but Peter Tarnoff, undersecretary for political affairs. A little checking showed that "Deputies Committee" was something of a misnomer, since not all members were deputy secretaries and the undersecretary of state for political affairs had often participated in the past. Nevertheless, when Warren Christopher invited Dolores and me to travel with him to the funeral of Supreme Court justice Thurgood Marshall at the end of January, I raised with him my hope for a more substantial involvement with the Deputies Committee. Typically phlegmatic, he did not say yes or no, just asked me to send him something in writing. I had known that Tarnoff had been Christopher's man during the Carter administration. But when I found out that he had also been Christopher's first choice for deputy secretary until Clinton intervened, I decided not to press the issue. In retrospect, saying nothing further was probably a serious mistake, though a more forceful and persistent argument might have provoked a major breach at the very beginning of my tenure. Christopher never changed his mind about my attending the meetings of the Deputies Committee.

▪ ▪ ▪ ▪

On February 5 Warren Christopher presented a plan for reorganizing the department at a meeting of its officers and staff in the Dean Acheson Auditorium. I sat on the stage with him. Outlining his changes, he assigned me three major tasks. Placing my office within his own, he said that "the deputy secretary shall share major policy responsibilities with the secretary and in the absence of the secretary shall serve in an acting capacity. In addition, [he] shall: (a) Coordinate the management of international affairs resources, especially on an interagency basis; (b) Oversee the process of ambassadorial appointments; (c) Assume other tasks and responsibilities at the request of the Secretary of State, such as reviewing organizational structures.

"In a time of tight budgets and increasing demands on international affairs resources," Christopher's statement continued, "clearer priorities must be established for the International Affairs Budget Function 150 Account if administration initiatives are to be realized. Under the direction of the Deputy Secretary, who will coordinate management of international affairs resources, the Policy Planning Staff shall provide policy guidance so that general spending priorities may be established.

"I have asked the Deputy Secretary," Christopher concluded, "to oversee the implementation of these changes in a manner consistent with the orderly functioning of the Department. In doing so, he will work with the Undersecretary for Management, who will coordinate the implementation of the directive. I have asked that all affected officials be consulted so as to achieve the changes in a timely and non-disruptive fashion. I have also asked the Deputy

Secretary to conduct a review of the operations and mandate of the U.S. Agency for International Development and to report his findings within sixty days so that we may propose to Congress a reorganization plan for this agency." Two weeks later I had a private lunch at the Pentagon with the outgoing chairman of the Joint Chiefs of Staff, General Colin Powell, who gave me some excellent advice based on his Washington experience.

I took Christopher's description of my major duties at face value. In practice, I soon found there were two responsibilities that rarely came up. I was never allowed "shared policy responsibilities," and the secretary rarely asked me to take on "other tasks." There was one channel that did offer regular exposure to foreign policy issues, though without my direct involvement. Early every morning there was an intelligence briefing with Jim Woolsey, director of the CIA, and his deputy, Admiral William O. Studeman, which I attended regularly with Christopher and Peter Tarnoff. But the meetings didn't often provide more information than the department's own global intelligence assessments every morning—four to six single-spaced memos covering countries throughout the regions of the world. Both sources were helpful for staying abreast of foreign policy "hot spots," but they were a poor substitute for direct personal involvement in dealing with the issues. The departmental memos in particular were simply a day or two ahead of information in the news and on TV, and they were very terse. I suspected they weren't much different from summaries given to the president.

Christopher was overseas for sixty-two days, almost a quarter of the period I served in the department. When Christopher was traveling there was some chance for at least indirect involvement with policy. Whenever the secretary left Washington the procedure was for him to send me a "handoff" memo, outlining the moment's issues and crises; on his return, I sent him a "handback" memo of a similar nature. During the secretary's absence I assumed responsibility for approving the talking points developed for daily press briefings by Mike McCurry, the department's press secretary. His raw material came from bureau heads' reports, which were then distilled into "hot topics" to be covered, plus suggested answers to questions that reporters were likely to ask. McCurry was adept at working the press both on and off the record, but beforehand his presentations had to be approved by the secretary or, when on duty, by me. Although I wasn't privy to the department's inner policy circles, my interactions with Mike provided valuable insights on what was happening at the cutting edge of our international relations.

Though I was "acting secretary" when Christopher was away, the reach of modern communications made it something of a formality—the secretary was rarely unreachable when circumstances warranted. As acting secretary I did attend a couple of Anthony Lake's troika lunches with himself and defense secretary Les Aspin.

· · · · ·

I hosted several "bilateral" meetings with visiting dignitaries, including Sodyq Safayev, the new foreign minister of Uzbekistan (March 11); Ali Alatas, the Indonesian foreign minister

(April 29); Javier Solana, Spain's minister of foreign affairs (March 15); and Gonzalo Sanchez de Lozada, president of Bolivia (October 1). Unlike "multilaterals," the bilateral meetings were between the U.S. State Department and the representatives of a single other nation. The intent was to deal directly with the top policy issues for the country involved, though in reality the actual conferences were usually rather stilted. The department participants sat on one side of a table and the foreign visitors on the other, with small national flags strategically ranged along the center line. Discussions rarely got much beyond previously prepared talking points. Occasionally there would be a joint press conference at the end. I also subbed for Christopher at a couple of White House meetings—a February visit hosted by Clinton for British prime minister John Major and an April 5 dinner for Hosni Mubarak, president of Egypt, hosted by Al Gore at Blair House.

My regular ceremonial duties included receiving the credentials of new foreign ambassadors to the United States. Technically, the "letters of credence" were addressed to the president, but because of the large number of diplomats and the president's own incredibly busy schedule, the formal acceptance protocol often had to be postponed. In such cases the secretary of state acted as substitute, or the deputy secretary when required. I met regularly with new U.S. ambassadors, occasionally briefing them (especially the political appointees) and officiating at their swearing in. In addition I hosted or spoke at receptions for newly appointed or promoted senior officers, including ambassadors. During my brief period of service as deputy secretary, I swore in fourteen U.S. ambassadors and four senior officers.

Washington is a tight company town, with often mysterious hierarchies and mores. It took a while to realize the rigidity of the "pecking order" and my place in it. For example, if I had accepted the U.N. ambassadorship originally offered, its Cabinet status would have carried more clout and prominence than the position I actually took—even though the U.N. ambassador was technically subordinate to both the secretary and deputy secretary of state. (This protocol became apparent when the ambassador to the U.N. accompanied the secretary of state and other Cabinet officers to the president's annual State of the Union address.)

Throughout Washington there was an informal network from which the administration tapped people for foreign policy jobs. Many came from the "in-crowd," that is, those who had worked in previous administrations (particularly Carter's), and some had also participated actively in Clinton's presidential campaign. In power or out, they knew each other well and stayed in touch over the years. Anthony Lake, Peter Tarnoff, Frank Wisner, and of course Christopher himself had ties stretching back to the days of the war in Vietnam.

It didn't take long to realize I wasn't part of the inner circle. A few recognized my former experience in Southeast Asia, as well as on presidential missions and in international economic development. One was Winston Lord, former president of the Council on Foreign Relations, now assistant secretary of state for East Asia. Not so Anthony Lake and Sandy Berger, his deputy. After all, they were the ones who had advised Clinton on foreign policy during the campaign. I was just a Johnny-come lately. Lord was a Republican, thus not part of the in-group himself. Ironically, I had been a trustee of the council when Warren Christopher maneuvered to have Peter Tarnoff become Lord's successor. I began to wonder if I had been chosen as "window dressing," not to contribute to foreign policy across the board—or was I being overly sensitive?

Another complication was the dramatic difference between the department's political appointees, often large donors, and the career civil servants. The former group often had a hard time shifting from "campaign mode" to an administrative/managerial role.

There also were old political grudges or historical conflicts that affected decisions and actions. A good example was Timothy Wirth, a former U.S. senator named to a newly created post of undersecretary of state for global affairs. The way had been paved using the position of the department's incoming general counsel by reducing his rank and lowering the salary category, thus avoiding the need to seek a new "line" from Congress. The incoming general counsel, Conrad K. Harper was a distinguished Black former partner with Simpson Thacher & Bartlett, before which he had been an attorney with the NAACP Legal Defense and Education Fund. He had also served as president of the Bar Association in New York City, as well as a trustee of the New York Public Library and the Metropolitan Museum of Art.[10] The administration's downgrading of his position made me wonder whether Clinton's vaunted 'inclusiveness" might be more expedient than real. When Jesse Helms put a hold on Wirth's appointment—there was history between the two—Wirth insisted on the opportunity to confront the issues in a public hearing and eventually won out. With his own prior Senate credentials, Wirth soon was part of a group of high administration appointees who met regularly for breakfast with Vice President Gore—a startling circumvention of the chain of command, but apparently common in the Washington playbook.

Another incident with troubling racial overtones was the selection of the assistant secretary of state for Latin American affairs. The leading candidate was Mario Baeza, a Cuban American attorney from New York. At age twenty-nine he had become a partner at Debevoise & Plimpton, the first minority to do so. (A Phi Beta Kappa graduate of Cornell with a triple major in economics, government, and psychology, he had earned his law degree from Harvard.) Baeza's possible appointment raised alarm with the Cuban American establishments in Miami and New Jersey, where he was seen as an advocate of dialogue with the Castro government—based solely on his having visited Cuba and met with some of Castro's associates. Having a brilliant, successful Cuban American as the first Hispanic to fill the region's assistant secretaryship might well have been welcomed throughout the hemisphere. But despite my protests, the Clinton apparatus bowed to the powerful Cuban American lobby—though it was clear the Cubans' main interest was in having someone who shared their anti-Castro views.

Another shock was the rapid decline of cooperation among leaders in Washington. When I first served on the State Department's East Asia and Pacific advisory committee, as well as during my seventeen years at MSU and SUNY, I had worked with political leaders from both sides of the aisle. Later, as chairman of the Board for International Food and Agricultural Development, I interacted frequently with congressional leaders, particularly BIFAD sponsors Senator Hubert Humphrey (D-MN) and Representative Paul Findley (R-IL). Over the years I had found that you could usually count on statesmanship from key leaders of both parties, who collaborated on critical problems regardless of ideological differences. But after I retired from BIFAD in 1983, I visited Washington considerably less often, and ten years later I found things strikingly different. The corrosive effects of ideological conflict and the never-ending cycle of fund-raising were everywhere apparent. In my early interaction with other Clinton appointees, it wasn't uncommon for someone to exult, "Now that we've won the election, let's really stick it to 'em!" The yardstick was no longer whether an action or decision was in the nation's best interest, but whether it would give the party and its candidate an advantage in the next election. Senators Hubert Humphrey and Jacob Javits were gone, and many Senate centrists such as Nancy Kassebaum, Warren Rudman, and Alan Cranston had decided not to run for reelection. There were a few who still stuck to the old ways—Senators Sam Nunn (D-GA) and Richard Lugar (R-IN) were two—but their numbers and influence were ebbing steadily. It was a depressing development particularly for foreign policy, which flourished best in a climate of bipartisanship.

Of course, Washington still had its engaging moments. One event I found especially memorable was a black-tie dinner at the beautiful British embassy residence in celebration of Pamela Harriman's designation as U.S. ambassador to France.[11] The guest list was a veritable D.C. who's who—congresspersons, Supreme Court justices, Cabinet officials, lobbyists, and foreign dignitaries. In her after-dinner remarks, Harriman coyly noted that she planned to decorate the American embassy in Paris with her collection of French impressionists— "bringing them back home," as she put it. Then she took from her purse a flimsy page from which she read a letter of congratulations on her marriage to Randolph Churchill, written and signed by General Charles de Gaulle!

Such soirees sometimes provided the backdrop for private negotiations, often subtle messages dropped into "casual" conversation, and to operate effectively you had to understand the nature of the milieu. As Vernon Jordan once said to Dolores and me, "There's a difference between being *in* Washington and *of* Washington." The "of" set were the ones who mattered. Despite my having served five presidents in foreign policy areas, I was definitely not considered part of the "of Washington" set. Nevertheless, I still thought that I should try to be a team player and eventually break into the "inner sanctum."

. . . .

New administrations are often swamped by job seekers, and the process of identifying qualified nominees and getting them confirmed can be overwhelming. Even before leaving for Washington I had gotten over a hundred letters from people asking about or offering recommendations for ambassadorships. When I arrived, one of my first meetings concerned key staffing.

An important duty of the deputy secretary is to chair the department's "D committee," which chooses career foreign service officers for ambassadorial appointment—but not the political candidates. Every recent administration had faced criticism over the balance between political appointees versus nonpolitical ambassadors, and Warren Christopher had vowed to reform the system. But it was a delicate problem, complicated by the preferences of the host countries. For example, Saudi Arabia insisted on an ambassador who was demonstrably close to the president. Great Britain always wanted a person of public prominence—and wealth, because the costs of the London embassy were never fully covered by the official U.S. appropriation. The director of the Foreign Service and I worked together to decide which vacant posts should be deemed political, with an eye toward both overall balance and special circumstances. There were always marginal cases, though the political category tended to predominate in such instances. An additional problem was that there were many career foreign service officers reaching the point where under the department's promotion policies they had to become ambassadors or retire, which made for intense pressure to protect as many nonpolitical slots as possible.

Among those interested in an ambassadorship was Don Blinken, former chair of the SUNY board, who had spoken with me about it even before Clinton's election. Don's preference was for Hungary, birthplace of his wife Vera. Since the political appointments were made by the president, vice president, secretary of state, and appropriate White House aides, I attended only one of the relevant meetings. Fortuitously, Blinken's name came up at that session in connection with the posting to Hungary. Al Gore objected, claiming Don was a Republican. His comment was surprising, since during the campaign the *New York Times* had published (July 19, 1992) a startling photograph of Gore dancing with Vera Blinken, bending her backward in a tango-like position. The Blinkens had been hosting a party for Gore at Manhattan's Barbetta restaurant, with guests including Russian ambassador Vladimir Lukin. When I protested that Blinken was a staunch Democrat, others spoke up, pointing out that Don's brother Alan, who had chaired Gore's finance committee in New York, had already been promised the ambassadorship to Belgium. Then the argument became that the administration should not appoint two brothers as ambassadors. I reminded the group that Don's wife Vera was a Hungarian naturalized American, who could make an unusually valuable partner and communicator in the country where she had been born.

Less than a week later the *New York Times* unveiled several ambassadorial nominees; many had been discussed at the meeting just past.[12] One was Richard Holbrooke, who called me almost daily pressing his interest in the posting to Japan. According to the *Times* article, Warren Christopher had called Holbrooke to say that he had been chosen for Germany instead. (I knew that Clinton had wanted the Japanese spot for Walter Mondale.) Several other nominees were mentioned, including my Harvard friend Richard Gardner, who was being sent to Spain. Surprisingly, the Hungarian ambassadorship had gone to a career foreign service officer, not Don Blinken. Both Don and Alan Blinken eventually got their ambassadorships, though in Don's case it took much pressure from Senator Pat Moynihan and Representative Tom Lantos (D-CA), a Holocaust survivor from Hungary.

An aspect of the White House appointment process that bothered me was the deliberate leaking of possible nominees. Most commonly in the *Washington Post*'s "Heard" column, tidbits would appear that "Mr. Brown" or "Ms. Blue" might be about to be named ambassador to "Ugarundi." Then if I happened subsequently to run into Mr. Brown or Ms. Blue at a reception or dinner somewhere, I would find myself confronted by the putative nominee, wanting to know if the leak were true—and if so, why no one had bothered to get in touch directly. When I complained about the practice to the political operatives, they said the leaks were often trial balloons, floated just to see what kind of fire they attracted. Anyway, I was told, people should be flattered for the public to see that they were under consideration. But I was aghast at the power brokers' callousness. It was one thing for people who were actively seeking office and who were willing to take their chances having their names painted on the side of a trial balloon. But it was something else again to subject others to the embarrassment (or worse) of being "turned down" for a position they had never applied for or perhaps even heard of.

As of March 1, 1993, there were forty-five vacant ambassadorships. The slow filling of vacancies was regular fodder for the media, particularly outlets that wanted to paint the new administration as lackadaisical or incompetent. Much of the delay came from the pace of background and security checks. But the number of slots that had to be filled increased every four years, a result of government's inexorable metastasis.

. . . .

My relationship with Warren Christopher was odd from the very beginning. After my confirmation I had suggested that we meet briefly every day to review whatever I was working on and see if there were any new assignments he wanted to me to take on. Although Christopher agreed, our daily "wrap-ups" rarely lasted more than ten or fifteen minutes. Christopher's comments were nearly always perfunctory if not vague, and he showed no interest in delegating anything beyond the three responsibilities he had outlined at his February address to the department staff—handling the department reorganization, reforming the 150 account, and reviewing the USAID foreign assistance program.

So my assignments were clear, if limited in scope, beginning with reorganizing the department. I drew up a plan addressing five key problems. First, the department had been slow to address a set of "cross-cutting" issues President Clinton had identified as foreign policy priorities: democratization, weapons nonproliferation, environmental protection, peacekeeping, and promoting American business abroad. Second, departmental bureaus were sometimes less than fully used, with professional staff isolated from senior leadership. Third, functions and responsibilities had been parceled inefficiently if not indiscriminately among bureaus and special offices, leading to confusion and redundant efforts. Fourth, excessive layering clogged the department's clearance and decision-making hierarchy, with too many deputy assistant secretaries and senior management staff aides. Finally, there were problems targeting departmental priorities with available resources, particularly in the 150 account.

Communication patterns at State mirrored those at many other traditional organizations. At the upper levels the chain of command was clear. For example, I sent Christopher a daily report, supplemented by our end-of-day wrap-up meetings. The secretary himself sent the president (or Mack McLarty, his chief of staff) a weekly report on recent developments, usually organized geographically. Frequently he supplemented the weekly reports with "Night Notes" or specials on fast-breaking issues.

But it was the internal communications flows that principally concerned me. Hence I set about personally visiting the major departmental bureaus, with special attention to the seven regional political bureaus and the four global bureaus. In each visit, I asked both line and staff personnel for candid assessments of their needs and problems, as well as their best judgments about how to improve. The meetings varied in quality, but on the whole I learned a good deal. Among other things, it was clear that direct consultation and information sharing were limited among the different bureaus and assistant secretaries. Overwork and the press of successive "crises" left little time for peer interaction. Like so many organizations, the department had developed into a cluster of insulated silos.

My visits also uncovered stark policy inconsistencies between different regions or countries, even on issues that seemed similar if not identical. For example, I asked about the Communist governments in Cuba, China, Vietnam, and North Korea. Why did U.S. foreign policy vary so widely among them? Was it because of differences in population? Prosperity? History? Proximity to the United States? Military power and/or aggressiveness? The point wasn't to suggest a one-size-fits-all foreign policy, but to be sure that variations were based on fact and analysis, not accident or caprice. My questions opened a useful dialogue among bureau chiefs and specialists, the goal of which was a more rational framework for U.S. foreign policy as a whole.

In one case I went beyond my stipulated portfolio. My assistant Anna Borg had been concerned over conditions for the Yugoslav desk, and she asked me to look into it. I was frankly shocked to learn that this critical group, which was central to the pivotal U.S. effort to damp hostilities in the Balkans, was cramped into tight quarters with woefully inadequate funding. Two Bosnia desk officers had resigned, and the four remaining ones were stuck at student-sized desks under which they could barely fit their legs. I did my best to improve things for them.

A longstanding organizational problem was the scarcity of younger Black and Hispanic diplomats. Not long into my tenure I got a visit from Horace Dawson, chair of the Association of Black Ambassadors. The association had been working aggressively to boost the number of minorities in the Foreign Service, and they hoped that with my appointment the department would take the issue more seriously. The main problem was our inability to attract the most qualified Blacks and Hispanics to enter the profession. Any young Black or Hispanic with the intelligence to pass the Foreign Service exams and the talent to be a successful diplomat could easily find much better prospects outside of government, where salaries were much higher and opportunities for advancement more plentiful. Moreover, Blacks and Hispanics already in the department faced no shortage of problems (though hardly on the scale my father had dealt with).

As always, the key was leadership at the top. I knew that improving the situation would take time, but if the U.S. Army could build a solid, broad-based cadre of Blacks in top leadership positions, why not the Department of State? Unfortunately, after a few months I began to be uneasy about Warren Christopher's personal feelings on race. His reputation was positive enough, going back to the days as vice chairman of the California governor's commission on the Los Angeles race riots of 1965–66. More recently he had chaired a commission investigating the Los Angeles Police Department after the riots following the police abuse of Rodney King in 1991. But there had been countercurrents, as well. In 1967–68, as deputy attorney general in the Johnson administration, he had been part of the Pentagon "war room" that ordered the secret surveillance of political dissidents, civil-rights activists, and antiwar protestors. Moreover, after the assassination of Martin Luther King Jr., he helped draw up surveillance plans to contain civil, racial, and political disorders in cities such as Detroit and Newark.

Christopher's service in the cause of racial justice seemed at odds with his involvement with the secret surveillance of protesters, and I began to wonder about his racial liberalism when it came to individuals who were his Black peers. My concerns weren't allayed by the Conrad Harper vs. Timothy Wirth imbroglio. Later Vernon Jordan confided that he and Christopher had clashed as codirectors of Clinton's transition committee, when Jordan had to brace Christopher firmly to keep from being frozen out of important meetings and discussions.

• • • •

On March 4 President Clinton ordered a national performance review called "Reinventing Government," headed by Vice President Gore.[13] They proposed a six-month assessment of all units of government, aimed at streamlining and increasing the efficiency of all operations. Besides seeking ideas from a hundred or so upper managers, the Gore plan asked for input from federal workers and citizens at large. It seemed much in keeping with our reorganization efforts at the Department of State, where I was moving as rapidly as possible. Drawing in part on recommendations from an earlier "State 2000" task force of foreign and civil service staffs, I launched a number of changes. A few would require congressional action, but most could be implemented administratively. Within a few weeks, for example, we had made a preliminary reduction in the number of deputy assistant secretaries by 40 percent—even the *Washington Post* was impressed.[14]

· Reforming Aid _____

Reforming the Agency for International Development was a high priority not only in the Department of State but also among the foreign affairs leadership in Congress. Senate foreign relations chair Claiborne Pell (D-RI) began a regular dialogue with me on the topic. Lee Hamilton (D-IN), chair of the House Foreign Affairs Committee, was especially interested, as was Paul Sarbanes (D-MD), the senior Democrat on the Senate Foreign Relations Committee. Senator Jesse Helms (R-NC) had been known for years as an obstructionist, but I suspected I might be able to bring even him aboard the reform bandwagon, especially with help from Senator Pell.

One of my first goals was to help select AID's new head administrator. Among the names that surfaced was Matthew McHugh, a former nine-term congressman from New York and a respected lawmaker who had made foreign assistance a principal interest. He also had been helpful to me in the SUNY battle for engineering at New Paltz. Warren Christopher's initial choice was Brian Atwood, the Department's undersecretary for management, but he reluctantly agreed that McHugh's legislative connections might be an advantage as we pushed for change. Although at the time McHugh was considering an offer from the World Bank, he told me he would definitely prefer the AID position. Unfortunately, the train was immediately derailed by Tom Harkin, the Democratic senator from Iowa, who was pressing for the appointment of his wife. The mini-flap dragged on and McHugh couldn't wait it out. In March, Clinton named Harkin's wife as president of the Overseas Private Investment Corporation, and a few months later Brian Atwood took over at AID.

As I launched a plan to restructure AID, I was surprised to learn of a new unit being proposed in the Defense Department under Mort Halperin, the controversial foreign policy guru who had been on Nixon's enemies list. Although he had been nominated as assistant secretary of defense for democracy and peacekeeping, it was clear that the new position would revolve around foreign development assistance. The rumor was that Halperin's proposed unit budget would be larger than the total U.S. foreign assistance appropriation, plus the State Department's entire operational expenditures. Such large amounts were often described as mere "rounding errors" in the massive defense budget. Fortunately the unit didn't get funding, and Halperin was never confirmed. (A typical Washington survivor, Halperin soon found a home as special assistant to the president and senior director for democracy at the National Security Council.)

Meanwhile, to work on restructuring AID I created a special task force composed of representatives from each of State's departments and agencies responsible for programs funded through the 150 account. There were five working groups that targeted overall goals, organization, functions, policy development, and implementation. Ultimately thirty-five officials took part, including people from the congressional Office of Management and Budget, the National Security Council, and the National Economic Council (see appendix 10). Beginning on April 2, the group met six times during the month, preparing a basic "discussion draft." After discussion and review, the report was revised into a "final draft," completed on May 7. In January I had promised in my congressional hearing to bring back a report in May, but that plan would soon run into a brick wall.

I was also responsible for preparing and submitting to Congress the Department of State's 150 account, which supports the majority of U.S. international assistance. Its programs include the Agency for International Development, multilateral development banks, nonproliferation and disarmament funds, the Peace Corps, the Overseas Private Investment Corporation, the Development Fund for Africa, and more, with programs ranging from aid to the former Soviet Union to refugee assistance and counternarcotics. My first reading of the budget showed no clear relationship between program priorities and dollars being allocated. It was just a disorganized aggregation of policies and programs that had accumulated over the last forty years. Dollars allocated are usually a good gauge of a program's importance, so I decided to develop a totally new budget format that tied funds requested to a simplified list of foreign policy goals articulated by the president and his administration.

My key staff on this effort were with the department's policy and resource office, including Dan Speckhard, Brian McCleary, and Ann Richards, plus Anna Borg from my office. In the left column we listed categories and subcategories of priorities: building democracy, promoting and maintaining peace, promoting economic growth and sustainable development, addressing global problems, providing humanitarian assistance, and other—each had subcategories. Boxed headings at the top identified the different departments and agencies involved. These involved eleven major categories ranging from economic assistance and military assistance to development banks and international organizations/peacekeeping. In the right-hand columns were entered the dollars associated with each program, which at least in theory should have reflected its relative importance in the overall scheme of things. But in point of fact the document we produced showed no such thing—the disparities were almost shocking. Many areas the administration claimed to be critically important were seriously underfunded, while other clearly secondary efforts were immoderately endowed. Moreover, too many programs were spread across and divided up among several agencies, an obvious waste of effort, expertise, and public money.

Our findings had painful implications across the whole structure of the federal government's international programs, but I decided that was a confrontation for another time. For now I concentrated on preparing the 150 account, using the new format. Then I submitted a preliminary draft to Leon Panetta, director of the Office of Management and Budget, and his deputy, Alice Rivlin. Both agreed that it was a far clearer picture than before of explaining where appropriations were going, what they were being used for, and how priorities were being reflected. I mused that in this area my prior management experience was doing some good—and unwittingly it would have a lasting impact.

Twelve years later I was surprised to learn that my budgeting method was still being used in the Department of State, and that some of the department's officers considered it one of my major contributions. I was told that Secretary of State Hillary Clinton repeated my approach of aligning objectives with resource allocation and the creation of interagency groups during the conduct of her Quadrennial Diplomacy and Development Review in 2010.[15]

. . . .

My first trip abroad as deputy secretary of state was in late April, to attend the state funeral for Turgut Özal, the president of Turkey. There had been a last-minute flurry of concern over the need to have someone of higher rank represent the United States, and since former secretary of state James Baker was traveling in the area already, the White House asked him to lead the delegation. The central event of the trip was a funeral procession through the teeming streets of Ankara, with the Americans surrounded by a tense U.S. security detail on the watch for Turkish terrorists. Anxiety was running high because of the attempted assassination of former president George H. W. Bush by Iraqis as he spoke at Kuwait University on April 13.[16] Later, at a reception for all the foreign dignitaries, Secretary Baker made a point of taking Dolores and me around, introducing us again and again to ambassadors, foreign ministers, and numerous foreign acquaintances. He made every effort to help us establish genuine contacts, and Dolores and I were grateful for his generosity. In one hour, James Baker and his wife showed more professional courtesy to us than Warren Christopher would do during our entire stay in Washington.

A second trip came in early June, to attend the twenty-third annual meeting of the Organization of American States, in Managua, Nicaragua. Warren Christopher couldn't go, and with my Spanish fluency I was designated to substitute. The previous month I had already delivered one speech, originally written for Christopher, to the Americas Society and David Rockefeller's Council of the Americas. Its main theme was the Clinton administration's shift away from the last two Republican presidents' policies, which focused overwhelmingly on fighting communism in Cuba and Central America. Freed from the obligation to check communism on many fronts, a post–Cold War United States could concentrate on helping Latin America build democratic institutions. While opposing military dictatorships, we would now work hard to promote democracy and human rights. The speech ended with a strong reaffirmation of support for the North American Free Trade Agreement, which was under attack in Congress.

A month later I delivered much the same message in Managua. To the delight of the audience, I gave the first half of my speech in Spanish, touching on some points my past experience suggested would resonate well among the delegates. Describing the Clinton administration's new vision for the hemisphere, I said that the United States hoped to revitalize inter-American relations on the basis of common interests and mutual respect. The days of paternalism and quasi-colonialism were past, I said, and the United States would respect and support the aspirations of the people of Latin America and the Caribbean.

Overall the speech was well received,[17] with several Latin American delegates commenting favorably on the message about the need for mutual changes in North-South relations—a carefully crafted phrase the Latinos understood fully. But afterward a U.S. reporter insisted on asking about possible shifts in the U.S. stance toward South Africa. The shift I had been talking about, I pointed out, was in the U.S. approach to South *America*. "Well," the reporter said, "that speech was written for you. I want your thoughts as a Black about how Nelson Mandela is going to handle his massive problems."

I could only shake my head. In the past I had been repeatedly and prominently involved with apartheid issues for years both at SUNY and TIAA. But right then, though I was a U.S. deputy secretary of state speaking in Spanish to the Organization of American States, the reporter wanted my thoughts on Black South Africa, eight thousand miles away. The press fixation must be honored.

While in Managua I had lunch with Violeta Chamorro, Nicaragua's first woman president, with whom I established quick rapport. I also met the influential Roman Catholic cardinal Obando y Bravo. The Central American trip ended with a brief in Guatemala for an audience with President Ramiro de León Carpio.

Taking a quick break from Washington, Dolores and I went back to East Lansing in May 1993. Acting president Gordon Guyer had invited us to the unveiling of a plaque with our photograph and brief biographies in the Wharton Center's Great Hall vestibule. In 1992, Dolores had made a $1 million gift to the Clifton and Dolores Wharton Center for Performing Arts using the special director's insurance program of the Kellogg Company.

▪ ▪ ▪ ▪

Even more than most would suspect, the media influences every administration, and press criticism of Clinton's conduct of foreign policy was blistering almost from the beginning—a May 15 *New York Times* editorial was typical, lambasting the administration's human rights "failures" in China, Haiti, and Bosnia. A few weeks later a controversy blew up over remarks by Undersecretary of State Peter Tarnoff. In a press backgrounder, he tried to defend Warren Christopher's failure to gain international support, especially from Russia, for an arms embargo in the Balkans. The problem, Tarnoff argued, had to be seen in the context of U.S. fiscal constraints, as well as a shift from virtual U.S. dominance in global affairs to a broader multilateral approach. Tarnoff's claim that U.S. failure to lead stemmed from domestic economic troubles set off a furor. Three days later Warren Christopher publicly contradicted Tarnoff, stating that the United States would continue to lead the way in international affairs.

"The president makes foreign policy, and I make foreign policy," he proclaimed, "and it is not made by other officers of the department, no matter how valuable and effective they are." The secretary also said that he had had no advance notion of what Tarnoff would say, unfortunately reinforcing perceptions of disarray within the department.

By June several other salvos had appeared in the news. In an interview with the *New York Times* Christopher tried to show that he was enjoying (and up to) the challenges, but the article still managed to rehearse all the department's recent missteps. The ever-acerbic William Safire said that "Warren Christopher may be the most inept Secretary of State since Edward Stettinius." Another writer said that the president's rocky start and sharply dipping polls were causing concern abroad, and yet another argued that the administration's foreign policy was "weak and vacillating."

Though I had been excluded from the policymaking process, I thought I might be able to help, bringing my years of experience to bear on the administration's goals in Southeast Asia. Though the region wasn't at the top of the State Department's list of priorities, there were a number of matters that warranted being addressed. Among them were the U.S. role in regional security, the status of the Khmer Rouge in Cambodia and Cambodian refugees in Thailand, Malaysia's interest in buying American fighter jets, the U.S. position on the proposed East Asian Economic Caucus, and Indonesian human rights violations in East Timor.

When I scheduled a two-week mission to Southeast Asia to begin in mid-June, I little realized what consternation the plan would unleash. First came the red tape of getting use of Air Force 2 for the trip, a bureaucratic nightmare finally dispelled by Christopher's assistant Marc Grossman. Then came the wrangling over itinerary and the composition of the group that would accompany me. My assumption that Dolores would go along made for still more hand-wringing. While there was a long-standing practice permitting official travel by the spouse of the secretary of state, I was told that no similar practice had yet been developed in the case of the Deputy Secretary's spouse. (We knew otherwise—Dolores had previously spoken with Marcia Dam, wife of the deputy secretary in the Reagan administration, who said that she had regularly traveled with her husband.) So a legal counsel drafted a memo of procedures to be followed for Dolores's travel to be approved. Jim Thessin, our previous nemesis, presented us with a complicated manifesto stipulating that "when the department determines that travel by the Deputy Secretary's spouse would further official governmental purposes in specific circumstances, such travel on a government aircraft under Circular A-126. . . . Section 8(a)." The clincher: The "department should particularly ensure that her travel unambiguously furthers official purposes, and that she carries out a comprehensive program of representational activities . . . and that these activities are appropriately documented." Ironically during all this legal argument my brother William was head of legal assistance for the passport office.

Eye-rolling as it was, Thessin's memo would have been acceptable, except that it implied that Dolores was not to be present at my official meetings with foreign leaders—unless she had her own "comprehensive program" of a U.S. foreign policy goal. Without being satirical, I pointed out that many of the leaders knew Dolores well from our years of residence in Southeast Asia; others she had met on her own through her corporate and nonprofit board activities. (Did that constitute a "program" related to the promotion of U.S. interests abroad, as long as she did not promote the corporations where she was a director? I dared not go that far to ask.) My wife and I had always been seen as a team, and she also had had her own activities in the region. Hence, I would inevitably be asked, "Where's Dolores?" Clearly the State lawyers were unable to understand or accept the idea that her presence on the mission went far beyond that of spousal companionship and even that her independent role could be recognized as a "representational activity" in itself. I felt like I was in the middle of a Molière play.

The sour taste of nit-picking faded away when we arrived at Andrews Air Force Base on the morning of June 17. Following diplomatic protocol, the ambassadors (*and* their spouses) from six countries on our itinerary appeared to bid us bon voyage.

▪ Southeast Asian Tour

We had been assigned a U.S. Air Force jet C-137B Stratoliner that accommodated sixty persons, including a "stateroom" area with two couch/beds where Dolores and I could sleep. Our mission or "delegation" included my immediate staff plus key department officers.[18]

The first stop was Bangkok, on June 19. Though I had cabled U.S. ambassador David Lambertson requesting no meetings until we had had time to recover from jet lag, he insisted on a small reception at his residence the evening after we arrived. Five Thai dignitaries were there, two of whom demonstrated exactly what I had been saying about our prior relationships in the region. One was Kamphol Adulavidhaya, president of Kasetsart University, whom I had sent for his master's (Oregon State) and PhD (Purdue) under an ADC fellowship. The other was Amnuay Viravan, the deputy prime minister, with whom I had also worked during my ADC years. The two Thais jokingly reminded me of my speech in 1962 to the Agricultural Economics Society of Thailand—"The Inelasticity of Southeast Asian Agriculture: Problems of Monocultural Perennial Export Dominance," which they said had precipitated a major internal policy debate in the Thai government. After all these years, I couldn't believe they remembered the speech, much less its jaw-breaking title.

A subsequent dinner turned out to be almost an "alumni reunion" of ADC fellows I had sent to the United States or given study grants: Arb Nakajud, now vice rector of Kasetsart University; Chaiwat Konjing, deputy rector at the university; Sopin Tongpan, director of the university's Center for Applied Economic Research; and Pantum Thisyamondol, a former university dean now in the Thai Department of Cooperative Promotion. The U.S. ambassador was surprised that many of his guests knew the Whartons so well.

On June 11 we breakfasted with the board of governors of the American Chamber of Commerce, then met with Wichit Sukmak, minister of defense, followed by Prime Minister Chuan Likphai, with whom we discussed a number of issues. The most contentious arose from something Winston Lord had said the week before, testifying in the U.S. Congress that Thailand was a key supporter of the Khmer Rouge in Cambodia. The Thai government strongly disputed Lord's remark. Part of the conflict had to do with claims that the Thais were either lax or complicit in Khmer Rouge border crossings for the purpose of selling contraband. I told Likphai that the United States shared the Thais' hopes for democracy in Cambodia, but the administration was still worried about the Khmer Rouge and their continued violations of the Paris Peace Accords.

A more complex and sensitive issue was whether the Khmer Rouge should be allowed to take part in the new Cambodian government. Lord had testified that the United States was strongly against it, even in the interests of national recognition. When asked if the United States would recognize a Cambodian government that included the Khmer Rouge, I said that I wouldn't attempt to predict what the Clinton administration would or wouldn't do. The horrific depredations of the Khmer Rouge violated every international law and standard of human decency, but the reality was that the Cambodians needed to make their own decisions on how to come to terms with the past. It was well enough for the United States to make its position clear, but experience working in the region convinced me that pressing too heavy-handedly would prove self-defeating. We had already tried that in pushing the Thais for permission to overfly the border to gather intelligence, which they had been unwilling to grant. Similarly, they had refused our request to visit Burmese refugee camps on the Thailand-Myanmar border.

I acknowledged that the Thailand-Cambodia border was a long one, and even with its best efforts the government couldn't be expected to prevent every infiltration. After the discussion was over, Deputy Foreign Minister Surin Pitsuwan told the press that "the question of Thailand's position was not raised by the U.S. administration, but by its legislative wing . . . [and] the legislative officials may have received unclear information. . . . Their comments are not based on the truth. The administrative branch appreciates this."[19] The chief of the Thai National Security Council, General Charan Kullavanijaya, confirmed that his nation was adhering to U.N. resolutions on Cambodia and that it "no longer had special relations with the four Cambodian factions [of] the Khmer Rouge."

The highlight of the day was an audience Dolores and I had with King Phumiphon Adunlayadet at Chitlada Palace. The king was interested in my agricultural development background and enthusiastically recounted his own efforts with rural cooperatives. The visit lasted twice as long as scheduled, which his aides told us was a sign that the king had particularly enjoyed the meeting.

The next day we went on to Cambodia for a one-day visit. I spent some time being briefed by Lieutenant-General John Sanderson, an Australian who commanded the U.N. transitional authority in the country. UNTAC had been commissioned in February 1992 as a peacekeeping mission, the U.N.'s first over a sovereign country. It was also the first time the organization had taken over administering an independent state, organizing and conducting an election.[20] In April 1993, despite a boycott and attacks by the Khmer Rouge, 89.6 percent of Cambodians had voted in the nation's first national elections for a constituent assembly. The winner was the royalist FUNCINPEC party, which supported Prince Norodom Sihanouk.

I was impressed by UNTAC's success in bringing stability and democracy to the country. Though it got little public attention in the United States, it was an amazing feat for so small (22,000-member) a U.N. force. Although they hadn't managed to disarm the Khmer Rouge, they succeeded with the local militias, reducing the violence and insurgency to a level that allowed broad popular participation in the national election.

Two years before, Prince Norodom Sihanouk had returned from thirteen years in exile to become king. He and his wife, Princess Monineath, greeted Dolores and me at the top of the stairs of his beautiful palace, where he gently prevented the two women from separating themselves. "We don't stand on such protocol here in Phnom Penh," he said. Of course, the princess (née Paule Monique Izzi) was known throughout the country as the power behind the throne. She and Dolores sat with the prince and me throughout the interview.[21]

Though in an indirect manner, Sihanouk himself raised the question of national reconciliation through offering the Khmer Rouge a role in his new government. In response to the insurgents' genocidal "killing fields," where two million people[22] had been tortured and butchered, the U.S. Congress had absolutely forbidden any economic aid to the group. Sihanouk's concern was that bringing them into his government could jeopardize much-needed assistance, including U.S. support for UNTAC. Whether the Khmer Rouge should be allowed to take part in the new Cambodian government was a complex and sensitive issue. Assistant Secretary Lord had testified that the United States was strongly against it, even in the interests of national recognition.

When asked if the United States would recognize a Cambodian government that included the Khmer Rouge, I again said that I wouldn't attempt to predict what the Clinton administration would or wouldn't do. After complimenting the prince on the nation's progress toward a final settlement, I pointed out the depth of U.S. repugnance at the Khmer Rouge's reign of terror, but the reality was that the Cambodians needed to make their own decisions on how to come to terms with the past. The United States would not try to dictate Cambodia's course, I concluded, but democracy in Cambodia was still fragile, and every step was fraught with peril.

Though Sihanouk was well known to be mercurial, he listened courteously. How he took my remarks was uncertain—it wasn't a message he hadn't heard before.

On the way to the airport Dolores and I reminisced about days past in Cambodia. We recalled the annual Loi Krathong festival, when people festooned small paper boats with flowers, incense, and candles, then floated them down the Mekong River, bidding goodbye to all their past problems. At night the flotilla of flickering candlelight looked magical. It was a much happier thing to think about than the Khmer Rouge's five years of executions, starvation, "reeducation," and forced labor, which left a pall that would take decades to fade.

Our next stop was Kuala Lumpur, Malaysia, where we looked forward to seeing some of our many friends and former associates. With a roaring motorcycle escort we raced through the city, officers stopping traffic at cross streets—it was embarrassing, but efficient in getting through the congestion. The foreign minister, Abdullah Ahmad Badawi, and his wife Endon hosted a large buffet for us, with a profusion of favorite Malay and Indian dishes. Later on, Dolores and I hosted a lunch for our friends and colleagues from the University of Malaysia.

My session with Prime Minister Dr. Mahathir Mohamad was predictably prickly. His antipathy toward U.S. foreign aid was well known, as was his ideology of "Look East," espousing the need to shift focus to the region rather than the West. I had known Mahathir since my ADC days, when he was a physician and former elected state official with UMNO, Malaysia's dominant political party. Now I deliberately avoided discussing the exclusive free trade organization (the East Asia Economic Caucus, or EAEC) he had championed after the failed Uruguay Round in 1990. Instead I concentrated on what was happening with the country's latest five-year development plan. After talking with Mahathir I met with the late former prime minister Tun Razak's son, Najib, now minister of defense, who was interested in purchasing U.S. military jets. (He later became prime minister.)

Malaysian press coverage of the visit was extensive, especially commenting on my long-term residence and relationship with the country.[23] Particular attention was given to U.S. acknowledgment of the Association of Southeast Asian Nations position as the fourth largest market for American products. Noting my use of the Bahasa phrase *wawasan baru*, signifying a new spirit to reinvigorate U.S.-Malaysian relations, reporters appreciated a more conciliatory approach to the EAEC concept as a positive signal. A prominent article concluded that "Malaysia has grown hoarse with having to shout in vain to be heard by the previous Bush administration. . . . Wharton has given the impression that the Washington of today is more open-minded and more willing to listen to others."[24]

In Singapore I made a brief courtesy call with "Senior Minister" and former prime minister Lee Kuan Yew, whom Dolores and I had known since our residence in 1958. During a subsequent press conference, I welcomed Singapore's decision to allow the United States to continue using its military facilities, stressing our firm security commitments to allies in the region.[25] Although the strategic situation had changed with the fall of communism and the Soviet Union, ethnic and religious rivalries were emerging that could lead to regional conflicts, endangering the well-being of peace-loving peoples. I noted that the United States was following developments closely and adjusting its force deployments accordingly. A highlight of the visit was a dinner hosted by the National University of Singapore Society on June 25 attended by my former economics students.

Immediately after landing at the Indonesian airport, Dolores and I traveled to Bogor Agricultural University, where we met old friends, including some who had participated in my ADC econometric workshop in 1968. We also toured former president Sukarno's summer palace before returning to the capital.

The simmering issues for Indonesia were labor rights and human rights violations in East Timor. Toward the end of the Bush administration, congressional concern had heightened over the massacre of Timorese by Indonesian troops. In October 1992 Indonesian officials seemed to admit that the killings had been an act of government policy. Congress cut off military training aid to Indonesia, despite protests from the Bush administration and lobbyists for many prominent U.S. corporations. (During his presidential campaign Bill Clinton had criticized the U.S. stance on East Timor as "unconscionable.") Three months before my visit, Congress pushed the Department of State to reverse its pro-Jakarta stance; it also cosponsored a successful resolution at the U.N. human rights commission, criticizing Indonesian abuses.

Accompanied by U.S. ambassador Robert L. Barry, I visited President Suharto on June 27. Just the week before a group of U.S. senators had sent a petition to President Clinton demanding that he press Indonesia to improve its human rights practices. There was also a threat that the United States might suspend special trade benefits under the Generalized System of Preferences because of the country's violations of labor protections. (Indonesia had been given eight months to improve or lose their ability to ship goods to the U.S. duty-free.) I spoke candidly with Suharto on both topics, but he responded with typical Malay/Indonesian deflection—a gentle but firm *pelan-pelan*, "slowly." It would take much more pressure to bring a change in the nation's behavior. A month later, sure enough, bowing to Congress, the State Department blocked a transfer of F-15 fighters from Jordan to Indonesia, citing human rights violations as one of the reasons.

Brunei was another one-day visit. On the north coast of Borneo, the oil-rich nation was home to the sultan of Brunei, then reputed to be the world's wealthiest man. His fabulous palace had 1,788 rooms, 257 bathrooms, and a floor area of 2,152,782 square feet. Gold leaf was everywhere—on the walls, the furniture, even woven into the rugs and draperies. While I met with the sultan, Hassanal Bolkiah Mu'izzaddin Waddaulah,[26] Dolores called upon his two wives in separate audiences, one a former airline stewardess. (Dolores and I had still been living in Malaysia when the sultan and his brother had attended Victoria Institution, a private secondary school in Kuala Lumpur. Their residence had been a miniature, gold-domed palace, two roads over from our house on Jalan Damai.)

Brunei was largely a courtesy call, and talks with the sultan touched only lightly on foreign policy. Although he spoke perfect English, the sultan insisted upon using a translator, perhaps to give him time to reflect on his responses. I couldn't resist a bit of fun. Knowing that he was an ardent collector of automobiles (especially Rolls-Royces), I mentioned that I had been a director of Ford Motor Company and hoped he would try to add at least one

Lincoln to his collection. I gave him a wink, and he burst out laughing, while the translator looked on in confusion.

In the Philippines we called at Malacañang Palace compound, where I spent time with President Fidel Ramos while Dolores met the first lady, Amelita "Ming" Martinez-Ramos. We agreed that relations between our two nations were entering a new phase, based more on trade than security alliances. Despite the closing of U.S. bases in the Philippines, I assured him that America would remain an active partner in the region, economically as well as militarily. I also conveyed a personal invitation to Ramos from President Clinton to visit the United States.[27]

Dolores and I got back to Washington on July 1 fatigued but exhilarated. Though it had not been the aim of our trip, our observations of the Agricultural Development Council programs throughout the region inspired great pride in the creative contributions of the John D. Rockefeller 3rd Foundation. From 1953 to 1985, ADC supported advanced degree studies for a total of 588 men and women from seventeen countries. In country after country, former ADC fellows and grantees were now in leadership positions. They were university presidents, deans, department chairs, national planners, bankers, extension experts, ministers, and cabinet officers—a huge reservoir of human capital for their countries to draw on. Especially considering the program's relatively modest costs compared to its astonishing return, it was a striking demonstration of how well-designed technical assistance and philanthropy could have a dramatic and lasting impact.

On the broader purpose of our mission, I had three general observations. First, the nations of Southeast Asia were becoming more important within the larger Asia-Pacific sphere, and they needed more U.S. foreign policy attention. Most of them had moved well beyond postcolonialism. Malaysia, Singapore, and Thailand were experiencing explosive economic growth, and it was clear there would soon be more than the four "Asian tigers" of the 1960s and 1970s. Second, the United States wasn't dealing effectively with the region's efforts at self-determination and self-expression, such as the Association of Southeast Asian Nations (ASEAN) and the Asia-Pacific Economic Cooperation organization (APEC). (The regional free trade proposal by Malaysia's Mahathir, which excluded U.S. participation, required especially delicate handling.) Particularly given China's drive for hegemony, most Southeast Asian nations still wanted our protective military umbrella, but they bristled at attempts to leverage it to influence their internal politics or regional relationships. Old ideas about falling dominoes and cheap imports needed to make way for a more mature, less paternalistic role for the United States.

Finally, Dolores and I had been struck by the dramatic changes in the role of women and their emergence from behind the veils of tradition into positions of leadership in education, business, the professions, and politics.

On the whole it had been a highly productive two weeks, but when I returned to work at the Department of State, Warren Christopher merely asked if I had had a nice trip. He had enjoyed reading my reports, he said. And that was that. No follow-up questions; no probing about possible next foreign policy steps based on what I had done. The reaction was as though I had been on a vacation sightseeing tour, not a mission involving the key leaders of an important region.

Two weeks later, however, I talked to two reporters from the *Washington Post* who wanted information about Cambodia. I stuck to the talking points used for my visit to Phnom Penh that had been prepared by the Office of East Asian and Pacific Affairs. The next day, the *Washington Post* article trumpeted, "Aid Is Out if Khmer Rouge Is In, U.S. Tells Cambodia," with a sharp negative slant to the story following.[28] It was hardly a new position, and it had been publicly and previously articulated by Winston Lord, assistant secretary of state for East Asia and Pacific affairs. The wily Prince Sihanouk immediately canceled his talks with the Khmer Rouge. Sihanouk was known for frequently changing his mind, and there was speculation that he was trying to pressure the United States to be more flexible.[29]

Though the article reported that I had told Sihanouk clearly that the United States wasn't going to interfere in his peace efforts, Warren Christopher was upset. He said nothing to me at the time, but when he visited ASEAN in Singapore on July 23–24, he took the opportunity to "clarify" U.S. policy. An unidentified official accompanying him intoned that "recent statements by officials [i.e., me] have been oversimplified. The impression was developing, not only in the media but among some of our partners out here in the region, that we were ruling out flatly any Khmer Rouge participation or any aid to a government that included them."[30] The anonymous spokesman added, "Our suspicion of the Khmer Rouge and/or repugnance at their past history [remains] a constant. . . . We would not give aid, in any event, directly to the Khmer Rouge, because we'd be prohibited [by U.S. law] from doing so and would have no desire to do so." He concluded that if key conditions were met concerning arms and violence, there might be ways of working out the problem, but without ever allowing U.S. support to go directly to the Khmer Rouge. Diplo-speak at its finest, I thought. No wonder the United States was struggling to deal with the area.

. . . .

On July 30 the White House announced that the office of the national security adviser would conduct a comprehensive review of *all* U.S. foreign activities, including foreign aid. In a presidential review directive (PRD 20), a thorough overhaul of foreign assistance programs was recommended, on the grounds that they were often wasteful, incoherent, and inconsistent with broad U.S. objectives.

Though embracing an even wider universe, the directive seemed to supplant my own almost finished review of U.S. foreign aid—a task I had been handed very publicly before Congress and in Warren Christopher's address to the Department of State. (The main culprit in the bureaucratic end-run was Richard A. Clarke.[31]) Bill Montgomery had left his post as my executive assistant and on July 11 and been replaced by James "Jock" Covey, who had recently been deputy assistant secretary of state for political affairs,[32] Working with my AID and Foreign Assistance Task Force, and with Brian Atwood, AID's new administrator, we had already developed a preliminary report. I had spoken generally about the report to the Senate Foreign Relations Committee on July 14. Now our work was to be subsumed under the PRD 20 umbrella, and I was to delay issuing any report pending completion of the new survey. Not surprisingly, I wasn't happy. The State Department task force had nearly finished its work, while the PRD 20 report wouldn't be ready for many months. There was no reason to think our recommendations would conflict with or undercut Clarke's project. Moreover, I had already promised to share our final draft with congressional leaders, including the chairs and minority leaders of the House and Senate foreign relations committees. In March Senator Patrick Leahy (D-VT) had given a major speech on foreign aid reform and referred explicitly to our work on reforming AID: "The Deputy Secretary . . . says he will have a proposal . . . by the end of April. I have met with the Deputy Secretary to discuss foreign aid reform and *appreciate his willingness to consult closely* with the Congress. . . . I welcome the efforts the Deputy Secretary has made to begin a new era of cooperation" (emphasis added). (Leahy had served with me on the Linowitz Hunger Commission.) Did the Clinton administration and Christopher want to achieve a significant change in international assistance or just go through the motions? I could not tell, but it certainly seemed wishy-washy.

When I asked to be allowed to keep my promise to Leahy and others in Congress, the national security adviser, Anthony Lake, rejected the request out of hand, forbidding even preliminary contact with the Democratic leadership. It was a sad example of how Washington's turf wars could swamp genuine efforts on behalf of the national interest, and perhaps a partial explanation of why so many honorable politicians were leaving both the Senate and the House of Representatives. I felt trapped.

By coincidence, however, I was scheduled to substitute for the vacationing Warren Christopher at one of Tony Lake's regular lunches with defense secretary Aspin on August 25. While there, I broached the subject with Lake once again. I pointed out that the charge Christopher had given me specifically called for reporting findings within sixty days. We were already well past the deadline, and the draft report was finished. I was anxious to complete the assignment and turn to the process of working with Congress to implement our recommendations. "Tony," I concluded, "I'll abide by your decision. But I made a public promise, and this will be the first time in my professional life that I won't have kept my word."

Rather to my surprise, the White House and Secretary Christopher very reluctantly came around. A grotesque compromise was hammered out, allowing me to read portions of the draft to the congressional leaders but not to give them an actual copy. I didn't particularly like it but decided to give it a try. My first stop was with Senator Paul Sarbanes, a bright Rhodes Scholar with a law degree from Harvard. Almost as soon as I began explaining the awkward situation, I felt ridiculous—sitting there with a draft in hand, telling Sarbanes what was in it, but unable to give or even show it to him. Disgusted, I stopped and apologized—I had never operated this way before, and I thought it insulting to the senator. In his understated way, Sarbanes said he agreed, but understood the White House fear of congressional preemption. Even so, he promised to keep pushing for the reforms my group was proposing, and my already high regard for this son of Greek immigrants went up a few more notches. Once again, if it were not for the seriousness of the effort for U.S. international assistance policy, I would have considered the situation to be a laughable Rube Goldberg construction. But I was still determined to do my utmost to bring the report to fruition.

By September my task force had completed its report—"Preventive Diplomacy: Revitalizing A.I.D. and Foreign Assistance for the Post–Cold War Era." Across the top of the cover page was stamped "For Official Use Only," and at the bottom, "Release Pending."

The core of the report lay in restructuring the department's 150 account around new foreign policy priorities. It used two charts—"Department/Agency Responsibility by Current Function 150 Program Category" and "Department/Agency Responsibility by Foreign Objective"—to categorize activities and match them against the responsible entity. The goal was to clarify responsibilities as a basis for improved administration and coordination.

A touchy issue was whether to consolidate the Agency for International Development into the Department of State reporting structure. During the Cold War, AID had often been seen as a CIA proxy, and in many parts of the globe the perception persisted. Now the agency saw an opportunity to target selected countries where it could help plant and nurture democratic values, building a foundation for lasting prosperity. Brian Atwood, the new administrator, strongly backed the change. The question at hand was whether AID should be a solid line or dotted line relationship to the secretary of state, who under the law already had authority. The solid line is a direct report; a dotted, indirect. When there is conflict in direction between a solid line leader and dotted line leader, the solid line leader typically has final authority. To a subordinate the solid line leader will always prevail. There were also questions at the Department of State regarding consolidating two other agencies, the Arms Control and Disarmament Agency and the U.S. Information Agency, but these were not the subject of the task force report.

While the AID task force report struggled to see the light of day, reorganization of the Department of State itself continued.[33] With Brian Atwood shifted to the Agency for International Development, Richard M. Moose took over as undersecretary for management to oversee finishing the task. Already thirteen bureau plans had been approved, five more approved provisionally, and six returned for revisions. Staff reductions for department had hit our 4 percent target, with further reductions ahead. Deputy assistant secretaries had been reduced by almost 30 percent. I had also cut my own office staff by about the same fraction.

Meanwhile, I stepped up efforts to push ideas and recommendations from our unreleased task force report. I gave an overview of the document to BIFAD—now called BIFADEC,

NEW FORMAT 150 BUDGET TABLE FY 1994

FY 1994 International Affairs Programs
(Budget Request—Function 150)
(Budget Authority—$ Millions)

	FY 1994 BUDGET REQUEST
BUILDING DEMOCRACY	2,723
Former Soviet Union	704
Central and Eastern Europe	409
Information and Exchanges	1,439
Other	171
PROMOTING AND MAINTAINING PEACE	6,236
Peace-Keeping and Related Activities	735
Non-Proliferation and Arms Control	197
Middle East Peace	5,172
Defense Cooperation and Regional Security	132
PROMOTING ECONOMIC GROWTH AND SUSTAINABLE DEVELOPMENT	5,269
Bilateral Development	1,696
Developing Human Capital, Building Markets and Income Opportunities, Expanding Science and Technology, Building Institutions	
Multilateral Development	2,343
Trade Promotion	1,230
[Program Activity]	[17,412]

the Board for International Food and Agricultural Development and Economic Cooperation—and spoke to the Association of Professional Schools of International Affairs on "U.S.
National Interests in the Post–Cold War Era." The Congressional Black Caucus invited me to
address the "foreign affairs brain trust" of the Constituency for Africa, where I advocated the
need for a stronger commitment to alleviating poverty—not only abroad but also at home.[34]
I argued that poverty efforts had failed "to distinguish between economic development . . .
and the elimination of poverty. The former is a process; the latter a condition." Congressman
Charles Diggs, Ambassador Terence Todman, and several other Black leaders seemed proud

ADDRESSING GLOBAL PROBLEMS	1,488
Counter-Narcotics and Counter-Terrorism	308
Environment	397
Population	663
AIDS	120
PROVIDING HUMANITARIAN ASSISTANCE	2,031
Refugees and Migration	690
Disaster Relief	149
Child Survival	252
Other	940
ADVANCING DIPLOMACY	3,720
State Department Salaries and Expenses	2,198
Foreign Buildings	421
United Nations and Other Affiliates (Assessed)	341
Other International Organizations (Voluntary)	86
Conferences and Miscellaneous	122
USAID Operating Expenses	552
OTHER	100
Total	21,567

Source: "Preventive Diplomacy: Revitalizing A.I.D. and Foreign Assistance for the Post–Cold War Era," September 10, 1993 (final).

of my State Department appointment. Others, I sensed, were disappointed that I didn't tackle the traditional "Black" concerns. In fact, I had just given an interview to the *Lansing State Journal* in which I pointed out that at the time only five Blacks held U.S. ambassadorships, all to African nations, with two others awaiting confirmation to posts in Africa and Asia. Of the Department of State's 162 nonpolitical ambassadors, only three were Black, all stationed in Africa. It reminded me of my father's complaint thirty-five years before, that the department was "exporting discrimination abroad in the Foreign Service."[35] I also took my campaign to the Black Professionals in International Affairs, with whom I again stressed the importance of economic assistance in "preventive diplomacy," as well as the need to demonstrate more clearly to the American public how foreign aid promoted their own interests.

Yet at the end of the day, all attempts were fruitless to extract the AID task force report from the tentacles of the White House policy advisers. A perceptive analysis summarized the situation: "Early drafts of the 'Wharton Report' demonstrated a shift in the direction of supporting a more sustainable development process. . . . Before long, however, the task force got embroiled in a battle with an interagency working group that Clinton had set up under the more conventional leadership of the National Security Council. . . . [T]he failure to act quickly and decisively in a new direction killed a great deal of the momentum for change."[36]

The so-called "Wharton Report" was never officially released. Bizarrely, neither was the PRD 20 report! It was territoriality at its finest, and both documents were consigned to the Washington dustbin. The outcome was a perfect instance of where a laudable goal to serve the national interest was defeated by the petty machinations of the Washington "in-crowd."

▪ ▪ ▪ ▪

In September the Department of State began drafting its fiscal 1995 budget request. The effort was sometimes called the "Big Pie Exercise" because it cut up the appropriations request to conform to the new goals in the foreign aid budget. The slices and categories were precisely those I had developed with my task force, and I was quietly pleased that our approach was working. Then, abruptly and unexpectedly, the process was handed off to Lynn Davis, undersecretary for arms control and international security affairs and an experienced national security expert with a PhD in political science from Columbia. I was puzzled—why not the undersecretary for management, as previously done? Perhaps, I thought, it was because Richard Moose was new in the job, having replaced Brian Atwood only a month before.

But a major problem was that the department's initial budget allocation from the Office of Management and Budget was only $19.6 billion—woefully inadequate to meet President Clinton's stated goals. Our new framework for the 150 account made the gap dramatically clear—we would have to either secure much greater funding or make hard choices about program reductions. Yet instead of discussing with Richard Moose and me what Christopher wanted to do and how we might be able to increase our appropriation, he turned to someone else entirely. I was baffled. A month later, Christopher launched a fierce campaign with Clinton and his White House to increase the department budget.

This time Christopher's actions gave me serious pause: what was he trying to accomplish? Although I had given my utmost with the administrative tasks Christopher assigned me, I had always rued that I had not been part of senior deliberations on foreign policy. My discomfort had sharply increased when, despite my history in and recent mission to Southeast Asia, Christopher left me out of the briefing prior to the president's upcoming participation in an ASEAN meeting in Singapore. I probably had more personal and professional familiarity with the region than any other senior government official, but I wasn't asked to help prepare the president for his trip. A few months later, when Clinton was planning for a meeting in Seattle of the Asia-Pacific Economic Cooperation (APEC), I suggested to Warren Christopher that Clinton consider offering to move the session to Southeast Asia as a gesture of Asian-style deference. The secretary waved the idea off.

On September 30 the U.S.-ASEAN Council hosted a dinner honoring Dr. Mahathir, the Malaysian prime minister. I sat at Mahathir's table, along with Hank Greenberg, CEO of AIG and the council's chair, and Carla Hills, a former U.S. trade representative. Mahathir was planning to boycott the forthcoming APEC meeting, but I hoped to persuade him to change his mind. I tried to couch my points in the subtle, indirect manner of Asian-Malay discourse, and Mahathir seemed to be listening attentively. Then Greenberg broke in with his usual bluntness, commanding Mahathir, "You must go!" The prime minister's face hardened, and so did his resolve. I still might have been able to rescue the situation later, but I was never consulted by either Clinton or Christopher.

Meanwhile, mid-autumn witnessed escalating public criticism of Clinton's maladroit foreign policy and Christopher's competence as secretary of state. On October 2, the *Economist* published an article called "Rules of Engagement," lambasting the president's recent speech at the U.N. for "making up his foreign policy as he goes." That very day came the news of the military debacle in Somalia, when a small force of 160 U.S. peacekeepers suffered eighteen deaths, eighty-four wounded, and one captured at the hands of a mob in Mogadishu. The televised images of downed Black Hawk helicopters and the sight of dead U.S. soldiers dragged savagely through the town's filthy streets cast a cloud over Clinton's entire administration, especially Les Aspin, the secretary of defense.

Shortly afterward the *Economist* returned to the fray with "Four Characters in Search of a Doctrine," with quotes from Clinton, Christopher, Tony Lake, and U.N. ambassador Madeleine Albright. Two weeks later, "Foggy Bottom Fumbling" strongly suggested that the president needed to overhaul his foreign policy team. On October 23 a Knight Ridder article pummeled Christopher for equivocation and lack of clear vision. The next day, a blistering op-ed appeared in the *New York Times* by Frank McCloskey of Indiana, a senior Democrat on the House Foreign Affairs Committee. McCloskey demanded Christopher's resignation outright, saying that the secretary had "severely damaged the U.S. national interest through his leadership failure." It was hard to know whether these were just the standard media attacks on a still-new administration or something more serious. But they didn't have anything to do with my own assignments, so I didn't see any personal reason to be concerned, except that the team from which I had been deliberately excluded was foundering.

What did trouble me personally was an October 22 television program, PBS's *Washington Week in Review*. Discussing the administration's troubles, the independent journalist Hedrick Smith commented, "But watch . . . over time, for some changes at the deputy level, say Clinton Horton [*sic*] at the State Department. Now it was the Deputies Committee, which is right under the secretary of state and secretary of defense, national security adviser, which made a number of operational decisions. And I think there are likely to be some changes there. You know, Larry Eagleburger was the deputy secretary of state. A very experienced man, in the Reagan and Bush years. And they may be looking for somebody like that to help Christopher . . . but they don't want to have any heads roll and appear to be scapegoating people."

What the devil? I thought. Was that *me* Smith was talking about—"Clinton Horton"? I wasn't a member of the Deputies Committee. Much to my regret, I had never attended a meeting of the Deputies Committee and rarely made any "operational decisions" on foreign policy. Somebody had obviously been whispering in Smith's ear—but who? I would have brought it to Warren Christopher's attention, but he had just left for a six-day trip to the former Soviet Union. I did reach Thomas E. Donilon, his top aide, to whom I expressed my concern. Donilon seemed to think the story was just one of those things that happen in Washington and that I shouldn't pay it much heed.

Nothing further occurred for a few days, so I was beginning to think Donilon was probably right. But on October 25, an item came out in *Newsweek*'s "Periscope" column claiming that I was at the "epicenter" of a Department of State shake-up.[37] The article belittled my foreign affairs experience, alleged that I was "prickly and unreliable," and said that Warren Christopher was "exasperated" with me. An anonymous White House source said there was a general consensus that I "had not been the best fit" in my job. The article ended with the suggestion that Christopher needed more help "from a veteran in the mold of Lawrence Eagleburger, James Baker's deputy," and that I would be offered another post.

Taken together, the PBS and *Newsweek* pieces were starting to look like the beginnings of a concerted attack. The magazine wouldn't have carried its piece without a high-level source. Clearly it was being pushed by someone with an agenda. Such deliberate leaks are legion in Washington, where a stab in the back is usually easier than a face-to-face confrontation. Whether it came from the White House or the State Department didn't matter much—the damage had been done.

I called Dolores, who was fifty miles away on Maryland's Eastern Shore, conducting her FCI meeting at the Aspen Institute Wye River Conference Center. "Fasten your seat belt," I told her, and described the turn of events. Dolores wasn't exactly surprised. She had never been enthusiastic about Washington's hothouse political culture, and of course we had talked before about my systematic exclusion from the Clinton administration's foreign policy apparatus.

On the same day, ironically, I pinch-hit for the traveling Christopher at a working lunch with President Clinton and Egyptian president Hosni Mubarak. At the time Egypt was receiving around a billion dollars annually in foreign aid, not including substantially more in military assistance. Rumors were in the air that the nation's aid amounts were about to be reduced, and one purpose of Mubarak's White House visit was to seek reassurances that no cuts were in the offing. When the Egyptian president raised the question, I looked down the table at national security adviser Tony Lake and his deputy, Sandy Berger. Neither seemed to have anything to say. I was concerned that Clinton might inadvertently make an untenable commitment. I was also concerned because given my role with the 150 account, there had been times when "principals" had made funding promises to foreign leaders for which there were no budget dollars, and I had to transfer funds around to honor their promises. So I spoke up, explaining that Egypt's support was merely being stretched over a slightly longer period. I promised Mubarak that we would discuss things more fully the next morning, at our bilateral meeting at the State Department. After the lunch ended and Clinton bid Mubarak farewell, the president took me aside to thank me for stepping in with my helpful comment.

Meanwhile, the *Newsweek* article was so worrisome that I called some close confidants. Phil Talbot was shocked at the news. Vernon Jordan was similarly concerned (we agreed to meet for breakfast the following Sunday). Sol Linowitz was frankly puzzled. If Christopher were really so dissatisfied, why wouldn't he tell me to my face—much less wait so long to do it? He urged that I confront the secretary and speak candidly about my own frustrations. Sol then asked who was handling my press relations. When I said no one, he asked if there was someone I could call upon. I told him about Bob Perrin, and he thought it might be wise to have Bob come to Washington for a couple of months to help out. When I said I suspected the situation had already unraveled too far, Sol said, "If you have to leave, you owe it to yourself that it not be done precipitously but on your own timetable."

Dolores was also getting feedback from some of her contacts, such as columnist Carl Rowan, her fellow director at Gannett, who recommended that we "just batten down the hatches and keep on going."

After thinking it over, I took Linowitz's recommendation and called Bob Perrin, who had come out from Michigan from time to time to work with me on departmental projects. He was as shocked as everyone else. I asked whether he could join me again for a few months to help me with communications, and he promised to talk with his wife Barbara and get back to me right away.

As soon as Warren Christopher returned from Russia, I met with him, on Thursday, October 28, at 10:00 A.M. When I brought up the leaks, he responded with a rambling commentary. He had been giving a lot of thought, he said, to recent foreign developments. He and I were not giving the president the support he deserved—we were doing fine in some areas, but not others. He took "full responsibility," even though he had been working flat out. The department mirrored a broader pattern, he remarked, citing an upcoming meeting of undersecretaries where we needed to do "a better job."

Then Christopher got down to brass tacks. He said he and I should have a better division of labor. I had been waiting for him to take projects on, rather than taking my own initiatives. He needed me to go after substantive policy issues, and this was a void only I could fill.

I was stunned. If that was what he wanted, I started to ask, why had he excluded me from the Deputies Committee and policy formulation from the beginning—and why had he waited so long to ask me? But I decided to let him finish.

He needed more follow-up, Christopher continued, calling the department reorganization plan "adrift"—another shocker, since the plan was already under way and had received very positive coverage in the department's own magazine. I also needed to travel more—though he could not authorize travel for Dolores, he added, for legal and political reasons. The secretary concluded that I had a "perception problem" at the White House—though he stressed "that does not include the president. . . . People feel that you are not giving me as much help as you should. They say you are not effectively managing the role of deputy."

At this point I began for the first time to think that Christopher really was looking for a sacrificial lamb for his own and Clinton's botched foreign policies. I told Christopher that if he were "exasperated," so was I, since I had been doing precisely what he had asked—AID and budget reform, plus reorganization of the department. In several cases, my efforts had been deliberately undercut—I cited the problems getting the AID report released to Congress. As for being more help on foreign policy, I reminded Christopher that I had been excluded again and again from such deliberations. All the leaks were laying the administration's foreign policy failures at my footsteps, and now he was doing the same thing.

What made things even more incomprehensible was that when the secretary was in Washington, we had near-daily meetings—almost seventy-five since the beginning of February. Not once in any of them had Christopher mentioned the slightest concern with my performance. He had given no indication of displeasure, nor suggested any change in my stipulated assignments. He certainly never mentioned wanting me to step into foreign policy development—and now I couldn't help wondering to myself if he had kept silent deliberately all these months to lay the groundwork for me to "fail." Although they don't let you on the team to play, they then ironically try to get rid of you by saying that the losses are your fault.

At the end of the meeting I said that I had come to Washington only to be helpful to President Clinton, and I still hoped to do so. In response to Christopher's comments I would prepare a plan for altering my role, which he and I could review when he returned from a trip for his daughter's wedding in California.

When I repeated the conversation to Dolores, she was livid—Christopher's actions, she said, were unconscionable. Not supporting his own appointees showed weakness of character. She reminded me of a conversation she had had with Gay Vance, wife of the former secretary of state Cy Vance, when Christopher was his deputy secretary. Gay had said Christopher was a very secretive man, and he particularly didn't like wives' participation in their husband's activities. Dolores was certain that Christopher was looking for a fall guy for his own failures of leadership.

The next evening former Deputy Secretary of State John Whitehead and his wife Nancy joined Dolores and me in cohosting the Department of State's thirty-third annual reception for the United Nations Association,[38] where I offered brief remarks. After that there was a dinner at the National Building Museum. One honoree was U.N. secretary-general Boutros Boutros-Ghali. The diplomat's own relations with the Clinton administration were tense, and his feisty remarks reflected it. Other award recipients were Senator Pat Moynihan, lawyer-diplomat Max Kampelman, and Vice President Al Gore. No one said anything about either the *Newsweek* article or the *Week in Review* leak, and I said nothing about my showdown with Christopher.

On Sunday, October 31, I had a long, enlightening breakfast with Vernon Jordan. He was sympathetic, describing his confrontations with Warren Christopher during Clinton's transition period. Though Jordan considered Christopher a person who wanted to "do the right thing," his best guess was that the secretary was unlikely to take decisive action, allowing things to "peter along" until I did something myself. He also thought the administration's foreign policy straits would probably get worse—"The process in place will be hard to change." Anthony Lake, Sandy Berger, Peter Tarnoff, Richard Holbrooke, Madeleine Albright, and others had been together since the days of Jimmy Carter, plotting their return to power. "They worked on the campaigns for Mondale, Dukakis, and Clinton, parceling out the jobs." They were part of Clinton's inner team and clearly had excluded me from making the contribution that I could make.

Jordan wasn't able to give me any clue who might be leaking tales to the press. He recommended that I put my own interests first, either finding another job in the administration or working out a graceful exit. He promised to check into the World Bank presidency, my first choice when approached by the Clinton team, but said there was still no reason to think that the current president of the Bank was planning early retirement.

At lunch the next day, I told Sol Linowitz I thought I should resign. Linowitz recalled that Douglas Dillon had once told him, "Never for a day let them forget that you can pick up your marbles and go home."[39] But I doubted whether Christopher or Clinton much cared whether I did or did not "pick up my marbles." Whoever was pushing for me to leave, it had to be with either Clinton's or Christopher's concurrence.

The leaks continued. A Hearst News Service release led to an article in the November 3 *Washington Times*: "Senior White House officials say Clifton Wharton Jr., the deputy secretary of state and one of the Clinton administration's highest ranking blacks, is expected to resign within six months. . . . The officials say Mr. Wharton will leave amid White House and State Department dissatisfaction with his *day-to-day management of the nation's diplomacy* [emphasis added]. . . . The officials stressed that Mr. Wharton is not being fired, nor is there any timetable for his departure. White House officials traditionally use such leaks to signal displeasure with top appointees in hopes that they will step down."[40]

Now I was mishandling day-to-day foreign policy! Well, at least the *Washington Times* spelled my name right. When questioned about the article, the department's press secretary,

Mike McCurry, told reporters that he "was not aware of any truth to that item. I think the secretary highly regards Dr. Wharton, both professionally and personally, and I'm not aware of any plans of change in his status as deputy secretary." White House press secretary Dee Dee Myers chimed in, "Rumors, rumors, rumors." Then she added, "Of course, some rumors become true even though they're not true when they start." President Clinton and Warren Christopher kept their own counsels.

The Hearst release had a couple of points that hadn't been picked up by the *Washington Times*. One was an allegation that I had an imperious style "that hasn't meshed well with the easygoing camaraderie of many of Clinton's other top aides." The other was that "Wharton also may be shouldering blame for Presidential Directive 13, a draft policy document committing the United States to wider involvement in United Nations peacekeeping operations. Wharton was a *key member of the 'Deputies Committee'* [emphasis added], the interagency panel made up of second-ranking national security officials at the White House, State Department, Pentagon, and Joint Chiefs of Staff. Christopher, Wharton's boss, revised the deputies' draft and eventually shelved the effort after 18 GIs were killed in an ill-fated raid in Somalia as part of a U.N. operation." This was a shocking total fabrication since I had never heard of, much less seen, PRD 13!

As the leaks continued, other outside observers began to challenge the often-vacillating and erroneous claims. A November 4 article in the *Albany Times Union* repeated several allegations but quoted a number of angry rebuttals from SUNY colleagues and New York legislators, based on their previous association with me.[41] The article also concluded with a review of my successes at the State Department. Two days later, the paper published a supportive editorial headlined, "Mr Wharton as Scapegoat. . . . If true, he's taking the fall for Warren Christopher's disarray."

Dolores's no-nonsense advice was "If Christopher won't give you his support, let's get the hell out of here!" I agreed. Unless the secretary or the president unambiguously refuted the leaks, I would never regain any effectiveness in my job. On November 5, I asked Bob Perrin to draft a possible letter of resignation. That evening he sent me two versions. The first was a four-sentence blast, saying in effect that I was being undermined, and I quit. The second was a careful, detailed explanation of why I had joined the Clinton administration, my reaction to the faceless, unfounded attacks, and the absence of support from the administration.

I saw Christopher again on Saturday, November 6. As promised, I brought a plan for stepping more actively into the policy arena. But Christopher's first few words made it clear he would issue no unequivocal rebuttal to the leaked allegations and would prefer that I fade gracefully from sight. I told him I would be submitting my resignation promptly. He asked if there was anything else I might like to pursue in the Clinton administration, mentioning the ambassadorship to Great Britain's Court of St. James, among the most prestigious U.S. embassies. I politely declined.

After letting Bob Perrin know, I called my close friends to get any advice they had for the letter of resignation. Vernon Jordan said that if Dolores and I were comfortable with the decision, he was too, but warned that anything I said would be subject to close scrutiny by the press. Phil Talbot urged that I state the record as I saw it. "This early in an administration," he remarked, "they can't afford to fire the secretary, so the typical Washington ploy is to let the deputy go." Sol Linowitz gave sound counsel: 90 percent of the people in Washington wouldn't know anything about what had been going on, so I needed to explain myself dispassionately to avoid looking thin-skinned. "Facing a foreign policy crisis Clinton had to choose between firing Christopher or you. You gave it your best shot, but you were confronting faceless leaks that undercut your effectiveness. Just don't bang the door too loudly."

I didn't want my departure to occasion a media frenzy to skewer President Clinton's administration, but if I had had any reservations about their deviousness, the handling of my resignation's press coverage dispelled them. A draft of my letter went over to the White House for clearance. Several hours later they sent back their revisions, which removed what they thought were overly critical.

I officially submitted the letter on Monday, November 8. In it I pointed out that "in the past two weeks, it became unmistakably clear that I was being subject to the classic Washington practice of sustained, anonymous leaks to the media. Therefore I decided to resign, rather than permit my effectiveness to be further eroded. I am confident that those who know me well would never accuse me of quitting in the face of adversity."

About a quarter past 4:00 P.M., President Clinton called to express his regret that I was leaving and to thank me for my service. It was a short conversation, neither warm nor particularly chilly. I hardly remember what was said by either of us. Meanwhile, the White House communications staff held up approval of my letter of resignation until after the evening news hour to blunt its impact. I was told afterward that the delaying tactic was David Gergen's idea. He was an acquaintance of mine from the Aspen Institute, so I was especially disappointed by his action.

Exactly one week later, Dolores and I had left our Watergate Hotel suite and were back in our home at United Nations Plaza in New York City.

My departure didn't end the controversy. After my resignation became public, the White House and Department of State shifted their message back to their early false allegations of my "limited foreign policy background" and Christopher's need for a broadly seasoned professional. Department spokesman Mike McCurry said that I had done "enormously good work as it relates to the restructuring of AID, the whole large issue of how do we configure a budget in the post–Cold War era." He added, "Dr. Wharton's reasons for leaving had nothing to do with hot spots around the world, but had everything to do with his view of the job and the secretary's view of the job." Other officials sought to head off the perception that I had been sacrificed to appease the administration's critics, alleging that I had "never mastered the bureaucratic intricacies of the department and was slow in making decisions, such as producing a plan to revamp the Agency for International Development."[42] That charge left me fuming. I had completed the AID review on time, and its release had been delayed first by the White House, then by Christopher's disagreement with my proposal to change AID's reporting structure.

By now I thought nothing more could surprise me—but the day after I resigned, the *New York Times* reported that the decision to force me out of office was by the State Department alone, not the White House. According to the usual unnamed senior officials, "Christopher had long complained about [my] lackluster performance" and had informed Clinton of his intention to replace me. This meeting had taken place on October 19—three days before the leaks had begun and nine days before meeting with me for the first time to discuss them.[43] So much for Christopher's claim that I "had a problem with the White House." Christopher himself had made the decision, never mentioned to me his prior meeting with the president, and afterward continued to act as if we might be able to "work things out." I was astonished.

The other distressing aspect was the behavior of President Bill Clinton. He had asked me to take the job as deputy secretary of state, but his lack of support made it hard not to feel betrayed.[44] His letter accepting my resignation and complimenting my efforts as "outstanding" was small comfort.

By now the media was starting to catch on. The *New York Times* declared that I had been "dumped" to foster the impression that Warren Christopher was "setting his department in order" and that "the administration had a coherent foreign policy."[45] The *Chicago Tribune* called me a "scapegoat" for a faulty foreign policy. Representative Frank McCloskey, who had already called for Christopher's resignation, said that the secretary should "look in the mirror. He is the major part of a severe problem in the administration."[46] A. M. "Abe" Rosenthal wrote an op-ed in the *New York Times* that was especially hard-hitting, coming from the paper's former executive editor. "Pieced together," he said, "it is a story of how an Administration failed to do its duty to itself and an American achiever. . . . People with outstanding lifetime records may consider the Wharton case if they are asked to work in the Administration."[47]

While the leaks were under way and afterward, I was strongly defended by three syndicated Black columnists—Carl Rowan, Chuck Stone, and Chester Higgins Jr. All of them skewered the allegations that I lacked foreign policy experience or managerial skills. They also raised questions about whether there had been a racial undertone to the attacks. For Rowan, it was a "sordid bureaucratic assassination." My friend Chuck Stone went so far as to call the episode a "lynching." Their support was a welcome contrast to the limited reaction from Blacks in Congress. After I announced my resignation, I heard from just three of them. Senator Carol Moseley Braun (D-IL) belatedly called to ask if there was anything she could do. Representative Donald Payne (D-NJ) and my cousin, Representative Charles Rangel, merely said they were sorry I was leaving.

The process of choosing my successor was worthy of a Marx brothers movie. Seeking a "career Foreign Service type" to be the next deputy, the names most frequently mentioned in the press were Tom Pickering, Mike Armacost, Frank Wisner, and Stephen Bosworth. All four had impressive career foreign policy credentials, including multiple ambassadorships, but those contacted declined. Armacost was especially favored and repeatedly pressed—first by Strobe Talbott (speaking for the president), then by Christopher himself, and finally by David Gergen.[48] But Armacost declined, indicating that he did not think he was the right person for the job, especially because there was a "significant political component" that he had observed with prior deputies—an indirect reference to my departure. Finally chosen was Strobe Talbott (Clinton's Rhodes Scholar roommate at Oxford). A former *Time* editor-at-large, Washington Bureau chief, and a specialist on Russia, Strobe certainly was not a seasoned career officer with broad experience. The press "spin-masters" at State tried to make it appear that he had been the sole candidate for the position even before I resigned. "Senior officials said Christopher considered Talbott a candidate to replace Clifton R. Wharton Jr. even before the former deputy resigned under fire. During a trip to the Middle East last month, Christopher spoke with Talbott about the job, interviewed him again upon returning and offered him the job formally on Sunday."[49]

The most insightful sequel came when I learned from General Powell's autobiography[50] that Christopher had seriously thought of retiring in 1994 and that Powell had been approached by Vernon Jordan to be the new Secretary of State.[51] Despite a direct inquiry from the president himself,[52] Powell declined, reflecting later, "Left unspoken were my reservations about the amorphous way the administration handled foreign policy." Eventually, Christopher changed his mind about resigning. This anecdote made me wonder whether Christopher's possible insecurity as secretary led him to deliberately exclude me from policy making.

In retrospect, the best symbol for my nine months in Washington was a bright red telephone that had been installed inside a special safe in our apartment at the Watergate. The hot line was connected to the Department of State operations center to be used for totally secure communications with foreign policy officials in the United States and abroad. Opening the safe required a secret combination. Only once in all my time at the State Department did I receive a hot line call. I never had occasion to make one.

Strangers and close associates alike inevitably wondered if racism played a part in my troubles at State. I never encountered anything overt—certainly nothing approaching the challenges my father faced as the sole Black officer in the department, nor the disgraceful discriminatory manner in which his early postings were handled. But assuredly there were some people who believed that my only qualification as deputy secretary was the color of my skin—that I had been selected mainly in the interest of show-case "diversity" in high-level presidential appointments. The latter point was covered by the distinguished Black reporter Lee Daniels with an in-depth interview where he also surmised I may have been seen as a threat to Christopher's position as secretary of state." In addition I suppose that the old negative expectations syndrome probably played a part, as it did so often in my earlier careers. Regardless of my considerable foreign policy background, there were those who saw only my Blackness. Expected to make no major contribution, I had been excluded from the venues where I might have done so—a vexing, self-fulfilling prophecy.

The Black publication *Emerge* confronted the issue head-on. "Wharton believed the press did not delve further into the reason why he left the State Department because he was perceived in some circles from the beginning as being a 'token' black appointment," commented George E. Curry, *Emerge*'s editor in chief. "Dr. Wharton . . . has been successful without relying on race as a crutch. [His resignation proves that] race matters a lot. And as long as race matters, being good won't be good enough."[54]

My conclusion at the time was that all these speculative factors were probably involved, but assigning relative weights would be difficult or impossible, if not pointless. I should have said no to Clinton as I had to Cabinet inquiries from two previous presidents!

Although I had left the Department of State, I did not avoid discussing the experience. At the November 11, 1993, annual dinner of the National Association of State Universities and Land-Grant Colleges, I gave a talk titled "Foreign Policy and Preventive Diplomacy: Redefining U.S. Development Assistance after the Cold War." On February 21, 1994, I gave an address to the American Council on Education called "Preventive Diplomacy: The Other Dimension of National Security." Both speeches got a warm reception, and the ACE presented me with its Distinguished Service Award for Lifetime Achievement. It was very moving to accept the award from ACE's president, my old friend and colleague Bob Atwell, and an honor to join the company of the prior recipients, including Clark Kerr, Father Ted Hesburgh, John Gardner, Benjamin Mays, and David Riesman.

The outpouring of support for me from former colleagues and friends was gratifying, especially those who saw the State Department as scapegoating me despite my long career of success and failing to use my talents in public service. Most telling was a telephone call from my friend and colleague Bill Friday, who encouraged, "Clif, don't let those SOBs in Washington diminish you one iota. Your record and past is the proof of who you are and what you have done."

Thus my reaction to the Washington brief interlude, while disappointing, could not overcome my long history of positive achievements. This feeling was reinforced by a virtual avalanche of inquiries and offers of new positions. They ranged from endowed chairs (Michigan State, Cornell, and Ohio universities) to professorships and fellowships (Syracuse, Minnesota, and Harvard) and even a presidential search (Texas A&M). There were invitations to join a number of corporate and nonprofit boards. Most I declined with heartfelt thanks. I rejoined the boards of Ford Motor Company (on which I would serve a total of twenty-four years, until May 1997), the New York Stock Exchange, and the Overseers of TIAA-CREF

(1994 to 2001). Eventually, two new corporations, Tenneco and Harcourt General, were added. I also became a trustee of the American Assembly, Winrock International (successor to my old ADC), the Clark Foundation, and Bassett Healthcare Network (Cooperstown). All these calls gave me a strong sense of personal validation.

The temptation to return to teaching was strong, and Peter McPherson, then president of Michigan State, pressed me enthusiastically to do so. Teaching had been my first and in many ways my best-loved vocation. Dolores and I continued to regard the campus in East Lansing very fondly. But I resisted the temptation.

After considering all the options, I decided that my new major activity would be to write my autobiography.

. . . .

Back in New York, I had an office provided by TIAA-CREF. Dolores continued her corporate and nonprofit activities. At the Kellogg Company she served for twenty-two years, until 1997, and at the Gannett Company for nineteen years, until 1998. She joined COMSAT corporation in 1994 and National Public Radio (NPR) the same year. In 1995 she was a founding director of the Capital Bank & Trust Company (Albany, NY), serving until 2002. She also continued for many years as a trustee of the Aspen Institute, the Asia Foundation, Center for Strategic and International Studies (CSIS), the SUNY Fashion Institute of Technology, New York City Center, and Glimmerglass Opera (Cooperstown, NY).

Before we left Washington, Dolores had begun the process of handing off her Young Executive Program to the Aspen Institute. In October 1993 she initiated an "FCI Fellows" program, which brought selected alumni together for seminars designed to provide more intensive reinforcement of business acumen and leadership skills, with added focus on the global marketplace. The new program received support from the Ford, Volvo, and Gordon and Llura Gund foundations. (A major gift to FCI was given by the Kellogg Company upon Dolores's retirement from the Kellogg board.) In 1994 the Aspen Institute assumed full responsibility for the Young Executive Program. Over the next several years Aspen tried hard to rekindle the energy and enthusiasm that had been so marked among the program's earlier participants. But by then many corporations had begun to develop their own internal programs for mentoring their high-potential inside talent. After several years the effort no longer attracted enough interest, and the Aspen version of FCI would close officially in May 2001.

So, our lives continued to be active and rewarding. And our sons were living their own independent lives, with our help when needed and ever constant love.

Clifton 3rd continued at the Pratt Institute in Baltimore, where his childhood affinity served him wonderfully well as the children's services librarian. He had enrolled in the University of Maryland's MA Library Science program, receiving his degree in 1988. Dolores and I attended the ceremonies and were elated to watch Clifton 3rd beaming with pride as he walked across to receive his diploma. In October 1989, Pratt promoted him to the post of automation coordinator. His first marriage had ended, and on July 29, 1991, he married Mary Kovacevich, who had worked at Pratt.

In May 1990, Bruce received his BA degree in business and human resources from SUNY College of Technology. He joined the ITT Sheraton New York and Manhattan Hotel Complex from July 1990 to December 1992, working as employment coordinator and then as reservations and communications manager. The position required him to service 2,500 rooms at the two hotels and supervise a staff of sixteen reservation agents and twenty-four telephone operators. But next he decided to pursue an MBA degree at the Broad College of Business at Michigan State. At MSU, he became a teaching and research assistant to Professor Bonnie Knutson, which gave him an inside experience and exposure to the academic world.

Both Dolores and I found ourselves in a new mode of retirees who were wanted and pursued for involvement with various institutions, while enjoying the more leisurely tempo of expanded social and cultural life. We were back relishing the dual pleasures of country living in Cooperstown and the vibrancy of our beloved New York city "habitat."

CHAPTER THIRTEEN

The Retiree: Roles, Recognitions, and Reflections

The past two decades of retirement introduced a new lifetime course as an elder statesman. I was offered and carefully selected opportunities to contribute in areas of my previous interest—primarily chairing study groups, commissions, and special panels. Four of these endeavors involved my professional areas—Asia, New York higher education, New York Stock Exchange, and intercollegiate athletics. (My corporate boards continued until their mandatory retirement ages.[1])

▪ Retirement Roles

In 1996, the Asia Society approached me about heading a study mission to Southeast Asia, our former operational area. Both Dolores and I had served as Society trustees—I served from 1967 to 1977 and Dolores from 1982 to 1987. They had already undertaken several similar studies, and for the present wanted to focus on the economic impact of Taiwan in East and Southeast Asia.[2] My cochair was William Donaldson, founder of Donaldson, Lufkin and Jenrette, and former chairman and CEO of the New York Stock Exchange. The society appointed eight other knowledgeable and experienced persons to the mission (see appendix 11).

After travel in the region, our 1997 report encouraged Taiwan to pursue increased direct investment and trade in eastern and southeast Asia, while adopting policies to encourage stronger economic relations with the People's Republic of China, including cross-straits dialogue; increased contacts of an academic, professional, and quasi-official nature; and eventually a bilateral meeting of leaders. Our recommendations included Taiwan's reaffirming a more straightforward commitment to a one-China policy and to correlate that reunification by peaceful means.

One of our mission's more disturbing findings was that

The post cold war period has been marked by a distinct lack of consistency in [U.S.] Asia policy and the United States prestige in the region has suffered as a result. The maintenance of a forward United States military presence will act as a damper on tension in the region and demonstrate the U.S. commitment to the peaceful evolution of relations among the powers throughout the region. However, this must take place in the context of a clear, consistent, and bi-partisan set of policies. Taiwan matters cannot be considered independently of relations with the PRC and cannot become a partisan issue. A consensus for a productive relationship with the People's Republic of China needs to be restored throughout all branches of the U.S. government, including Congress.

This observation on the growing international ascendancy of China made almost two decades earlier appears prescient in retrospect.

▪ New York Student Financial Aid ─────────────────────

My SUNY and higher education experience was reengaged in 1998. Senator Ken LaValle, chairman of the New York Senate Higher Education Committee, approached me about his wish to have a review of the state's student financial aid structure. The state took great pride in having the largest and most generous program of student aid in the nation. This was a reflection of the state's history and the composition of its higher education sector. Because New York enrolled fewer students in its public colleges and universities than other states, it spent less per capita on higher education. New York ranked forty-first among all fifty states. Therefore, given this profile, the previous ten years had seen a decline in the level of higher education funding, which affected the two critical goals of aid—student choice and student access. Further, the quality of both public and private sectors had suffered.

LaValle and I discussed the idea of a special commission being appointed by the New York Senate, which I would cochair with Paul Volcker, former chairman of the Federal Reserve Board. At my request, Paul agreed to serve. I identified nine other national academic leaders and former government officials to serve on a commission that included both public and private higher education luminaries as well as corporate and civic leaders (see appendix 12).

Just before our report was due, state senate majority leader Joseph L. Bruno decided to offer up his own proposal on student financial aid. LaValle had no explanation for Bruno's unexpected action. Nevertheless, we went ahead and issued our report. Our final report[3] noted that New York's economy and society had "benefitted hugely" from the state's Tuition Assistance Program.

More than 78 percent of TAP recipients in 1989 were still living in New York seven years later, investing their talents and hard work in the state had helped them attend college. The commission noted that while New York spent $700 million—more than any other state—on scholarships, the grants had not kept pace with inflation. We discussed ways to expand financial aid to college students and proposed that New York State sharply expand its financial aid to college students, continuing to concentrate on low-income families rather than the middle class. We recommended that the state pay 100 percent of the tuition for the neediest students at SUNY and the City University of New York, rather than the 90 percent then being provided. Our panel also suggested that for private colleges the state raise the maximum annual grant in the Tuition Assistance Program, its primary financial aid program, by more than 20 percent, to $5,000 for undergraduates and $1,500 for graduate students.

At a press conference, Paul Volcker remarked, "I was struck by the unanimity of the commission that the TAP program was worth keeping and strengthening and that the emphasis really ought to be on the underprivileged. . . . Now that [the senate and assembly have] come up with their own initiatives, I have more hope that they are going to take some action."[4] Among other recommendations, the commission called for the state to eliminate a policy that reduced TAP awards to students in their last two years of college and to raise support to private colleges to at least $75 million, an increase of $27 million.[5] In the end, the report had some impact on future student financial aid changes by the state.

. . . .

A third activity involved the New York Stock Exchange, which I had rejoined after leaving Washington. In 1999 Dick Grasso, NYSE CEO, asked Alex Trotman, CEO of Ford Motor Company, and me to cochair an NYSE board Committee on Market Structure (see appendix 13). The title was a catchall for a range of issues, including decimalization (pricing in pennies instead of eighths of a dollar), the future role of specialists, liquidity versus fragmentation, traders versus individuals, and cost and speed versus price improvement. While arcane topics to the general public, the issues dealt with the critical lifeblood of Wall Street. Our general goal was to identify a process to further the computerization of exchange processes while avoiding serious disruptions or other negative consequences.

The committee of twelve directors met seven times, reviewing basic papers, holding hearings, and interviewing key leaders. The economic interests affected by our agenda were huge and powerful. Among our several recommendations, the one that attracted the greatest attention was the proposal to eliminate the Intermarket Trading System.[6] Although our original key mandate was to review the NYSE governance and ownership, including the feasibility of becoming a for-profit company, I reported that the committee had decided to "wait until after the switch from fractional to decimal pricing of stocks."[ ] The major contribution of the study was providing a base and guideline for the next evolution of the Exchange.

▪ Knight Commission Again

Intercollegiate athletics became once again a demanding and important activity. From 1989 to 1992 I had served on the first Knight Commission on Intercollegiate Athletics, chaired by Father Ted Hesburgh, president of Notre Dame, and William Friday, president of the University of North Carolina. The commission's initial goal was to address the commercialization of college sports and the manner in which it often undercut academic values and overshadowed the underlying goals of higher education. In its 1991 first report, *Keeping Faith with the Student Athlete*, the commission proposed a "one-plus-three model," with complete presidential control of athletic programs as the "one" central factor. We stated that "presidents are accountable for the major elements in the university's life. The burden of leadership falls on them for the conduct of the institution, whether in the classroom or on the playing field. The president cannot be a figurehead whose leadership applies elsewhere in the university but not in the athletics department." We therefore recommended that presidents regain control of both the NCAA and regional athletics conferences, and that university trustees affirm presidential authority over athletic program administration. The commission's recommendations to restructure the NCAA were largely completed, taking six years. Presidents were given full authority for the governance of intercollegiate athletics at the national level. (Previously it had been in the hands of a council of athletics administrators and faculty representatives.)

Then in 2000 the Knight Foundation decided that, although most of the original recommendations had been implemented, college athletics still had major problems. The "arms race" of differential expenditure rates between intercollegiate athletics and academics had continued to escalate. Coaches' salaries at big-time colleges were beginning to outpace the salaries of administrators and faculty. Student athletes especially in football and basketball had seriously low academic grades and graduation rates. Athletics was beginning to corrupt academic standards. Consequently the commission was needed once again, and Bill Friday called, urging me to reenlist. This time I eventually served as vice chair (in 2005), then as cochair (in 2006–7).

The commission's second major report was *A Call to Action: Reconnecting College Sports and Higher Education* (2001). The report focused on the ten years since its predecessor, calling for an even stronger commitment to academic standards in college sports. As a result of the restructured governance system and presidential engagement, the presidents were able to push through sweeping academic reform legislation in 2004. The most meaningful outcome was the development of a national standard for measuring academic progress and graduation rates of athletes and institutional sanctions for those college programs that fell below the minimal acceptable standards.

By 2010, many issues and problems that concerned the commission had in fact grown even worse, particularly as regarded the impact of college athletics upon the fundamental missions of higher education.[8] The situation was aptly captured by the title of the commission's 2010 report, *Restoring the Balance: Dollars, Values, and the Future of College Sports.* Many institutions' big-time sports (football and basketball) had become more than university "subsidiary enterprises." Coaches and the athletes functioned in their own separate world within the academy. Athletic programs had become virtually independent adjuncts whose role and impact upon their universities had grown enormously, despite their relatively small proportion of an institution's total budgets. This process had spawned a serious imbalance.

The worst aspect of these developments, then and now, is that the relative growth rate of financial expenditures in college athletics at most big-time major institutions was faster than that of the regular university budgets. There was a growing "arms race." The distortion was such that, "according to the National Collegiate Athletic Association (NCAA), over the past decade, spending on athletics has been rising at a rate three to four times faster than the rate of increase of academic budgets among institutions competing in the NCAA's Division I."[9] The Delta Cost Project and American Institute for Research found that "Division I schools with football spent $91,936 per athlete in 2010, seven times the spending per student of $13,628."[10] The study also found that "between 2005 and 2010, on a per capita basis . . . athletic costs increased at least twice as fast as academic spending at institutions with top-tier athletic programs." The commission recognized that universities could not sustain this distorted pattern indefinitely. All this was occurring in the broader context of continuing decline in regular academic funding and against a backdrop of increasing cost burdens placed upon students and their parents. When and how does this growth inequality stop?

Unfortunately, as of today most universities their leaders, boards, alumni, students, and fans—fully believe the major myths about college athletics. Many still believe that college athletics make a "profit" and keep athletics budgets in the "black," that it increases the quality and number of student applicants and improves fund-raising, or that it is the best way for economically disadvantaged students to acquire a higher education and helps create greater "diversity" on the campus. Most of these views are untrue or only partially true. All have become justifications for the status quo, preventing or obstructing needed reforms.

I had previously pushed the Knight Commission on the myths of athletic success increasing donations and enrollments, which led to a report by Cornell economist Professor Robert Frank, *Challenging the Myth: A Review of the Links among College Athletic Success, Student Quality and Donations* (May 2004). Frank's findings had generally confirmed my views. He found no significant correlation between winning teams and an increase in private giving, nor did he find increased enrollments (though sometimes applications increased temporarily following a single spectacular season—the so-called Flutie effect, after Boston College's Heisman Trophy–winning quarterback Doug Flutie). But the myth that a winning football or basketball season equals bigger donations to the nonathletic side of the university still persists to this day.

Despite other arguments about university "brand," image, and alumni loyalty engendered by intercollegiate athletics, the collateral negative consequences to the university's fundamental mission are serious. I believe that in far too many colleges and universities big-time college athletics steadily erodes institutional values and ethics. Almost every other month a newspaper headline blares about a college or university violation of NCAA regulations. The scandals of athletic student arrests for impropriety or illegalities pale in comparison to the outrage from Penn State's assistant coach's behavior toward minors and his convictions.[11]

A more recent shock was the disclosure of academic improprieties at the University of North Carolina. At that campus as many as 560 unauthorized grade changes were suspected of having been made—often with forged faculty signatures—dating back to 1997. Many students enrolled in the courses were student athletes. The faculty involved have been indicted by a grand jury for actions described by the *New York Times* as "one of the biggest cases of academic fraud in North Carolina history. That it has taken place at Chapel Hill, known for its rigorous academic standards as well as an athletic program revered across the country, has only made it more shocking."[12] This is a dramatic example of athletics producing corruption in basic academic standards.

The academy has traditionally played a vital role in setting both intellectual and moral standards for itself and the student body.[13] Colleges and universities have special values that give answers to important questions: Is published research truthfully performed and accurately reported? How is plagiarism dealt with? Does research follow the accepted canons of verification, testing, replication, and transparency? Does a professor give honest grades to students, or are some given preferential treatment? Do students cheat on their exams or papers? Does a university president maintain his or her integrity under the pressure of outside forces that would adversely impact the institution?

Intercollegiate athletics, as a subset of the academy, also raises ethical/values questions. What is the difference between a "booster" who cheats by providing secret benefits to recruit a prize student athlete who helps a team win and a corporate CEO who encourages back-dating of stock options to raise the level of compensation for his corporate "team"? Or do both believe that winning is everything? What is the difference between a college coach who turns a blind eye toward steroid use among his players and a professional league commissioner who does the same thing, all in the name of top performance to satisfy the fans—and, yes, to keep the revenue flowing?

Most egregious, what is the implication of the stratospheric salaries paid to superstar college coaches whose reputations are partially built upon student athletes whose allowed financial payment is equivalent to a minimum wage? (Or compared with faculty salaries?) In 1999 only five coaches in college football made $1 million or more per year.[14] By 2010, 42 of the 119 coaches in college football made $1 million or more. By 2013 the number had changed even more dramatically.[15] Nick Saban of the University of Alabama made $5,545,852 and Mack Brown of University of Texas Austin, $5,453,750. Fifteen other coaches make more than $3 million, and seventy coaches make more than $1 million.[16] Every year the number of millionaire coaches and the size of their salaries grow larger and larger.[17] Most of these numbers do not include hidden "bonuses," "special incentives," "perks," and unreported "deferred compensation arrangements." A typical example was the recent University of Michigan hiring of its new football coach.[18]

Are the college head coach salaries reflective of true academic values? How can these salaries be morally justified when they are based upon the performance of poorly compensated athletes—"student" athletes? This is almost a form of indentured servitude defended as building college student morale and adding luster to the college brand! For the majority of student athletes, even from the elite teams, their hoped-for ultimate financial rewards are a mirage.

In a speech before the Andrew W. Mellon Foundation in 2006 I listed some numbers from the NCAA's 1982–99 Participation Statistics Report detailing how many college athletes make it to the pros:

- Of the 12,600 NCAA senior student athletes in *football,* only 250 were drafted—2 percent. What happened to the other 98 percent—the 12,350 former student athletes?
- Of the 3,500 NCAA senior student athletes in *basketball*, only 44 were drafted—1.3 percent. What happened to the other 98.7 percent—the 3,456 former student athletes?

These percentages have not significantly changed in the years since.[19]

Lately the exploitation of college athletes and their compensation has drawn considerable fire,[20] including legal action by athletes against the NCAA for the right to unionize.[21] The vaunted amateur student athletic model is under attack.[22] Congressional action is imminent, and calls for major reform are escalating, but the response from the athletic leadership has been tepid at best or has added further commercialization at worst.[23]

Basketball has been especially flagrant in its practices and is perhaps unintentionally likely to produce corrective action. A growing number of basketball "powers" are adopting a "one-and-done" approach, where top-tier high-school athletes enroll for one year and then leave for the pros. This practice is attributable to the NBA rule that players are not eligible for its draft until they are a year removed from high school. As a result, highly rated prospects flock to certain colleges to spend only one year, hopefully on a team that will be in the Elite Eight or Final Four or win a national championship, enhancing their professional prospects and astronomical salaries. The athletes are known euphemistically as "one and done." They enroll as Freshmen in the Fall semester, but don't worry about the Spring semester courses because as soon as the season is over, they are off to the NBA. In these situations the myth of athletes as students is beyond laughable. Are they truly student athletes or merely pseudostudents whose sole goal is winning a lucrative professional slot after only one year of playing, not an education? Why do colleges and universities allow, even encourage, the practice? If they are not truly students, why shouldn't they just be paid? Meanwhile, the universities are fully complicit in this disgraceful charade of educational practice. The additional damage is that academe has allowed an external business association (the NBA) to intrude adversely into the internal operation of a university through the cooperation of some coaches.

The ultimate inescapable question that no one wants to ask or everyone is afraid to ask is this: What does *this particular kind* of intercollegiate athletics have to do with the mission of higher education?[24] Are universities part of the corporate universe, the entertainment business, or the education world? The commercialization of college athletics has drawn criticism even from former university presidents with big-time programs,[25] but action for serious fundamental reform is still lacking. Not so well known is that even the non-big-time colleges and universities are also suffering from these problems. *The Game of Life: College Sports and Educational Values*, by former Princeton president William Bowen and James Shulman, uses hard historical data to show the influence of athletics upon class composition and campus ethos of even selective schools.[26]

Admittedly, not all intercollegiate sports are subject to this disease. Many are not, but the tendency has continued to seep into them less visibly. Ignoring the problem areas is no different than dismissing a fast-growing cancer in a leg or arm by assuming it has no effect on the rest of the body.

The problems of the relationship between big-time intercollegiate athletics and universities have continued to escalate. Despite the noble efforts of the Knight Commission, little seems able to stop the behemoth of exploding growth accompanied by infractions, corruption, and misconduct within the institutions of higher education. Nowhere is this more evident than in the new "Power Five"—that is, the five "major" conferences—ACC, Big Ten, Big 12, Pac-12, and SEC. These five conferences are now dominating the rules and conduct of the 128 team NCAA Football Bowl Subdivision (FBS). Their role is capped by the concluding championship playoffs in six bowl games—the Rose, Sugar, Orange, Cotton, Fiesta, and Peach.[27]

The competitive commercialization race is further reflected in the continuing escalation in interconference membership shifts and the stadium building booms.[28] Larger stadiums feed larger revenue streams—provided of course they host winning seasons. Most important is that the overhang of needed revenue to pay off any capital construction bonds produces huge pressures to recruit top athletic talent, especially where academic eligibility is questionable. The force to bend is fierce, and academic standards are often severely weakened. There is nothing wrong with "special admissions" for students who require supportive help in order to graduate, whether student athletes or not. The problem arises when the real goal of the athlete is not graduation or when the level of academic support and tutoring far exceeds that which is provided to other nonathletes who are academically weak.

At the very first meeting of the original Knight Commission in 1989, I commented that in addition to the valuable "one-plus-three" model of presidential leadership, there was an additional issue: how to achieve "arms control" in the continuously escalating expenditures on college athletics. I argued that the "arms race" could not be solved by "unilateral disarmament" by any single institution or even by a single conference. It could only be done through total collective disarmament (i.e., proportionate expenditure reduction) by the entire academic intercollegiate "athletic industry." To those who say this is unrealistic and impossible, I say if nations can disarm ballistic missiles and atomic bombs that are far more dangerous, why should college sports be more difficult? My belief then and now is that if such a drastic collective proportionate reduction were made, the outcomes in the game scores and the championships would be exactly the same as before the reduction. I am still waiting for that Nirvana.

The irony is that I am a die-hard fan of intercollegiate athletics. As a former college athlete, I can still recall the joys of participation in track and field—the excitement of the competition, the exuberance of a team effort, and the rewarding sense of well-being at trying to do my best. There is for me a difference between college and professional athletics, not just in the skill level but in the attitudes and spirit of the college athletes. This difference is still there, though perhaps hidden, even in the big-time sports and colleges. In trying to correct and reform the current problems, that spirit is what we need to strengthen, protect, and achieve.

When properly conducted, amateur athletics does have a place in higher education, but its current high status and influence is damaging and adversely affecting academe. It need not be so.

▪ Recognitions

Recognitions and awards for both Dolores and me continued into the retirement years.[29] By this time Dolores had received nine honorary doctorates—the first one from Central Michigan University in 1973. I received fifteen more honorary doctorates, bringing the total to sixty-three—a fair number, but less than half of Father Hesburgh's *Guinness Book of World Records* title with 150 degrees.

▪ ▪ ▪ ▪

The year 2000 was our fiftieth wedding anniversary. Dolores and I decided to have the celebration in New York City at the University Club on April 7. It was a splendid affair including relatives and hundreds of friends. Ray Lamontagne was master of ceremonies with very brief remarks by Phil Caldwell, Eleanor Sheldon, and Chuck Stone. All this was topped off by a wonderful music set by cabaret singer and pianist Bobby Short. Both sons, were there—Clifton 3rd with his new girlfriend Kate Niemczyk (he was getting a divorce from his second wife) and Bruce, then manager of college relations at Starwood Hotels & Resorts headquarters in Stamford, Connecticut.

Two days later we received the devastating news that our eldest son Clifton 3rd had died of a brain embolism at age forty-eight. The sudden shock from Clifton's death left Dolores and me distraught with grief. Everyone he knew at the Enoch Pratt Free Library in Baltimore, where he had worked for sixteen years, was desolate. Pratt director Carla Hayden closed the central library and all Baltimore city branches for the morning of April 19 for a memorial service in the main library's Wheeler Auditorium. The turnout from across the city was a touching display of how much our son had meant to his colleagues. The program included reminiscences from six of Clifton's colleagues and a marvelous tribute from his closest friend there, Ellen Riordan, coordinator of children's services.

At the end Dr. Hayden announced the creation of a CRW 3rd Fund for Children's Reading Program, to which we and hundreds of our friends and family contributed. Based on our initial gift and other contributions, our donations to the Fund over the next ten years totaled almost a quarter of a million dollars.

With these funds, Dolores and I worked closely with Ellen Riordan on an experimental program to improve the reading skills of primary schoolchildren in selected Baltimore public schools. Clifton had always had a special affection for children's reading, a reflection no doubt of his own childhood. Riordan's efforts proved successful and ran for ten years, culminating in a report titled *Good Books in the Right Hands: Making a Difference*.[30] Dolores and I were happy that this tribute to our son had made a difference. We believe that Clifton 3rd would also have been pleased. Nevertheless, anyone who has experienced the death of a child before his or her own passing has a stark awareness of its causing a ragged tear in the normal order of life. It leaves scars on your soul that never fade, never stop aching.

. . . .

The most moving and repeated recognitions came from Michigan State.

On October 27, 2000, MSU held an unusual convocation to celebrate the thirtieth anniversary of my appointment as president.[31] The organizer and promoter of the event was James Spaniolo, my former assistant. (Dolores and I suspected that his unspoken motivation was to mitigate the loss of our son Clifton 3rd.) There were speeches by President Peter McPherson and Provost Lou Anna Simon, followed by a brief video on the "Wharton Years." Provost Simon confessed that in preparing her remarks she had gone back to read my very first speech given to the MSU faculty on January 20, 1970—the same one that had been criticized by the *State News* as "a rehash of old adages and clichés. . . . and at worst an abysmal failure."[32] I had

BILLY TAYLOR EULOGY FOR CLIFTON 3ᴿᴰ

When you lose a son, there's an empty space which cannot be filled by the words or actions of others. There is so much left to be said and done. You anticipated so much life. Now he's gone. And no one else will do what he could have done in the way that he would have done it. You remember so much . . . little things, big things, personal things, private things, no one else knew. You want to remember everything about him. Memories. You often relive some of the special times your shared. Your baby . . . learning to talk, learning to walk . . . laughing, acknowledgments, happy, sad, confused, determined, earnest, sincere. Into everything, searching, experimenting, testing, growing up. The child now a man . . . so mature in so many ways . . . smart, sensitive, unselfish, caring, curious, strong, adventurous . . . still searching, now finding his own way. Making a life of his own. To his parents he will always be that unique individual—rare, unequaled, distinctive, and matchless. Your son, he made you proud. You try to be consoled by the fact that his spirit lives in all those whose lives he touched. In his spirit we play this *In Loving Memory*.

—Billy Taylor, *Urban Griot* (CD, Soundpost Records, August 28, 2001)

a singular sense of validation when she cited that inaugural address as laying the foundation for all my subsequent initiatives and actions as president of MSU. (She would become MSU president in January 2005.)

Then a panel of former colleagues looked back on my time at MSU, moderated by Jim Spaniolo, then dean of the MSU College of Communication Arts and Sciences.[33] The panelists were agricultural economics professor Jim Bonnen; art professor Irv Taran; former vice president for business and finance Roger Wilkinson; and former presidential fellow Carl Taylor, now a national expert on urban gangs and MSU professor of family and child ecology. The insightful reminiscences by the panel concluded with brief acknowledgments by Dolores and me.

After dinner in the evening, our friend jazz pianist Billy Taylor performed a new work commissioned by the university, which included a piece "In Loving Memory" dedicated to our older son, Clifton 3ʳᵈ.[34] Before playing the piece, Taylor spoke from the Wharton Center stage, offering an empathetic eulogy about our son that reflected the earlier loss of his own adult son, Duane, in 1988. The capstone to an incredible day.

· · · ·

The twenty-fifth "birthday" celebration of the Wharton Center began on Sunday, October 14, 2007, with a performance in the Cobb Great Hall by the Chicago Symphony, which had played at the Center's original dedication. (Our Chicago friends Madeleine Condit and Joe

Glossberg, devoted supporters of the Chicago Symphony, were instrumental in arranging its return to East Lansing.) The Wharton Center twenty-fifth commemorative extended through an entire year, ending on Saturday, April 26, 2008, with a special world premiere. The MSU Symphony Orchestra, along with the two-hundred-strong University Chorale and the State Singers, performed a commissioned work in our honor.[35] Michigan State University alumnus and award-winning Black composer Adolphus Hailstork conducted a *Serenade: To Hearts Which Near Each Other Move.* The centerpiece for the text was a poem by Percy Bysshe Shelley that had been suggested to Dolores by her friend Irene Dusenbery. "*Serenade,*" said Hailstork, "was written in direct response to Mrs. Wharton's statement that she wished their love story could be told." The performance that evening was a magical moment for both of us.[36]

In October 2009, the MSU Black Alumni Association organized a dual celebration—the thirtieth anniversary of the creation of MSUBA and the fortieth anniversary of my election to the presidency of MSU. Since I was unable to attend due to my recovery from surgery, the MSUBA instead published a special statement about Dolores and me in the Homecoming football program, followed by an edition of Carl Taylor's e-mail newsletter commemorating the event.

• • • •

A unique recognition came in October 2007 at the end of MSU's successful campaign raising $1.44 billion. At the closing event, President Lou Anna K. Simon announced that she and her husband Roy had made a contribution to join the newly created donor society Clifton R. Wharton Jr. Fund at the $2.5 to $3.75 million level.[37] Their personal generosity, coupled with the demonstration of high personal regard of us, left us speechless.

Dolores and I were jointly honored in 2009 when our longtime friend Ray Lamontagne, then chairman of the New York City Center, named us winners of the Fiorello H. LaGuardia Award for distinguished service to the Center and the City of New York. Although it was Dolores who had been a Center trustee from 1994 until 2007, it was nice to be included. Bill and Judith Moyers made the presentations, which were attended by a large number of our friends and colleagues, filling the 2,750-seat theater.

These and other recognitions are far less occasions for ego gratification than expressions of high regard and approbation from one's colleagues and peers.

▪ Reflections on Leadership ─────────────────────────

I have been a leader in philanthropy, higher education, and business.[38] Also I have been involved in selecting and observing leaders in these three fields. Hence, I am often asked two questions: What lessons or principles have I learned that made me a successful leader? And are there any common similarities in successful leaders in these three areas?

Such questions make me uneasy, suggesting some formula or schematic that will produce effective leaders by rote. But leadership is much more art than science, and the basics—competency, knowledge, management proficiency, interpersonal skills, vision, goals, and prioritizing—are merely the preconditions rather than the essence of success. Techniques differ, as do circumstances; there is no universal template. All that can be offered by an experienced leader are personal reflections on what seems to have worked.

I have found six key principles—though underlying all of them is the basic given of being willing to listen and learn from your experiences along the way—to be a leadership lifetime learner.

First, from my father and my earliest jobs, I learned the value and importance of *relying upon individual talent and initiative*. For example, my father was the "chief of mission" at most of his Foreign Service posts. Throughout his career, he exercised independent judgment, taking personal responsibility for his decisions. A sequence of opportunities for exercising and acquiring leadership capabilities enabled him to grow and flourish, preparing him for posts of ever-increasing difficulty and consequence. I tried to follow his example throughout my various careers.

In 1948, as a trainee in Nelson Rockefeller's nonprofit technical assistance initiatives in Latin America, I was allowed to observe all the operations "from the top." I gained exposure to the management style of a premier philanthropic family. I was able to study and learn how their efforts were managed, as well as how different personalities interacted and a little about what made them succeed or fail. Similarly my first boss at AIA, Pete Hudgens, gave me an important glimpse of how to nurture and rely upon individual talent. Pete had faith in me—even more significant, he let me learn and grow in the process.

In my work with Art Mosher in Asia I learned the value of choosing the best people and giving them the opportunity to use their own intelligence, rather than fitting them into a predetermined mold. I also learned to recognize and take advantage of different circumstances in all their complexities, rather than trying to impose preconceived, one size fits all solutions. The best leadership requires thinking clearly, writing clearly, and speaking clearly one's vision. But most important of all, Mosher reinforced what I had already been learning along the way: the central importance of human capital in personal and economic development.

Second, the greatest leaders *cherish and protect their reputation for honesty and integrity*. As a result they are widely perceived as persons their "followers" can trust. Although my lessons on honesty started in childhood, the virtue of integrity was sharply etched by my mentor Theodore W. Schultz with his handling of the inquisitorial methods used during the 1950s McCarthy witch hunt incident, which left an indelible impression.

Third, very few leaders have a monopoly on insight, much less wisdom—yet more than a few believe they do. A frequent failing is their sense of omnipotence and infallibility. Although the best leaders usually do have an uncommon capacity for making sound decisions, they also recognize that their decisions are strengthened and implementation is improved by *relying upon the collective wisdom of their colleagues and subordinates — they listen*. At Michigan State University, at the State University of New York system, and at TIAA-CREF, my reliance upon and the support of a collective team made a critical difference time and again. Handling student demonstrations at Michigan State, especially in 1970, required effective marshaling of the collective wisdom within the campus. The same lesson applied in SUNY when the need arose to override a gubernatorial veto of the university system budget funds. When all the campuses worked together toward a common goal rather than operating unilaterally, we could build unprecedented political clout.

My dramatic program reforms and changes in different settings were often based upon collective wisdom and listening. Whether it was the use of board trustees coupled with officers for the *Future Agenda* at TIAA-CREF or the statewide constituent representations on the MSU Commission on Admissions, the model worked.

Fourth, one of the greatest derelictions of leaders is their failure to prepare or nurture their successors. Ted Schultz and Art Mosher shared an important characteristic I tried to make my own: their instinct for *nurturing the next generation of leaders*. Schultz and Mosher did it for me, and I have tried to do it wherever and whenever I could. At Michigan State University one of my early acts was to develop a program of presidential fellows. Today many of the former fellows are college or university presidents and vice presidents, foundation executives, university provosts and professors, government officials, and business executives. At TIAA-CREF, I created a similar program of rotating special assistants—mid-level, high-potential officers—who spent five months in my office. They had a chance to see firsthand my part in setting the future directions of the company.

Succession planning—preparing for your CEO successor—is vitally important, but there is another dimension that is even more neglected: nurturing leaders who will *not* become CEOs but who will make up the second and third tiers of leadership that are so vital to the success of any institution. They too are leaders, and they should not be overlooked.

One unlisted lesson about leadership has been my policy of what *not* to do when you are the ex-leader. I regularly followed a policy of not commenting publicly on my successors, though I stood ready to respond to any of their private requests for guidance or advice. My reason was that as a departed CEO you quickly lose your understanding of the forces and issues faced by the new leader, and any critical or negative comment from you can have an adverse effect on a successor. I violated this practice only once, when the new TIAA-CREF chairman and CEO Herb Allison attempted to eliminate the Board of Overseers. In 2004, he and the boards commissioned former U.S. attorney general Nicholas deB. Katzenbach to investigate the handling of an auditor independence matter at TIAA-CREF that had arisen in the summer and fall of 2004. His report blamed the problems on the company's governance structure because the Board of Overseers is over separate boards of directors for TIAA and CREF.[39]

He argued that the arrangement created the "constant risk of potential and actual conflict." Based upon the Katzenbach report, the law firm of Shearman and Sterling LLP was engaged by the Overseers to provide an analysis of the governance structure of TIAA-CREF, arguing incorrectly for the elimination of the Overseers as a solution. In my judgment this attempt was a serious contradiction to the founding charter of TIAA, which asserted the Overseers, the sole owners of TIAA stock, ultimately had the oversight role of judging actions or policies of the two operating boards.[40] This egregious proposal could not be ignored. I organized a letter signed by twelve of the living former TIAA retired Overseers and CEOs that strongly objected to any attempted change in the role of the TIAA Overseers.[41] The current Overseers concluded that the current structure should be retained.

Fifth, when I speak at business schools, the audience sometimes asks how comprehensive change came to TIAA-CREF so rapidly, yet without major disruptions of people and operations—new internal governance structures, new policies on handling of pension accumulations, implementation of new policies and funds, and best of all, rebuilding customer confidence while staving off market competition and doubling the company's assets in six years. A critical factor was *avoiding what I call the "power syndrome."* In higher education, centralized power is tempered by some degree of sharing across the institution, including the traditional faculty canon of "participatory democracy." In the corporate world, the thrust is more strongly toward an authoritarian model, making the "power syndrome" more acutely dangerous. I worked very hard to avoid or mitigate any such tendencies while I moved to build a new management and governance structure for TIAA-CREF.[42] As a corporate director, I had seen how power can change people, especially those newly elevated to positions of high authority. Power all too often becomes a virus that feeds on its host, eating away at a leader's effectiveness. I had repeatedly witnessed how being in a position of power could induce arrogance and high-handedness. As the leader, you can become convinced that you alone are responsible for all success, while all failures can be traced to the inadequacies of those beneath. Imperiousness leads to insulation from critical or divergent views, undercutting channels of communication. Worst of all, if your closest advisers unfailingly agree with your every pronouncement, it is little wonder that your ego becomes dangerously inflated.

Another element of power corruption is the compulsion to produce instant change. A new leader feels an irresistible urge to make an immediate imprint. Over the years, I have never ceased to be amazed at those newly elevated leaders who fell into the trap of trying to impose their own mold on organizations in their first months. All too often, they acted as though everything in the past was wrong, dismissing their predecessors out of hand; only what they were pushing for the future was right. Worse, some imperial CEOs acquire an insensitivity to human costs that borders on sheer cruelty. Even at its best, rapid change affects personnel morale, in part due to job uncertainty. Some of the worst cases are where massive personnel reductions are cruelly made with instant same-day effect and with security escorts out of the headquarters to the outside sidewalk. More is lost than the long years of service from a company's "memory bank"; the morale of those employees who survive can take years to recover—if it ever does. This approach can become such a fixation within the enterprise that the regular business or activities of the enterprise suffer. I sometimes refer to this danger as trying to "change the fan belt while the engine is still running." Too many leaders have lost more than their fingers in the process—all because they opted to coerce and compel rather than step back, attend to the knowledge and insight within the organization, develop a program of change rooted in existing institutional memory and wisdom, and then generate wider support of those to carry out the changes required.

Any heedless authoritarian leader—whether a foundation president, an elected official, a university chancellor, or a corporate CEO—can execute well for a time at least, even if only through fear. But such a leader inevitably fails to galvanize subordinates and convert them into eager followers. Listless, fearful, resentful execution always brings unplanned losses or unrealized gains. In contrast, thoughtful and humane exercises of power can unleash the vitality and creativity of entire workforces, magnifying by many multiples a leader's effectiveness. My colleague Bob Perrin, when interviewed at MSU, gave a probably biased assessment of my leadership strengths, mentioning "decision making ('He doesn't like to let things drag on'), ability to grasp problems, sensitivity to the effects his decisions will have on people, and ability to articulate his concerns and problems. . . . 'He wants results but he understands you're human.'"[43]

In each of my roles as a leader, I have tried to avoid falling into the "leadership power syndrome."

The eagerness to please (and the occasional sycophancy) of subordinates can be seductive. Hence, an important counterbalance to the "power syndrome" is a leader's willingness to listen to constructive criticism and contrarian views. I have always had at least a few direct reports who were willing to disagree with me or to criticize my ideas openly, because they knew I wanted to hear their honest opinions—whether I enjoyed it at the time (I sometimes didn't), as well as whether I ultimately agreed. This is the reason why I so strongly cherished top advisers like Bob Perrin and Al Ballard who would always tell me what they truly thought, not what they thought I wanted to hear. A related key attribute is that all successful leaders seem to keep their sense of humor—a strong antidote to the pomposity of the "power syndrome."

Sixth and finally, the very best leaders have personal characteristics that infuse what they do and how they do it. They treat subordinates fairly and equitably, realizing that it creates faith and trust. They "share the glory" of an institution's achievements, recognizing that they do not accomplish their goals operating alone. (Somewhat less commonly but much to be desired, they do what they can to "take the heat" of failures on their own shoulders.) *Change leaders must treat people humanely and have the trust of followers*, especially in institutions and organizations that are labor intensive. Articulating and directing change must be believed, and followers can easily tell the absence of honesty or trustworthiness in a leader. A leader cannot "fake it."

Great leaders don't lose their humaneness or forget what it was like when they started at the bottom. They are tough minded but not mean spirited. They truly care about the human beings in their institution or company—not as a faceless agglomeration, but as individuals, with all their uniqueness, to be treated with respect for their hard work, their dedication, and their loyalty. Whether a Pulitzer Prize–winning professor or a campus groundskeeper, a shop-floor mechanic or the genius information technology group president—they all deserve the respect and consideration that should be everyone's birthright.

A humane CEO is a revered CEO and becomes the inspirational leader throughout the corporation or institution.

▪ Reflections on Higher Education _____

Developments in higher education are an ongoing concern during my retirement, even though I am no longer directly involved. My interest reflects my lifelong view that higher education is a critical component in the creation of human capital.

First and foremost, my reflections begin from a belief in the unchangeable basic nature and cardinal goals of higher education. Its primary goals are to discover new knowledge, conserve past knowledge, transmit knowledge to successive generations, and meet the challenge of revising itself continuously without diminishing or destroying its core functions. The overall goal of postsecondary education is nurturing human competence in the broadest sense. This means much more than just preparing graduates for specific jobs. To succeed, higher education must foster critical thinking and engage deeply with the "humanizing" disciplines—literature, languages, philosophy, history, mathematics, theater, music, and the arts. A society that disdains the civilizing mission of higher education does so at its own great risk.

Current higher education institutions in the United States face an unprecedented number of challenges.[44] Some are the result of economic, social, and political changes in the general environment. Others are the result of dramatic technological inventions and fiscal shifts that have created a dynamic that must be dealt with. Yet others are reflections of the above forces upon the personnel structure, course offerings, pedagogic methods, and learning timetables or processes. The plethora of these forces are beyond the purview of this chapter, but let me mention a few that I deem especially important.

Knowledge institutions have usually adapted new technological inventions successfully to improve their functions. But this is true only if the changes recognize and are compatible with their fundamental natures. A new technology that violates core values will weaken if not destroy the institution. Moving from hand-illuminated texts to the Gutenberg press enhanced rather than constricted the growth of human capital, and so in large part today did moving so many educational resources to the computer. These changes remind me of my own experiences as a child living abroad with the Calvert correspondence courses. My lessons took two weeks to come by ship to the Canary Islands, then it took another two weeks for my tests to go back to Baltimore for review and grading and a third two weeks to return by ship before I knew my marks. Today this form of long-distance learning has been replaced by an instantaneous Internet. One feature in this comparison I believe has continued to be critical to the process—a direct physical interaction with a human being who is knowledgeable about the subject. Best of all is the role of that human interaction, to respond and guide the individual student throughout, to stimulate excitement in learning, and to produce the intangible dynamics that self-learning can never fully replicate.

One of today's challenges is the massive growth of instant worldwide communication. The problem is more than the latest new technological advances, such as e-courses and MOOCs (Massive Open Online Courses). Although colleges and universities with their traditional models do not have a monopoly on human capital formation, they still are the dominant actor. But the dangers of misleading alternatives for knowledge acquisition provide a heightened level of concern. In many cases, the availability of access to nearly endless, often anonymous information sources—regardless of their accuracy, impartiality, or completeness—distorts if not eviscerates traditional models of how human capital is formed.

Sixty years ago from my "bully pulpit" in East Lansing, I trumpeted the need for lifelong education because of the exponential growth in knowledge. The explosion, I said, made lifelong education vital to personal progress after formal degrees. The accuracy and legitimacy of new knowledge touted in those "sermons" met the tests of accuracy and "truth." Today, with its blogs, social networks, tweets, and a Pandora's box of other communication outlets, most vehicles of information transmission are without any significant test for their accuracy or even a nod to scientific method for judging their validity. Even traditional media—newspapers, radio, and television—have found it increasingly difficult to use or rely upon their mantra of multiple source checks. Add to this the more instantaneous nature of current communication and the tasks of "gatekeeper of the truth" could soon become an extinct as the dinosaurs. This situation cries out for providing individuals with the ability and mental training to evaluate this explosion of information flow. Absolutely central to this process is being armed with an understanding of techniques of evaluation and the value of the scientific method that underlies the trust in any flow of new information.

There is a closely related issue: the role of scientific methodology. This method of inquiry is based on empirical and measurable evidence subject to specific principles of reasoning. The ability to acquire new knowledge and to revise past knowledge is based upon the march of research using this methodology. It is a powerful process and a hallmark of higher education that must be protected. Advances in human knowledge require an environment that values the freedom to challenge accepted or dogmatic ideas, even if new theories are controversial or against conventional wisdom or religious dogma.

Societies and nations that attempt to circumscribe intellectual inquiry based upon flawed ideological thinking rather than a rational and scientific method seriously jeopardize human capital development and hence their own economic and social progress. Too often, those persons who object to the process or dislike the results of academic freedom and such research seek to modify, control, or even destroy the institutions that embody it. For example, today's increasing shift toward religious fundamentalism and away from empiricism and the scientific method is a very dangerous trend. Similarly, when legislatures pass laws based on ideology rather than verifiable facts, college or universities are caught in the crossfire and weakened in carrying out their responsibilities.

Maintaining adequate financial support for the human capital sector is a greater challenge today than ever before. Much has been made particularly in the last decade of the skyrocketing price of college attendance, but in reality at least three distinct though related issues are involved.

First are the rising costs of education delivery itself, which stem from factors as disparate as the challenge of keeping scientific equipment up to date to the competition among campuses to tempt prospective students with the richest—often most luxurious—campus experiences. Given prevailing circumstances, the really astonishing fact may be not how fast college prices have been rising but rather that they have not gone up even more.

Second is the changing mix among sources of institutional support, with students and their families contributing ever larger finances (and taking on increased private debt) as state and federal dollars have steadily waned. "Revenue from tuition paid for 44 percent of all operating expenses at public colleges and universities in 2012, the highest share ever. A quarter century ago, the share was just 20 percent."[45]

Third is the decline in state and federal support of higher education, which has been partially allayed by an increase in private funding—both individual donors and corporate. For example, when I arrived at Michigan State University in 1970, student tuition covered one-third of the university's costs, and two-thirds came from state and federal sources. Today, those ratios have exactly reversed. The 2011–12 General Fund Budget was 27.8 percent from state appropriations, 8.4 percent other funds, and 63.8 percent student fees. Private universities are not immune from this phenomenon due to their dependence on federal funds, especially for research. Ten of the twenty largest recipients of federal grants are private universities.

As private contributions become increasingly critical, corporate and donor influence increases. Of course, not all private funding is toxic to a university's mission and operation. Many sources are useful supplements for valuable activities that otherwise would not be provided. But in many cases the problems created, especially corporate, go far beyond the issue of ownership and copyrights of discoveries. Such funding can often skew the focus and mix of a department or college priorities, reflecting the donors' values above the traditional ones of the university. The growth of private funding is frequently predicated on donor stipulations that compromise fundamental academic prerogatives or tie contributions to institutional litmus tests based on partisan positions. Opinions that are counter to scientific evidence then are used to eviscerate the development of knowledge, giving precedence to false ideas, and in turn actions.

Changing societal perceptions of the value of education for the improvement of the community and the individual inevitably affect both absolute levels of financial support and the sector's claim on resources relative to other priorities. (For example, in many states the growth of spending on prisons and corrections has outpaced that on higher education for decades now. This reflects major conflicting national priorities—do we really value prisons more than colleges?) Such shifts have particularly invidious effects on the quality of public infrastructure, including human capital infrastructure—that is, education.

The shifting mix of financial support sources raises the perennial question: Who should pay for higher education? Economic studies have found that education creates a public or social benefit that we receive collectively, which must be included in the sum of income and other benefits received by the individual graduates. Yes, the individual derives benefit in a higher personal income. But education is likewise an investment by society and from which society receives returns beyond the training of its workforce. In other words, education is also society's investment in itself—and its future. It must be recognized as a means of aggregate empowerment, not a luxury or consumer product. Yet the steady shift of cost-bearing toward the individual has produced ever higher tuition levels for students, reducing educational access not only for low-income but also middle-class families. As Brit Kirwan, chancellor of the University of Maryland system, pointed out, "A child born into a family in the highest quartile of income (in the United States) has a roughly 85 percent chance of earning a college degree. A child born into a family in the lowest quartile of income has a less-than 8 percent chance of earning a degree."[46] Higher tuition is today creating a huge national loss of future human capital—those persons who could have gone but didn't, thereby reducing their contributions. Until society recognizes the fact that higher education contributes to future growth, we will continue to neglect this decisive key to our nation's future.

These funding issues are producing a *disinvestment* in higher education and human capital. The first lesson I learned as a youthful agricultural economist when studying small farmers in the less developed regions of Latin America and Southeast Asia was their rule to never eat your seed corn[47]—that is, always conserve the seed you need to plant next year's crop, even if it means going hungrier for now. In the United States, continuing state and federal government disinvestment in the underlying foundation of colleges and universities, public and private, represents nothing less than eating—more accurately, throwing away—our nation's economic and intellectual seed corn. This is lessening excellence in higher education and weakening its fundamental mission. It is little wonder that our nation's global rankings are no longer "number one" and falling behind other nations.

Great societies that have prospered in the past have always invested in human capital because both the individual and society received benefit. Our present course is a major peril to our future.

Epilogue

I am often asked which of my several vocations I liked best. The most enjoyable and immediately rewarding was teaching, a direct and personal channel for investing in human capital. Education, in its broadest sense, is the vehicle whereby each generation bequeaths guidance and wisdom to the next. Sometimes it takes place in a classroom, seminar, workshop, laboratory, or office. Sometimes it is through informal conversation and dialogue. And sometimes it is by way of personal example through attitudes, behavior, and values. Most important, its consummation is finest when one person is willing to provide and another person is willing to learn. Throughout our lives, Dolores and I have tried to provide counsel or support for those who will follow us. In every instance, the hope has been to reach out and share what we could of ourselves, our experience, and our knowledge. There were those who did it for us, and we owed it to do likewise for others. This is the experience that both Dolores and I have had and the richest legacy we could hope to leave behind.

I did not consciously set out to become a Black pioneer. Nevertheless, this book is an attempt to share the experiences of someone who had thrust upon him the fate to forge racial breakthroughs in three different careers. I hope the successes outnumbered the failures, and that the record of accomplishments speaks for itself.

My life is a story of being born to privilege and of surmounting prejudice to achieve new paths. I strived to compete in a fully integrated fashion within the dominant society, without special help or favor due to my race. It is also a story about the importance of not allowing racial discrimination or negative expectations to poison one's sensibilities or deflect one from a chosen path. While obstacles for Blacks and other minorities regretfully continue to exist in our nation, I believe these obstacles are less pernicious today than in my parents' day.

But I am also deeply pained that for too many segments the struggle against hidden or more subtle barriers continues. Still, I hope progress will continue apace for future generations. In any event, it is possible to surmount such barriers if you are willing to seize the opportunities that abound and the challenges they entail. Even for optimists, preparation, confidence, persistence, and a willingness to stand up to discrimination head-on will remain critically important in the years ahead.

Striving for excellence in every arena, being constantly prepared to listen and learn, maintaining integrity, and always trying to act humanely and compassionately were my fundamental life standards. To the best of my abilities I have tried to work with others whenever possible and on my own when I had to, without compromising more than seemed fair and reasonable. In many respects I have been enormously fortunate—though fortune, as they say, favors a prepared mind. My good fortune in parents, teachers, mentors, friends, and colleagues helped me beyond measure along the way.

My greatest good fortune lay in having Dolores as my incomparable spouse and strong life partner, who helped me meet every challenge and rise to every occasion. She and our successful marriage have been at the heart of whatever I have achieved. My life would not have been possible without my marriage to a wonderful woman. So above all else, my autobiography is at heart a story of two people in love.

The choral symphony composed and dedicated to Dolores and me by Adolphus Hailstork and performed at MSU used several poems by Percy Bysshe Shelley. One poem that beautifully captures our love ended with these words:

> To hearts which near each other move
> From evening close to morning light,
> The night is good; because, my love,
> They never say good-night.

Appendices

John Allison, former U.S. Ambassador to Indonesia

Hugh Borton, President of Haverford College

Claude A. Buss, Professor of History, Stanford University

Russell H. Fifield, Professor of Political Science, University of Michigan

Caryl Haskins, President of the Carnegie Institution

Alice Hsieh, Rand Corporation

Walter H. Judd, former U.S. Representative and medical missionary to China

Lucien Pye, Professor, Center for International Studies, MIT

Edwin O. Reischauer, Professor at Harvard and former U.S. Ambassador to Japan

A. M. Rosenthal, Metropolitan Editor for the *New York Times* and former foreign
correspondent in India, later Editor in Chief

Howard Rusk, contributing editor of the *New York Times*

Robert A. Scalapino, Chairman of the Department of Political Science, University of
California–Berkeley

Arch T. Steele, journalist in Portal, Arizona

George Taylor, Director of the Far Eastern and Russian Institute, University of
Washington

Frank N. Trager, Professor of International Relations, New York University

Robert E. Ward, Professor of Political Science, University of Michigan
Clifton R. Wharton Jr., acting Executive Director, Agricultural Development Council
Kenneth Young, President of the Asia Society and former U.S. Ambassador to Thailand

APPENDIX 2: FRIENDS AND PROFESSIONAL COLLEAGUES AT AFRICAN-AMERICAN DIALOGUES, NAIROBI, NOVEMBER 1968

John Brademas, U.S. Representative

Osborn Elliott, Editor, *Newsweek*

Wayne Fredericks, Ford Foundation and former deputy assistant secretary of state for African affairs

Charles V. Hamilton, Professor, Roosevelt University

Ed Hamilton, recent National Security Council aide in the White House

Arthur A. Houghton Jr., CEO Steuben Glass

Jane W. Jacqz, Secretary to the Conference

Andrew M. Kamarck, World Bank

David E. Lillienthal, of TVA fame and later Development and Resources Corp.

Brad Morse, U.S. Representative

Bill Moyers, Publisher, *Newsday*

Christopher H. Phillips, U.S. International Chamber of Commerce

Bayard Rustin, A. Philip Randolph Institute, organizer of the 1963 civil rights march on Washington

R. Peter Straus, Agency for International Development

Marietta Tree, U.S. delegate to the U.N. Commission on Human Rights

APPENDIX 3: MSU ALL-UNIVERSITY PRESIDENTIAL SEARCH AND SELECTION COMMITTEE, 1969

Chair, Professor Dale Hathaway (Agricultural Economics)

Prof. Arthur Adams (History)

Dr. John E. Cantlon (Botany) who resigned from the committee in July when he became Provost; Dr. Robert Ebel (Counseling)

Prof. Donald J. Montgomery (Metallurgy & Materials Science)

Prof. Dozier Thornton (Psychology)

Prof. Phil Johnson (Mathematics, Oakland)

Walt Chappell (graduate student in education)

Sue Gebelein (undergraduate)

LaMarr Thomas (Black student, junior), later replaced by Michael Hudson (undergraduate, Black Student Liberation Front)

Francis Ferguson (MSU Alumnus and CEO, Northwestern Life)

Five alternates: Jack Kinney (director, Alumni Association); Prof. William H. Pipes (Black faculty and American Thought and Language); Michael Geezer (undergraduate); Richard S. Allen (Black students and senior); Edward LaDue (graduate students). Dr. William Knisely (Institute of Biology and Medicine) was also a later replacement.

APPENDIX 4: MSU PRESIDENTIAL FELLOWS REUNION, MAY 31–JUNE 2, 1996

Dr. Robert A. Brooks, dentist, Village Dental Center in Arizona

Dr. R. Judson Carlberg, President, Gordon College

Linda A. Terrey Conklin, a licensed marriage and family therapist in Florida

Dr. Neil H. Cullen, Chief Financial Officer, Phillips Andover Academy

Dr. Dale M. Herder, Vice President, Lansing Community College

Dr. Ronald W. Richards, Program Director, Health Programming, Kellogg Foundation (subsequently Professor of Public Health at the University of Illinois, Chicago)

Delois R. Robison, Executive Director, Ujamaa Associates, Detroit

Dr. Teresa A. Sullivan, Vice President and Dean of Graduate Studies, University of Texas at Austin (subsequently Provost at the University of Texas System, Provost at the University of Michigan, and President of the University of Virginia)

Dr. Carl S. Taylor, Professor, Department of Family and Child Ecology, Michigan State University

Dr. James C. Votruba, Vice Provost, University Outreach, Michigan State University (later President, University of Northern Kentucky)

Eugene Wilson, Specialist, Family Independence Agency of Oakland County, Michigan

The two who were absent: Dr. Gary L. Reinhardt, Veterinary Center of Sarasota, Florida; Dr. Dale E. Work, Vice President, Research and Development, Phillips Lighting

APPENDIX 5: MSU COMMISSION ON ADMISSIONS, 1970–71

From the Academic Council: Norman Abels, Daniel Cowan, Mildred Erickson, Henry Kennedy, Mordechai Kreinin, Clifford Pollard, and Chitra Smith.

From the Educational Policies Committee: William Hicks, Willard Warrington.

From the Equal Opportunity Program: James Hamilton.

From the Graduate Council: Charles Blackman and James Pickering.

From ASMSU: Elizabeth Grebenschikoff, Jerry Rupley, William Rustem, David Snyder, and Walter Thomas.

From the Council of Graduate Students: Kwong-Yuan Chong (a former student of mine in Malaysia), William Greene, and Stanley Sibley.

From the alumni: Pat Carrigan and Louis Legg.

Members at large: Dorothy Arata (Honors College), Frank Beadle (a former state senator), and James Shaffer (agricultural economics).

Public members: Paul Bader (President, Michigan School Counselors Association), Robert Cahow (Executive Secretary, Michigan Association of Community Colleges), John Hoekje (President, Association of Independent Colleges and Universities of Michigan), Ronald Jursa (Director of Financial Aids, Bureau of Higher Education, Michigan Department of Education), and Benjamin Leyrer (Michigan Association of Secondary School Principals).

APPENDIX 6: ROCKEFELLER FOUNDATION BOARD OF TRUSTEES, 1970

John D. Rockefeller 3rd, Chairman

Barry Bingham (newspaper magnate)

John S. Dickey (President of Dartmouth College)

Robert H. Ebert (Dean of Harvard Medical School)

C. Douglas Dillon (President Kennedy's Secretary of the Treasury and Chairman of Dillon, Read)

Lord Oliver Franks (British leader in the Marshall Plan)

Robert F. Goheen (President of Princeton University)

Father Theodore M. Hesburgh (President, University of Notre Dame)

Arthur A. Houghton Jr. (CEO of Corning Glass)

Clark Kerr (former President of University of California)

Alberto Lleras Camargo (former President of Colombia)

Bill Moyers (journalist and former aide to President Lyndon Johnson)

John D. "Jay" Rockefeller IV (then Secretary of State in West Virginia, soon to be Governor)

Robert V. Roosa (partner, Brown Brothers Harriman)

Frederick Seitz (President of Rockefeller University)

Frank Stanton (President of CBS)

Thomas J. Watson Jr. (President of IBM)

W. Barry Wood Jr. (Chairman, Department of Microbiology, Johns Hopkins)

Whitney M. Young Jr. (President of National Urban League, died tragically March 11, 1971)

APPENDIX 7: U.S.–LATIN AMERICAN COMMISSION, 1974–76

Sol Linowitz, former CEO, Xerox, U.S. Ambassador to OAS, Chair

W. Michael Blumenthal, Chairman and CEO, Bendix Corp

Harrison Brown, Professor of Science and Government, California Institute of Technology

C. A. Constanzo, Vice Chairman, First National City Bank

Albert Fishlow, Chairman, Department of Economics, University of California–Berkeley

J. George Harrar, former President, Rockefeller Foundation

Henry J. Heinz 2nd, Chairman and CEO, H. J. Heinz

Andrew Heiskell, Chairman and CEO, Time Inc.

Rev. Theodore M. Hesburgh, President, University of Notre Dame

Lee Hills, Chairman and CEO, Knight Newspapers

Samuel P. Huntington, Professor of Government, Harvard University

Nicholas deB. Katzenbach, General Counsel, IBM, former U.S. Attorney General

Thomas Messer, Director, Guggenheim Museum

Charles A. Meyer, Vice President, Sears Roebuck, former Assistant Secretary of State for Inter-American Affairs

Arturo Morales-Carrion, President, University of Puerto Rico

Peter G. Peterson, chairman, Lehman Bros., former Secretary of Commerce

Eliot L. Richardson, Fellow, Woodrow Wilson International Center and former U.S. Attorney General; Secretary of Defense; Secretary of Health, Education and Welfare; Undersecretary of State

William D. Rogers, attorney, Arnold, Fortas & Porter (resigned when appointed Assistant Secretary of State for Inter-American Affairs)

Nathaniel Samuels, Partner, Kuhn, Loeb, former Undersecretary of State for Economic Affairs

Kalman Silvert, international division, Ford Foundation

Clifton R. Wharton Jr., President, Michigan State University

APPENDIX 8: PRESIDENTIAL COMMISSION ON WORLD HUNGER, 1978

Norman E. Borlaug, University of Minnesota, director of the Wheat, Barley and Triticale Research and Production Programs at the International Center for Maize and Wheat Improvement in Mexico

David W. Brooks, Chairman of the Policy Committee of Gold Kist

Harry Chapin, recording artist and founder of World Hunger Year

John Denver, recording artist and film producer, *I Want to Live,* on the problem of world hunger

Walter P. Falcon, Director of the Food Research Institute and Professor of Economics at Stanford University

Sol Linowitz, Washington attorney and ambassador, Chair

Jean Mayer, President of Tufts University and nutrition expert, Vice Chair

Steven Muller, President of Johns Hopkins University and Johns Hopkins Hospital, Vice Chair

Bess Myerson, newspaper columnist and former Commissioner of Consumer Affairs for New York City

Howard A. Schneider, Director of the Institute of Nutrition and Professor of Biochemistry and Nutrition at the University of North Carolina

Adele Smith Simmons, President of Hampshire College in Amherst, MA

Raymond G. Singletary Jr., President of Blakely Peanut

Eugene L. Stockwell, Associate General Secretary for Overseas Ministries of the National Council of the Churches of Christ in the U.S.A.

Clifton R. Wharton Jr., Chancellor of the State University of New York and a specialist in economic development

APPENDIX 9: INDEPENDENT COMMISSION ON THE FUTURE OF SUNY, 1984–85

Ralph P. Davidson, Chairman of the board at Time Inc., Cochair

Harold K. Enarson, President Emeritus of Ohio State University, Cochair

W. Michael Blumenthal, Chair and CEO, Burroughs, former U.S. Secretary of Treasury

Flora Mancuso Edwards, President, Hostos Community College (CUNY)

Murray H. Finley, President, Amalgamated Clothing and Textile Workers

William C. Friday, President, University of North Carolina

Rev. Timothy S. Healy, SJ, President, Georgetown University

Victor Marrero, senior partner, Tuffo and Zucotti, former Undersecretary, U.S. Department of Housing and Urban Development

Donald B. Marron, Chair and CEO, Paine Webber

Barbara Newell, Chancellor, State University System of Florida

W. Clarke Wescoe, Chair and CEO, Sterling Drug, former Chancellor, University of Kansas

John C. Whitehead, senior partner, Goldman Sachs, soon to become U.S. Deputy Secretary of State

Malcolm Wilson, Chair and CEO, Manhattan Savings, former Governor of New York
Don Blinken served ex officio, chair SUNY trustees

APPENDIX 10: DEPARTMENT OF STATE, USAID TASK FORCE MEMBERS, 1993

Clifton R. Wharton Jr., U.S. Deputy Secretary of State, Chair
Ray Albright, Senior Vice President, International Lending (Export-Import Bank)
Brian Atwood, Administrator, Agency for International Development
Peter Ballinger, Director, Investor Services for Asia, Latin America & Africa (OPIC)
Rodney Bent, Branch Chief of International Affairs (Office of Management and Budget)
Anna Borg, Special Assistant to the Deputy Secretary (DOS)
Esther Brimmer, Special Assistant to Undersecretary for Political Affairs (DOS)
Thomas Buckley, Special Assistant to the Undersecretary for International Security (DOS)
Mary Chambliss, Acting Associate Administrator, Office of International Cooperation and
    Development (Department of Agriculture)
Gene Clapp, international economist, Office of Multilateral Development Banks
    (Department of Treasury)
Brian Crowe, Deputy Director, Office of Multilateral Development Banks (Department of
    Treasury)
Phil DuSault, Deputy Associate Director for International Affairs (OMB)
Thomas Engle, financial economist, Office of Monetary Affairs (DOS)
Charles Ford, Deputy Assistant Secretary for International Operations, U.S. and Foreign
    Commercial Service (Department of Commerce)
Anthony Gillespie, Advisor to Undersecretary for Global Affairs (DOS)
Christopher Goldthwaite, Advisor to Secretary for Global Affairs (DOS)
Monica Healy, Senior Policy Adviser (AID Transition Team)
Matthew Hennessey, Director, Office of Multilateral Development Banks (Treasury)
Harvey Himberg, Director, Development Policy and Environmental Affairs (OPIC)
Cheryl Jones, Program Evaluation Officer, African Development Foundation
Kelly Kammerer, Mission Director, U.S. Economic Assistance Program to Nepal (AID)
Diane La Voy, Search Manager for AID, White House Office of Presidential Personnel
Robert M. Lester, Assistant General Counsel for Legislation and Policy (DOS)
Dick McCall, Senior Policy Advisor to Deputy Secretary (DOS)
Brian McCleary, Policy Resources Adviser, Office of Deputy Secretary (DOS)
David N. Merrill, Deputy Assistant Administrator for Europe (AID)
Anne Pence, Special Assistant to the Deputy Secretary (DOS)
Edward L. Saires, Acting Director for the Policy Directorate (AID)
Ronald Silberman, economist, Office of International Affairs (OMB)

Ralph Smuckler, Director, Center for University Cooperation in Development (AID)

Dan Speckhard, Director, Policy and Resources, Office of Deputy Secretary (DOS)

John Stremlau, Deputy Director, Policy Planning Staff (DOS)

Sandra Vogelgesang, Member, Task Force 2000 (DOS)

Helen Walsh, Director for International Economic Affair (National Security Council, White House)

Julie S, Wechser, Regional Director for Guatemala, Mexico, and Caribbean (Inter-American Foundation)

Ernest Wilson, Director of International Programs and Resources (National Security Council, White House)

APPENDIX 11: ASIA SOCIETY STUDY GROUP ON TAIWAN IN EAST ASIA, 1996

William Donaldson, founder Donaldson, Lufkin, and Jenrette and former President NYSE, Cochair

Clifton R. Wharton Jr., former Chairman and CEO, TIAA-CREF and former Asia Society Trustee, Cochair

Peter F. Geithner, Director, Asia Programs, Ford Foundation

Ellen M. Hancock, Chief Technology Officer of Apple Computer

Andrew Kim, Founder President and Chief Investment Officer, Sit-Kim International and Asia Society Trustee

Wan Kim, President, Kim Family Foundation

Linda Y. C. Lim, Director, Southeast Asia Business Program, University of Michigan (and wife of our old friend Pete Gosling)

Michael Miles, Special Limited Partner, Forstman Little

Dolores Wharton, Chairman and CEO, Fund for Corporate Initiatives and for Asia Society Trustee

Staff director was Dr. Robert W. Radtke, an Asia Society officer.

APPENDIX 12: COMMISSION ON NEW YORK STATE STUDENT FINANCIAL AID, 1998–2000

Paul Volcker, former Chairman, Federal Reserve, Cochair

Clifton R. Wharton Jr., former Chancellor, SUNY System, Cochair

Robert H. Atwell, President, American Council on Education (1984–96) and former President, Pitzer College (1970–78)

Mario Baeza, Chairman and CEO, TCW/Latin American Equity Partners, former senior
   partner, Debevoise & Plimpton (1974–94), trustee, Cornell University (1985–92)

Barber B. Conable Jr., President, World Bank (1986–91), U.S. Representative from the
   Thirtieth Congressional District (1965–85)

Judith S. Eaton, President, Council for Higher Education Accreditation (1997 to present),
   former Chancellor, Minnesota State Colleges and Universities (1995–97)

Maureen A. Fay, President, University of Detroit Mercy (1990 to present)

William C. Friday, President, University of North Carolina (1956–86), TIAA Board of
   Overseers (1986–95), member of Independent Commission on the Future of SUNY
   (1984–85)

John F. McGillicuddy, Chairman and CEO, Chemical Banking Corp. (1991–93), trustee
   emeritus, Princeton University

Adele S. Simmons, President, John D. and Catherine T. MacArthur Foundation (1989 to
   present), former President, Hampshire College (1977–1989)

Donald M. Stewart, Special Adviser to President, Carnegie Corporation of New York
   (1999 to present), President, College Board (1987–99), former President, Spellman
   College (1976–86)

APPENDIX 13: NEW YORK STOCK EXCHANGE SPECIAL COMMITTEE ON MARKET STRUCTURE, GOVERNANCE, AND OWNERSHIP, 1999–2000

Alex Trotman and Clifton Wharton, cochairs

Public directors from NYSE Board:

Geoffrey C. Bible, Philip Morris Companies Chairman and CEO

Stephen M. Case, America Online Chairman and CEO

Maurice R. Greenberg American International Group Chairman and CEO

Mel Karmazin, CBS Corp. President and CEO

Gerald M. Levin, Time Warner Chairman and CEO

Lord Marshall, British Airways Chairman

H. Carl McCall, former New York State Comptroller

Leon E. Panetta, Leon and Sylvia Panetta Institute for Public Policy President, former
   Chief of Staff to President Clinton

Linda J. Wachner, Warnaco Group Chairman, President, and CEO

Kathryn Whitmire, James MacGregor Burns Academy of Leadership, University of
   Maryland

.

Notes

CHAPTER ONE. THE BEGINNING: GENESIS AND YOUTH

1. Carter G. Woodson, *Free Negro Heads of Families in the United States in 1830* (Washington, D.C.: Association for the Study of Negro Life and History, 1925).

2. Richard H. Smith Jr., *Accomack County Virginia, Free Negro Records, Register of Free Negroes, 1807 to 1863 and List of Free Negroes—1804* (Woodsboro, MD: Firewood Treasures, 2007). Peter Wharton's listing is No. 905.

3. *Ladies Home Journal* 70, no. 3 (April 1963): 77.

4. The genealogical lineage of John Wharton 3rd and his ancestors was later verified by Dr. Dan Wharton's genealogical study of the Whartons.

5. There were similar inroads at the federal level, such as U.S. senators Hiram Revels in 1870 and Blanche Kelso Bruce (Mississippi) in 1875. In the Forty-Second Congress (1870–71) there were five Negro representatives; the Forty-Third and Forty-Fourth had six each. One of my wife Dolores's great-great-uncles, Samuel L. Duncan, was elected a member of the Fiftieth and Fifty-First General Assemblies of South Carolina (1872–76) and then in the Senate (1876–80). N. Louise Bailey, Mary L. Morgan, and Carolyn R. Taylor, *Biographical Directory of the South Carolina Senate, 1776–1985*, vol. 1 (Columbia: University of South Carolina Press, 1986).

6. Mark Curriden, "A Supreme Case of Contempt," *ABA Journal*, June 2009, data in sidebar "A Shameful History."

7. "Four Persons Dead in a Truro St. Fire. Two Women, a Girl and an Infant Cut Off by Rapidly Spreading Midnight Flames. Victims All of Top Floor. Several Escape Over Roof, Stairways Filled with Smoke. Most Occupants Aroused from Sleep. Incendiary Origin Seems Probable," *Boston Globe*, March 18, 1911, front page.

8. Clifton R. Wharton Sr., letter to the author, July 7, 1944. Note: Unless otherwise indicated, all subsequent correspondence and interviews are in my personal archives, eventually to be placed in the Michigan State University Archives.

9. Boston University Law School, Clifton R. Wharton, Grade Summary for LLB, June 16, 1920, and LLM, June 18, 1923.

10. This is the same fraternity and chapter that Dr. Martin Luther King Jr. joined in 1952 when he was a graduate student in theology at Boston University.

11. Years later, in 1939, the two Richardson spinster sisters were improbably living in the next block to our home on Walnut Avenue in Roxbury.

12. Dorothy McCardle, "Keeping Posted: Ambassador's Fete," *Washington Post*, June 29, 1975.

13. Eugene Gordon, "The Negro's Inhibitions," *American Mercury* 13, no. 50 (February 1928): 161–62.

14. *State Magazine* (U.S. Department of State), "Celebrating Blacks in Foreign Affairs," February 1998.

15. The composer of the Negro national anthem "Lift Every Voice and Sing," in 1899; it was set to music by his brother John Rosamond Johnson in 1900.

16. The traditional posts for politically appointed Negro diplomats were in Africa, Liberia in particular, and other undesirably tropical countries. Negroes occasionally went to the Azores or Oporto, Calais, and the predominantly Black nations of the Caribbean.

17. Homer Calkin, *Women in the Department of State: Their Role in American Foreign Affairs* (Washington, D.C.: U.S. Department of State, 1978), 72.

18. "Government Foreign Service School is Lily White, Mystery Disclosed Surrounding Quick Appointment of Liberian Sec'ty, Discrimination Victim Former Baltimorean, Trail of Race Prejudice Leads from Door of White House," *Afro-American,* May 9, 1925.

19. Known as the "Pepper Coast" or "Grain Coast," the region had Portuguese, Dutch, and English trading posts beginning in the mid-fifteenth century until the arrival of free Blacks from the United States.

20. Aldas Ridgely and John Garrett, two slightly older Negro boys who lived next door, at 71 Highland Street, escorted me to school each day. Later Garrett attended Boston Latin School a few years ahead of me and became a highly successful dentist.

21. Barbara Kevles, 1978 interview materials, in Clifton R. Wharton Jr. Archives, Michigan State University.

22. Ignacio Rivero, interview taped by the author, March 28, 1995.

23. Beginning in AD 711, the Muslim Moors from North Africa invaded and conquered Spain and Portugal and parts of France. Their occupation lasted for seven hundred years.

24. George Forsythe, letter to the author, May 2, 1997.

25. Maria's white father was probably Dr. James Henry Wise (b. 1830, d. 1896), a distinguished physician in Accomack.

26. In 1806 Washington College was merged with Jefferson College by act of the Pennsylvania legislature; it is now Washington and Jefferson College.

27. Charles Warren, *History of the Harvard Law School and of Early Legal Conditions in America*, vol. 3 (New York: Lewis Publishing Company, 1908), 27, 371. See also *Quinquennial Catalogue of the Officers and Graduates of Harvard University, 1636–1930* (Cambridge: The University, 1930) (listed as "Louis Cray Hamersly Finney" for his LLB).

28. Craig Simpson, "Political Compromise and the Protection of Slavery: Henry A. Wise and the Virginia Constitutional Convention of 1850–1851," *Virginia Magazine of History* 83, no. 4 (October 1975): 399.

29. While writing this book, I received a DNA report of a close genetic relative Willard R. Finney, also a lawyer, with whom I exchanged ancestral information and even met.

30. Stewart E. Tolnay and E. M. Beck, *A Festival of Violence: An Analysis of Southern Lynchings, 1882–1930* (Urbana: University of Illinois Press, 1992), ix.

31. This area was near where the current Route 13 ends and the Chesapeake Bay Bridge Tunnel crosses to

Norfolk, Virginia.

32. Curtis J. Badger, *Virginia's Eastern Shore: A Pictorial History* (Norfolk, VA: Donning Co., 1983), 79.

33. Gunnar Myrdal, *An American Dilemma: The Negro Problem and Modern Democracy*, 2 vols. (New York: Harper & Brothers, 1944).

34. *The Jazz Singer* movie in 1927.

35. William J. Roche, letter to the author, May 9, 1985.

36. "Big Cohen" later became president of Clark University; president of Queens College, CUNY; and a distinguished member of the New York State Board of Regents.

37. Dennis J. Curran, "Outstanding Alumnus, Clifton R. Wharton Jr. '42 [*sic*]," *Boston Latin School Bulletin* (Spring 1980). The occasion was at a conference of high school students from around the state of Massachusetts held at Boston Latin School.

38. Will Cloney, "English, Mechanics Open Reggie Battle," *Boston Herald*, March 11, 1941.

39. Tom Fitzgerald, "English Leads in Reggie Meet," *Boston Globe*, March 12, 1941; "New Mark Hung Up by Schoolboys: Two Tie for Record in High Jump at Reggies," *Boston Post*, March 12, 1941.

40. "Over and Over," *Boston Daily Record*, March 12, 1941.

41. *Liber Actorum*, Boston Latin School, Class of 1943.

CHAPTER TWO. THE STUDENT: COLLEGE YEARS

1. Recalling the 1923 photograph of my father and his fraternity brothers in the Boston Alpha Phi Alpha chapter, I realized progress on this front was snail-like.

2. Years later Carlos told me that as a scholarship student Hext told him he couldn't be too choosy about whom he roomed with. Carlos Blanco, interview by the author, August 9, 1994.

3. Pepe returned to Cuba and became a famous author and movie producer. He joined the Communist Party in 1948 and took part in Castro's revolution. At last count he had made thirty-eight films, received seventeen film festival awards, written several books, and become president of the association of Cuban writers and artists. The last time I spoke with him he begged me to send him a new Harvard pennant to replace one damaged by his children. I sent the banner, a Harvard T-shirt, and a school cap.

4. Harvard made suspended students spend a year at manual labor before applying for readmission.

5. "Galaxy Gazer: William Liller '48, Adams House Master, 1969–73," *Gold Coaster*, Adams House Alumni Magazine, vol. 1, no. 2, Spring 2011.

6. Much of the material in this section is based upon the "Crimson Network Comment Books," volumes 9 through 15, in the Harvard University Archives. Providentially these "comment books" had been saved. These were legal-size, bound books on whose pages we wrote notes, letters, and memos to Network members.

7. July 17, 1944, WHCN Comment Books, vol. 10, 246–47.

8. Writing in the comment book: "my term marks came out so badly that I stand a chance of losing two scholarships . . . I suggest that my assistant production director 'HNG' [Hartford Gunn] take over."

9. "Crimson Relay Quartet Conquers Rhode Islands," *Harvard Service News* (published by the *Harvard Crimson*), vol. 4, no. 18.8, January 16, 1945.

10. Lawrence P. Scott and William M. Womack Sr., *Double V: The Civil Rights Struggle of the Tuskegee Airmen* (East Lansing: Michigan State University Press, 1994).

11. Anne Stuart, ed., "War Stories: Clifton R. Wharton, Jr. '47," *Harvard Magazine*, January–February 2004.

12. The base commander when I arrived was Major H. C. Magoon, later succeeded by another white, Col. Noel F. Parrish.

13. Gunnar Myrdal, *An American Dilemma: The Negro Problem and Modern Democracy*, 2 vols. (New York: Harper and Brothers, 1944). The book became instantly a popular read within the Negro community since its conclusions resonated with the Negro experience.

14. Harold later graduated from Harvard Medical School in 1951, became chief of surgery at the Albert Schweitzer hospital in Haiti for eleven years, and became professor of surgery at the HMS and director of community medical care programs at Peter Bent Brigham in Boston in 1971.

15. Perry Young was one of a handful of Negro civilian instructors the Air Corps brought in to supplement the military cadre. In 1956 Young became the first Black pilot for a U.S. commercial airline, New York Airways.

16. Years later I mentioned the incident to a white southern acquaintance, a wartime veteran of the Air Corps, who thought it might have been the instructor's crude but effective way of finding out whether a future pilot would be able to control his emotions under fire. There might have been a grain of truth in that; I have no way of knowing. Either way, I was in a strange sense indebted to Kominic for one thing—the opportunity to see and deal with racism in its most virulent form.

17. Charles E. Francis, *The Tuskegee Airmen: The Men Who Changed a Nation* (Boston: Branden Publishing Co., 1993), 209.

18. Scott Jaschik, "New Evidence of Racial Bias on SAT," *Inside Higher Education*, June 21, 2010.

19. Bruce Ashcroft, *We Wanted Wings: A History of the Aviation Cadet Program* (HQ AETC Office of History and Research, 2005), 51.

20. The phrase "talented tenth" originated in 1896 among northern white liberals whose goal was establishing black colleges to train Negro teachers and elites. Du Bois, the first Black PhD from Harvard, used the term "talented tenth" to describe the likelihood of one in ten black men becoming leaders of their race in the world, through methods such as continuing their education, writing books, or becoming directly involved in social change. He strongly believed that blacks needed a classical education to be able to reach their potential, rather than the industrial education set forth by Tuskegee president Booker T. Washington in his Atlanta speech "Cast Down Your Bucket Where You Are," September 18, 1895.

21. Washington focused on having education for real-life jobs and not seeking equality from whites. W. E. B. Du Bois focused on the exact opposite—gaining equality through education. Du Bois cofounded the National Association for the Advancement of Colored People in 1909.

22. For a definitive description of the founding of the National Student Association, see Eugene G. Schwartz, ed., *American Students Organize: Founding the National Student Association after World War II; An Anthology and Source Book* (Westport, CT: American Council on Education/Praeger Series on Higher Education, 2006).

23. Committee for the Chicago Conference, printed letter to "Fellow [University] Students," n.d. 1946.

24. *Harvard Crimson*, December 13, 1946.

25. "Elliott Asks Wariness of Communists at Chicago; Student Conference Must Fight Minority 'Capturing' Tactics, Seek Democratic Principles," *Harvard Crimson*, December 19, 1946.

26. Cater's father served several terms as an Alabama state senator. Before college Doug had been a page in the Alabama legislature, no breeding ground for leftists. He subsequently became the Washington editor of *Reporter* magazine (1950–64). From 1964 to 1968 he served as a special assistant to President Johnson and played a key role in developing and passing the legislation that created the Corporation for Public Broadcasting and its spinoffs PBS and NPR. From 1982 to 1990 he was president of Washington College.

27. "Elliott's Charges Scored by Conference Delegate; Cater Denies Kremlin Control of Student Representatives at International Conference," *Harvard Crimson*, December 20, 1946.

28. Allan Ostar later became president of the American Association of State Colleges and Universities (AASCU) from 1965 to 1991.

29. *Daily Worker*, January 6, 1947.

30. Bill Ellis graduated from Harvard Law School and became a successful lawyer in New York City.

31. Carter retired on December 31, 1942. My father arrived in Tananarive in April 1942.

32. Clifton R. Wharton Jr., "The Constitutional Convention, Madison, September 1947," section 3, in Schwartz, *American Students Organize*, 144–49.

33. Bill Welsh subsequently served as aide to U.S. senators Herbert Lehman and Phil Hart. From 1969 to 1972 he was executive director of the National Democratic Committee.

34. "Birth of the NSA," *Newsweek* 30, no. 12 (September 22, 1947).

35. In 1950 SAIS affiliated with Johns Hopkins University.

36. Ronald D. Palmer, the second Black to graduate from SAIS, reported that Professor Linebarger regularly stated that I had been a problem because I had a chip on my shoulder and that I was "too proud, intellectually sharp and haughty." Palmer, e-mail message to the author, September 8, 1999. This characterization of me was disputed by Priscilla Mason. Mason, interview by the author, September 20, 1999.

37. Hans N. Tuch, "Epilogue: Conducting Diplomacy; Political and Cultural Change in Berlin, Bonn, and Washington, D.C.," in *Washington, D.C. Interdisciplinary Approaches*, edited by L. Hönnighausen and Andreas Falke (Tübingen, 1992), 221.

38. Robert S. Willis and Clifton R. Wharton Jr., "Flota Mercante Grancolombiana," *Inter-American Economic Affairs* 2, no. 1.

39. Ernie Howell went to work for the Asia Foundation in South and Southeast Asia, and Chuck Stone worked for CARE in India.

40. Many years later Clifton Garvin, CEO of Exxon (Esso successor), approached me about joining their board of directors. I declined because of a legal conflict due to my board membership with Ford Motor. When I laughingly told him about my failure to be hired from SAIS, he was shocked.

41. Jamieson had won a Pulitzer for his reporting on the Lindbergh kidnaping.

42. In addition to the nonprofit AIA, the two for-profit firms were the Venezuelan Basic Economy Corporation and the International Basic Economy Corporation. There were initially three trainees, but Nelson soon added a second one to IBEC so there were four of us: Richard S. Aldrich (Nelson's cousin), Richard Greenebaum (a cousin of my classmate Phil Stern), Jim O'Neill (a Dartmouth graduate), and myself.

43. Later Herter was governor of Massachusetts (January 8, 1953–January 3, 1957), under secretary of state (February 21, 1957–April 22, 1959) and U.S. secretary of state (April 22, 1959–January 20, 1961) when John Foster Dulles became ill.

44. Ron Palmer, the second SAIS graduate (1957), had an outstanding thirty-two-year career in the U.S. Foreign Service and later became U.S. ambassador to Malaysia, 1981–83. Another outstanding Black graduate was Frank Savage, SAIS MA 1964, chairman emeritus of Alliance Capital Management International, a subsidiary of Equitable Life Insurance Company.

45. Donald was the less notorious brother of Alger Hiss, a key officer in the Department of State and secretary-general of the 1945 San Francisco conference that created the United Nations. He was accused of being a Soviet spy in 1948 and convicted of perjury in connection with this charge in 1950.

CHAPTER THREE. THE YOUNG ECONOMIST; THE AIA, DOLORES DUNCAN AND CHICAGO

1. Bowser was just starting a writing career that would eventually include senior editing jobs at *Saturday Evening Post* and *Science Digest*.

2. Built by John D. Rockefeller Jr. and named for the famous Black poet, the Dunbar was one of New York's first cooperative housing complexes for Negroes. In the Great Depression it converted to rental apartments.

3. The best summary on the AIA program is Martha Dalrymple, *The AIA Story: Two Decades of International Cooperation* (New York: American International Association for Economic and Social Development, 1968). See also Margaret Carroll Boardman, "The Man, the Girl, and the Jeep. AIA: Nelson Rockefeller's Precursor Nonprofit Model for Private U.S. Foreign Aid," *Mexico and the World* 6, no. 1 (Winter 2001); and Margaret M. Carroll, "The Rockefeller Corollary: The Impact of Philanthropy and Globalization in Latin America," PhD diss., University of California, Los Angeles, 1999.

4. Nelson Rockefeller's other two (for-profit) businesses were on the same floor: the International Basic Economy Corporation and the Venezuelan Basic Economy Corporation.

5. Clifton R. Wharton Jr., "Aiding the Community: A New Philosophy for Foreign Operations," *Harvard Business Review* 32, no. 2 (March–April 1954); Clifton R. Wharton Jr., "Corporate Philanthropy: An Historical Vignette," *New Century Philanthropy* (Committee to Encourage Corporate Philanthropy), Spring 2004, 8.

6. J. W. Hisle, letter to the author, July 12, 1954.

7. From the sidelines I got a clear view of their consummate skill during the multiyear dissolution of the marriage between Winthrop Rockefeller and Barbara "Bobo" Sears, the daughter of a Pennsylvania coal miner who became a *Vogue* model and actress. The divorce scandal began in 1948, ending in 1954.

8. Spaulding had been hired in early 1947 (and remained until the end of 1982). He was a member of the famous Spaulding family in North Carolina, who founded the largest Negro insurance company of the period.

9. From a Black elite family, Alexander became a successful lawyer, businessman, and government official. President Carter appointed him secretary of the army (1977–81).

10. "Funeral of Tom Bradford, One of the Best Known Baltimore Colored Men," *Baltimore Morning Herald*, February 13, 1887, 3.

11. Richard Rodgers and Lorenz Hart, the 1925 revue *Garrick Gaieties*.

12. Founded in 1809 as the Free African Church of St. Philip's, in 1818 St. Philip's Episcopal Church became the first African American Episcopal parish in New York City. Vertner Tandy, the first African American architect registered in the state of New York, and George W. Foster Jr., one of two Black architects registered in New Jersey in 1908, designed the church. At its peak it had a congregation of over four thousand parishioners.

13. "Danbury Girl to Wed Son of U.S. Diplomat," *Amsterdam News* (New York), January 7, 1950; Bali Schalk, "Bali Talks about Boston Society," *Pittsburgh Courier*, January 14, 1950.

14. The 24 foot by 20 foot studio was saved in 1999 by the Connecticut Trust for Historic Preservation and was relocated to the Danbury Museum and Historical Society.

15. Gerri Major, "Top Society Wedding Solemnized at Anderson Estate; Miss Dolores Duncan Weds Clifton Wharton of Boston," *Amsterdam News* (New York), April 22, 1950, 21. The *Amsterdam News* had a full-page spread of photographs ("In the Spotlight: A Connecticut Wedding," *Amsterdam News*, April 22, 1950, 9).

16. "Eastern Seaboard Society Is Getting Ready for the Wharton-Duncan Wedding Ceremony Which Will Be Performed in the Studio of Marian Anderson on Her Connecticut Estate," Gerri Major, "Town Topics," *Amsterdam News*, April 1, 1950.

17. The Riverton, at 135th Street and Fifth Avenue, was a seven-building complex of 1,232 apartments built by the Metropolitan Life Insurance Company in 1947 for middle-class Negroes.

18. Rich became the *New Yorker* music critic and Marty Bookspan the voice for symphony on New York's WQXR. Hartford Gunn eventually became the head of WGBH in Boston.

19. At this time my father was deputy chief of mission in Lisbon, Portugal, Brazil's former colonial power. Dad attended the NATO (North Atlantic Treaty Organization) meeting in Lisbon on February 20. Clifton R. Wharton Sr., letter to the author, February 9, 1952.

20. Gilberto Freyre, *The Masters and the Slaves (Casagrande & Senzala): A Study in the Development of Brazilian Civilization*, trans. Samuel Putnam, 2nd ed. (New York: Alfred A. Knopf, 1956). Freyre is considered the main source of the myth that Brazil was a country without racism. This theory was later challenged by other scholars.

21. It is also referred to as "do-nothing farming" or "the Fukuoka Method" (named after the philosopher-farmer who first developed the system).

22. Things improved considerably after Juscelino Kubitschek de Oliveira became governor of Minas Gerais. Later elected president of Brazil in 1955, he became the prime mover for the new capital in Brasília. Nelson Rockefeller and he admired one another, and people who saw the Empire State Plaza that Rockefeller built during the 1960s in Albany detected strong echoes with the modernist style of Oscar Niemeyer, Brasília's principal architect.

23. John R. Camp, interview by the author, August 16, 1996.

24. Theodore W. Schultz, "The Supply of Food in Relation to Economic Development," *Economic Development and Cultural Change* 1, no. 4 (December 1952): 244–49.

25. A third Black student, Percy Luney, transferred into economics from the University of Kentucky during my second semester.

26. Also published as Wharton, "Aiding the Community."

27. Kemper's appointment had been based on his prior business ties to Latin America and his cofounding of the Inter-American Council of Commerce and Production.

28. M. L. Mosher, "History of the Family of Stephen and Ruth Mosher" (prepared for the Iowa Centennial Reunion, July 26, 1953). The manuscript was provided by Richard Mosher.

29. Some key texts were James G. Maddox, *Technical Assistance by Religious Agencies in Latin America*; Arthur T. Mosher, *Technical Cooperation in Latin American Agriculture*; and Philip Glick, *The Administration of Technical Assistance: Growth in the Americas* (all publications by the University of Chicago Press in 1956 and 1957). My own contribution was an article, Clifton R. Wharton Jr., "The Nature of Economic Development," *Economic Development and Cultural Change* 6, no. 2 (January 1958): 109–28.

30. Clifton R. Wharton Jr., "The Economic Impact of Technical Assistance: A Brazilian Case Study," *Journal of Farm Economics* 42, no. 2 (May 1960): 252–67. My doctoral dissertation was also mentioned in Dalrymple, *The AIA Story*, 50–51.

CHAPTER FOUR. THE DEVELOPMENT ECONOMIST I: THE ADC IN SINGAPORE, KUALA LUMPUR, AND SOUTHEAST ASIA

1. Arthur T. Mosher Jr. et al., *The Life and Work of Arthur T. Mosher* (Philadelphia: Xlibris, 2001), 76–77.

2. Russell Stevenson and Virginia O. Locke, *The Agricultural Development Council: A History* (Morrilton, AR: Winrock International Institute, 1989).

3. One of the staffers was agricultural economist J. Lossing Buck. His wife, Pearl S. Buck, became famous for

her novel *The Good Earth*, which was the best-selling book in the United States in 1931 and 1932, and won a Pulitzer Prize in 1932.

4. In 1964 the organization's name changed to the Agricultural Development Council, or ADC. Since the later name became far more familiar to everyone involved, I have chosen to use "the Council" or "ADC" hereafter, even though for much of the time the older name was in place.

5. John Ensor Harr and Peter J. Johnson, *The Rockefeller Conscience: An American Family in Public and Private* (New York: Macmillan, 1991).

6. Douglas Overton, president of the Japan Society; Harold Loucks, president of the China Medical Board (the inheritor of the funds and activities of the earlier Rockefeller activities in mainland China); Lloyd "Shorty" Elliott, executive vice president of Standard Oil; Phillips Talbot, executive director of the American Universities Field Staff and an outstanding Asian specialist; and J. Norman Efferson, a rice expert and then chairman of the Department of Agricultural Economics at Louisiana State University, who subsequently became dean of agriculture at LSU. Talbot, with his extensive experience in India, would later become ambassador to Greece and assistant secretary of state for the Near Eastern and South Asian Affairs.

7. "Wharton Sworn as Minister to Rumania after Mix-Up Results in 2 Ceremonies," *New York Times*, February 8, 1958.

8. Homer L. Calkin, "A Reminiscence: Being Black in the Foreign Service," *U. S. Department of State Newsletter*, February 1978, 28.

9. Michael L. Krenn, *Black Diplomacy: African Americans and the State Department, 1945–1969* (Armonk, NY: M. E. Sharpe, 1999), 25.

10. A. T. Mosher Memorandum to CECA Board of Trustees, September 1957.

11. Clifton R. Wharton Jr., letter to Dolores Wharton from New Delhi, India, April 26, 1958.

12. Clifton R. Wharton Jr., *The U.S. Graduate Training of Asian Agricultural Economists* (New York: Council on Economic and Cultural Affairs, 1959).

13. Barbara J. Walton, "Research on Foreign Graduate Students: A Review of the Literature," in *The Foreign Graduate Student: Priorities for Research and Action*, Wingspread Conference, June 16–17, 1970 (New York: College Entrance Examination Board, 1971), 86.

14. Clifton R. Wharton Jr., "The Economic Impact of Technical Assistance: A Brazilian Case Study," *Journal of Farm Economics* 42, no. 2 (May 1960); Clifton R. Wharton Jr., "Recent Trends of Output and Efficiency in the Agricultural Production of Brazil, Minas Gerais, and São Paulo," *Inter-American Economic Affairs* 13, no. 2 (Autumn 1959); Clifton R. Wharton Jr., "Processing Underdeveloped Data from an Underdeveloped Area," *Journal of the American Statistical Association* 55, no. 289 (March 1960). Translated into Spanish as "Elaboraciòn de Datos Subdesarrollados en Una Regiòn Subdesarrollada," *Estadistica, Journal of the Inter-American Statistical Institute*, March 1962.

15. Felder, who had a PhD in agricultural economics from Ohio State, was another Negro who had moved into international work as a fertile place to use his professional skills. In New Delhi he represented the Cooperative League of the U.S.A.

16. The title "Ungku," or Prince, signified his hereditary (paternal) title from one of the lineages of the royal family of Johor (a Malaysian state).

17. Written by Negro minstrel James A. Bland, the song generated a great deal of controversy over whether it reflected a slave's nostalgic longing to return to his master or a satirical spoof on slavery in the guise of describing a slave's positive attitudes toward slavery.

18. When Groves became president of Central State University, he asked me to give the keynote speech at his 1966 inauguration. He later became dean of law at North Carolina Central University and Henry Brandis Professor of Law at the University of North Carolina, Chapel Hill.

19. Other staff conferences were held in Penang, Malaysia, 1961, and in Bangkok, 1963, attended by JDR 3rd.

Each meeting regularly included a few members of the ADC board of trustees.

20. His title, "Tjokorda Gede," indicated that Soekawati belonged to the highest of the four noble castes in Bali.

21. My visit in November 1959 was a reunion with Asia Foundation representative Curt and Ellie Farrar, both friends from my National Student Association days. It was clear that the country was not yet ready to take advantage of our ADC programs. (Dolores and Clifton 3rd visited Angkor Wat in January 1964 as a Christmas present before it closed.)

22. Ralph H. Smuckler, *A University Turns to the World: A Personal History of the Michigan State University International Story* (East Lansing: Michigan State University Press, 2003).

23. This scandal was the subject of a famous article, "University on the Make," in *Ramparts* magazine (April 1966). The cover featured a garish cartoon of Madame Nhu as a cheerleader waving a green-and-white "S" pennant.

24. Brown had a successful subsequent academic career in the United States and overseas. Besides teaching at University of Illinois, Iowa State University, and Texas A&M, Dave spent almost two decades living and working abroad in more than twenty countries ranging from Indonesia and Pakistan to Ethiopia and Tanzania, working for the Food and Agriculture Organization of the United Nations, the United Nations Development Programme, and the World Bank.

25. "The Teaching of Economics in Southeast Asia," *Malayan Economic Review* 4, no. 2 (October 1959): 6–15.

26. T. H. Silcock, "The Teaching of Economics in Southeast Asia: A Reply to Dr. Wharton," *Malayan Economic Review* 4, no. 2 (October 1959): 16–20.

27. Art Mosher and his family had been the architects and actual builders of their home at 118 N. Sunset Drive.

28. Clifton R. Wharton Jr., "Economic and Non-economic Factors in the Agricultural Development of Southeast Asia: Some Research Priorities," *A/D/C Paper*, August 1962–June 1963.

29. The Federation of Malaya, officially created in August 30, 1957, was composed of eleven states states—Perlis, Kedah, Penang, Perak, Selangor, Negeri Sembilan, Malacca, Johore, Pahang, Trengganu, and Kelantan. Nine of the states had hereditary Malay sultan rulers who rotated the national post of Paramount Ruler or *Yang di-Pertuan Agong*, commonly referred to as the king, and who were selected for five-year terms by the sultans.

30. Clifton R. Wharton Jr., "Marketing, Merchandising, and Moneylending: A Note on Middleman Monopsony in Malaya," *Malayan Economic Review* 8, no. 2 (1962).

31. The institute program was administered by the Institute of International Education with an advisory board nominated by the American Economic Association. See "Notes," *American Economic Review*, March 1960.

32. Clifton R. Wharton Jr., "Human Capital and Socio-cultural Values: Implications for Economic Development," Regional Conference, Young Presidents Organization, Kuala Lumpur, Malaysia, September 24, 1998.

33. Somewhat like silk-screening, the technique involved drawing a picture on cloth, then covering all areas with wax except one, then dipping the cloth into dye, and drying. The process is then repeated until a full-color painting is achieved. *Peasant and Bullock* was used on the cover of my book *Subsistence Agriculture and Economic Development* (Chicago: Aldine, 1969).

34. "Malam Irama Is an Imaginative Show," *Malayan Times*, October 27, 1963.

35. "Not Quite the Same as in Grandpa's Time . . . ," *Straits Times*, October 23, 1963.

36. Managing Director of *Malayan Times,* letter to Dolores Wharton, September 3, 1962.

37. The painting became part of selected Malaysian paintings we donated to the Johnson Museum at Cornell University in 1999.

38. Yap Pow Veng, letter to Dolores Wharton, August 10, 1963.

39. "University Gets a Rockefeller Research Grant," *Straits Times*, January 25, 1962; "$18,500 for Varsity to

Conduct Survey," *Malay Mail*, January 27, 1962.

40. Augustine Hui-Heng Tan, "Natural Rubber: Problems and Techniques of Stabilization," master's thesis, Department of Economics, University of Singapore, November 1965.

41. Francis Chan Kwong Wah, "A Study of Supply Response by Malayan Rubber Estates," honors thesis, University of Malaya in Singapore, September 1961.

42. The supply curve of labor shows how the change in real wage rates affects the amount of hours worked by employees. If wages increase, then workers will obtain a greater "utility," due to their higher incomes. Hence, they would be willing to increase their hours worked—so as wages go up the labor supply increases, or gives the supply curve a positive slope forward. On the other hand, if the wage increases but the number of hours worked falls, this is because the income effect has now become greater than the substitution effect, or the utility gained from an extra hour of leisure is greater than the utility gained from the income earned working. In simple terms, the workers are being paid enough to sustain their current lifestyle without having to work more hours, which creates a backward bend in the supply curve.

43. I was clearly influenced by my Chicago classmate Marc Nerlove's *The Economics of Supply: Estimation of Farmer Supply Response to Price* (Baltimore: John Hopkins University Press, 1958). In 1969 Marc was awarded the John Bates Clark Medal in economics.

44. Clifton R. Wharton Jr., "Rubber Supply Conditions: Some Policy Implications," in *The Political Economy of Independent Malaya*, ed. T. H. Silcock and E. K. Fisk (Canberra: Australian National University Press, 1963), chap. 6.

45. Francis Chan Kwong Wah, "Economic Aspects of Malayan Rubber Supply after the Second World War, 1946–61," master's thesis, Department of Economics, University of Malaya in Singapore, July 1962. See also Francis Chan Kwong Wah, "A Study of the Supply Response of Malayan Rubber Estates between 1948 and 1959," *Malayan Economic Review* 7, no. 2 (October 1962).

46. While Bauer, as a young economist, had rejected the colonial administrators' stereotypic view of peasants as lazy, unambitious, and risk averse, he later adopted a cultural explanation for these characteristics. Bruce M. Knauft, ed., *Critically Modern: Alternatives, Alterities, Anthropologies* (Bloomington: Indiana University Press, 2002), 95.

47. Han Suyin was the pen name of Elizabeth Comber, born Rosalie Matilda Kuanghu Chou. In 1952, she married Leon F. Comber, a British officer in the Malayan Special Branch, Johor, Malaya.

48. Clifton R. Wharton Jr., letter to Harriette B. Wharton, September 14, 1962.

49. Under President Kennedy's Special International Program for Cultural Presentations.

50. Milton Friedman and Rose Friedman, *Two Lucky People: Memoirs* (Chicago: University of Chicago Press, 1998), 329–30.

51. Clifton R. Wharton Jr., "The Economic Meaning of Subsistence," *Malayan Economic Review* 8, no. 2 (October 1963).

52. George Dalton, ed., *Economic Development and Social Change: The Modernization of Village Communities* (Garden City, NY: Natural History Press, 1971).

53. Clifton R. Wharton Jr., letter from Professor Robert Bates, Harvard Institute of International Development, November 13, 1999.

CHAPTER FIVE. THE DEVELOPMENT ECONOMIST 2: BACK IN THE UNITED STATES

1. My father had received an honorary doctorate in civil law from Morgan State University and attended a reunion of his English High School class (June 4, 1963), which presented him with a Paul Revere Silver Bowl.

2. Clifton R. Wharton Sr., letter to the author, August 6, 1963.

3. Stewart L. Udall, Secretary of the Interior, letter to the author, June 19, 1963.

4. Kennedy also recognized the overwhelming Black voter support he had received, which led to the high-level appointments of Carl Rowan as deputy assistant secretary of state, Thurgood Marshall as judge of the Second Circuit, and Wade McCree, my Boston Latin School fellow alumnus, as judge of the District Court for Eastern Michigan.

5. My participation later led to my joining the MIT Visiting Committee, Center for International Studies.

6. "Isle Parley Hopes to Aid Subsistence Farmers," *Honolulu Star Bulletin*, February 26, 1965.

7. "Aid to Subsistence Farmer Held Vital," *Honolulu Advertiser*, March 1, 1965.

8. Wharton, *Subsistence Agriculture and Economic Development* (Chicago: Aldine, 1969).

9. They included Orville Bentley, dean of agriculture at the University of Illinois; C. Brice Ratchford, vice president of extension at the University of Missouri; Robert R. Nathan, Robert Nathan Associates and former chair of ADA; and C. Harold Joiner, president of the Newspaper Farm Editors Association. Only Nathan and I had any experience in Vietnam or Southeast Asia.

10. Clifton R. Wharton Jr., "Visit to Cai-San," *International Agricultural Development*, Monthly Newsletter no. 18, U.S. Department of Agriculture, April 1966.

11. In 1967 Habib became deputy assistant secretary of state for East Asian and Pacific Affairs, and in 1968 he was part of the U.S. delegation to the peace talks with Vietnam.

12. Orville L. Freeman, U.S. Secretary of Agriculture, letter to the author, February 28, 1966.

13. Bill was the older brother of McGeorge Bundy, who had been dean of arts and sciences at Harvard before coming to President Kennedy's National Security Council.

14. Clifton R. Wharton Jr., "The Green Revolution: Cornucopia or Pandora's Box?" *Foreign Affairs*, April 1969, 464–76.

15. Borlaug won a Nobel Prize for his work in 1970.

16. Gordon Parks, *A Choice of Weapons* (New York: HarperCollins, 1966).

17. Clifton R. Wharton Jr., letter to Kenneth W. Thompson, Vice President, Rockefeller Foundation, April 17, 1968.

18. Clifton R. Wharton Jr., letter to Kenneth W. Thompson, April 17, 1968.

19. A few parts of this early idea were later initiated by Dolores through her Fund for Corporate Initiatives to increase the upward mobility of mid-level minorities and women in the corporate world.

20. AAI developed graduate-level and professional training scholarship programs for Africans in fundamental capacity-building fields, including agriculture, business and finance, education, government, health care, science, and technology. It also created opportunities for policymakers, business executives, government officials, and opinion leaders from Africa and the United States to gain a more complete understanding of each other and to explore, debate, and work collaboratively on issues of mutual interest.

21. Nelson's protest resignation was matched by his prior unknown support of the civil rights movement. During the May 2, 1963, Birmingham demonstration, the infamous police chief Bull Connor had arrested hundreds of young children who had marched. Their bail was $160,000, to which Nelson secretly contributed $100,000 personally in the vault of the Chase bank to Reverend King's lawyer, Clarence Jones, who signed a promissory note. Three days later the note was returned to Jones signed "paid in full."

22. I am grateful to Darwin Davis for providing me with a copy of the plan. His career at Equitable exemplified this process of purposeful upward mobility in the company, rising from an agent to manager of their Detroit office. He then, in 1974, became vice president in charge of field development, the first Black to reach the company's senior executive level, finally becoming a corporate senior vice president in 1987. Davis died in

2006.

23. Milton Friedman, letter to the author, December 27, 1968.

24. Joseph H. Boyd and Charles R. Holcomb, *Oreos and Dubonnet: Remembering Governor Nelson A. Rockefeller* (Albany: Excelsior Editions/State University of New York, 2012), chap. 7; Joseph E. Persico, *The Imperial Rockefeller: A Biography of Nelson A. Rockefeller* (New York: Simon and Shuster, 1982); Richard Norton Smith, *On His Own Terms: A Life of Nelson Rockefeller* (New York: Random House, 2014), chap. 22.

25. Gloria Steinem, "Nelson Rockefeller: The Sound of One Hand Clapping," *New York* magazine, August 11, 1969; Smith, *On His Own Terms*, 555.

26. In 1962, the Foreign Assistance Act of 1961 was amended by the Republican senator from Iowa, Bourke B. Hickenlooper, who proposed it. The law not only restricted aid to Communist countries, but to any country that nationalized U.S. corporate property without full compensation.

CHAPTER SIX. THE PRESIDENT OF MSU 1: THE START AND STUDENT DEMONSTRATIONS

1. Gayl had also worked closely with me in the Asia Society's Southeast Asian Development Advisory Group (SEADAG).

2. Three months earlier, coincidentally, I had been scheduled to sponsor and attend a conference, "Land Settlement and Development in the Tropics," at the University of Michigan, but had to cancel due to my trip for President Johnson's agricultural mission to Vietnam.

3. Robben W. Fleming, *Tempests into Rainbows: Managing Turbulence* (Ann Arbor: University of Michigan Press, 1996).

4. David A. Thomas, *Michigan State College: John Hannah and the Creation of a World University, 1926–1969* (East Lansing: Michigan State University Press, 2008).

5. There is controversy over which was the first land-grant institution. Kansas State University claims that it was "founded in 1863 as the country's first operational landgrant university." Iowa State was created by its state legislature, accepting the designation under the Morrill Act in March 1864. Michigan State was chartered under Michigan state law as a state agricultural land-grant institution on February 12, 1855, but designated a land grant in 1863 along with Penn State. Since Michigan Agricultural College (later MSU) was the first school to open, it claimed to be the model on which later ones were based.

6. The largest single-campus institution in the country was Ohio State. There were ongoing disputes over the rankings, in part because the University of Minnesota wanted to count its two branches in Minneapolis and St. Paul as a single "campus." Another disagreement was whether to measure students by head count or FTEs, full-time equivalent enrollments. MSU in fall 1969 listed 40,820 exclusive of Oakland University. *This Is Michigan State University*, "1970 Facts Book," 30.

7. William H. Sewell, letter to the author, August 18, 2000.

8. Hathaway had chaired a Commission on the Future of MSU in 1969 and had been a highly respected vice president of the American Farm Economics Association.

9. In 2004, on the fiftieth anniversary of the ADC, Winrock created the John D. Rockefeller 3rd Scholars Program to recognize Rockefeller's lifelong contributions to international development.

10. Dale Hathaway, interview by the author, April 5, 1995.

11. "Four Weighed as Chief of Michigan State," *New York Times*, August 29, 1969.

12. Thomas J. Noer, *Soapy: A Biography of G. Mennen* (Ann Arbor: University of Michigan Press, 2005), 515.

13. Oakland University would soon become independent in 1970, and Varner would leave to become president

of the University of Nebraska. Varner would be succeeded at Oakland by Donald O'Dowd.

14. *MSU State News*, October 15, 1969.

15. Other public campuses in Michigan follow the more conventional model—no constitutional autonomy and substantially regulated by the state department of education.

16. Years later Hannah told Professor Jim Bonnen that he thought he had make a serious mistake in changing from the previous arrangement, under which the governor selected board members.

17. The incident was later broadcast in the PBS documentary *Eyes on the Prize: America's Civil Rights Years (1954–1965)*, 1987.

18. George Colburn, "Dr. Adams—Support and Non-support," *Towne Courier* (East Lansing), October 14, 1969.

19. Ibid.

20. John F. A. Taylor, "Being Dealt With in Contempt," *MSU State News*, October 16, 1969.

21. Helen Clegg, "Adams Reaffirms His Non-candidacy," *Lansing State Journal*, October 16, 1969.

22. Lee, who attended Camp Atwater with me in 1943, was an early Black graduate of West Point and the winner of a White House Military Fellowship (1965–66).

23. Barbara Parness and Marilyn Patterson, "3 Trustees Stall Wharton Vote," *MSU State News*, October 19, 1969, giving details of the executive session. (Note: the paper was incorrectly dated October 12, 1969.)

24. MSU Board of Trustees Minutes, October 17, 1969.

25. Healy was the first American Negro to earn a doctorate from the University of Louvain, in Belgium. His brother James was the first Black Roman Catholic bishop in the United States, and a third brother, Michael, was a captain in the U.S. Revenue Cutter Service, the forerunner to the Coast Guard.

26. "Negro Economist Is Named Head of Michigan State U.: Clifton Wharton, Aide on Development Council, to Succeed Hannah," *The New York Times*, October 18, 1969.

27. "He's Known as 'Quiet Firster,'" *MSU Faculty News* 1, no. 4 (October 21, 1969).

28. Linda Lewis, "Wharton—Life as President, Father, Husband," *MSU State News*, November 3, 1969.

29. Joseph E. Wolff, "New MSU President: A Man of Many Firsts," *Detroit News*, October 17, 1969.

30. Bernard Bard, "Clifton Wharton: Things Are Changing," *New York Post*, October 25, 1969.

31. William Grant, "Wharton: Diplomacy at MSU," *Detroit Free Press*, October 26, 1969.

32. WJIM-TV (Lansing), November 12, 1969.

33. "A New Generation of College Presidents," *Time*, February 9, 1970. This article also profiled Harold Brown (Cal Tech), Terry Sanford (Duke), Martin Meyerson (University of Pennsylvania), and John Kemeny (Dartmouth).

34. George Colburn, "Black Faculty Back Wharton," *Towne Courier* (East Lansing), October 21, 1969.

35. "Reaction to New U of M [*sic*] President Is Divergent," *Three Rivers (Michigan) Commercial*, October 18, 1969.

36. Clifton R. Wharton Jr., remarks at funeral service for Don Stevens, St. John's Student Parish, East Lansing, MI, March 26, 2002.

37. John Ensor Harr and Peter J. Johnson, *The Rockefeller Conscience: An American Family in Public and Private* (New York: Charles Scribner's Sons, 1991), 283.

38. Helen Clegg, "Wharton Pledges 'Assistance to All' at MSU, Links Campus Activism to Concern," *Lansing State Journal*, October 24, 1969; UPI, "Extra Pressure? Wharton Says He Expects It as MSU President," *Lansing State Journal*, October 25, 1969.

39. Marilyn Patterson, "'U' Deans React Favorably to Wharton as President," *MSU State News*, October 27, 1969.

40. Charlie Hass, "'Spartan' Wharton Scores. Homecoming Crowd Cheers MSU First Family," *Lansing State Journal*, November 2, 1969.

41. Helen Clegg, "White Charges Collusion: Naming Wharton, Porter Called Plot to Defeat Austin," *Lansing State Journal*, November 5, 1969; Glenn Engle, "Hiring of Wharton Called Gribbs Plot," *Detroit News*, November 5, 1969.

42. Helen Clegg, "Wharton Pledges Disclosure: MSU President-Designate Calms Trustee Meeting," *Lansing State Journal*, November 22, 1969; "Wharton to Make Taxes Public, Trustees Approve," *State News*, November 23, 1969; and William Connellan, "Wharton Ends MSU Dispute over Salary," *Detroit News*, November 22, 1969.

43. "Board Makes Dr. Adams President of Michigan State for Three Weeks," *Flint Journal*, December 13, 1969. Adams later wrote a book on his experiences during the period, *The Test* (New York: Macmillan, 1971).

44. The others were the Asia Society, the Overseas Development Council, the American Agricultural Economics Association, an advisory board to my alma mater, the School of Advanced International Studies, and the Science and Technology Board for Agricultural Development at the National Academy of Sciences.

45. Two key people on the business side were Ted Simon, assistant vice president for physical plant, and Emory Foster, manager, Dormitories and Food Service, both of whom I courted assiduously, knowing that the nonacademic side of MSU venerated their leadership. Foster was due to retire, and I persuaded him to remain with a promotion to assistant vice president for business operations.

46. When President Lincoln signed the Morrill Act, July 2, 1862, higher education in the United States was totally dominated by private institutions. The land-grant approach was deliberately designed to provide higher educational opportunities to the underserved population of its day.

47. Elaborate inauguration ceremonies should be added to Hannah's list of "don'ts" for new university presidents. Many have stumbled, almost before starting, by holding expensive events, which are seen largely for the gratification of presidential egos.

48. Clifton R. Wharton Jr., "A Presidential Credo: A Personal Word," MSU Faculty Club, January 20, 1970.

49. Minutes of the Informal Meeting of the MSU Board of Trustees, January 15, 1970.

50. The push for participation in academic governance had already been recommended in the university's (Professor) McKee Report, which was pending Academic Council action.

51. Jacqueline Korona, "Loot Bag Dinner Wednesday, Legislators Start with Full Stomach," *Jackson Citizen Patriot*, January 13, 1970; "Farmer's 'Loot Bag' Still a Hit," *Detroit Free Press*, January 14, 1970.

52. There were "Eight" originally, a who's who of the radicals of that period: Abbie Hoffman, Jerry Rubin, David Dellinger, Tom Hayden, Rennie Davis, John Froines, Lee Weiner, and Bobby Seale. Seale's trial was detached from the others, creating the Chicago Seven.

53. He had been director of the Student Union, director of the Hotel and Restaurant Management School, director of the Kellogg Center, and director of the Continuing Education Program.

54. *MSU State News*, January 19, 1970.

55. Barbara Parness, "Huff Asks Wharton to Clarify Questions on VP Appointment," *MSU State News*, January 30, 1970.

56. Ann Hodge, "First Lady 'Tunes In' Area with Art," *MSU State News*, January 7, 1970; "MSU's First Lady a Graffiti Lover," *Detroit Free Press*, January 11, 1970.

57. Clifton R. Wharton Jr., "The University Environment: City of Youth" (speech, Michigan Municipal League Annual Convention, September 9, 1970).

58. The material on the MSU demonstration is based on a detailed daily chronology in my archival version,

which was developed using my calendar, newspaper clips, and fortunately the personal diary of my assistant James Spaniolo.

59. Among them were Bob Grossfield, head of the Associated Students of Michigan State University; Hal Buckner of the Men's Hall Association; and Terry Kerry, representing the People's Park "residents."

60. "MSU to Shut Down All Classes Friday," *Lansing State Journal*, May 7, 1970.

61. "MSU, U-M, WSU Heads Asked to Quit, Resolution in House," *Lansing State Journal*, May 8, 1970.

62. John Gillespie Magee Jr., "High Flight," 1941.

63. Helen Clegg, "Strikers Demands Added to MSU Council Agenda," *Lansing State Journal*, May 12, 1970.

64. Ibid.

65. He later became an assistant deputy in the Michigan attorney general's office.

66. Panel discussion, "Trial and Triumph: The Wharton Years," MSU Thirtieth Anniversary Convocation, Wharton Center, Michigan State University, October 27, 2000, videotape.

67. Norman Sinclair, "Police Arrest 132 on MSU Campus," *Lansing State Journal*, May 10, 1970.

68. Laura R. Wascha, "Wharton to Welcome Pupils from Garfield," *Flint Journal*, May 24, 1970.

69. "132 Arrested in Union File Suit against Officials," *State News*, July 3, 1970.

70. "Man of the Year," *Boston Herald-Traveler*, November 25, 1970.

71. "Report Chronicles a Campus in Crisis," *MSU Faculty News*, January 19, 1971.

72. Gerald Elliott, "Clifton Wharton: A Diplomat's Son Becomes a Pioneer—from Harvard to Malaysia to MSU," *Grand Rapids Press*, July 5, 1970; John Borger, "Wharton—Focal Point for Contacts with 'U,'" *MSU State News*, July 9, 1970; "Clifton Wharton's First Six Months," *Michigan Chronicle*, July 25, 1970. The Black media also provided significant coverage. *Ebony* devoted six pages to a photo-laden essay ("New Boss Takes Over at Michigan State," *Ebony* 25, no. 9 [July 1970]: 60–70); and *Jet* had me on its cover with an article (Valerie Jo Bradley, "Black President Runs Michigan State University, Gets Demanding Position Which Is One of Many Firsts," *Jet*, May 21, 1970).

73. Robert Berg, "MSU's Black Prexy Maintains His Calm in First Six Months," *Detroit News*, July 5, 1970.

74. Tom Tiede, "Wharton Fits New Image Established at MSU," *Detroit News*, October 1, 1970.

75. Dave Short, "Strike Tests New Leadership," *MSU State News*, September 19, 1970.

76. Doug Huston, *MSU State News*, June 5, 1970.

CHAPTER SEVEN. THE PRESIDENT OF MSU 2: DEVELOPING A PLURALISTIC UNIVERSITY

1. Janice Hayhow, "President Wharton Tackles Time Study," *MSU New Bulletin*, April 7, 1977.

2. Clifton R. Wharton, letter to James Jones, March 18, 1976.

3. Allan J. Mayer with James C. Jones, "Executives: The Flying Whartons," *Newsweek*, April 12, 1976.

4. Paul Hanson, "Cowles House Opened to 'U' Faculty Art Works," *State News*, July 20, 1970.

5. MSU Presents, "Cowles House: Art in Residence," 1971, Michigan State University Television, MSU Development Fund, producer Thomas L. Turk, director James C. Lau.

6. Virginia Redfern, "'Arts in Residence' Film Shown," *Lansing State Journal*, June 2, 1971.

7. The subjects revealed my major concerns for key target audiences: six on the "pluralistic university" and higher education; four specifically on MSU, including one on the role of women; four on Black affairs; three

on agriculture; three on students and youth; three on business and economics; and two on U.S. foreign policy.

8. Clifton R. Wharton Jr., "The Pluralistic University: New Directions for Higher Education in the Seventies," Detroit Economic Club, March 30, 1970; "The Pluralistic University: The Concern for Human Values," University of Michigan Commencement, Ann Arbor, May 2, 1970; "The Pluralistic University: The University's Quest for a Social Role," Michigan Academy of Arts and Sciences," Kalamazoo, Michigan, April 23, 1971.

9. "The Role of the University in Public Affairs," sponsored by the National Association of State Universities and Land Grant Colleges and the Carnegie Corporation, from 1968 to 1971.

10. David C. Pollock and Ruth E. Van Reken, *Third Culture Kids: Growing Up among Worlds* (Boston: Nicolas Brealey, 1999).

11. Four decades later I reflected on this concept's applicability to the newly elected president, Barack Obama. My thought was to write an Op Ed. I even spoke with his mother's doctoral thesis adviser at the University of Hawaii seeking confirmation, but I decided not to add fire to the attacks about Obama's birthplace and citizenship.

12. Jim Spaniolo would leave in 1972 to enroll in the University of Michigan Law School.

13. Deborah Krell, "Orientation—Presidential Style," *MSU Faculty News*, July 28, 1970.

14. Justin Morrill College was one of three MSU residential colleges; the others were James Madison and Lyman Briggs. Modeled on the British Oxbridge "living-learning" model, these colleges were located in the residential halls, thereby improving student access to faculty and facilities, as well as giving a feeling of smallness in the larger university.

15. Founded in 1964, the program typically gave fellows a year as a full-time, paid assistant to senior White House staff, Cabinet secretaries, and other topranking government officials in Washington, D.C.

16. Open Admissions is usually defined as nonselective enrollment where the only criterion for college entrance is a high school diploma or a General Educational Development (GED) certificate.

17. *The Report to the President of Michigan State University from the Commission on Admissions and Student Body Composition* (East Lansing: Michigan State University, 1971), 35.

18. The report also developed definitions of minority students and physically handicapped students (*Commission on Admissions*, 37).

19. Clifton R. Wharton Jr., "Women at Michigan State University: Past and Future," speech, MSU Business Women's Club, April 16, 1970.

20. Clifton R. Wharton Jr., "Women at Michigan State University."

21. "Women Hail New MSU Tuition Policy," *Towne Crier* (East Lansing), March 19, 1970.

22. "Women's, Minority Programs Name Assistant Directors," *MSU News-Bulletin*, May 3, 1973.

23. They both became our lifelong friends. Jim sadly died May 18, 1994, from Amyotrophic lateral sclerosis (ALS, or Lou Gehrig's disease). Ruth would subsequently become a highly influential trustee of TIAA-CREF.

24. Dr. Tom Freeman, e-mail message to the author, October 28, 2013.

25. "Keep Races Separated, Clay Tells MSU Students," *Detroit News*, February 28, 1970.

26. He replaced Don Coleman, a legendary MSU football star, on Nonnamaker's staff.

27. Tom Haroldson, "Unit Studies Faculty Union Flaws," *MSU State News*, October 3, 1972.

28. "Board Meeting Features Unscheduled Appearance by Officials of Chicano Group," *MSU News-Bulletin*, October 21, 1971.

29. Beckie Hanes and Michael Fox, "Between 'U,' Chicanos: Debate Request Denied," *MSU State News*,

October 12, 1971; Michael Fox, "'U'-Chicano Debate 'Irrational,'" *MSU State News*, October 15, 1971.

30. Mike Wagoner, "Chicanos Will Use 'Proper' Channels," *Lansing State Journal*, October 16, 1971; Michael Fox, "Trustees Promise Help to Chicanos for Projects," *MSU State News*, October 18, 1971.

31. Mike Wagoner, "Bylaw Amendment Sought, Try to Clip Wharton's Wings Fails," *Lansing State Journal*, July 17, 1971; John Borger and Steve Waterbury, "Board Clash Ends in Triumph for Wharton," *MSU State News*, July 19, 1971; "MSU in a Huff," *Detroit Free Press*, June 29, 1972.

32. "Bickering Game," *Lansing State Journal*, November 1, 1972; "Hollow Theatrics by Warren Huff," *WJIM*, October 25, 1972.

33. Report of Select Committee on the Condition of the University, 2 House Documents 1840 (p. 470) quoted in Michigan Supreme Court, *Sterling v. Regents of the University*, 110 Mich. 369, 375 (1896).

34. Bob Hoerner, "Dr. Green Seeks Black Equality," *Lansing State Journal*, February 20, 1972.

35. Mike Wagoner, "Wharton Requests Discussion of Issues at Big 10 Meeting: Reforms Not Aimed at MSU Teams," *Lansing State Journal*, February 11, 1972.

36. Bob Hoerner, "Protest by Black Students Delays Start of MSU Game," *Lansing State Journal*, February 27, 1972.

37. "Disruptions Intolerable, Dr. Wharton Issues Get Tough Policy," *Lansing State Journal*, March 3, 1972.

38. Riddle's later life and career were of a nature the word "checkered" was invented for. After getting a law degree from the University of Michigan, he practiced in Detroit, and in the early 1980s he even worked for Phillips Petroleum Company while Dolores was a member of the board of directors. He later ran unsuccessfully for the Michigan State Senate and headed Jesse Jackson's 1984 presidential campaign in Michigan. Eventually he became a "political consultant" in Detroit, where in 2009 he was arraigned and convicted for corruption.

39. Underwood later became deputy commissioner of the Big Ten and returned to MSU as athletic director, 1999–2002.

40. "4 Trustees Oppose Choice of MSU Dean," *Detroit News*, March 8, 1972.

41. "Board Okays Urban Proposal, University Adds Its 17th College," *MSU News Bulletin*, May 25, 1972.

42. Ira Polley, "National Merit and National Achievement Scholar," memorandum to the author, November 6, 1975.

43. "Grant Will Support Task Force Study of Lifelong Education," *MSU News-Bulletin*, November 24, 1971.

44. The task force report was later incorporated into a book edited by Father Theodore Hesburgh, president of Notre Dame, Paul Miller, president of Rochester Institute of Technology, and me, *Patterns for Lifelong Learning* (San Francisco: Jossey-Bass, 1973).

45. Their pursuit and conviction was due to the unyielding determination of a then-young officer named James Dunlap, who later became chief of the MSU Department of Police and Public Safety. Margaret Harding, "Arrests Made in 32-Year-Old Case," *State News*, October 10, 2005; Kelly Hassett, "Ingham Co. Cold Case Squad Arrests 2 in '73 MSU Slaying," *Lansing State Journal*, October 10, 2005.

46. Don Stevens led the pressure because he wanted an honorary degree for Gus Scholle, president of the Michigan AFL-CIO, who was ill and dying.

47. Robert Perrin, *To Talk of Many Things: A Life Story* (Ann Arbor, MI: Malloy, 2008), 211.

48. Eleanor Breitmeyer, "Van Cliburn, Mrs. Marcos, Visit Ford Estate in G.P.," *Detroit News*, December 9, 1974.

49. Sheila O'Brien, "Van Cliburn Speaks of Music . . . and Love," *Lansing State Journal*, December 8, 1974.

50. Norman Sinclair, "Police Arrest 132 On MSU Campus," *Lansing State Journal*, May 19, 1970; Marcia Van Ness, "Decrease in Michigan State Appropriation Anticipated," *Lansing State Journal*, May 19, 1970.

51. After a few years, the controversy was finally settled when the East Lansing fire marshal reopened an old

complaint that the room used for showings wasn't compliant with codes governing a theater. (Although he denied it, I always thought university attorney Lee Carr might have called in a favor.) With great sadness, we had to notify the Beal group that no comparably suitable facility existed on campus.

52. "Three First Ladies Tour," *MSU News Bulletin*, September 23, 1976.

CHAPTER EIGHT. THE PRESIDENT OF MSU 3: ENRICHMENT, ATHLETICS, AND POLITICS

1. Henry Weinstein, "Phillips Petroleum Agrees to Change in Reply to Suit, Rearranges Board to Settle Stockholder Action on Gifts—Nixon's Personal Acceptance of $50,000 Is Disclosed," *New York Times*, February 19, 1976.

2. "Group to Review U.S. Latin Policies," *New York Times*, May 15, 1974.

3. David Binder, "Ford Gets Report Urging End to Cuban Embargo," *New York Times*, October 30, 1974.

4. David Binder, "Commission Favors New Panama Treaty, Carter Urged to Take Added Steps on Ties to Latin America," *New York Times*, December 19, 1976.

5. "Policy for the Americas," *New York Times*, December 21, 1976.

6. Clifton R. Wharton Jr., Testimony Hearings House Committee on Foreign Affairs, July 21, 1975.

7. "Building Plan Stirs Furor: MSU Groups Question Need," *Lansing State Journal*, January 16, 1970.

8. Dolores Wharton, "Arts Provide Joy," Point of View, *Lansing State Journal,* July 14, 1974.

9. Iris Wescott, e-mail message to the author, July 7, 2010. For the memorial Wendell played, as usual, brilliantly.

10. She replaced me on the Museum of Modern Art board and also joined the China Medical Board.

11. "Retiree Honored, Degree Flown to Tecumseh," *Lansing State Journal*, December 15, 1970.

12. "Ford Gives MSU $1.5 Million," *Lansing State Journal*, October 6, 1977; also, *Detroit News, Flint Journal, Ann Arbor News*. "Boost for MSU Arts Plan," *Lansing State Journal*, October 12, 1977.

13. "MSU: Great News for Arts," *Lansing State Journal*, January 14, 1978.

14. "Mott, Nisbet Receive New MSU Award," *Flint Journal*, May 25, 1972.

15. William E. Cote, "Wharton: Sports, Academics Mix, but Sometimes Stirring Is Hard," *Flint (Michigan) Journal*, March 7, 1976.

16. "Wharton Casts Eye at Health Care," *MSU State News*, November 1, 1972.

17. Clarence Underwood with Larry Paladino, *Greener Pastures: A Pioneer Athletics Administrator Climbs from Spartan Beginnings to the Top at Michigan State* (n.p., December 2005).

18. Joe Falls and Howard Erickson, "How One MSU Gridder Violated Rules," *Detroit Free Press*, April 28, 1975.

19. The fiftieth "allegation" was a simple statement that the NCAA would appreciate any comments or information we might have on the case.

20. Located in Clifton R. Wharton Jr. Archives.

21. "Final Word from Wharton," *Lansing State Journal*, July 9, 1975.

22. Warren Brown, letter to the author, June 5, 1975 (emphases added).

23. "Michigan State Wins, 16 to 13, as Clock Halts Ohio State on 1," *New York Times*, November 10, 1974.

24. *MSU State News*, November 11, 1974, p. 1.

25. Gordon S. White Jr., "Big Ten Powers Meet Today in Battle of Antagonists," *New York Times*, September 13, 1975.

26. President Enarson eventually did what many thought impossible: he fired Hayes after Hayes punched an opposing football player in a Gator Bowl game. Paul Winfield, "Coach Hayes Ousted by Ohio State for Punching Player; Gator Bowl Melee Ends His Reign, Interception Starts Incident, Leaves with Police Escort, Hayes Dismissed by Ohio State," *New York Times*, December 31, 1978.

27. Located in Clifton R. Wharton Jr. Archives.

28. Denny Stolz, letter to the author, May 14, 1975.

29. Patricia M. Carrigan, letter to the author, October 21, 1975.

30. Clifton R. Wharton Jr., letter to Walter Byers, January 30, 1976; Walter Byers, letter to the author, February 9, 1976.

31. Doug Underwood, "Details of MSU Probe Released," *Lansing State Journal*, October 1, 1978.

32. NCAA Infractions to NCAA Council, January 18, 1976.

33. MSU Select Committee, "Recommendations Pertaining to the Athletic Program," confidential memorandum to the author, January 27, 1976.

34. MSU Select Committee, "Special Audit Review of Firms Which Contributed to Mr. Kenneth Erickson for 'MSU Football Bust,'" Confidential Memorandum for the Record, June 14, 1976.

35. MSU Select Committee, "Unauthorized Bank Accounts Established by Kenneth Erickson," Confidential Memorandum for the Record, April 13, 1976.

36. Edward L. Ronders, "Recruiting Fund Linked to Departure of Stolz," *MSU State News*, March 31, 1976; Charlie Vincent, "Conflicting Stories Cost Denny Stolz His MSU Job," *Detroit Free Press*, April 1, 1976.

37. Report of Commissioner on Michigan State University to Big Ten Compliance Group, December 1, 1976.

38. Charlie Vincent, "Wharton Forces Resignation, Besieged Stolz Quits as MSU Coach," *Detroit Free Press*, March 17, 1976; Jack Berry, "Big Sweep by MSU Tied to Slush Fund," *Detroit News*, March 17, 1976; Lynn Henning, *Spartan Seasons: The Triumphs and Turmoil of Michigan State Sports* (South Boardman, MI: Croft on Creek Press, 2003).

39. The board action was unanimous and not the impulse of one trustee in a closed session as reported elsewhere. Henning, *Spartan Seasons*, 45.

40. Corky Meinecke, "Stolz Near End of Climb Back, Ex-MSU Coach Feels Wanted after Guiding BG to Success," *Detroit News*, December 11, 1985.

41. The removal of basketball coach Gus Ganakas was totally unrelated to the NCAA investigation as some reporters mistakenly believed. Henning, *Spartan Seasons*, 46.

42. "Ex-A.D. Seeks Old Job, Smith Wants $3.5 Million," *Lansing State Journal*, December 28, 1977; "Smith Sues MSU to Get Job Back," *Detroit Free Press*, December 29, 1977; Gary Miles, "The Forgotten Spartan, Former Athletic Director Burt Smith Lived Publicly but He Died Privately," *Lansing State Journal*, October 17, 1991.

43. For a detailed description of this event, see Henning, *Spartan Seasons*, chap. 8.

44. Jack Breslin, letter to Burt Smith, May 19, 1975; Burt Smith, letter to Jack Breslin, June 2, 1975.

45. Jack Breslin, memorandum to the author, March 12, 1976.

46. Mike O'Hara, "Firing Comes as Surprise to Ganakas," *Detroit News*, March 17, 1976. However, Charlie Vincent did correctly report that Ganakas had been criticized for failing to demand discipline on his squad in the January 4 incident and that there had been rumors of his removal in the summer of 1975. Charlie Vincent, "MSU Fires Cage Coach," *Detroit Free Press*, March 17, 1976.

47. Lynn Henning, "'Probation Handled Terribly,' Duffy Rips Administration," *Lansing State Journal*, November 23, 1977.

48. Dave Matthews, "Rogers a Sharp Cookie," *Lansing State Journal*, August 7, 1976.

49. U.S. House of Representatives, Committee on Interstate and Foreign Commerce, *Enforcement Program of the National Collegiate Athletic Association* (Washington, D.C.: U.S. Government Printing Office, December 1978).

50. Clifton R. Wharton Jr., statement before the Sub-Committee on Oversight and Investigations, Committee on Interstate and Foreign Commerce, U.S. Congress, February 28, 1978; Gordon S. White Jr., "NCAA Policies Criticized," *New York Times*, March 1, 1978.

51. White, "NCAA Policies Criticized."

52. Steve Smith, "Congress Begins Probe of NCAA," *Chronicle of Higher Education*, March 6, 1978; White, "NCAA Policies Criticized"; Tom Siler, "Wharton Issues Warning against No. 1 Syndrome," *Sporting News*, March 25, 1978; Doug Underwood, "'Mockery of Due Process,' Wharton Says NCAA Violated Rights, Used Hearsay," *Lansing State Journal*, March 1, 1978.

53. "Questions of Abuse," *Sports Illustrated*, March 13, 1978.

54. "Congress Urged to Act if NCAA Doesn't Reform," *Chronicle of Higher Education*, March 20, 1978.

55. "Former Employee Accuses NCAA of Abuses," *Higher Education Daily* 6, no. 40 (February 28, 1978).

56. Willard Baird, "MSU Ready for Law School Push," *Lansing State Journal*, March 21, 1974.

57. Daniel Dever, "'U' Funding OK Said Likely—Not Law School," *State News*, February 8, 1974.

58. "Law School Stirs Controversy among Michigan Legislators," *Big Rapids Pioneer*, March 25, 1974; "Law School Chance This Year? Legislation Viewed 'Likely,'" *Kalamazoo Gazette*, March 26, 1974.

59. Willard Baird, "Law School 'Won't Hurt Medicine,'" *Lansing State Journal*, March 26, 1974.

60. Daniel Dever, "Medical School's Priority May Doom College of Law," *State News*, March 27, 1974.

61. John Lindstrom, "Legislature Late with MSU Budget, but Outlook Hopeful for Law School," *State News*, June 28, 1974.

62. "Senate OKs School Budget," *Lansing State Journal*, July 4, 1974.

63. Diane Silver, "Law School Gets OK, No Funds," *State News*, July 5, 1974.

64. John Lindstrom, "MSU Suffers 3rd Straight Setback: No Chance Seen to Get a Law School," *State News*, July 12, 1974.

65. Two decades later, in 1995, the Detroit School of Law affiliated with MSU in a unique public-private partnership that resulted in an independent college integrated into a public university. After moving to the East Lansing campus, in April 2004 the school changed its name to the Michigan State University College of Law. Although it operates as a constituent college of the university, it remains financially independent and receives no state or university funding.

66. Richard E. Sullivan, "Time is Now to Show Commitment," *MSU State News*, April 10, 1975; Clifton R. Wharton Jr., "Arts Center to Be for All," *Lansing State Journal*, April 13, 1975.

67. There also were objections to the selection of Bennett and Horne. "Some Objections to Benefit," *Towne Courier* (East Lansing), week of March 20–27, 1975.

68. Jeanne Whittaker, "Tony Bennett and Lena Horne at MSU Benefit, Concert Raises $85,000," *Detroit Free Press*, April 21, 1975.

69. Pat Nardi, "Wharton Contributes $40,000 to Defray PAC Concert Costs," *State News*, April 14, 1975.

70. Frances Brown, "Board Affirms '76–'77 Budget, Called Austere, Disaster Plan," *State News*, August 2, 1976.

71. MSU Board of Trustees minutes, April 21–22, 1977.

72. Bob Ourlian, "'Priorityism' Permeating MSU as Economics Take the Reins," *State News*, February 22, 1977.

73. Larry Paladino, "Spartan Boosters Take a Few Jabs at Wolverines," *Detroit Free Press*, December 8, 1978.

74. Carole Leigh Hutton, "Board Hears 300 Protest Iran Project," *State News*, May 27, 1977.

75. W. Kim Heron and Mary Flood, "Iran Film Rebuff Brings on Sit-in," *Lansing State Journal*, June 4, 1977; W. Kim Heron, "Masked Protesters, MSU Officials Hit an Uneasy Impasse," *Lansing State Journal*, June 5, 1977; W. Kim Heron, "200 MSU Protestors End Sit-in Peacefully," *Lansing State Journal*, June 6, 1977.

76. With my encouragement Pee had received his MA at the University of Hawaii. After receiving his doctorate at MSU, he worked with the Rubber Research Institute for eleven years and then worked for twenty years at the World Bank in Washington, D.C.

CHAPTER NINE. THE CHANCELLOR OF SUNY 1: BUILDING A HIGHER EDUCATION SYSTEM

1. P. A. Rohman, "MSU's First Lady: From the Little Red Schoolhouse to the Big Green Multiversity," *MSU Alumni Magazine*, January–February 1975.

2. She had served on my Admissions Commission and was the first woman to become manager of a GM auto assembly plant.

3. "The Harvard 23: One for President," *Time*, December 14, 1970; John Borger and Diane Petryk, "Wharton Included on List for Harvard Presidency," *MSU State News*, December 3, 1970; "Harvard Drops 40 from List to Succeed Pusey," *Boston Globe*, December 3, 1970; Robert Reinhold, "Naming of Harvard President Near after Exhaustive Search, 23 Are Considered by Governing Board to Succeed Pusey—Campus Favorite Is Derek Bok, Law School Dean," *New York Times*, December 19, 1970.

4. Pat Nardi, "Wharton Cited as Candidate for Top U-C Position," *MSU State News*, January 18, 1975; "MSU President Says He Has Not Discussed U. of California Job," *Flint Journal*, January 28, 1975; "California Post Hopefuls Named," *Ann Arbor News*, February 12, 1975.

5. William Robbins, "Shift in Farm Policy under Carter Is Seen, "*New York Times*, November 26, 1976.

6. "MSU's Wharton Rejects 2 Offers for Carter Posts," *Detroit Free Press*, January 6, 1977.

7. Developed largely by John Mitchell (later President Nixon's attorney general), the so-called full faith and credit or moral authority bonds were not formally issued by the state. Therefore they required no legislative approval, and their debt service escaped restriction under New York's constitutional balanced budget requirement.

8. The Maritime College is located in historic Fort Schuyler, on the Throggs Neck peninsula, where the East River meets Long Island Sound.

9. Patricia LaCroix, "SUNY Considers Wharton for Chancellor, Recent Visits for Personal Interviews Confirmed," *State News*, October 5, 1977.

10. W. Kim Heron, "Wharton Remains 'Loyal Spartan,'" *Lansing State Journal*, October 27, 1977.

11. Judith Cummings, "Wharton Named Chancellor of State U.," *New York Times*, October 27, 1977.

12. David Bird, "An Identity with Achievement," *New York Times*, October 27, 1977.

13. Rev. Father James Goode, quoted in "Wharton Named SUNY Chancellor," *New York Amsterdam News*, November 5, 1977. He was referring to the *New York Times* "Man in the News" profile, which repeated a quote from their earlier profile of 1969.

14. Louis Martin, "Clifton Wharton on to N.Y. State Univ.," *Michigan Chronicle*, November 19, 1977.

15. W. Kim Heron, "'The Wharton Years,' Progress . . . and Holding MSU Together: New Colleges, New Buildings, Rhodes Scholars," *Lansing State Journal*, January 22, 1978.

16. Frank Angelo, "MSU Loss: Wharton Takes a Message to New York," *Detroit Free Press*, December 5, 1977.

17. Dean Richard Sullivan, "Clifton R. Wharton, Jr.—an Assessment" in "The Whartons at MSU," *MSU News-Bulletin*, Special Supplement, December 1977.

18. Rockefeller had already led a major renewal project in Albany, razing a large area of urban blight and replacing it with the massive South Mall complex of state offices (later named in his honor).

19. John T. Moore, "New Boss Deans at SUNY—but Is Cool toward Housewarming," *Knickerbocker News* (Albany), November 8, 1977.

20. Paul J. Browne, "Wharton Remodeling Costs State $145,000," *Watertown Daily Times*, May 17, 1978; "Bruno in Protest of Wharton Requests," *Albany Times Union*, May 19, 1978; "Legislators Ask Wharton House Probe," *Albany Times Union,* May 17, 1978.

21. Lois Uttley, "Taxpayers Unscathed by $150,000 SUNY Chief's Home," *Knickerbocker News* (Albany), October 24, 1978.

22. Frances Ingraham, "The Whartons Meet a Decorating Challenge," *Albany Times Union*, December 12, 1985.

23. "New Headquarters for State University Are Dedicated," *New York Times*, June 6, 1978.

24. Ari L. Goldman, "A Forthright Wife Accompanies New State Education Chancellor," *New York Times*, November 20, 1977.

25. Clifton R. Wharton Jr., "Education and Black Americans: Yesterday, Today and Tomorrow," New York State Association of Black and Puerto Rican Legislators, Sixteenth Annual Dinner, Albany, February 19, 1978.

26. Ari L. Goldman, "Peripatetic State U. Chancellor: 12 Campuses Down and 52 to Go," *New York Times*, April 3, 1978.

27. This program had been recommended by the Select Committee on the Future of Private and Independent Higher Education chaired by McGeorge Bundy. A. M. Farber, "Aid to All Colleges Urged," *New York Times*, January 31, 1968.

28. See Sanford H. Levine, "The Empire State Creates a University," in *SUNY at Sixty: The Promise of the State University*, ed. John B. Clark, W. Bruce Leslie, and Kenneth P. O'Brien (Albany: State University of New York Press, 2010), 16–29.

29. Edward B. Fiske, "State Regents vs. the State U., Board Victory in Ending 2 Doctoral Programs Is Merely Latest Round in a Power Struggle," *New York Times,* February 14, 1977.

30. Vernon Jordan, interview by the author, April 9, 1999.

31. The delayed choice of a president was covered by the press. Kathleen Teltsch, "Rockefeller Foundation Fails to Pick a President," *New York Times*, December 5, 1979.

32. Kathleen Teltsch, "Rockefeller Foundation Screening 5 for President," *New York Times*, January 1, 1980.

33. Kitty Teltsch, "Rockefeller Group Selects a New Head; Philanthropic Foundation Names Lyman, President of Stanford, as Knowles's Successor, Four Candidates Remain," *New York Times*, January 27, 1980.

34. Albin Krebs and Robert McG. Thomas Jr., "Notes on People, a First (but Not Last)," *New York Times*, December 9, 1981.

35. Edward B. Fiske, "Its Boom Years Over, State U. Now Strives for Excellence with Less Money, "*New York Times,* July 3, 1981, B2.

36. Key contributors to these early efforts were Hugh Tuohey, Richard Gillman, and Jim Van Houten.

37. A. M. Farber, "Aid to All Colleges Urged," *New York Times*, January 31, 1968.

38. Gene I. Maeroff, "Debate over Engineering Courses," *New York Times*, November 8, 1983.

39. Memo from SED Deputy Commissioner Don Nolan to SUNY Executive Chancellor Donald O'Dowd, June 1983.

40. Gene I. Maeroff, "Regents Split in Rejecting Engineering School," *New York Times*, November 21, 1983.

41. Governor Cuomo, letter to Board of Regents, December 13, 1983.

42. Gene I. Maeroff, "Regents, in Reversal, Pass Plan Sought by Cuomo," *New York Times*, May 26, 1984.

43. *Poughkeepsie Journal*, April 26, 1984.

44. Maeroff, "Regents, in Reversal."

CHAPTER TEN. THE CHANCELLOR OF SUNY 2: EXCELLENCE, FLEXIBILITY, AND INDEPENDENCE

1. In 1986 LeMelle became president of Mercy College.

2. The Communist People's Republic of China became the government of China on October 1, 1949, after Mao Zedong defeated the Kuomintang Nationalist Army of General Chiang Kaishek, which then fled to Taiwan.

3. "Indonesia Settles on State U. to Train Its Schoolteachers," *New York Times*, December 11, 1983.

4. Dartmouth College, Rockefeller's alma mater, had already established a Rockefeller Center for the Social Sciences, but the SUNY plan was for a broader program with greater potential for state and national impact.

5. Clifton R. Wharton Jr., letter to Laurance Rockefeller, December 26, 1980.

6. Laurance Rockefeller, letter to the author, February 23, 1981.

7. When Dolores and I left SUNY several years later, the trustees surprised us by the naming the 411 State Street building the Clifton and Dolores Wharton Research Center.

8. Rick Karlin, "UAlbany to Oversee Think Tank: Rockefeller Institute Shift Comes with Arrival of New SUNY Chancellor," *Albany Times Union*, August 28, 2009.

9. Clifton R. Wharton Jr., letter to Chancellor Zimpher, September 18, 2009.

10. Clifton R. Wharton Jr., "Public Universities and Public Service: A Productive Past, a Powerful Future," New York State Publishers Association, Fifty-Seventh Annual Meeting, Syracuse, March 6, 1978.

11. Clifton R. Wharton Jr., "SUNY'S Third Mission: A Progress Report on Public Service," Keynote, Annual Harpur Forum, SUNY–Binghamton, June 16, 1978.

12. Dennis Petroskey, "Arts Center on Its Way," *State News*, July 20, 1979; Patrick J. Fitzgerald, "State MSU Art Center in July?" *Lansing State Journal*, June 22, 1979.

13. Kenneth C. Beachler, tape recording excerpt; Kenneth C. Beachler, e-mail message to the author, October 12, 2009.

14. Rose Wojnar, "Black Faculty Wants McGoff Name Removed," *State News*, November 8, 1983.

15. Jennifer Harsha, "Margaret McGoff: Remove My Name from Center," *Lansing State Journal*, December 15, 1984.

16. "Audit Questions Wharton Center Construction," *MSU News-Bulletin*, October 14, 1982.

17. James A. Harris, "MSU Names Arts Center for Whartons," *Lansing State Journal*, April 3, 1982; Marji Hess, "Performing Arts Center Named After Wharton," *MSU State News*, April 5, 1982; "Fitting Tribute: Wharton PAC," *State News*, April 7, 1982.

18. Denice Anderson, "Happy Accidents Boost MSU Sculpture," *Lansing State Journal*, March 30, 1978.

19. The Carnegie Foundation for the Advancement of Teaching; the Agricultural Development Council; the National Council on Foreign Language and International Studies; and the National Academy of Science's Committee on Research Grants, Board of Science and Technology for International Development.

20. The Committee for Economic Development (1980–2004); Aspen Institute (1980–93); the Council on Financial Aid to Education (1983–86); the MIT Board of Overseers (1984–86); the Council on Foreign Relations (1983–93); the Foreign Policy Association (1983–87); and the Academy for Educational Development (1985–86).

21. Press release, September 12, 1978.

22. *Overcoming World Hunger: The Challenge Ahead* (March 1980); also, Sol M. Linowitz, *World Hunger: A Challenge to American Policy* (New York: Foreign Policy Association, 1980).

23. Walter P. Falcon, "Reflections on the Presidential Commission on World Hunger," *American Journal of Agricultural Economics* 63, no. 5 (December 1981).

24. My exaugural speech summarized the work that had been accomplished during my tenure. Clifton R. Wharton Jr., "BIFAD'S Sixth Birthday: A Personal Exaugural," AID Administrator's International Development Leaders Forum, U.S. Agency for International Development, Washington, D.C., March 30, 1983.

25. U.S. Agency for International Development, *Report to Congress on Title XII: Famine Prevention and Freedom from Hunger* (Washington, D.C.: U.S. Agency for International Development, April 1, 1982).

26. John Hillkirk, "Deal Seals Lips, Director Couple Shuns Merger Talk," *USA Today*, March 3, 1989.

27. The term "glass ceiling" wasn't then commonplace. Many point to the term's first use in an article by Carol Hymowitz and Timothy Schellhardt, "The Glass Ceiling: Why Women Can't Seem to Break the Invisible Barrier That Blocks Them from the Top Job," in the March 24, 1986, issue of the *Wall Street Journal*.

28. Students came from campuses such as SUNY–Albany, Union College, SUNY–New Paltz, Russell Sage College, College of Saint Rose, and Rensselaer Polytechnic Institute.

29. Clifton R. Wharton Jr., "U.S. Business Can't Change South Africa," *Newsday*, November 30, 1978.

30. Clifton R. Wharton Jr., "U.S. Firms Should Leave South Africa," *Newsday*, November 18, 1984.

31. "South African Divestment Voted by State U. Trustees," *New York Times*, September 25, 1985.

32. Dolores D. Wharton, "Personal Report and Observations on Visit to South Africa," presented to Kellogg Board of Directors, July 25, 1988, 4–5.

33. The bill, which passed the U.S. House and Senate in June 1986, was vetoed by President Reagan, but the veto was overridden in October 1986.

34. Marion B. Folsom, John W. Gardner, and Henry Heald, *Meeting the Increasing Demand for Higher Education in New York: A Report to the Governor and the Board of Regents* (Albany, NY: State Education Department, November 1960.)

35. Wells loved to correct those who failed to recognize that his middle initial "B" legally had no period. "It's Herman 'B' no period Wells," he would announce proudly.

36. Herman Wells, James Perkins, and G. R. Clark, *The Legislature and Higher Education in New York State: A Report by the Legislative Consultant on Higher Education* (New York: Academy for Educational Development, 1964), 17–18.

37. Clifton R. Wharton Jr., "Administrative Flexibility: Accountability's Point of Diminishing Returns," Annual Regional Conference, American Society for Public Administration, Albany, NY, October 6, 1978.

38. Edward B. Fiske, "Panel Suggests SUNY's System Be Reorganized," *New York Times*, January 17, 1985; "Panel Says State Strangling SUNY; Urges Restructuring," *Binghamton Press*, January 16, 1985; John Hildebrand, "Rules Strangle SUNY, Panel Says," *Newsday*, January 17, 1985; "SUNY Red Tape: A Study Urges a Freer Structure," *Time*, January 28, 1985.

39. Lise Bang-Jensen, "SUNY Corporation Idea To Be Aired," *Knickerbocker News* (Albany), January 17, 1985.

40. Jeffrey Schmalz, "Cuomo Calling for Flexibility in Public University Budgets," *New York Times*, February 24, 1985.

41. "A Cuomo Plan for State, City Universities: Trustees Discussing Governor's, Commission's Proposals for Greater FISCAL Flexibility," *Knickerbocker News* (Albany), February 26, 1985.

42. "No Half-Measures for SUNY," *New York Daily News*, February 27, 1985; "Trying to Cut Bureaucracy:

Cuomo, Trustees Vie on SUNY Plan," *Albany Times Union*, February 27, 1985.

43. Rekha Basu, "SUNY Board OKs Operational Changes," *Knickerbocker News* (Albany), March 27, 1986.

44. Sharon Gazin, "SUNY Shuffles Officers to Stimulate Challenge," *Albany Times Union*, September 11, 1986.

45. Upon my departure from SUNY, Komisar became acting chancellor (February 1, 1987–July 31, 1988). In 1990, he assumed the presidency of the University of Alaska system, serving in that role for eight years.

46. Penney had previously been associate provost at Yale (1976–82).

47. Haffner's position was filled by SUNY–Binghamton president Clifford D. Clark.

48. Tim Spofford, "Community Colleges Rescue Plan Offered," *Albany Times Union*, December 17, 1986.

49. Vincent O'Leary, *The Improbable President* (Burlington, IN: Author House, 2004), 185–88.

50. Clifton R. Wharton Jr., "The Tiresome Tuition Game at SUNY," *New York Times*, February 8, 2003.

51. Chapters 552 through 555 constituted the 1985 flexibility legislation.

CHAPTER ELEVEN. THE CHAIR AND CEO OF TIAA-CREF: PROMOTING A FUTURE AGENDA

1. Stephen Frank, "Clifton Wharton: Life at the Top, Reaping the Rewards of Pride and Prodigy," *Albany Times Union*, September 14, 1986.

2. *Pension and Investment Age*, January 1986; *Pension and Investment Age*, January 1988.

3. Fellow Ford Motor director Ambassador Carter Burgess strongly urged Caldwell to make this move.

4. Hesburgh, Roosa, and Hardin were trustees with me on the Rockefeller Foundation board.

5. Samuel Weiss, "State U. Chief to Resign to Become Head of $50 Billion Pension Fund," *New York Times*, October 16, 1986.

6. Tim Spofford, "Wharton Praised as Leader," *Albany Times Union*, October 18, 1986.

7. Tim Spofford, "Economist Wharton's Career Move Seen as Logical," *Albany Times Union*, October 16, 1986.

8. Sharon Gazin, "Ex-SUNY Trustee: Wharton Met the Challenge," *Knickerbocker News* (Albany), October 16, 1986.

9. Editorial, *Albany Times Union*, October 18, 1986.

10. "SUNY's First Lady Looks Back," *SUNY Forum*, January 1987.

11. Frances Ingraham, "Not Goodbye," *Albany Times Union*, February 1, 1987.

12. Tim Spofford, "Building Renamed for Whartons, Departing SUNY Chancellor Feted," *Albany Times Union*, January 29, 1987.

13. The naming was a clever way to circumvent SUNY board policy of not naming a university building until five years after the departure of a SUNY employee.

14. Stephen Frank, "Clifton Wharton Life at the Top Reaping the Rewards of Pride and Prodigy," *Albany Times Union*, September 14, 1986.

15. *The Guardian* (UK) July 7, 1989.

16. This was the same Oscar Ruebhausen who had worked with me on the draft report for Nelson Rockefeller's Latin American mission in 1969.

17. Dan Fastenberg, "Top 10 Worst Bosses—Al Dunlap," *Time Magazine*, October 18, 2010.

18. The four white papers were "New Accumulation Funds and Pay-out Vehicles," "Transferability of

TIAA-CREF Annuity Accumulations," "Reporting, Services, and Planning for Policyholders and Institutions," and "Corporate Governance."

19. Forty-five years later AAU member presidents included two Blacks (one male and one female), one Hispanic, three South Asians, and thirteen women. L. Norton, assistant to AAU president, e-mail message to the author, September 4, 2014.

20. L. J. Davis, "Precious Cargo: The $60 Billion Challenge; Clifton Wharton Struggles to Preserve a Pension Fund," Business World, *New York Times Magazine*, March 27, 1988.

21. November 18, 1987.

22. John Kifner, "Armed Negroes End Seizure; Cornell Yields; Armed Negro Students End 36-Hour Occupation after Cornell Capitulates," *New York Times*, April 21, 1969.

23. The unit combined metric measures of the annual growth of all assets under management by TIAA-CREF as well as the company's Capital Account. The focus was on the company's annual investment performance relative to portfolio benchmarks and its annual net client flow performance. The goal was superior investment performance relative to portfolio benchmarks in a given performance measurement period. In this fashion participants' investment returns would increase relative to benchmarks over meaningful time horizons. Thus the employee experience and rewards were aligned with the investment experience of participants through their portfolios.

24. Alfonso A. Narvaez, "Clifton R. Wharton, 90, Is Dead; Pioneering U.S. Diplomat," *New York Times*, April 25, 1990.

25. Bruce D. Wharton, "A Life Remembered," Encanto Community Church, Phoenix, Arizona, May 6, 1990.

26. Clifton R. Wharton Jr., remarks, commemorative stamp of Ambassador Clifton R. Wharton Sr. celebration unveiling, Washington D.C., May 30, 2006.

27. Theodore W. Schultz, letter to the author, May 31, 1991.

28. Clifton R. Wharton Jr., "Theodore W. Schultz," *Proceedings of the American Philosophical Society* 147, no. 3 (September 2003): 311–15.

29. By "governance" I mean the structures that shape the rights of and relationships among the principal stakeholders in corporations: shareholders (if any), management (led by the chief executive officer), and trustees or directors. Secondary stakeholders include customers, employees, suppliers, creditors, and the community.

30. Steven C. Mason and Clifton R. Wharton Jr., *Three Realities: Minority Life in the United States* (Washington, D.C.: Business-Higher Education Forum, 1990).

31. William Raspberry, "For Minorities, Different Realities Call for Different Remedies," *Orlando Sentinel*, June 11, 1990; "Report Defines Three Levels of Black Life," *Jet*, July 2, 1990.

32. David Broder, "Will We Turn Our Attention to 'Three Realities' about the U.S.?" *Washington Post*, June 28, 1990.

33. Michelle Osborn, "The Wharton School, Clifton Wharton Gives Pension Fund Giant a Lesson in Turnarounds," *USA Today*, October 2, 1991.

34. After my retirement the company named it the Clifton R. Wharton, Jr. Auditorium.

35. Davis, "Precious Cargo," *New York Times*.

36. President John Biggs and I were "inside" trustees on both boards; Jim Martin, executive vice president, was an inside trustee on the CREF board.

37. The section of Harvard Yard bounded by University Hall, Memorial Church, Widener Library, and Sever Hall where annual commencements are held.

38. "Bok, Updike to Get Degrees—Violinist, Economist, Physicist Are among 11 Honorands," *Harvard*

Crimson, June 14, 1992.

39. Harrell had also been with Senator David Pryor (AK) throughout his career, serving as press secretary, chief of staff, confidant, and overall adviser.

40. President-elect Clinton Economic Summit, Little Rock, Arkansas, "International Economic Discussion," tapes 1 and 2, Video C-Span Cable, December 14, 1992.

41. "The Transition: Excerpts from Clinton's News Conference Introducing His Latest Nominees," *New York Times*, December 23, 1992.

CHAPTER TWELVE. THE SECRETARY: DEPARTMENT OF STATE

1. For the next two years Jones served as vice chairman at TIAA-CREF, but then he was lured away by Sandy Weill to Travelers Group and eventually became chairman and chief executive officer of Citigroup Inc.'s Global Investment Management from 1999 to 2004.

2. Marc Levinson, "That Old College Try: The World's Largest Private Pension Scheme Is Booming. But Can It Fend Off the Mutual Funds?" *Newsweek*, January 11, 1993.

3. Michael Useem, "Clifton Wharton Restructures TIAA-CREF," in *The Leadership Moment: Nine True Stories of Triumph and Disaster and Their Lessons for Us All* (New York: Three Rivers Press, January 1998), chap. 6.

4. Bill McAllister, "Wharton Is Well-Established in Foreign Policy, Education, Business," *Washington Post*, December 23, 1992.

5. Rowland Evans and Robert Novak, op-ed, ". . . And Teacups?" *Washington Post*, December 25, 1992; "Some Old, Some New, Some Borrowed . . . Clinton Strains to Finish Building a Cabinet That 'Looks Like America,'" The Week, *Time*, December 20–26, 1992; Leslie Gelb, "The Diversity Trap, Neo-cons, Jews, Blacks . . . Trouble," *New York Times*, January 7, 1993.

6. John Sewell, letter to the editor, *Washington Post*, January 2, 1993; Abe Weisblat, letter to *Time*, January 8, 1993. Sewell was president of the Overseas Development Council; Weisblat was an associate at the Agricultural Development Council.

7. Alison Mitchell, "The Twin Towers: The Sect; Suspect in Bombing Is Linked to Sect with a Violent Voice," *New York Times*, March 5, 1993.

8. Elaine Sciolino, "Egypt Warned U.S. of Terror, Mubarak Says," *New York Times*, April 5, 1993; Zina Hemady, "Mubarak Said to Call Radical Cleric a 'CIA Agent,'" *Washington Post*, May 29, 1993.

9. The proper formal title is "Permanent Representative of the United States of America to the United Nations, with the rank and status of Ambassador Extraordinary and Plenipotentiary."

10. Harper later was an overseer at Harvard who resigned in 2005 due to President Summers's comments on women and Blacks. Alan Finder, "Raise for Harvard's President Led Board Member to Quit," *New York Times*, August 2, 2005.

11. Karen De Witt, "Pamela Harriman Chosen for Paris," *New York Times*, March 23, 1993.

12. Steven Holmes, "Mondale (Tokyo), Holbrooke (Bonn) Surprised," *New York Times*, June 10, 1993.

13. Ann Devroy and Stephen Barr, "Gore Heads Latest Government Evaluation; Clinton Orders 'National Performance Review' to identify What Works and What Doesn't," *Washington Post*, March 4, 1993.

14. Steven A. Holmes, "Executive Brief: The State Department; They Talk Not of Bosnia, but of Plans to Cut Jobs," *New York Times*, February 4, 1993.

15. Anna Borg, e-mail message to the author, March 3, 2013.

16. Kuwaiti officials disarmed a bomb and arrested the suspected assassins. Secretary Christopher talked

President Clinton into a retaliatory strike on Iraq, and on June 16 the United States launched twenty-three Tomahawk missiles against the country's intelligence headquarters in Baghdad.

17. The Cuban Foreign Ministry put out a statement detecting "a more moderate tone" but still treated my speech as close to past U.S. "aggressive and hostile" policy. Two steps forward, I thought, one step back.

18. The Deputy of State's immediate staff were William D. Montgomery, senior policy adviser; Wynetta Kelly, staff assistant; Kathryn Sartori, personal assistant; and Marjorie Soltis, staff assistant. The Department of State officers were Jessica Matthews, deputy to the undersecretary for global affairs; Thomas C. Hubbard, deputy assistant secretary of East Asian Affairs; Richard Hecklinger, principal deputy assistant secretary for economic and business affairs; Kenneth Quinn, deputy assistant secretary for East Asian and Pacific Affairs; Kent Wiedemann, senior director for Asian affairs; George Laudato, acting assistant administrator, Bureau for Asia, Agency for International Development; and George Beasley, deputy director East Asia and Pacific, U.S. Information Agency. The support staff were Patrick O'Boyle and James Cronin, diplomatic security; Gail Cleveland, executive secretary; Lynn Sweeney, computer specialist; and James Williams, trip coordinator.

19. "U.S. Softens Accusations on Khmer Rouge," *Bangkok Post*, June 22, 1993.

20. Trevor Findlay, *Cambodia: The Legacy and Lessons of UNTAC*, SIPRI Research Report No. 9 (New York: Oxford University Press, May 1995).

21. Sihanouk would be re-elected king on September 24, 1993.

22. Estimates of the total number of deaths resulting from Khmer Rouge policies, including disease and starvation, range from 1.7 to 2.5 million out of a 1975 population of roughly 8 million.

23. Datuk Dr. Kamal Salih, "A Man of Distinction in Whom We Have a Tremendous Friend," *New Straits Times*, June 26, 1993.

24. Anna Taing, "More Conciliatory US Stance toward EAEC Proposal," *Malaysian Business Times*, June 25, 1993.

25. "US Will Maintain Security Commitments to Its Allies," *Indonesia Times*, June 28, 1993.

26. His full name was Sultan Haji Hassanal Bolkiah Mu'izzaddin Waddaulah ibni AlMarhum Sultan Haji Omar Ali Saifuddien Sa'adul Khairi Waddien.

27. Marc Logan, "Clinton Invites Ramos to Visit US," *Philippines Times Journal*, July 1, 1993.

28. Thomas W. Lippman, "Aid Is Out If Khmer Rouge Is In, U.S. Tells Cambodia," *Washington Post*, July 19, 1993.

29. "Sihanouk Irked at U.S.," *Washington Post*, July 21, 1993.

30. John M. Goshko, "U.S. Eases Stance on Cambodia Aid; Official Sees Assistance Even If Government Includes Khmer Rouge," *Washington Post*, July 25, 1993.

31. Clarke was the anti-terrorism czar under presidents George H. W. Bush and Clinton becoming famous with his book *Against All Enemies: Inside America's War on Terror* (New York: Free Press, 2004).

32. A career State Department officer, Covey had previously served as special assistant to the president and senior director of the NSC office of Near East and South Asia (1990–92) and had been deputy chief of mission at the U.S. embassy in Egypt (1986–89).

33. A subsequent book by Professor Vernon Ruttan recognized the political tug-of-war between the task force report and the PRD 20 project. Vernon W. Ruttan, *United States Development Assistance Policy: The Domestic Politics of Foreign Economic Aid* (Baltimore: Johns Hopkins University Press, 1996).

34. Clifton R. Wharton Jr., "The Third World: Where America's Foreign and Domestic Interests Meet," September 17, 1993.

35. Richard A. Ryan, "Clifton Wharton: Diplomat Seeks Bigger Role for Blacks," *Lansing State Journal*, August 29, 1993.

36. John Cavanaugh, Robin Broad, and Peter Weiss, "The Need for a Global New Deal," *The Nation*, December 27, 1993.

37. Though the magazine was dated November 1, it was available on the newsstands on October 25. Two days later it was reprinted on the front page of the *Lansing State Journal* (October 27, 1993).

38. Whitehead was also president of the UNA.

39. Linowitz told me of a confrontation he had had with Lyndon Johnson, who had asked him to serve as ambassador to the Organization of American States. At a meeting, Johnson had (probably accidentally) embarrassed Linowitz in a way that might have undercut his effectiveness before he even began. Linowitz saw the president immediately afterward and followed Dillon's advice. Johnson instantly returned to the group and corrected his inadvertent offense.

40. "State Department Deputy to Resign," *Washington Times*, November 3, 1993.

41. Stewart M. Powell, "Insiders Expect Wharton to Quit, State Department's Management Is Criticized," *Albany Times Union*, November 4, 1993.

42. Thomas W. Lippman, "Wharton Resigns at State Department, Deputy Secretary First Top Member to Quit Foreign Policy Team," *Washington Post*, November 9, 1993.

43. Elaine Sciolino, "With Foreign Policies under Fire, Top State Department Deputy Is Ousted," *New York Times*, November 9, 1993.

44. David Maraniss, who wrote a biography of Clinton, told me that when in trouble Clinton had always looked immediately for someone else to blame.

45. "The Limits of Ad Hockery," editorial, *New York Times*, November 12, 1993.

46. Martin Fletcher and Wolfgang Munchau, "Christopher Critics See Sacked Black Deputy as Scapegoat," *Times* (London), November 10, 1993.

47. A. M. Rosenthal, "On My Mind: The Wharton Case," *New York Times*, December 3, 1993.

48. Michael Armacost, e-mail to author, November 1, 2010.

49. Daniel Williams, "Coping with Shortcomings at State; Talbott's Selection Made with Two Weaknesses of Secretary in Mind," *Washington Post*, December 29, 1993.

50. Colin Powell and Joseph Persico, *My American Journey* (New York: Random House, 1995), 586.

51. "Powell Memoirs Reveal Overtures from Clinton," *Los Angeles Times*, September 4, 1995.

52. Evan Thomas, John Barry, and B. Cohn, "Powell on the March (General Powell May Run for President)," *Newsweek*, September 11, 1995.

53. Lee A. Daniels, "Abrupt Exit: Racism, Leaks and Isolation Drove Clif Wharton to Resign from the State Department," *Emerge*, February 1994.

54. George E. Curry, *Emerge*, March 1994, 4.

CHAPTER THIRTEEN. THE RETIREE: ROLES, RECOGNITIONS, AND REFLECTIONS

1. Ford Motor (until 1997) and TIAA Overseers (1994–2001). I added Tenneco (1994–99) and Harcourt General (1994–2001).

2. A year earlier I had served as a member of the Council on Foreign Relations Task Force on Taiwan. Stephen Friedman, "Managing the Taiwan Issue, Key Is Better U.S. Relations with China," Council on Foreign Relations, January 1995.

3. Paul A. Volcker and Clifton R. Wharton Jr., *Report of the Commission on New York State Student Financial Aid* (Albany, NY: The Commission, 1999).

4. Andrew Brownstein, "Panel Seeks College Aid for Low-Income Families," *Albany Times Union*, March 10, 2000.

5. Paul A. Volcker and Clifton R. Wharton Jr., "State Higher Education Challenge, New York Needs to Fix Its Aid System," *Albany Times Union*, April 9, 2000.

6. Alex Berenson, "Big Board Suggests Ending Links among Exchanges," *New York Times*, April 7, 2000.

7. Greg Ip, "NYSE, in a Break with Heavyweights, Calls for End to System Linking Markets," *Wall Street Journal*, April 7, 2000.

8. Clifton R. Wharton Jr., "Ethics, Values, and College Athletics," College Sports Project, Andrew W. Mellon Foundation, New York, NY, December 11, 2006.

9. William E. "Brit" Kirwan and R. Gerald Turner, "Changing the Game: Athletics Spending in an Academic Context," *AGB Trusteeship* 18, no. 5 (September–October 2010).

10. Tamar Lewin, "At Many Top Public Universities, Intercollegiate Sports Come at an Academic Price," *New York Times*, January 16, 2013.

11. Joe Drape, "Sandusky Guilty of Sexual Abuse of 10 Young Boys," *New York Times*, June 22, 2012.

12. Sarah Lyall, "A's for Athletes, but Charges of Fraud at North Carolina," *New York Times*, December 31, 2013; Paul M. Barrett, "The Scandal Bowl: Tar Heels Football, Academic Fraud, and Implicit Racism," *Bloomberg Businessweek*, January 3, 2014.

13. "Million-Dollar Coaches Move into Mainstream," *USA Today*, November 16, 2006.

14. Wharton, "Ethics, Values, and College Athletics."

15. Allie Grasgreen, "Coaches Make More Than You," *Inside Higher Education*, November 7, 2013.

16. At least one basketball coach, Mike Krzyzewski at Duke University, tops all these, with $9.7 million in 2011. "At Private Colleges, 33 Coaches and Athletic Directors Top $1 Million," *Chronicle of Higher Education*, December 16, 2013.

17. Jim Baumbach, "College Football Coaches' Salaries and Perks Are Soaring," *Newsday*, October 4, 2014.

18. Roger Groves, "The Jim Harbaugh Total Pay Package Will Be Much Bigger than It Looks," *Forbes*, December 30, 2014; Adam Kilgore, "Jim Harbaugh's Contract with Michigan Continues College Football Arms Race," *Washington Post*, December 30, 2014.

19. If the statistics had been drawn solely from the major "powers," the percentages would have been somewhat higher, since more student athletes are drafted from those conferences.

20. Andrew Zimbalist, *Unpaid Professionals: Commercialism and Conflict in Big Time College Sports* (Princeton: Princeton University Press, 2001).

21. Ben Strauss and Steve Eder, "College Players Granted Right to Form Union," *New York Times*, March 26, 2014.

22. Editorial Board, "Fairness for College Athletes," *New York Times*, November 12, 2013.

23. "Can Congress (Yes, Congress) Help NCAA Find Solutions?" *CBS Sports*, August 18, 2014; C. Thomas McMillen, "Could the Government End the Mess in College Sports? A Bipartisan Commission to Reform Amateur Athletics Is Vitally Needed Now," *Chronicle of Higher Education*, August 15, 2014; Ron Morris, "'Power' Move Shows Who's in Charge," *The State* (South Carolina), August 16, 2014.

24. The commission chairman, the late Bill Friday, wrote an op-ed decrying college athletic "entertainment" as antithetical to the founding mission of higher education. William C. Friday, "To Teach or to Win?" *Charlotte Observer*, November 30, 2006.

25. James J. Duderstadt, *Intercollegiate Athletics and the American University: A University President's Perspective* (Ann Arbor: University of Michigan Press, 2003); Derek Bok, *Universities in the Marketplace: The Commercialization of Higher Education* (Princeton: Princeton University Press, 2004).

26. James L. Shulman and William G. Bowen, *The Game of Life: College Sports and Educational Values* (Princeton: Princeton University Press, 2002).

27. Pete Thamel, "After Much Debate, College Football's Postseason Future Is Still Cloudy," *New York Times*, December 31, 2006; Dan Wolken, "Questions and Answers for the College Football Playoff," *USA Today*, April 25, 2013.

28. Greg Bishop, "Television Revenue Fuels a Construction Boom in the Pac-12," *New York Times*, November 29, 2013.

29. Among the significant ones: Michigan State University, College of Education, Crystal Apple Award and Featherstone Award (2000); Johns Hopkins University Alumni Association, Woodrow Wilson Award for Distinguished Government Service (2002); Africare Legacy Award (2005); the John Hope Franklin Award, Diverse Issues in Higher Education (2005); New York City Center Mayor Fiorello H. LaGuardia Distinguished Service Award (2009); and the New York University, Stern School of Business, Haskins Award (2013). In addition to my status as MSU president emeritus, the SUNY Board of Trustees, then chaired by Carl F. McCall, appointed me chancellor emeritus on May 10, 2012.

30. E. Christine Potts, *Good Books in the Right Hands: Making a Difference, The Clifton R. Wharton, 3rd Designated Reader Program*, Enoch Pratt Free Library, Baltimore, Maryland, 2010.

31. *Trial and Triumph: The Wharton Years: 1970–1978, A Tribute to Clifton and Dolores Wharton* (video).

32. "What else is new, Pres?" *MSU State News*, January 21, 1970.

33. Spaniolo became an executive officer with Knight Ridder and then vice president and chief program officer of the Knight Foundation. He would next serve as president at University of Texas–Arlington (2004–13).

34. Billy Taylor, "In Loving Memory," *Urban Griot*, CD, Soundpost Records, August 28, 2001.

35. Commissioned by the Michigan State University College of Music and Wharton Center for Performing Arts.

36. During 2008–9 the Wharton Center was refurbished with a new facade and internal extensions. On October 10–11, 2009, Dolores and I were delighted to take part in the rededication.

37. MSU has a series of named donor societies, many for former presidents, at different contribution levels. The highest is the William J. Beal Society ($10 to $15 million); the second highest is named for the first president, Joseph Williams ($5 to $7.5 million). Mine is the third largest.

38. Clifton R. Wharton Jr., "Personal Reflections on Leadership: Common Findings in Diverse Settings," Global Leadership Forum on Governance, Abshire Inamori Leadership Academy, Center for Strategic and International Studies, Washington, D.C., October 21, 2003.

39. "An Open Letter from Herb Allison to TIAA-CREF Participants," May 5, 2015.

40. As previously described the TIAA charter definitively states that Overseers have the final governance responsibility regarding whether or not the broad corporate mission is properly and adequately being met. This duty was more than perfunctory since it meant that the Overseers were in the position to challenge any major policy or action that they judged to deviate from the original mission or purpose of TIAA. While this power to challenge or countermand either of the two operating boards was rarely used, it meant that major changes in policies or programs were submitted to the Overseers and carefully reviewed by them.

41. Letter to TIAA Board of Overseers from Robert H. Atwell, Lucius J. Barber, John H. Biggs, Thomas C. Edwards, William G. Friday, Theodore M. Hesburgh, Juanita Kreps, G. G. Michelson, Jack W. Peltason, Paul A. Volcker, Clifton R. Wharton Jr., and John C. Whitehead, June 27, 2005.

42. Michelle Osborn, "The Wharton School: Clifton Wharton Gives Pension Fund Giant a Lesson in Turnarounds," *USA Today*, October 2, 1991; Michael Useem, *The Leadership Moment: Nine Stories of Triumph and Disaster and Their Lessons for Us All* (New York: Crown, 1998), chap. 6.

43. Francis Ward, "Michigan State University's Clifton Wharton Facing the Knowledge Explosion," *Chicago Tribune*, May 12, 1974.

44. Goldie Blumenstyk, *American Higher Education in Crisis: What Everyone Needs to Know* (New York: Oxford University Press, 2014).

45. Robert Hiltonsmith and Tamara Draut, "The Great Cost Shift Continues: State Higher Education Funding after the Recession," *Demos*, March 6, 2014; see also chart 1, State Higher Education Finance Report 2013, State Higher Education Executive Officers Association.

46. William E. Kirwan, "The Completion Imperative: Harnessing Change to Meet our Responsibilities," 2013 Atwell Lecture, American Council on Education Ninety-Fifth Annual Meeting, March 3, 2013.

47. Clifton R. Wharton Jr., "Never Eat Your Seed Corn," Haskins Award Lecture, Stern School of Business, New York University, April 24, 2013.

Index